INVESTMENTS

INVESTMENTS

NINTH EDITION

HERBERT E. DOUGALL

C.O.G. Miller Professor of Finance, Emeritus
Stanford University

PRENTICE-HALL, INC., Englewood Cliffs, N.J.

Library of Congress Cataloging in Publication Data

Dougall, Herbert Edward.
    Investments.

    First- ed. by D. F. Jordan, published 1919–1941 under
title: Jordan on investments.   –7th ed., by D. F.
Jordan and H. E. Dougall, published 1952–1960 under
title: Investments.
    Includes bibliographies.
    1. Investments. I. Jordan, David Francis
Jordan on investments.
HG4521.D65 1973   332.6'78   73–1825
ISBN 0-13-504563-0

© 1973, 1968, 1960, 1952, 1941, 1934, 1924, 1920
by PRENTICE-HALL, INC.
Englewood Cliffs, N.J.

PRINTED IN THE UNITED STATES OF AMERICA

10   9   8   7   6   5   4   3

Prentice-Hall International, Inc., *London*
Prentice-Hall of Australia, Pty. Ltd., *Sydney*
Prentice-Hall of Canada, Ltd., *Toronto*
Prentice-Hall of India Private Limited, *New Delhi*
Prentice-Hall of Japan, Inc., *Tokyo*

To Louise

Contents

30 Stocks of Insurance Companies   559

Preface

Since the publication of the eighth edition of this book in 1968, the whole investment scene has changed dramatically. Some of the developments in a period that could appropriately be called revolutionary are: a massive increase in the accumulation of savings; a relative decline in individuals' interest in stocks together with their renewed interest in bonds; new high levels in stock prices, followed by one of the longest and sharpest breaks in stock market history; the continuing passage of the ownership of stocks into institutional hands, and the domination of institutions in the trading in securities; the enormous growth in assets of institutions in general and the decline in the appeal of mutual funds; new tax laws affecting investors and investment policy; the rise and wane of the "performance cult" of institutional investment portfolio management; an enormous expansion of corporate and government debt; a second postwar "credit crunch" that saw bond and mortgage yields at their historical highs, and their continuation at relatively high levels; the continued decline in stock yields; massive Federal deficits with their impact on markets and yields; a great increase in financing by Federal credit and other agencies; the burgeoning of real estate investment trusts and other methods of participation by individuals in real estate ownership and financing; reorganization of the organization and management of securities exchanges, together with new services and new commission schedules; back-office problems of securities firms followed by the failure or merger of brokerage houses, and the new public ownership of stock exchange member firms; the electronic mechanization of securities quotations and other improvements in the dissemination of market information; the movement toward unified national securities markets; the rise, decline, and renewed interest in speculation; the development of more sophisticated methods of measuring investment performance, and the growing practice of disclosure of and competition for performance results on the part of institutional investors; new approaches to the analysis and valuation of corporate securities; new problems of corporate liquidity, the failure of Penn Central, and the renaissance of interest in the corporate balance sheet; the transfer of railway passenger service to Amtrak; the development of financial conglomerates that offer a variety of financial and investment services; the changing investment appeal of industrial, railway, public utility, bank, and insurance stocks.

These developments, and many others, are discussed in the ninth edition, and have required a very thorough revision. All factual information, regulation, taxation, and innovations in investment theory and practice are updated through 1972. The lists of references at the end of each chapter have been revised to include the most important new books for further reading.

I am again indebted for ideas and information to many individuals and organizations, and especially wish to express my thanks to those that provided early information: the Federal Power Commission, the Federal Deposit Insurance Corporation, The United States Savings and Loan League, and the Institute of Life Insurance. I wish also to thank the various investment services and firms for permission to cite data drawn from their publications; all sources have been faithfully indicated. Lastly, I am grateful to Professor Christopher U. Light of the University of Utah for a thoughtful review of the manuscript.

This edition contains a dedication to my wife, whose interest and patience have supported me through the pains, perils, and pleasures of a challenging writing assignment.

HERBERT E. DOUGALL

INVESTMENTS

1 The Nature of Investment and Investment Media

SCOPE: This chapter discusses the concept of investment and outlines the major types of investment media that are available to individuals and institutions. The order of discussion is (1) the financial and economic meaning of investment, (2) investment versus speculation, (3) classification of investment media, and (4) the scope of the book.

Financial and Economic Meaning of Investment

From the point of view of investors or suppliers of capital, investment is the commitment of present funds for the purpose of deriving future income in the form of interest, dividends, rent, or retirement benefits, or of appreciation in the value of the principal.

From this financial standpoint whether the money saved and invested is devoted to a "productive" use in the economic sense is not important. A government bond whose proceeds are used for destructive missiles is just as much an investment as a new share of stock sold by a corporation to finance plant expansion.

Nor from the financial standpoint does it matter whether the investor is purchasing a security from someone else, or whether the funds are to be used for new assets. The purchase in the open market of a "secondhand" instrument such as a bond, a share of stock, or a mortgage, is just as much an investment as the purchase of a security issued for new capital. In fact, most investments, in the popular sense, are mere transfers of property or rights to income from one person to another.

These ideas on the nature of investment in the financial or popular sense should be contrasted with its meaning in the economic sense. In this latter context the term implies the formation of *new* and *productive* capital in the form of new construction, new producers' durable equipment, or additional inventories. It forms an integral part of the Gross National Product. The Gross National Product is the value of all goods and services produced in the country in a given period, or its equivalent, the total expenditures for

goods and services, which fall into four main categories: (1) personal consumption expenditures, (2) gross private domestic *investment,* or business
expenditures for plant, equipment, and increased inventories, (3) net foreign
investment, or the difference between the spending by foreigners for American exports and the spending by America on its imports, and (4) government
purchases of goods and services.

However, the financial and economic meanings of the term are connected.
Part of the savings of individuals, which flow into the capital market, either
directly or through institutions, are devoted to new permanent capital
financing. Investors as suppliers and investors as users of long-term funds
thus find a meeting place in the market. The interrelations between supply
and demand for investment funds are developed further in Chapter 2. In
most of the discussion in this book, however, the term *investment* will be used
in its financial sense, and investments will include those media or instruments
into which savings are placed.

Investment versus Speculation

Discussions of the process of investment often seek to sharpen its meaning by
contrasting it with speculation. But the line of demarcation is difficult to
draw. Traditionally, investment involves minimum risk and is, therefore,
confined to media whose future income is relatively certain and whose
principal is "safe," whereas speculation involves taking possibly high risk.
This concept of investment is frequently used in the financial services where
one may find one list of recommended securities classed as "investment
grade" whereas another is labelled "speculative."

One difficulty with this distinction is that, owing to the uncertainties of
the future, all commitments for future income and return of principal involve some risk. Risk is a matter of degree, and the line between low risk
and high risk is often purely arbitrary. If all securities were ranked in order
of risk, from a short-term Federal obligation to the weakest common stock,
where would the line between investment and speculation be drawn?

Another difficulty with this distinction is that the degree of uncertainty
must be measured differently for different types of media. For many bonds
and mortgages the probability of receiving the future stream of interest payments, and the principal at maturity, may be appraised accurately and an
appropriate yield may be offered that will reward for risk. But in the case of
equities, principal is ordinarily recoverable only in the marketplace, and
income is a distribution of profit at the discretion of the issuer. How does one
measure the "safety" of a stock? Only by estimating the future course of stock
market values and dividends. Furthermore, the reward for risk-taking, in the
form of a "reasonable" rate of return must, in the case of many stocks, include future appreciation; even Treasury bonds produce higher yields than
most widely held stocks.

The distinction between investment and speculation on the basis of risk is
faulty for other reasons. A marketable Federal bond—a riskless investment

insofar as payment of interest and principal at maturity is concerned—involves risk of two other types: (1) the purchasing-power risk, or possibility of decline in the real value of the interest and principal, and (2) the money-rate risk, or risk of decline in market value when interest rates rise. When one buys a fixed-dollar obligation, is he not "speculating" on the future value of money and on the future market value of his security?

Another distinction was formerly made between investment and speculation, namely, that an investment must be represented by a contract by a responsible debtor to repay the original money outlay at a definite date with a definite return in the meantime. For many years stocks were excluded from the investment category because they represented ownership and not a contract to repay a definite sum. The assumption was that such instruments involve such inherent risk as to place them beyond the pale of investment thinking. Certainly the record of stocks as a class, with respect to dollar loss, is not as strong as that of bonds; yet some high-risk bonds are virtually worthless and many stocks have an eminently respectable record. One cannot logically dignify a poorly secured bond as an investment and ignore a strongly entrenched stock merely because it represents ownership and hence has possibilities of loss (and of profit).

Another distinction between the two terms is still frequently drawn on the basis of the period for which the commitment is made. The speculator is said to be interested in trading for the quick turn, the investor in long-run holding. There is an element of validity in this position. But many corporations and individuals make short-term commitments that afford a high degree of protection, and many "speculators" hope for very material gains over a period of years.

Another distinction is found in the *motive* of the supplier of funds. The investor is said to be interested in income; the speculator, in capital appreciation. The difficulty with this concept is that it would exclude from investment common stocks which yield little or no current return but which represent a steady growth through reinvestment of earnings and an increase in principal value and eventual payment of substantial dividends. It would include in investment both stocks and bonds of very high risk which are currently yielding a very high income that may disappear tomorrow.

To deal with this problem, the concept of "income" is expanded by some to include relatively long-term price appreciation so as to justify low- or even no-dividend stocks in an investment program. This makes sense to the investor in higher income tax brackets who avoids dividend income and prefers the reinvestment of corporate earnings. When he needs cash, he can sell off some of his shares and pay the lower long-term capital gains tax.

A final distinction is found in the role of analysis. The investor's appraisal of the qualitative and quantitative factors will permit him to make a rational choice and even a precise valuation of the security; the speculator is interested in market action apart from its validity. The investor asks, what is the security worth? The speculator asks, how will the price move? Close inspection of this concept reveals that even the "speculator" may investigate a situation thoroughly; to do otherwise would be to gamble. And no analysis will remove all of the uncertainties.

Analysis of these customary distinctions between the two concepts reveals that an exact line of demarcation is difficult, if not impossible, to draw. Nevertheless, they are not without value. Thinking about them requires the investor to identify his financial objectives, to decide how much risk he is willing to assume, and to plan his course of action for both the near and the longer term. Some investors can take little or no risk and must be content with a modest return; others can assume considerable risk and can base their plans on the possibility of a high return. Some investors must concentrate on high-grade bonds and other relatively safe commitments in order to assure the income that their plans require; others can logically acquire equities, provided that the selection, timing, pricing, and diversification are adequately handled. Some investors can reasonably acquire short-term holdings at little or possibly large risk, while others must frame a long-range program that minimizes risk, emphasizes income, and relies on little or much capital appreciation.

An old saying holds that a good investment is a successful speculation. The end result determines the distinction. Such a concept is useful in that it suggests that risk is a matter of degree and that some degree of risk is inevitable. The concept is dangerous, however, in that it suggests that intelligent planning and selection may not be worthwhile. There is a very wide range of securities and other media to fit a wide range of investment goals. The problem of investment is to relate the media and the goals in an intelligent fashion.

Investment Media

Many investors are not aware that many types of investment media are available. Yet no investment program can properly be constructed unless the investor has familiarized himself with the various alternatives. The very form in which funds are committed in some instances encourages, and in other cases discourages, the selection of a type. Some investment media are simple and direct, others present complex problems of analysis and investigation. Some are familiar, some are relatively strange. Some are more appropriate for one type of investor than for another.

The major investment media are described in Part II of this book, and their use in the investment programs of individuals and institutions is described in Part IV. Part V provides an approach to analysis of corporate securities, the category which presents the greatest problems of selection and valuation. At this point, however, we shall examine briefly the various forms in which investment media are classified.

Classification of investment media.

A. Classification by general form
 1. Insurance and retirement group
  (a) Life insurance
  (b) Annuities: fixed and variable

      (c) Government retirement plans; Social Security
      (d) Private pension plans: insured and trusteed
   2. Deposit group
      (a) Savings and time deposits in commercial banks
      (b) Deposits in mutual savings banks
      (c) Accounts in savings and loan associations
      (d) Shares in credit unions
   3. Securities group
      (a) Bonds, notes and stocks of business or commercial corporations
         (1) Industrial companies
         (2) Public utility companies
         (3) Transportation companies
      (b) Securities of financial companies
         (1) Investment companies: bonds and shares
         (2) Commercial bank debentures and stocks
         (3) Insurance company stocks
         (4) Securities of finance and loan companies
      (c) Government and government-sponsored securities
         (1) U.S. Government obligations: marketable and nonmarketable
         (2) State and municipal bonds
         (3) Securities of foreign governments
         (4) Bonds of federal agencies
   4. Real estate group
      (a) Real estate
         (1) For occupancy
         (2) For income and/or gain
      (b) Obligations secured by real estate
         (1) Mortgages
         (2) Mortgage-backed securities
         (3) Shares in mortgage investment trusts
   5. Business group: direct investment in business property
 B. Other classifications
   1. By investor status
   2. By security
   3. By maturity features
   4. By degree of marketability
   5. By tax status
   6. By degree of management required
   7. By degree of risk
   8. By degree of protection against price changes

Insurance group. Life insurance should be an integral part of most investment programs. Indeed it should have top priority in most financial plans. Insurance is the only means by which most investors can provide a substantial estate for dependents. And most types of contracts contain a savings or investment element that is available during the life of the insured. These aspects of insurance, and the means by which provision for retirement may be made through annuities, Social Security, and pension plans, are discussed in Chapter 3.

Deposit group. This group includes the banking-type investments held primarily for liquidity but producing some income. Four investment media belong in this group: savings and time deposits in commercial banks, deposits in mutual savings banks, accounts in savings and loan associations, and shares in credit unions. These claims on institutions provide liquidity, modest income, and (under ideal circumstances) little or no risk of dollars of principal. They are discussed in Chapter 4.

United States Savings bonds may logically be discussed in the section devoted to deposit-type investments. For millions of investors they are real rivals of banks and other depositories for liquid savings, and they offer almost the same liquidity, and certainly equal or even greater safety than deposits offer; therefore, a discussion of their characteristics is included in Chapter 4.

Securities group. Many thousands of securities of all kinds are available to the investor. The following classification is based on type of issuer, without attempt at this point to discuss the investment qualifications of the securities.

SECURITIES OF BUSINESS CORPORATIONS. These are of two general types: bonds and stocks (preferred and common). A widely used classification involves a threefold division: (1) industrials, including manufacturing, merchandising, extractive, and service concerns; (2) public utilities, including companies in electric light and power, gas, gas transmission, telephone, telegraph, water, and local transit; and (3) transportation, including railroad, trucking, airline, and bus companies. Each of these main groups can be further subdivided.

Other useful methods of classifying business corporation securities are (1) by legal status of owner: bonds (and corporate notes) and stocks; (2) by type of pledge or lien, if any: secured bonds and mortgages, and unsecured instruments, debenture bonds and stocks; (3) by purpose of issue— whether issued for specific purposes or used to finance general working capital and capital expansion needs; (4) by degree of participation in earnings—whether they bear a fixed or an uncertain income. Most bonds and preferred stock bear a fixed rate of return, while common stock has no fixed rate, receiving the net income, large or small, distributed as dividends at the discretion of directors; (5) by maturity and redemption features. Stocks, both preferred and common, have no maturity date, since they involve no promise to pay principal. However, the call feature in preferred stock, and to a certain extent its fixed liquidating value, limit the amount of any payment of capital to its holders under certain conditions. Bonds, with very few exceptions, have a definite maturity date and usually include provisions for redemption before maturity at the option of the corporation.

The above classifications are suggestive of many that may be used in studying and comparing corporate securities. Chapters 7 and 8 describe the characteristics of bonds and stocks, and offer general conclusions concerning their investment merits. A general approach to the analysis of corporate securities is set forth in Chapter 24, while Chapter 25 deals with the difficult problem of their valuation. The analysis of individual industrial, utility, and railroad securities is the content of Chapters 26–28.

SECURITIES OF FINANCIAL COMPANIES. The securities issued by four main types of private financial institutions play an important part in many investment programs: debentures, preferred stock, and common shares of investment companies; debentures and shares of commercial banks; shares in insurance companies, including nonmutual life, property, and liability companies; and bonds and shares of finance companies. Through these institutions the investor can make an indirect commitment in a portfolio of securities and other instruments. Investment companies are discussed in Chapter 9. The analysis of bank and insurance stocks, while different from that of corporate securities in general, is included in Part V (Chapters 29 and 30) so as to utilize the general approaches to analysis developed earlier in that section of the book.

GOVERNMENT SECURITIES. From the standpoint of volume, government securities take first place in the investment scene. Their importance to individual and institutional investors can scarcely be overemphasized. In addition to all banks, all insurance companies, many thousands of trust estates, endowment funds, business corporations, government agencies, and investing concerns, millions of individuals own government securities.

Three classes of government obligations are discussed in this volume: (1) direct and guaranteed debt of the United States (Chapter 5); (2) bonds of states and municipalities (Chapter 6); and (3) dollar bonds of foreign governments (Chapter 10). The first group can be subdivided by maturity, by tax status, by ownership, by marketability, by purpose of issue, and by other characteristics. State and municipal bonds are likewise divisible into various categories. A fourth category, the unguaranteed bonds of Federal agencies, are included in this group because they have the moral, if not the actual backing of the Federal government. They are discussed in Chapters 5 and 11.

Real estate group. Direct investment in real estate proper plays an important role in many investment programs. The most important form is the ownership of domestic property for occupancy. The most significant single investment that most families make is in a home. The investment aspects of home ownership are not the only ones that must be taken into consideration by the homeowner, but they are too often given scant attention. Consideration is given in Chapter 11 to the investment factors in the ownership of real estate for occupancy.

Investment in real estate for income and/or capital gain has enjoyed increasing popularity in recent years. The equity may be held directly, or indirectly through ownership in shares of real estate companies and real estate investment trusts. Because of the highly specialized characteristics of real estate investments, only slight attention is given this group in this book, and the emphasis is on income rather than capital appreciation.

Obligations secured by real estate hold an impressive place in many investment portfolios, especially those of institutions. Mortgages and other instruments are discussed in Chapter 11.

Business group. The savings of many thousands of individuals are directed toward the purchase or expansion of business ventures, especially in smaller concerns. But discussion of this type of investment would involve a discussion of business operation and management itself. Furthermore, funds invested by proprietors are not subject to rapid recovery in the marketplace. For these reasons no attempt is made in this volume to discuss this type of investment.

Other classifications. A variety of other classifications of investments is possible:

By INVESTOR STATUS. The investor is a creditor when he holds corporate and government bonds, has a savings account in a bank or other institution, owns a mortgage, or has a life insurance or annuity contract. For the most part these might be called "fixed-income obligations." The investor is an owner of "equities" when he owns preferred and common stocks or real estate or has a share in a business. (Preferred stock belongs in the ownership category, but most investors in this type of security place it in the fixed-income category because of its usually limited return and fixed liquidating value.)

By SECURITY. All equities are unsecured. Some debt instruments, such as debenture bonds of corporations, and all direct obligations of Federal, state, and local governments have no lien on specific assets, but represent general promises to pay and so are secured only by general assets and earnings. The lack of specific security does not necessarily represent a weakness. The strongest unsecured corporate obligations, together with government bonds, may receive the highest rating. Bank deposits, and claims against insurance companies, are likewise "unsecured." Secured bonds, such as mortgage bonds, have a claim to specific assets pledged for their support, in addition to a general claim.

By MATURITY FEATURES. Equities lack a maturity date because they do not represent promises to pay. As noted previously, however, preferred stocks have certain features that give them a semblance of maturity, especially the call feature by which they mature at the option of the corporation. Shares in investment companies of the open-end (mutual) type represent equity, but are redeemable on demand. This gives them maturity of a sort but not a fixed value. Perhaps we might better say that they enjoy *liquidity* rather than a definite maturity. Debt instruments, with rare exceptions, mature at a ·specified time or at optional dates, as in the case of Treasury bonds. Most life insurance contracts and annuities mature at death or retirement age.

By DEGREE OF MARKETABILITY. Marketability means access to ready purchase and sale without substantial loss owing to imperfections of the market itself. (It does not imply liquidity in the sense of little risk of loss). In the case of securities, it is measured roughly by volume of trading. Investments differ considerably with respect to marketability. Listed securities and those traded actively over-the-counter enjoy superior marketability. But many bonds and stocks have no ready market. Deposit-type investments also enjoy marketability in the sense that they are liquid. One disadvantage of mortgages and of real estate is a relative lack of marketability. The benefits of insurance and annuity contracts are transferable only under limited conditions, although the cash-surrender value of an insurance policy is available on demand.

The need of marketability varies greatly among investors. It is often most essential, and income may have to be sacrificed to obtain it.

BY TAX STATUS. The tax status of investments becomes more important as the rates of income and estate taxes increase and as the investor gets into higher tax brackets. The search for total or partial exemption plays an important part in the planning of many investors and has a significant effect on the prices and yields of certain securities. The tax status of securities is discussed in Chapter 18.

BY DEGREE OF MANAGEMENT REQUIRED. Investors differ in the degree to which they are willing and able to assume the responsibility of managing their investments. The appeal of different types of investments is, therefore, affected by their relative freedom from care. Whether the investor need spend little or much time and effort in selecting and managing his investments depends upon (1) the relative safety of the investment; (2) the degree to which the problems of management are turned over to others because of the investor's lack of time, interest, or ability; and (3) the extent to which the investment has a specialized character. United States Savings bonds are carefree because they are simple and straightforward. An annuity is carefree because of its relative safety and because the insurance company assumes the problems of portfolio management. Real estate lacks the carefree quality because it needs constant attention and requires special training and experience.

BY DEGREE OF RISK. Classification by degree of risk can be incomplete at best. With the exception of U.S. Savings bonds, risk of loss of dollars of income or principal is found in all investments. Even Treasury bonds rise and fall in market value. Deposits in insured banks and savings and loan associations may approach being riskless insofar as principal is concerned, but the income derived from deposited savings varies with the times. Life insurance companies "guarantee" a rate at which their reserves are built up, and the strong companies have a remarkable record. Corporate securities run the whole gamut from very high-grade short-term obligations to worthless stocks. Bonds as a group have a stronger record than stocks as a group. Yet each group contains a wide range of quality.

BY DEGREE OF PROTECTION AGAINST PRICE CHANGES. All investments that involve promises to pay income, principal, or both, in a fixed number of dollars, are vulnerable to the changes in the purchasing power of the dollar. Only equities (common stocks and real estate) and debt securities that are low grade or that have participation or convertible clauses offer protection against the rise in the price level, and these only imperfectly or in varying degrees. One of the tragedies of savings and investment is that the greater the need for a "hedge against inflation," the less able the investor is to afford such a hedge. The assurance of dollars of income and principal is so important to the investor of limited means that the risks involved in holding most equities is an expensive luxury.

Common stocks, shares of investing institutions such as fire insurance companies and investment trusts that hold portfolios of common stocks, and weak and speculative bonds and preferred stocks or those selling at a substantial discount, and real estate, offer possibilities of appreciation and of increased income as prices rise and thus may protect the buying value of the investor's funds and income to a certain extent. This factor is very important whenever the investment fund is designed to provide an income for living purposes. It constitutes a strong appeal for including securities of these types, along with fixed-income obligations, in many investment portfolios.

Scope of the Book

This chapter has introduced our subject by defining the nature of investment and investment media. Chapter 2 will develop further some of the economic aspects of the subject, emphasizing the flow of funds into and out of the capital market, the interrelation among the different segments of that market, and the basic influences that determine the rates of return on investments.

Intelligent planning of an investment program requires a considerable background, including knowledge of the alternative types of investment media that are classified earlier in this chapter. Chapters 3 through 11 (Part II) describe and evaluate these media. A general description of corporate securities is included here, but the more detailed approach to their analysis is reserved for later chapters.

Additional background information is provided in Part III (Chapters 12 through 18). Investors should be acquainted with the basic mathematical language used in investment calculations. Particularly important is the concept of investment yield, or rate of return expressed as a percentage of the capital investment, which in the opinion of the market, reflects the degree of risk in any investment situation. The basic concepts of investment mathematics form the subject matter of Chapter 12.

As aids to investment planning and management, the investor should be acquainted with the sources of investment information and with the types of advice that are available. These are discussed in Chapters 13 and 14.

The procedures by which investments—particularly corporate securities—originate, and the operations of the securities markets, are important segments of investment knowledge without which the investor cannot act intelligently. These matters are described in Chapters 15 and 16, while Chapter 17 is designed to acquaint the reader with the procedures through which his actual securities orders are effected.

To an increasing extent tax considerations are entering into investment planning and selection, and this situation promises to persist for many years to come. Tax matters have been singled out for special attention in Chapter 18 and are also referred to elsewhere wherever important.

We are now ready (Part IV) to consider the planning and executing of an investment program. The first step is to determine the goals toward which savings will be directed and then to analyze the various types of risks that confront the investor (Chapter 19) and the means of minimizing or avoiding them (Chapter 20). The principles that should guide the investment policy and portfolio management of individuals and institutions form the subject matter of Chapters 21 through 23.

After the goals and general media have been determined, the specific investments are selected. The major media of investments, including corporate securities, are described in Part II. However, because of their greater complexity and lack of homogeneity, a special section on the analysis of corporate securities comprises Part V of the book.

REFERENCES

AMLING, FREDERICK, *Investments: An Introduction to Analysis and Management,* 2nd. ed., Chapter 1. Englewood Cliffs, N.J.: Prentice-Hall, Inc., 1970.

BADGER, R. E., H. W. TORGERSON, AND H. G. GUTHMANN, *Investment Principles and Practices,* 6th ed., Chapter 1. Englewood Cliffs, N.J.: Prentice-Hall, Inc., 1969.

GRAHAM, BENJAMIN, *The Intelligent Investor,* 3rd. rev. ed., Chapter 1. New York: Harper & Row, Publishers, 1965.

GRAHAM, BENJAMIN, D. L. DODD, AND SIDNEY COTTLE, *Security Analysis,* 4th ed., Chapters 4, 8. New York: McGraw-Hill, Inc., 1962.

2 The Capital Market

SCOPE: This chapter describes the forces at work in the long-term segment of the investment market and its major subdivisions, and provides the economic background for an understanding of the movement of the prices and the returns available on the more important types of investment media. More detailed discussion of some of these forces is reserved for later chapters. We should note at this point that in addition to the factors associated with the particular security, mortgage, or other investment— such as its quality and marketability—general economic factors play an important part in determining its value and income. These factors include those which affect the flow of funds into and out of the capital market as a whole, and those which influence particular segments of the market. The order of discussion is (1) definition and distinctions among the capital, money, and investment markets, (2) scope of the capital market, (3) supply of funds seeking investment, (4) demand for investment funds, (5) relation of supply and demand factors to the returns available on investments, and (6) shifts or changes in actual investment yields in recent years.

The Capital, Money, and Investment Markets

In the economic sense, capital formation is the change in the stock of the capital goods represented by producers' durable equipment, new construction (including residential nonfarm construction), and business inventories. In 1971 the gross private domestic capital formation was $152 billions. After capital consumption allowances, such as for depreciation and depletion, the net figure was $58 billions, or 5.5 per cent of Gross National Product of $1,050 billions.

In a modern capitalistic economy, capital formation would be impossible without a market or group of markets for the transfer of savings (mainly through a variety of institutions) to those seeking funds for investment in economic goods and services. To effect such a transfer, a variety of instruments representing money and claims to money are employed. The savers provide the funds and expect to receive interest, dividends, or rent. The users—investors in the economic sense—offer the hope of income, price appreciation, or both.

12

In the financial sense, the *capital market* is the market for the instruments that represent longer-term funds, as distinguished from the *money market* for obligations with a year or less to maturity. It consists of a sprawling complex of institutions and mechanisms whereby intermediate-term funds (represented by loans say up to ten-year maturity) and long-term funds (represented by longer-maturity loans and corporate stocks) are pooled and made available to business, government, and individuals, and where outstanding instruments are transferred.

In the economic sense, investment means the commitment of funds to capital assets. In this sense, investors are the *users* of funds—their own or those acquired in the market. In the sense in which we shall use the term, however, investors are on the other side of the transaction. They supply the funds by acquiring debt and equity instruments with their savings, and they also transfer these instruments among each other. In financial terminology, the *investment market* includes the market(s) for funds, both short and long term. To many this term involves only the organized securities exchanges.

We shall use the term in the broad sense. Our emphasis is on the long-term segment of the investment market, including the primary sale and purchase of, and secondary transactions in, the instruments classified in the previous chapter. We shall not be concerned with short-term borrowing or lending (save by the Federal government), consumer credit, general agricultural credit, or highly specialized forms of real estate credit.

As contrasted with the capital market, the money market provides facilities for the transfer of short-term debt instruments. The direct or customers' market is found wherever banks and other financial firms supply short-term credit to customers. The open market is mainly the complex of facilities in New York where idle funds, drawn from all over the country, are transferred through intermediaries. The suppliers of such funds are the Federal Reserve Banks, commercial banks, business corporations with idle funds, insurance companies, foreign banks and investors, financial companies, state and local governments, and individuals. The users are other commercial banks, finance companies, business firms, the Federal Reserve Banks, state and local governments, the U.S. Treasury, securities brokers, and dealers in "street" loans. The institutions serving as intermediaries are chiefly the Federal Reserve Banks, large commercial money-market banks, and dealers in government securities. The instruments used are chiefly Federal funds (excess member bank reserves), short-term government securities, bankers' acceptances, and prime commercial paper.

Any firm distinction between the money and capital markets is somewhat arbitrary. Suppliers of funds may direct them to one or to both markets, and users of funds may draw funds from either market. Furthermore, funds flow back and forth between the two. And some institutions serve both markets. Rates in the two are interrelated with changes in the general demand for and supply of funds.

Perhaps the chief characteristic distinguishing the two markets is the liquidity and quality of the instruments that are issued and transferred. Federal funds are real money. Short-term government and commercial paper are "near-money" instruments, subject to very slight price risk. The longer-

term instruments issued in or traded in the capital market, especially corporate stocks, show considerable price variation.

Scope of the Capital Market

The financial importance in 1950–1971 of the long-term or capital market is
indicated by the data in Table 2-1 on the size of the major components
that compete for funds. The government debt figures include all maturities
unless otherwise noted.

Table 2-1. SELECTED MEDIA IN THE CAPITAL MARKET, 1950–1971
(at year-end, in billions of dollars)

	1950	1955	1960	1965	1968	1971
U.S. Govt. debt						
Total	$257	$281	$290	$321	$358	$424
Marketable	153	163	189	215	237	262
Due in over 1 year	99	97	105	121	128	143
Federally sponsored agency debt						
(nonguaranteed)	2	3	8	14	22	43
State and local govt. debt						
Total	27	48	75	107	133	172
Long-term securities	24	44	67	95	115	147
Corporate long-term debt						
Net long-term	60	90	139	209	281	392
Bonds outstanding (domestic)	37	59	85	116	157	217
Domestic corporate stock						
(market value)						
Total	160[a]	283	395	709	968	995
Listed	111	239	335	573	760	796
Over-the-counter	39[a]	37[a]	53[a]	120	168	137
Mortgage debt						
Total	73	130	207	326	398	500
Residential (1–4 family)	45	88	141	213	251	308

[a]Estimated.

SOURCES: *Federal Reserve Bulletin* (including flow-of-funds tables); *Survey of Current Business;*
Securities and Exchange Commission, *Annual Reports* and *Statistical Bulletin; Treasury Bulletin;* U.S.
Department of Commerce, Bureau of the Census, *Summary of Government Finances* (Annual).

Bonds. At the end of 1971, the direct Federal government debt (including guaranteed obligations of the Federal Housing Administration) stood
at $424 billions, a record-high figure. And this total was expected to increase
substantially in 1972. Excluding U.S. Savings bonds and other nontransferable obligations, the marketable debt was $262 billions. Of this amount,
$173 billions was held by "the public"—commercial banks, other institutions,
and individuals. Longer-term debt moves steadily into the short-term category. And all maturities are so closely interrelated with respect to both
supply and demand that attention to only the long-term portion is somewhat
arbitrary. But it is interesting to note that at the end of 1971 only $143

billions or 54 per cent of the marketable debt had a maturity of over one year, that is, belonged in our "capital market" category. The reasons for the emphasis on shorter-term financing are discussed in Chapter 5.

The unguaranteed debt of Federal credit agencies represents obligations of high quality whose yields are only slightly above those of Federal securities of equal maturity. (See Chapter 5).

State and local government debt has expanded greatly in the postwar period. Of the total of $172 billions at the end of 1971, $147 billions of long-term securities were outstanding.

Net corporate long-term debt of $392 billions at the end of 1971 includes debt over one year to maturity, including bonds, mortgages, term loans, and net long-term trade credit, but excludes intercorporate debt. The figure of $217 billions of bonds (domestic corporations) is the most important for our purposes. We should note that listed domestic corporate bond issues, with a total par value of approximately $131 billions, constituted about 60 per cent of total bonds outstanding. But in terms of number of issues, most publicly held corporate bond issues are traded over-the-counter (see Chapter 16).

Corporate stocks. The estimated value of all domestic corporate stocks outstanding was $995 billions at the end of 1971. There are about 1½ million active business corporations in the United States, but most of these are relatively small. Stocks of the major corporations are listed on the organized exchanges or traded on the over-the-counter market. At the end of 1971, listed corporate stocks, both preferred and common, had a market value of $796 billions. Unlisted stocks were worth about $137 billions, exclusive of shares of investment companies and foreign companies.[1]

Real estate mortgages. Real estate mortgages outstanding at the end of 1971 totalled $500 billions. Of this, $33 billions was farm debt; the balance represented the financing of one- to four-family residential properties ($308 billions), multifamily residences ($67 billions), and industrial and commercial properties ($92 billions).

The above are the major components of the investment market. Long-term funds also flow into and out of unincorporated businesses, into and out of real estate ownership, and into and out of foreign governments and businesses.

Supply of Investment Funds

Funds for investment are derived from five main sources: (1) individual savings, (2) business savings, (3) bank credit, (4) government funds, and (5) foreign funds. These funds flow mainly into the purchase of homes, the

---

[1]Source: Securities and Exchange Commission, *Statistical Bulletin*. April 1972, p. 22. The total of $995 billions is net after intercorporate holdings, but includes closely held (untraded) stock ($179 billions).

expansion of business capital assets and inventories, and the financing of government activities.

Individual savings. Individual savings find their way into real estate, into durable consumer goods, into claims against institutions which invest in a variety of assets, and into securities. But some savings are "negative"; that is, they are used to repay mortgage, consumer, and other debt (such funds can be reloaned or reinvested by creditors). And as we saw in Chapter 1, most securities purchased do not represent new capital. They are "secondhand" securities already outstanding, so that transactions in them represent merely a transfer of funds from one investor to another.

The most familiar measure of personal savings is the U.S. Department of Commerce figure of disposable personal income less personal outlays shown in Table 2-2.

Table 2-2. TRENDS IN "PERSONAL SAVING," 1950–1971
            (in billions of dollars)[a]

Item	1950	1955	1960	1965	1966	1967	1968	1969	1971
Personal income	$227.6	$310.9	$401.0	$538.9	$587.2	$629.3	$688.9	$750.3	$861.4
Less personal tax and nontax payments	20.7	35.5	50.9	65.7	75.4	83.0	97.9	116.2	117.0
Disposable personal income	206.9	275.3	350.0	473.2	511.9	546.3	591.0	634.2	744.4
Less personal outlays[b]	193.9	259.5	333.0	444.8	479.3	506.0	551.2	596.3	683.4
Equals personal saving	13.1	15.8	17.0	28.4	32.5	40.4	39.8	37.9	60.9
Personal saving as a percentage of disposable income	6.3%	5.7%	4.9%	6.0%	6.3%	7.4%	6.7%	6.0%	8.2%

[a]Statistical discrepancies are the result of rounding.

[b]Personal consumption expenditures, consumer interest payments, and transfer payments to foreigners.

SOURCES: U.S. Department of Commerce, *Business Statistics*, 1965, and *Survey of Current Business*.

The ratio of personal saving to disposable personal income has varied from year to year. During World War II it climbed to over 20 per cent, largely because people were unable to buy many types of consumer goods. It ran between 5 and 6 per cent in the early 1960s, but increased greatly in 1967–1970, and reached over 8 per cent in 1971. This reflected individuals' reluctance to spend and contributed substantially to the economic stagnation within that period.

The fact that individuals "saved" a certain total amount according to U.S. Department of Commerce figures does not mean that they added only that much to their holdings of cash assets, securities, and insurance and pension reserves. These assets can be increased by funds diverted from other uses. Table 2-3 shows the annual gross increase in financial assets 1950–1971. The figure rose sharply in 1965–1971 as funds were poured into deposit-type investments and into reserves. In 1971, for example, gross financial savings were $100 billions, compared to "personal saving" of $61 billions. But a large amount of debt was also paid off. The net financial savings, plus in-

Table 2-3. "INDIVIDUALS' SAVINGS," 1950–1971
         (in billions of dollars)

Item	1950	1955	1960	1965	1968	1971
Currency and demand deposits	$ 2.2	$ .8	$ −1.9	$ 7.3	$ 12.8	$ 8.6
Savings accounts	2.5	8.8	12.4	26.4	30.4	73.5
Securities						
U.S. Savings bonds	.3	.3	−.3	.6	.4	2.4
Other U.S. Govt. and agency	−.5	2.2	−.2	1.5	4.2	−25.1
State and local govt. bonds	.6	3.4	3.4	2.3	−.2	4.9
Corporate and foreign bonds	−.8	1.1	.2	.7	6.8	7.6
Investment company shares	.2	.9	1.5	3.1	4.7	1.3
Other corporate stock	.4	.2	−1.9	−5.0	−12.3	−10.4
	.2	8.1	2.6	3.3	3.5	−19.2
Misc. financial assets	1.9	1.9	3.0	1.9	5.9	6.5
Private insurance and pension reserves	5.1	6.6	8.4	12.4	13.9	17.2
Govt. insurance and pension reserves	1.8	1.8	3.3	4.8	6.0	9.8
Gross increase in financial assets	13.7	27.9	27.7	56.0	72.4	96.3
Increase in debt						
Home mortgage debt	7.4	12.2	10.8	15.2	14.9	24.5
Other mortgage debt	1.8	2.1	2.4	6.6	6.6	11.3
Consumer credit	4.1	6.4	4.6	10.0	11.1	10.4
Other debt	3.4	4.7	3.0	7.3	10.8	13.4
	16.7	25.4	20.7	39.2	43.3	59.6
Net financial saving	−3.0	2.5	7.0	16.8	29.1	36.7
Net investment in tangible assets	30.3	31.1	21.7	35.8	37.2	46.4
Individuals' savings	$ 27.3	$ 33.6	$ 28.7	$ 52.6	$ 66.3	$ 83.1

SOURCES: Securities and Exchange Commission, *Statistical Bulletin; Federal Reserve Bulletin.* Data may not add due to rounding.

creased investment in tangible assets, produced a figure of $83 billions of total "individuals' savings." This figure includes savings of farms, unincorporated business, trust funds, and nonprofit institutions.[2]

As indicated in the table, a large part of the savings of individuals does

[2]A reconciliation of the Securities and Exchange Commission and the U.S. Department of Commerce series appeared in the April 1970 issue of the S.E.C. *Statistical Bulletin.*

not flow directly into securities and mortgages but is invested by financial institutions serving as intermediaries between the savers and the money and capital markets. The growth of savings institutions is discussed in Chapters 3 and 4. The flow of savings into securities is discussed in Chapters 5–9.

Business savings. Savings of farmers and unincorporated businesses were included in personal savings as discussed above. The major portion of business savings, however, is produced by nonfinancial corporations and is represented by retained profits. Depletion and depreciation allowances, while not savings in the technical sense, also provide funds for replacement and expansion. Funds from these internal sources, together with the proceeds of sale of new securities and the incurring of other debt, are used to finance the increases in operating assets, cash assets, and investments in other companies, and to reduce debt.

Table 2-4. SOURCES AND USES OF FUNDS, NONFARM NONFINANCIAL CORPORATIONS, 1950–1971

(in billions of dollars)

Item	1950	1955	1960	1965	1968	1971
Sources of funds:						
Internal						
Retained profits	$ 14.3	$ 13.9	$ 10.0	$ 23.1	$ 19.9	$ 14.5
Inventory valuation	−5.0	−1.7	.2	−1.7	−3.3	−4.7
Depreciation and depletion	8.6	17.0	24.2	35.2	45.1	57.3
Total internal	$ 17.9	$ 29.2	$ 34.4	$ 56.6	$ 61.7	$ 67.1
External						
Stocks	1.4	1.9	1.6	—	−.8	13.4
Bonds	1.6	2.8	3.5	5.4	12.9	19.4
Mortgages	.9	1.8	2.8	3.9	5.8	11.2
Bank and other loans	3.5	4.0	3.8	11.2	12.9	4.5
Trade debt	8.2	7.9	3.6	9.4	10.4	3.4
Other (mainly short-term)	8.4	6.6	1.8	6.8	7.0	7.7
Total external	$ 24.0	$ 25.1	$ 13.7	$ 36.5	$ 48.1	$ 59.6
Total sources	$ 41.9	$ 54.2	$ 48.1	$ 93.1	$109.8	$ 126.7
Uses of funds:						
Fixed assets	19.3	26.6	36.0	54.8	69.7	84.1
Increase in inventories	4.8	5.1	3.0	7.0	6.4	1.1
Increase in cash and govt. securities	4.4	5.1	−4.6	.8	2.4	7.8
Increase in trade credit	11.8	11.4	5.3	15.1	13.9	4.0
Increase in other financial assets	1.6	2.1	4.1	7.3	·7.1	9.9
Total uses	$ 41.9	$ 50.1	$ 43.7	$ 85.9	$ 99.5	$ 106.9
Discrepancy (uses less sources)	$ .0	$ −4.2	$ −4.3	$ −7.2	$ −10.3	$ −19.8

SOURCE: U.S. Department of Commerce, Bureau of the Census, *Survey of Current Business*. Data may not add due to rounding.

As shown by Table 2-4, the internal sources, including "savings," have been much more important in financing business expansion than the external sources. But although retained profits and funds representing depreciation are placed directly in corporate assets, and thus circumvent the investment market, they nevertheless have an effect on the market. When corporations choose to finance their needs from such sources, fewer securities are sold. By the same token, funds which might otherwise have been distributed to stockholders are placed in business assets just as if they had been paid out and then reinvested by the stockholders.

Our main interest lies in that portion of corporate savings which, together with long-term external sources, is devoted to relatively permanent uses and thus directly or indirectly affects the flow of funds into and out of the capital market.

Bank credit. Commercial bank credit is a basic source of funds for use by industry and government. It serves as an interim or temporary source pending more permanent financing, and as a supplementary source of investable funds when the flow of savings is inadequate in relation to expansion of capital equipment, inventories, and governmental services.

Commercial bank credit is used chiefly for short-term purposes. But banks also play a secondary but nevertheless important role as suppliers of intermediate- and long-term credit. A substantial portion of bank assets is represented by mortgages, term loans, and bond investment.

Thus banks not only channel into productive use the individual and business savings left with them, they also supply additional credit that increases the supply of capital and makes possible increased total spending by business and government.

The limits to bank credit expansion affect the supply of long-term as well as short-term funds. These limits are set by the reserve position of the banking system, and this in turn is affected by the banks' own liquidity, and more importantly, by Federal Reserve policy. Thus the "tight money" policy of the Federal Reserve in 1955–1959, 1965–1966, and 1969–1970 restricted the flow of bank funds into investments and was one of the two main causes of increasing interest rates. The other was the pressure of demand for investment funds in all segments of the capital and money markets that was not matched by the flow of savings. The whole pattern of prices and yields on securities, mortgages, bonds, and, to a certain extent, stocks, is influenced by the money supply and its regulation. Insofar as bond prices and yields are concerned, the open-market operations of the Federal Reserve and, to a lesser extent, the discount rate, are the most effective weapons of bank credit control.[3]

Government funds. A fourth source of investment funds is the flow of tax money into Federal and municipal bonds and corporate securities

---

[3]Changes in the discount rate are one of three major "indirect" methods by which the Federal Reserve influences the supply of bank credit; the others are (1) open-market operations, the purchase or sale of Treasury bonds by the Federal Reserve Banks so as to increase or diminish the member banks' reserve account positions; and (2) changes in the member-bank legal reserve account (deposit at the central bank) ratio, expressed as a percentage of bank deposits. Reductions in the reserve ratio mean that bank loans and deposits can be increased with no increase in the dollar amount of legal reserves.

acquired by government trust and retirement funds, and of funds invested in mortgages and securities by Federally sponsored agencies and corporations.

Foreign funds. Foreign investors provide a fluctuating and occasionally substantial supply of net funds to the American economy. This flow is directed mainly to short-term instruments, but the foreign demand for American business securities is growing.

Demand for Investment Funds

The demand for investment funds (or, the supply of available investments) comes from three major users: individuals, business, and government. Each of these may be subdivided into different categories.

Individuals use long-term funds chiefly for the financing of residential real estate. The significance of this demand during the period following World War II is indicated by Table 2-5. (The data do not include com-

Table 2-5. PRIVATE RESIDENTIAL REAL ESTATE FINANCING, 1950–1971
(dollar figures in billions)

Item	1950	1955	1960	1965	1968	1971
Number of private housing starts (in thousands)	1,908	1,627	1,252	1,473	1,508	2,052
Nonfarm mortgage recordings ($20,000 and under)	$16.2	$28.5	$29.3	*a*	*a*	*a*
Less: Repayments on mortgages	8.6	15.9	18.9	*a*	*a*	*a*
Annual increase in mortgages outstanding:						
One- to four-family	$ 7.6	$12.6	$10.4	$15.4	$15.2	$27.6*b*
Multifamily	1.5	.8	1.6	3.6	3.4	8.8*b*

*a*Not available.
*b*Preliminary.
SOURCES: *Federal Reserve Bulletin*, flow-of-funds tables; Federal Home Loan Bank Board.

mercial or farm mortgages.) The first postwar peak figure of $28.5 billions of new home mortgage debt was reached in 1955. This great demand for mortgage money, together with other demands for individual, business, and government use, was not matched by the funds available, and late in 1954 interest rates in general began a rise that by the autumn of 1957 carried them to their highest level in twenty-six years. After a decline in demand in 1958, mortgage financing contributed to a pressure on total available capital market funds that brought yields to a new postwar peak late in 1959. Thereafter, although real estate financing increased each year, the supply of institutional funds was substantial enough to prevent an equivalent increase in yields until 1966, when "tight money" conditions again prevailed, housing starts dropped sharply, and mortgage yields again reached new highs. In early 1967 there was a modest decline in yields as more funds became available, but the second "credit crunch" in 1969–1970 drove mortgage yields to the highest levels in history. (See Chapter 11.)

In 1971–1972 a substantial reversal took place. Savings flowed into mortgage-lending institutions at a high rate, and mortgage yields declined. Private housing starts reached the annual rate of over 2 millions by mid-1971, and this level continued through 1972.

Business demand for investment funds is reflected mainly in the increase in corporate security offerings when internal sources are not sufficient to finance expansion. As shown by Table 2-6, during the period since World War II total new corporate security offerings have steadily increased as a means of financing increased inventory and plant requirements. Bonds

Table 2-6. NEW CORPORATE SECURITIES OFFERED FOR CASH, 1950–1971

(in millions of dollars)

		Bonds				Total	Total Net
	Total	*Publicly Offered*	*Privately Offered*	*Preferred Stock*	*Common Stock*	*Gross Proceeds*	*"New Money"*
1950	$ 4,920	$ 2,360	$2,560	$ 631	$ 811	$ 5,342	$ 4,006
1955	7,420	4,119	3,301	635	2,185	10,240	7,957
1960	8,081	4,806	3,275	409	1,664	10,154	8,758
1965	13,720	5,570	8,150	725	1,547	15,992	13,063
1966	15,561	8,019	7,542	574	1,939	18,074	15,806
1967	21,954	14,990	6,964	885	1,959	24,798	22,230
1968	17,383	10,732	6,651	637	3,946	21,966	a
1969	18,347	12,734	5,613	682	7,714	26,744	a
1970	30,315	25,384	4,931	1,390	7,240	38,945	a
1971	32,123	24,775	7,354	3,670	9,291	45,084	a

*a*Not available.

SOURCE: Securities and Exchange Commission, *Annual Reports* and *Statistical Bulletin*.

played an increasing role until 1968–1969, when the volume of this financing fell off somewhat with the growing credit strain that culminated in the "credit crunch" of 1969–1970. The immense increase in bond financing in 1970 is, at first sight, somewhat surprising in view of the high interest rates with which the year opened. The fact that bond interest (unlike dividends on stock) reduces taxable corporate income was an important factor. Even with yields on high-grade corporate bonds at 8 to 9 per cent, the after-tax cost of borrowed capital was still substantially lower than that of common stock, for most companies.

The rise in volume of bond financing was maintained through 1971–1972, reflecting the need on the part of many companies to bolster their cash positions after the "liquidity crisis" of 1970. It is interesting to note that privately placed (unregistered) bond issues have declined in volume in recent years. Their chief buyers, the life insurance companies, have turned, in part, to other less traditional types of investments. (See Chapter 23.)

The decline in preferred stock offerings until 1964–1965 reflects the relative disadvantage of this type of financing from the standpoint of the issuer's tax position as compared to long-term debt, and its waning appeal to investors who increasingly prefer either the safety of debt instruments or the appreciation possibilities of common stock. The substantial amount of preferred stock financing in 1965–1969 is accounted for primarily by a large volume of convertible issues, whose main appeal lies in the holder's option to exchange for common. In 1969–1971 the need of public utility companies for equity financing that at the same time offered some advantages of fixed cost of capital led them to issue preferred stock in order to relieve high-debt financial structures. (See Chapter 27.) The very substantial increase in 1971 is mainly attributable to the $1,375,000,000 issue of American Telephone and Telegraph Co. convertible preferred stock in June of that year.

The volume of common stock financing has varied with the changing need for new capital, the economic outlook, the pattern of interest rates, and the general level of stock prices. In 1955–1957, in 1959, and especially in 1961, stock financing was significant. Lower volume in 1958, and 1960 reflects the recessions in those years, and the great decline in 1962 resulted from the break in stock prices in that year which discouraged new stock issuance. Even in 1963, in spite of continued economic expansion, there was no shift to this type of equity financing. Debt continued to have appeal and internal sources of funds, bolstered by accelerated depreciation, provided ample funds for corporate growth. The large increases in 1968–1971 reflected the use of conservative financing to retire short-term debt, improve financial structures, and help finance continued investment in new capital assets.

Because some new securities are issued for refinancing purposes, the proceeds of securities sold for "new money," shown in Table 2-6, are substantially less than the gross volume of financing. Nevertheless, when a company sells a refunding bond issue this affects the market because it must compete for funds with other issues.

Business demand for long-term funds is also reflected in the annual volume of multifamily (apartment) and commercial mortgage financing which reached an all-time high of $19 billions in 1971, or 30 per cent of total mortgage financing.

Public or government demand for funds is indicated by the offering of new Federal, state, and local securities and by bond issues sold by federal agencies and foreign governments (see Table 2-7).

A large part of the public securities are issued to retire existing debt. Nevertheless, they compete for funds in the capital market and thus have a significant effect on the general pattern of interest rates.

The large volume of Federal government and agency financing in years like 1967, 1970 and 1971 is explained in Chapter 5. When this has been accompanied by high municipal government and corporate bond sales, the great total demand for borrowed funds helps to explain the record high bond yields that have prevailed in recent years (see p. 26). New public financing continued very high in 1971 and 1972, but the substantial increase in funds available for investment produced some decline in required yields.

We should note in passing the increasing significance of financing by state

Table 2-7. NEW ISSUES OF PUBLIC SECURITIES, 1950–1971
GROSS PROCEEDS

(in millions of dollars)

Issue	1950	1955	1960	1965	1966	1967	1969	1971
U.S. Govt.	$ 9,687	$ 9,628	$ 7,906	$ 9,348	$ 8,231	$19,431	$ 4,765	$17,325
Federal agencies[a]	30	746	1,672	2,731	6,896	8,180	8,617	16,283
State and local govt.	3,532	5,977	7,230	11,148	11,089	14,268	11,460	24,370
Other[b]	282	182	579	889	815	1,817	1,531	2,165
Total	$13,531	$16,533	$17,387	$24,116	$26,941	$43,716	$26,373	$60,143

[a]Nonguaranteed issues.

[b]Includes foreign government and World Bank bonds.

SOURCES: Securities and Exchange Commission, *Statistical Bulletin*; *Federal Reserve Bulletin*.

and local governments, which, in recent years, has accounted for a growing percentage of total government and corporate securities issued.

But newly issued mortgages and securities make up only a small part of the total supply of investments. They only add to the existing securities already outstanding—the "secondhand" securities that are also available. The significance of this "secondhand" market is indicated by Table 2-1 at the beginning of this chapter.

Return on Investments

Rates of return in the various segments of the capital market tend to rise and fall together, reflecting the conditions of supply and demand prevailing in the whole market. In addition, investment funds are frequently shifted from one segment of the market to the other; each segment thus competes to a certain extent with each of the other segments. However, special influences, both of supply and demand, and of regulation and control, make each main type of investment somewhat independent, and thus the available returns are seldom if ever uniform.

Later we shall discuss the special influences that determine the yields available on each of the major types of investments. At this point only some of the major factors will be outlined. These influences are over and above the ebb and flow of supply and demand for investment funds in general.

U. S. Government securities. The chief special influences on this group are the monetary policy of the Federal Reserve system and the fiscal and debt management policy of the Treasury (see Chapter 5). Federal Reserve policy influences the prices and yields on Government securities directly through the changing holdings of securities by the Federal Reserve Banks. More indirectly, policy influences the relative appeal of Government securities as commercial bank assets, compared to loans. Fiscal and debt management by the Treasury is influential through the amount and maturities of Government securities offered or retired. Yields on marketable Federal obligations would be "pure interest" rates if it were not for the impact of these special influences. In addition, the rates of return on U.S. Savings bonds and other nonmarketable types of Federal debt are fixed by legislation, and may or may not match the going rates on marketable bonds.

Corporate bonds. The course of prices and yields of high-grade corporate bonds is discussed in Chapter 7. These movements are influenced chiefly by the "bellwether" Government bond yields, and by the volume of new financing and the supply of funds in this segment of the market. The spread between yields on Government bonds and high-grade corporate bonds reflects the fact that the latter are private obligations and, in many cases, have much poorer marketability. A special influence on this category of investments is the institutional market. Life insurance companies, banks, corporate trustees, pension funds, and other institutional buyers are the major market for high-grade corporate bonds, and the ebb and flow of savings into and out of these institutions has an important impact on the whole bond market. Also, these institutions may shift their funds from one category of investments to another within the limits set by governing regulations.

Prices and yields of second-grade corporate bonds are also influenced by the trend of long-term interest rates. But since the payment of their interest and principal is less certain, they are also affected by the outlook for corporate profits. And within the whole category of corporate bonds, the quality of the individual issues, their marketability, maturity, and special features cause their prices and yields to differ at any one moment of time.

State and local government bonds. Prices and yields in this group reflect supply and demand conditions in the bond market as a whole, as well as three special factors: (1) the volume and timing of new offerings, (2) the exemption of interest from income taxation (Federal and that of the issuing jurisdiction), and (3) the vacillating demand by commercial banks. (See Chapter 6.) The outpouring of state and municipal bonds in the postwar period would have lifted the yields on these bonds to a *relatively* high level except for their tax appeal and the increasing bank demand. Yields did reach record highs in 1970 in line with the high level of bond yields as a whole, but in 1971–1972 were substantially lower.

Mortgages. This category is more specialized than any of the others. The rise and wane of savings and the special institutional demand for mortgages and the fluctuating demand for funds needed for real estate financing are the important influences. Government restrictions also affect the available yields of certain types of mortgages such as FHA-insured and VA-guaranteed mortgage loans. (See Chapter 11.) And yields on all mortgages are consistently higher than those on high-grade bonds because of their specialized character, poorer marketability, and awkward denominations. Mortgage interest rates also reflect substantial regional differences, although widespread institutional demand has tended to reduce the local differentials somewhat.

Corporate stocks. While bonds and stocks in general appeal to different types of investors, all have the privilege of choosing between the two. And many users of capital also have a choice between borrowing and selling stock. Thus, some relationship should exist between the yields on "bond money" and "stock money," and this is true in so far as preferred stocks are concerned. Dividends on common stock can also be regarded as a return on capital. As bond prices and yields rise and fall, so, theoretically, should common stock prices and yields rise and fall, to the extent that stock prices are influenced by general forces of supply and demand for long-term capital. And one would expect a rather consistent spread between the yields on the two types of securities.

For over three decades, from the early 1930s to the mid-1960s, this relationship failed to appear. Except in occasional years the two series went their separate ways. The dividend yield on the Standard & Poor's Industrial Stock Series declined from nearly 300 per cent of the yield on the same service's high-grade bond series in 1950 to 40 per cent in late 1972. In the "credit crunch" years of 1966 and 1969–1970, however, bond and stock prices both declined, and yields on both types of securities increased. A major cause of weakness in stock prices was the high level of interest rates that made bonds attractive to both individuals and institutions. But improved stock prices, and declining bond yields, in 1971–1972, still left stock yields far below those on fixed-income securities.

The prices and yields of stock are swayed by factors that are even more potent than the supply of or demand for investment funds in general, notably the outlook for the economy as a whole, and for corporate profits in particular. These forces will be discussed in greater detail in Chapter 8.

As we shall see, preferred stocks represent investments that, like bonds, usually provide a fixed return. However, because they represent ownership, preferred stocks should command a higher return than high-grade bonds with similar earnings protection. But their special income tax advantage to corporate owners depresses their yields below those of bonds of equal quality (see p.135). Changes in prices and yields through time are caused chiefly by (1) the general factors affecting bonds and (2) the earnings prospects of their issuers. Very high-grade preferred stocks move in the market like bonds; the lower the quality of the preferred stock, the more its price and yield movements resemble those of common stocks.

The Course of Investment Yields

The general discussion above of the factors at work in the investment market has been confined to the broad categories of investments without taking into account the substantial differences that exist, in almost all of the major categories, with respect to quality and individual features. Methods of analyzing individual securities from the standpoint of quality, as well as more detailed attention to their special characteristics, are reserved for later chapters.

But the impact of the general factors discussed above can be seen at work in data that show the changing pattern of investment returns. Table 2-8 shows representative interest rates and yields in various segments of the

Table 2-8. VARIATIONS IN INTEREST RATES AND SECURITIES YIELDS, 1961–1971

Investment Medium	Mid-1961	Sept. 1966	May 1967	Jan 1970	Mar. 1971	Sept. 1972
Short-term credit						
Federal funds	1.10%	5.40%	3.95%	9.00%	3.70%	4.50%
U.S. Govt., 3-month bills	2.25	5.35	3.60	7.90	3.40	4.85
U.S. Govt., 9 to 12-month issues	2.80	5.80	3.90	7.50	3.60	4.60
Prime commercial paper, 4–6 months	2.70	5.90	4.65	8.80	4.20	5.40
Prime bankers' acceptances, 90-day	2.75	5.75	4.40	8.65	3.80	5.10
Stock exchange call loans	4.50	6.25	5.25	8.75	5.50	4.85
Bank prime rate	4.50	6.00	5.50	8.50	5.25	5.25
Federal Reserve discount rate	3.00	4.50	4.00	6.00	4.75	4.50
Medium-term credit						
U.S. Govt., 3- to 5-year issues	3.70	5.60	4.70	8.15	4.75	6.15
Municipal bonds, high-grade, 5 years	2.50	3.80	3.50	5.80	4.25	4.00
Corporate bonds, high-grade, 5 years	3.90	6.30	5.35	8.80	7.00	6.75
Term loans to business, prime	4.75	6.25	5.75	8.75	7.50	6.25
Long-term credit						
U.S. Govt., Treasury bonds	3.90	4.80	4.75	6.85	5.70	5.65
Municipal bonds, long-term (Moody's Aaa)	3.35	3.95	3.70	6.40	5.00	5.20
Corporate bonds, long-term (Moody's Aaa)	4.40	5.50	5.25	7.90	7.20	7.10
Corporate bonds, long-term (Moody's Baa)	5.10	6.10	6.00	8.85	8.45	8.10
Mortgage loans, FHA-insured (nominal rate)	5.50	6.00	6.00	8.50	7.50	7.00
Mortgage loans, residential, conventional	6.00	6.65	6.45	8.35	7.60	7.60
Savings institutions						
Commercial bank passbook accounts	3.00	4.00	4.00	4.50	4.50	4.00
Mutual savings bank accounts	3.50	4.50	4.75	5.00	5.00	4.50
Savings and loan assoc. passbook accounts	4.50	4.75	4.75	5.00	5.00	5.00
U.S. Savings bonds, Series E, to maturity	3.75	4.15	4.15	5.00	5.50	5.50
Stocks						
Preferred (Standard & Poor's)	4.70	5.25	5.20	7.00	6.50	7.00
Common stock (Standard & Poor's)	3.00	3.75	3.20	3.55	3.10	2.80

financial markets in the 1961–1972 period. The dates selected are those at which yields in general were at the extreme highs and lows. Although we are mainly concerned with the course of yields on long-term instruments, short- and intermediate-term rates are included, along with returns available at savings institutions.

In mid-1961 relatively easy credit conditions prevailed. The economic expansion into 1965 brought a modest increase in rates, which culminated in "tight money" conditions and the "credit crunch" of 1966. By the autumn of that year, most short- and long-term rates reached their highest postwar peaks. Nonmarket rates such as the Federal Reserve discount rate, the nominal (contractual) yield on FHA-insured mortgages, and yields on savings had also been adjusted upward.

With the lessening of the credit crisis, yields declined in early 1967. But renewed economic expansion and enormous demands for credit and capital funds, and a severe shortage of both long- and short-term money, drove most yields to their highest levels in history by the beginning of 1970, in the second postwar "crunch." Severe liquidity problems of corporations aggravated conditions in the financial markets and helped to produce an almost panic condition, of which the "prime" rate of 8½ per cent was ample evidence.

The subsequent decline in some yields, especially the short-term, in the first quarter of 1971, was steeper than in any equivalent period in history. More bank credit was available. Federal Reserve policy was one of easing credit, and savings available for long-term investment were greatly expanded. But, as discussed later, all yields did not change in like degree. Continued large demands for long-term funds, depressing political and social developments, and continued concern about corporate liquidity (especially after the bankruptcy of the Penn Central Company in June) produced wide differentials among the rates on different types of financial instruments. During the remainder of 1971 most market yields vacillated around a lower average. Short-term rates were eased by continual expansion of the money supply. That the "credit crunch" was over is well evidenced by the decline in the prime rate to 4½ per cent in early 1972. Rates paid on savings deposits also began to weaken at that time. Yields on long-term bonds and mortgages held fairly steady. Then short-term market rates and the prime rate increased in the remainder of 1972.

The table reveals the variations in the general rate structure of the total money and capital markets from time to time. It also shows that ordinarily, regardless of the height or depth of the general pattern of interest rates, shorter maturities bear lower yields than longer maturity obligations of the same type. The table also shows, however, that as interest rates rise, the influence of the difference in maturity declines. Indeed, in periods of very "tight money" conditions, such as in 1966 and 1970, some short-term rates push above long-term rates. In 1959, for example, yields on one-year Treasury bonds had exceeded those on long-term Federal obligations. More normal relationships between short- and long-term rates prevailed until late 1965—mid-1966, although, as a result of the Administration policy of keeping short-term rates high to prevent gold outflow, and long-term rates low to encourage expansion, the spread between maturities was smaller than in previous "normal" periods. By the middle of 1966, the "yield curve" again showed higher short-term than long-term yields, and very little difference between intermediate- and long-term yields; that is, the curve was flat after an early hump. Although all yields declined in early 1967, the hump persisted.

The "crunch" of 1970 shows that during and after periods of severe credit and capital crisis, although all yields change dramatically, the greatest variation takes place in the short-term group. The yield on 91-day Treasury bills rose from 3.60 per cent in May 1967 to 7.90 per cent in January 1970, then fell to 3.40 per cent in March 1971. Normally, over any extended period, long-term instruments bear higher yields than short-term paper of equal quality. But panic conditions reverse this relationship. The 9.00 per cent rate on Federal funds (excess member bank reserves borrowed for possibly only a few hours or days) in early 1970 is a dramatic example. During most of 1971 and 1972, the normal pattern of higher long- than short-term rates was restored.

Differences in the quality of investments have an obvious influence on the returns that will satisfy investors. Other things being equal, the higher the risk, the higher the rate. As the table shows, U.S. Government obligations, with their "riskless' characteristics, bear the lowest rates (with the exception of municipal bonds) in any particular maturity group and at any time, regardless of the general level of rates. High-grade bonds yield lower rates of return than medium-grade bonds. Bankers' acceptances (drafts honored by banks) and prime commercial paper (short-term unsecured notes of large firms with high credit standing) bear lower rates than prime direct short-term business loans. Marketable good-grade and high-grade bonds bear lower rates than real estate mortgages except under the unusual circumstances that prevailed in 1970–1971. (See Chapter 11.) In relating quality to yields, however, two special factors should be mentioned. The lower yields of municipal bonds, as compared to Treasury obligations, are attributable to the exclusion of municipal bond interest payments from income subject to federal income taxes. Yields on high-grade preferred stocks are similarly depressed by their tax advantage: Taxed *corporate* investors enjoy an 85 per cent deduction on preferred dividend income. The normally higher yields on mortgages than on bonds reflect in part the poorer market for mortgages as compared to securities.

As mentioned previously, although a very considerable flow of funds occurs between the various segments of the whole investment market, certain barriers or special factors tend to "departmentalize" the market to some extent and prevent uniformity of returns even when maturity and quality are similar. The rates paid by savings institutions tend to change at much less frequent intervals than open-market rates. The yields on Savings bonds are fixed by the government and not by the market, so that the influence of competition shows up only in occasional revisions of these yields some time after rates on other media have changed. And the mortgage market is influenced by regulations and restrictions on institutional investors, by geographical differences in the flow and demand of investment funds, and to a certain extent by legislation, as in the case of the nominal rates on FHA and VA mortgages.

The influence on interest rates of the credit control policies of the Federal Reserve, while very real, is not too apparent in Table 2-8. The rise in the discount rate (the rate at which member banks can borrow at the central bank and thus increase their legal reserves) accompanies the rise in interest rates in the period shown. In other years, not shown on the table, several adjustments were made in the discount rate, both upward and downward. Usually this rate is changed after money-market conditions have changed; at other times, the change is designed to influence the course of rates, and it does so to varying degrees. For example, in 1966 and 1970 the rate was reduced to encourage the continued reduction in market yields after these had already softened. In contrast, the rate was increased in February 1969 to evidence the desire of the Federal Reserve System for tighter credit. Periodic reductions were made in 1971 and 1972 to encourage bank lending. The commercial bank prime rate (on unsecured loans to strongest clients) took a dramatic fall from 8½ per cent in mid-1969 to 4½ per cent two years later, and stood at 6 per cent in late December, 1972.

As suggested previously, the yields on preferred stocks change with those of bonds, since both are fixed-income types of securities. The yields on the high-grade preferred stock series rose to a peak in early 1970 and declined thereafter when interest rates declined. (The relatively low yield on preferred stocks, as compared to bond yields, is explained by their tax advantage to corporate owners and by their short supply.)

The relation between bond yields and common stock yields is not as direct, however. Dividends on common stocks are a distribution of profits and hence depend not only on net earnings, but also on dividend policy. Yields are the net result of a number of variables on both the income and the price sides. Stock yields can rise when interest rates are declining, and contrariwise. Nevertheless, a very sharp change in interest rates is also reflected to a certain extent in a change in dividend yields, since the latter are a return on capital. However, this influence may be entirely overcome by others of much greater importance. Stock yields are more volatile, rising and falling as prices reflect changing estimates of corporate earnings and dividends and the valuation of these basic factors. But in very recent years bond and stock prices, and hence their yields, have often trended together. Prices of both types of securities rose during most of 1970, declined together in the spring of 1971, then rose dramatically with President Nixon's announcement of controlled wages, prices, and imports in August. Yields of both types followed a contrary course. However, in the autumn of 1971 the relationship between bond and stock prices, and yields, reverted to a more traditional pattern as bond prices rose with declining yields, while stock prices fell.

Yields on common stocks, in general, have been much lower than bond yields, and the spread between the two widened to record proportions in 1970–1972. The explanation is that stock prices reflect the outlook for earnings, and their reinvestment, more than their dividend payout. The preference of most investors for appreciation over current income from stocks is strikingly evident. There is almost an inverse relationship between the valuation of earnings (as measured by the price-earnings ratio) and the share of earnings distributed in dividends. The high-ratio high-priced "glamor stocks" offer little or no yield. The major factors affecting stock prices are discussed in Chapters 8 and 25.

This very general account of the play of forces in the investment market provides only a broad explanation of a complicated subject. In later chapters of this book, the influences affecting the returns from particular types of investments will be discussed more specifically.

REFERENCES

BADGER, R. E., H. W. TORGERSON, AND H. G. GUTHMANN, *Investment Principles and Practices,* 6th ed., Chapter 1. Englewood Cliffs, N.J.: Prentice-Hall, Inc., 1969.

BANKERS TRUST COMPANY, *The Investment Outlook.* New York: Bankers Trust Company, annual.

BOARD OF GOVERNORS OF THE FEDERAL RESERVE SYSTEM, *Flow of Funds Accounts, 1945–1968,* Washington D.C.: The Board, 1970.

DAWSON, J. C., *A Flow-of-Funds Analysis of Saving-Investment Fluctuations in the United States.* Princeton, N.J.: Princeton University Press, 1965.

DOUGALL, H.E., *Capital Markets and Institutions,* 2nd ed. Englewood Cliffs, N.J.: Prentice-Hall, Inc., 1970.

FEDERAL RESERVE BANK OF CLEVELAND, *Money Market Instruments,* 3rd ed., 1970.

FEDERAL RESERVE BANK OF RICHMOND, *Instruments of the Money Market,* 1968.

GOLDSMITH, R. W., *A Study of Saving in the United States,* Three volumes. Princeton, N.J.: Princeton University Press, 1955.

———, *The Flow of Capital Funds in the Postwar Economy* New York: Columbia University Press, 1965.

———, *Financial Institutions.* New York: Random House, Inc., 1968.

HOMER, SYDNEY, *A History of Interest Rates.* New Brunswick, N.J.: Rutgers University Press, 1963.

Institutional Study Report of the Securities and Exchange Commission, Supplementary Volume No. I, Chapter 4. 92nd Congress, 1st Session, House Document No. 94–64, 1971.

KESSELL, R. A., *The Cyclical Behavior of the Term Structure of Interest Rates.* New York: Columbia University Press, 1965.

KUZNETS, SIMON, *Capital in the American Economy: Its Formation and Financing.* Princeton, N.J.: Princeton University Press, 1961.

MEISELMAN, DAVID, *The Term Structure of Interest Rates.* Englewood Cliffs, N.J.: Prentice-Hall, Inc., 1962.

NADLER, MARCUS, SIPA HELLER, AND S. S. SHIPMAN, *The Money Market and Its Institutions.* New York: The Ronald Press Company, 1955.

POLAKOFF, M. E., et al., *Financial Institutions and Markets,* Chapters 1, 4. Boston: Houghton Mifflin Company, 1970.

ROBINSON, R. I., *Money and Capital Markets.* New York: McGraw-Hill, Inc., 1964.

3 Life Insurance, Annuities, and Retirement Plans as Investments

SCOPE: The purpose of this chapter is to discuss the investment aspects of life insurance and of various arrangements for retirement income that are usually based on formal contracts with institutions. The order of discussion is (1) investment aspects of life insurance, (2) types of policies, (3) investment merits, (4) fixed-dollar annuities, (5) variable annuities, (6) private pension funds, (7) individual tax-free pension plans, (8) state and local government retirement funds, (9) and (10) Federal Social Security.

Discussion of life insurance in a work on investments is appropriate for several reasons : (1) The reserve liabilities of life insurance companies represent the largest single collection of individuals' savings in any one type of institution ; (2) these savings are invested in securities and mortgages so that insurance company investments are a large share of institutional investments in general ; (3) millions of individuals invest through insurance companies and are, therefore, greatly concerned with insurance company investment policy.

Provision for retirement is an important investment objective, and a substantial volume of savings is devoted to acquiring income from institutions that contract to make fixed or semifixed payments after an agreed time has elapsed. In addition to the premiums on annuities sold by life insurance companies, the annual contributions to uninsured private pension funds, Social Security, and Federal and state retirement plans total approximately $55 billions per year.

We are concerned in this chapter with what these institutions do for the investor. The investment policies of the institutions themselves are discussed in later chapters.

Life Insurance as an Investment

The life insurance companies have long provided one of the most important forms of savings in the country. At the beginning of 1972 their assets totalled $222 billions, and their policy reserves about $179 billions. In 1971 their annual income exceeded $54 billions, of which nearly 75 per cent was derived from premium payments. (Additional data on the industry are given in Chapters 23 and 30.)

The investment aspects of life insurance. Life insurance enters into investment planning in three major respects: (1) Insurance provides the only feasible method by which most investors can provide an adequate immediate estate for dependents; (2) most insurance contracts have a substantial investment element in the form of a policy reserve that represents savings and that is available in the form of cash values or policy loans; (3) the insured may create a retirement fund for himself after the need of protection for dependents has declined or disappeared. An extensive discussion of the principles of insurance and of the various types of policies would be out of place in this volume, but the following summary may prove useful. Discussion of government, group, and industrial insurance and many special combination-type policies is omitted.

The premium paid for insurance is usually a level premium that is the same each year even though the risk of death increases with age. It is fixed at the time the policy is issued and is based on the age of the insured. It consists of three elements: (1) a sum contributed toward the company's operating expenses—the "office premium" or "load," (2) an amount necessary to reimburse the insurance company for carrying the risk of premature death of the insured, and (3) an amount added to reserves and invested at a "guaranteed" rate so as to cover future death loss at the more advanced age. Disregarding the first item, we see that part of the premium goes for current *protection* and part into the policy reserve or *investment* element. It is this latter element that constitutes the cash value that is available (after a stated period, possibly the first two or three years) through cancellation of the contract or in the form of a policy loan. The reserve may also be used to extend the term of the insurance or to purchase a paid-up policy for a reduced amount of insurance if the insured wishes to stop paying premiums on the original policy. Or it may be used to provide an annuity at retirement.

The premium is calculated on the basis of (1) the probability of death age by age as indicated by a mortality table, (2) an assumed rate of earnings on invested reserves (as low as $2\frac{1}{2}$ to $3\frac{1}{2}$ per cent), (3) expected selling expense, office expenses, and taxes of the company, and (4) the type of policy issued. Savings on the first three of these may be substantial, and in the case of mutual companies (and participating policies of stock companies) may be returned to the policyholder in the form of "dividends." Or the "dividends" may be left with the company at interest, be used to reduce the annual premium or to purchase additional paid-up insurance. The dividend is, of course, not a true profit but simply a return of excess premium paid.

Types of policies. In comparing the cost of similar policies issued by different companies, one should make sure that their provisions and benefits are identical and then compare the *net* cost over a period of years, that is, premiums less any dividends. Another and perhaps preferable method of determining the net cost is to compare the total premiums paid in, less "dividends," less the cash-surrender value, at the end of a given period. The cost may be zero, or even a negative amount. Dividends are not paid in regular amounts and are not assured, but depend on the company's experience.

The following annual gross premiums at age twenty-five for various types of policies and the cash-surrender values at age sixty-five were representative in 1972 on contracts of $10,000 or more. Premium on participating policies were somewhat higher:

	Premium per Thousand	*Cash Value Age 65*
Five-year term[a]	$ 5.00	—
Straight life	14.00	$ 588
Family income (20 years)	17.20	592
Twenty-payment life	23.70	706
Retirement income at 65	26.20	1,635
Twenty-year endowment	45.40	[b]

[a]Renewable and convertible.
[b]Paid off at $1,000 at age forty-five.

Since the year-to-year cost of protection for each $1,000 of insurance is the same for each age of issue, the difference in gross premiums on various policies (at the same age) depends on the investment element (reserve) in the policy. This varies according to the type of policy purchased. The *term* policy is renewed annually at an increasing premium, or issued at an annual level premium for a certain term such as five years, ten years, "term to sixty-five," and so forth. The face value is paid only if death occurs within the stipulated period in very much the same way as a fire insurance policy protects property for a certain period. It has no recovery value at the end of the term. Since nothing is paid for survival, the insurance company need not accumulate a reserve for that purpose. Longer-term contracts, say, for fifteen to twenty years, have a small reserve element that increases during the earlier years, but declines to zero at the expiration of the period. To the investor desiring the greatest temporary protection at the least outlay, the term policy is the best choice. As shown by the schedule of rates, at age twenty-five an annual premium of $100 would buy about $20,000 of protection for five years through a five-year term policy (renewable and covertible into permanent protection), $7,140 in straight-life protection, $5,810 through a twenty-year "family-income" policy, $4,220 in twenty-year paid-up life insurance, $3,820 in a retirement-at-sixty-five income policy, and $2,200 in in twenty-year endowment insurance. (Deducting the "dividends" or rebates, the actual cost of each type might, of course, be considerably reduced.)

Arguments for the use of term insurance include (1) maximum protection per dollar of premium outlay when needs are greatest (for example, when children are young and the insured's income is modest); (2) the possibility of investing the difference between the premium on term insurance and a higher-premium form at a higher rate than would be earned by the insurance company; (3) the possibility of converting into a permanent form of insurance without medical examination within a certain period of time before the expiration of the term policy if permanent protection is needed; (4) the possibility of exercising an option to renew the contract for a further period without medical examination; (5) the use of the term policy to insure the payment of debt in case the borrower dies before the debt matures, the nonrenewable and declining term insurance associated with mortgage financing.

Arguments against term insurance are (1) the inability of many people to save systematically unless compelled to save in order to keep insurance in force; (2) the lack of a reserve that would be available in cash in emergencies and that would keep the policy in force if the insured were unable to meet his premiums; (3) the high cost or even impossibility of renewal at the expiration of the period; (4) the natural lethargy that leads to failure to convert or renew and hence to expiration of the protection. Perhaps the best plan for the young man is to take out convertible term insurance to the full amount of his need and change to permanent insurance as soon as he can afford to do so. To offset the practical difficulties that this plan involves, the family-income policy is recommended.[1] This combines ordinary life with decreasing term insurance and pays a monthly income upon the premature death of the insured until the expiration of a specified date (say, ten or twenty years from date of issuance) and the face of the policy as of that date. The annual premium is somewhat greater than that for term insurance and less than that for whole-life insurance.

Whole-life policies provide permanent protection. The *straight-life* policy requires premiums until the insured dies or reaches age ninety. Advantages of this form are (1) the insured is never without protection; (2) the savings or investment element is substantial; (3) the premium remains constant, whereas the premium for a term policy increases with each renewal; (4) at retirement or when the insured no longer has dependents, the reserve value may be taken in cash or used for an annuity; (5) if at a later age continuing the premiums become difficult or if the need for protection declines, the paid-up values may be used to extend the insurance for a term or to buy a reduced amount of protection for life. The chief disadvantages are (1) the the maximum amount of temporary protection, say, during the establishment of a family by a younger man, is not obtained; (2) to keep the full amount of insurance in force, payments must be continued long after the earning years have ceased.

Preferred-risk straight-life policies are issued at lower than regular rates to persons willing to buy a minimum of $5,000 or $10,000 at one time and who have excellent medical histories and are not engaged in hazardous occupations. The premiums are usually lower and the cash values higher than for the corresponding straight-life policies.

Limited-payment life policies are also whole-life policies but premiums are paid at a higher rate for a period (say, for twenty or thirty years), after which the policy continues in force for life without further payments. Advantages of this form are (1) protection is obtained for life; (2) premium payments are made when the policyholder is most capable of earning and do not become a burden on retirement income; (3) there is a more substantial investment element of cash value because reserves are accumulated

---

[1]Not to be confused with the "family-maintenance" policy under which all members (and prospective members) of a family are covered by one contract, with varying amounts of protection per member.

in the twenty or thirty years that will protect against death loss after premium payments are no longer required. The major disadvantage is that the insured has substantially less protection per dollar of premium than is afforded by term or straight-life insurance during the period when the protection may be most needed (in other words, the possible overemphasis on savings and underemphasis on protection).

Endowment policies offer protection for a specified period of time (say, twenty or thirty years), at the end of which the policy matures and the amount of the policy is paid to the insured himself. They combine relatively small current protection with a relatively large investment element. The endowment policy combines an increasing savings fund protected by decreasing term insurance. If the insured dies during the period, the beneficiaries are paid the face amount; if he lives, he collects it himself. Advantages of endowment insurance are (1) where the need for protection is small and the need for savings is predominant, the insured is forced to save to keep his policy in force; (2) the goals of insurance may be met whether the insured lives or dies; (3) the very substantial cash value provides a cash fund or fund for conversion into retirement protection. The main limitations or disadvantages are (1) protection expires when the policy matures; (2) low current protection is afforded per dollar of premium; (3) the difference between the premium on "cheaper" insurance and on endowment insurance of the same amount could be invested safely and, in the event of the insured's death before the policy expired, would also increase the estate.

The *retirement-income* policy combines whole-life insurance with a life income payable in units (say, $10 per month for each $1,000 to $1,500 of insurance) at the selected retirement age. These are expensive policies because they build up savings even faster than endowment policies maturing at the same age. (In the previous table the retirement-income policy assumes retirement at age sixty-five, whereas the endowment policy matures at age forty-five; an endowment policy maturing at age sixty-five would require a much lower annual premium.) This type of policy is really a retirement annuity with death benefits added. The cash value can be substantial.

Investment merits. Life insurance policies offer, in various degrees, a valuable combination of protection and investment. However, many feel that the two should not be combined in one contract. The rate of return on that part of the premium which represents an investment commitment is substantially below that which an individual can get on sound securities. However, the lower rate of return assumed by the insurance company is *compounded*—something the individual investor may not accomplish. In addition, that portion of the investment income that goes to build up the reserve is tax-free. The compulsory savings requirement, the encouragement to systematic thrift, the safety of the funds derived from the caution and skill and degree of diversification with which the large insurance companies make their investments, and the convenience and freedom from managerial care on the part of the insured are strong arguments for substantial investment values in life insurance contracts for the majority of investors.

A major disadvantage of life insurance is that its fixed-dollar benefits suffer from declining purchasing power during periods of inflation. Protection can be obtained by the purchase of additional coverage, but only at higher premiums as age increases, and if medical requirements can be met. The insurance industry has been investigating the possibilities of variable life insurance, in which the beneficiary would receive at least the policy's face value, and possibly a higher benefit from the appreciation of equity investments held as reserves. Such policies are already permitted in several states including New York, although none have been sold as yet (1972). They are available in Canada.

Annuities as Investments

Fixed-dollar annuities. The traditional *annuity* is designed to produce a fixed return with safety at or prior to retirement age. The contract provides for the receipt of a series of equal annual dollar installments at once or after an agreed age, usually so long as the annuitant lives, in return for a lump-sum payment or regular annual premiums. The basis of calculation is the age of the annuitant. The longer the annuitant lives in comparison with the average, the more he receives in relation to what he has paid. If he is short-lived, he may receive back much less than he has invested. The life annuity is simply a means of making sure that a given sum of capital will provide an income which cannot be outlived. Since a part of the principal, in addition to the interest earned, is returned each year, the return to the annuitant is larger than that which would be produced by interest income from the fund alone. The penalty of this higher income is the complete liquidation of principal at the death of the annuitant, at least in the straight-life annuity described below. The more important types of annuities can be described very briefly. A *single-premium* annuity is purchased by the payment of one lump sum, the payments to begin at a stipulated age for the life of the annuitant. *Installment-payment* annuities call for premiums periodically over a period of years to the date of retirement, after which the annuitant receives an income for life. A *life insurance* annuity is purchased by the proceeds of a life insurance policy which are distributed as an annuity in lieu of a lump sum. Most life insurance policies provide for this type of settlement option.

From the standpoint of receipt of benefits, annuities can be classified as *immediate,* which pay a given sum periodically for life following purchase, or *deferred,* in which income does not begin until some time in the future, usually at the estimated end of the annuitant's income-producing period. Possibly the most common type of annuity is the installment-payment type whose income will be deferred until retirement age. In such annuities, death benefits and possibly cash-surrender values are available prior to, but not after, retirement. *Joint and last-survivorship* annuities pay an income to two or more persons, such as husband or wife, as long as either survives.

A *straight-life* annuity provides income to the annuitant for his lifetime. When death occurs, the income ceases. Under such an arrangement, in case of early death, the annuitant may have received only a fraction of what has been paid in. The annuitant, and more especially his heirs, may fail to appreciate that this is the price paid for the income that would have been received if he had lived longer than the average. Consequently, straight-life annuities are not so common today as annuities with special features attached, such as the *life-annuity with installments certain,* which pays an income for life but guarantees to make a minimum number of payments, such as for ten or twenty years certain, irrespective of the time of death of the annuitant. An *installment-refund* life annuity pays an income for life but provides for a continuation of installments to beneficiaries or estate until the payments total the premiums paid, should the annuitant die before that time. A *cash-refund* life annuity is similar but provides for the payment in cash of the balance of the premiums paid. Such annuities often contain substantial cash values. The advantage of the refund type is that income or principal is available for dependents in the event the annuitant should die before the dependents have economic independence. The *retirement-income* (insurance-plus-income) *policy* was described above.

The cost of annuities and the income received from them depend on the age and life expectancy of the annuitant, the rate earned by the insurance company, and the form of the policy. The following rates show the amount of a monthly straight-life *nonparticipating* annuity that could be purchased from a prominent company with an immediate lump-sum payment of $1,000, based on rates quoted in 1971, assuming an interest rate of 3 per cent.

| | Annuity per Month | |
Age at Purchase	Male	Female
50	$5.24	$4.69
55	5.83	5.15
60	6.63	5.76
65	7.65	6.60
70	9.10	7.86

The annuity payment increases as the age at time of purchase increases and the life expectancy decreases. When interest rates are low, the above payments would be attractive. At age sixty-five, for example, a male annuitant would receive about three times the interest income from an investment at 3 per cent that produced $2.50 a month. This was because the return consisted of both principal and interest. But in recent years such annuity payments have been unsatisfactory. In 1972, $1,000 invested in a fairly high-grade bond produced interest income of 8 per cent or $6.67 a month, and the principal remained intact. Under such conditions only those fixed annuities whose benefits are increased through participation in "dividends" would have much appeal, save to the very aged.

Ordinary annuities have the advantage of certainty of a fixed income, convenience, freedom from care, and compulsion to save. Most important, they offer the assurance that the annuitant will not outlive a definite dollar income. For the investor of limited means, a definite income for retirement is assured. For the man of wealth, the purchase of fixed-dollar annuities will provide a fixed income (using part of capital) and leave a larger portion of his total fund free for other investments. But in addition to their loss of appeal during periods of high interest rates, fixed annuities suffer, as do all fixed-income investments, from the reduced purchasing power resulting from inflation. The interest rate at which the reserves are compounded is low. And premium rates have been increasing in recent years to reflect the increase in the average life-span. Fixed annuities lack the appeal of common stock investments that has been reflected in the growth of corporate pension funds, mutual investment funds, and other vehicles for sharing in an expanding economy. The number of *individual* annuities in force dropped from its previous peak of 1,279,000 in 1952 to 1,140,000 in 1965, but rose to 1,830,000 in 1971, and the annual income rose to $1.4 billions in 1971. Group annuities covered 7.5 million persons in 1971.[2]

Variable annuities. Under the variable annuity the annuitant's premiums are invested in a diversified list if common stocks, as are the dividends on the stocks. Each annuitant acquires, as his share in the accumulated reserve, an increasing number of "accumulation units" or "premium units" that vary in value with the value of the total portfolio. Upon retirement, the accumulation units are transferred to the annuity fund, all of which is still invested in common stocks. The annuitant thereafter receives periodically the dollar value of the number of "annuity units" attributable to him. Such units are calculated on the basis of assumed and actual mortality experience, income, and expense. In the event of death prior to retirement, the total value of the accumulation units is paid to the beneficiary.[3]

The purposes of the variable annuity are to provide a hedge against expected long-term inflation, to increase annuity income by sharing in the rising values and dividends of common stocks, and to provide a steady increase in living standards. The company engages in dollar-cost averaging in common stocks that are expected to rise in value, over the long run, more than the cost of living—in short, to preserve and increase *real* retirement income. The first such annuity was offered in 1952 by College Retirement Equities Fund, an affiliate of Teachers Insurance and Annuity Association, and is available only to personnel of college, university, foundation, and research organizations. Table 3-1 shows, for July 1952-December 1971, the average annual value of C.R.E.F. accumulation units and the value of annuity units (calculated annually), compared to the average monthly value of Standard & Poor's 500 Stock Index and the annual average of the Bureau of Labor Statistics Consumer Price Index. During this period the rise in the value of the C.R.E.F. units, and of stocks in general, greatly exceeded the increase in the cost of living.

The growth of the variable annuity was slowed by problems of jurisdiction as well as by resistance on the part of some large life insurance com-

[2]Institute of Life Insurance, *Life Insurance Fact Book 1972*. New York: The Institute, 1972, pp. 55–57.
[3]For formulas used in calculating the value of accumulation and annuity units, see R. I. Mehr, *Life Insurance: Theory and Practice*, 4th ed., Chapter 6. Austin, Texas: Business Publications, Inc., 1970.

Table 3-1. C.R.E.F. UNIT VALUES V. STOCK AND CONSUMER PRICES

	C.R.E.F. Values Accumulation Unit	Annuity Unit	Standard & Poor's 500 Stocks (1941–43 = 10)	B.L.S. Consumer Price Index (1967 = 100)
	(average of monthly values)	(annual)[a]	(average of monthly values)	(monthly average)
1952	$10.06[b]	$10.00[c]	$25.06[b]	$ 79.5
1953	9.87	9.46	24.73	80.1
1954	12.59	10.74	29.69	80.5
1955	16.44	14.11	40.49	80.2
1956	19.09	18.51	46.62	81.4
1957	18.83	16.88	44.38	84.3
1958	20.40	16.71	46.24	86.6
1959	25.72	22.03	57.38	87.3
1960	25.85	22.18	55.85	88.7
1961	30.71	26.25	66.27	89.6
1962	26.38	26.13	62.38	90.6
1963	28.93	22.68	69.87	91.7
1964	32.98	26.48	81.37	92.9
1965	36.69	28.21	88.17	94.5
1966	36.96	30.43	85.26	97.2
1967	41.64	31.92	91.93	100.0
1968	43.44	29.90	98.70	104.2
1969	42.89	32.50	97.84	109.8
1970	35.98	28.91	83.22	116.3
1971	43.18	30.64	98.29	121.3

[a]As of May 1.
[b]Six months, July-December.
[c]As of July 1.
SOURCE: Annual Reports, T.I.A.A.-C.R.E.F.

panies. In 1959 the U.S. Supreme Court ruled that such contracts were securities and thus were subject to the Federal securities laws—especially the Securities Act of 1933, which imposes registration and prospectus requirements, and the Investment Company Act of 1940, under which the contracts would be regulated as mutual investment funds.[4] They were also subject to supervision by state insurance departments. Eventually, however, the Securities and Exchange Commission set up stipulations whereby life insurance companies could sell variable annuities if the assets in which the reserves were invested were segregated in special accounts. A number of companies now offer these contracts either directly or through subsidiaries, sometimes in connection with the sale of mutual funds.[5] An important legal provision in most states is that once annuity payments begin, they must be fixed-dollar annuities.

[4]*S.E.C.* v. *Variable Annuity Life Insurance Co.* (Valic), 359 U.S. 65 (1959).
[5]For a summary of the legal history of the variable annuity as sold by life insurance companies see *Institutional Investor Study Report of the Securities and Exchange Commission*, Chapter VI. 92nd Cong., 1st Sess., House Document No. 92–64, 1971.

Variable annuity plans sold to individuals must be registered under all major Federal securities acts, and are also subject to state "blue-sky" regulations and to the control of insurance commissioners. They are still prohibited in some states; in others some companies specialize in writing this form of contract. Life insurance - companies offer individual contracts but their chief interest is in group annuities for pension plans (see p. 43).

This new type of annuity has much to commend it. If over the long run the course of the market value of the common stocks (and reinvested dividends) coincides with or exceeds the cost of living, a hedge against inflation is obtained both while the premiums are being paid and after retirement. In the meantime, by dollar-cost averaging, advantage is taken of the variations in the market price of stocks, and much of the risk of fluctuations is minimized. Another advantage lies in the fact that the investor enjoys a tax-free accumulation of dividend income and capital gains until retirement payments begin; at retirement age his income presumably falls in a lower tax bracket. The investor must understand, however, that shorter-run fluctuations in the value of the fund can take place (as in 1962, 1966, and 1970) and possibly cause sharp variations in the value of his accumulation units before retirement, and of his dollar income after retirement. The whole assumption is that the *long-run* increase in the cost of living will be more than matched by the *long-run* increase in common stock values.

Arguments raised against the variable annuity, especially against its sale by life insurance companies, are (1) common stocks inevitably involve risk, and no insurance company should engage in the sale of retirement benefits that are not guaranteed and that pass the risk along to the investor; (2) there have been and will likely continue to be periods of substantial length during which common stocks have declined very sharply in value whereas the cost of living has increased or remained relatively stable, or declined in much lesser degree (for example, September 1929—July 1932; March 1937 —March 1938; October 1939—April 1942; May 1946—February 1948; April 1956—October 1957; December 1961—June 1962; February—October 1966; May 1969—June 1970); (3) during a real recession period many investors will be unwilling to continue to pay premiums in the face of shrinking income and declining stock prices, thus losing the benefit of averaging.

Many investors will be attracted by the advantages of the variable annuity. In the case of individuals, the best arrangement would be the purchase of a *combination* of fixed- and variable-annuity benefits, from a company which has demonstrated its superior ability to manage a growth fund, and without the freedom to "cash out" the accumulated values prior to retirement, or at least for a waiting period of several years. Investors must be prepared to see the value of their units rise and fall with the course of the stock market, and to continue to pay their premiums through faith in the dollar-averaging process and the long-run rise in stock values.

Many investors participate in variable annuities on a group pension plan basis. These are growing steadily in acceptance as life insurance companies develop experience in the legal and practical aspects of their management (see p. 43). The sale of variable annuities will probably expand not only because of their attractiveness to employee groups but also as a result of the

Smathers-Keogh Act of 1962 which provides tax exemption of self-employed and small-company retirement plans (see p. 44).

Retirement Funds as Investments

Private pension funds. A large and growing number of companies and nonprofit organizations now provide pension and retirement benefits to employees in both executive and rank-and-file levels. Most of these plans are voluntary; others have arisen as features of union bargaining. At the beginning of 1971 some 30 million employees—about 48 per cent of the private work force—were covered by over 200,000 private retirement plans. The more important reasons for the great growth of private pension plans are (1) the growth in employment; (2) the increase in the number of persons over sixty-five years of age; (3) the use of such plans to increase productivity and attract and hold employees; (4) a company sense of social responsibility; (5) union bargaining for fringe benefits; (6) concern over inflation (and hence the growth of investment of pension funds in common stocks); (7) the tax structure, which permits tax deductible contributions by employers, under qualified plans, tax-exemption of the income and capital gains of the funds, and tax-deferment of employee benefits.

Most corporate pension plans can be classified as (1) insured (administered by insurance companies), (2) self-administered (or trusteed), and (3) "pay-as-you-go." Insured plans involve the purchase by the company of annuity contracts; the investments of the fund are managed by insurance companies. Self-administered funds are usually placed in the hands of a bank as trustee who may act as a mere custodian, or may make the investment decisions. Some trusteed plans are "actuarial" in the sense that the retirement benefits are known in advance; monthly payments are based on previous career average pay or on final year's pay. Others are "final-account-balance" funds; that is, the employee's balance is not known until his retirement. This is especially the case for plans which are based in whole or in part on profit-sharing contributions; on retirement the balance to the employee's credit is invested in an annuity or distributed according to some other system of payment. A few plans operate on the "pay-as-you-go" basis, and are not insured or funded in advance.

Pension plans vary widely with respect to the type of employees covered, the service and age requirements for eligibility to participate, the retirement age involved, the proportion of employees' versus employer's contributions, and the type of benefits received. Plans also differ as to whether the employer's contributions include a varying profit-sharing element. Wide variations also exist with respect to the number of years of credited service at which the employee is fully "vested," that is, can leave the company's service without forfeiting any of the company's contribution; his benefits would still be in effect only on retirement. Where a severed employee has contributed to the fund, the plan usually provides for repayment of his own contribution, with interest, on early retirement or severance.

The importance and growth of private pension funds in the years 1950–1970 are indicated in Table 3-2. The data include multiemployer and union-administered plans and plans of nonprofit organizations but are dominated by those of corporate employers.

Insured plans are administered, and their benefits paid, by life insurance companies to which funds are remitted regularly for the purchase of annuities. During his employment, the employee's claim is adjusted to changes in pay and in the company's contribution. Two main types of insured plans are administered on a group basis for each contracting employer. Under the "group deferred annuity" arrangement, the contracting employer buys a paid up annuity or contributes a specific amount for its purchase in each year for each employee. Under the "group deposit administration" plan, contributions are not made according to a predetermined fixed schedule but are adjusted according to the plan's experience, and benefits can be flexibly determined.

A number of smaller insured plans are operated on an individual pension trust basis; that is, separate policies are maintained for each employee. Life insurance companies also administer "tax-sheltered" plans under the Keogh Act (see below) and other special arrangements for the self-employed and for small businesses.

Table 3-2. PRIVATE PENSION FUNDS, 1950–1970

	1950	*1955*	*1960*	*1965*	*1970*
Persons covered[a] (in millions of persons)					
Insured plans	2,600	3,800	4,900	6,200	9,300
Noninsured plans	7,200	11,600	16,300	19,100	20,400
	$ 9,800	$15,400	$21,200	$25,300	$ 29,700
Contributions (in millions of dollars)					
Insured plans	$ 920	$ 1,380	$ 1,490	$ 2,100	$ 3,150
Noninsured plans	1,160	2,460	4,040	6,270	10,790
	$ 2,080	$ 3,840	$ 5,530	$ 8,370	$ 13,940
Benefit payments					
Insured plans	$ 80	$ 180	$ 390	$ 720	$ 1,330
Noninsured plans	290	670	1,360	2,650	6,030
	$ 370	$ 850	$ 1,750	$ 3,370	$ 7,360
Reserves or assets (book value)					
Insured plans	$ 5,600	$11,300	$18,800	$27,300	$ 40,100
Noninsured plans	6,500	16,100	33,100	59,200	97,000
	$12,100	$27,400	$51,900	$86,500	$137,100

[a]Exclusive of annuitants receiving benefits.

Sources: U.S. Department of Health, Education and Welfare, Social Security Administration, *Social Security Bulletin;* Securities and Exchange Commission, *Statistical Bulletin;* Institute of Life Insurance, *Life Insurance Fact Book.*

The size of the pension fund reserves of the various insured types was as follows at the end of 1971:[6]

[6]Institute of Life Insurance, *Life Insurance Fact Book 1972*, p. 40.

Group deferred annuities	**$13.3** billions
Deposit administration group annuities	24.3
Individual policy pension trusts	3.6
Other	5.1
	$46.3 billions

The data in Table 3-2 show that until recently insured private plans lagged steadily behind trusteed or uninsured plans for several reasons: (1) it was difficult to tailor the plans to suit the needs of different employers because the type of plan in vogue—deferred annuities—did not allow flexible timing or size of contributions nor shifts in reserves among different types of investments; (2) insured plans showed a low rate of return compared to that produced by trusteed plans because their reserves were mingled with general insurance company assets and were subject to the restrictions on investment policy; (3) investment earnings of qualified insured pension plans were subject to federal income taxes until the formula for calculating insurance company taxes was changed in 1959.

In recent years insured plans have regained much lost ground. There has been a considerable shift to the more flexible deposit administration type of plan. This has been accelerated by the authorization of separate accounts for different employers' reserves rather than merging these reserves with general assets and liabilities. Separate accounts were legalized in Connecticut and New Jersey in 1959 and in New York in 1962, and are now authorized in all but a few states. They have also been made exempt from the Investment Company Act and are no longer regulated as mutual funds.[7] Separate accounts grew from $100 millions in 1964 to $7.2 billions in 1971.[8]

The separate account has made possible the investment of life insurance company pension reserves in common stocks and has made insured plans much more competitive with the uninsured. Group and individual variable annuities have also given the insurance companies a more attractive package of pension wares.[9]

Uninsured (trusteed) pension and profit-sharing portfolios are managed by company committees, professional investment advisors, or the banks that serve as trustees. Frequently two or more managers are engaged to manage portions of a fund on a competitive basis. Most portfolios are free from legal restrictions with respect to the types of investments permitted. Some funds are conservatively invested, and must meet strict actuarial requirements. Others are invested at considerable risk. Generally speaking, the employer's pension or retirement committee determines the general nature of the portfolio and the goals to be achieved. Investment principles and policies of uninsured funds are discussed in Chapter 23.

---

[7]*Institutional Investor Study Report of the* S.E.C., *op. cit.*, Chapter VI. This source contains detailed information on insured pension plans and especially on the history, organization, characteristics, and management of separate pension accounts.

[8]S.E.C. *Statistical Bulletin*, April 1972.

[9]At the beginning of 1972, there were 9,969 group variable plans covering 746,000 persons. Institute of Life Insurance, *Life Insurance Fact Book* 1972, p. 56.

At the end of 1971 the assets of uninsured private pension funds reached $106 billions at book value and $125 billions at market value. Insured fund reserves totalled $45 billions at book value.[10] Total private pension fund assets are expected to reach $150 billions by 1975 and cover possibly two-thirds of the private work force. Thus a major financial institution has developed in response to social needs.

Individual "tax-free" pension plans. The tax-exempt feature of corporate pension plans has been extended to self-employed individuals under the Keogh Act. Owners of businesses (proprietors or partners holding more than a 10 per cent interest) may establish plans for themselves (and must include all full-time employees who have three or more years of service) whereby half of the owner's contributions to his own plan (to a maximum of $2,500 annually) and all of his contributions for employees may be deducted from taxable income. The earnings from the plan accumulate tax-free until withdrawn, and participants are not taxed on their benefits until distributions are actually made.

The owner or partner may contribute to the plan up to 10 per cent of his "earned income" each year, or $2,500, whichever is less. Contributions for covered employees are a percentage of their compensation at the same rate. Funds withheld under the Keogh plan may be invested in (1) special U.S. Retirement Bonds which yield 3.75 to 5 per cent; (2) bank trust accounts; (3) life insurance company annuities; (4) shares in qualified mutual investment companies, held by a bank as custodian (see p.172). At the end of 1971, about 260,000 self-employed plans had been approved.[11]

State and local government retirement funds. A   great   increase in retirement coverage of state and local government personnel has accompanied the growth of government functions at the non-Federal level. At the end of 1970, about 7 million persons were covered by over 2,000 separate plans. One cannot generalize about the size and adequacy of the benefits received by individual members, because of the variety of plans and types of employees covered. The assets of these plans totaled $65 billions at the end of 1971. Government securities and corporate bonds predominate as investments, although a growing number of plans are now introducing some common stocks into their portfolios to provide growth and protection from inflation. The emphasis, however, remains on long-run safety of principal and assurance of income. The assets of these funds grow much more rapidly than their payout requirements. Thus in fiscal 1971 total receipts amounted to $11.3 billions while only $4.2 billions were paid out in benefits.[12] Like corporate pension funds they need little immediate recovery of principal, and what is needed is amply provided by the type of assets held. (See Chapter 23.)

[10]S.E.C. *Statistical Bulletin*, April 1972. The total assets of all private and public pension funds, including insured and noninsured private funds, state and local government retirement funds, and Federal retirement funds including Social Security reserves, was $287 billions. *Ibid.*

[11]Arthur Wiesenberger, *Investment Companies*, 1972 ed. New York: Wiesenberger Services, Inc., p. 83.

[12]U.S. Department of Commerce, Bureau of the Census, Finances of Employee-Retirement Systems of State and Local Governments in 1970–71. Washington, 1972.

Federal retirement systems. Not including Social Security, there are over a dozen retirement systems for civilian employees of the Federal government, covering 3.3 million persons and holding assets (at book value) of $28 billions at the end of 1970.[13] The largest of these is the U.S. Civil Service Retirement System with over 2.7 million active workers on its roll in 1969. The Federal government also administers the Railroad Retirement System covering 1,088,000 workers and holding assets of $4.4 billions (1971). The reserves of all of these plans are mainly invested in U.S. Government obligations (see p.426).

Summary of pension plans. The growth of all pension plans (excluding Social Security) is summarized in Table 3-3. Over 41 million persons participated in these plans in 1970, and assets (at book value) totalled over $223 billions—an increase of 150 per cent since 1960. Assets at the end of 1971 were estimated at $247 billions.[14]

Social security. At the end of 1971, 73.8 million persons including self-employed, had Old Age, Survivors, and Disability Insurance (OASDHI) wage credits under the Federal Social Security Act. In addition to retirement income, the legislation provides for disability insurance and other family

Table 3-3. PRIVATE AND PUBLIC PENSION FUNDS, 1960–1970

(numbers in millions; dollars in billions)

	Persons Covered		*Assets (book value)*	
	1960	*1970*	*1960*	*1970*
Private[a]				
Insured funds	4.9	9.3	$18.8	$ 40.1
Noninsured funds	16.3	20.4	33.1	97.0
	21.2	29.7	$51.9	$137.1
Public				
State and local	5.1	7.0	19.6	57.9
Federal[b]	2.6	4.4	16.4	28.3
	7.7	11.4	$36.0	$ 86.2
Total	28.9	41.1	$87.9	$223.3

[a]Includes funds of corporations, multiemployer and union funds, and those of nonprofit organizations.

[b]Includes Civil Service Retirement program (various) and Railroad Retirement funds. Excludes Old Age, Survivors, and Disability Insurance.

SOURCES: Institute of Life Insurance, *Life Insurance Fact Book;* Securities and Exchange Commission, *Statistical Bulletin.*

benefits before retirement, survivors' life insurance, and hospital-medical benefits. During working years employees and their employers, and self-employed persons, pay Social Security contributions which are placed in special funds. Monthly cash benefits are paid when the worker retires, dies,

[13]Institute of Life Insurance, *Life Insurance Fact Book 1972*, p. 43.

[14]S.E.C. *Statistical Bulletin*, April 1972, p. 28.

or becomes disabled. At the end of 1971, OASDHI reserves totalled $34 billions.

For persons who meet the eligibility requirements (the required number of "quarters" of covered earnings), the maximum monthly retirement benefits at age sixty-five, based on average annual earnings after 1950 (to a maximum of $9,000), were $295.40 a month (as of 1972).[15] The maximum monthly income to survivors (widow with two or more minor children) was $517.00. Workers who have become disabled are entitled to disability benefits that are functions of age and years of credited work. The system also provides a lump-sum death benefit of three times the monthly retirement payment with a maximum of $255.[16]

In 1965 hospitalization ("Medicare A") was added to the Social Security program. With few exceptions, persons aged sixty-five or over become automatically eligible for hospital insurance. Additional medical (doctor bill) insurance ("Medicare B") is obtained (as of 1973) with a premium of $6.30 a month which is matched by the Federal government.[17]

The cost of Federal Social Security, including hospitalization, is financed by an employment tax that, in early 1972, was 5.2 per cent paid by both employer and employee on the first $9,000 of income. Self-employed persons are eligible for benefits and pay 1½ times the employee tax.[18] "Medicare B" premiums are an additional $6.30 a month in 1973.

Social Security benefits form the foundation on which the investor can expand his provision for insurance and retirement income. Many private retirement plans have been adjusted to make Social Security the first portion of a larger plan, since for many investors the benefits are more generous than they would be if based on actuarial calculations.

REFERENCES

BANKERS TRUST COMPANY, *1971 Study of Industrial Retirement Plans.* New York: Bankers Trust Company, 1971.

BIEGEL, H. C., et al., *Pensions and Profit Sharing,* 3rd ed. Washington, D.C.: BNA, Inc., 1964.

BOGEN, J. I., ed., *Financial Handbook,* 4th rev. ed., Sec. 19. New York: The Ronald Press Company, 1968.

CAMPBELL, P. A., *The Variable Annuity.* Hartford, Conn.: Connecticut General Life Insurance Company, 1969.

[15]Benefits at this level are not payable until later, because it will take some time for average earnings to reach $9,000 and the maximum creditable earnings for earlier years are at lower levels.

[16]For details on qualifications for coverage, benefits, conditions producing full or partial benefits after retirement, definition of "self-employed," and other provisions, see U.S. Department of Health, Education and Welfare, *Social Security Handbook on Old-Age, Survivors, and Disability Insurance.* Washington, D.C.: Government Printing Office, 1969. All changes through 1972 are explained in Commerce Clearing House, Inc., 1973 *Social Security and Medicare Explained.* New York, 1973.

[17]For details, see U.S. Department of Health, Education and Welfare, Social Security Administration, *Your Medicare Handbook,* available at Social Security offices.

[18]In July, 1972, President Nixon signed a bill that raised Social Security benefits by 20 per cent. The tax rate, paid by both employer and employee, is 5.85 per cent on the first $10,800 of income in 1973. The base will increase to $12,000 in 1974, and will rise each year according to a formula linking it with the general price level in the economy.

CASEY, W. J., *Life Insurance Planning*. New York: Institute for Business Planning, Inc., 1965.

COMMERCE CLEARING HOUSE, *Medicare and Social Security Explained*. Chicago: Commerce Clearing House, 1968.

CORBETT, R. M., *Pension Trends and the Self-employed*. New Brunswick, N.J.: Rutgers University Press, 1961.

DEARING, C. L., *Industrial Pensions*. Washington, D.C.: The Brookings Institution, 1954.

DONALDSON, E. F., AND J. K. PFAHL, *Personal Finance*, 3rd ed. New York: The Ronald Press Company, 1961.

FRICKE, C. V., *The Variable Annuity: Its Impact on the Savings-Investment Market*. Ann Arbor, Mich.: Bureau of Business Research, School of Business Administration, University of Michigan, 1959.

GREENOUGH, W. C., *A New Approach to Retirement Income*, New York: Teachers Insurance and Annuity Association, 1964.

HAMMOND, J. D., AND A. L. WILLIAMS, *Essentials of Life Insurance*. Glenview, Ill.: Scott, Foresman and Company, 1968.

HASKINS AND SELLS, *The Pension System in the United States*. New York: Haskins and Sells, 1964.

HOLLAND, D. M., *Private Pension Funds: Projected Growth*. New York: Columbia University Press, 1966.

HUEBNER, S. S., AND KENNETH BLACK, JR., *Life Insurance*, 7th ed. New York: Appleton-Century-Crofts, 1969.

Institutional Investor Study Report of The Securities and Exchange Commission, Chapter VI, and Supplementary Volume I, Chapters 2 and 5. 92nd Congress, 1st Session, House Document No. 92–64, 1971.

JACOBS, DONALD, et al., *Financial Institutions*, 5th ed. Homewood, Ill.: Richard D. Irwin, Inc., 1972.

JERING, J. J. *The Investment and Administration of Profit Sharing Trust Funds*. Evanston, Illinois: Profit Sharing Research Foundation, 1957.

JOHNSON, G. E., *Variable Annuities*. Washington, D.C.: The Reprint Company, 1970.

KELSEY, R. W., AND A. C. DANIELS, *Handbook of Life Insurance*, 4th ed. New York: Institute of Life Insurance, 1969.

LASSER, J. K., AND SYLVIA F. PORTER, *Managing Your Money*, new rev. ed. Garden City, N.Y.: Doubleday, 1963.

LUDTKE, J. B., *The American Financial System; Markets and Institutions*, 2nd ed. Boston: Allyn and Bacon, Inc., 1967.

MACKIN, J. P. *Protecting Purchasing Power in Retirement: A Study of Public Employment Retirement Systems*. New York: Fleet Academic Editions, Inc., 1971.

MATTESON, W. J., *What Will Social Security Mean to You?* Gt. Barrington, Mass.: American Institute for Economic Research, 1962.

———, *Life Insurance and Annuities from the Buyer's Point of View*. Gt. Barrington, Mass.: American Institute for Economic Research, 1969.

McGILL, D. M., *Fundamentals of Private Pensions*, 2nd ed. Homewood, Ill.: Richard D. Irwin, Inc., 1964.

MEHR, R. I., *Life Insurance: Theory and Practice*, 4th ed. Austin, Texas: Business Publications, Inc., 1970.

MURRAY, R. F., *Economic Aspects of Pensions: A Summary Report*. New York: National Bureau of Economic Research, 1968.

PHILLIPS, E. B., AND SYLVIA LANE, *Personal Finance*, 2nd ed. New York: John Wiley & Sons, Inc., 1969.

PRESIDENT'S COMMITTEE ON CORPORATE PENSION FUNDS AND OTHER PRIVATE RETIREMENT AND WELFARE PROGRAMS, *Public Policy and Private Pension Programs*. Washington, D.C.: U.S. Government Printing Office, 1965.

Private Pension Plans. Hearings before the Subcommittee on Fiscal Policy of the Joint Economic Committee, 89th Congress, 2nd Session, 1966. Washington, D.C.: U.S. Government Printing Office, 1966.

SCHOTTLAND, C. I., *The Social Security Program in the United States*, 2nd ed. New York: Appleton-Century-Crofts, 1970.

TAX FOUNDATION, *State and Local Government Employee Retirement Systems: A Summary*. New York: The Foundation, 1969.

UNGER, M. A., AND H. A. WOLF, *Personal Finance*, 2nd ed. Boston: Allyn and Bacon, 1969.

U.S. DEPARTMENT OF COMMERCE, BUREAU OF THE CENSUS, *Finances of Employee Retirement Systems of State and Local Governments*. Washington, D.C.: The Bureau, annual.

————, *Employee-Retirement Systems of State and Local Governments,* 1967 Census of Governments Topical Volume 6, Studies No. 2, Washington, D.C., 1968.

U.S. DEPARTMENT OF HEALTH, EDUCATION, AND WELFARE, SOCIAL SECURITY ADMINISTRATION, *Social Security Programs in the United States*. Washington, D.C.: Government Printing Office, 1966.

WERBEL, B. G., *Life Insurance Primer*, 4th ed. Greenlawn, N.Y.: Werbel Publishing Co., 1961.

4 Deposit-type Investments; U.S. Savings Bonds

SCOPE: This chapter discusses the investment aspects of claims against institutions that hold the liquid savings of individuals, pay a modest return on those savings, and stand ready to provide cash on demand or on short notice. Following the presentation of data on total savings, the order of discussion is (1) savings and time deposits in commercial banks, (2) deposits in mutual savings banks, (3) accounts in savings and loan associations, (4) claims against credit unions, (5) the "Hunt Commission" Report, and (6) U. S. Savings bonds.

United States Savings bonds differ from deposits in form, and are the obligations of the U. S. Government. But they have many characteristics of deposit-type investments and the general motives behind their purchase are similar to those pertaining to the deposit group; hence they are included here.

Other major "savings" media—life insurance, annuities, private pension plans, and government retirement funds—were discussed in the previous chapter.

The Growth of Institutional Savings

The liquid portion of the great and growing accumulation of personal savings referred to in Chapter 2 is represented in large part by the increase over the years in the accounts of the institutions that receive such savings and that in turn make them available to the investment market. The year-end figures given in Table 4-1 are indicative of the trend.

The data in Table 4-1 reveal the enormous accumulation of financial savings in deposit-type and other major financial intermediaries, and in U.S. Savings bonds. Intermediaries are institutions that pool savings and funnel them into the money and capital markets. The deposit-type or "thrift" institutions appeal chiefly to the smaller investors who seek safety and liquidity but who have difficulty gaining access to the markets directly, or prefer not to invest directly. Such investors also value the deposit insurance feature. Insurance-type institutions serve all types of investors. Savings bonds appeal chiefly to the small investor.

In this chapter as in Chapter 3, we are concerned with the investment aspects of placing money with intermediaries. In Chapters 22 and 23 we shall see what the intermediaries do with the money.

Table 4-1. INSTITUTIONAL SAVINGS, 1950–1971
   (in billions of dollars)

	1950	1955	1960	1965	1971
Deposit-type					
Commercial bank savings and					
time deposits[a]	$36.3	$48.4	$71.6	$146.7	$267.8
Mutual savings bank deposits[a]	20.0	28.1	36.3	52.4	81.4
Savings and loan association					
accounts	14.0	32.1	62.1	110.4	175.4
Credit union shares and deposits	.9	2.4	5.0	9.2	18.1
Postal Savings deposits	2.9	1.9	.8	.3[b]	—
U.S. Savings bonds					
(redemption value)	58.0	57.9	47.2	50.3	54.9
Insurance-type					
Life insurance company reserves[c]	54.7	74.8	97.7	126.2	174.0
Uninsured private pension fund					
reserves (book value)	6.5	16.1	33.1	59.2	106.4
State and local govt. retirement					
fund reserves	5.0	10.7	19.6	33.1	64.7
Federal insurance and retirement					
fund reserves[d]	12.7	15.8	17.4	21.4	37.0

[a]Excludes interbank time deposits.
[b]The Postal Savings System was discontinued in March 1966.
[c]Includes insurance, annuity, and pension fund reserves.
[d]Excludes Social Security Fund.

SOURCES: *Federal Reserve Bulletin*; National Association of Mutual Savings Banks, *National Fact Book*; United States Savings and Loan League, *Savings and Loan Fact Book;* Credit Union National Association, *Credit Union Yearbook*; Institute of Life Insurance, *Life Insurance Fact Book;* Securities and Exchange Commission, *Statistical Bulletin*; *Treasury Bulletin*.

Interest-Bearing Deposits in Commercial Banks

Most of the 35,000 banking offices in the United States operated by the 13,800 commercial banks furnish savings facilities. About half of interest-bearing deposits consist of ordinary savings accounts, which have no specific maturity, are not subject to check, are available only to individuals, and on which the bank has the legal right to require thirty days' notice of intention of withdrawal. Bank passbook savings accounts may legitimately be classed as investment media. They bear interest at modest rates—now (1972) a maximum of 4½ per cent with some banks dropping to 4 per cent in early 1972. Immediate liquidity is obtained, for although the bank has the right to demand notice of withdrawal, such right is rarely exercised. In some states the assets of the savings department must be segregated from the other assets of the bank. The state authorities restrict the amount and type of loans permitted and issue an approved list of securities in which savings funds may be invested. No such specific segregation occurs in the case of national banks.

In addition to ordinary savings accounts, two other major types of interest-bearing deposits are available: (1) time deposits in various denominations that have specific maturities ranging from six months to over two years. During 1972 banks were offering up to $5\frac{1}{2}$ per cent on such accounts, depending on size, location, and maturity; (2) negotiable certificates of deposit (CD's) in large denominations (generally $100,000 and over) issued to corporations and other large investors. These short-term investments bore yields as high as $6\frac{1}{2}$ per cent during 1972; the most common rates were 5 to $5\frac{1}{2}$ per cent.[1]

The interest rates paid on savings and time deposits are subject to the regulation of the Board of Governors of the Federal Reserve System, insofar as member banks are concerned. At the present time (early 1973) under Regulation Q, the maximum interest rate is set at $4\frac{1}{2}$ per cent on ordinary passbook savings accounts, $4\frac{1}{2}$ to 5 per cent on time deposits, and $7\frac{1}{2}$ per cent on negotiable CD's, depending on size and maturity. The rate payable by a member bank may not in any event exceed the maximum rate payable by state banks on like deposits under the laws of the state in which the bank is located. In recent years the competition for funds among banks has been working to the advantage of the saver, for interest rates on savings and time accounts have shown substantial increase. Because they must maintain greater liquidity, commercial banks neither earn nor pay as much on their thrift accounts as do savings and loan associations.

All national and most state banks are members of the Federal Deposit Insurance Corporation (F.D.I.C.), which insures individual accounts up to $20,000. For this reason most depositors in insured banks need not be concerned about the ultimate safety of their funds. They have liquid assets drawing a modest rate of return. At the end of 1971, 98 per cent of all commercial banks were insured. These banks held 99 per cent of all commercial bank deposits. The proportion of all fully protected accounts in insured banks was 64 per cent.[2]

The savings account offers safety, immediate recovery of principal, convenience, and modest income. No tax advantages are enjoyed, as interest on accounts is fully taxable. Such accounts, together with time accounts, are mainly useful as a cash reserve and for accumulating funds to be invested later in other types of investment media. Negotiable certificates of deposit bear higher yields and are more comparable to short-term securities as an investment medium.

How commercial banks invest the funds placed with them in savings and time deposits is discussed in Chapter 22.

Deposits in Mutual Savings Banks

Importance of the group. The 490 mutual savings banks (with 1,100 branches) are chartered in eighteen states, primarily in the New

---

[1] *Time deposits* include (a) open account deposits, (b) savings certificates, and (c) nonnegotiable CD's. For an analysis of their relative importance compared to negotiable CD's, their maturities, and variations in rates of interest, see *Federal Reserve Bulletin*, April 1972, pp. 363–374. In September 1966 regulatory authorities (the Federal Reserve and the F.D.I.C) were instructed to impose a 5 per cent interest ceiling on bank deposits under $100,000.

[2] *Annual Report of the Federal Deposit Insurance Corporation*, 1972.

England and Middle Atlantic States. Nearly three-quarters of the banks are located in New York, Massachusetts, and Connecticut, and over 80 per cent of savings deposits are located in these three states. There are only nine banks in the Middle West and twelve on the Pacific Coast (Washington, Oregon, and Alaska). Such institutions appeal especially to the small investor who requires a maximum of safety. As explained in Chapter 22, savings banks are permitted to invest their deposits solely in those securities and mortgages that are approved by law.

Although mutual savings banks comprised only 3.5 per cent of all banks in the United States at the end of 1971, they held 23 per cent of the nation's savings and time deposits. Table 4-2 shows their combined assets and liabilities.

Table 4-2. CONDENSED STATEMENT, MUTUAL SAVINGS BANKS
DECEMBER 31, 1971

(in millions of dollars)

	Amount	Percentage of Total
Assets		
Cash and balances with banks	$ 1,389	1.7%
U.S. Govt. and agency obligations	5,531	6.2
Municipal bonds	390	.4
Corporate and other bonds	12,785	14.3
Corporate stocks	2,983	3.3
Mortgage loans (net)	61,770	69.0
Other loans	2,810	3.1
Real estate and other assets	1,711	2.0
Total	$89,369	100.0%
Liabilities		
Deposits[a]	$81,440	91.1
Other liabilities	1,810	2.0
General reserve accounts	6,119	6.9
Total	$89,369	100.0%

[a]Virtually all deposits are time deposits.

Sources: National Association of Mutual Savings Banks, *National Fact Book* (New York: The Association, 1972); *Federal Reserve Bulletin.*

Of interest here is that the ratio of capital funds to deposits was 7.5 per cent; cash and U.S. Government and agency obligations covered deposits by 9 per cent.

Character of deposits. Mutual savings banks are organized without capital stock, and net earnings are distributed to depositors as interest. Earnings over and above established interest rates are carried to the general reserve (surplus) account, which belongs to the depositors. Each depositor has an equitable share in the surplus, irrespective of the period of his deposit. The mutuals operate under the direction of self-perpetuating boards of trustees and are chartered and supervised by state banking authorities.

Nearly 80 per cent of deposits are ordinary passbook accounts. The remainder are "special" deposits including time or term accounts with specific maturities. No deposits are payable on demand. In the case of passbook accounts, the right is reserved to require notice of intention of withdrawal, varying from ten days to ninety days in the various states. This right is rarely exercised. Over their long history, mutual savings banks have maintained an excellent safety record. And while only a portion of the mutuals have chosen to join the Federal Deposit Insurance Corporation,[3] their enviable record, financial strength, insurance of deposits (in some cases), and strict state regulation provide the same safety and liquidity that can be enjoyed through commercial bank savings accounts. Only a few mutuals have chosen to join the Federal Reserve System. In New York State the banks have, however, subscribed to stock in two central organizations of their own, both formed in 1933—the Savings Banks Trust Company, which advances funds to members on the security of bond investments, and the Institutional Securities Corporation, formed to purchase mortgages from member banks.

The amount of deposits that can be accepted from one person by any one bank is limited, for example, to $15,000 (exclusive of accrued interest) in New York and to $25,000 in New Jersey. This discourages large "investment" accounts that might be withdrawn in full on short notice. The rate of interest paid on deposits varies with changes in money and capital market conditions. Competition for funds was especially severe from the period of the "credit crunch" of 1966 through the next "crunch" in the spring of 1970. Ceiling or maximum rates are set by the individual states and range (1973) from $4\frac{1}{2}$ to $5\frac{1}{2}$ per cent on ordinary passbook deposits to as high as 6 per cent on time deposits of one year or more to maturity, depending on size. Rates usually exceed those paid on commercial bank time and savings accounts and are about equal to those paid by most savings and loan associations on accounts of similar size and maturites.

Summary and recent developments. The mutual savings bank provides a safe place for small savings, legal protection, modest income, and a convenient means of accumulating a reserve fund. Although the savings departments of commercial banks provide substantially the same service, they often pay a lower rate of interest.

A growing development in the savings bank field has been the sale of life insurance policies by savings banks in Massachusetts (since 1907), New York (since 1938), and Connecticut (since 1941). Such policies have the advantages of lower premiums (owing to lack of sales commissions and a lower rate of lapse) and a higher initial cash-surrender value. At the beginning of 1972, $4,545,000,000 of such protection was in force.[4]

[3]As of December 31, 1971, 327 mutual banks were insured by the F.D.I.C., while all but one other were insured by state funds. [National Association of Mutual Savings Banks, *National Fact Book* (New York: The Association, 1972)].

Balances in mutual savings banks in Massachusetts are insured by the Mutual Savings Central Fund and in Connecticut by the Savings Banks Deposit Guarantee Fund.

[4]National Association of Mutual Savings Banks, *National Fact Book*, 1971.

Like savings deposits in commercial banks, mutual savings bank deposits are safe, liquid, convenient, and produce modest income. The income is fully taxable. How the deposits are invested by the banks is discussed in Chapter 22.

Accounts in Savings and Loan Associations

General characteristics. Savings and loan associations are devoted almost entirely to the accumulation of funds in savers' accounts and the investment of these funds in urban mortgage loans. There were approximately 5,500 savings and loan associations with combined assets, at the end of 1971, of $206 billions. They are currently the source of 45 per cent of the dollar amount of all home loans. The old building and loan associations, chartered only by states, were organized primarily for the purpose of cooperative home financing. Since the early 1930s, however, the savings-depository function has grown in importance, and today the savings and loan associations are actively competing with banks and insurance companies for the thrift funds of individuals. Their rapid growth is indicated by the data on savings in Table 4-1.

Savings and loan associations operate under both state and Federal charters. Federal associations are chartered under legislation passed in 1932 which set up the Home Loan Bank Board. All Federal associations are mutual in type, that is, owned by depositors who elect the directors. They are examined and supervised by the Federal Home Loan Bank Board, and must have their accounts insured by the Federal Savings and Loan Insurance Corporation (F.S.L.I.C.). At the end of 1971, 2050 associations, or 37 per cent of all associations, were operating with federal charters. They controlled 55 per cent of the total assets of the industry.

State-chartered associations (3,495, or 63 per cent of the total) now control 45 per cent of industry assets. They are supervised and examined by their respective banking or savings and loan departments or commissioners. 2780 state associations are mutuals; the other 715 are organized in some twenty states, notably California, Illinois, Ohio, and Texas, whose statutes permit "permanent stock associations," owned and managed by shareholders. This type had $40 billions of assets at the end of 1971.

Status of the accounts. Originally, savings and loan associations were not depositories. Savers placed funds in associations, invested in "shares," and became owners of the institution, whereas depositors in banks were legally creditors and had creditors' rights in the event of default. Depositors in banks received interest; accountholders in savings and loan associations received dividends, after provision for operating expenses and reserves. In the course of time, state-chartered associations developed the passbook account. And in many states court decisions confirmed the concept that accounts in savings associations and in banks were identical in that the holder is a creditor. Under the Housing and Urban Development Act of 1968, federally chartered associations are permitted to describe accounts as "deposits" and to refer to earnings on accounts as "interest." In short, associations are real depository institutions.

Associations are permitted to offer a variety of accounts. Regular pass-book accounts comprise about 60 per cent of deposits. (Some associations issue variable rate accounts bearing higher rates than those paid on ordinary accounts and which must be maintained for at least a year.) The certificate account is the other major type of savings instrument. Certificates are issued in fixed maximum amounts with fixed maturities.

Interest rate ceilings, set by the Federal Home Loan Bank Board and/or state authorities, are presently (that is, early 1973) 5 per cent on regular passbook accounts, $5\frac{1}{4}$ to 6 per cent on certificates of from 90 days to ten years in maturity (with various minimum denominations), and $6\frac{1}{2}$ to $7\frac{1}{2}$ per cent on various maturities with a minimum denomination of $100,-000. Actual rates paid vary from state to state to reflect different competitive conditions. The great flow of savings funds into savings and loan associations in 1971–1972, together with the decline in interest rates earned on mortgages, put downward pressure on interest rates paid on deposits, and some associations began lowering rates or issuing shorter-term time deposits in the spring of 1972.

The savings and loan account is not a demand account; checks cannot be written against it. From 80 to 85 per cent of the assets of the typical association consist of mortgage loans on owner-occupied homes which the borrower pays back in regular monthly installments. The liquidity provided by a commercial bank is not to be expected under these conditions. Associations are prepared to meet ordinary withdrawals (retirements of shares) on demand; some require thirty days' notice for withdrawals, except in cases of real emergency. When unable to meet withdrawals, the Federal- and most state-chartered associations require the holders of accounts to file written applications for withdrawal. The institution must then either pay the amount of withdrawal requested within thirty days or apply at least one-third and in some states as much as two-thirds of cash receipts to the holders of accounts in the order of filing; holders of an account in Federal associations applying for more than $1,000 receive that amount and their applications are renumbered and placed at the end of the list. The right is also given to the board of directors to repurchase not more than $200 of any one account in any month without regard to other provisions.

In recent years almost all associations have been meeting requests for funds in full on demand or on relatively short notice; such a condition should continue except in periods of severe economic depression or local distress and mismanagement. Cash reserves, availability of loans from the Federal Home Loan Banks (F.H.L.B.), and the large holdings of government securities provide sufficient liquidity for ordinary purposes. However, the generally less liquid character of the assets should not be overlooked. Since September 1950 the manner of insurance settlement in case of default has been virtually identical for insured banks and insured savings and loan associations. In either case, the laws now provide that the F.D.I.C. (or the F.S.L.I.C.) pay insured deposits (or accounts) either (1) by cash or (2) by making available to each insured depositor (or accountholder) a transferred balance in a new insured institution in the same community or in another insured institution. All Federal savings and loan associations and about 2,200 state associations carry and pay for insurance (up to $20,000 per account) with the F.S.L.I.C., established in 1934. Together such associations carry about 97 per cent of the entire savings and loan resources of the country.

As of January 1, 1972, the F.S.L.I.C. had assets of $3,040 millions, of which nearly 90 per cent consisted of cash and U.S. Government obligations. It insured accounts of 4,270 institutions with combined assets of $200 billions. The savings in these institutions totalled $169 billions, of which 96 per cent was fully insured.[5]

The well-managed savings and loan association provides a safe place for savings. The major part of its funds are invested in mortgage loans. The investor cannot expect to receive the higher returns paid by associations as a result of their earnings on mortgages (in comparison with rates paid on bank savings accounts) and be assured of the same liquidity.

Statement of condition. The statement (Table 4-3) for all savings and loan associations and cooperative banks at the end of 1971 indicates the character of their work and the protection afforded accountholders.

Table 4-3. COMBINED STATEMENT OF CONDITION OF ALL SAVINGS AND LOAN ASSOCIATIONS, DECEMBER 31, 1971

(in millions of dollars)

	Amount	Percentage of Total
Assets		
Cash on hand and in banks	$ 2,783	1.4%
Investment securities	18,293	8.9
Mortgage loans	174,385	84.5
F.H.L.B. stock	1,550	.7
Real estate owned	700	.3
All other assets	8,592	4.2
Total	$206,303	100.0%
Liabilities and Reserves		
Savings balances	$174,472	84.5
Borrowed money	9,048	4.4
Loans in process	5,072	2.5
All other liabilities	4,524	2.2
General and unallocated reserves	13,187	6.4
Total	$206,303	100.0%

SOURCE: Prepared by the United States Savings and Loan League from reports of the Federal Home Loan Bank Board and state supervisory authorities.

Cash and government bonds were 10 per cent of accounts. Of course, the showing of individual associations in these respects would cover a wide range. The investor should obtain a recent statement of his local association

[5]United States Savings and Loan League, *Savings and Loan Fact Book*, 1972.

and inquire carefully into its conditions and management. Of special importance is the proportion of reserves and undivided profits to share capital, the liquidity position, and the quality of the mortgage portfolio.[6] Associations whose accounts are insured by the F.S.L.I.C. are required to allocate to reserves each year an amount that will meet minimum "benchmark" and other requirements.[7] In addition, the Federal Home Loan Bank Board is authorized to establish "liquidity requirements" (cash and U.S. securities) within a range of 4 to 10 per cent of total savings and borrowings payable. This rate has varied with the times and was 7 per cent in 1972.[8]

Federal home loan banks. The Federal Home Loan Bank Board supervises Federal savings and loan associations, the F.S.L.I.C., and the eleven regional Federal Home Loan Banks. All Federal associations are required to hold stock in the Federal Home Loan Banks; other stockholders consist of state associations electing membership, and a few savings banks and insurance companies. The original capital of the Federal Home Loan Banks was provided by the government; member institutions subscribed to stock in the amount of 1 per cent of outstanding home mortgage loans, purchase contracts, and similar obligations. In 1950 provision was made for the retirement of the Government-owned stock by increasing the required member institution stockholdings to 2 per cent of outstanding home mortgage assets. This has since been reduced to 1 per cent, plus 1/12 of the debt to the regional Bank (if debt equals or exceeds 12 per cent of total loans). The chief source of funds of the Federal Home Loan Banks has been the issuance of consolidated notes and debentures, of which $7.1 billions were outstanding at the end of 1972 (see p.72). This represented a substantial decline from the peak figure of over $10.2 billions at the end of 1970. The reduction reflects the influx of new funds into the associations in late 1970 and in 1971, part of which was used to reduce borrowings.

An important function of the Federal Home Loan Banks is to make loans to members against home mortgages, government bonds, or stock in the Banks assigned as security. The charter of a Federal association permits it to borrow up to one-half of its capital (savings accounts plus earnings credited thereto). The amount which may be borrowed from sources other than a Federal Home Loan Bank is limited to one-tenth of such capital. However, with prior approval of the Federal Home Loan Bank Board, the association may borrow an unlimited amount from its Federal Home Loan Bank, upon such terms as may be required by the Bank. This gives the Banks considerable control over the supply of mortgage credit.

The Federal Home Loan Bank Board sets limits on the rates paid by

[6]The investment policy and restrictions on investments of savings and loan associations are discussed in Chapter 22.

[7]These are determined by the ratio of net worth to specified assets (balance due on conventional mortgage loans plus 20 per cent of the balance due on VA and FHA loans). By the end of the thirtieth year, and for each year thereafter, accumulated reserves must equal at least 5 per cent of total savings accounts. In addition, an association must maintain a net worth equal to its benchmark reserves plus 20 per cent of "scheduled items" (loans delinquent 90 days or more).

[8]In addition, short-term Government securities must equal $2^1/_2$ per cent of savings and borrowings payable on demand or due in one year or less.

associations on savings accounts, by withholding bank loans for those that do not abide by its maximum requirements, and, as we have seen, establishes reserve and liquidity requirements.

Shares in Credit Unions

Credit unions are nonprofit Federal- or state-chartered thrift organizations formed to serve the members of a particular group such as the employees of a business firm or government office, or members of a church, trade union, or fraternal organization. The credit union is managed by officers and directors elected by the members, and its activities and accounting are subject to strict governmental regulation. The essential purpose is to pool the savings of the members and make them available to members through loans. Savings are represented by shares in the union. Installment loans are made for a variety of consumer purposes, and any earnings remaining after expenses and legal reserves are returned in the form of dividends.

Although legally a sixty-day notice of withdrawal may be required, most credit unions make a practice of repurchasing shares on demand, so that the shares are considered savings accounts by most members. The investor should check the management of the union, its cash and government bond holdings, and the adequacy of its reserves. (Federal credit unions are required to add 20 per cent of annual net earnings each year until they are built up to a total of 10 per cent of shares outstanding.)

In October 1970, by Federal statute, federally chartered unions were required, and state-chartered unions could elect, to apply for share account insurance of $20,000 per account through the new National Credit Union Administration. This will place the shares of insured unions on the same protected basis as the deposits of banks and savings and loan associations. By October 1971, all but a few Federal unions had qualified for insurance, but most state-chartered organizations had not joined. In some states, state insurance systems have been set up.

The National Credit Union Administration replaces the former Bureau of Federal Credit Unions under the U.S. Department of Health, Education, and Welfare. The Administration, through six regional offices, will examine and supervise all aspects of federally chartered unions' operations.

As of December 1971, there were 23,375 credit unions operating in the United States and Territories, with total assets of $20.6 billions. Total savings (shares and deposits) amounted to $18.1 billions. These provided funds for loans to 24 million members amounting to $15.5 billions.[9]

The commission report. In a report issued in December 1971, the Report of the President's Commission on Financial Structure and Regulation ("Hunt Report"), there was a comprehensive list of recommendations concerning the four types of depository institutions described previously in

---

[9] *The Credit Union Magazine*, January 1972, p. 35. Annual data are available from Credit Union National Association, *International Credit Union Yearbook* (Madison, Wisconsin, annual).

this chapter. The following is a summary of the major points in which all of these institutions are involved:

1. Orderly phasing-out of the differentials in the rates paid on savings by the four, over a five-year period.

2. Abolishment of the rate ceilings on all time and savings deposits and shares of $1,000,000 or more.

3. Requirement, after a five-year phase-in period, of the same deposit reserves of all savings institutions.

4. Abolishment of legally required reserves of all savings institutions on time and savings deposits, share accounts, and certificates of deposit.

5. Equalization of the real estate lending powers of commercial banks, savings banks, and savings and loan associations.

6. Permission for any institution to change its charter to that of any other type: state or Federal, stock or mutual.

7. Abolishment of statutory and regulatory restrictions on all types of mortgage loans, and abolishment of geographical lending limits.

8. Development of uniform standards for all deposit-insuring agencies for meeting claims of failing deposit institutions.

9. Enactment of legislation to produce a uniform income tax formula for all depository institutions.

10. Reorganization of the functions and responsibilities of the regulatory agencies (and rename them), but preserve the independence of the Federal Reserve System.

These and many other recommendations to eliminate specialization and reduce competition will be hotly debated before actual legislation is accomplished (see also p.206).

U.S. Savings Bonds

Although Savings bonds could logically be considered in Chapter 5 on Federal obligations, it seems more appropriate to discuss them in the section of the book devoted to savings types of investments because Savings bonds "compete" with the deposit types of investments for the liquid savings of millions of investors.

Amount outstanding. United States Savings bonds were first issued in 1935 to furnish a medium of investment for the savings of individuals and to help meet Federal deficits. During World War II great emphasis was placed on the accumulation of these bonds, and in the post-World War II and post-Korean War periods the Treasury Department has persisted in maintaining the interest of investors in these securities. New forms have been developed, and the terms of the older bonds have been changed to make them more attractive.

The growth in importance of this medium of saving is indicated by Table

4-4 showing the amounts outstanding (at redemption value) and the character of ownership at the end of selected years.

Following the large issuance during the war, the outstanding amount of Savings bonds, particularly Series E bonds, continued to increase until 1951, when new sales and the current accrual of redemption values began to fall behind redemptions, reaching the low point in 1960. Since then a modest annual excess of new sales over redemptions has resulted in a moderate increase in the outstanding total.

Types.   Savings bonds are now issued in only two series: E and H. Sale of two other series of the original types first offered in 1935—Series F and G—was discontinued in May 1952; these were replaced by two additional series—J and K. Issuance of these latter series was in turn discontinued April 30, 1957, but a substantial volume of these is still outstanding. Series H bonds were first issued in 1952.

Table 4-4. SAVINGS BONDS OUTSTANDING
(in billions of dollars)

| Year | Held by | | Total |
(December 31)	Individuals	Others	Outstanding
1940	$ 2.8	$ .4	$ 3.2
1945	42.9	5.3	48.2
1950	49.6	8.4	58.0
1955	50.2	7.7	57.9
1960	45.7	1.5	47.2
1965	49.7	.6	50.3
1966	50.3	.5	50.8
1967	51.2	.5	51.7
1968	51.9	.4	52.3
1969	51.8	.4	52.2
1970	52.1	.4	52.5
1971	54.4	.5	54.9
1972 (Oct.)	57.1	.4	57.5

SOURCES: *Treasury Bulletin; Federal Reserve Bulletin.*

SERIES E BONDS.   The distinctive features of the Series E bonds are:

1. These bonds are issued in denominations ranging from $25 to $1,000 maturity value.

2. The bonds do not bear any stated rate of interest, but are sold at 75 per cent of face value. The 25 per cent accumulation when the bond is due represents its interest to maturity. Bonds issued to May 1, 1952, had a maturity of ten years and produced 2.9 per cent at maturity. The maturity period was reduced and the yield to maturity was increased six times from 1952 to 1969 in order to make the bonds more attractive in competition with yields available elsewhere. In 1969, the maturity was established at five years and ten months, to produce a yield of 5 per cent to maturity. In

August 1970, the maturity remained the same but a special bonus was added that increased the redemption price to 102.72 (per $75 cost) at maturity, on bonds bought after May 31. This increased the yield to 5.5 per cent.

3. The bonds are redeemable at the option of the holder at any time after two months from the date of issue at a fixed price schedule under which the redemption price gradually increases from the purchase price to the face value at the end of the last year. Under this plan, the investor is protected against any depreciation in the dollar value of his investment during the entire period. If the bonds are redeemed well before maturity, the rate of income return as indicated by the established redemption prices will be substantially less than that obtainable if the bonds are held until the maturity date. Moreover, if the bonds are redeemed, the rate of yield voluntarily surrendered on the unexpired period of the bonds will be higher than the maturity rate. As shown in Table 4-5 (which applies to bonds issued June 1, 1970 and after), if a bond is redeemed just after being held for five years, the redemption price of $94.70 (per $100 of face value) would afford a yield of 4.84 per cent for the five-year period; however, a yield of 9.47 per cent would be required from an alternative investment to equal

Table 4-5. UNITED STATES SAVINGS BONDS (SERIES E)
Redemption Values and Income Yields

Period After Issue (beginning June 1, 1970)	Redemption Value	Yield Gained (if held)	Yield Lost (if redeemed)
First $^1/_2$ year	75.00%	0.00%	5.50%
$^1/_2$ year to 1 year	76.20	3.20	5.72
1 to $1^1/_2$ years	78.04	4.01	5.81
$1^1/_2$ to 2 years	79.80	4.18	5.96
2 to $2^1/_2$ years	81.60	4.26	6.15
$2^1/_2$ to 3 years	83.52	4.35	6.37
3 to $3^1/_2$ years	85.56	4.44	6.63
$3^1/_2$ to 4 years	87.72	4.52	6.97
4 to $4^1/_2$ years	90.12	4.64	7.38
$4^1/_2$ to 5 years	92.64	4.75	8.05
5 to $5^1/_2$ years	95.28	4.84	9.47
$5^1/_2$ to 5 years, 10 mo.	98.04	4.93	15.12
At maturity (5 years, 10 mo.)	102.92	5.50	—

that which would have been obtainable through holding the bond to just over 5½ years. The remarkable rate of 15.12 per cent (annual rate) would be lost if the bond were redeemed just before maturity date.

4. To discourage redemption of previous issues, their redemption values and yields have been increased whenever new issues have been offered on a more attractive basis. There is now a somewhat bewildering variety of redemption price schedules which should be carefully checked by holders of the bonds. For example, bonds that were issued (for $75) in June 1943 had a redemption value of $213.68 on June 1, 1973 (after two ten-year extensions).

5. Owners of bonds have the option of retaining matured bonds for extension periods as long as twenty years. No savings bond ever issued has reached final maturity, if the owner has chosen to hold it.

6. The bonds are nontransferable (except to heirs) and are redeemable only by the registered owners, thus protecting the holders against loss from theft, forgery, fire, and similar causes.

7. The bonds may be purchased by any investor other than a commercial bank. They may be registered in the name of one individual or of two individuals as co-owners (either of whom may redeem the bond), or as owner and beneficiary.

8. The maximum purchase permitted any individual investor is now $5,000 (issue price) for each calendar year of issue. Of course, several times the limit could be bought in the same family through the use of joint ownership.

9. The bonds may be purchased at commercial, savings, Federal Reserve banks, and savings and loan associations, or directly from the Office of the Treasurer of the United States.

SERIES H (CURRENT INCOME) BONDS. These bonds were first issued June 1, 1952, and are available in denominations ranging from $500 to $5,000. Unlike the E's, they are sold at 100 per cent of face value and pay interest semiannually by check for their maturity of ten years. They are redeemable at par six months from the issue date, at one month's notice. Their yield to maturity is now (1973) 5.50 per cent compounded semiannually. If redeemed before maturity, the yield is reduced because the semiannual interest checks are lower in the first year than in the later years. Like the E bonds, they are issued to all investors except commercial banks. Investors' purchases are limited to $5,000 maturity value each calendar year. The transfer provisions are the same as those of the E bonds. Interest is subject to Federal but not to state income taxes.

Former issues. Series F bonds were twelve-year bonds bought at $74 per $100 of maturity value, originally yielding 2.53 per cent if held to maturity. They were withdrawn from sale in 1952, and replaced by Series J bonds priced at $72 to yield 2.76 per cent if held to maturity. Sale of the J's was terminated in 1957.

Series G bonds were twelve-year bonds originally paying interest at the rate of 2.5 per cent if held to maturity. They were withdrawn from sale in 1952 and replaced by Series K bonds yielding 2.76 per cent if held to maturity. Sale of the K's was terminated in 1957.

Holders of Series E, F, and J bonds may exchange them for the present E's and H's. Those retained have extension privileges and their redemption values have been increased to provide yields comparable to those on the adjusted E's and H's.

Investment characteristics. The advantages of Savings bonds may be summarized as follows:

1. They are as safe as any investment can be, and they do not suffer from market-price fluctuations. Their exact redemption value is known at all times. They provide complete liquidity (after the initial waiting period).

2. They are redeemable at the option of the holder. This enables the investor to switch to higher-yielding investments when interest rates rise.

3. Interest is automatically compounded semiannually. To achieve this with corporate bonds requires the immediate reinvestment of the interest at the yield rate.

4. Two income tax advantages are enjoyed: (1) interest is free from state and municipal levies, and (2) on Series E and J bonds, the interest may be reported as income currently as it accrues or all at once when the bond is redeemed. Under the latter option, interest is tax-free until redemption, and the redemption date may be chosen so as to place the income in a lower tax bracket, say after the investor has retired, or in a year in which other income is lower. (However, if substantial amounts of bonds mature or are redeemed in one year, especially if the taxpayer's other income in that year is high, the interest may be taxed at a higher rate.)

5. Owners of outstanding E bonds may exchange $500 or more at current redemption values, for H bonds which pay interest by check. The appreciation of the older bonds is not taxed until the H bonds are cashed in or mature. This privilege was extended to J bonds beginning in April 1964.

6. The maturity value of G and K bonds is payable in full to the estate on the death of the owner.

7. Automatic transfer to co-owners, heirs, and beneficiaries is permitted.

8. Registration permits ease of replacement in the event the securities are lost or destroyed.

9. Bonds are easily purchased and redeemed without any commission charge.

10. Many businesses cooperate with the Treasury Department by withholding, on request, wage or salary increments for the regular purchase of Savings bonds.

11. Occasionally, yields on Savings bonds have been competitively attractive.

Chief disadvantages are:

1. Savings bonds are not transferable (except to estates) and so may not be used as collateral.

2. The fixed returns on Savings bonds usually lag behind those of alternative investments, and even when increased to induce more new sales and fewer redemptions, improvement is usually too late. Thus in early 1970, interest rates on deposit-type investments ran from 4½ per cent on bank passbook accounts to as high as 6 per cent on smaller time deposits with two-year maturities, and marketable Treasury bonds were yielding over 8 per cent. But the yield on Savings bonds ran only 3.6 per cent to 5.5 per cent depending on issue date and maturity. The major decline in market

yields in 1970–1971, however, reduced interest rates on intermediate Treasury obligations to 4.75 per cent by March 1971, and some banks reduced passbook savings rates to 4 per cent. Under these conditions the 5.5 per cent yield to maturity on Savings bonds became relatively attractive, and for the first time in several years, more of these were sold than were redeemed. This trend continued in 1971–1972, although open market yields firmed in the former year.

3. Some investors object to the fact that E and J bonds do not provide current income. The objection is probably not serious in most cases, with H bonds available by new purchase or through exchange.

4. Yield is sacrificed if the bonds are redeemed before maturity.

5. These bonds have the same disadvantage as all fixed-principal and fixed-income investments, namely, that their real value in terms of purchasing power declines with the rise in the price level.

REFERENCES

AMERICAN INSTITUTE OF BANKING, *Savings and Time Deposit Banking*. New York: The Institute, 1968.

CONWAY, L. V., *Savings and Loan Principles*, 3rd ed. Chicago: American Savings and Loan Institute Press, 1965.

COOKE, G. W., et al., *Financial Institutions: Their Role in the American Economy*. New York: Simmons-Boardman Publishing Corp., 1962.

COX, A. H., JR., *Regulation of Interest Rates on Bank Deposits*. Ann Arbor, Mich.: Bureau of Business Research, Graduate School of Business Administration, University of Michigan, 1966.

DUBLIN, JACK, *Credit Unions: Theory and Practice*. Detroit: Wayne State University Press, 1971.

Federal Savings Institutions. House Committee on Banking and Currency, Report No. 1642, 90th Congress, 1st Session. Washington, D.C.: U.S. Government Printing Office, 1967.

FRIEND, IRWIN, *Study of the Savings and Loan Industry*. Submitted to the Federal Home Loan Board (Washington, 1969).

GOLDSMITH, R. W., *A Study of Saving in the United States*, three volumes. Princeton, N.J.: Princeton University Press, 1955–1956.

———, *Financial Intermediaries in the American Economy Since 1960*. Princeton, N.J.: Princeton University Press, 1958.

———, *Financial Institutions*. New York: Random House, Inc., 1968.

GREBLER, LEO, *The Future of Thrift Institutions*. Danville, Ill.: Joint Savings and Loan and Mutual Savings Banks Exchange Groups, 1969.

JACOBS, DONALD, et al., *Financial Institutions*. 5th ed. Homewood, Ill.: Richard D. Irwin, Inc., 1972.

KENDALL, L. T., *The Savings and Loan Business: Its Purposes, Functions, and Economic Justification*, a monograph prepared for the Commission on Money and Credit. Englewood Cliffs, N.J.: Prentice-Hall, Inc., 1962.

LUDTKE, J. B., *The American Financial System: Markets and Institutions*, 2nd ed. Boston: Allyn and Bacon, Inc., 1967.

MOODY, J. C., AND G. C. FITE, *The Credit Union Movement*. Lincoln, Nebraska: University of Nebraska Press, 1971.

NATIONAL ASSOCIATION OF MUTUAL SAVINGS, *Mutual Savings Banks: Basic Characteristics and Role in the National Economy*, a monograph prepared for the Commission on Money and Credit. Englewood Cliffs, N.J.: Prentice-Hall, Inc., 1962.

PRATHER, W. C., *Savings Accounts*, 4th ed. Chicago: American Savings and Loan Institute Press, 1970.

REPORT OF THE PRESIDENT'S COMMISSION ON *Financial Structure and Regulation*. Washington, D.C.: U.S. Government Printing Office, 1971.

THE FIRST BOSTON CORPORATION, *Securities of the United States Government*. New York: The Corporation, *biennial*.

WELFLING, WELDON, *Mutual Savings Banks: The Evolution of a Financial Intermediary*. Cleveland: Press of Case Western University, 1968.

5 U.S. Government and Agency Securities

SCOPE: This chapter discusses the investment characteristics of the obligations of the Federal government and its agencies and explains the predominant position that they have attained in the investment field. The order of discussion is (1) short history of the Federal debt, (2) types of Federal debt, (3) Federal agencies, (4) territorial bonds, (5) investment tests—ability to pay and willingness to pay, (6) other criteria, (7) tax position, (8) price and yield record, (9) ownership, and (10) market for government bonds.

The importance of Federal debt is indicated by its size—the amount outstanding at the end of 1972 totalled $445 billions—and by the fact that this amount represented about 70 per cent of the total public debt (Federal, state, and local) at that time. Federal obligations support the liquidity and solvency of the financial institutions that are its chief owners. Individuals, who own over $74 billions or over 16 per cent of the Federal debt, also have a very substantial stake in this medium of investment. The impact of the monetary and fiscal management of the Federal debt on the market prices and yields of securities affects all types of investors and all segments of the capital market.

Short History of the Federal Debt

At the beginning of the present century, the total debt of the Federal government amounted to slightly over $1 billion ($16 per capita) with an annual interest charge of $33.5 *millions*. As of December 1972, the comparable figures were $445 billions ($2,125 per capita) with annual interest of nearly $22 billions. How did the Federal debt grow to such astronomical size, and what types of issues appeared during the seven decades?

During the first decade of the century, total debt was reduced to $913 millions. In addition to general financing, Panama Canal bonds were issued as direct obligations for the purpose of financing the construction of the interocean waterway.

During the second decade, war financing increased Federal interest-bearing debt to a peak of $25.2 billions in 1919, with annual interest of $1.1 billions. The main components of the debt by 1920 were the Liberty and Victory Loan bonds, which have now been retired, and the shorter-term

Table 5-1. NATIONAL DEBT OF THE UNITED STATES, DECEMBER 31, 1971

(in millions of dollars)

Direct debt	
Public issues	
Marketable issues	
Treasury bills	$ 97,505
Certificates of indebtedness	—
Treasury notes	113,965
Treasury bonds	50,568
Total marketable	$262,038
Nonmarketable issues	
U.S. Savings bonds	54,275
(at current redemption value)	
Treasury bonds, Savings and investment series	2,320
Foreign series securities and other	18,019
Total nonmarketable	$ 74,614
Special issues	$ 85,656
Total interest-bearing direct debt	422,308
Matured debt on which interest has ceased	304
Debt bearing no interest	1,518
Total direct debt	$424,131
Guaranteed debt	
Federal Housing Administration	490
Total direct and guaranteed debt	$424,621

SOURCE: *Treasury Bulletin*, February 1972.

Treasury notes and *certificates*. In addition, two new types appeared: (1) the *Postal Savings* bonds, which are no longer sold but which were used to enable depositors in the Postal Savings System to invest more than the maximum of $2,500 permitted in a savings account; (2) *Federal Land Bank* and *Joint Stock Land Bank* bonds, which were issued under the Farm Loan Act of 1916 as *instrumentalities* rather than obligations of the Government.

During the prosperous 1920s, almost $10 billions were pared from the Federal debt, which totalled $15.9 billions in 1930 with annual interest charges of $660 millions. *Treasury bonds,* issued primarily for the purpose of refunding higher-interest war loan bonds, were prominent in this period.

The 1930s produced a great increase in Federal debt resulting from the deficits of that period. In 1940 interest-bearing debt reached the unprecedented figure of $42.4 billions, an amount regarded by many at the time as about the maximum that could be supported (the legal debt limit was set by Congress at $45 billions in 1941). However, interest rates were maintained at a low level, so that the annual interest charges in 1940 amounted to only $1 billion, the same as on the $24-billion debt of 1920. Decline in the demand for funds on the part of business, the sale of Federal obligations to banks, and emphasis on short maturities were the chief explanations for the phenomena of increasing debt and decreasing interest rates.

During the 1930s, a variety of issues of Federal agencies and instrumentalities appeared. The *Federal Home Loan Banks* were created in 1931 with authority to issue so-called instrumentalities. In 1932, the *Home Owners'*

Loan Corporation was created with authority to issue bonds guaranteed by the Federal government in exchange for home mortgages in default. In the same year, the *Federal Farm Mortgage Corporation* was established with similar authority to issue guaranteed bonds in exchange for farm mortgages in default. The *Reconstruction Finance Corporation* (since liquidated) was also established in 1932 with power to issue obligations backed by Federal guarantee for the purpose of making loans to business organizations in need of financial assistance. Subsequently, the *Commodity Credit Corporation,* the *Federal Housing Administration,* and the *U.S. Housing Authority* were created with power to make loans bearing Federal guarantees. In 1935, *U.S. Savings* bonds were authorized to be sold directly to investors. In addition to these new issues sold to the public, several special types were created for internal fiscal purposes, such as the unemployment insurance and old-age retirement trust funds authorized under the Social Security Act of 1935.

World War II produced an astronomical increase in debt resulting from the Federal deficits of the war and immediate postwar periods. The peak of $278 billions in interest-bearing debt (including guaranteed obligations) was reached in February 1946 with annual interest charges of $5.4 billions. This tremendous total was composed of all types of obligations—marketable Treasury bonds, notes, certificates of indebtedness, and bills; nonmarketable issues including Savings bonds and Savings notes; and a variety of special issues for special fiscal funds. Again the generally low rates of interest in the capital market, the sale of nonmarketable issues to banks and individuals, and emphasis on short maturities, together with fiscal control of money rates, kept the interest charges low in relation to the principal.

The fiscal year ending June 30, 1947 saw the first Federal surplus after sixteen consecutive years of deficits. By June 1948, interest-bearing debt had been reduced to $250 billions. In the whole 1948–1971 period, however, surpluses appeared in only six fiscal years—1951, 1955, 1956, 1957, 1960, and 1969. During that period the debt increased $172 billions to $425 billions by the end of 1971.[1] Even during the booming 1960s deficits were the order of the day, and the recession years of 1968 and 1970–1971 made necessary an unusual volume of Federal financing. The very large deficit in fiscal 1971–1972 reflected the Government's attempt to stimulate the economy and the extraordinary costs of the Vietnam war. Changes in debt reflect not only budget surpluses and deficits but also changes in the Treasury's cash balances and the effect of certain trust fund transactions.

Types of Debt

Treasury bills. Treasury bills are sold at auction through the Federal Reserve Banks at rates that reflect the condition of the short-term money market at the time of offering. They are issued on a discount basis, with a maturity of between three months and one year. They are payable to the bearer, and denominations range from $1,000 to $1,000,000. Federal Reserve

---

[1]To legalize the great growth in debt, Congress has successively raised the debt limit from $45 billions in 1940 to $465 billions (November 1972).

and commercial banks are the chief market, but individuals, and especially corporations, find in them a liquid investment for short-term funds. In January 1970 yields on representative three-month bills were 7.90 per cent— the highest in history. They declined to 3.4 per cent in March 1971, rose to 4.80 per cent in September 1971, stood at 3 per cent in early 1972, and 5.2 per cent in January 1973.

Certificates of indebtedness. Certificates of indebtedness are bearer instruments issued with a maturity of one year or less and carry one coupon providing for payment of interest and principal at maturity. Denominations range from $1,000 to $1,000,000. Banks, individuals, and corporations find in them a liquid investment. At the end of 1972, none were outstanding.

Treasury notes. Treasury notes are coupon instruments issued with maturities of from one to seven years. They are chiefly owned by the Federal Reserve and commercial banks. The yields to maturity on representative three- to five-year maturities reached 8.30 per cent in January 1970—the highest on record, but declined to 4.7 per cent in March 1971, rose to 6.80 per cent in July 1971, and stood at 6.20 per cent in January 1973.

Treasury bonds. Treasury bonds are issued with maturities of over five years. They fall into two main classes: fully marketable issues eligible for purchase by all investors, including banks, and nonmarketable "Investment Series" bonds. The latter bear interest at 2¾ per cent and are issued in denominations ranging from $1,000 to $10,000,000. They are convertible at the owner's option into five-year 1½ per cent marketable Treasury notes. They are designed primarily for large institutional investors, but those in a deceased individual owner's estate can be applied to the payment of Federal estate taxes. Other minor types of nonmarketable issues are held by foreign governments and their monetary authorities.

Marketable Treasury bonds are available in denominations ranging from $50 to $1,000,000 and in a wide range of maturities. Until 1971 the statutory limit of 4¼ per cent for coupons prevented the issuance of such bonds when market yields exceeded that rate. In the spring of 1971, Congress removed the limitation from $10 billions of bonds. Yields on outstanding Treasury bonds have varied widely through the years, reflecting the rise and fall of long-term interest rates. In May 1970, the yield on representative issues reached an all-time high of 7.2 per cent but declined to 5.33 per cent in November 1971, only to rise again reaching 5.82 per cent in January 1973. Different maturities bear different yields. On January 19, 1973, yields ranged from 4.80 to 6.85 per cent. The lowest yields are available on "deep discount" bonds bearing low coupons, reflecting their advantage from the standpoint of capital gains taxes, and on certain issues acceptable at par in payment of Federal estate taxes.

U. S. Savings bonds. These bonds are nontransferable and hence nonmarketable. Their redemption prices are so arranged as to provide yields at lower rates than are obtainable if held to maturity. In December 1972, $58.1 billions were outstanding (at current redemption value). Two different classes are available to investors (other classes are still outstanding, but are no longer issued) :

Series E Savings bonds issued beginning June 1, 1970 have a maturity of 5 years, 10 months. Each purchaser is limited to amounts of not more than $5,000 face (maturity) value within a calendar year. These bonds are sold on a discount basis at 75 per cent of maturity value, and yield 5.50 per cent if held to maturity. They are redeemable at any time (after the first sixty days of issue) at values stated on the bonds, and may be exchanged at any time for Series H bonds.

Series H Savings bonds are issued at par and are redeemable at par. Interest is payable semiannually by check. On bonds bought beginning June 1, 1970 the yield, if held to maturity, is also 5.50 per cent.

Further details concerning these issues and their investment characteristics are found in Chapter 4.

Special issues. These are issued by the Treasury directly to various Government trust funds (for example, Social Security and Federal Employees' Retirement funds) and may be redeemed whenever such accounts need funds. Coupon rates range from 2 to 4 per cent.

Miscellaneous types. Other nonmarketable obligations include the following: (1) *Retirement-plan bonds* are available for purchase only in connection with bond-purchase plans and pension and profit-sharing plans under the Self-Employed Individuals Retirement Act of 1962 [Keogh Act (see p. 44)]. They bear denominations of from $50 to $1,000. Values increase each six months according to a special table. Interest (reaching 4.15 per cent to maturity) is paid only on redemption. (2) *Depository bonds* (2 per cent) are issued to banks in compensation for the cost of servicing government payrolls. They are acceptable as collateral for deposits of Federal funds.

Guaranteed debt. In recent years, the Federal Housing Administration has been the only Federal agency to borrow funds through the use of securities that are fully guaranteed as to principal and interest by the U.S. Government. Certain other agencies, such as the Commodity Credit Corporation, the Federal Farm Mortgage Corporation, the Reconstruction Finance Corporation, and the Home Owners' Loan Corporation, have issued guaranteed securities in the past, but these have been retired. The fact that bonds are fully guaranteed by the Federal government gives them an investment status essentially equal to that of direct obligations. (Their tax status is discussed in Chapter 10.)

Federal Agencies

The term "Federal agency" is used rather loosely to denote corporations or organizations controlled by the Federal government, or sponsored by the government even though their shares are privately held. Even the latter are operated under Federal supervision. The bonds of these "agencies" are not guaranteed by the Government, but its strong moral obligation gives them an investment standing that is second only to that of direct Federal debt. Yields are slightly higher than those on Federal obligations with similar maturities. Interest on agency bonds is fully taxable by the Federal government but is exempt from state and municipal income taxation. Bonds outstanding at the end of October 1972 are shown in Table 5-2.

Table 5-2. FEDERAL AGENCY BONDS, October 31, 1972

(in millions of dollars)

Federal Intermediate Credit Banks—collateral trust debentures	$ 5,976
Federal Land Banks—collateral bonds	8,181
Federal Home Loan Banks—consolidated notes and bonds	7,949
Federal National Mortgage Association—notes, debentures, and mortgage-backed bonds	18,724
Government National Mortgage Association—participation certificates for which GNMA is trustee	4,885
Federal Home Loan Mortgage Corporation—mortgage-backed bonds	615
Banks for Cooperatives—debentures	1,859
Tennessee Valley Authority—debentures	1,995

SOURCE: *Treasury Bulletin, Federal Reserve Bulletin.*

The twelve Federal Intermediate Credit Banks were created in 1923 to rediscount paper of and make loans to production credit and cooperative associations. Noncallable *consolidated debentures* are issued as the joint and several obligations of the twelve banks, which (since 1968) own the Banks' stock. Their chief market is financial institutions. Debentures usually have a maturity of nine months.

The Federal Land Banks were created under the Farm Loan Act of 1916 for the purpose of supplying long-term credit to farm owners. An eligible loan must represent a first mortgage on unencumbered farm property in an amount not exceeding 65 per cent of the appraised normal value, repayable in installments over a period of between five and forty years. These loans become the collateral security for bonds issued by the banks.

Loans handled by the Federal Land Banks are made principally through local Land Bank Associations, which own the Banks' shares. The borrowers must buy stock in their local associations to the extent of 5 per cent of the loan. The associations, in turn, guarantee each loan, which they pass on to the Federal Land Bank in which they share ownership. The present practice is to issue *Consolidated Federal Farm Loan bonds* representing the joint obligation of the entire group. Commercial banks and individuals hold the bulk of Land Bank bonds.[2] The Federal Home Loan Banks were described

[2]The Farm Loan Act also provided for Joint Stock Land Banks as private ventures for the purpose of making loans to farmers. Bonds issued by the Joint Stock Land Banks had the same type of collateral security as those of the Federal Land Banks, but they represented only the obligation of the issuing bank. In all, eighty-eight banks were chartered. Many of them were poorly managed, and nine of them went into receivership. Under legislation passed in 1933, they were ordered to cease making new loans, and since then have been liquidated.

in Chapter 3. They issue bonds secured by the mortgages offered as collateral by borrowing members aggregating 190 per cent (in unpaid principal) of the bank bonds. Although these bonds may be issued by separate banks, in which event the other banks are jointly liable, the present practice is to issue *consolidated bonds* as the joint liability of all eleven banks.

The Federal National Mortgage Association ("Fannie Mae") was first organized in 1938 to purchase and sell FHA-insured and VA-guaranteed mortgages. Fannie Mae is entirely privately owned (since 1968), but it is subject to regulation by the Secretary of Housing and Urban Development. Its purpose is to provide a secondary market for mortgages insured by the FHA or guaranteed by the administrator of Veterans Affairs. Fannie Mae originally bought or sold mortgages to supply or soak up funds depending on the supply of and demand for mortgage credit. It now deals in commitments rather than in mortgages, by holding weekly auctions of forward commitment funds with the prices and yields determined by the bidders. It is still the only substantial secondary market for Federally supported mortgages.

Fannie Mae finances its operations by selling short-term discount notes, unsecured debentures, and mortgage-backed bonds, mainly to institutions, and its shares are traded on the New York Stock Exchange.[3]

The Government National Mortgage Association ("Ginny Mae") was formed in 1968 as a corporate entity within the U.S. Department of Health, Education and Welfare to take over the special-assistance programs and liquidating functions formerly performed by the Federal National Mortgage Association. It buys mortgages that meet institutional standards but for which market funds are not freely available and is also engaged in liquidating the original Fannie Mae portfolio. A new activity that may become very important in financing home building is its guarantee of securities issued by mortgage bankers and other qualified investors. These "pass-through" certificates are secured by pools of FHA and VA loans.[4] Ginny Mae raises funds by selling participation certificates on its mortgage portfolio, using the proceeds to repay advances by the Federal government.

The Federal Home Loan Mortgage Corporation ("Freddie Mac") was created in 1970 to strengthen the existing secondary market in FHA and VA mortgage loans and to develop a new secondary market for conventional mortgages. It buys mortgages from the Federal Home Loan Banks and their member banks, and from other institutions whose deposits are insured by agencies of the Federal government. Its capital stock is held by the Federal Home Loan Banks. The corporation issues bonds backed by pools of mortgages, but its operations are not yet substantial.

The Farm Credit Act of 1933 provided for the formation of a District Bank for Cooperatives in each of the twelve Farm Credit Districts. These banks, under the supervision of the Farm Credit Administration, make loans to eligible farmers' cooperative associations that own their stock. Consolidated debentures of all twelve banks, or bonds in which a Central Bank for Cooperatives participates, are sold to provide funds for loans.

[3]See Chapters 2, 5, and 11 for further discussion.
[4]See Chapter 11.

The Tennessee Valley Authority was established in 1933 to develop power and the economy in the Tennessee River and adjacent areas. It is authorized to issue bonds and notes that are a fixed charge against net power proceeds (ahead of interest and depreciation). Discount notes of four-month maturity are sold at auction. Bonds are offered at competitive bidding, similar to the practice in public utility financing. (See Chapter 27).

World Bank Bonds

The International Bank for Reconstruction and Development was established in 1945 under the Bretton Woods Agreement Act to assist in the reconstruction and development of the production facilities and resources of the nations belonging to the Agreement. It is not an "agency" of the Federal government. Of the capital stock of $26.6 billions subscribed by the member nations as of June 30, 1972, 10 per cent has been paid in. World Bank dollar bonds were outstanding in the amount of $3,500 millions as of June 30, 1972.[5] Until the amount of bonds outstanding reaches $6.35 billions, they are backed in full by the commitment of the U.S. Government, because that is the portion of the subscribed capital for which the United States is subject to call.

World Bank bonds are fully subject to taxes imposed on resident holders. A large number of states have approved their purchase by commercial banks, mutual savings banks, insurance companies, and trust funds.

Territorial Bonds

The only bonds of this class are those of the Commonwealth of Puerto Rico, of which $525 millions were outstanding as of June 30, 1971. Their interest and principal are solely the responsibility of the Commonwealth. They are, however, exempt from all U.S. Federal and state income taxes. Since December 1961, debt service in any fiscal year may not exceed 15 per cent of average annual revenues of the Commonwealth's treasury during the two preceding fiscal years.

Investment Tests

The safety of the bonds of the United States depends entirely upon the ability and willingness of the American people to carry the debt, that is, to provide, through taxation, funds sufficient to assure the payment of principal and income when due. Other desirable investment qualifications include ready marketability and collateral value and *relative* stability of price and

---

[5]In addition, bonds payable in Canadian dollars, Netherlands guilders, pounds sterling, Belgian francs, German marks, Italian lire, Japanese yen, and Swiss francs were outstanding. For additional discussion of this institution, see Chapter 10.

hence of yield, compared to other types of securities. But actual stability has been notably absent in recent years.

Ability to pay. The burden of public debt, while enormous in terms of its dollar amount, is best measured by reference to its relation to national wealth and income, and to the likelihood of its continued increase or its reduction. Certain data that help to point up these comparisons are given in Table 5-3.

The enormous Federal debt reached its immediate postwar peak in 1946 in terms of amount outstanding and per capita, and interest as a per cent of national income. The general reduction of debt from 1947 through 1951 was accompanied by a decline of principal per capita and as a per cent of national income, and of interest in relation to national income. Except for a pause 1956–1957, debt rose steadily to its all-time peak in 1972. On a per capita basis, however, it declined to less than $1,600 by 1957 and levelled off at about that figure until the recent increases in 1968–1972. Its relative decline in terms of national income continued steadily to a new low figure in 1970, but as a percentage of national income, the interest burden remained around 2 per cent until 1968. In terms of the burden on the economy, the interest expense is more significant than the principal. The real test of ability to pay lies not so much in the dollar amount of debt and annual interest, but in the size of these items in relation to wealth and income, and in the ability of the American people to carry an annual Federal budget of over $250 billions. Of greatest concern is that, reflecting increased borrowing and higher interest rates, the annual interest bill now approaches 10 per cent of the Federal budget outlays.

An analysis of the annual Federal budget reveals that three-quarters of the expenditures are associated with wars—past conflicts, present outlays resulting therefrom, and preparedness for and prevention of future wars. The elimination of fear of war would be the greatest single aid to the debt situation. But, some additional steps can be taken to place the debt in a manageable position, including economical management of government expenditures, retirement of some debt in times of peak prosperity, and wider distribution of debt outside of the banking system to reduce its inflationary influence. There is no danger of debt repudiation, in terms of dollars. In terms of what the dollar will buy, each dollar of debt and interest has become steadily less valuable with successive increases in the price level.

The Test of Willingness to Pay

An axiom of the investment business is that the "will to pay" must be present in every good loan. Even though unwilling debtors can at times be forced to pay, no investor voluntarily buys into a law suit. Bonds of national governments, moreover, are issued by sovereign powers, which are usually immune from suits by creditors. Thus the only real basis for national government loans is confidence in the good faith of the borrowing nation. The best test of good faith is found in the simple record of past transactions. Unfortunately

Table 5-3. DATA ON FEDERAL FINANCES AND DIRECT DEBT[a]

Fiscal Year ended June 30	Budget Receipts[b] (millions)	Budget Outlays[b] (millions)	Surplus or Deficit (millions)	Public Debt[a] (millions)	Public Debt per Capita ($)	Computed Annual Interest on Public Debt (millions)	Public Debt as a Percentage of National Income	Computed Interest as a Percentage of National Income	Computed Interest Rate on Public Debt
1940	$ 5,144	$ 9,062	$− 3,918	$ 42,968	$ 326	$ 1,095	52.9%	1.3%	2.58%
1945	44,475	98,416	− 53,941	258,682	1,849	4,964	142.5	2.7	1.94
1950	36,495	39,617	− 3,122	257,357	1,702	5,613	106.7	2.3	2.20
1955	65,469	68,509	− 3,041	274,374	1,670	6,387	82.9	1.9	2.35
1956	74,547	70,460	+ 4,087	272,751	1,630	6,950	77.7	2.0	2.58
1957	79,990	76,741	+ 3,249	270,527	1,588	7,325	73.9	2.0	2.73
1958	79,636	82,575	− 2,939	276,343	1,594	7,245	75.1	2.0	2.64
1959	79,249	92,104	− 12,855	284,706	1,613	8,066	71.2	2.0	2.87
1960	92,492	92,223	+ 269	286,331	1,591	9,316	69.1	2.2	3.30
1961	94,389	97,795	− 3,406	288,971	1,579	8,761	67.6	2.1	3.07
1962	99,676	106,813	− 7,137	298,201	1,604	9,519	65.1	2.1	3.24
1963	106,560	111,311	− 4,751	305,860	1,621	10,119	63.5	2.1	3.36
1964	112,662	118,584	− 5,922	311,713	1,629	10,900	60.1	2.1	3.56
1965	116,833	118,430	− 1,596	317,274	1,637	11,467	56.2	2.0	3.68
1966	130,856	134,652	− 3,796	319,907	1,633	12,516	51.5	2.0	3.99
1967	149,552	158,254	− 8,702	326,221	1,649	12,953	50.0	2.0	4.04
1968	153,671	178,833	− 25,161	347,578	1,739	15,404	48.8	2.2	4.50
1969	187,784	184,548	+ 3,236	353,720	1,752	17,087	46.4	2.2	4.89
1970	193,743	196,588	− 2,845	370,919	1,816	20,339	46.2	2.5	5.56
1971	188,392	211,425	− 23,033	410,292	2,050	20,254	48.0	2.4	5.14
1972	208,649	231,876	− 23,227	438,154	2,124	21,545	47.5	2.3	5.09

[a]Public debt excludes guaranteed securities.
[b]1940–1945: Administrative budget; 1955–1972: Unified budget.

SOURCES: *Treasury Bulletin; Annual Report of the Secretary of the Treasury; Federal Reserve Bulletin.*

nations which do not desire to repay their loans usually find a convenient method of evasion. The experience of American investors with foreign government loans has been most unhappy in this respect.

In a relative sense, the debt record of the Federal government of the United States has been excellent. At no time in the history of the nation has there been a dollar default in the payment of interest or principal on a Federal bond. The record, however, is not perfect. A blemish was the cancellation in 1933 of the gold payment clauses in the Government bonds. These clauses had been placed in the bonds as a method of guaranteeing buyers against loss from the decline of purchasing power of their money in the event that the nation should either reduce the gold content of the dollar or abandon the gold standard entirely. In fairness, we should state that when the gold clauses were cancelled, holders of bonds which were not then due were permitted to have their bonds redeemed immediately at face value. Holders were thus permitted to employ their money in any alternative commitment which might seem preferable in the light of possible monetary inflation.

The virtual abandonment of gold in August 1971, when the value of the dollar was allowed to "float" in terms of foreign currencies, and the subsequent devaluation in 1972 from \$35 to \$38 an ounce, did not represent a default situation. Dollar obligations, both foreign and domestic, are paid in dollars. What the dollar is worth, however, is another matter.

Other Investment Criteria

Federal securities meet the highest standards of recovery of principal (at maturity), assurance of income, and collateral value (with the exception of Savings bonds). The marketable issues are free from care with respect to ultimate payment, but not from price risk. While there is an immediate and active market, prices can and do move sharply in reflection of interest rate changes. Savings bonds provide absolute recovery of principal at a schedule known in advance.

Tax Position of Government Bonds

The income tax status of Government securities is explained in Chapter 18. Federal obligations do not enjoy any special advantages insofar as Federal income taxes are concerned. They are on a par with the obligations of states and municipalities in being exempt from state income taxation, but lack the exemption from Federal income taxes enjoyed by the latter. The fact that income from a certain Federal bond is fully taxable whereas that from a municipal bond is nontaxable explains why the latter, if high-grade and of the same maturity, produces a lower yield to maturity.

Price and Yield Record

Through time, the yield (and hence the price) of marketable Government securities varies with the rise or fall of the interest rates on short- and long-term money. Because Federal securities are the closest to being riskless of all obligations, the yield represents the nearest thing to "pure interest" known to the money and capital markets. They would represent pure interest if they were not subject to special government influence. Such influence takes two forms: (1) Treasury department debt management, including the use of nonmarketable issues, variation of maturities, and purchase and sale of securities by Treasury investment accounts; and (2) Federal Reserve System policies, which influence the prices and yields of bonds through open-market operations, and more indirectly through discount-rate policy and "moral suasion."

Table 5-4. YIELDS ON HIGH-GRADE BONDS

	Long-Term Treasury Bonds		*High-Grade Corporate Bonds—Average Yield (Moody's Series)*
	Average Price	*Average Yield*	
1920	85.9	5.32%	6.12%
1930	108.8	3.29	4.55
1932	88.9	3.68	5.01
1936	101.3	2.65	3.24
1940	107.2	2.21	2.84
1944	100.3	2.48	2.72
1946	104.8	2.19	2.53
1948	100.8	2.44	2.82
1950	102.5	2.32	2.62
1953	93.9	2.94	3.20
1954	99.5	2.55	2.90
1956	93.0	3.08	3.36
1957 (old series)	96.0	3.47	3.89
1957 (new series)	93.2	3.47	3.89
1958	94.0	3.43	3.79
1959	85.5	4.07	4.38
1960	86.2	4.01	4.41
1961	87.6	3.90	4.35
1962	86.9	3.95	4.33
1963	86.3	4.00	4.26
1964	84.5	4.15	4.40
1965	83.8	4.21	4.49
1966	78.6	4.66	5.13
1967	76.6	4.85	5.51
1968	72.3	5.25	6.18
1969	64.5	6.10	7.03
1970	60.5	6.59	8.04
1971	67.7	5.74	7.39
1972	68.7	5.63	7.21

SOURCES: Treasury bonds: *Federal Reserve Bulletin*; Corporate bonds: *Moody's Bond Survey*.

Yields on Government bonds have varied through time to reflect the changes in money rates, and their prices have changed accordingly. Table 5-4 shows the course of average annual yields and prices of Treasury bonds in selected years (1920, 1930–1941, partially tax-exempt; 1942–1972, taxable). To provide a comparison, the average yield on high-grade corporate bonds (Moody's series) is also shown.

Note that the prices and yields of long-term Government bonds have been by no means stable. The average price declined twenty points in 1930–1932. From the peak of 111.0 in 1941, the average price declined to 93.0 in 1956, the lowest level in over two decades. This decline in the middle 1950s reflected the substantial stiffening of interest rates in a "tight money" situation that brought them, by 1957, to the highest level in over two decades. Toward the end of 1957 the rates turned downward, and the prices of "money bonds" turned up.

Yields dropped slightly in the depression year of 1958, but rose to a new peak in the tight money period of late 1959, and prices reached the then historical low. After a decline in 1961, yields again took an upward, and prices a downward, course, so that in 1970 the former reached their highest level, and the latter their lowest level on record.

Historically, at any one time the yields on different marketable issues have differed primarily as a result of different maturities—the longer the maturity, the higher the yield. But the sharp rise in interest rates that was especially acute in 1955–1957, 1959, 1966, and 1969–1970 was accompanied by an even greater rise in short-term and intermediate-term rates, so that the usual spread reflecting differences in maturities was greatly diminished and at times disappeared altogether, so that investors had little incentive to purchase the long maturities with their greater price risk. The sharp break in interest rates in 1970 and early 1971 sent short-term yields well below the long-term, and the more normal pattern of yields-maturities was resumed. But the spread narrowed again later in 1971. Table 5-5 shows the changing relationships in yields at interest rate peaks and lows in recent years.

Table 5-5. YIELDS ON U.S. GOVERNMENT SECURITIES,
           SELECTED DATES

	May 1961	Sept. 1966	June 1967	Jan. 1970	Mar. 1971	July 1971	July 1972
Three-month bills	2.29%	5.36%	3.53%	7.87%	3.38%	5.39%	4.00%
Six-month bills	2.44	5.79	3.88	7.78	3.50	5.62	4.50
Nine- to twelve-month issues	2.72	5.80	4.40	8.82	3.66	5.73	4.90
Three- to five-year issues	3.28	5.62	4.96	8.14	4.74	6.77	5.85
Long-term issues	3.73	4.79	4.86	6.86	5.71	5.91	5.57

SOURCE: *Federal Reserve Bulletin.*

The Ownership of Government Bonds

With approximately $445 billions in direct and guaranteed bonds outstanding, U.S. Government issues have a dominant position in the American investment market. They comprise a very important earning asset of the banks of the country, second only to total loans, and are the chief asset of the Federal Reserve Banks. They also form a very substantial proportion of the portfolios of the leading financial institutions and are also popular with individuals desiring maximum safety and liquidity.

The ownership of outstanding Federal direct and guaranteed debt at the end of 1955, 1965, and 1971 is seen in Table 5-6.

Table 5-6. OWNERSHIP OF FEDERAL SECURITIES
(dollars in billions)

	Dec. 31, 1955		Dec. 31, 1965		Dec. 31, 1971	
	Amt.	%	Amt.	%	Amt.ᵃ	%
Total outstanding	$280.8	100.0%	$320.9	100.0%	$424.1	100.0%
Held by:						
Commercial banks	62.0	22.1	60.7	19.0	65.3	15.4
Federal Reserve Banks	24.8	8.8	40.8	12.6	70.2	16.6
Total banks	$ 86.8	30.9%	$101.5	31.6%	$135.5	32.0%
Individuals	65.5	23.3	72.1	22.5	74.0	17.4
Insurance companies	14.3	5.1	10.3	3.2	6.6	1.5
Mutual savings banks	8.5	3.0	5.3	1.6	2.7	.6
Other corporations	23.4	8.4	15.8	4.9	12.4	3.0
State and local governments	15.1	5.4	22.9	7.1	25.0	5.9
U.S. government agencies and trust funds	51.7	18.4	59.7	18.6	106.0	25.0
Other investorsᵇ	15.5	5.5	33.3	10.4	61.9	14.6
Total nonbank investors	$194.0	69.1%	$219.4	68.4%	$288.6	68.0%

ᵃExcludes guaranteed debt.

ᵇIncludes savings and loan associations, dealers and brokers, nonprofit institutions, corporate pension funds, foreign investors, and miscellaneous.

SOURCE: *Treasury Bulletin.*

Commercial banks are big holders of Treasury notes and intermediate-term bonds; they also have a substantial investment in Treasury bills. The Federal Reserve Banks are interested primarily in the short-term bills and certificates. Individuals hold the bulk of the savings bonds and are important holders of long-term marketable bonds. Insurance companies and mutual savings banks concentrate their holdings in Treasury bonds, particularly in the medium- and longer-term maturities. United States Government agencies and trust funds own special issues and long-term marketables. Business corporations concentrate on short maturities.

Primary and Secondary Markets

The Federal Reserve Banks serve as agents of the Treasury in issuing and redeeming government securities. Banks and a relatively small number of dealers form the chief primary market.

Trading in marketable U.S. Government securities takes place primarily in the over-the-counter market, through dealer specialists and banks. So active is the market that the trading range on any day is very narrow. No securities are more liquid in the sense of immediate recovery of principal. To the institutions mentioned above, and to individuals seeking liquidity, they have a prime appeal. Also of interest is that trading in Government securities is exempt from Government regulation, including exemption from the standard margin requirements of the Board of Governors of the Federal Reserve System.

REFERENCES

BOARD OF GOVERNORS OF THE FEDERAL RESERVE SYSTEM, *Treasury-Federal Reserve Study of the Government Securities Market.* Washington, D.C.: U.S. Government Printing Office, 1960.

BREAK, G. F., et al., *Federal Credit Agencies,* research studies prepared for the Commission on Money and Credit. Englewood Cliffs, N.J.: Prentice-Hall, Inc., 1963.

COPELAND, M. A., *Trends in Government Financing.* Princeton, N.J.: Princeton University Press, 1961.

DOUGALL, H. E., *Capital Markets and Institutions,* 2nd ed., Chapter 7. Englewood Cliffs, N.J.: Prentice-Hall, Inc., 1970.

FEDERAL NATIONAL MORTGAGE ASSOCIATION, *Background and History of FNMA.* Washington, D.C.: The Association, 1969.

FIRST BOSTON CORPORATION, *Securities of the United States Government and Federal Agencies.* New York: The First Boston Corporation, *biennial.*

GAINES, T. C., *Techniques in Treasury Debt Management.* New York: Free Press, Inc., 1962.

LEVY, M. E., *Cycles in Government Securities. I. Federal Debt and its Ownership,* Studies in Business Economics No. 78. New York: National Industrial Conference Board, 1963.

MELTZER, A. H., AND GERT VON DER LINDE. A *Study of the Dealer Market for Federal Securities.* Materials prepared for the Joint Economic Committee, 86th Congress, 2nd Session. Washington, D.C.: U.S. Government Printing Office, 1960.

ROOSA, R. V., *Federal Reserve Operations in the Money and Government Securities Market.* New York: Federal Reserve Bank of New York, 1956.

SCOTT, I. O., JR., *The Government Securities Market.* New York: McGraw-Hill, Inc., 1965.

6 Bonds of State and Local Governments

SCOPE: This chapter discusses the investment position and methods of analyzing the bonds of the states and their political subdivisions. The order of discussion is (1) amount and growth of debt, (2) classification of borrowing units, (3) sources and uses of revenues, (4) purposes of bond issues, (5) types of debt: general, special assessment, revenue, warrants, (6) difficulties of analysis, (7) tests of ability to pay, (8) willingness to pay, (9) legality, (10) bond ratings, (11) form of bonds, (12) tax status, (13) yields, (14) municipals market, and (15) investment position.

Amount and Growth of Debt

As of June 30, 1971, gross state debt was $47.8 billions and local government debt $110.0 billions, or a total of $158.8 billions.[1] Table 6-1 shows relative growth of the three main types of public debt—Federal, state, and local—for selected fiscal years (as of June 30).

In comparison with the Federal debt, the volume of state and local debt does not appear alarming. But in the postwar period it has grown much faster than the Federal debt, both in amount and on a per capita basis. Prior to World War I, state debt was very small, and municipal debt was substantial in amount. The expansion of state and municipal services caused both types to increase severalfold by 1940. During World War II retirements exceeded new issues. Since the war the great expansion of debt has reflected the growth of state and local public services, the increase in population and its steady urbanization, and the rising operating and capital costs of government.

---

[1]Total debt before deduction of sinking funds. Net long-term debt was $133 billions.

Table 6-1. GROSS PUBLIC DEBT

	Federal[a]		State[b]		Local[b]	
	Amount (millions)	*Per Capita*	*Amount (millions)*	*Per Capita*	*Amount (millions)*	*Per Capita*
1932	$ 19,487	$ 156	$ 2,832	$ 23	$ 16,373	$131
1940	42,968	326	3,590	27	16,693	127
1945	258,682	1,849	2,425	17	14,164	101
1950	257,357	1,702	5,285	35	18,830	125
1955	274,374	1,670	11,198	68	33,069	201
1960	286,331	1,591	18,543	103	51,412	286
1965	317,274	1,637	27,034	139	72,478	374
1966	319,907	1,633	29,564	151	77,487	395
1967	326,221	1,649	32,472	164	81,185	410
1968	347,578	1,739	35,663	178	85,492	478
6669	353,720	1,752	39,553	196	93,995	466
1970	370,919	1,816	42,008	206	101,563	496
1971	410,292	2,050	47,800	238	111,034	538

[a]Exclusive of guaranteed debt.
[b]1960–1971 data include Alaska and Hawaii.

SOURCES: U.S. Department of Commerce, Bureau of the Census, *Historical Summary of Governmental Finances; Governmental Finances*, annual.

Classification of Borrowing Units

Including special tax districts, United States has over 81,000 state and local governmental units.[2] Of these, possibly 30,000 have issued bonds from time to time. One method of classifying state and local governments is by the character of the obligor:

    A. Regular governmental units
        1. States
        2. Counties and parishes
        3. Cities, towns, boroughs, and so forth
        4. Townships
    B. Special tax districts
        1. School districts
        2. Water districts and sanitary (sewer) districts
        3. Road districts and street improvement districts
        4. Park districts and the like
        5. Drainage, irrigation, and levee districts
    C. Statutory authorities
        1. Bridge authorities or commissions
        2. Port authorities
        3. Toll road commissions or authorities
        4. Miscellaneous (hospital, college dormitory, parkway, etc.)
    D. Municipal utilities departments (electric, water, etc.)
    E. Special housing authorities

[2]U.S. Department of Commerce, Bureau of the Census, *1967 Census of Governments, Vol. 1: Government Organization*, p. 1, 1968.

Bonds of the first two above categories are classified as *general obligations* supported by the power to tax. Those of the third and fourth groups are ordinarily called *revenue* or *nonguaranteed* bonds. Housing authority issues are a special type of revenue bond, although they are further supported by state or Federal guarantee.

Bonds issued by the states are the obligations of sovereign powers. Under the Federal Constitution, each state arranges its financial affairs without interference from the Federal government. With the exception of New York, where the state constitution specifically grants such permission, state governments may not be sued by individuals or corporations, although one state may sue another state. Investors must, therefore, rely principally upon the good faith of the states. That most state bonds are accorded high investment rating despite the legal disability feature is a testimonial to the importance of intangible factors in contrast to tangible property and legal protection.

The political subdivisions include not only counties and cities, but also towns, villages, and numerous varieties of districts, many of which overlap. Municipalities have certain powers that have been delegated by state authority in order that they may act as agencies for local administration. They are incorporated under a general state law or receive special charters under separate legislative acts. The powers usually delegated are (1) police power for the maintenance of law and order, (2) taxing power, from which necessary revenues are secured, and (3) eminent domain, which confers the right to take private property, at fair compensation, for public use.

Regular governmental units possess broad general powers. Their activities produce little revenue, and taxes are their principal source of income. They ordinarily issue bonds by pledging their general credit; but they may also pledge specific revenues or may create a special district or an authority to issue revenue bonds. Districts are similar to regular governmental units in that they have the power to tax, but they are usually organized to promote a specific activity. Statutory authorities and municipal utilities or departments are public corporations without the power to tax, which are organized for the purpose of operating revenue-producing projects.

Sources of Revenue

The sources of the revenues from which state governments meet their general obligations include Federal aid and the various taxes levied by the respective state legislatures (see Table 6-2). At one time a share of the general property tax collected by local authorities was an important source of state revenue, but in most states this has been replaced by revenue from special taxes imposed for state purposes. Retailers' occupational taxes (sales taxes) have sprung into prominence, along with individual and corporate income taxes, and the very important gasoline taxes and automobile licenses. Other sources include cigarette taxes, inheritance and estate taxes, special taxes on public utilities, and a variety of miscellaneous types. The relative importance of these sources differs according to the laws of the various states. Federal aid

**Table 6-2. REVENUES AND EXPENDITURES OF STATE AND
LOCAL GOVERNMENTS, 1970**

(Year ended June 30; dollars in millions)

Revenues	States Amt.	%	Local Govts. Amt.	%
Intergovernmental revenue (net)	$20,248	22.9%	$29,525	33.1%
Taxes				
Property	1,092	1.2	32,963	37.0
General sales	14,177	16.0	1,951	2.2
Selective sales and gross receipts[a]	13,077	14.7	1,118	1.3
Individual income	9,183	10.3	1,630	1.8
Corporate income	3,738	4.2	—	—
Motor vehicle and operators licenses	2,728	3.1	176	.2
All other taxes	3,966	4.4	995	1.1
Total taxes	$47,961	53.9%	$38,833	43.7%
Current charges and misc. revenue	9,545	10.7	12,558	14.0
Utility revenue	—	—	6,608	7.4
Liquor store revenue	1,748	1.9	258	.3
Insurance trust revenue	9,437	10.6	1,299	1.4
Total revenue	$88,939	100.0%	$89,082	100.0%

Expenditures[b]	States Amt.	%	Local Govts. Amt.	%
Education	$30,865	36.3%	$38,970	42.0%
Highways	13,483	15.8	5,426	5.9
Public welfare	13,206	15.5	6,700	7.2
Health and hospitals	5,355	6.3	5,010	5.4
Public safety and correction	2,223	2.8	583	.6
Natural resources	120	.1	2,116	2.3
Housing and urban renewal	6,010	7.0	6,405	7.0
Insurance trust expenditure	7,273	8.5	1,263	1.3
Interest on general debt	1,499	1.8	2,875	3.1
Other expenditures	5,021	5.8	23,174	25.1
Total expenditures	$85,055	100.0%	$92,522	100.0%

[a]Chiefly motor fuel, alcoholic beverages, tobacco products, and public utility taxes.
[b]Includes capital outlays: state, $13.3 billions; local, $16.4 billions.
SOURCE: U.S. Department of Commerce, Bureau of the Census, *Governmental Finances in 1969–1970.*

to states has taken a sharp increase since World War II. The grants have been mainly for highways and public welfare.

The types of taxes levied to pay state expenses and to service its debt are of considerable importance to the investor. Generally, the absence of any predominant source affords a diversification that tends to promote stability of income.

The most important single source of revenue for local governments is the general property tax, but to an increasing degree special taxes and aid from state and Federal governments are relied upon for income.[3] The relative

[3]In the fiscal year ended June 30, 1971 states contributed $31.1 billions to local governments, mainly for education and public welfare.

importance of these sources varies from place to place. As of June 1970, local governments obtained their general revenues (aside from general borrowings) from the sources noted in Table 6-2.

Uses of Revenue

The uses or expenditures to which state revenues are applied are also indicated in Table 6-2. Of the total, the most important single type of expenditure is aid to local governments. Interest and debt retirement make only a modest drain on revenues. Ideally, the annual revenues of the state should more than cover each year's operating expenses and, in addition, provide adequately for debt service. Debt service includes the annual interest charge and the provision for repayment of principal, either by redemption of serial issues or by sinking fund. Although the debt service legally ranks equally with operating expenses, expediency usually places it in a subordinate position.

The revenues of municipalities are used for the purposes indicated in Table 6-2. Public safety, public welfare, highways, and education predominate. General revenues are insufficient to take care of substantial capital expenditures as the need arises. Hence the municipalities must issue debt instruments whose carrying costs and retirement are spread over the years and charged to current receipts.

Purposes of Bond Issues

States have traditionally borrowed principally to finance the construction of long-term improvements, although important exceptions to this pattern appeared in the extensive borrowing to provide funds for emergency relief in the 1930s and in the heavy bond emissions for veterans' bonuses after World War II. More modern debt has been incurred for educational facilities, highway construction, park development, state institutions, grade-crossing elimination, social service and health programs, veterans' bonuses, and housing (guarantee of local housing authority notes and bonds), and to meet special types of operating expenses. The relative importance of the financing by state governments of the major types of durable improvements and other functions is shown in Table 6-3.[4]

The debt of New York State as of March 31, 1970 (Table 6-4) provides an example of borrowing purposes in an old, highly industrialized, and heavily populated area. The gross debt at this date was $2,523 millions, including temporary debt.

Municipalities constantly face extraordinary expenditures that cannot conveniently be met from current revenues, and so loans are arranged to spread the cost over a period of years. The variety of purposes for which

---

[4]*Federal Reserve Bulletin* reports the purposes of issues for new capital on an annual basis.

**Table 6-3. PURPOSES OF LONG-TERM STATE DEBT OUTSTANDING
JUNE 30, 1970**

(dollars in millions)

	Amt.	%
Education	$10.8	27.7%
Highways	12.6	32.4
Hospitals	.6	1.6
Water transportation	.6	1.6
Veterans Administration	.3	.7
Other	14.0	36.0
Total	$38.9	100.0%

Source: U.S. Department of Commerce, Bureau of the Census, *State Government Finances in 1970*, p. 41.

Table 6-4. NEW YORK STATE DEBT

	Amount
Highways	$1,148,700,000
Housing and urban renewal	838,190,000
Mental health construction	159,700,000
Pure waters	85,600,000
Parks, forest preserves	80,280,000
Mass transportation	68,500,000
Higher education construction	67,100,000
Other	74,540,000
Total	$2,522,610,000

Source: Moody's Investors Service, *Municipal and Government Manual* (1971).

bonds are issued by municipalities is suggested by the following list:

Bridges	Libraries
Buildings	Parking facilities
Emergencies and catastrophies	Police facilities
Fire equipment	Public utilities
Funding of floating debt	Public welfare
Grade crossings	Recreation and parks
Harbor improvements	Schools
Highways	Sanitation and sewage disposal
Hospitals	Street improvements
Housing	Urban renewal

As shown by Table 6-3, education facilities and municipal utilities still comprise the most important purposes for local municipal loans. Streets, sanitation, housing, and urban renewal are also important. Special types of operating expenses are also funded, and considerable refunding takes place annually. Although no exact relationship exists between the amount of debt financing and capital expenditures, most debt is incurred to anticipate, then to fund, part of the cost of new fixed assets. The balance of capital cost is currently financed from special taxes and Federal grants.[5]

Types of Debt

Bonds of states and local political subdivisions can be classified into principal groups.

GENERAL OBLIGATIONS. The interest and principal of general obligations or "full faith and credit bonds" are supported by the full taxing power of the governing unit. In the purchase of state bonds, investors prefer the unlimited tax obligations of states that pledge their "full faith and credit" and whose constitutions provide for unlimited taxation for debt service. The New York State Constitution provides that the legislature shall annually provide by appropriation for the interest and maturing principal of state debts as they fall due; failing such an appropriation, the Comptroller must set aside from the first revenues thereafter received a sum sufficient to meet such payments.

Other full faith and credit bonds are payable primarily from certain special pledged sources of revenue, but in addition, the unit agrees unconditionally to cover any deficit that may later develop in the special fund. Thus, a water bond might be issued by a municipality with the pledge of its full faith and credit but with the expectation that the bond would be serviced from the earnings of the water department. If these earnings are insufficient, the issuing unit must levy taxes to make up the deficit. Similarly, bonds payable initially from a specific tax, but which rest ultimately on the power to levy taxes, belong in this category.

As of June 30, 1971, of the total long-term state debt of $44.3 billions, $21.5 billions or 48 per cent were full faith and credit obligations. Of gross long-term local debt totalling $99.3 billions, $62.5 billions or 63 per cent fell in this category.

While all general obligations are backed by the pledge to levy taxes, this levy may or may not be limited as to rate or amount. The power of taxation may be limited by either a constitutional or a statutory provision to, say, a certain number of dollars per thousand of property valuation. (For example, Alabama has a constitutional limitation on *state* property taxes of $6.50 per $1,000 of property assessed at 60 per cent of market value.) The issuer is obliged only to exercise its powers of taxation up to this limit for the payment of the obligation or to make good any deficiency in a special fund primarily pledged for its payment. Such bonds are known as *limited tax bonds*.

Because most states have tax-limit legislation in effect, most bonds of local governments deserve the *limited tax* title. In many states, however, the tax limit does not apply to debt service, for which payment unlimited taxes may

---

[5]In fiscal 1971 the capital outlay by states and local governments totalled $33.1 billions. But the net long-term debt issued in that year (after retirements) totalled only $11.6 billions. U.S. Department of Commerce, Bureau of the Census, *Government Finances in 1970–1971*.

be levied. Property taxes levied by municipalities in New York State are limited to a legal maximum of 2 per cent (2½ per cent in New York City), but rates actually in effect in most New York municipalities are in excess of $2.00 per $100 annually, after the inclusion of the debt service. All New York State municipal obligations are, therefore, regarded as no-tax-limit bonds. An even smaller tax limit in Ohio (1 per cent of "true value"), which also does not exclude the debt service, has resulted in bonds being issued both inside and outside the tax limit. Accordingly, both classes of bonds may be issued by cities of this state.

The term *general obligation* applies to any obligation for the service of which the issuing governmental unit has pledged its entire tax revenues, whether such revenues are raised by a general property tax or by a special tax from a special source, or from a limited area of property. Thus *tax district* bonds belong in the category of general obligations although the district may be established for the promotion of only one activity and only the property within the district may be subject to levy. Some special districts have been formed for the purpose of avoiding the tax limits that prevail for the municipality.

In the educational development of the United States, school districts have been established to serve communities beyond existing incorporated areas. These districts have issued bonds for the purpose of erecting school buildings, payable out of taxes levied on all property in the areas served, irrespective of whatever towns might be included therein. The bonds are general lien obligations of the entire district and, as such, have gained favorable investment ratings. But the generally favorable experience with school district obligations has not always extended to other types such as irrigation and road district bonds. The quality of tax district bonds is far from uniform.

The restriction of a low debt limit tends to encourage financing by district bonds which are not part of the legal debt of an included municipality. Even in New York State, where the debt limits of 5 to 10 per cent of the five-year average full value of taxable realty are usually adequate for local municipal credit, the legislature faces continual requests for the establishment of new tax districts.[6] In Illinois, where the local debt limit is set at 5 per cent and where appraisal values are much lower than in New York, the inducement to establish tax districts is almost irresistible. At one time in Cook County, more than 400 units of government had power to levy general property taxes. This extreme overlapping contributed greatly to the financial difficulties of the Chicago area during the 1930s. California permits tax districts to be formed for such purposes as the following: airport, boulevard, cemetery, fire protection, sanitation, water, garbage disposal, highway lighting, irrigation, library, health, memorial, mosquito control, parks, museum, utility, recreation, and transportation.

The investment position of tax district bonds depends upon the purpose for which the district was created, as well as the wealth, income, and *total* debt burden of the included area. The existence of overlapping tax districts

---

[6]Different limits apply to different classes of municipalities, for example: 10 per cent for Nassau County, 7 per cent for other counties; 10 per cent for New York City, 7 to 9 per cent for other cities; 5 per cent for school districts.

greatly complicates the problem of financial analysis. In 1970, the City of Albany, New York reported a bonded debt of $25.5 millions. This statement, however, did not include Albany's share (87.89 per cent) of the debt of the Albany Port District ($1,802,000), but it did include the school debt. In the same year, the City of Seattle, Washington reported net debt figures which did not include a share either of the Port of Seattle debt (about 66 per cent) or of the King County School District No. 1 debt (about 97 per cent). At the end of 1970, the net bonded debt (general obligations) of the City of Chicago was reported at $278,138,000, but this did not include $43,807,000 in park bonds, $157,940,000 in school district bonds, nor $62,-000,000 in sanitary district bonds, all general obligations. Investors in tax district bonds should realize that the published financial statements do not include the debts of underlying municipalities. Buyers of regular municipal bonds, in turn, should understand that the financial statements of cities do not include the proportionate debts of overlapping tax districts, which, as shown previously, may exceed the internal debt.[7] The short prospectuses issued by municipal bond dealers sometimes include, sometimes exclude, data on overlapping debt.

Special assessment bonds. When loans are made to improve facilities in certain parts of the city, such as street pavements and the extension of water and sewer lines, it is often the practice to place the cost upon the property owners who are directly benefited, through assessments (usually spread over a series of years) in addition to their regular taxes. Assessment or "improvement" bonds are issued whose interest and amortized principal are payable, not from the general tax levy, but from these assessments. Although the payment of assessments is just as mandatory as the payment of general taxes, a claim against some of the property in a city is less secure than a claim against all the property. Accordingly, assessment bonds are regarded as inferior to general-lien local bonds, and bear higher yields. As a practical matter, however, city credit is at stake in the payment of assessment bonds, and cities usually supply funds from other sources for the payment of charges on these bonds when assessment collections prove temporarily inadequate. New York City follows the unusual practice of paying bonds, including those of an assessment nature, from general tax collections. Such bonds are thus properly classed as general obligations and are known as *general-specials*.

Unless specifically backed by the credit of the community, the special assessment bond is suitable only for local investment funds. It has the advantage, along with other local debt, of exemption of interest from Federal income taxes.

---

[7]The effect of overlapping districts upon comparative tax rates was clearly illustrated by the contrast of the two leading California cities in 1965–1966. The tax rate in San Francisco (city and county) in 1970–1971 was $75.43 per $1,000 of assessed valuation, plus $47.12 for the unified school district with the same area limits, and $5.65 for the rapid-transit district, or a total of $128.20. However, no separate school district bonds were outstanding—all bonds for school purposes were the general obligations of the city and county. The city rate in Los Angeles was $25.16 per $1,000, but the total rate was $123.73 after including five overlapping districts. Each city used an assessment basis of 50 per cent of true value.

Revenue bonds. Revenue bonds are payable solely from revenues derived from the operation of a public facility or from some special source of revenue (such as motor fuel taxes), rather than from general tax collections. The use of the revenue bond to finance the construction or acquisition of public works has become popular in all parts of the country for a variety of projects as varied as toll bridges, express highways, electric light and power plants, gas plants, water works, sewer systems, swimming pools, parking areas, and, in at least one instance, a crematorium. State toll highway obligations have become increasingly important. Between 1950 and 1971 the outstanding amount of revenue obligations and other nonguaranteed long-term debt increased more than twentyfold and at the middle of 1971 accounted for 42 per cent of total state and local long-term debt. Revenue bonds reflect the attitude that the users of a public facility should support it. More important, they offer a means of financing public projects or services without tax increases and without violating the debt limits that apply to "full faith and credit" debt.

Most revenue bonds are issued by special authorities, departments, or commissions rather than by regular governmental units. Their major purpose is to keep down the direct debt and the tax rate. Other reasons are (1) to make the project self-supporting, (2) to avoid having to refer an increase in debt to the electorate, (3) in some cases to obtain a lower interest rate where the general credit of the municipality is not strong, (4) to avoid setting up a special district in which all taxpayers would not receive equal benefits from the facility, and (5) to finance the construction of industrial facilities to be leased to private enterprise.

Because the position of these bonds depends solely upon the earning power of the project or on special taxes, they should be regarded as distinctly different from ordinary municipal bonds payable from general tax collections. However, revenue bonds may be in a stronger position and bear lower yields than those of privately owned public utility companies for four important reasons. First, the rates charged for the use of the facility can be raised, in most states, without securing the approval of the public utility commission. Second, the enterprise is usually tax-free, and thus avoids the burden of corporation taxes, which take as much as 20 per cent of the gross revenues of private utility companies. Third, income from revenue bonds is exempt from Federal income taxes. Fourth, the enterprise is in little, if any, danger from competition or expiration of a franchise privilege.

Some argue that revenue bonds are entitled to as good rating as general-lien bonds because the projects are self-supporting, self-liquidating, and independent of tax collections. In certain cases, interest on revenue bonds has been maintained by cities in default on their bonds payable from taxes. During periods of recession, however, the argument loses much of its validity when declining revenues impair interest payments. The City of Seattle defaulted in the payment of charges due on street railway revenue bonds in 1937 and required the bondholders to accept a substantial loss on their holdings in the reorganization of the enterprise in 1940.

Under recent practice, revenue bonds are frequently issued under a corporate title differing from the name of the municipality or area wherein the project is located. Examples are the Triborough Bridge and Tunnel Authority (New York City) and the Calumet Skyway (Chicago).

Many projects financed by revenue bonds operate beyond the limits of one municipality, for example, the San Francisco-Oakland Bay Bridge (California Toll Bridge Authority) and the Port of New York Authority (various bridges, tunnels, airports, and terminals with a twenty-five-mile radius). The most prominent of these to appeal to the national market in recent years have been the toll-road bonds issued by a number of express roads linking cities in the East, the Middle West, and the South. Some examples are the New York State Thruway Authority, the Ohio Turnpike Commission, the Illinois State Toll Highway Commission, and the Maine Turnpike Authority.

Revenue bonds have become an important part of public finance. When issued in connection with soundly conceived and well-managed projects, they are entitled to a good investment rating. We should recognize, however, that not all projects offer equally attractive investment opportunities. The list of projects regarded as suitable for revenue bond financing includes, in addition to the traditional gas and electric utility, water, and sewer purposes, such enterprises as airports, urban transportation hospitals, parking, public markets, college dormitories, and various types of recreational facilities.[8]

Of note is the New York City practice of issuing bonds for many revenue-producing purposes, such as rapid transit, docks, and water supply, and designating such bonds as general obligations payable from general revenues including tax collections. However, these bonds issued by the city are issued through "authorities," rather than by the city directly.

The strength of the revenue bond depends mainly on the coverage of interest and maturing principal afforded by earnings, with a sufficient margin of safety allowed for contingencies. The ratio of the investment in plant to the outstanding net debt is an indicator of asset protection, and in a few states revenue bonds may be specifically secured by a mortgage lien on the property. The revenues from the project go into a revenue fund, from which the following are provided, in order, for (1) operating expenses, (2) depreciation fund, (3) debt service, and (4) special reserves. Any surplus revenues after these items may revert to the city or be used for additions or for special bond retirements. An unusual arrangement is found in the case of the bonds of the California Toll Bridge Authority; the Highway Department of the State of California pays the maintenance expenses of the San Francisco-Oakland Bay Bridge and other bridges operated by the Authority so that the *gross* revenues are available for other operating expenses and debt service.

Occasionally a revenue bond may be backed by both taxing power and derived revenues, but this arrangement is exceptional and contrary to the usual objective of providing a capital improvement without adding to the general tax load.

The quality of revenue bonds ranges from first rate to mediocre or worse. Some are strong enough to sell at yields that are as low as those of the general bonds of the jurisdiction that set up the authority. Some of the toll-road or

---

[8]For a list of issuers of public enterprise revenue bonds, classified by states, see Moody's Investors Service, *Municipal and Government Manual*, blue section, *annual*.

turnpike bonds issued since World War II have remained high grade. Others have fallen in investment status because of sadly discouraging revenues. One of the poorest toll-road situations in recent history has been that of the West Virginia Turnpike Commission. Regular interest on bonds was paid through 1957. Thereafter payments ran one to four years late. As of June 30, 1971, overdue coupons and accumulated interest on same totalled $22.4 millions, and in 1972 the bonds sold flat in the low 80's.

The range in quality of revenue bonds is indicated by the spread between their yields and those of high-grade general obligations. In early January 1973 the yield on Moody's series of long-term Aaa general municipals was 4.95 per cent, and Baa municipals yielded 5.45 per cent. At the same time, however, a sampling of long-term revenue bonds of general investment interest disclosed yields ranging from 5.00 per cent to 8.00 per cent. Nevertheless, some revenue bonds show such adequate coverage of interest and debt retirement as to make them eligible for purchase by banks and other institutional investors under the regulations of a limited number of states.[9]

TAX-ANTICIPATION WARRANTS. Tax-anticipation warrants or notes represent current debt issued in anticipation of a tax levy to meet the financial needs of the state or municipality until the taxes are collected. They are ordinarily a first claim against incoming tax revenues. Their investment quality depends on the credit of the issuing municipality and its taxcollection status. They are frequently without fixed maturity, with payment date depending on tax receipts.

SPECIAL TYPES. Hybrids or combinations of the first three types described above represent *special types* of revenue bonds that are difficult to classify. These include bonds issued by cities or districts with pledge of special utility revenues or receipts from special taxes in addition to the pledge of general credit; revenue bonds further supported by assessments; bonds on which payment is pledged only from specified taxes without unconditional promise to pay; and bonds supported by both project net revenues and the guarantee of the state or municipality.

The obligations of public housing authorities have special characteristics making them different from ordinary revenue bonds. Of particular importance are the bonds now being issued in very large volume by local public housing authorities created under the laws of the states and authorized to cooperate with the Federal government in carrying out the expressed policy of providing safe and sanitary low-rent housing. Under the U.S. Housing Act of 1937, as amended, the faith of the United States is pledged to the payment of annual contributions to the local housing agency sufficient, with other funds of the local agency, to pay the principal and interest of the bonds when due. The bonds are also secured by a pledge of the net revenues of the housing projects. The Federal Act provides that the bonds and interest thereon shall be exempt from Federal taxation; with a few exceptions, the

[9]States in which qualified revenue bonds are "legals" include California, Connecticut, Florida, Illinois, Maryland, Massachusetts, Michigan, New Jersey, New York, Ohio, Pennsylvania, and Texas.

bonds are also exempt from property and income taxes of the states where issued.

Difficulties in Analysis of Municipals

The analysis of state and local government securities presents a number of problems. Among these are (1) the selection of pertinent material from the mass of economic and political information available, (2) the lack of absolute standards for measuring risk, and the consequent reliance on the *comparative* merit of an issue either in the light of similar situations or of the past record of the government studied, (3) the difficulty of keeping in touch with the changing and complex field of municipal operations and finance, (4) the unsatisfactory and incomplete character of specific credit information, and (5) the complex legal considerations that are often involved. Nevertheless, in spite of these complications, a survey of the most important factors will at least serve to determine whether a bond is high grade, borderline, or low grade. The advice of dealers and services specializing in tax-free bonds is necessary to enable the investor to determine a more exact rating and the appropriateness of a particular bond in his own portfolio.

Ability to Pay

The three general tests of the investment position of a municipal bond are the ability to pay,[10] willingness to pay, and legality.

Seemingly, because the sovereign position of a state, in contrast to a political subdivision, places it in a position to pay or default on its debt as it sees fit, willingness to pay is the most important test. The fact is that willingness is largely dependent on ability to levy and collect the necessary taxes to meet expenses and debt service.

The analysis of the capacity of a state or of a local municipality to meet its obligations involves an examination of its fiscal condition as shown in its financial statement, together with budgetary material and economic and industrial information. The financial statements are quite different from those of business enterprise, and cover primarily such factors as assessed valuation of taxable property, debt outstanding, tax collections, and debt in relation to property and population.

Financial statements of local municipalities sometimes provide more detail. In any case, the first major item is the assessed value of the taxable property located in the jurisdiction. In the 1970 New York statement (Table 6-5), this item is listed at $56.2 billions, and on the local municipal statement in Table 6-6 at $180.0 millions. The use of this figure has limited direct

[10]A comprehensive and detailed checklist of the factors to be considered in analyzing the credit of local municipalities is given in Investment Bankers Association of America, *Fundamentals of Investment Banking* (Englewood Cliffs, N.J.: Prentice-Hall, Inc., 1949), pp. 374–76.

Table 6-5. STATE OF NEW YORK FINANCIAL STATEMENT, MARCH 31, 1970

Assessed valuation of taxable real property (50.78% of full value)		$56,242,330,000
Net bonded debt	$1,798,660,000	
Temporary debt	723,944,000	
Total debt[a]		$ 2,522,604,000
Population (1970)	18,190,740	
Net debt as a percentage of assessed valuation	2.23%	
Net debt per capita	$138.70	

[a]In addition, the state guaranteed $439,000,000 of bonds of New York State Thruway Authority.

Table 6-6. LOCAL MUNICIPAL FINANCIAL STATEMENT SPECIMEN FIGURES—DECEMBER 31, 1971

Assessed valuation (**90%** basis) of taxable property		
Real property		$180,000,000
Franchise values		4,500,000
Personal property		27,000,000
Total		$211,500,000
Gross bonded debt		$ 16,750,000
Water bonds	$2,125,000	
Sinking fund	375,000	2,500,000
Net bonded debt		$ 14,250,000
Population (1970 census)	121,600	
Tax rate per **$1,000** of assessed valuation	$21.20	
Ratio of net debt to assessed value	6.74%	

Tax Collections	% Uncollected at End of Year	% Uncollected on Dec. 31, 1971
1968	15.8%	3.1%
1969	11.6	3.6
1970	10.2	4.6
1971	6.3	6.3

significance in states such as New York, where neither real nor personal property is taxed for state purposes. In addition, assessment methods vary greatly throughout the country, so that comparison of states is difficult. Nevertheless, property is a measure of wealth, and property produces income that is taxable.

The value of property has more significance in the case of local municipalities, since their chief source of general revenue is property taxes. In our local municipal financial statement, the *total* property value of $211,500,000 does not include exempt private property or nontaxable city property. Franchise valuations are the values of that part of the property of public utility companies located on public property. Such property is usually subject to the same tax rate as real estate and is regarded as equally productive. Of the three classes of property listed, the value of real property (and buildings), is of outstanding importance. In most communities, tax officials find the problem of appraising personal property extremely difficult, so that payment is readily evaded. Real estate is, therefore, generally relied upon to provide the bulk of tax revenue. The basis upon which property is assessed for tax purposes varies widely. Some jurisdictions use a basis of 100 per cent of "true" value, others use a basis as low as 20 per cent.[11] A study made in 1971, covering the principal cities in the United States, showed considerable variation, as indicated in Table 6-7.

Table 6-7. RATIOS OF ASSESSED TO REAL VALUE,
SELECTED CITIES, 1971

City	Basis	City	Basis
New York	100%	Buffalo	54%
Chicago	100	Savannah	40
Richmond	90	Atlanta	30
Honolulu	70	Spokane	25
Los Angeles	50	Wichita	20

Source: Moody's *Municipal and Government Manual (1971).*

With such variations in practice, debt percentages, as well as tax rates, for different municipalities are comparable only after adjustment for differences in assessment methods. A debt ratio (per cent of net debt to property value) of 6 per cent and a tax rate of 2.40 per cent in a city employing a 100 per cent assessment basis are equivalent to a debt ratio of 9 per cent and a tax rate of 3.60 per cent in a city using a 67 per cent assessment basis.

Although property taxes provide the main source of local income, an increasing share of the total city revenue comes from rents for the use of city properties, fees for various services, and shares in state revenues from special taxes, such as mortgage, bank, and corporation taxes. Such revenues, however, are regarded as being primarily available for operating expenses of the city rather than for debt service.

The tax power of local jurisdictions is limited by economics as well as by law. An unlimited legal power to tax might result in excessively high rates beyond the economic capacity of the taxpayers, thereby becoming ineffective. Tax power does not guarantee safety to investors. In most states, however, a maximum annual tax rate, restricting the charge to a reasonable limit, is imposed by law upon municipalities. Because of the general rule that operating expenses take precedence over debt service, this tax limit seriously impairs the position of municipal bonds in the states which have imposed tax limits without excluding the cost of debt service on bonds.

The gross debt, as stated, may or may not include temporary obligations to be paid out of tax revenue receivable in the near future. In the illustrative local statement, the gross debt figure of $16,750,000 did not include

[11]Actual market values may be considerably higher than "true" values; an assessment ratio of 50 per cent of "true" value may be in fact only 30 to 40 per cent of market value in a growing and desirable community.

$1,160,000 in tax-anticipation warrants. In like manner, the gross funded debt of New York City on June 30, 1970, which amounted to $5.1 billions, did not include $820 millions of temporary debt issues, such as tax-anticipation notes and budget notes.

The New York City debt included $5.1 billions of public-enterprise bonds for revenue-producing purposes such as rapid transit, water supply, and public docks. However, only that part ($1.9 billions) which was actually self-sustaining or otherwise exempt was properly deductible in the computation of net debt. A further deduction of $700 millions should be made for sinking funds that have been appropriated for the nonexempt debt. These funds are held in cash and marketable securities, principally some of the same New York City bonds that are included in the gross debt total.

The remaining funded debt, $2.5 billions, is added to the amount of net miscellaneous debt, $800 millions, to arrive at the *net debt* for this example. This amount, $3.3 billions, is the total tax-supported liability within the debt limit and can be compared with New York City's total debt-incurring power as of July 1, 1970, which was calculated to be $5.6 billions. To obtain the real debt burden on the property of New York would require the addition of overlapping debt.[12]

More specific tests of ability to pay, some of which are indicated by the illustrative statements, are as follows (these apply to general obligations rather than to revenue bonds).

1. Ratio of net debt to assessed value. The debt of a state should bear a reasonable relation to its taxable property, even though the state itself may not levy a tax on property. A suggested conservative maximum debt ratio is 3 per cent of true (not necessarily appraised) value. As shown in the New York State statement (Table 6-5), the net debt amounted to 2.23 per cent of the assessed value of the real property in the state. As the assessed value averaged about 50.78 per cent of the full value, the true debt percentage was about half of the figure shown. One should not assume, however, that the state debt here shown comprises the entire public debt against the property, since the reported indebtedness does not include the local municipal debts.

The ratio of net tax-supported debt to the assessed value of the taxable property of a local municipality (shown by Table 6-6 as 6.74 per cent) is a useful indicator of municipal credit. However, in comparing cities the ratio of net *overall* (including overlapping) debt to estimated *true* value (adjusted for the appraisal basis) is mandatory. In view of the widely accepted belief that, because of the increased stability of revenue that comes from diversified properties, large cities are better credit risks than small cities, one cannot apply any inflexible rule to the maximum acceptable net debt percentage. Although 5 per cent may be regarded as a fair standard for a medium-sized city, 4 per cent would not be an unreasonably low limit for a small city, and 6 per cent would not be excessive for a large city.

The population figure shown in Table 6-6 is 121,600, reflecting an in-

[12]In addition to its bonded indebtedness, New York City unconditionally guaranteed (as of June 30, 1970) the principal and interest of $468,000,000 of bonds issued for housing and urban renewal.

crease of nearly 11 per cent in the past decade. As the average increase for the nation over the decade was considerably greater, evidently this city has not made favorable progress in this respect. Although rapid growth is a favorable sign, it is not without its disadvantages. City expenditures must keep pace with this increase in population, with the result that bond issues are almost continuous, and new issues often come on the market before the previous ones have been absorbed. A condition of financial indigestion tends to harm the position of all bonds of the city.

2. Net debt per capita. This is another widely used "short-cut" indicator of debt burden and, hence, of ability to pay. This figure has serious limitations unless viewed along with statistics on government finance and on the wealth and income of the area. But when accompanied by figures on per capita assessed values and per capita tax receipts, it suggests whether a large debt can be amply supported.

For all fifty states in 1971, the long-term state debt outstanding amounted to $232 per capita, $104 of which was represented by general credit obligations.[13] A maximum of $100 of general debt per capita is often suggested as a criterion. Many of the states are well below this figure, but in others, such as Massachusetts and Delaware, the figure is much higher and suggests a situation of weakness that might have serious repercussions in a period of economic distress.

In analyzing local municipalities, the combined (including overlapping) per capita net debt should be used, especially when comparing different cities.

The per capita debt shown in the illustrative municipal statement (Table 6-6) is $117. While consideration must be given to the relative wealth and income of the community in the use of this item for comparative purposes, a per capita debt of $400 is too high for convenient repayment by any municipality and $300 is a reasonable maximum.

3. Debt service requirements. The relationship of annual debt service requirements (interest plus principal to be retired) to total annual revenues indicates the ability of the state or municipality to cover its fixed charges. The debt service charge for New York State in 1970 amounted to $139.2 millions, or approximately 2.4 per cent of general state revenues. A maximum of 5 per cent is suggested as a useful criterion for a state. For a municipality, the ratio should not exceed 15 per cent of the annual budget.

4. Trend of debt; debt retirement policy. The trend of the debt of a state or municipality furnishes a good indication of the fiscal policy of the unit. The debt may not have reached unusual proportions up to the present, but if it has been increasing steadily for a number of years, the result may be a decline in its value and rating.

Policies and requirements concerning debt retirement should be examined carefully. The retirement of about 25 per cent of the outstanding debt

---

[13]U.S. Department of Commerce, Bureau of the Census, *Government Finances in 1970–1971*, p. 28.

within the ensuing five years is highly desirable. Where debt can be retired at this rate within a debt service ratio of 15 per cent of the annual budget, sound financial administration is evident. The use of serial bonds contributes greatly to regular retirement and a balanced debt structure.

5. Limitations of debt and tax rate. Reference has been made to the statutory debt limits, in terms of assessed value of taxable property, that are imposed on local municipalities in most states. These would seem to impose restrictions that would keep the debt within conservative limits. But in some cases the legal limits have been set so high that they provide little restraint upon the issue of debt. And even when the limits are reasonable, evasion is often relatively easy. Assessments can be raised, special districts can be created (unless the state has set an overall debt limit), or revenue bonds may be issued by the unit itself or by an authority created especially for this purpose. Nevertheless, a net debt limitation of 10 per cent of assessed valuation is desirable, for it precludes unlimited borrowing.

Of more importance are the limitations on taxing power, expressed as a per cent of valuation or in dollars per $1,000 of valuation, that are imposed on municipalities in many states, either in the constitution or by special statute or by municipal ordinance. The purpose of such limitation is to keep the tax rate down and to keep the borrowing of the municipality within reasonable bounds. But the result may be to impair its credit. If the municipality has reached the limit, it must either increase the assessment or turn to other forms of taxation, or to borrowing.

In appraising the tax limitations, one should note whether they apply to taxation for all purposes, including payment of debt, or whether debt service is excluded. Nevada prescribes a limit of 5 cents per dollar of assessed valuation for all purposes; but New York exempts the debt service from the limitation of a total tax rate of 2 per cent ($20 per $1,000).

From the standpoint of the investor, *unlimited*-tax bonds, which permit the municipality to draw adequately on its resources, are, of course, to be desired, provided that total debt-incurring power is restricted and that the affairs of the unit are managed efficiently. Limited-tax bonds may produce a higher yield, but the restrictions they impose may be too serious to be compensated by a slightly higher income.

6. The actual tax rate. If there is any legal limit on the amount of tax levied for operating purposes, the present rate may be so close to that limit as to create embarrassment if expenses increase or assessed values decline. But even if there is no limit, a high or increasing rate may indicate trouble. If the rate is at an all-time high, there may be resistance on the part of taxpayers, with a resultant lowering of the rate of tax collection, and of the investment quality of the bonds.

The nominal tax rate must, of course, be adjusted for the bases on which property is assessed. The tax rate of $21.20 per $1,000 shown in Table 6-6 is based upon an assessment rate of 90 per cent of full value and is, therefore, equal to a tax rate of $19.10 at full value. Comparisons of rates are misleading unless proper adjustment is made for different bases. An overall tax rate of $30 per $1,000 of true valuation is suggested as a maximum.

7. The tax-collection record. It is one thing to levy taxes and another to collect them. The investor should examine both the amount and the trend of the deficiency in tax collections. The data in the specimen local statement indicate that collections have been improving throughout the four-year period. The city collected in 1967 about 84 per cent of the taxes levied during that year, about 88 per cent in 1968, about 90 per cent in 1969, and over 93 per cent in 1970. By the end of 1971, the city had collected 97 per cent of the 1968 levy, 96 per cent of 1969 taxes, and 95 per cent of 1970 taxes. A tax collection record of 90 per cent during the year of levy is regarded as favorable. The older the delinquencies become, the harder they are to collect. A large volume of taxes over a year old may indicate faulty collection machinery, unaggressive collection policy, insufficient income in relation to government expenditures, or the presence of unproductive real estate. In most cases at the present time, the tax-delinquency figures are low.

8. General economic factors. Where information is available, the general economic condition, resources, and growth of the state or municipality, as indicated by income, wealth, types and diversification of industries, payrolls, population, and other factors, should be examined. Information on such matters in the typical prospectus describing an offering of municipal bonds is very sketchy indeed. The investment manuals often provide considerable detail, but it is difficult to relate to the appraisal of a particular bond at a particular yield. Here again, the investor is likely to rely on the investigation of the issue that has been made by the offering house.

9. The character of public administration. The standing of the public officials, their training, experience, and record, the completeness and frankness of their financial reports, and the stability of local administration are important factors in municipal analysis. The more tangible tests applied to the unit may reveal a sound basic credit situation, but mismanagement of the unit's affairs may lead to difficulties in the future.

Willingness to Pay

The second major test of the quality of municipal bonds is *willingness to pay,* as measured by past record and present conditions. This test is particularly important in the case of state debt, for the state may not be sued without its consent.

Since the Civil War period, the record of state bonds has been free of actual default. The State of Arkansas, in 1933, attempted to force holders of 4¼, 4½, 4¾, and 5 per cent bonds of that state to exchange them for 3 per cent bonds at par by refusing to continue interest payments on the former issues. This difficulty, however, was adjusted through a refunding program adopted in 1934, which provided for eventual payment of interest in full. But the action was a severe blow to the credit of the state and suggests that repudiation is not without possibility. The best protection is the restriction of debt to modest proportions relative to wealth and income.

Valid local government bonds are enforceable obligations. Creditors holding bonds in default can sue in a court of jurisdiction and obtain judgment. If no property is available for attachment, a writ of mandamus can be obtained, requiring the city authorities to levy and collect additional taxes to cover the claim. Although such power of collection seems complete, even the final alternative proved ineffectual in certain instances in the 1930s.

Willingness is a matter of convenience and good faith. Convenience is largely a matter of capacity, whereas good faith is a matter of character. Capacity may best be judged from the financial condition of the city and character from its financial history. A strong financial statement and an excellent debt record are, therefore, the best indication of willingness to pay. This is well illustrated by experience with defaults by numerous Florida cities after the collapse of the land boom in 1926. Chicago was brought to the brink of receivership in 1932 because of delays in tax collections between 1928 and 1931.

Inability to pay because of inadequate revenues arising out of tax-limit legislation could just as properly be termed unwillingness to pay. As was previously indicated, investors should prefer the bonds of those communities that are obligated to pay their bonds with no limitation as to taxes for such purpose.

In contrast to the many illustrations that might be cited of unwillingness to pay on the part of municipalities, numerous examples might be cited to the contrary. Many cities have maintained the integrity of their credit ratings, through a drastic reduction in operating expenses, and, at the same time, actually lowered the tax burden upon property owners. In many instances even grave disasters such as fires, floods, and earthquakes did not prevent the full payment of maturing obligations. Good faith is an excellent municipal asset.

Unlike ability to pay, specific indicators of willingness to pay are difficult to pinpoint. The debt record, the tax-collection record, the fiscal policies of the municipality's administration in the face of adversity are suggestive, however. Cities like Detroit, Mobile, and Atlantic City were forced to default in the early 1930s but subsequently put through refunding programs, and their credit has been redeemed. Since World War II relatively small losses have been suffered by owners of direct municipal debt. Defaults of revenue bonds have been much more serious.

Legality of Issue

The third test of the investment position of state and local bonds is *legality of issue*. Although the state is the sole judge of the legality of state debt, practically all states now limit their debt-creating capacity through voluntary restrictions written into the state constitution. These restrictions vary in the different states; in general, they are: (1) no state credit for private benefit, (2) bonds essentially for long-term improvements, and (3) referendum approval on large issues.

New York further requires that all state bonds must be issued in serial form, that each bond issue mature within the estimated life of the improvement, and that the proceeds of each issue be segregated into a special fund to be used only for the designated purpose and not combined with the general funds of the state.

In the case of bonds of local jurisdictions, legality is of prime importance, first, because creditors are allowed to sue municipalities to compel payment, and, second, because a municipal bond that has been illegally issued is invalid and noncollectible. Although instances may be found where courts, to protect innocent investors who have acted in good faith, have held some municipal bonds with minor technical defects as valid obligations, the general rule is that buyers of local bonds do so at their own risk and may not plead ignorance if illegality should later be established. Because all negotiations involving the issuance of municipal bonds are open to public inspection, and the laws regarding such issues are matters of record, a plea of ignorance of any defect would be an acceptable basis in a suit for collection.

Cases involving illegality of issue of local government bonds may be divided into four groups. The *authority of issue* may be inadequate under the powers granted to the city. The *purpose of issue* may be outside the legitimate purposes for which bonds may be issued. The *process of issue* may have violated any one of a score of minute details required by law. The *restriction of issue* may have been ignored in the issuance of bonds to an aggregate amount beyond the legal debt limit of the city. Since the investor is rarely in a position to pass upon such questions, he must rely upon the advice of qualified attorneys.

The procedure followed in the issuance of municipal bonds must be in strict accord with legal requirements. The enabling ordinance must be properly drafted and introduced at a legal meeting of the city council, approved in turn by the finance committee, the council, and, in many cases, a public referendum. The bond offering must ordinarily be advertised for public sale, sealed bids submitted, and the award properly made. The bond instruments must agree in all details with the provisions of the ordinance. Failure to observe any of the many technical requirements of the law endangers the validity of the obligation.

Investors should be assured not only that outside counsel has carefully checked and approved the legality of issue, but also that the particular counsel has a recognized reputation in municipal finance. So important are both of these phases that experienced investors in municipal bonds will buy only those issues that have been approved by certain attorneys. Fewer than 100 law firms in the entire United States have gained a national reputation in this field.

Municipal Bond Ratings

Two financial services—Moody's Investors Service and Standard & Poor's Corporation—provide a valuable service to investors by publishing quality ratings on a large number of state and local general obligations and revenue bonds.[14]

The small investor may be content to rely on bond ratings for his appraisal of quality. When substantial sums are involved, however, the investor should make his own analysis as a check against the ratings, which are not infallible and are subject to change. Table 6-8 shows selected examples of ratings, by types of issuer.

Examinations of rating lists reveals many bonds of smaller cities, counties, school districts, and local utility revenue bonds, running from Aaa to ratings of C or lower. Size and rating are not well correlated. With few exceptions, ratings of general obligations of local governments seldom exceed those of the state in which the jurisdiction is located, but they are often as high.

Form of Municipal Bonds

The leading features of state and local government bonds are usually prescribed by statute. They are issued in both coupon and registered forms; in some cases, the denominations of the latter type run as high as $1,000,000. Most bond issues mature serially, especially where the proceeds are used to finance depreciating assets. Sinking fund bonds are becoming generally less popular. It is, of course, in the interest of the investor that the sinking fund appropriations be used principally to retire the precise bond issues for which the funds are established.

Many municipal bonds include the call feature, making possible redemption before maturity for general or sinking fund purposes, as well as advanced refunding.[15]

Tax Position of Municipal Bonds

Income from all classes of municipal bonds, whether general lien, assessment, or revenue obligations, issued by states, municipalities, special districts, or authorities is exempt from all Federal income taxes. This feature is of particular value to investors whose incomes are subject to heavy tax rates (see Chapter 18). Repeated efforts have been made to remove this exemption feature from such issues, but with no success.[16]

[14]Moody's ratings are found in Moody's *Municipal and Government Manual* (annually), and *Moody's Bond Survey*; the symbols used are Aaa, Aa, A-1, A, Baa-1, Baa, Ba, B, Caa, Ca, and C. Ratings below B are rare. Many small issues are unrated.

Standard and Poor's uses the symbols AAA, AA, A, BBB, BB, B, CCC, CC, C (reserved for income bonds) and DDD-D (bonds in default). Ratings are found in Standard & Poor's *Bond Guide* (monthly). Ratings below B are rare.

Most revenue bonds are unrated. Very few have the top rating, unless they are guaranteed or are supported by special taxes such as motor fuel taxes.

[15]The purpose of refunding in advance of maturity is to take advantage of a decline in interest rates. A refunding issue may even be sold some weeks or months before outstanding bonds are called. The proceeds are invested in short-term Federal obligations.

[16]For a complete discussion, see the citation to Ott and Meltzer in the references at the end of this chapter.

Table 6-8. SELECTED MUNICIPAL BOND RATINGS

	Ratings	
States (general obligations)	*Moody's*	*Standard & Poor's*
Missouri	Aaa	AAA
Arkansas	Aa	AA
California	Aa	AAA
Massachusetts	Aa	AAA
New York	Aa	AAA
Hawaii	A-1	AA
Rhode Island	A	AA
Alaska	Baa-1	A
Large cities (general obligations)		
Milwaukee	Aaa	AAA
Rochester, Minn.	Aaa	AA
Cincinnati	Aa	AAA
Dallas	Aa	AA
San Francisco	Aa	AAA
St. Louis	Aa	AAA
Chicago	A-1	AA
Baltimore	A	AA
Honolulu	A	A
Miami	A-1	A
Philadelphia	Baa-1	BBB
Boston	Baa	A
Detroit	Baa	A
New York City	Baa-1	BBB
Nonguaranteed revenue bonds		
Burlington, Vermont utility	Aa	AA
Rhode Island Turnpike and Bridge Authority	Aa	AA
Port of New York Authority	Aa,A	AA
New York State Thruway Authority	A	A
Ohio Turnpike Commission	A-1	—
Virginia Highway Commission	Baa	—
Indiana Toll Road Commission	Ba	BBB
Los Angeles Metropolitan Transit Authority	Ba	BBB
Dade County, Florida, Causeway	Ba	BBB
Makinac Bridge Authority	Ba	—
Chicago-Calumet Skyway	Caa	—
West Virginia Turnpike Commission	Caa	—
Bellevue Bridge Commission, Nebraska	Ca	—
Dunbar Bridge, West Virginia	Ca	—

SOURCE: Moody's ratings from *Municipal and Government Manual* (1972), which shows year-end 1971 ratings; Standard & Poor's from *Bond Guide* (March 30, 1972). The differences in dates may partially explain different ratings by the two services.

The position of municipals with respect to state personal property or intangible taxes, and state personal and corporate income taxes, is not uniform. Although there are some exceptions, a state obligation or the income therefrom is not usually taxed in the state of issue, nor are the obligations of subdivisions in that state. Interest on obligations of other states and subdivisions thereof is sometimes taxed in other states, sometimes exempt. Exemption from local taxes is particularly valuable in Pennsylvania, Massachusetts, New York, and Virginia where taxes upon holders of out-of-state issues are relatively severe. There is no exemption from Federal or state estate and inheritance taxes.[17]

Because any profit on resale of a municipal bond is taxable at the capital gains rate applying to the investor, buyers of municipal bonds should prefer those bearing coupon rates that approximate the yield to maturity—in other words, bonds priced around par. The income from these bonds is tax-exempt, and such income constitutes most or all of the yield of the bond. If bonds are bought at a substantial discount, any subsequent rise in value is taxable on resale.

Yields

Table 6-9 shows the *average* annual yields on Moody's Aaa and Baa state and local government bond series as compared with the "riskless" yield on

Table 6-9. AVERAGE ANNUAL YIELDS

	Long-term Treasury	State and Local Government		Spread	Spread
	(1)	*(2)* *Aaa*	*(3)* *Baa*	*(1) over (2)*	*(3) over (2)*
1960	4.01%	3.26%	4.22%	.75	.96
1961	3.90	3.27	4.01	.63	.74
1962	3.95	3.03	3.67	.92	.64
1963	4.00	3.06	3.58	.94	.52
1964	4.15	3.09	3.54	1.06	.45
1965	4.21	3.16	3.57	1.05	.41
1966	4.66	3.67	4.21	.99	.54
1967	4.85	3.74	4.30	1.11	.56
1968	5.25	4.20	4.88	1.05	.68
1969	6.10	5.45	6.07	.65	.62
1970	6.59	6.12	6.75	.47	.63
1971	5.74	5.22	5.89	.52	.67
1972	5.63	5.04	5.60	.59	.56

U.S. Treasury long-term bond series, for the years 1960–1972. The last two columns show the spread between yields on the highest grade and good-grade municipals.

The yields on state and local government bonds as a group are the result of five main influences:

1. *Interest rates in general.* The previous data show that rises and declines in the yields on Treasury bonds are accompanied by changes in the same direction for municipals. By midsummer 1970, both had reached record levels. Long-term Federal bonds yielded 7.25 per cent, and Aaa municipals

[17]For the tax status within each state of issues, see Moody's Investors Service, *Municipal and Government Manual*, blue section.

6.95 per cent. These astronomical rates were dramatic evidence of the "credit crunch" that had begun in 1969. Yields on these two categories stood at 5.80 and 4.95 per cent, respectively, in early January, 1973.

2. *The supply of new securities of this type.* The net annual increase in long-term municipal public debt (after refinancing) for the years 1960–1971 was as follows (in billions of dollars) :[18]

1960	1961	1962	1963	1964	1965	1966	1967	1968	1969	1970	1971
$5.0	$5.0	$5.1	$5.5	$5.2	$6.7	$5.1	$6.5	$9.4	$5.4	$10.0	$15.6

The relation between net new debt and yields, although crude, is apparent. The first "credit crunch" period of tight money that culminated in high yields in 1966 was accentuated insofar as municipal bonds were concerned by the large new financing that had been building up since the early 1960s. Then in 1967–1968 and again in 1970, the huge volume of municipal offerings, accompanying tight money in general, was partly responsible for the record-breaking yields that peaked in mid-1970. Municipal financing continued at a high level in 1971–1972 but easier money conditions more than offset this influence, and yields declined substantially. The highest-grade issues yielded 4.95 per cent in early 1973.

3. *The supply of funds available for purchase of tax-free bonds.* New issues are absorbed primarily by taxed institutions, especially commercial banks, insurance companies, and by individuals. Bank acquisitions have shown the greatest variations. In 1959 and 1960, for example, their buying fell off sharply because of rising demand for loans, and municipal bond yields rose. Renewed large scale buying in 1962–1964 drove yields down. Demand again fell off in 1965–1966 as bank funds were diverted to loans, and yields rose. Again in 1966 commercial bank acquisitions of municipal securities dropped to $1.9 billions from $5.1 billions in 1965, as banks diverted funds to ease the tight short-term loan situation. Banks were back in the municipals market in 1967 and 1968, and their supply of funds helped to ease the yield level. But in 1969, they again deserted the tax-exempt market in the face of the credit strains of that year. Heavy buying began later in 1970, after the main crisis had passed, and continued in 1971–1972.

4. *The value of the tax-free privilege.* This factor is a major influence, as revealed by the spread between Treasury and Aaa municipal yields in Table 6-9. The changes in the spread reflect the forces that forced up Treasury yields until 1970–1972 and those that caused the relative decline in tax-free yields in recent years. It appears that the decline in income tax rates in 1964 and 1970 did nothing to disturb the increasing appeal of state and local government bonds.

5. *Individual characteristics.* Yields on individual issues are affected by their investment quality or rating, their marketability (largely a function of size), and their state income tax status. The declining spread in yield be-

[18]Investment Bankers Association, *Statistical Bulletin*; Bankers Trust Company, *The Investment Outlook*, annually; *Federal Reserve Bulletin*.

tween good-grade and high-grade municipals reflects the increasing value of the tax-free privilege as more individuals and institutions seek this benefit; it also reflects the fact that the supply of lesser-rated issues has been declining.

The difference in quality among state bonds is narrow, so that bonds of different states, of equal maturities, sell in a close yield range. Bonds of local municipalities present a wide range of quality, and, therefore, present a wide range of yields; this is especially true in the case of revenue bonds. The average investor should confine his purchases to the general-lien bonds of states and of the larger and stronger cities. The lower grades should be bought only by investors skilled in municipal bond analysis or especially familiar with the issuing unit, and able to assume more risk.

The Market for Municipal Bonds

New issues of general obligations are sold by competitive bidding to the some sixty investment houses that specialize in such obligations and to commercial banks, which are permitted, under the National Banking Act as amended, to act as principals (underwriters) in the purchase of municipal bonds (with respect to *general* obligations only). Revenue bonds are frequently sold on a negotiated basis. The dealers and "dealer banks" then retail the bonds to investors and maintain an over-the-counter market in them.

After the details of an issue, including its denomination, maturities, and other aspects of its form, have been determined by the administrative officials of the issuing unit, an official notice is published that offers the issue for sealed competitive bidding. The *Daily Bond Buyer* is widely used in this connection to reach the bond trade. Unless the offer is accompanied by a legal opinion that the bonds are legally and regularly issued, bidders generally bid subject to subsequent approval of legality. Usually the bid of the house or joint account (syndicate) that shows the lowest net interest cost to the issuer is accepted.

The next step is for the successful bidder to reoffer them (at a slight markup). The offering circular provides a bare minimum of information, including the financial statement of the municipality and possibly some data on the industry and the general economic condition of the area. The brevity of municipal bond circulars is in sharp contrast to the completeness required in new corporate security offerings under the Securities Act of 1933.

Municipal bonds are usually offered (and later traded) on a *yield basis,* that is, the price is indicated as a yield to maturity rather than in dollars. When short-term interest rates are lower than long-term, the early maturities sell at lower yields than the later ones.

Trading in outstanding state and municipal bonds is carried on over-the-counter through dealer houses specializing in these securities and through municipal bond brokers who serve as contacts between dealers. For trading purposes, the daily *Blue List of Current Municipal Offerings* is of great value in that it lists the current offerings of most municipal houses; between 2,000 and 3,000 issues may be available. The minimum round-lot unit of trading is $5,000 par value.

Municipal bonds of good quality enjoy a ready market, although they are never listed on any exchange. They are much in demand on the part of individuals seeking an income tax exemption. Their other major market is among institutions such as commercial banks, insurance companies, and trustees. State bonds may be used by banks in lieu of surety bonds to guarantee the safety of deposit of state funds and by insurance companies under state laws requiring policy guarantees. Bonds of state and local units are also purchased by individuals seeking the highest quality of investments regardless of tax-exemption. Table 6-10 shows estimates of the ownership of interest-bearing state and local government bonds as of December 31, 1971.

Investment Position of Municipal Bonds

In general, bonds of states enjoy an investment position second only to that of Federal obligations. The spread in yield between the strongest and the weakest bonds is small. Yet the market does make a distinction between the bonds of states with a good past record, a sound economic trend, and stable political management, and those of inferior record, poor economic development, and unreliable leadership. As we have seen, bonds of local municipalities, and revenue bonds, range in quality from mediocre to excellent.

Table 6-10. OWNERSHIP OF LONG-TERM MUNICIPAL DEBT, 1971
(in billions of dollars)

Ownership	Amount	%
Commercial banks	$ 82.4	56.0%
Individuals and personal trusts	33.6	22.8
Non-life insurance companies	19.3	13.1
Life insurance companies	3.4	2.3
State and local governments	2.1	1.4
State and local retirement funds	1.9	1.3
Mutual savings banks	.4	.3
Others	4.2	2.8
Total	$147.3	100.0%

SOURCES: Citations in Chapters 4, 22, 23, 29, 30; *Federal Reserve Bulletin*, flow-of-funds tables.

The investor in the lower income brackets who is interested in buying bonds should ordinarily avoid municipal obligations, because their yield reflects their exemption from income taxation. He would be paying for a feature he does not need. But a growing number of investors, even those in moderate income brackets, should calculate the comparative after-tax yields of taxable and tax-exempt bonds. (See Chapter 18.) The higher the taxable income, the greater the value of the exemption and the lower the acceptable yield. Since 1961 investors who wish to avoid making their own selection of bonds have been able to purchase the shares of a number of funds whose portfolios consist of tax-free bonds and whose income is tax-free. Because these funds do not make a continuous offering of shares, their shares represent an interest in a fixed portfolio. Such funds are a type of "unit trust" whose shares sell for asset value plus a sales charge. (See Chapter 9.)

REFERENCES

BOLLENS, J. C., *Special District Governments in the United States.* Berkeley, Calif.: University of California Press, 1963.

CALVERT, G. L., ed., *Fundamentals of Municipal Bonds,* 7th ed. Washington, D.C.: Investment Bankers Association, 1969.

CURVIN, W. S., *A Manual on Municipal Bonds,* rev. ed. New York: Smith, Barney & Co., 1964.

DAVIS, E. H., *Of the People, By the People, For the People,* rev. ed. Chicago: John Nuveen Co., 1958.

DOUGALL, H. E., *Capital Markets and Institutions,* 2nd ed, Chapter 8. Englewood Cliffs, N.J.: Prentice-Hall, Inc., 1970.

FRIEND, IRWIN, et al., *The Over-the-Counter Markets.* New York: McGraw-Hill, Inc., 1965.

HEMPEL, G. H., *The Postwar Quality of State and Local Debt.* New York: National Bureau of Economic Research (distributed by Columbia University Press), 1971.

INVESTMENT BANKERS ASSOCIATION OF AMERICA, *Fundamentals of Investment Banking,* Chapters 11, 12. Englewood Cliffs, N.J.: Prentice-Hall, Inc., 1949.

LENT, G. E., *The Ownership of Tax-Exempt Securities, 1913–1953.* New York: National Bureau of Economic Research, Inc., Occasional Paper 47, 1955.

LOLL, L. M., AND J. G. BUCKLEY, *The Over-the-Counter Securities Markets,* 2nd ed. Englewood Cliffs, N.J.: Prentice-Hall, Inc., 1967.

MAXWELL, J. A., *Financing State and Local Governments.* Washington, D.C.: The Brookings Institution, 1965.

OTT, D. J., AND A. H. MELTZER, *Federal Tax Treatment of State and Local Securities.* Washington, D.C.: The Brookings Institution, 1963.

RABINOWITZ, ALAN, *Municipal Bond Finance and Administration.* New York: John Wiley & Son, Inc. (Interscience Division), 1969.

ROBINSON, R. I., *The Postwar Market for State and Local Government Securities.* Princeton, N.J.: Princeton University Press, 1960.

TAX FOUNDATION, INC., *Facts and Figures on Government Finance.* New York: The Foundation, annual.

U.S. DEPARTMENT OF COMMERCE, BUREAU OF THE CENSUS, *City Government Finances; State Government Finances; Governmental Finances.* Washington, D.C.: U.S. Government Printing Office; all reports annual.

7 Characteristics of Corporate Bonds

SCOPE: This chapter discusses the general characteristics of corporate bonds from the viewpoint of the investor. The order of discussion is (1) general characteristics, (2) reasons for use, (3) importance of bond financing, (4) bond indentures, (5) the bond instrument, (6) classification of bonds, (7) market for corporate bonds, (8) bond yields, (9) investment position of bonds.

General Characteristics

Bonds represent long-term debt, as contrasted with stocks, which represent ownership. Claims of all bondholders have priority over the interest of stockholders, both preferred and common. Particular bond issues may enjoy preferred claims over other issues, but only when the nature of the preference is definitely stated in the instrument, as in the case of first mortgage issue. Bonds usually contain a promise to pay a fixed rate of interest, and their principal is payable on a definite date. The bondholder is ordinarily entitled to the fixed income and principal but to no more.

Bonds normally give the holder no voice in management, except in case of default. Failure to meet the terms of the issue gives the bondholder, through the trustee named in the indenture, the right to take legal action—either to foreclose on any pledged property or to sue for breach of contract. In a majority of cases, however, default leads to financial reorganization rather than to liquidation.

The position of the bondholder contrasts sharply with that of the stockholder or owner. The bondholder takes risk—but *relatively* less risk than the stockholder, in the same corporation. He has made a loan, he expects a fixed rate of income, and he anticipates a full return of the face value of the bond at a definite future date. The quality of his bond, as reflected in price and yield, depends on the degree to which the debtor can be expected to fulfill these promises.

Reasons for Issuing Bonds

When governments are unable to meet their expenses from current tax income, they have no choice but to borrow. Corporations, on the other hand, have a wider choice of methods with which to finance their operations. Among other ways, they may sell stocks or grow from retained earnings and other "internal" sources. Why do they incur the risk of borrowing? Five main reasons explain the use of bonds.

1. *To lower the cost of funds.* Investors are usually satisfied with a lower return from the bonds than from preferred stock of the same company.[1] Bond financing is also often cheaper than common stock financing. The cost of common stock financing is properly measured by the relation between earnings and market price.[2] The corporation is willing to incur the risk of borrowing in order to save on the cost of part of its capital.

2. *To gain the benefit of leverage.* In financial parlance *leverage* means the use of funds bearing a fixed cost in the hope of earning a higher rate than that cost. Thus if a company can borrow at 5 per cent, and put the funds to work to earn 10 per cent, the earnings on the owners' investment are increased. The leverage effect of borrowing can, however, lead to loss to the owners when the borrowed capital earns less than the fixed charge for its use.

3. *To widen the source of funds.* Funds can be attracted from individual investors and especially from investing institutions that are unwilling or are not permitted to purchase stock.

4. *To preserve control.* Since bonds ordinarily carry no voting rights, an increase in debt does not disturb the voting power of present owners, at least as long as the bonds are not in default.

5. *To effect tax savings.* The interest on bonds is deductible in figuring corporate income for tax purposes, whereas dividends on stock are not.

Borrowing also has definite limitations that the wise corporate management feels obliged to follow. When these limitations are disregarded, the investment position of the bonds suffers, and the cost of borrowed money increases; very substantial overborrowing may lead to default and bankruptcy. In the later sections of this book attention will be given to the tests of sound financial policy from the investor's standpoint.

---

[1]An exception is found in the case of high-grade preferred stocks, which because only 15 per cent of their dividends are subject to Federal corporate income taxes, have a special appeal to taxed institutional investors, and so produce market yields below those on high-grade bonds, even of the same issuer.

[2]The whole subject of the relative costs of debt and equity capital is discussed in works dealing with corporate financial policy; see references at the end of this chapter.

Importance of Bond Financing

The data in the tables in Chapter 2 (Tables 2-4 and 2-6) show the use of bond financing by corporations since World War II. The latter table shows that bonds have far exceeded stocks as means of raising new money by the issuance of securities. However, the former reveals that when retained earnings are added to new stock issues, equity capital financing has exceeded the use of long-term bonds by a large margin. Large use has, however, been made of other types of long-term debt such as mortgage notes and term loans.

Bond Indentures

When a corporation issues bonds, the basic document is the *indenture* or trust agreement. This is the contract between the borrowing company and the trustee (usually a bank) or trustees representing the bondholders. It contains all of the provisions of the borrowing, and hence, especially in the case of mortgage bonds, is often a long and formidable document. It also includes the duties of the trustee and his relation to the issuer and the bondholders. The trustees' chief duties are to authenticate the bonds, to represent the bondholders by enforcing the terms of the indenture, especially in the event of default, and to handle the details of sinking fund payments, interest payments, and bond redemption.

The Trust Indenture Act of 1939 requires corporations to file trust indentures with the Securities and Exchange Commission in the case of debt securities registered under the Securities Act of 1933. It sets forth the qualifications of the trustee and outlines the material concerning the trustee's actions that must be included in the indenture.

The Bond Instrument

The bond certificate itself contains only a summary of the main provisions of the borrowing. It is in effect a long-term promissory note. Its title usually indicates the name of the issuer, the rate of interest, the date of maturity, and some suggestion of the nature of any pledged property. The face amount or denomination of each bond is customarily $500 or $1,000 and represents part of a large issue that has been divided into small units for convenience in distribution. A fixed annual interest rate is stated on each bond; interest payments are usually made semiannually. Interest is collected by the owner through the presentation of coupons detached from the bond or of a check from the issuer. Practically all bonds bear definite maturity dates; few American corporations have issued perpetual debt.

Bonds may be *secured,* that is, enjoy a lien on specific assets pledged, or *unsecured,* that is, have a claim on assets in general and junior to any secured issues. Some of the highest-grade issues are unsecured bonds.

Although all bonds are essentially similar in that they all represent long-term debt, many variations are found in practice. The chief difference lies in the nature of the claim the bondholder has against the issuer. The issue with a prior claim on valuable assets naturally represents the safer security, taking precedence over any other bonds issued by the same debtor. The title of the bond is usually taken from the nature of the security, such as *first mortgage, collateral,* or *debenture;* or from the purpose of issue, such as *adjustment, refunding,* or *consolidated;* or from some special feature, such as *sinking fund,* or *convertible.* In numerous cases, a combination title is used, such as *first consolidated, adjustment income,* or *first and refunding.* The title, however, serves to describe the issue more than to reflect the investment position. Even when correctly named, some first mortgage bonds are inferior to unsecured issues of other companies.

A single company may have several bond issues outstanding. Moreover, one company with numerous bonds of its own may be directly or indirectly responsible for the payment of bonds issued by affiliated companies. The Penn Central Transportation System had outstanding in 1972 thirty bond issues or series, in addition to its equipment obligations. Each one of these fits into a definite sequence of claim upon earnings. Industrial companies usually have relatively few issues, and these are of a correspondingly simpler nature.

Classification of Bonds

Titles based upon security. The customary bond title indicates the nature of the security behind the obligation (or lack of it), the promised rate of interest, and the maturity date, such as First Mortgage 4's, 1980; Collateral Trust 5's, 1994; Debenture (unsecured) 6's, 2001. However, some issues avoid reflecting a junior claim in their titles; or where they are little better than an unsecured claim, some harmless title such as *refunding* 5's or *sinking fund* 4½'s may be adopted.

Mortgage bonds are the most common form of secured issues. A mortgage bond is secured by a lien on specific fixed assets described in the indenture, and the extra protection afforded by the mortgage depends on the priority of the lien and the value of the property pledged. This may be the entire fixed property or only a certain section of it, as in the case of railroad divisional bonds. If the mortgage is *closed,* no more bonds may be secured by the same lien. However, corporations have found that such issues may make future financing difficult. The *open-end* mortgage is designed to meet this situation. Under this arrangement, more bonds secured by the same lien may be issued, but certain protective provisions are required to prevent the dilution of the original security: (1) that additional bonds be limited to a proportion (often 75 per cent) of new property added and (2) that additional bonds be issued only when aggregate interest charges on new and old bonds are adequately earned (say, twice). The effects of expansion of debt (usually in successive series) are also limited if the open-end mortgage contains an *after-acquired-property clause,* which provides that all fixed property "hereinafter acquired" be included in the property pledged.

A further covenant of importance is the penalty clause for failure to meet the various covenants in the indenture, under the terms of which default in any specified promise renders the entire principal immediately due and payable.

Mortgage bonds may be classified as *senior* and *junior liens,* according to priority of claim. The senior liens, which hold the first claim upon both earnings and (designated) assets, comprise first mortgages. The Duquesne Light Company (Pittsburgh) First Mortgage bonds illustrate such an issue. At times the senior issues are called *prior liens,* illustrated in the Missouri-Kansas-Texas Railroad Company Prior Lien bonds which are senior with respect to part of the property but which constitute a second lien on other parts of the main line. The senior group also includes a good number of nominally junior issues, which are, in many cases, a combination of a large senior claim and a small junior position, or which are preceded by a small amount of prior bonds, or which have gradually advanced in rank with the retirement of earlier claims. The former Pennsylvania Railroad Company General Mortgage bonds are now a senior issue.

Secured junior bonds have a secondary claim upon the designated corporate property. It would be most helpful if every bond bore a numerical adjective indicating the position of the security. Corporations, however, are reluctant to disclose thus openly the position of junior issues; they prefer less significant and, in some cases, misleading titles, such as *general,* or *unified,* or *consolidated,* or *first refunding.*

Bonds secured by the deposit of other bonds and stocks are generally termed *collateral* or *collateral trust bonds.* In the event of default the collateral can be seized and sold. The most frequent users of this type are holding or parent companies which have as their main assets securities of other companies. Industrial and public service companies sometimes issue collateral bonds when all of their fixed property is pledged, or they may issue bonds secured by both mortgage and the deposit of securities.

Three main factors determine the investment standing of collateral trust bonds: (1) the nature and value of the securities pledged, (2) the general credit of the issuer, and (3) the specific protective provisions of the indenture. There should be an ample spread between the value of the collateral and the amount of the debt, and the issuer should be required to maintain this differential. If the value of the collateral is doubtful, the investor must rely chiefly on the general earning power of the company, for if the specific security is worthless, the bonds become in effect a general claim along with unsecured debt. Any clause in the indenture that permits substitution of collateral should be given special scrutiny. The investor should be particularly wary of collateral trust bonds that are secured by common stocks of companies that themselves have bonds and preferred stocks outstanding, and so are in reality junior securities.

A third group consists of those secured by the promise to pay of a company other than the issuer, and includes *guaranteed, assumed,* and *joint* bonds. The guarantee may be direct, covering interest, or interest and principal, or it may arise through a lease contract whereby the lessee agrees to pay to the lessor a sum sufficient to cover the interest and/or sinking fund on the bonds. *Assumed* bonds are issues of a company that has been acquired by another by merger or as a result of the reorganization of the original issuer. In taking over the property of the original issuer, the debt of the issuer has been assumed by the successor company. *Joint* bonds are the direct joint obligation of two or more concerns or, more likely, obligations of a company that operates property used by both, such as a terminal, and whose bonds are jointly guaranteed by the users.

Assumed, guaranteed, and joint bonds depend, for their quality, on (1) the property and earnings of the original issuer and (2) the value of the additional promise to pay of the guaranteeing or successor concern. If both of these elements are very strong, the issue will command high investment respect. The best examples are found in the railway field, where the issues of small corporations that have long since ceased to operate their own properties have been guaranteed or assumed by a large company. If the property is important to the system, such issues rank with the senior issues of the system.

Although these types of bonds have been discussed under the heading of secured issues, we should note that they may be either mortgage bonds or unsecured bonds. The factor that gives them special interest is the addition of the credit of a second corporation, or possibly of several other corporations, as in the case of Cincinnati Union Terminal Company First Mortgage bonds, which have a first lien on the terminal property and in addition are jointly and severally guaranteed by seven railroad companies.

A fourth group comprises the *debenture* issues, which are not secured by a lien or any specific assets but rank with the general debt of the issuer. A common provision in the indentures of modern debenture bonds provides that, if the company should issue any mortgage debt, the debentures will be similarly secured. Thus, a debenture issue may move up into the secured category and still be designated by the original title.

Debentures are issued by companies with credit standing ranging from very strong to weak. The debenture issues of the American Telephone and Telegraph Company are considered high grade. The strongest industrial corporation bonds are debentures. The fact that bonds are unsecured does not weaken their investment status if they are the only long-term debt of the issuer and if the general assets and earning power of the issuer provide ample protection. The main strength of any bond issue, secured or unsecured, lies in the earning power of the borrower. But because debentures lack a specific lien on assets, their position may deteriorate if excessive equal or prior debt is issued, or if their backing by general assets, and working capital in particular, is weakened by subsequent developments. The investor should check carefully the protective provisions in the debentures that are designed to protect their status. Common provisions include (1) the equal-coverage clause mentioned above, providing for securing the debentures equally with any new mortgage debt, (2) provision against the payment of dividends that would reduce net assets below a certain figure, (3) requirement of the issuer to maintain a certain ratio of current assets to current liabilities before dividends may be paid, and (4) limitation of the *total* funded debt, including the debentures, to a certain proportion of the total assets or of the capital stock or, more frequently, to an amount on which the interest is earned a certain number of times.

Debentures frequently include a sinking fund to provide for regular reduction in the amount outstanding and, to give them a speculative touch, are often made convertible into common stock.

Debentures are used most frequently by industrial and financial corporations. Railroads and public utilities customarily issue mortgage bonds. Except in unusual cases, the debenture bond of a railroad is preceded by layers of secured debt and is, therefore, a junior security of secondary quality.

A relative newcomer to the family of bonds is the *subordinated debenture*. This is payable after other designated unsecured debt and is the "low man on the totem pole" of bonds. It is widely used by finance companies as a means of increasing the junior capital base so as to support a higher amount of short-term bank debt, while still gaining the interest and income tax advantages that bonds provide. A number of industrial companies have used this type of issue in recent years, for example, Crane Company Subordinated Sinking Fund Debenture Series B 7's, 1994, and (J. C.) Penney Company Subordinated Debenture 4¼'s, 1994. To add to their appeal, subordinated debentures usually include the convertible feature.

Titles based upon purpose of issue. The purpose for which the bonds have been issued forms a second basis for the selection of a title. The underlying reason may be to take advantage of a favorable investment attitude toward certain classes of securities, as in the case of equipment trust certificates, or to avoid the admission of a junior lien through the use of a title such as *adjustment mortgage*. This method of styling bonds is, however, not without advantages, irrespective of the motive. Investors should be very interested in the use to which their funds are put since that is an important test of safety.

Adjustment bonds are issued in the reorganization of companies in financial difficulties. In practically all cases, they are received by investors in exchange for old securities retired in the new plan, under conditions whereby interest is payable only if earnings permit. They are a leading type of *income* bond (see below). Although these bonds are usually issued under clouded conditions, the eventual success of the company, as shown in the case of the Atchison, Topeka, & Santa Fe Railway Adjustment Mortgage 4's of 1995 (issued in 1895) may place the bonds in the investment category. The Adjustment Income 5's of the Hudson and Manhattan (issued in 1913) fared less auspiciously. They were defaulted in 1955 and the company was placed in bankruptcy. Adjustment bonds are usually protected by a junior mortgage. Foreclosure or reorganization is ordinarily permitted following default in the payment of principal and in the payment of interest if it has been earned.

Consolidated mortgage bonds are issued to consolidate into one issue several separate bond issues. They are ordinarily the result of refunding operations and often involve a first mortgage on one part and second or other mortgages upon other parts of the company's property.

Divisional bonds are railway mortgage bonds secured by a first lien on a division or section of the system. Since they precede other mortgage issues with respect to a claim on a certain division, they are also classified as *underlying* bonds.

Equipment obligations are issued to finance the purchase of equipment —notably railway rolling stock—on the partial-payment plan. Funds for the payment of such purchases are obtained by paying an advance rental or down payment of from 20 to 25 per cent and securing the balance through the sale of serial obligations payable over a period usually of fifteen years. For example, in August 1971 Seaboard Coast Line Railroad Company bought forty-two 3,600-h.p. locomotives and ten locomotive units at a total cost of $13,388,000. The company made a cash payment of about 20 per cent and issued $10,650,000 of 8 per cent equipment trust certificates maturing at the rate of $710,000 annually for fifteen years.

Under one method, known as the Philadelphia plan, the equipment is leased to the road for the period by a bank acting as trustee, the installment payments are regarded as rent, and the investors receive "dividends" on their equipment trust *certificates.* The certificates represent a beneficial interest in the trust and are usually guaranteed as to principal and interest by the railroad. The trustee leases the equipment to the railroad at an annual rental sufficient to pay the expenses of the trust, dividends on the certificates, and the principal of the certificates as they mature serially. The railroad also agrees to maintain the equipment in good order. The lease expires after all the certificates have been paid, and at that time title to the equipment is transferred to the railroad. In the event of default, the trustee may take possession of the equipment and sell or rent it for the benefit of the certificateholders.

Under another method that is increasingly in favor, the railroad makes a down payment under a conditional sales contract and borrows the balance from a bank or insurance company, paying this off in installments.

Equipment obligations have traditionally been regarded as excellent investments and bear relatively low yields, owing to (1) the essential nature of the equipment, (2) the mobility that would facilitate repossession and ready sale or rent of standardized equipment to another road, (3) the gradual increase in the value of the equity owing to the liquidation of the debt on a scale faster than the wearing-out of the equipment, which normally lasts well beyond fifteen years, (4) the adequacy of the cash "throw-off" from depreciation charges, especially if accelerated, to meet the installments, (5) the fact that receivers and trustees in charge of companies in insolvency usually continue to pay interest charges on equipment obligations even though they may allow the mortgage bonds of the company to remain in default, and (6) the excellent investment record of these securities. In only one instance in modern railroad history, that of the Florida East Coast Railway, was the lease disaffirmed and the equipment sold (1936). In this case payments totalling $593.54 per $1,000 certificate were distributed. In three other cases in the 1930s, maturities were extended, and two roads exchanged their certificates for other obligations bearing a lower rate of interest.

The decline in railroad earnings in the latter 1960s reduced the investment status of equipment trust obligations considerably, and many of them sold to yield as high as 8 or 9 per cent. But such rates also reflected the generally high level of bond yields. Ratings of the obligations of weak railroads fell to Baa or B, and those of some normally strong companies to as low as A (from Aaa). A substantial improvement in earnings will be necessary to restore equipment debt to its previous high investment position.

Formal equipment obligations are occasionally used by other types of carriers. In January 1972, American Airlines placed with an institutional investor an issue of eighteen-year "equipment trust loan certificates" in the amount of $19,500,000. This was 60 per cent of the cost of two McDonnell Douglas DC-10 aircraft leased to the airline for eighteen years.

Receivers' certificates are the obligations of a company being operated by a receiver in equity. With proper court approval, they enjoy priority over other obligations, although technically they are not secured by any lien. They are issued as a means of improving the property and the working capital position of the failed company, pending a reorganization. Receivership in equity has largely given way to reorganization under bankruptcy proceedings, and *trustees' certificates* are the modern type of issue.

Refunding bonds are those issued for the more obvious purpose of getting new capital on a favorable basis. Just as the conversion of a short-term debt into a long-term debt is known as a *funding* operation, the payment of debt at or before maturity with the proceeds of a new loan is called *refunding*. The main reason for refunding before maturity is to save on interest charges when interest rates have fallen or the credit of the issuer has improved. Refunding at maturity takes place when the company has made no provision for redemption. The investor must examine a refunding issue to determine whether the use of that name is for the purpose of disguising a junior issue. Senior issues are usually labelled "First and Refunding."

Terminal bonds are issued for the purpose of financing the construction of terminal facilities in large cities to be used by one or more railroad companies. These companies, either separately (severally) or collectively (jointly), usually assume proportionate responsibility for the debt of the terminal company, either by direct obligation or by guarantee. The fifteen companies which own the Terminal Railroad Association of St. Louis and guarantee its bonds include several of the most important systems in the country.

Titles based upon form of issue. Bonds are issued in either *coupon* or *registered* form. Some are interchangeable for a small service fee. *Coupon* bonds are payable to bearer and carry detachable interest coupons. *Registered* bonds are payable only to the registered owner, to whom interest checks are mailed, except in the case of bonds registered as to principal only. The coupon bond, being more negotiable to the bearer, may be more conveniently transferred and hence may command a price slightly higher than that of the registered bond.

Interim bonds are temporary certificates issued pending the preparation of the *definitive* bonds. Some months are required for the preparation, engraving, and printing of the regular bonds. Meanwhile the interim certificate evidences ownership and may be readily transferred.

Titles based on redemption.
The title of a bond is sometimes taken from some feature with respect to redemption. In such cases, the bond may be a secured or an unsecured obligation; if secured, the claim is usually a junior lien, since the company would naturally select a more indicative title for a senior obligation.

Perpetual bonds are those that represent permanent obligations and might more properly be termed *perpetual interest-bearing certificates,* as in the case of the Canadian Pacific Railway Perpetual 4 per cent Consolidated Debenture Stock.[3] Some long-term domestic issues, such as the West Shore Railroad 4's of 2361 and the Elmira and Williamsport Railroad Company Income 5's of 2862, might readily be classed as annuity bonds for all practical purposes.

Redeemable bonds, also known as *callable,* are those which may be paid at the option of the issuer during a specified period prior to maturity. Most modern bonds contain the call feature. The price at which the bonds may be repaid is usually computed on a sliding scale providing for a premium of as much as $4 to $8 per $100 of principal in the event of early redemption and declining to zero just before maturity. Unfortunately from the investor's viewpoint, the life of callable bonds is uncertain and they are most likely to be called when interest rates are low. The buyer of a redeemable bond may be forced to accept less income if interest rates fall but may not be able to obtain more income if interest rates rise. Since most bonds are callable, the investor has little choice in the matter. And the call price acts as an upper peg or platform through which the price of the bond is not likely to break except in a very strong bond market and when the chances of call are unlikely.

When money is "tight," as in 1966 and 1969–1970, corporations have to offer investors special inducements to attract their funds. In addition to attractive interest rates, many issues are made noncallable for a period of years, so as to assure the investor of his high return. An example is Eaton Corporation Debenture 6's of 1996 offered in September 1971. These bonds are not callable by the company until 1981.

Serial bonds are those on which the maturities are spread over a succession of years rather than in a single year. The Southern Railway Equipment 9's were issued in 1970 in the total amount of $9,465,000 repayable at the rate of $631,000 semiannually from 1971 to 1985. Most municipal bonds are retired serially, but corporate examples are unusual.

Series bonds are issued in sequential series under an open-end mortgage. Although all bonds thus issued have the same security, each series has dis-

---

[3]*Debenture stock* is a British term for an unsecured long-term debt. It is rarely used in American practice.

tinctive features such as interest rate, maturity date, and call price. This type of financing gives the corporation a maximum degree of flexibility and allows each new issue to meet the prevailing conditions in the market. In 1972 the Pacific Gas and Electric Company had thirty-six series of open-end mortgage bonds outstanding, designated "M" to "XX" with different coupon rates (from $2\frac{3}{4}$ to 9 per cent) and maturities (1977 to 2003).

Sinking fund bonds are those that require the establishment of a fund, to be built up during the life of the issue to sink, or liquidate, the debt. Such bonds are more prevalent in industrial issues than in railroads or public utilities, although there is a growing tendency, through the force of regulation, to insert sinking fund requirements in these latter types. The amounts annually appropriated for the sinking fund may be (1) fixed annual amounts—either a certain amount in dollars or a percentage of the bonds issued, or (2) varying annual amounts, increasing or decreasing each year, or (3) an amount varying with earnings, or (4), in the case of extractive industries, an amount proportionate to physical output. The sinking fund may be used (1) to redeem, either by purchase in the open market or by call, outstanding bonds of the same issue, or (2) to invest in other securities. From the investor's viewpoint, the first method stated in each case is preferable. The expression "subject to call for sinking fund only" applies to bonds which are otherwise nonredeemable.

Bonds which are called for sinking fund purposes are drawn by lot and must be surrendered if loss of interest is to be avoided. A source of irritation to investors is the return to them of unpaid interest coupons which are deposited for collection after that particular bond has been called for redemption for the sinking fund. Corporations keep no record of the owners of unregistered bonds, and so there is no notification of redemption other than by newspaper advertising. Such notices are often missed by bondholders, although they can protect themselves by using bank or broker safekeeping service. In partial compensation for the loss of interest and the trouble of reinvestment, the bonds are called at a premium, although such premiums are usually lower than those paid for ordinary refunding.

Sinking fund requirements are particularly important in the bond issues of corporations with uncertain earnings and those whose property is depleted or depreciated through time, such as extractive and real estate companies. Many debenture bonds include the words "Sinking Fund" in their titles to indicate that, although lacking specific security, they must be retired on a regular schedule.

Sinking funds should not be confused with so-called "capital improvement" funds whereby a public utility is permitted to substitute increased investment in property for definite retirement of debt.

Titles based upon participation. Some bonds whose interest payments are directly or indirectly contingent upon the earnings of the issuer bear a title reflecting that condition. As a general rule, these bonds are unsecured debts, although they are occasionally secured by a junior lien.

Income bonds are those on which the payment of interest is contingent upon the amount of current earnings and is not a mandatory charge. They are generally issued as part of a reorganization plan under which bond interest charges are "scaled down" to an amount within the reasonable capacity of the enterprise. Income bonds have been used to a large extent in connection with railroad reorganizations. The practice of replacing fixed-interest bonds with income bonds has also been employed extensively in real estate reorganizations. The payment of interest is contingent upon and proportionate to earnings available, up to a maximum rate. The interest is often cumulative; that is, if not earned and paid in one year, it must be paid later before any dividends may be declared. But if the interest is earned, it must be paid, in contrast to preferred stock dividends, which are contingent on earnings *and declaration*. One difficulty is the possible difference of opinion that may prevail as to whether the interest has been earned, in spite of the definition of earnings contained in the indenture. The real earnings of a company, after allowance for maintenance, depreciation, and other items, can be a matter of controversy.

The reputation which income bonds have gained by having been associated with failure, together with their inherently weak characteristics, has prevented their frequent use for raising new capital. Their real nature is difficult to explain to investors, and they lack the straightforward features of ordinary bonds or preferred stock. Even the tax advantage enjoyed by the corporation arising from the fact that their interest, unlike preferred dividends, is deductible for tax purposes has not often led to their wide use for ordinary financing. There have, however, been a few exceptions. In 1963 TransWorld Airlines sold $112 millions of Subordinated Income Debenture $6\frac{1}{2}$'s of 1978. A review of the use of income bonds, other than in reorganization, reveals that most have been issued to refinance preferred stock. Those sold for new capital have in the main been placed privately rather than offered to the general public.

Participating bonds are those that are entitled to share in the net earnings of the company in addition to receiving interest. A participating bond is an anomaly, since it seems to combine stock income with bond safety. Very few such bonds are now outstanding. The modern method of bond participation is through the indirect procedure of conversion or stock-purcase warrants.

Convertible bonds may be exchanged for stock at the option of the holder at a ratio and during the period stated in the indenture. These bonds make a strong appeal to investors who like a privileged opportunity to share in the future earnings, and are popular methods of financing during rising stock markets. In 1971, for example, convertible bonds totalling $3,607 millions constituted nearly 20 per cent of new corporate bonds sold for cash.[4]

The conversion feature may extend over the entire life of the bond, as in the case of Phillips Petroleum Convertible Subordinated Debenture $4\frac{1}{4}$'s of 1987, or over a limited period during the early life of the bond, as in the case of the J. C. Penney Company Convertible Subordinated Debenture $4\frac{1}{4}$'s of 1977, which will lose their conversion privilege in 1977. The conversion ratio may be par for par, or one $1,000 bond for ten shares of $100

[4]Securities and Exchange Commission, *Statistical Bulletin.*

par stock. Or it may be expressed in terms of a conversion price for the stock. The Southern California Edison Convertible Debenture 3⅛'s, 1980, are convertible at $43.50 per share, which means that one $1,000 bond may be exchanged for 22.99 shares.

Frequently the conversion price increases (with fewer shares in exchange per bond) in stages over the life of the issue, and occasionally conversion may call for some cash payment when the bond is exchanged. Thus, to convert United Air Lines Convertible Subordinated Debenture 4¼'s of 1992, the bondholder must turn in a $1,000 bond plus $260 cash in exchange for 16.2 shares of common stock.

A convertible bond should possess inherent strength so that in a weak market its value will not fall below what it is worth as a good bond without any reliance on the conversion feature. (See Chapter 12.) In a rising stock market, it will advance at least in proportion to the price of the stock into which it is convertible, or even sell at a premium to the conversion value. Thus, in December 1972, Lucky Stores Convertible Debenture 5's of 1993, convertible at $10 a share, were quoted at 165 to yield 3 per cent, when the common stock was selling at 15¾. At the same time the company's Sinking Fund Debenture 8½'s of 1996 were selling at 105⅛ to yield 8.0 per cent.

Where the value of the common stock into which the bond may be converted is well below conversion price, or where the prospects of increase are remote, the convertible bond sells at its "investment value" as a straight bond. Thus, Memorex Corporation 5¼'s of 1990 sold in January 1973 at 45¾ to yield 13 per cent. The bonds were convertible at 17 but the value of common stock to be received on conversion was 12.

In summary, then, with respect to price and yield, convertible bonds (and preferreds) may be classified in three groups: (1) those selling at a premium above their conversion value, and often producing a very low or even a negative yield; (2) those selling at their conversion value; (3) those selling at "investment value". In a weak or falling stock market, especially when interest rates are high, as in 1970–1971, the prices of bonds in the first group are particularly vulnerable. Thus, for example, Data Processing 4¾'s of 1987 fell from 300 in 1969 to as low as 50 in 1970.

The circumstances under which conversion is likely to take place are explained in Chapter 12. We should note here that, while conversion is at the option of the bondholder, a corporation may force conversion by exercising the right to call the bonds at a price lower than the market value of the bond or of the stock into which it is convertible.

Provided the investor does not pay too much for the privilege, the convertible feature may have real advantages. The owner of the convertible bond remains a creditor as long as he holds the bond. When it is to his advantage to do so, he may convert into stock with its possibilities for higher earnings and price appreciation. As indicated above, convertible bonds have a special appeal under bull market conditions because of their possibilities for sharing in the upward course of stock prices. However, the investor should remember that once conversion has taken place, the step cannot be retraced. Moreover, although he may choose not to convert, or if it is never profitable for him to do so, he has nonetheless probably paid something for the conversion option that he has not exercised. And, as we have seen, the prices of convertible bonds can be very volatile.

Bonds *with warrants* bear stock-purchase option warrants giving the holder the privilege of buying a certain number of shares of stock at a fixed price. The warrants may or may not be detachable, and may be valid for a limited or an unlimited period. (See Chapter 12.) The warrants attached to the TransWorld Airlines Subordinated Income Debenture 4's of 1992 are detachable and give the holder the right to purchase, up to December 1, 1973, twenty-seven shares per $1,000 bond at $22 per share.

Although many warrants become highly valuable during active stock markets, investors should realize that in warrant bonds, as well as in convertible bonds, the speculative feature has usually been added mainly to enhance the marketability of issues that may lack fundamental investment quality.

Stock-purchase option warrants have often been used in connection with bonds issued in corporate reorganizations. The purpose of the warrants is to give bondholders who have accepted a drastic reduction in interest payments an opportunity to share in any subsequent improvement in the earning power of the enterprise. They are presently becoming widely used in public financing of real estate.

Market for Corporate Bonds

At the end of 1971, an estimated $217 billions of domestic corporate bonds were outstanding.[5] This in contrast to the $85 billions outstanding at the end of 1960. The average annual net increase (after refunding) of $12 billions per year in the 1960s and early 1970s reflects the economic growth of the period and the growing willingness of corporations to borrow so as to enjoy the advantages of long-term debt financing indicated early in this chapter. The annual average increase in corporate bonds outstanding does not, however, tell the whole story. A much higher annual volume appeared in 1966–1967 and 1970–1971. In 1970 the increase was over $22 billions, and in 1971 it was $25 billions. The great demand for corporate funds contributed substantially to the record interest rates that prevailed in 1966–1971. A special factor in the 1970–1971 period was the need by corporations to improve their cash position after the "liquidity crisis" in 1969 and early 1970.

Corporate bonds, especially the high grade, have not been attractive to most individual investors until recent years because their yields were seldom higher than, and were often lower than, the rates paid by savings institutions. And the latter offer no price risk. To wealthier investors, tax-free municipal bonds provide higher after-tax yields. Thus, the main buyers have traditionally been financial institutions. But the weakness of the stock market in

[5]*Federal Reserve Bulletin*, flow-of-funds tables.

1969–1971, accompanied by record-breaking yields on bonds (see Table 7-2), turned many individuals towards bonds. The net purchases of households, personal trusts, and nonprofit organizations rose from $2.0 billions in 1966 to $12.4 billions in 1970 and $7.7 billions in 1971; in these two years they absorbed over 40 per cent of the net increase in corporate bonds outstanding.[6] Table 7-1 shows the ownership of *domestic* corporate bonds at the end of 1971.

Table 7-1. OWNERSHIP OF DOMESTIC CORPORATE BONDS, 1971
(in billions of dollars)

	Amount	%
Life insurance companies	$ 74.7	34.4
Uninsured private pension funds	25.9	12.0
State and local government retirement funds	36.2	16.7
Mutual investment companies	4.9	2.2
Mutual savings banks	12.8	5.9
Non-life insurance companies	9.3	4.3
Commercial banks	4.3	2.0
Individuals, trustees, and minor institutions	48.9	22.5
	$217.0	100.0

SOURCES: *Federal Reserve Bulletin*, flow-of-funds tables. See also sources cited in institutional balance sheets, Chapters 3, 4, 22, 23.

Life insurance company ownership is still first in importance. These companies acquire the bulk of their higher-grade industrial bond investments by direct placement. Pension plans and other institutional owners likewise seek to secure a higher long-term yield than that available on Federal obligations. Ownership by individuals rose very substantially with the higher yields in 1969–1972.

Yields

The factors that determine the yields on bonds of various quality ratings, and on individual issues, will be discussed later in this book. Bond yields are one type of long-term interest rates, and they change with the general pattern of interest rates. The spread between yields on high-grade straight corporate bonds and Treasury bonds, and between corporate bonds with different ratings, represents the margin for greater risk and poorer marketability (most corporate bonds are unlisted). As Table 7-2 shows, the premium for risk and poorer liquidity tends to rise as yields in general rise. But this relationship has been by no means uniform.

Yields on high-grade corporate bonds, together with other long-term interest rates, reached record levels in 1970, reflecting the tight situation then prevailing in the capital market. This situation was the result of a tre-

[6] *Federal Reserve Bulletin*, flow-of-funds tables.

Table 7-2. BOND YIELDS AND RISK PREMIUMS

| | Corporate | | | U.S. Treasury | |
	Baa (1)	Aaa (2)	Spread (1) over (2)	Long-Term (3)	Spread (2) over (3)
1960	5.19%	4.41%	.78	4.01%	.40
1961	5.08	4.35	.73	3.90	.45
1962	5.02	4.33	.69	3.95	.38
1963	4.86	4.26	.60	4.00	.26
1964	4.83	4.40	.43	4.15	.25
1965	4.87	4.49	.38	4.21	.28
1966	5.67	5.13	.54	4.66	.47
1967	6.23	5.51	.72	4.85	.66
1968	6.94	6.18	.76	5.25	.93
1969	7.81	7.83	.78	6.10	.93
1970	9.11	8.04	1.07	6.59	1.45
1971	8.56	7.39	1.17	5.74	1.65
1972	8.16	7.21	.95	5.63	1.58

SOURCES: Corporate bond yields: *Moody's Bond Survey*; U.S. Government series: *Federal Reserve Bulletin*.

mendous demand for funds, on the part of both governments and corporations, and the inadequate supply of savings available for long-term investment. Bond yields also reflected the tightness of credit in the money market. (See Chapter 2). As more funds became available, bond yields declined substantially in 1971 and levelled off in early 1972.

The Investment Position of Bonds

Bonds have traditionally been regarded as the most conservative form of corporate security investment. To the investor who has complete freedom in the choice of his commitments, they provide a combination of dollar safety and convenience surpassing that available in any alternative form of security. To the investing institution which, for reasons of fiduciary safety, is restricted in the choice of securities, bonds provide a satisfactory medium of investment, as evidenced in the billions of dollars carried by these institutions in bondholdings.

Yet no investor can afford to assume that just because a security is a bond, it has inherent strength. Corporate bonds vary greatly in investment quality, from worthless to almost riskless. The investor must examine each security on its own merits, regardless of its legal form. Generalizations concerning any large class of securities are usually dangerous. That some common stock yields are lower than bond yields is not evidence of their superior safety of income and principal but of the regard in which they are held by investors seeking price appreciation rather than current income. Nor can the investor expect stability in bond prices. As yields on outstanding bonds increase, their prices decline. The average value of AAA corporate bonds was 97.0 in March 1961. In July 1970 it reached 59.0, a decline of 39 per cent, but stood at 66.1 in December 1972.[7] It should be noted that these are prices of a series of long-term bonds. Shorter maturities suffered a smaller variation.

Another aspect of bond price action should be noted. As yields in general increase, the prices of low-coupon bonds decline the most, and in periods of high yields reach very low levels. But they have the greatest potential for appreciation in the event of a market turnaround that reflects declining yields. The investor also enjoys a locked-in yield because the chances of call by the corporation are virtually nil. A further advantage is that any subsequent gain on resale is taxable at capital gains rates.

As to whether bonds are "better investments" than stocks, the answer is that most bonds are *safer* insofar as dollars of interest and principal are concerned. Like all debt instruments, their fixed-dollar character provides no protection against the declining purchasing power of their interest and principal.[8] Whether corporate bonds in general, or a certain bond in particular, should be purchased depends on the bond, on the needs and purposes of the investor, and on conditions in the bond market. General principles of bond valuation are set forth in Chapter 25, and much of the material on corporate security analysis in Part V is applicable to the task of determining the investment strength of corporate bond issues.

REFERENCES

ATKINSON, T. R., *Trends in Bond Quality*. New York: Columbia University Press, 1967.

BOGEN, J. I., ed., *Financial Handbook,* 4th rev. ed., Section 14. New York: The Ronald Press Company, 1968.

CHILDS, J. F., *Long-Term Financing,* Chapter 5. Englewood Cliffs, N.J.: Prentice-Hall, Inc., 1961.

COLLIER, R. P., *Purchasing Power Bonds and Other Escalated Contracts.* Taiwan: Buffalo Book Company, 1971.

DEWING, A. S., *Financial Policy of Corporations,* 5th ed., Book I, Chapters 7–9. New York: The Ronald Press Company, 1953.

DOUGALL, H. E., *Capital Markets and Institutions,* 2nd ed., Chapter 9. Englewood Cliffs, N.J.: Prentice-Hall, Inc., 1970.

GERSTENBERG, C. W., *Financial Organization and Management,* 4th rev. ed., Chapters 6–8. Englewood Cliffs, N.J.: Prentice-Hall, Inc., 1959.

GRAHAM, BENJAMIN, D. L. DODD, and SIDNEY COTTLE, *Security Analysis,* 4th ed., Chapters 22–26, 29. New York: McGraw-Hill, Inc., 1962.

GUTHMANN, H. G., and H. E. DOUGALL, *Corporate Financial Policy,* 4th ed., Chapters 10–12. Englewood Cliffs, N.J.: Prentice-Hall, Inc., 1962.

HESS, A. P., and W. J. WINN, *The Value of the Call Privilege.* Philadelphia: University of Pennsylvania, 1962.

[7] *Federal Reserve Bulletin.*

[8] Some advocate the use of purchasing-power bonds whose interest and principal are adjusted to the changing purchasing power of money. Such obligations would present serious actuarial and accounting problems.

HICKMAN, W. B., *Corporate Bond Quality and Investment Experience*. Princeton, N.J.: Princeton University Press, 1958.

HUSBAND, W. H., and J. C. DOCKERAY, *Modern Corporation Finance*, 6th ed., Chapters 7–10. Homewood, Ill.: Richard D. Irwin, Inc., 1966.

KENT, R. P., *Corporate Financial Management*, 3rd ed., Part IX. Homewood, Ill.: Richard D. Irwin, Inc., 1969.

PILCHER, J. C., *Raising Capital with Convertible Securities*. Ann Arbor, Mich.: Bureau of Business Research, School of Business, University of Michigan, 1955.

STREET, D. M., *Railroad Equipment Financing*. New York: Columbia University Press, 1959.

VAN ARSDELL, P. M., *Corporation Finance*, Chapters 14, 15. New York: The Ronald Press Company, 1968.

WESTON, J. F., and E. F. BRIGHAM, *Managerial Finance*, 3rd ed., Chapter 19. New York: Holt, Rinehart and Winston, Inc., 1969.

8 Characteristics of Stocks

SCOPE: This chapter discusses the general nature of corporate stocks from the viewpoint of the investor. Investment policy involving stocks is reserved for later attention. The order of discussion is (1) general characteristics, (2) legal position of the stockholder, (3) stock terminology, (4) preferred stock—general nature, (5) preferred stock protective provisions and voting, (6) classified common stock, (7) preferred stocks as investments, (8) preferred stock yields, (9) guaranteed stocks, (10) common stock—general nature, (11) dividend policies, (12) large stock dividends and stock splits, and (13) common stocks as investments.

The form and title of a security do not determine its investment quality. Many common stocks have had very superior records, and many preferred stocks have become worthless. Nevertheless, the basic distinctions are important, and some general conclusions may be set forth concerning the relative attractiveness of the two classes of stocks. The reader will realize, however, that in the case of any individual security, it is the price, earnings and dividend record and prospects and the amount and character of the assets that support the stock that determine its investment appeal.

General Characteristics

Stock, whether preferred or common, involves no promises. The owner of a share of stock is part owner of the corporation. His stock gives him the right to share in the *net* assets of the business (if any), the *net* income (if any), and management.

The capital stock is divided into units, called *shares*. At the end of 1971 the outstanding stock of J. C. Penney Company comprised 53,265,197 shares, each of which represented 1/53,265,197 share of the net assets or *net worth* of the company. The evidence of ownership of shares is the *stock certificate*. The name of the owner appears on the face of the certificate, together with the number and kind of shares represented by the certificate. The certificate is always a registered instrument; the owner's name is registered on the books of the company. Only the registered owner can assign the stock by signing the blank form on the back of the certificate. The registered owner is the one who receives the dividends, has the right to vote, and otherwise enjoys the privileges of ownership.

Stock certificates are written evidences of ownership of shares of stock and are transferable if properly endorsed and delivered. When stocks are sold, the usual practice is for the owner to endorse them in blank. They may pass through many hands before being registered on the corporation's books in the name of the new owner. The actual registration and transfer is usually handled by a transfer agent appointed by the company.

Corporation stock may have a *par value,* of from a few cents to several hundred dollars per share, or *no par* value. The par value is a purely nominal amount which is supposed to show the original investment per share. When the par value has been paid in to the corporation, the stock certificate is designated "full-paid and nonassessable." For many years the customary par value was $100. Today the trend is toward low par value stock, or stock without par value, which is full-paid when the original consideration set for each share has been received by the company.

To the investor, no-par stock has a real advantage in that each share simply represents a certain fractional ownership in the corporation without any confusion as to nominal value. A stock with a par value of $50 (Reading Company) may sell, as it did in 1972, as low as $1 per share. Probably few of its owners knew that at one time the company had received the equivalent of $50 per share in cash or other assets for this stock. Neither the market value nor the *book value* (dollars of net assets per share of stock) is influenced by the nominal par value after the company has been in operation for some time.

Table 8-1 shows the par value (if any), the book or net asset value at the end of 1971, and the range in market value of selected common stocks for the year 1971. The selection reveals that the market value, based primarily on the prospects for earnings and dividends, is usually very considerably different from nominal and book values.

Legal Position of the Stockholder

As the owners of corporations, stockholders have certain well-defined rights and obligations, depending upon the corporation laws of the state in which the company is chartered. Although state laws differ widely with respect to powers of corporations, the position of the stockholder is fairly uniform in most states.

The stockholder has a right to receive dividends when earned and if declared by the directors. The income claim of a stockholder is contingent, differing fundamentally from that of the bondholder, who has a fixed claim and who can take action in the event of default. The stockholder shares in the fortunes of the business, large or small. In the case of common stocks, there is no theoretical upper limit, while most preferred stocks can receive only a maximum stated dividend. Even when earnings are large, stockholders only rarely compel dividend payments if the management decides to reinvest the profits in the business. This is true even of preferred stock, except that the preferred has a right to dividends before the common.

Table 8-1. SELECTED COMMON STOCK VALUES

Company	Par Value, Dec. 31, 1971	Book Value Dec. 31, 1971	Price Range 1971
Cinerama, Inc.	$ .01	$ 1.60	2–6
Merck & Co., Inc.	.05-5/9	14.17	94–131
Digitronics Corp.	.10	.85[a]	3–14
Chock Full o' Nuts	.25	5.12[b]	8–14
Sperry Rand Corp.	.50	22.58[a]	22–38
Memorex Corp.	1.00	6.64	19–80
Glenmore Distilleries, B	1.00	31.68	10–14
General Motors Corp.	1.6667	36.75	60–91
Signal Companies, Inc.	2.00	28.82	14–22
Superior Oil Co.	2.50	77.50	138–221
El Paso Natural Gas Co.	3.00	15.97	16–22
International Business Machines Corp.	5.00	57.49	283–366
Union Pacific Corp.	10.00	66.16	47–66
Crane Co.	25.00	58.04	34–50
Reading Co.	50.00	69.00	2–9
United N.J. R. R. & Canal Co.	100.00	272.52	47–53
Raychem Corp.	No par	26.70[c]	62–123
Proctor & Gamble Co.	No par	16.87[c]	56–81
RCA Corp.	No par	13.79	26–41
Chicago, Milw. Corp.	No par	134.20	9–20

[a]March 31, 1971.
[b]July 31, 1971.
[c]June 30, 1971.

The stockholder has the right to share in the net assets of the corporation in the event of dissolution. This right vanishes in practical value in the case of failed concerns, even in the case of preferred stocks, which ordinarily have a set liquidating value that must be paid before anything goes to the common. But where there is nothing to distribute, such priority is meaningless.

Unless denied him by the charter of the company, the stockholder usually has the *preemptive* right to subscribe to new issues of common stock in proportion to his existing holdings, so that he may preserve his relative share of the assets, earnings, and voting power that might be diluted if the shares were sold to new investors. Because convertible bonds and preferred stock may eventually be exchanged for common and thus increase the common stock outstanding, the stockholder is usually given preemptive rights to subscribe to new convertible securities. Since the subscription price is below market price, the rights to subscribe may have considerable value. The method of calculating the value of rights is given in Chapter 12.

The stockholder has a right to inspect the corporate books. This right applies to the general books, such as the minutes of the stockholders' meetings and the list of stockholders, rather than to the ledgers and the books of financial record, and is restricted by certain requirements that make it of little value to the investor unless he wishes to stage a proxy battle with management.

The stockholder has a right to vote in the selection of the board of directors and on all matters affecting the corporate property as a whole, such as sale or merger or liquidation of the business.[1] The voting right is exercised at the annual or special meetings of stockholders in person or by the use of proxies which delegate voting rights to designated parties. When a stockholders' meeting is called, the management accompanies the notice with a proxy form, which the stockholder may sign and thus convey his votes to the committee acting for management.

Other fundamental rights of the stockholders include the right to receive a certificate representing his shares, to transfer his shares, and to take action against the wrongful acts of the management and the majority of stockholders.

The stockholder is liable for the debts of the corporation only to the amount of unpaid subscriptions to the capital stock, and to the difference between subscription price and par value, in the event the former is lower. This limited liability feature is one of the great advantages afforded by the corporate form of organization.

The stockholder is also generally liable for wages of employees for limited periods. This provision applies to employees in subordinate positions, for periods not exceeding three months, under somewhat technical conditions.

Stock Terminology

The *authorized* stock is the maximum number of shares of each type that may be issued, as specified in the certificate of incorporation. To change this number, or the provisions of any class of stock, requires the formal approval of stockholders. *Issued* stock is the amount of shares that have been issued for cash, property, or services. Stock reacquired by the company by purchase or donation and not reissued or cancelled is called *treasury* stock. Treasury stock is ordinarily deducted on the balance sheet from the issued stock to show the amount of *outstanding* stock. *Full-paid stock* is, as we have seen, stock for which the corporation has received full payment up to par value, or up to the amount established as the selling price of no-par shares. *Part-paid* stock is stock that has been issued for less than par value or the agreed subscription price. Under the laws of most states, stock cannot be issued unless fully paid.

Preferred Stock—General Nature

The capital stock of a company is often divided into two classes, *preferred* and *common*. The provisions of the preferred stock are set forth in the corporate charter. The universal characteristic of preferred stock is that it has priority over the common stock with respect to dividends, that is, no dividends may be paid on the common stock in any year in which the full

---

[1]The ordinary voting right, that is, to vote for directors, is sometimes denied the holders of preferred stock (see section below on preferred stock voting rights).

preferred dividend has not been paid. The amount of the annual preferred dividend, which is limited, is stated either in dollars per share or as a percentage of par value. The preferred dividend is not a fixed charge in the sense that the company is required to declare it. Preferred dividends, like common dividends, are contingent upon the discretion of the management as represented by the board of directors. Even though the available profits may be adequate for the payment and the cash position may be strong, the directors may decide to conserve the funds in the business. However, where the preferred dividend is earned, a strong inducement exists to pay it in order to keep the record clean and to clear the road for common dividends.

Cumulative preferred stock is that type under which dividend payments omitted at any time accumulate in the form of arrearages. These arrearages, although not corporate liabilities, must be paid in full before any dividend may be paid on the common stock. *Noncumulative* preferred stock has no prior claim on dividends, except on those for the current year. Past dividends are lost forever. The advantage of cumulative over noncumulative preferred stock is not so great as it might seem. A prolonged period of poor earnings may result in an accumulation of dividend arrearages beyond the capacity of the company to pay. In such a situation a solvent company is almost permanently enjoined from paying any dividends to the common stockholders. Even when the amount of arrearage is not discouragingly large, the holders of cumulative preferred stock are usually persuaded to accept other securities or part cash in lieu of cash in full.

Companies that regularly use preferred stock financing often issue two or more series that share the same rank of priority over the common. But their dividend rates, call prices, and even sinking fund provisions may differ because the several series were sold at different times and under different market conditions. Pacific Gas and Electric Company has eleven classes of preferred stock, all ranking equally in priority but having dividend rates ranging from 4.36 to 9.28 per cent (on $25 par). Flintcote Company has three classes, one of which, carrying a rate of $4, is known as Preferred and has dividend priority over the second, of which there are three series, known as Convertible Second Preferred. The term *prior preferred* is sometimes used to designate the particular preferred stock which has priority of claim, although the term *first preferred* is more generally used for this purpose. In such cases, the senior issue is entitled to its full dividend rate before any payment may be made on the junior issue. A rather extreme example of the use of issues of preferred stock with different priorities is found in Commonwealth Edison Company (Chicago), which has (1972) three "layers" of preferred ahead of the common: 9.44 per cent Cumulative Prior Preferred, par value $100; $1.45 Convertible Preferred, no par value; and $1.90 Cumulative Preferred, no par value.

Preferred stocks usually have priorities also in the distribution of assets (in the event of dissolution). The amount of the preference is usually stated in dollars per share and generally approximates the original value of the stock, plus any accumulated dividends. This "preference as to assets" is rarely of practical value. Failure usually finds the creditors in possession of the assets, with little if anything available to the stockholders.

Redeemable or callable preferred stock may be retired by the issuing company upon the payment of a definite price stated in the instrument. Although the call price provides for the payment of a premium, which may range from $2 to as much as $10 above the face value of the stock, the provision is more advantageous to the corporation than to the investor. When money rates decline, the corporation is likely to call in its preferred stock and refinance it at a lower dividend rate. When money rates rise, the value of the preferred declines so as to produce a higher yield. And the call price tends to act as an upper peg or plateau through which the price will break only in a very strong market.

Noncallable preferred stocks are issued in periods of high interest rates such as 1966 and 1969–71. The issuer is barred from redeeming them later in the event of generally falling yields, or for a certain period, so that the investor has important protection against declining income. Examples include Pacific Telephone and Telegraph $6 preferred, selling at 90 to yield 6.7 per cent, and Universal Leaf Tobacco $8 preferred, selling at 114 to yield 7.0 per cent. Pacific Gas and Electric 9.28 per cent preferred, issued in 1970, is noncallable until 1980.

Convertible preferred stock may be exchanged into common stock at the option of the holder. Preferred stocks which carry this privilege are likely to be deficient in quality, because ordinarily adding this feature to attract investors to a stock that is strong in its own right is unnecessary. However, in periods when common stocks are in demand and rising in value, even strong companies may add the convertible feature to attract investors who would not be enthusiastic about ordinary preferred stock.

The exchange ratio is stated in the instrument and is often on a sliding scale whereby the conversion price increases during the conversion period. The longer the investor waits, the less common stock he will receive on conversion.

The American Telephone & Telegraph Company financing in June, 1971 was unique in two respects: (1) it was the company's first issue of preferred stock, and (2) it was the largest single offering of stock in history. The company offered $1,375,000,000 (27.5 million shares) of $4.00 convertible preferred to stockholders through rights. Details of the offering are described in Chapter 12.

The convertible feature may have real appeal to investors looking for a compromise type of security. The circumstances under which conversion becomes profitable are discussed in Chapter 12. Further discussion of convertible securities is also found in Chapter 7 under the heading "convertible bonds."

Participating preferred stock is entitled to a further share in any dividends after the payment of the regular preferred dividend. The most common arrangement permits the preferred to share with the common stock in further dividend distributions after the common has received a stated rate. Very few important preferred stocks contain the participating feature. It is usually a speculative inducement to bolster the attractiveness of a preferred stock that lacks strength on its own merits. The same is true of preferred stock to which *stock-purchase warrants* are attached at the time of sale. These give the owner the right to purchase common stock from the

company at a stipulated price during a specified period, and are usua
substitute for sound investment quality in the preferred stock itself.

Preferred Stock Protective Provisions and Voting Rights

In addition to the two basic features of preferred stock noted previously—
preference (over the common stock) as to dividends and as to assets—other
features may give it investment strength. These are especially important in
the case of preferred stock that lacks ordinary voting rights. The more important are (1) a repurchase or sinking fund that requires the steady reduction in the amount of preferred outstanding, (2) required approval by the
preferred stockholders of the issuance of any funded debt or of additional
preferred, and (3) restriction on the payment of common dividends unless
a certain working capital position is maintained.

Although the right to vote for the board of directors and thus to participate in management is a fundamental right adhering to all stock, it is
often withheld from preferred stock. No great harm is done so long as the
company's earnings, dividends, and general financial strength are well
maintained. The investor in preferred stock, although a part owner of the
corporation, regards himself as an "outside" investor. However, if dividends
are not paid, and if he has no voice in management, he is in an impotent
position. Therefore, the preferred usually has the right to vote under certain conditions, even if normal voting power is lacking. The preferred may
be given one vote per share after a certain number of quarterly dividends
(often four or six) have been omitted. Or the preferred as a class may
receive the right to elect a certain number of directors, or, in some cases,
to elect a majority or even all of the directors. Such contingent voting power
is a strong inducement to management to earn and pay the preferred dividends and avoid an accumulation. In addition, the preferred usually has
the right to vote on certain questions that affect its status considerably, such
as on the dissolution of the company, the mortgaging or sale of its property,
and merger with another concern.

Classified Common Stock

In the 1920s, a hybrid type of security was developed by the issuance of
more than one type of "common" stock, and today the balance sheets of
some corporations still show "Class A" and "Class B" common, or "Class
A common" and "Common." In some cases the only difference between the
two classes of common is that one is devoid of voting rights. Control of
the corporation is thus concentrated in one issue.[2] In recent years the trend

[2]An interesting current example of classified common stock is Ford Motor Company's Common
(voting) Class A, nonvoting (held by the Ford Foundation), and Class B (voting), with $2.50 par
value. These were issued in 1956 as a result of the recapitalization when Ford stock was first made
available to the public (by the Foundation).

has been away from nonvoting common. It may not be listed on the New York Stock Exchange, and it is frowned upon by the Securities and Exchange Commission insofar as gas and electric companies are concerned.

Other issues of so-called classified common stock are, in fact, merely weak preferred stocks, with preference as to assets and dividends but without the other protective provisions ordinarily found in true preferred. A description of such provisions is readily obtained in the investment manuals.

Preferred Stocks as Investments

In general, preferred stock occupies an intermediate investment position offering more income but less safety than bonds, and less income but more safety than common stocks. It is designed to attract investors who desire a favorable rate of return and who are willing to assume the attendant risk. Some preferred stocks resemble bonds in their investment position, but many issues might more properly be placed in the category of common stocks as far as investment quality is concerned. Until recent years many well-known companies had no long-term debt outstanding, so that their preferred stocks had claims on earnings which were not subordinate to or lessened by bond interest payments. So long as this condition continued, these preferred stocks were the senior securities of the enterprise, and this position is reflected in their low yields. There are very few important companies in this category today.

Other preferred stocks belong, in terms of safety, in the bond category because of the prosperity of the issuing companies. Certain railroad companies, such as Union Pacific and Santa Fe, certain public utility companies, such as Cleveland Electric, Pacific Telephone, many small public utility operating companies, and certain industrial companies, such as General Motors, W. T. Grant, and Standard Brands, have established impressive records of earnings over long periods of years, thus placing their preferred stocks in a strong investment position.

Many other preferred stocks, however, especially of industrial companies, belong, in effect, in the common stock category because of inadequate earnings protection. Investors who have bought preferred stocks upon the assumption that the payment of dividends was as certain as the payment of bond interest have found that dividends may be passed and that in liquidation or in reorganization the preferred stockholders are in a very weak bargaining position.

Some preferred stocks are very high grade, and many are of low-grade quality. It is not the *form* of a security that gives it value and stability, but the earnings and assets that support it. Nevertheless, because preferred stock lacks the legal claim of the bondholder and the profit and appreciation possibilities of a common stockholder (because of the customary fixed dividend rate, stated liquidating value, and call feature), it has a questionable investment status that is clearly revealed when hard times appear. Were it not for their tax appeal to corporate investors, even the highest-grade preferred issues, well protected by assets and earning power, would yield more than high-grade bonds of long maturity.

Preferred Stock Yields and Prices

The price and yield action of a preferred stock is determined by four fundamental factors: (1) the general level of long-term interest rates (the preferred dividend being a fixed annual amount), (2) the earnings and asset strength of the issuer, (3) the special appeal of preferred stocks to the taxed *corporate* investor, and (4) the shortage of high-grade preferred issues. The influence of the first two factors is discussed elsewhere in this volume, as are the methods of appraising them and applying them to specific securities.

The third or tax factor deserves some mention here, and helps to explain the data on yields given below. Only 15 per cent of the dividends on preferred stock owned by taxed corporations are subject to the Federal corporate income tax. This tax-exclusion feature gives preferred dividend income an advantage over bond interest income, and largely explains why the yields on very high-grade preferred stocks, held mainly by institutional owners, have been as low as, and even lower than, the yields in bonds of the same companies, since 1960. Another tax influence applies to the dividends not covered by the 85 percent tax-exclusion. The dividends on these preferred stocks, notably public utility issues, are not taxable in part or sometimes not at all because they represent a return of capital. This situation arises when a company that charges accelerated depreciation for tax but not for "book" purposes reports no taxable income, so that its dividends are unearned.

The data in Table 2-6 reveal the relative unimportance of preferred stock financing until recent years. The small flow of new issues, accompanied by the demand for preferred stocks on the part of taxed institutional investors, has contributed to the special price and yield pattern found in the preferred stock market in very recent years. The increase in preferred stock financing in 1967 and especially in 1970–1971 is explained by three factors: (1) the appeal of convertible preferred, especially as issued for mergers, (2) the need by public utility companies to balance their capital structures after very heavy debt financing, and (3) the large issue of American Telephone preferred referred to previously.

The data in Table 8-2 show the course of average annual high-grade and good-grade preferred stock yields, 1960–1972, compared to those of bonds of the same rating, using Moody's industrial series. Both preferred and bond yields rise and fall with general long-term interest rates. The yields on high-grade preferreds would be higher than on high-grade bonds were it not for their tax appeal. The spread between the yields on high-grade and good-grade preferred stocks reflects the greater risk of the latter.

The price action of preferred stock is, of course, the opposite of the change in yield. The prices of even the highest-grade preferreds are, like bonds, subject to substantial variations as interest rates change. For exam-

Table 8-2. PREFERRED STOCK YIELDS

	High-Grade Industrials		Good-Grade Industrials		Spread	
	Aaa Bonds	Low-Dividend Preferreds	Baa Bonds	Medium-grade Preferreds	(2) over (1)	(4) over (2)
	(1)	(2)	(3)	(4)	(1)	(2)
1960	4.28%	4.48%	5.11%	4.80%	.20	.32
1961	4.21	4.36	5.10	4.68	.15	.32
1962	4.18	4.21	4.98	4.60	.03	.39
1963	4.14	4.04	4.90	4.41	−.10	.37
1964	4.32	4.05	4.87	4.38	−.27	.33
1965	4.45	4.07	4.92	4.38	−.38	.31
1966	5.12	4.67	5.68	4.95	−.45	.28
1967	5.49	5.13	6.21	5.39	−.36	.26
1968	6.12	5.62	6.90	5.83	−.50	.21
1969	6.93	6.15	7.76	6.38	−.78	.23
1970	7.77	7.03	9.00	7.25	−.74	.23
1971	7.05	6.55	8.37	6.84	−.50	.29
1972	6.97	6.53	7.99	6.87	−.44	.34

ple, W. T. Grant Company 3 3/4 per cent preferred sold as high as 112 in 1937, but as low as 48 in 1970 when extremely high interest rates prevailed, although the dividend was covered over 100 times. Changes in quality have of course always affected yields.

High-grade preferred stocks, with their relatively low yields, are not attractive to individual investors. Individuals interested in income would do better to choose savings types of investments, corporate bonds, or tax-free municipal bonds. In addition to the yield disadvantage, most preferred stocks, being unlisted, lack good marketability.

Guaranteed Stocks

Guaranteed stocks are those upon which dividend payments are guaranteed by some company other than the issuer. The guarantee usually arises out of a consolidation of properties under a lease. Such stocks, confined almost entirely to the railroad field, may be preferred or common. They are more like bonds, however, since dividend payments are fixed, rather than contingent, charges. The amount of the guaranteed dividend is either the regular rate stated on the preferred certificate or a contractual rate in the case of common stock.

The investment position of guaranteed stock depends upon the nature of the guarantee, the value of the underlying property to the guaranteeing company, and the financial responsibility of the guaranteeing company, but most especially the latter. A $5 dividend is guaranteed by the Penn Central Transportation Company on the common stock of the New York & Harlem Railroad Company which owns the entrance to New York and terminal properties of the former Pennsylvania Railroad Company. The stock sold as high as 180 in 1960 but as low as 40 in 1970 following the bankruptcy of the lessor, although the dividend continues to be paid.

Common Stock—General Nature

Common stock represents the basic ownership of the company. The claim of the common stockholders to income and assets is subordinate to all other claims, except in the relatively few instances where preferred stock is not preferred as to assets. Ordinary common stock always has voting rights. Common stocks are often called residual *equities,* since they usually represent only part of the total capitalization as contributed by the owners, in contrast to the remainder supplied by creditors and preferred stockholders.

After a corporate reorganization, the shares of the new company are often placed in trust with a small group of trustees for from five to ten years. *Voting trust certificates* are issued to the stockholders. These certificates have all of the characteristics of the common stock itself except voting rights.

Income payments to stockholders are in the form of dividends, which, as the term implies, represent a division of profits. Dividend payments are usually made quarterly and in cash.[3] The payments may be semiannual or annual, and are occasionally in some form other than cash. In some instances, dividends are declared in the form of short-term promissory notes, called *scrip.* In rare cases, certain of the corporate assets are distributed as property dividends.

Investors are often confused by dividends in the form of stock, since the distribution is in reality a division of the ownership into a larger number of units, and, therefore, not a true distribution of earnings. The result would not be different if the disbursement were made in cash and the money reinvested in new stock. "Stock dividends" are the external evidence of reinvestment of profits in the business. Stockholders who do not wish to increase their investment in the company may sell their stock dividends. In doing so, of course, they are parting with a portion of their equity.

Dividends in the form of stock have a strong appeal to many investors. Where the company is earning a high rate of profits, the stockholder may prefer to have his earnings reinvested at such a rate. The tax advantages of stock dividends are also appealing to many investors. No income tax is paid when the dividend is received, and only a capital gains tax if the dividend shares are ultimately sold at a profit.

Dividend Policies

Some common stocks are bought primarily for income, others primarily for price appreciation. In the former case, the stockholder wants some assurance that the current or future return of his common stock will be sufficiently

[3]The American Telephone & Telegraph Company pays a cash dividend on the tenth of January, April, July, and October to all stockholders who were listed on the corporate books on the tenth of the preceding month. The interval between the *record date* and the *dividend date* is provided in order to allow the checks to be prepared for mailing. The magnitude of this task is indicated by the fact that more than 3 million separate stockholders receive checks quarterly from this one company. A mailing schedule is prepared under which all stockholders throughout the country receive their checks at the same time, irrespective of place of residence.

higher than the return on bonds and preferred stock to compensate for the additional risks of common stock ownership. In the latter case, he wants assurance that the retained earnings are employed at a rate that will lead to growth in capital value.

Dividend policies may be divided somewhat arbitrarily in the following fashion:

Regular dividend irrespective of current earnings. This policy, as followed by the American Telephone & Telegraph Company for many years, is regarded as the investment ideal by many. The disadvantage is that the dividend rate may be maintained too long after earning power has declined. The Penn Central Transportation Company had large losses in 1967–1969 and went into bankruptcy in 1970. But it had paid dividends of $2.40, $2.40, and $1.80 in the three years prior to bankruptcy.

Regular dividend proportionate to current earnings. This policy of distributing substantially all earnings in dividends is followed by many operating utility companies and by industrials not seeking to expand from internal sources, as in the case of United Brands (formerly United Fruit). The wage-price "freeze" of 1971–1972 limited increases to 4 per cent.

Regular dividend at minimum rate. This policy permits companies to pay a small but dependable dividend at all times and to reinvest most of current earnings for expansion purposes. It is characteristic of International Paper and other companies in the paper industry, and of the stronger steel companies, and forms the basis for occasional extra distributions, sometimes in the form of stock.

Regular dividend payable in stock. This policy enables companies to make a distribution to stockholders which they may convert into cash if they desire, but which allows the retention of cash in the business. Current industrial examples are found in Columbia Pictures and Litton Industries. Savings and loan associations and their holding companies typically follow this practice.

Regular dividend payable partly in cash and partly in stock. This policy, which represents a combination of two methods, is used by a few companies. The cash payments are made quarterly, but the stock payments are made either semiannually or annually to avoid the effect of rapid compounding. Examples are found in Boise Cascade and Walt Disney Productions.

Experience has taught corporate stockholders two important considerations respecting dividends. The first is that common stockholders should not always expect to receive all or even a major part of available earnings as dividends. The management is almost certain to retain part of the profits in the business, a practice that has been especially evident since World War II. That such a policy is favored by the majority of stockholders is indicated by the fact that in the 1960s and early 1970s growth stocks have sold at higher price-earnings multiples than income stocks. Table 8-3 shows the earnings and dividends per share on Standard & Poor's 425 Industrial Stock Index. The data indicate the tendency for industrial corporations as a group to retain a substantial portion of earnings. Great variations are of course to be found among individual companies.

The chief reason for the conservative dividend policy of many companies has been the purpose of raising funds for expansion. In addition to short-term borrowing for working capital purposes, three major sources of long-term funds have been available: (1) long-term loans, as represented by bond issues and term loans; (2) the sale of stock; and (3) internal sources, as represented by depreciation reserves and by reinvested profits. (See Chapter 2.)

The use of the second of these sources is greatly influenced by the level of prices in the common stock market in relation to the company's earnings and assets. When stock prices are low, to sell stock at less than book value may result in a considerable dilution of the existing stockholders' equity. But even when prices are high in relation to earnings, many corporations prefer to avoid public financing with stock in favor of the easier route of reinvestment. Internal sources and debt financing may provide all of the funds needed for expansion. And management may not wish to increase the number of outstanding shares for fear of dilution.[4]

Table 8-3. EARNINGS AND DIVIDENDS ON STANDARD & POOR'S INDUSTRIAL STOCK INDEX

	Earnings	*Dividends*	*Dividends as a Percentage of Earnings*
1960	$3.39	$2.00	59%
1961	3.37	2.08	62
1962	3.87	2.20	57
1963	4.24	2.38	56
1964	4.83	2.60	54
1965	5.50	2.85	52
1966	5.89	2.98	51
1967	5.66	3.01	53
1968	6.15	3.18	52
1969	6.17	3.27	52
1970	5.36	3.28	61
1971	5.96	3.18	53
1972 (est.)	6.08	3.17	52

SOURCE: Standard & Poor's *Trade and Securities Statistics.*

Many corporations have, therefore, turned to retention of profits as a major source of funds, and their dividend payments have suffered as a result. Such a policy makes for a more conservative capital structure (unless offset by increased debt), but it may have a corresponding disadvantage to the stockholder in that the value of the retained earnings, as represented by

[4]The meaning and importance of dilution is discussed in Chapter 25.

a growing retained earnings account, may not be reflected in an equal growth in market price. If, however, market price does grow in relation to a high current or expected rate of earnings, many stockholders should approve a modest dividend payout because the corporation can invest funds at a higher rate than can the owners who also avoid income taxes on current dividend income.

With the general rise of common stock prices (as measured by the averages) to their then all-time peak in 1961, and their 1962–1966 recovery from the 1962 decline, some companies again turned to the sale of common stock for new money. Nevertheless, retained earnings and funds representing depreciation continued to be even more important sources. (See Table 2-4.) With the subsequent stock price decline in 1966, internal sources became even more important, in spite of substantial price recovery in 1967. Corporations turned to common stock financing to an unusual extent in 1969 and in 1970, although stocks had suffered the worst bear market in a generation (see p. 21). Stocks as well as bonds were sold to reduce current liabilities and improve liquidity. In 1971–1972 utility and communications companies especially continued to rely on common stock financing of large new plant requirements.

Large Stock Dividends and Stock Splits

When a company declares a dividend in the form of stock, additional shares with the same par or nominal value are issued, without any change in the total net worth. A 100 per cent stock dividend doubles the number of shares outstanding, and, other things being equal, each share should decline 50 per cent in price since the assets and earnings are divided among twice as many shares. A two for one split-up, which doubles the number of shares by reducing their nominal value 50 per cent, should have the same result.

Actually a large stock dividend or a split-up may make the stock more attractive, and cause a rise in price when the event is rumored or announced, for the following reasons: (1) A larger number of shares outstanding and a lower trading range per share may improve the marketability and distribution of the stock; (2) the cash dividend rate may not be reduced proportionally, resulting in a larger cash income per old share (as in the case of American Telephone whose old stock paying $9.00 was split in 1959 into three shares each paying $3.30 and again in 1964 into two shares each paying $2.00); (3) attention is dramatically called to the high price per share and to the growth and prospects of the company. Large stock dividends and split-ups are a feature of bull markets.

Common Stocks as Investments

Advantages. Although generalizing about the investment qualifications of any group of securities as a class is dangerous because of the wide variation in quality within any one group, certain observations concerning common stocks as investments may be hazarded.

Recent years have seen a growing interest in common stocks, on the part of both individual and institutional investors. Studies show that, given proper selection and timing, the long-run record of a diversified list of high-grade common stocks has been better than that of bonds from the standpoint of income and capital value.[5] The period selected and the securities making up any such studies have, of course, greatly affected the results obtained. But the overriding advantage of common stocks in general has been the actual and potential growth in market value and in dividends, combined in the total rate of return.

Wide differences between individual stocks with respect to quality, income, and price performance exist in any given period, regardless of general economic and market levels and trends. With these limitations in mind, however, let us review the major factors that were responsible for the long postwar rise in the stock averages that reached its peak in January 1973, although interrupted by several periods of weakness. Most of these factors are developed at greater length elsewhere in this book.

1. Confidence in the continued expansion of the economy;
2. Rising corporate earnings and dividends;
3. The short-lived nature and mildness of postwar recessions and the increasing potency of government action as a preventive against serious depressions;
4. The steady movement of stocks into institutional hands;
5. The great increase in individual ownership of common stocks (30,000,000 holders) and so in the demand for this type of investment;
6. The Federal income tax structure that favors investment for capital appreciation by applying lower taxes on long-term capital gains than on current income;
7. The slow increase (and in some very recent years an actual decline) in corporate stocks outstanding as a result of corporate financing policy;
8. The improved "quality" of reported earnings as a result of more uniform and revealing accounting methods;
9. The improvement in information and analytical techniques that make for better projections of earnings and more valid valuations;
10. The declining importance of current dividend yields to an increasing number of investors;
11. The continued desire for an inflation hedge.

Not all of these factors continued to be important in the later 1960s and the early 1970s, with the result that common stocks showed a volatile record and failed to reach the previous all-time high. The averages fell dramatically

[5]The first of these were Edgar L. Smith, *Common Stocks as Long-Term Investments* (New York: The Macmillan Company, 1926); C. C. Bosland, *The Common Stock Theory of Investment* (New York: The Ronald Press Company, 1937); and D. C. Rose, *Practical Application of Investment Management* (New York: Harper & Row, Publishers, 1934). More modern references include W. J. and D. E. Eiteman, *Common Stock Values and Yields, 1950–1961* (Ann Arbor, Mich.: Bureau of Business Research, Graduate School of Business, University of Michigan, 1962); and Lawrence Fisher and J. H. Lorie, "Rates of Return on Investments in Common Stocks," *The Journal of Business*, January 1964, pp. 1–21.

in 1966. Subsequent recovery was halted in the spring of 1969, when a very severe decline rode to 1970. Vascillating rise and fall was characteristic of 1970–1971. The secular expansion of the economy had levelled out. The recession of 1969–1970 did not halt continued inflation. And perhaps most important of all, the rise in bond yields to unprecedented levels in 1970, and the continuation of historically high levels, provided competition for stocks that deprived them of much of their appeal. But in late 1972 and January 1973 (when the Dow Jones Industrial Stock Average reached 1052) the prices of common stocks in general, reflecting the high level of economic activity and the expectation of peace in Viet Nam, reached all-time highs. However, they continued to fluctuate substantially.

Table 8-4 (using Moody's Industrial series) shows average annual prices, price-earnings multiples and their opposites, the "earnings yields", and dividend and bond yields, 1960–1972. The relationships among these factors will receive much attention later in the book. But the data reveal that the combination of fluctuating earnings and changing rates of capitalization of earnings produced sharp volatility in prices. The variations would show as even more marked if interim changes were indicated. Nevertheless, institutional ownership of stocks continues apace, and the number of individual owners broke through 30 millions in 1971.

The traditional advantage of common stocks with respect to dividend yield, as compared with bonds, was in recognition of the premise that the return on equities should exceed that on long-term credit instruments. This advantage declined steadily in the postwar period as common stock prices rose, until in 1959 the "spread" between average high-grade bond and average stock yields became negative. Table 8-4 shows the average annual divi-

Table 8-4. AVERAGE YIELDS ON COMMON STOCKS AND BONDS

	125 Industrial Stocks					*Aaa Industrial*	
	Earnings	P/E Ratio	Price	Earnings Yield	Dividend Yield	Bond Yield	Spread
					(1)	(2)	(2) over (1)
1950	$ 8.45	6.8	$ 57.83	14.60%	6.52%	2.55%	3.97%
1955	10.51	12.4	130.66	8.04	3.93	3.00	.93
1960	9.62	18.0	173.48	5.33	3.48	4.28	− .80
1961	9.61	20.8	199.90	4.81	3.04	4.21	−1.17
1962	11.10	17.1	189.95	5.84	3.39	4.18	− .79
1963	12.43	17.5	218.34	5.70	3.20	4.14	− .94
1964	14.35	18.0	258.55	5.57	2.98	4.32	−1.34
1965	16.42	17.3	284.32	5.78	2.98	4.45	−1.47
1966	16.78	15.9	266.67	6.37	3.44	5.12	−1.68
1967	15.76	18.4	290.05	5.40	3.11	5.49	−2.38
1968	17.58	18.0	315.86	5.55	2.93	6.12	−3.19
1969	17.53	19.0	313.15	5.55	3.14	6.93	−3.79
1970	15.30	17.7	270.80	5.68	3.60	7.77	−4.17
1971	17.54	18.2	318.75	5.53	2.98	7.05	−4.07
1972	19.90	18.2	362.44	5.49	2.65	6.97	−4.32

SOURCES: *Moody's Industrial Manual, 1972,* and *Moody's Stock Survey.*

dend yields on Moody's 125 industrial averages compared with the same service's index of high-grade industrial bonds, and the relation of bond and stock yields in the postwar period. Also shown is the common stock "earnings yield," or the ratio of earnings to price, and its complement, the price-earnings multiple. These latter data reveal that earnings, as well as dividends, received a higher valuation through the period, reaching a peak in 1961.

The relation between prices, dividends, and earnings remained fairly stable in 1962–1965. Stock prices, on the average, reached their then peak in early 1966. After the substantial decline in prices in 1966, common stock yields and earnings yield improved and price-earnings multiples were reduced, but bond yields also rose, so that the negative spread between bond and stock yields increased. Dividend yields declined with the rise in prices in 1967–1968, and rose somewhat in 1969–1970. But the precedent-setting increase in bond yields in 1966–1970 and the strong stock market in 1972 drove the negative spread between bond and stock yields to record figures in 1970–1972.

Such general movements should, however, not obscure the very important fact that different stocks have applied, and will continue to apply, different values to earnings and dividends. The relation between these factors is discussed in Chapter 25.

Disadvantages. The investor cannot afford to overlook the distinct disadvantages involved in commitments in common stocks, although we must again emphasize that the vast range in quality within the common stocks available for investment makes generalizations somewhat dangerous.

From a *technical* viewpoint, common stocks suffer the double handicap of being junior securities and of having only contingent claims upon earnings. The stockholder faces the probability of a reduction in dividend income and the possibility of a complete loss thereof in periods of economic stress, in contrast to the contractual right of the bondholder to be paid irrespective of prevailing earnings. This is not to say, of course, that *all* common stocks behave worse than *all* bonds in times of adversity.

From an *economic* viewpoint, common stocks suffer the double handicap of being subject, in varying degree, to the vicissitudes of the business cycle and to the adverse influences of industrial trends. In periods of prosperity, when earnings are good, dividends are regular and the price action is favorable; but in periods of recession, when earnings are poor, dividends may be irregular, prices may decline, and the situation of the stockholder may become unenviable. Prices also change because investors change their requirements for price-earnings ratios and dividend yields. Over longer periods, certain industries grow as others decline, making the selection of an industry as difficult as that of a particular corporation. A policy of alertness and adaptability is essential to protect capital investments under these changing circumstances.

From a *political* viewpoint, common stocks suffer the handicap of bearing the brunt of public regulation and increased and double taxation (on both the corporate net income and the dividends received by the investor). Even though the enterprise may not be under the restricting influence of a regulatory commission, as the railroad and utility companies are, the company may face increased costs in the form of heavy taxes and higher wage scales, which cannot all be passed on to buyers of its products and which reduce income available to stockholders.

Finally, and most important, the erratic and unpredictable action of the prices and yields of common stocks, that reflect the greater risk of equities both in individual situations and in the market as a whole, makes the problem of valuation of these securities particularly difficult.[6] Too much may be paid for even a good equity, and too little received for it when sold.

Nevertheless, in spite of their weaknesses, common stocks have a place in the portfolios of many investors, *provided* (1) the risk is lessened by adequate diversification of industries and companies; (2) all but the most skilled investors restrict their purchases to the stocks of large, prominent, and conservatively financed companies with a long record of continuous dividends or of price appreciation; (3) the prices paid for the stocks are reasonable in relation to the prospective earnings and dividends of the companies selected; (4) the purchases (and sales when sales are called for) are timed properly; and (5) most important of all, the investor is really in a position to take the risks that even a well-diversified, well-selected, well-timed portfolio of common stocks inevitably involves. Considerable attention is given to these problems in other sections of this book.

The vast majority of investors would do well to avoid attempting to "play the market" in short-term trades, and a great many of them would do well to avoid the direct purchase of common stocks for long-term holdings. Methods exist for indirect investment in common stocks which capitalize to a certain extent on the real advantages of common stocks, and minimize, to some degree at least, their equally real disadvantages. These are discussed elsewhere in this volume.

REFERENCES

The following sources provide descriptions of the characteristics of stocks, their ownership, and their price action. References on the use of common stocks in investment programming, and methods of their analysis, are cited in the bibliographies of Parts V and VI. The problem of common stock valuation is discussed in Chapter 25.

Bogen, J. I., ed., *Financial Handbook,* 4th rev. ed., Section 13. New York: The Ronald Press Company, 1968.

Childs, J. F., *Long-Term Financing.* Englewood Cliffs, N.J.: Prentice-Hall, Inc., 1961.

Cox, E. B., *Trends in the Distribution of Stock Ownership.* Philadelphia: University of Pennsylvania Press, 1963.

Dewing, A. S., *Financial Policy of Corporations,* 5th ed., Book I, Chapters 3–6. New York: The Ronald Press Company, 1953.

[6]The problem of valuation of common stocks is discussed in Chapter 25.

DONALDSON, E. F., *Business Organization and Procedure,* Chapters 23–25. New York: McGraw-Hill, Inc., 1938.

DOUGALL, H. E., *Capital Markets and Institutions,* 2nd ed., Chapter 11. Englewood Cliffs, N.J.: Prentice-Hall, Inc., 1970.

GERSTENBERG, C. W., *Financial Organization and Management,* 4th rev. ed., Chapter 5. Englewood Cliffs, N.J.: Prentice-Hall, Inc., 1959.

GRAHAM, BENJAMIN, D. L. DODD, and SIDNEY COTTLE, *Security Analysis,* 4th ed., Chapters 8, 30, 31. New York: McGraw-Hill, Inc., 1962.

GUTHMANN, H. G., and H. E. DOUGALL, *Corporate Financial Policy,* 4th ed., Chapters 8, 9. Englewood Cliffs, N.J.: Prentice-Hall, Inc., 1962.

HUSBAND, W. H. and J. C. DOCKERAY, *Modern Corporate Finance,* 6th ed., Chapters 5, 6. Homewood, Ill.: Richard D. Irwin, Inc., 1966.

KENT, R. P., *Corporate Financial Management,* 3rd ed., Chapters 17, 23. Homewood, Ill.: Richard D. Irwin, Inc., 1969.

LEFFLER, G. L., and L. C. FARWELL, *The Stock Market,* 3rd ed., Chapter 2. New York: The Ronald Press Company, 1963.

New York Stock Exchange, *Institutional Shareownership.* New York: The Exchange, 1964.

————, *Shareownership: 1970.* New York: The Exchange, 1970.

ROSE, D. C., *Practical Application of Investment Management.* New York: Harper & Row, Publishers, 1933.

SMITH, E. L., *Common Stocks as Long-Term Investments.* New York: The Macmillan Company, 1926.

VAN ARSDELL, P. W., *Corporation Finance,* Chapter 12. New York: The Ronald Press Company, 1968.

9 Investment Company Securities

SCOPE: This chapter describes a very important medium of indirect investment—the investment company—and suggests methods by which its securities may be analyzed. The order of discussion is (1) general nature and purpose, (2) classification of types, (3) size and scope, (4) growth of the industry, (5) regulation, (6) lesser forms of investment companies, (7) financial statements and prospectuses, (8) capitalization and leverage, (9) organization and management, (10) distribution and redemption of shares, (11) purchase and sales commissions, (12) investment policy, (13) general factors in selection, (14) specific tests of performance, (15) senior securities, (16) warrants, (17) special uses, (18) tax status, (19) prices, dividends, and yields, and (20) recent developments.

General Nature and Purposes

The investment company invests the funds of a large number of individual investors in a portfolio of securities, so as to obtain advantages that the individual might not enjoy through direct investment in securities of his own choosing. By operating a large collective fund contributed by a number of shareholders and possibly creditors, the investment company can offer each investor a stake in a variety of individual securities at possibly a very low total outlay.

The investment company is financed through the issue of shares (and in some cases, of bonds and preferred stock), the proceeds of which are distributed over a number of securities to obtain a spreading of risk. As indicated later, the aims of these companies differ as to emphasis on income or capital appreciation. In any event their hope is to produce results in one or possibly both of these respects superior to those the investor could obtain through managing his own funds with his limited capital and lack of expert knowledge. The true investment company is to be distinguished from the holding company, which through its ownership or control of subsidiaries, undertakes the management of the concerns in which it has an interest.

The purported advantages of the investment company may be summarized as follows:

1. Diversification for a small outlay. Through the purchase of one share in an investment company, the investor may obtain an interest in a portfolio that may contain a cross-section of types of securities, of industries, and of companies.

2. Selection of securities, industries, and companies by experts who have at their disposal research and talent facilities not available to the individual investor. Professional supervision should result in continuous adjustment to changes in market and business conditions.

3. Appropriate timing of purchases and sales within the portfolio, presumably on the basis of seasoned judgment.

4. Convenience through the handling by the investment company of all the details connected with the ownership of corporate securities.

5. Simplicity of estate management and settlement. Equal division of an estate may be made without a possibly disadvantageous conversion to cash.

These advantages, especially the first four, are of special interest to the small investor. The investor of means can obtain them through the employment of investment counsel, and can afford the fees required for such service. (Even so, studies of investment company ownership show an increasing percentage of large accounts.) But the companies differ greatly in some of these respects. Funds vary from widely diversified to highly specialized. The investment record of many leaves much to be desired. The "experts" have by no means always done a good job; some of them have done very poorly. Many funds have not excelled in the appropriate timing of transactions, or in becoming more or less liquid as conditions require. And in addition to the wide differences in performance, companies differ in their objectives (notably in the choice between price appreciation and current income), in customer options and services, in sales charges, and perhaps most important of all, in portfolio growth and stability. The investor's problem is to select the company or companies with superior records which will achieve for him the investment objectives that he would like to obtain by direct action but which are difficult or impossible through management of his own funds.

Types of Investment Companies

Investment companies may be classified by a number of criteria:

1. By degree of managerial discretion. In the *management* investment companies, the management has power to change portfolio securities at its discretion, subject to any specific restrictions that may be contained in their charters or in the law. *Unit* or *fixed* trusts have portfolios that are rigid, or nearly so, in which the power of substitution is either denied or rigidly limited. The fixed trust is an arrangement by which the shareholder purchases shares or units representing a proportional interest in a specific portfolio of securities.

2. By arrangements for issuance and redemption of shares. *Closed-end* companies have a fixed capitalization. The securities they have issued are purchased and sold on the market like those of other companies. They do

not make a continuous offering of shares nor do they agree to redeem their shares on demand. *Open-end* companies (known generally as mutual funds) stand ready to redeem their shares at net asset value, on demand, and make a continuous offering of shares at their net asset value (calculated at least daily) plus (in most cases) a commission or sales fee.

In late 1966 and early 1967, nine issues of a new type of closed-end company appeared—the so-called *dual-purpose* funds. While differing in details, these have a major feature in common: two kinds of shares—participating preferred and common—are issued. The preferred shares, representing one-half of the fund, receive all of the *income* from the total fund, with a minimum annual dividend, and are to be eventually retired. The common shares receive all of the *capital appreciation* from the total fund. Thus "2-to-1" "leverage" was introduced. Upon completion of the offerings, the shares were listed or traded over-the-counter, and sell at premiums or discounts depending on their expected performance.

Another newcomer to the closed-end group had appeared recently—the "letter stock" fund specializing in a portfolio of restricted (unregistered) securities (see p.176).

3. By type of long-term capital structure. *Nonleverage* companies (including all open-end funds with one or two exceptions) have only common stock outstanding, although they may gain some leverage benefit from short-term bank loans.[1] *Leverage* companies (closed-end) have outstanding senior capital in the form of bonds or bank loans and/or preferred stock. Consequently, any increases and decreases in asset value and in earnings are magnified insofar as their common stock is concerned. The significance of leverage is discussed in more detail later in this chapter.

4. By type of portfolio securities. The portfolio may consist entirely of common stocks, with various degrees of diversification. (By legal definition a *diversified company* is a management company in which holdings of one company do not exceed 10 per cent of the outstanding voting securities of that company or 5 per cent (at cost) of the investment company's total assets.) Or the portfolio may be *balanced*, that is, may contain bonds and preferred and common stocks of a variety of companies, with minimum proportions of each type stipulated by the investment company's charter. Some funds contain no restrictions. Other types invest solely in bonds, low-grade or high-grade, in preferred stocks, or in stocks of one industry (*specialized* funds). There are also funds which concentrate on convertible securities, in stocks representing foreign investment, and other special types.

5. By degree of risk, as measured by vulnerability to price change. Funds range from very conservative to very speculative. On the one extreme are funds invested in high-grade bonds; at the other are those emphasizing low-priced volatile common stocks and special situations. The investor should, of course, determine, from the announced policies of the management and the character of the portfolio, whether the fund is designed for safety or for high but uncertain income or capital appreciation.

6. By investment purpose. Closely allied to the foregoing is the classifica-

[1]Such loans must be covered by at least 300 per cent in asset value.

tion according to the objectives and purposes of the fund. Some funds are designed for regular or possibly maximum current income, others aim at capital appreciation, while still others hope to produce both reasonable income and growth in market value.

7. By tax status. Most investment companies have elected to be classed as *regulated* for tax purposes, in order to obtain the tax concessions provided by the Internal Revenue Act. Classification by tax purpose suggests two groups: (1) companies taxed like other corporations with respect to income derived from interest, dividends, and capital gains; (2) regulated companies choosing to pay out substantially all net income derived from interest and dividends and which may or may not retain realized capital gains and pay a tax on the same. The tax status of investment company securities is discussed in more detail later in this chapter.

8. By type of purchase contract. The shares of *unit* or *fixed* trusts, and of management funds, are purchased outright. Another arrangement is now seldom used: the purchase of face-amount installment certificates by which the investor agrees to make regular payments to the company over a period of years, and the company agrees to pay the investor a specific sum of money on a future date. The investor's installments are invested by the company in mortgages and in securities.[2]

9. By type of organization. Unit trusts and some of the earlier management trusts are trusts in fact; however, most investment companies are now organized as corporations. The use of the trust form of organization in Europe and in the early years in the United States led to the expression "investment trust"—a term which has given way to "investment company" or "investment fund" in recent years.

10. By method of sale or sponsorship (mutual funds). Most mutual funds are distributed through local brokers and dealers, thence to the investor. Some, however, have their own "captive" sales forces, which sell only the particular funds directly to the shareholders. Both of these types charge a sales load or commission. *No-load* funds, for which no dealer or representative system is employed, are offered by investment counselling firms which manage a mutual fund as a secondary activity, or by brokerage firms. There are over 200 active no-load funds.

11. By actuarial requirements. As indicated in Chapter 3, variable annuities sold commercially by other than life insurance companies must be registered as investment company securities and their issuers are regulated under the Investment Company Act of 1940. Although legally classified as such, these contracts are not ordinarily included in discussions of investment company instruments.

The variety of classifications listed above suggests that the investor has a wide choice in his selection of a fund, on a number of bases. A feasible reclassification by main types would be as follows:

---

[2]This arrangement should not be confused with the accumulation plans whereby shares in open-end funds are acquired regularly. See the discussion of special uses of investment company shares later in this chapter.

1. Unit investment trusts
2. Management companies
   (a) Open-end or mutual funds, with a range of types of portfolio and purposes
   (b) Closed-end, both leverage and nonleverage, with a similar range
3. Minor types: face-amount installment certificates

The above classifications are not mutually exclusive. On the contrary, certain logical combinations are to be expected.[3] For example, investment purpose, type of portfolio securities, and degree of diversification go hand in hand. The objective of capital appreciation usually involves a portfolio of common stocks, and these have varying degrees of risk in terms of stability of price and dividends. Maximum appreciation as a goal would invariably involve concentration on a specialized portfolio of high-risk equities (see p. 424). Similarly, where current income is the goal, bonds and preferred stocks, as well as dividend-paying common stocks, are acquired, diversification is emphasized, and much less volatility is tolerated.

Scope of the Group

Several methods of measuring the scope of the investment company group and its various classifications are available. The largest numbers are indicated by the Securities and Exchange Commission. As of June 30, 1971, 1,246 active companies were registered with the Commission under the Investment Company Act of 1940, with total assets (at market value) of $78 billions.[4] This represented a growth of over $70 billions since the middle of 1950.

	No. Active Companies	$Assets (billions)
Management, open-end		
No load	230	$ 6.1
Variable annuity-separate accounts	47	.5
Load funds	548	53.2
	825	$59.8
Management, closed-end		
Small business investment companies	52	.3
Dual-purpose (leverage) funds	8	.4
Other	127	7.1
	187	$ 7.8
Unit investment trusts	228	9.5
Face-amount certificate companies	6	1.0
Total	1,246	$78.1

[3]Such combinations of factors are used by Wiesenberger in the section of *Investment Companies* devoted to performance measurement. This source lists diversified open-end common stock companies as large and smaller, maximum gain with high volatility, long-term growth plus income with above-average volatility, and growth plus current income with average and with below-average volatility. See Arthur Wiesenberger, *Investment Companies* (New York: Arthur Wiesenberger Services, Inc., annually, with quarterly supplements.)

[4] *Thirty-Seventh Annual Report of the S.E.C.*, 1971, p. 142.

It should be noted that the above data include small business investment companies and variable annuities. Neither of these types is usually included in discussions of investment companies for ordinary purposes.

A useful classification breaks down the more important open-end or mutual funds into eight major categories as of the end of 1971:[5]

Type of Fund	*Number of Funds*	*Combined Assets (millions)*	*As a Percentage of Total Assets*
Common stock			
Maximum capital gain	192	$ 8,721	15.0%
Growth	174	18,419	31.7
Growth and income	130	19,807	34.1
Specialized	12	257	.4
Balanced	28	6,695	11.5
Income	29	2,354	4.0
Tax-free exchange	24	1,104	1.9
Bond and preferred stock	21	803	1.4
Total	610	$58,160	100.0%

Growth of the Industry

The major growth in the industry has taken place in the open-end or mutual category, whose assets increased from $2.5 to $57 billions in the 1950–1968 period, fell off to $51 billions at the end of 1970, and reached an all-time high of $58.0 billions in 1971. At that time 11 million shareholder accounts were owned by over 8½ million investors. Pertinent data are shown in Table 9-1. The information on mutual funds is confined to members of the Investment Company Institute, which represent 90 per cent of the industry's combined assets. The total assets of mutual funds in Table 9-1 are therefore somewhat lower than in the preceding schedule.

The great postwar expansion reflects a number of factors: the growth of individual savings available for investment, the increased interest in securities investment, the rise in market values of common stocks, and the aggressive promotion of the sale of mutual fund shares as a means of participating in economic growth and (through common stocks) of hedging against inflation.[6] Other factors include the increase in the number and variety of funds to meet different investment objectives, and the availability of a number of convenient features such as accumulation and withdrawal plans and dividend reinvestment arrangements.

The decline in sales of new shares that began in 1962, accompanied by a higher rate of redemption, produced a substantial drop in net sales in that year that reflected in part the severe break in stock prices in the first six months of the year. The continued decline in public interest through 1963 reflected the general apathy towards stocks in general and mutual

[5]Arthur Wiesenberger, *Investment Companies*. (New York: Arthur Wiesenberger Services, Inc., 1972), p. 45.

[6]For an analysis of the excess of sales of shares over redemptions, and the asset change attributable to change in market value during 1950–1968, see H. E. Dougall, *Capital Markets and Institutions*, 2nd ed., (Englewood Cliffs, N.J.: Prentice-Hall, Inc., 1970), p. 81.

Table 9-1. INVESTMENT COMPANIES ASSETS, SHAREHOLDERS,
AND SALES OF NEW SHARES, 1950–1971

(dollar figures in millions)

	Net Assets			Open-End Companies Only			
	Open-End	Closed-End	Total	No. of Shareholder Accts. (thousands)	Gross Sales	Redemptions	Net Sales
1950	$ 2,531	$ 872	$ 3,403	939	$ 519	$ 281	$ 238
1955	7,838	1,199	9,037	2,085	1,207	442	765
1960	17,026	2,084	19,110	4,898	2,097	842	1,255
1961	22,789	3,205	25,994	5,319	2,951	1,160	1,791
1962	21,271	2,783	24,054	5,910	2,699	1,123	1,576
1963	25,214	3,218	28,432	6,152	2,459	1,505	954
1964	29,116	3,523	32,639	6,302	3,403	1,874	1,529
1965	35,220	3,391	38,611	6,709	4,358	1,962	2,396
1966	34,829	3,163	37,992	7,702	4,672	2,005	2,667
1967	44,701	3,777	48,478	7,904	4,670	2,744	1,926
1968	52,677	5,171	57,848	9,080	6,820	3,839	2,981
1969	48,291	4,744	53,035	10,391	6,718	3,661	3,057
1970	47,618	4,024	51,642	10,690	4,626	2,988	1,638
1971	55,045	5,324	60,369	10,901	5,147	4,750	397

Sources: Investment Company Institute, *Mutual Fund Fact Book* (New York: The Institute, annually) and *News* (weekly); Arthur Wiesenberger, *op cit.* The data on open-end companies pertain to members of the Instrument Company Institute. Data on closed-end companies pertain to larger companies only.

shares in particular. In both years mutual companies' sales suffered from the criticism levied on their managements in the original "Wharton Report" (cited in footnote 10), and in the Securities and Exchange Commission's massive study of the securities markets.[7] Net sales recovered in 1964–1965 and reached a new high in 1966.

In 1967 the rate of redemption reflected the economic difficulties of that year and the weakness in the stock market. However, net sales showed increases to record heights in 1969 and 1970 as the equities market flourished into the spring of the latter year. Then followed the sharpest bear market for stocks in postwar history until May 1970, and disillusioned investors substantially reduced their purchases of mutual fund shares. The weakness in the market for such shares in 1971 reflected dissatisfaction with stocks in general and mutual fund shares in particular. Redemptions actually exceeded sales in several months of 1971—an unprecedented development which was accompanied by uncertainties in the economy and which fed the weakness in equities. The industry faced new problems of stagnation and the task of overcoming the disillusionment of investors over fund performance, especially that of the very aggressive funds which had shown the greatest vulnerability to price change. In the latter part of 1971 general

[7]*Report of the Special Study of the Securities Markets of the S.E.C.*, Part 4, Chapter XI, "Open-End Investment Companies," 1964.

stock market strength revived both prices of and interest in mutual funds, but in 1972 sales were again low and redemptions high.

The above comments apply mainly to mutual funds. The growth of closed-end funds in the postwar period has been modest as was shown (Table 9-1). The major long-term factor of growth has been the secular rise in the market value of portfolios rather than the issuance of new securities. A few older companies have done some new financing, and a number of new and specialized forms of closed-end companies such as the leveraged "dual-purpose" and "letter stock" funds have been promoted in recent years.

Regulation

Investment companies are subject to both state and Federal regulation. With a few exceptions, state "blue-sky" laws deal mainly with the distribution of securities rather than with company operation and management. Far more important is the Federal regulation under the Investment Company Act of 1940, which provides for the registration with the Securities and Exchange Commission of every investment company with more than 100 securityholders. Unregistered companies are forbidden to conduct an interstate business and are denied the use of the mails for purchase or sale of securities. The general purposes of the Act are to prevent major abuses and to assure the dissemination of accurate and adequate information. In addition to the regulations of this Act, companies offering shares to the public in interstate commerce or through the mails are also subject to the Securities Act of 1933, and those closed-end companies whose securities are listed must comply with the provisions of the Securities Exchange Act of 1934. Companies must also obtain permission for intrastate sale of shares from the securities departments or commissioners of individual states. Trading in unlisted shares (including all mutual funds) is regulated by the Maloney Act of 1938 which established control over over-the-counter transactions through the National Association of Securities Dealers, Inc.

The major provisions of the Investment Company Act, together with important rulings of the Commission, may be summarized as follows:

1. Registered companies must file with the Commission a registration statement covering their background, mode of operation, management advisory contracts, and intended investment policy. This information must be kept current by periodic revision.

2. For management companies, minimum capital is set at $100,000 before stock may be publicly offered; this discourages the formation of small and weak concerns.

3. Closed-end companies may issue funded debt or incur a bank loan only if it is covered three times by assets; preferred stock must be covered twice. Only one class of bonds and one class of preferred may be issued, and preferred stock must have voting rights. Open-end companies formed after

1940 may not issue senior securities, and any bank loans must be covered three times by assets. Face-amount certificate companies organized since 1940 must have a minimum capital of $250,000 and may not issue preferred stocks.

4. Each management company must clearly declare its basic investment policies, and, once stated, these can be changed only with majority stockholder approval. This restriction would prevent a declared "diversified" company from becoming nondiversified without notice.

5. Semiannual reports must be issued to stockholders. Some companies now issue reports quarterly. The reports must present balance sheets, income and surplus statements, the composition and value of portfolio items, the aggregate purchases and sales made during the period covered, and the remuneration paid to officers, directors, and advisers. The Commission has the power to require certification of statements by independent public accountants and to promulgate uniform accounting rules.

6. Dividends from any source other than undistributed net income must be accompanied by a written statement disclosing the source, so that stockholders may distinguish income and capital gains distributions.

7. Sales practices are largely self-regulated through the rules of fair practice of the National Association of Securities Dealers, Inc., an organization subject to the jurisdiction of the Commission. All sales of new securities must be made in compliance with the Securities Act of 1933.

8. Sales promotion literature is governed by the Statement of Policy issued in 1950, which deals with methods of stating performance results, claims in regard to management ability, and other items.[8]

9. Other provisions cover certain standards of conduct and operation, including intercompany investments, self-trading, dealings with sponsors, and custodianship of assets. An important clause is that at least 40 per cent of the directors must be persons who are not officers or employees of the investment company, its investment advisor, or principal underwriter.

10. Certain regulations governing the sales practices, financing, and operations of fixed trusts, installment plans, and face-amount certificate companies are included in the Act. Regulation of management fees and sales commissions, and other rules introduced in 1970, are indicated in the last section of this chapter.

11. The Act contains severe penalties for fraud, embezzlement, and willful violation of its provisions.

---

[8]Section (h) of the Statement of Policy states that it will be considered materially misleading for open-end company sales literature "to use any comparison of an investment company security with any other security or medium of investment or any security index or average without pointing out: (1) that the particular security or index or average and period were selected; (2) that the results disclosed should be considered in the light of the company's investment policy and objectives, the characteristics and quality of the company's investments, and the period selected; and (3) any factor necessary to make the comparison fair."

Other important provisions of the Statement include (1) approved method of showing the rate of return that distinguishes investment dividends and capital gains, (2) prohibition of statements concerning future returns, and (3) prohibition of extravagant statements concerning management ability.

The activities of the Investment Company Institute have had a salutary effect on the attitude of investors toward management companies. This organization has worked closely with the S.E.C. and with state and tax authorities to improve standards and public relations.

Regulation does not assure the investor of success in his use of the investment company as a medium of indirect placement of funds. It does, however, offer him reasonable protection against malpractices, and its disclosure provisions assure him of adequate information, on the basis of which he should be able to make his selections with intelligence.

Unit Trusts and Other Lesser Forms

Although major investment interest today centers on the management companies, there are still outstanding securities of a number of the lesser forms of investment companies.

In the creation of fixed or unit-type trusts which hold stocks, definitive blocks of certain dividend-paying stocks are purchased and are deposited with a trustee, and against them certificates of ownership are issued in small denominations. Ten shares each of thirty different common stocks of well-known companies might be purchased at a total cost of $12,000 and deposited with a trustee against the issue of 10,000 shares of stock. These shares might be sold at $1.32 each, giving the sponsors a gross profit of $1,200, out of which distribution expenses would be paid. As dividends are received by the trustee, a small fee is retained, and the remainder is distributed proportionately to the shareholders. After the first block of 10,000 shares is sold, the process is repeated indefinitely, the sales price being adjusted each day to prevailing quotations on the deposited securities. Thereafter, the certificateholder can redeem his shares for cash at their net asset value, or accept his proportion of actual portfolio securities.

The provisions of the unit trust usually require that the trustee make a complete distribution of all income received, whether in the form of cash, stock, or rights. Shareholders must distinguish those distributions that are not income but are return of capital investment.

Few unit trusts with common stock portfolios have been formed in recent years. But a number of "tax-free" funds have been formed that own portfolios of municipal securities and sell shares against specific different blocks of such bonds from time to time.

The other minor form of arrangement is the face-amount certificate plan whereby the investor buys a contract that provides for the return by the seller of a lump sum of money at a specific future date. The selling company invests the periodic payments toward this contract in mortgages and securities. The chief disadvantage of this arrangement is that if the investor should withdraw during the first few years before the maturity date, the cash surrender value of his contract is less than the accumulated payments that have been made. The Investment Company Act of 1940 requires that companies offering these certificates set up a reserve equal to at least 93 per cent of subscriber payments, and that the cash value of the contract shall never be less than 50 per cent of the reserve.

The remainder of this chapter will deal with management companies because of the relative unimportance of the lesser forms described above.

Financial Statements

Investment companies are required to issue to stockholders at least semi-annually reports containing detailed financial portfolio information. For closed-end companies the statements include (1) a balance sheet, (2) an income and expense statement, (3) a statement of surplus, and (4) in some cases, a summary of assets and liabilities. For open-end companies, the exhibits include (1) a statement of net assets, (2) an income and expense statement, (3) a statement of changes in net assets, and (4) the record of net asset value and distributions per share for at least the three preceding fiscal years.

The balance sheet of the closed-end company usually carries the portfolio at market value (with cost indicated in parentheses). The asset coverage of funded debt, preferred stock per share, and common stock per share, at the date of the statement, is usually shown elsewhere in the report. The statement of net assets of the open-end companies also shows investments at market value, so that, after deduction of liabilities, the net assets applicable to total outstanding shares and on a per-share basis are revealed.

For both types of companies, the statement of income must itemize each category of income or expense that represents more than 5 per cent of income or expense. The statement shows dividend and interest income from securities owned, less general expenses including investment and administrative expenses, and interest on any debt. Federal income taxes may be deducted before the figure for net income, depending on the policy followed with respect to tax status. Gains on securities, realized and unrealized, are excluded.

Statements of the American Express Investment Fund, an open-end balanced fund, as of December 31, 1971 are shown in Tables 9-2, 9-3, and 9-4.

The statement of changes in net assets found in the open-end report itemizes the investment income and dividends paid therefrom, as well as realized capital gains and dividends paid therefrom. The report thus explains the derivation of the total net assets figure exhibited in the statement of net assets. To the net assets at the end of the previous period are added any undistributed realized gains (or loss) on sales of investments (the net income from ordinary operations having all been distributed), the increase or decrease in unrealized appreciation of assets, and the net increase in shares outstanding.

The required reports also include a complete portfolio of securities held, usually classified by type and by industry and showing the percentage of each classification to the total. The amount and market value of each item owned on the date of the balance sheet are also shown.

The surplus statement of the closed-end company shows the derivation

Table 9-2. AMERICAN EXPRESS INVESTMENT FUND

Assets and Liabilities, December 31, 1971

Assets	
Investments at market quotations	
(identified cost, $146,124,913)	$167,508,273
Short-term obligations, at cost which	
approximates market	9,493,799
Cash on deposit with custodian	92,907
Receivable for shares sold	38,736
Receivable for investments sold	2,343,436
Dividends and interest receivable..................	1,336,240
Total assets	$180,813,391
Liabilities	
Accounts payable .... $ 264,313	
Capital gain distribution payable	
January 5, 1972 6,746,104	
Payable for shares repurchased............ 22,264	
Payable for investments purchased 3,637,658	
Total liabilities	10,670,339
Net Assets	
Net assets at market value applicable	
to 19,253,534 shares	$170,143,052
Net asset value per share	$8.84

No provision has been made for Federal income tax on net income or net realized gains from sales of investments, since it is the policy of the Fund to comply with the special provisions of the Internal Revenue Code available to investment companies and to make distributions from net income and realized gains sufficient to relieve the Company from all or substantially all such tax.

Reproduced by permission.

Table 9-3. AMERICAN EXPRESS INVESTMENT FUND

Income and Expense, Year ended December 31, 1971

Income		
Cash dividends	$3,741,791	
Interest	4,393,611	$8,135,402
Expense		
Management fee	840,014	
Stock transfer and dividend disbursement fees	163,523	
Custodian fee	22,023	
Legal, audit, and association fees	36,810	
Registration fee	1,100	
Printing and postage	52,666	
Taxes, other than income	27,346	
Miscellaneous	14,588	1,158,070
Net Income		$6,977,332

of the earned and capital surplus figures on the balance sheet, after adding to previous earned surplus the ordinary net income and any profit (or loss) on sale of securities and deducting the dividends paid during the reported period.

Table 9-4. AMERICAN EXPRESS INVESTMENT FUND

Changes in Net Assets, Year ended December 31, 1971

Net Assets (December 31, 1970)		
(including $547,096 undistributed net income)		**$164,864,670**
Income		
Net income	$ 6,977,332	
Less net accrued income included in price of shares issued		
and repurchased	34,920	
Remainder	6,942,412	
Less dividends paid (37 cents per share)	7,126,281	
(Decrease) in undistributed net income		(183,869)
Principal		
Net realized gain from sales on investments		
(average cost basis $7,036,280)....................	6,877,013	
Less distribution of 35 cents per share payable		
January 5, 1972	6,746,104	
Increase in accumulated gain from sales of investments		130,909
Increase in unrealized appreciation to $21,383,360		6,417,077
Shares issued and repurchased (exclusive of amount		
allocated to income above):		
Receipts for 912,512 shares issued	8,100,861	
Shares issued (279,713) as capital gain distribution		
paid January 5, 1971	2,371,965	
Cost of 1,305,731 shares repurchased	(11,558,561)	(1,085,735)
Net Assets, December 31, 1971		
(including $363,227 undistributed net income)		**$170,143,052**

In addition to the periodic reports, prospectuses are prepared by the closed-end company when it offers new securities; the open-end company issues a new prospectus regularly because it makes a continuous offering of new shares. In addition to financial statements, the open-end prospectus contains material concerning the history, functions, investment policies, capitalization, management, provisions for purchase and redemption of shares, price of shares, and dividend record of the company, together with a complete portfolio shown at both cost and market.

Capitalization and Leverage

The capitalization of the open-end company (with one or two exceptions) is simple, consisting of one type of stock. Some short-term bank debt may be used. In contrast, some closed-end companies have senior securities outstanding in the form of bonds and/or preferred stock, and may also have incurred bank debt. It is this senior financing that provides leverage. The senior securities have a fixed claim on assets and earnings, so that when these rise, the increases redound to the benefit of the common stock. Likewise, when total asset value and income (before interest and preferred dividends) decline, the shrinkage is magnified insofar as the common stock is concerned.

Leverage causes the common stock of some closed-end companies to increase or decrease in market value more than the market rises or falls as a whole.[9]

The effect of leverage is accentuated when the portfolio of the company includes common stocks that are themselves junior securities of their issuing companies. Thus, the least total leverage is found in companies with only common stock outstanding and with portfolios that are very conservative, and the highest is found in those which have issued bonds and preferred stock to a high proportion of total capital structure and have a portfolio consisting mainly of junior securities. The closed-end group includes a wide range in this respect.

Organization and Management

Investment companies are ordinarily organized as corporations. All fixed trusts and some management companies use the trust form.[10]

The directors (or trustees), officers, and staff may handle all of the affairs of the company including general administration, servicing of accounts, distribution of shares, and investment management. Ordinarily, however, in the case of mutual funds, the latter two functions are performed by the management firm that originally sponsored the fund or group of funds, or by separate subsidiaries of the sponsor, one for underwriting and distribution, the other for investment counsel.[11]

Management companies that underwrite and distribute mutual fund shares may be further classified with respect to method of distribution: (1) those that serve as wholesalers, distributing through local broker-dealers who in turn sell to the public, and (2) those with their own "captive" sales organizations which sell only the shares of the sponsored fund or group of

[9]A simple illustration will indicate the effects of leverage. Suppose that a fund starts with total assets of $10,000,000 and has a capitalization consisting of $5,000,000 in par value of bonds and preferred outstanding (the preferred having a liquidating preference of par value) and 500,000 shares common stock. The asset value per share of common is $10.00. If the value of the total assets increases 50 per cent to $15,000,000, the equity of the common stock becomes $10,000,000 or $20.00 per share, a 100 per cent increase. If the value of the total assets decreases 50 per cent to $5,000,000, the common stock has no equity at all.

Similar effects would be seen in any increase or shrinkage of total income available for interest and dividends. Variations in the return to the common stock, after fixed interest and preferred dividends, would be determined by (a) variations in the overall earnings and (b) the degree of leverage or ratio of senior capital to total assets.

[10]Of 156 open-end companies that replied to a comprehensive questionnaire for the Wharton study, 117 were corporations and 39 used the trust form of organization. *A Study of Mutual Funds*, prepared for the Securities and Exchange Commission by the Wharton School of Finance and Commerce, 87th Congress, 2nd Session, 1962. (Washington: U.S. Government Printing Office, 1962.)

[11]Of the 156 companies mentioned in footnote 9, all but 14 were parties to contracts with at least one outside organization that functioned as investment adviser, administrative manager, or both. *Ibid.*, p. 6.

The Wharton Study reports the results of a comprehensive questionnaire filed by 163 advisers of 232 mutual funds with total assets of $15 billions as of 1960. Of these, 73 were "independent" advisers that in some cases also wholesaled the shares, 36 were investment counselors or their subsidiaries, 27 were broker-dealers or their subsidiaries, 5 were subsidiaries of underwriters of shares, and the balance consisted of several minor arrangements. *Ibid.*, p. 27.

funds. In the latter case, the "complex" or completely integrated corporate organization enjoys the income from both the management fee charged to the fund or funds and the entire sales commission.[12]

The management fee generally runs one-half of one per cent of assets up to a certain amount, then often graduate to as low as one-quarter of one per cent on large assets. In a few cases compensation is a function of investment performance as measured against the market averages. No specific regulations governing management fees were introduced in the 1970 amendments to the Investment Company Act of 1940.

Most no-load mutual funds are sponsored and managed, for a fee, by investment counsel firms. These do not actively promote sales and charge no initial sales commission. Some charge a small fee for redemption of shares. Other no-load funds are operated by securities brokerage or investment banking firms. In all, about 150 no-load funds are of general public interest.

Closed-end companies are managed by their own officers and staff; they may, however, buy investment management, at a fee, from an affiliated firm or from an independent advisor.

In the late 1950s and early 1960s the shares of a number of management or sponsoring companies were made available to the general public. At the time of writing (mid-1972), shares in about twelve of such firms are available. With two or three exceptions, the shares are traded over-the-counter.

The affiliations and fee arrangements of the investment company with other concerns acting as sponsors, distributors, or investment managers are set forth in the prospectuses of mutual funds and indicated in the annual reports of the closed-end funds.

Distribution and Redemption of Shares

Like those of any corporation, the securities of closed-end companies remain outstanding in the same amount unless the company carries on new financing, retires its senior securities, or purchases common stock for the treasury. There is no continuous offering of new shares and no provision for redemption at the option of the investor. In contrast, new shares of open-end companies are, with a few exceptions, continuously offered at their net asset value plus a "loading fee"; hence, the supply is virtually unlimited and the investor can buy any quantity at any time. The shares of the open-end fund may be presented for redemption at any time to the company or its sponsor, at net asset value. (A few no-load funds charge a small redemption fee.) The company is obliged to redeem within the period stated in its prospectus, and in no case in more than seven days. In actual practice, most

[12]In addition to advisory and management fees and distribution income, some management concerns also derive brokerage commissions on the purchase and sale of portfolio securities held by their associated funds. Their total income is thus a function of the number of shares sold and value of the portfolio.

The whole matter of sales practices and commissions is very thoroughly explored in *Report of the Special Study of the Securities Markets of the S.E.C.*, *op. cit.*, Chapter XI, Part B, and it also has received special scrutiny by the S.E.C. in its 1966 report.

open-end companies repurchase very promptly, but the investor runs the risk of a loss in net asset value per share if he chooses to redeem during a period of rapidly declining security prices.

The above arrangements give the shares of the open-end company perfect marketability. Those of the closed-end companies that are actively traded on exchanges or over-the-counter have good marketability. The bonds and preferred stock of closed-end funds are usually traded over-the-counter.

Purchase and Sales Commissions

The purchase and sale of securities issued by closed-end companies involve the payment on listed issues of brokerage commissions identical with those charged for trading in any listed securities. For closed-end securities bought in the over-the-counter market, the investor pays the asked price.

In the case of shares of open-end companies, the buyer pays the net asset value per share (calculated daily) plus a commission or loading charge in the neighborhood of from $7\frac{1}{2}$ to $8\frac{1}{2}$ per cent of the offering price. On large orders there is usually a graduated scale at lower rates.[13] The bulk of this loading charge is retained by the local dealer as his sales commission or by the fund's allied distributing organization; in the former case, the balance goes to the principal underwriter or distributor. The investment company itself is not expected or allowed to shoulder any selling expenses. Ordinarily no charge is made for redemption.

If the shares are held for a long period, the initial load, amortized over a number of years, becomes a modest percentage of any income or capital appreciation received. But where the investor holds his shares for only a short period, the charge may consume any dividends or increase in capital value that may have been gained.

Investment Policy

As indicated previously, investment companies by no means follow a uniform investment policy. There is a great range in type of portfolio investments held—from the most conservative bond funds to low-priced and specialized common stock funds. There is an equally wide range in objectives—from funds seeking regular income to those frankly seeking capital appreciation. Between these two extremes are all sorts of combinations.

The order of thinking on the part of the investor should run as follows: (1) What portion of my funds may appropriately be placed in investment company securities? (2) Which investment company or companies have investment policies, as demonstrated by their announced objectives and their performance, that come closest to meeting my needs?

---

[13]Funds sponsored by investment counselling and brokerage firms apply no sales load, but their shares are not generally available through local dealers and are issued only on application to the company itself or its distributing affiliate.

New legislation pertaining to sales commissions is noted in the concluding section of this chapter.

Registered investment companies are obliged to state their broad investment policies in the prospectuses describing their shares. In these statements and in the actual operations of the company as indicated by their periodic reports, the policy decisions are revealed by (1) the general type of portfolio held, (2) the degree of actual diversification, (3) the investment quality of the portfolio, (4) the extent to which the fund remains fully invested, and (5) the relative emphasis on stability of income as against trading profits and/or appreciation.

The general portfolio may consist solely of common stocks, of preferred stocks, or of bonds, or it may be a balanced fund containing all three of these security types. The type of security held and the safety or appreciation prospects of the fund are not necessarily related, for an all-bond fund may be more speculative than an all-common-stock fund, depending on the character of the portfolio. But in general, the funds consisting of senior securities and the balanced funds aim at more stability of income and show less volatility in price action than the all-common funds. There are, however, gradations in all categories.[14]

Policy is also reflected in the actual degree of diversification, measured by the number of companies represented in the portfolio, which may range from 30 to 300, and the percentage distribution of the total dollar value of the fund in different companies and industries. In addition to the limitations set by the Investment Company Act of 1940, each fund has its own diversification policy, and this is announced in its prospectus and revealed by its portfolio. If the investment company is registered and publicized as a "diversified" company, it must by law meet the standards of the Act. Otherwise it may concentrate or spread its funds as it wishes, in accordance with announced policy. In general, wide diversification is sought if stability of income is a primary goal. The narrowest diversification is found in those funds that are invested in stocks of one industry or in highly selected "special situations."

Regardless of the type of securities in the fund and the degree of numerical diversification, the choice still has to be made between high-grade securities, speculative securities, or a combination of the two. That is, the fund may or may not be diversified from the standpoint of quality.

Policy must also be made with respect to full employment of funds. Some companies, especially those primarily interested in producing income, remain virtually fully invested. Others switch between cash and bonds, and common stocks, depending on the judgment of the management concerning the future course of the market.

The relative importance of income as against appreciation is revealed by the changing character of the assets (shifts between defensive and aggressive positions) and by the source of dividends as revealed in the income and surplus statements. The investor who is investing primarily for regular

[14]Keystone Custodian Funds has no balanced fund but makes available nine classes of portfolios: B1, high-grade bonds; B2, good and medium-grade bonds; B4, high-return discount bonds; K1, medium-grade (income) bonds and preferreds; K2, speculative or "appreciation" common stock; S1, high-grade common stocks; S2, good-grade "income" common stocks; S3, growth common stocks; S4, low-priced common stocks.

income should avoid those companies whose distributions depend primarily on realized capital gains.

In the discussion above, the distinction between open-end and closed-end companies was not clear-cut, nor was that between leverage and nonleverage companies. Although some relation exists between the general type of company, or the way in which it is financed, and its investment policies and objectives (for example, a closed-end fund may seek to magnify speculative gains through high leverage), there are some conservative closed-end companies and some very speculative open-end companies. And a few leverage companies follow a more conservative policy than some companies without senior financing. Possibly because the open-end company is under pressure to sell new shares and must be prepared to repurchase shares on demand, its investment policy is directed toward maximum appeal to the greatest number of investors; hence investment performance and marketability of holdings are given more emphasis than in the case of the closed-end company.

Most buyers of investment company securities are not willing or able to make a detailed examination of portfolios and portfolio changes. But they should at least be aware of the general nature of these policies and of their results in terms of actual performance. When an investor buys investment company shares, he is in effect saying, "Here's my money—you put it to work for me." He ought to know something of the type of concern to which he is entrusting his funds, and whether its aims and objectives coincide with his own. And he ought to apply some tests to determine whether, based on its past record, the fund is likely to prove to be good, bad, or mediocre for his specific purposes.

General Factors in Selection

Several important factors (other than investment performance) should be considered in selecting the securities of one or more investment companies.

Objectives and general character of the fund. The first step is to eliminate those companies whose announced purposes do not coincide with the investor's own objectives, and whose general policies and portfolio indicate more (or possibly less) risk than the investor is prepared to take. Investors requiring recovery of principal would avoid all but the most conservative companies. Investors requiring assurance of regular income would select shares in well-managed income, balanced, or tax-free, funds, or senior securities of closed-end companies. Investors seeking capital appreciation would determine what price (in terms of risk) they are prepared to pay and what type of fund portfolio is aimed at growth and with what degree of stability.

Age and size. The size, maturity, and rate of growth of the investment company deserve close scrutiny. The company should be large enough to provide adequate diversification (if this is a consideration) and be able to afford compensation for skilled management without consuming too large a proportion of income for managerial and operating expenses. The company should be old enough to be tested under periods of both prosperity and adversity. Any investment company (and most individual investors, for that matter) can show a good performance in a bull market; it is the record during both good and bad times that counts. The rate of growth of the open-end fund is important because it affects the expense ratio. It also indicates the general appeal the fund has had to the investment community.

Very large funds have the advantage of being able to obtain wide diversification in portfolio securities and to devote a large management fee to research and analysis. They are, however, handicapped by the sheer size of individual holdings. To divest a block of stock worth several millions may take weeks to accomplish.

Price volatility. Many investors require high stability of price; they may count on redemption or sale of shares for liquidity. Others are willing to assume price risk for the sake of high income and/or appreciation. The variations in price in periods of unusual general market change—as in the last six months of 1961, before the break, the first six months of 1962, when stock prices fell sharply, and in 1962, 1963–1965, 1966 and 1969–1970 can be obtained from the Wiesenberger manual and other sources.

Volatility of fund prices during "ups" and "downs" in the stock market is used by some services in classifying funds into different categories. This is a way of recognizing that risk as well as performance is a factor to be considered in the choice of the funds that are appropriate in a given investment situation. In recent years, measures of fund performance have been developed that incorporate risk into the specific tests. In these measures, risk is indicated by the volatility of the total rate of return rather than price alone. (See p.420 .)

Management fee and total expense ratio. The holder of investment company securities pays for the management of his funds. The management fee, together with other expenses involved in operating the company, should bear a fair relationship to income and to the assets managed. For open-end companies, expenses (not including interest and income taxes) range between 10 and 15 per cent of investment income and between .20 and 3.00 per cent of average net assets. Some closed-end companies with specialized activities show even higher rates. These ratios should be considered in the light of the size and the objectives of the fund. As a fund grows, its expenses do not rise proportionally. And the objectives of the fund may require unusually high research and management expense, as in those companies that delve heavily into special situations. The investor would prefer a company with a high expense ratio producing superior results to an economically managed fund that produces mediocre results.

A high ratio of expense to *income* may result from the fact that the portfolio deliberately includes a number of low or nondividend stocks, acquired for appreciation. In such a case the investor may be more than repaid by a good growth record.

Sales commissions. The investor should not select a fund or funds merely because the original sales commission or "load" is low or even nil. Performance is more important. He should, however, be aware of the initial sales charge and use it as a marginal factor in the selection process. Short-term trading in mutual fund shares is expensive, especially when small amounts are involved.

Conveniences and services. The investor should check the availability and terms of special services and arrangements offered by mutual funds.[15] They include

1. Automatic dividend reinvestment (including income and capital gains distributions) in new shares without a sales commission, that is, at their asset value.

2. Voluntary accumulation plans, in which the shareholder invests a certain number of dollars at regular intervals, usually along with reinvestment of dividends. The minimum dollar amount of original purchase and of subsequent regular investment in new shares is prescribed. This is an open-account arrangement involving no definite time period or total investment, and the shareholder may withdraw from the plan at any time.

3. Contractual accumulation plans, whereby the investor agrees to pay a fixed monthly or quarterly payment over a designated period of years. The minimum installment permitted by the Investment Company Act of 1940 is $10 a month. A typical plan involving $3,000 would call for 120 monthly payments of $25 each. In these plans a large portion of the total sales charges is paid in advance as a *front-end load*. Such a load cannot exceed 50 per cent of the first twelve installments. In the previous example, the total sales load at 8 per cent would be $240. Fifty per cent of each of the first twelve payments, or $12.50 per month, totals $150 and comprises 62.5 per cent of the total sales charge. The rest of the total sales load is distributed over the remaining payments at, of course, a much lower per cent of each. In addition, a custodian fee of from one to three per cent of the total payments is also deducted from the first payments, so that less than one-half the amount of the early payments is "working" for the investor.

The Securities and Exchange Commission has been very critical of contractual front-end-load plans, on the grounds that they do not represent the incentive to savings that is claimed for them, and that many investors do not understand the initial consumption of payments by sales expenses.[16] Legislation governing such plans was passed in 1970 (see p.175).

4. Withdrawal plans. After the investor has made a minimum initial investment in shares (often $5,000 or $10,000), the fund pays a certain amount to him each month. Some of the capital of the account may have to be withdrawn to make up the payments, depending on the earnings

---

[15]Arthur Wiesenberger, *Investment Companies*, has a special section where each of these arrangements, along with other information, is indicated for each fund reported in the manual.

[16]*Report of the Special Study of Securities Markets of the S.E.C.*, Chapter 11, Part IV, pp. 115–203.

on his shares, their increase or decrease in value, and the dollar size of the withdrawals.

5. Conversion privilege, which enables the shareholder to transfer from one fund to another within a group of funds managed by the same advisor, as his needs change—for example, from a growth to an income fund. A small fee, but no sales commission, may be charged for the transfer.

Specific Tests of Investment Performance

The past performance of investment companies may be measured by applying various specific tests so as to eliminate those firms that are unworthy of consideration. No one test is applicable to all companies. Tests should be selected in the light of the objectives of the companies studied. For example, balanced funds could not be expected to record changes in asset values similar to those of common stock funds. Income funds will yield different rates of return and different changes in asset values than growth funds.

Performance should be studied over a period of years. Short periods are not representative of varying business and market conditions. And even average annual performance over a period of years may have been affected by one or two especially good or bad years. The year-by-year and the cumulative performance are most important. And one must recognize that, although the past record is the only significant clue to the future, identical results may not be produced in the future.

The following tests apply to common stock. Senior securities of closed-end companies will be discussed later in the chapter.

Test of total earning power. For both closed-end and mutual funds, the total earning power derived from interest and dividends received on a portfolio is measured by the percentage of such income to the average value of the assets held during the year. In the case of closed-end companies, earnings before interest is the numerator. A consistently low rate of return does not necessarily reflect poor management. The fund may consist of high-grade securities that are expected to produce regular rather than large returns. Or the investment policy may be directed more toward capital growth than toward interest and dividend income.

Test of dividend yield. For the holder of mutual fund shares or of common stock in a closed-end company, the important current income test is the annual rate of return produced on the net asset value of his shares from net investment income after all expenses, interest, and taxes, and exclusive of realized capital gains from portfolio securities sold by the company. In the case of mutual fund shares, either the beginning, the average, or the year-end net asset value may be used as the base, and the actual investment dividends may be used rather than the net investment income, since virtually all net investment income is distributed. A further refinement would be to employ the offering price (net asset value plus any sales load) as the base.

Income yield based on the average value of the net assets per share has. the disadvantage of being affected by change in asset value during the year —higher where assets value has declined, lower where assets value has increased. This complicates the problem of comparing different funds.[17]

The yield on closed-end stocks is calculated like that on any common stocks, namely, by the relationship between market price and dividends.

The actual return as well as its stability are, of course, affected by the objectives of the fund, the composition of its portfolio, and in the case of closed-end companies, the degree of leverage and the size of any premium or discount from asset value at which the shares are bought. There is a wide range. The stocks of many diversified mutual common stock growth funds produced (in 1972) less than 2 per cent, some even less than 1 per cent. At the other extreme, yields of 5 to 6 per cent were found in the case of income funds. Until recent years, if shares bought primarily for current income could consistently offer a net investment return of 5 per cent and, in addition, produce modest capital gains, the fund was thought to be doing better than most investors could do alone. But with the rise of bond yields to record heights in 1969–1971, such yields on stocks became competitively unattractive. Managers of income funds were obliged to place more emphasis on appreciation of portfolio value to produce a satisfactory total rate of return. Convertible securities were frequently bought as a compromise. Also, a number of new funds were formed to take advantage of the high yields, and were restricted to corporate bonds or to tax-free municipal securities.

Amount and character of dividends. Because of the tax advantages accruing to investment companies that elect to declare themselves "regulated" companies for tax purposes, under the conditions described later in this chapter, most investment companies consistently distribute as dividends all net investment income and all or a part of realized capital gains. This may make the total dividend very erratic, since the capital gains portion varies considerably from year to year depending on the securities market and the rate of turnover of the portfolio. The company is required to state the portion of each dividend derived from each of the two sources. The investor primarily interested in income should measure the company chiefly by its ability to earn and distribute regular investment income. He should reinvest rather than spend that portion of the dividend derived from capital gains so as to preserve his capital intact.

Test of growth. Capital appreciation is more important than current income to many investors. This is measured by computing the percentage rate of change in net asset value plus distributed realized capital

[17]Wiesenberger reports the yield from dividend income on the year-end asset value.
Using DI for dividend income and NA for asset value, the following model may be useful:

$$\text{Yield on beginning asset value} = \frac{DI}{NA}$$

$$\text{Yield on average asset value} = \frac{DI}{(NA_t + NA_{t+1})/2}$$

gains, annually and for various periods.[18] In comparing companies, one must add back *distributed* capital gains to compensate for the fact that the amount of these varies from company to company and from time to time.

Measures of total performance. The total performance of an open-end company for a single year or over a longer period may be measured by combining the change in the net asset value per share and the dividends (from all sources) distributed during the period. If the net asset value per share of an open-end fund or of a nonleverage closed-end fund were $100 at the beginning of the period and it distributed $8 in total dividends, and the net asset value were $102 at the end of the period, the performance gain was 10 per cent for the period. The performance of an individual company should be compared with that of other companies with similar objectives. The performance of common stock funds should be compared with selected stocks or groups of stocks, and with a stock average or index such as the Dow-Jones composite index of 65 stocks or the Standard & Poor's index of 500 stocks as representing the market as a whole.[19]

A more refined measure is used by some services. The percentage change over a period (or alternatively, the growth in value of an initial investment in terms of dollars—say $10,000) is calculated by adding to the change in net asset value of the original shares the cumulative value of shares obtained by reinvesting realized capital gains in additional shares of the fund, plus investment income dividends in cash. Many annual reports of mutual funds display charts showing the results of an assumed investment (after sales commission) over a given period, calculated in this way. Some also present figures to show the ending value of the original investment assuming that *all* dividends are reinvested in shares.

More sophisticated measures of mutual fund performance have been developed that may be more widely used in the future, although those just mentioned are likely to dominate the performance data that are available for broad public use.[20] The more refined methods use volatility of rate of return, as the measure of risk of a fund, in relation to the market as a whole. The volatility coefficient "beta" described in Chapter 23 is the "char-

---

[18]Using NA for net asset value, and DC for distributed capital gains, the model for this test is

$$\frac{NA_{t+1} + DC}{NA_t} - 100\%$$

[19]The index of total performance may be calculated by the investor or found in an advisory service. It cannot be used or furnished by an investment company.

Using NA for net asset value, DI for income dividends, and DC for distributed capital gains the model for this test is

$$\frac{NA_{t+1} + DI + DC}{NA_t} - 100\%$$

Restrictions in the Securities and Exchange Commission Statement of Policy include (1) the period covered in any statement of performance must include at least ten years, (2) the sales charge, or total cost of the investment, must be shown, and (3) dividends from investment income and distribution from security profits may not be combined. However, "capital results" may be shown either by adding back security profit distributions or by assuming that these had been reinvested.

[20]For sources that publish performance information, see Chapter 13.

acteristic line". The characteristic lines of two or more funds are plotted, and for each fund the distance is examined on the vertical axis to the point where the fund's line intersects the line for a risk-free investment (such as a savings account). Funds are ranked, rather than measured in absolute terms, by this method.[21]

In another method of measurement, the average rate of return as well as its standard deviation is calculated for the period studied. Using the return from a risk-free investment, the "reward-to-variability" ratio is calculated. This is the fund's average return less the risk-free rate divided by the standard deviation of the rate of return. The ratio measures the amount of extra rate of return the investor receives for each unit of risk he takes.[22]

The concept of risk and its use along with rate of return is discussed at greater length in Chapter 23 in connection with pension fund management.

The usefulness of any index of performance for comparative purposes is limited by the period chosen for study. Performance in any one year is not very significant; performance over a period of years is affected by the course of the market as a whole. For these reasons emphasis should be placed on an examination of year-to-year results in the search for consistent superiority, and if a period of some years is used, the performance of the whole period should be viewed in the light of the trend in the market as a whole. A defect of data, charts, and graphs based on a selected period is that an investor cannot determine what his performance experience would have been if other particular stages of the period had been chosen.

Comparison of the performance of an individual company or of a group of companies with a general stock index also has decided limitations. "No one buys the averages." These represent a nonexpense, fully invested, non-managed position in common stocks with no particular policy involved. And in any period of generally rising (or falling) prices, their performance would have an upward (or downward) bias. The performance indexes are useful mainly for purposes of comparison of funds which have substantially the same objectives and types of portfolio. Any other comparisons, or comparisons with the averages, are likely to be misleading.[23]

The basic test. While somewhat intangible, the real test of the appeal of an investment company's shares lies in the answer to the question, "based on its record, is the company likely to do a better job for my purposes than I could do alone with respect to safety, income, appreciation, or other objectives?" A cold-blooded inspection of the records of investment companies reveals that some have fallen far short of the results to be expected of expert management. But there are many whose performance has been very satisfactory indeed, and some whose record has been clearly superior.

---

[21]J. L. Traynor, "How to Rate Management of Investment Funds", *Harvard Business Review*, January–February 1965, pp. 63–75. This approach has been carried further by Traynor and others in subsequent articles.

[22]W. F. Sharpe, "Mutual Fund Performance", *The Journal of Business*, January 1966, pp. 119–138.

[23]For the position of the Securities and Exchange Commission in this respect, see footnote 8 above.

Senior Securities

The preceding discussion has pertained mainly to the shares of open-end funds and the common stock of closed-end funds. The latter have steadily reduced their senior securities in recent years, by mandatory sinking funds or by using the call feature. Most debentures have been retired, but a few preferred stocks are still outstanding.

Five factors should be analyzed in the appraisal of investment company preferred stocks: (1) overall asset coverage, or ratio of assets to the sum of all liabilities plus the preferred stock at liquidating value; this proportion should be at least 400 per cent; (2) overall income coverage, or ratio of investment income to total interest plus preferred dividends; this proportion should be at least two times; (3) regularity of dividends derived from investment income as contrasted with realized capital gains; (4) special features, such as the convertible feature, and the advantages of same; (5) possibilities of price appreciation. An example of a high-grade issue is found in General American Investors Company $4.50 Preferred. The issue is preceded by no senior obligations and is well supported by assets ($6,700 per share at the end of 1971) and by earnings (dividends earned 17 times in 1972). The issue is callable at 105 plus accrued dividends and is nonconvertible. The yield at the November 1972 price of 76 was 6.0 per cent. Dividends have been paid regularly since 1929.

Warrants

At the opposite extreme from the senior securities of closed-end companies are the stock-purchase warrants that have been issued by a few concerns. These warrants carry an option to buy common stock from the company at a stipulated price during a specific period. The value of the warrant is theoretically determined by the excess (if any) of the market price of the common stock over the price at which the warrant may be exercised. Actually the warrant may sell at a considerable premium above its theoretical value, and may be in demand even if its theoretical value is zero or negative. This is because any rise or potential rise in the market value of the stock gives value to the option to purchase it at a set price. If the warrant is an option to buy at 10, and the market price of the stock is 10, the warrant has no theoretical value but may sell for $2 or $3 because, if the stock should rise to 15, the warrant would be worth $5. Variations in the price of the common stock are magnified in the market value of warrants, which tend to have marked price volatility. For example, the warrants of Tri-Continental Corporation give the holder the perpetual option of buying 3.03 shares of common stock at $7.46 per share. The price of the common stock ranged from 28 to 34 during 1972, and the price of the warrants (traded on the American Stock Exchange) ranged from 66 to 76. The price action of warrants, like that of common stock, is, of course, affected by the degree of leverage in the capitalization of the issuing company.

Special Uses of Investment Company Shares

In recent years much has been made of the advantages of investment company securities to the small investor. Certain other more specialized uses that pertain to investors in general should also be examined.

For dollar-cost averaging. The investor who wishes to avoid making decisions with respect to the swings in the market and who is steadily accumulating funds that can appropriately be placed in equities finds in the shares of investment companies an almost ideal vehicle for the device of dollar-cost averaging that is described in Chapter 20. The problem of selection of the fund or funds for this purpose still remains, but the diversification and management that are obtained are valuable additions to the advantages which the process of dollar averaging may produce. In recognition of this appeal, and in order to acquire a continuous market for new shares, most open-end companies provide "accumulation plans" whereby the investor enters into an agreement to invest a certain number of dollars at regular intervals, and in some cases all dividends and distributions can be automatically reinvested at asset value without a sales load on this portion of the accumulation. The minimum dollar amount of initial purchases and of subsequent regular investment in new shares is prescribed (see p.165).

For the operation of formula-timing plans. One of the problems in the use of the formula-timing device is the selection of the securities for the defensive and, more importantly, the aggressive components used in the plan. This problem may be met by the use of investment company issues. This approach has merit provided the investment company shares are appropriate for the purpose, and provided the investor is willing to pay the costs required by shifting between defensive and aggressive portfolios.

The investor may employ the formula-timing idea through the medium of investment company shares in several ways: (1) by operating his own plan, using selected investment company shares for the aggressive section of the plan, (2) by entering into an arrangement with an investment company under which the company operates the plan for him, using its own shares, or (3) by purchase of shares in companies whose *own* policy and portfolio holdings are based on formula timing; these are rare today.

For provision of a fixed cash income. Most open-end companies offer withdrawal plans whereby the shareholder may obtain a fixed monthly income. Where the dividend income is not large enough to cover the required amount, shares are liquidated for the balance (see p.165). In 1964 the Securities and Exchange Commission, for the first time, permitted mutual funds to issue literature showing the past results that such arrangements would have produced. Because of the secular rise in common stock prices, some funds have been able to show that a certain rate of cash income (such as 6 per cent) could have been distributed in the past, from income and liquidation of shares, and the erosion of capital could still have been offset by capital appreciation, leaving the fund larger at the end of a given period of years than at the beginning. Of course, such a performance is not guaranteed in the future.

For the investment of trust funds. Investment company shares are eligible for trust investment (1) where the trustee is empowered by the trust instrument to purchase investment company shares, (2) in the states where by law or court decision fiduciaries may purchase investment company shares, (3) in the other states that also follow the "prudent man" rule, and (4) where the "legal list" does not include equities but where general discretionary powers are provided by the instrument. Controversy concerning the appropriateness of including such shares in trust portfolios has been considerable. Originally, the main argument against the practice was that the purchase of such shares involved the improper delegation of trust powers to the management of the investment company that selects the portfolio. This is not the case, although the trustee must still apply rules of caution to the selection of the particular securities by investigating the policy, portfolio, and management of each company under consideration.

For the investment of pension and profit-sharing funds.[24] The rapid growth of corporate pension plans in the period since World War II, described in Chapter 3, has opened up another outlet for investment company securities that may reach very substantial proportions. Where the purchase of equities over a prolonged period is appropriate for such funds, investment company shares provide the opportunity to acquire an interest in a managed and diversified portfolio.

Tax Status of Investment Companies

If investment companies were taxed as ordinary corporations, triple income taxation would result. The corporation whose securities are held in the portfolio has paid taxes; the investment company would pay a tax on its earnings; and the holder of its shares would pay taxes on dividends received. The Internal Revenue Code recognizes this problem by permitting an investment company to elect to be a "regulated investment company" for tax purposes. To qualify as such, it must (1) be registered under the Investment Company Act of 1940, (2) derive at least 90 per cent of gross income from dividends, interest, and gains from sale of securities, (3) obtain less than 70 per cent of gross income from sale of securities held for less than three months, (4) have at least 50 per cent of assets in cash, Government securities, and a diversified list of securities, and (5) distribute as taxable dividends not less than 90 per cent of its net investment income (interest and dividend income less expenses) for any taxable year. It is not obliged to

[24]The Keogh Act of 1962 specifically authorizes the use of mutual fund shares in the tax-free retirement plans of self-employed individuals. (See Chapter 3.) Only a custodial account with a bank is required.

distribute any of its realized security profits. The few "nonregulated" companies pay regular corporate taxes on realized capital gains and the current corporate ordinary and surtax rates on 15 per cent of dividend income and 100 per cent of interest income after deducting expenses and general taxes.

The "regulated" investment company may retain long-term realized capital gains and pay a 25 per cent tax on them, *on behalf of the stockholder.* The stockholder reports this payment on his own income tax return. (If his top tax bracket is less than 50 per cent, in effect he receives a refund.) The shareholder then writes up the cost of his shares by three-quarters of the gain to reflect the fact that a capital gains tax has now been paid on part of the value of his holdings, just as if the net after-tax gain had been distributed and then reinvested.

Investment companies may thus be classified into two groups for tax purposes:

1. Nonregulated companies that are fully taxable.
2. "Regulated" companies that distribute substantially all of net investment income and pay taxes only on that portion retained (less than 10 per cent), and
   (a) pay out all realized capital gains (taxes on these to be paid by the shareholder), or
   (b) retain all or part of realized capital gains, and pay taxes on same as indicated above.

When the shareholder of a regulated investment company receives a dividend check, the company indicates that portion derived from net investment income and that portion derived from realized capital gains, so that the investor can report and pay the personal income taxes that apply to him.[25]

Two types of funds have been available to those seeking exemption or postponement of Federal income taxes: (1) funds whose portfolio consists of tax-free state and municipal securities and (2) tax-free exchange ("swap") funds. Swap funds, which first appeared in 1960, were formed to accept the investors' securities in exchange for their shares. No current capital gain was realized by the investor. The tax cost of the fund shares remains the same as that of the investor's original holdings, as does that of the fund itself. Later, if the fund sells portfolio securities, any realized capital gain is taxed on the same basis as that applying to other funds. However, since requests for redemption of fund shares can be honored by delivering portfolio securities instead of cash, the fund can avoid forced realization of capital gains and so these are further postponed as far as the investor is concerned.

Swap funds are closed-end—they do not make a continuous offering of shares; the securities contributed were held in escrow during the organiza-

[25]To avoid impairment of the capital at work, most open-end companies urge their stockholders to take their capital gains distributions in additional shares of stock. The individual shareholder has the same right as any investor to the normal dividend exclusion on *income* dividends received. (See Chapter 18.)

tion period, and shares in the fund were exchanged in a single transaction. At the beginning of 1973 twenty-eight such funds had been formed. By Federal law, no new exchange funds could solicit business after April 30, 1967.

Prices, Dividends, and Yields

As indicated previously, the buying price of a share of an open-end company consists of its net asset value plus, in most cases, a selling charge to cover distribution costs. The "bid" price reported in the financial columns is this net asset value. The "asked" price is virtually the net asset value plus the load.[26] The value of the share thus rises and falls with the value of the total portfolio, which is in turn determined by the composition of the portfolio and the condition of the securities market. The range of volatility in price action among the whole open-end group is very wide, reflecting the different purposes and objectives of the different funds and the investment policies followed.

Dividends derived from investment earnings on open-end shares likewise differ in amount and in stability depending on the character of the fund and the policies of the management. Just as with individual securities, the investor has a wide choice among funds emphasizing growth and appreciation, or those aiming at high but variable income, or those directed toward moderate but more stable income.

The price of shares in closed-end funds is affected by the same factors plus the influence of a high or a low degree of leverage. The difference between asset value per share and market value may be very substantial, just as the market price per share of a business corporation may differ considerably from its book value. In the postwar period the shares of many closed-end companies have sold at considerable discounts from asset value. Wiesenberger reports that at the end of 1971, there was an average discount of 15 per cent on the shares of ten diversified closed-end companies; the range was from 3 to 16 per cent discount. Including specialized funds and nondiversified companies, twenty-four sold at discounts and three at a premium.[27] In 1972–1973 discounts rose to record proportions.

A substantial discount does not necessarily indicate a bargain. It may reflect lack of confidence in the management, but is more likely to reflect the general condition of the market and the evaluation of earnings and dividends by appropriate capitalization of these factors. Unlike shares of open-end companies, the common stocks of closed-end companies sell for what the market thinks they are worth in terms of earning power, dividends, and prospects of appreciation.

Because of their more specialized nature, the fact that they can be re-

---

[26]Actually, the asked price is found by multiplying the bid price (net asset value) by 100 over 100 minus the load. Thus if the bid price is 10, and the load is 8 per cent, the asked price is 10(100/92) = 10.87.

[27]Arthur Wiesenberger, *Investment Companies*, 1971, p. 46. Prices and premiums or discounts are reported each Monday in *The Wall Street Journal*. See also United Business Service, Inc., *United Mutual Fund Selector*, (semi-monthly).

deemed only by sale in the open market, and (in some cases) the factor of leverage, the common stocks of closed-end companies in general have more price volatility than those of open-end companies. The greatest volatility is shown by those companies whose portfolios themselves are volatile and which have high leverage in their own capitalization.

The character of the closed-end fund is also reflected in its dividend policy and the yield action of its shares. Here again the investor has a wide choice. Earnings, and hence dividends, are affected by the objectives of the fund, the proficiency of its management, and the relative importance of investment income and capital gains. And the yield on these shares is determined by the factors affecting earnings and dividends, as well as by the market price action.

Recent Developments

A number of developments that have taken place in the investment company field in recent years, both in operation and regulation, are summarized as follows.

1970 Amendments to the Investment Company Act. After extensive investigation, in December 1966 the Securities and Exchange Commission released a comprehensive report on mutual funds.[28] The S.E.C. suggested that a number of important revisions be made in the Investment Company Act of 1940 and in the regulatory power of the Commission under that statute, relative to mutual funds. Its chief recommendations were (1) abolition of "front-end load" contractual plans, (2) limitation of sales charges to a maximum of 5 per cent (4.75 per cent of offering price), (3) requirement of "reasonable" management fees, and (4) control or elimination of "give-ups" whereby part of the sales commission earned by selling dealers are given up to other dealers who have provided research services to the funds' managers or to smaller dealers unable to develop a large volume of sales.

After long and controversial hearings, in 1970 Congress passed amendments to the Investment Company Act that fell considerably short of meeting the S.E.C. recommendations. The more important of these were

1. "Front-end load" plans were not eliminated, nor was the 50 per cent sales charge in the first year. But the investor can rescind the entire transaction within forty-five days, and during the first eighteen months the shareholder can get a refund of his payments less 15 per cent.

2. Sales charges were not limited to a specific maximum, but the offering price of mutual fund shares may not include "an excessive sales load."

[28]*Report of the S.E.C. on the Public Policy Implications of Investment Company Growth*, Report of the Committee on Interstate and Foreign Commerce, 89th Congress, 2d Session, House Report No. 2337 (Washington, D.C.: U.S. Government Printing Office, 1966).

Rules relating to the sales commission are to be formulated by the National Association of Securities Dealers.

3. Management fees are not specified. But fees based on performance are prohibited unless they increase or decrease proportionately with an appropriate index of securities prices used to represent the market as a whole.[29]

4. "Fiduciary duty," that is, the obligation to guard the interests of shareholders with honesty and prudence, is imposed on the officers and directors of investment companies and their advisors. Actions by shareholders to recover damages are enforceable only in a U.S. District Court.

Sale of mutual fund shares by life insurance companies. As indicated in Chapter 3, insurance companies have entered the mutual fund business directly or through affiliates. At the end of 1971 eighty-seven funds organized by insurance companies had assets of $900 millions. In addition, insurance companies or their parent companies owned sponsors that managed 60 funds with assets of about $8 billions.[30] Some of these offer a "funding" arrangement whereby the investor agrees to purchase a certain dollar amount of mutual fund shares and of life insurance, over a period of time, on a regular basis (monthly or quarterly). The shares are used as collateral for loans to purchase the insurance. The expectation is that the long-term increase in value of the shares will more than pay the interest cost on the loan.

The entrance of insurance companies into the mutual fund area was the result of several factors: (1) the need to meet the competition of equity-type securities that are more attractive than cash reserve life insurance policies in an inflationary setting; (2) as a step in the development of financial conglomerates offering a variety of financial services; (3) as a means of increasing life insurance sales; and (4) to increase agents' income.

Commercial banks and mutual funds. For some time commercial banks have wished to operate their own mutual funds. Their trust departments already manage common trust funds and serve as managers of individual agency accounts and of estates consisting of securities portfolios. In April 1971, in a case involving the First National City Bank of New York, the Supreme Court ruled that, based on the separation of commercial and investment banking required by law, banks may not operate commingled agency accounts.[31] But some bank holding companies have recently set up new closed-end investment companies as subsidiaries.

New types of funds. Letter stock funds (closed-end) specialize in acquiring restricted (unregistered) securities and in direct private placements. Securities are often bought at substantial discounts from the market

---

[29]For detailed information and analysis of management fees, see *Institutional Investor Study Report of the Securities and Exchange Commission*, Chapter IV. 92nd Congress, 1st Session, House Document No. 92–64. (Washington: U.S. Government Printing Office, 1971).

[30]Arthur Wiesenberger, *Investment Companies* (New York: Arthur Wiesenberger Services, Inc., 1972), pp. 418–419.

[31]401 U.S.617 (1971).

prices of registered shares of the same issuer. A problem arises in case of the need to liquidate portfolio assets.

"Hedge funds" and "offshore funds" have been discussed earlier in this chapter. Some of the latter, notably the Fund of Funds based in Switzerland, consist of shares in other funds, so that sales expense and management compensation are pyramided.

Closed-end dual-purpose funds (see p.148) have not lived up to expectations. Their double leverage feature resulted in very substantial declines in the market value of their capital shares in the 1969–1970 and the late 1971 periods of marked weakness in stock prices. Only a few (1973) are selling at or above net asset values, and in certain cases the latter have been substantially eroded.

Criticism of investment performance. Unlike pension funds, investment counsels, and bank trustees, the investment record of mutual investment companies is an open book. The asset values of the shares of widely held companies are reported daily, and their dividends are reported regularly. A number of services issue comparative reports on performance. Consequently, mutual funds have been subject to constant scrutiny, with resulting praise and blame. Funds are compared with each other, and with the general market indexes. During strong stock markets, most of them come off well, especially the more aggressive and speculative funds. In periods of weakness, many look bad and criticism mounts.

Two research studies have been especially critical: "The Wharton Study" in 1962,[32] and a Twentieth Century Fund study in 1970.[33] The former concluded that for the period 1953–1958, the average performance by mutual funds was not appreciably better than would have been achieved by a completely unmanaged (general market) portfolio with the same distribution between stocks and other assets. The second study, using the period 1960 through June 1968, compares the rate of return (dividends plus capital gain as a percentage of initial investment) with what could have been achieved by investing equal amounts in a random sample of all stocks listed on the New York Stock Exchange. In this study the factor of risk (volatility of monthly rates of return) was also taken into account and related to performance. The study concluded the following, based on elaborate statistical analysis: The funds demonstrated an inability clearly to outperform the stock market; management showed no particular ability to predict market trends; management fees and sales charges were excessive for the results obtained. It is not surprising that a high correlation was found between rate of return and risk.

Such criticisms, while perhaps relying too much on average performances, suggest that it is important to make a careful selection among the many funds that are available, and that the choice of a fund or funds should be made on the basis of long-run results. They also suggest the significance of

[32]See footnote 10.
[33]Irwin Friend, Marshall Blum, and Jean Crockett, *Mutual Funds and Other Institutional Investors: A New Perspective.* A Twentieth Century Fund Study (New York: McGraw-Hill, Inc., 1970.)

the period studied and of the choice of the types of companies that are studied for performance. These factors are emphasized by the fact that in two later studies mutual funds were given much better ratings. In its special study for the Securities and Exchange Commission, the National Bureau of Economic Research reported that in the period 1965–1970 the performance of the "growth" funds, measured by traditional methods, was distinctly better than that of the popular stock averages, in spite of the market losses in 1969–1970.[34]

In a thorough study of industry performance, the Commission found that 236 open-end funds with net assets of $30 billions (90 per cent of the industry) were well run in relation to risk. Measuring performance by the difference between the rate of return earned by the funds and that realized by standard portfolios which had shown the same risk (volatility), the group produced a higher return by 0.6 per cent annually in the ten year period 1960 through 1969.[35]

Unregulated investment companies. Two types of open-end funds have received considerable recent attention: "hedge funds" and "offshore funds." These were selected for special analysis by the Securities and Exchange Commission in its comprehensive 1971 report.

At the end of 1968 there were 140 hedge funds with assets of $1.3 billions. They are typically organized as limited partnerships, and quotations are available on only two or three publicly held funds. Their name derives from the fact that they attempt to hedge the effects of high leverage and margin trading (debt financing) with short selling, arbitrage, and the use of options, in order to take advantage of swings in stock market prices. They ranged in size from $50,000 assets to $118 millions. Two features distinguish their common stock portfolios from those of other aggressive funds: emphasis in investment policy on stocks traded on regional exchanges and over-the-counter, and willingness to buy initial stock offerings. The Commission found their investment performance to be mediocre. The Commission has also recommended that they be brought under its regulation.[36]

"Offshore" funds are incorporated in foreign countries and sell shares to foreign nationals. But they are often organized and managed by Americans and invest all or a substantial portion of their portfolios in American equity securities. Because they are not registered under the Investment Company Act and because their shares are not registered under the Securities Act, these cannot be sold in the United States. The reported value of their holdings in American securities, held by American custodians alone, reached $2.35 billions in December 1969, falling to $2.12 billions in February 1970.[37] In its lengthy study of offshore funds the Commission concluded that although they had been a significant vehicle for foreign investment in American equities, their faulty disclosure of operations and investment information, the doubtful quality of their portfolio management, and the substantial

[34]*Institutional Investor Study Report of the S.E.C.*, *op. cit.*, Supplementary Volume I, Chapter 5.

[35]*Institutional Investor Study Report of the S.E.C.*, *op. cit.*, Chapter IV.

[36]*Ibid.* See also *Fortune*, May 1971, pp. 269–270.

[37]*Ibid*, Chapter VII.

losses to investors in some funds all indicated the need for bringing the funds under its regulation. Although the funds themselves would be exempt, regulation could be applied to sales corporations based in the United States that sell shares in offshore funds abroad.[38]

Conclusions

Investment companies differ widely with respect to basic characteristics, size, rate of growth, investment policies and types of portfolios, income, dividend, and price performance. All of these factors deserve the closest scrutiny. In utilizing this indirect and delegated means of investment, the investor must first be sure of his own objectives. He must then select a fund or group of companies that appear to have the same objectives, keeping in mind that no investment company is "tailor-made" to fit a particular investment situation. He must then examine the statements and performance of these companies and, having selected one or more for a portion of his funds, must make a continued appraisal in order to know whether the company is doing a better job for him, at a cost to him, than he could do alone. He must not expect spectacular results. On the other hand, he is entitled to full value in services rendered.

REFERENCES

A Study of Mutual Funds, prepared for the Securities and Exchange Commission by the Wharton School of Finance and Commerce, 87th Congress, 2nd Session, 1962. Washington, D.C.: U.S. Government Printing Office, 1962.

BARNES, LEO, *Your Buying Guide to Mutual Funds and Investment Companies.* Larchmont, N.Y.: American Research Council, annually.

BULLOCK, HUGH, *The Story of Investment Companies.* New York: Columbia University Press, 1959.

CASEY, W. J., *Mutual Funds Investment Planning.* New York: Institute for Business Planning, Inc., loose-leaf.

DOANE, C. R., and E. J. HILLS, *Investment Trusts and Funds from the Investor's Point of View.* Gt. Barrington, Mass.: American Institute for Economic Research, 1970.

FRANK, ROBERT, *Successful Investing Through Mutual Funds.* New York: Hart Publishing Company, 1969.

FRIEND, IRWIN, M. BLUM, AND JEAN CROCKETT, *Mutual Funds and Other Institutional Investors.* A Twentieth Century Fund Study. New York: McGraw-Hill, Inc., 1970.

Institutional Investor Study Report of the Securities and Exchange Commission, Chapters IV, VII, and Supplementary Volume No. 1, Chapter 5. 92nd Congress, 1st Session, House Document No. 92–64. Washington, D.C.: U.S. Government Printing Office, 1971.

---

[38]For a complete survey of types, structure, management and sponsorship, tax status, and other aspects of offshore funds, including their significance in the balance of payments, see *Institutional Investor Study Report of the S.E.C. op cit.,* Chapter VII.

Investment Company Institute, *The Mutual Fund Shareholder.* New York: The Institute, 1966.

————, *The Money Managers: Professional Investment Through Mutual Funds.* New York: McGraw-Hill, Inc., 1967.

————, *Investment Companies, A Statistical Summary, 1940–1960.* New York: The Institute, 1961.

————, *Management Investment Companies,* a monograph prepared for the Commission on Money and Credit. Englewood Cliffs, N.J.: Prentice-Hall, Inc., 1962.

JACOBS, R. H., *Securities,* Volume 2: *Financial Planning and Mutual Funds,* 2nd ed. Washington: Kalb, Voorhis & Co., 1967.

JENKINS, DAVID, *How to Build Capital and Income in Mutual Funds.* Larchmont, N.Y.: American Research Council, 1961.

JOHNSON, H. A., *Johnson's Investment Company Charts.* Buffalo: Hugh A. Johnson Investment Co., annually.

MEAD, STUART B., *Mutual Funds: A Guide for the Lay Investor.* Morristown, N.J.: D.H. Mark Publications, 1971.

PALANCE, DEAN, *Mutual Funds—Legal Pickpockets?* New York: Vantage Press, Inc., 1963.

Report of the Securities and Exchange Commission on the Public Policy Implications of Investment Company Growth. Report of the Committee on Interstate and Foreign Commerce, 89th Congress, 2nd Session, House Report No. 2337, December 2, 1966. Washington, D.C.: U.S. Government Printing Office, 1966.

Report of the Special Study of the Securities Markets of the Securities and Exchange Commission, Part 4, Chapter XI. Washington, D.C.: U.S. Government Printing Office, 1963.

SHARP, W. F., *Mutual Fund Performance: Management and Prediction.* Santa Monica, Calif.: Rand Corporation, 1965.

SMITH, R. L., *The Grim Truth About Mutual Funds.* New York: G. P. Putnam's Sons, 1963.

STRALEY, J. A., *What About Mutual Funds?* 2nd rev. ed., New York: Harper & Row, Publishers, 1967.

WEISSMAN, R. L., *Investment Made Easy: Through Mutual Funds and Closed-end Investment Companies.* New York: Harper & Row, Publishers, 1962.

WIESENBERGER, ARTHUR, *Investment Companies.* New York: Arthur Wiesenberger Services, Inc., annually.

10 Foreign Securities

SCOPE: This chapter discusses the investment position of foreign securities in the United States. The emphasis is on foreign government bonds. The order of discussion is (1) types of foreign investment, (2) volume of private foreign investment, (3) government investment abroad, (4) reasons for purchase of foreign securities, (5) special factors in analysis, (6) tests of quality—foreign public issues, (7) the record of foreign public bond issues, (8) foreign corporate issues, (9) barriers to portfolio investments, (10) protective agencies, (11) bonds of the World Bank, (12) prices and yields, and (13) investment position of foreign bonds.

Types of Foreign Investment

Long-term private American investments in foreign countries are divided into two main classes: (1) *direct* investments, consisting of corporate and individual holdings of foreign properties and investments in foreign branches and subsidiaries, and (2) *portfolio* investments, consisting of foreign government bonds, bonds and stocks of foreign corporations offered in the United States, and banking and other claims. Control of portfolio investments is in other than American hands in the sense that the investor depends solely on the foreign obligor to pay them back.

Foreign government and corporate bonds can be classified as (1) *dollar* obligations, those whose interest and principal are payable in the United States in dollars—these are *external* loans from the standpoint of the borrower, and (2) securities payable in the currency of the issuer—these are *internal* bonds from the standpoint of the borrower. A few foreign government issues are payable in several currencies and are known as *multiple-currency bonds*. Most foreign government bonds are unsecured.

Volume of Private Foreign Investment

At the beginning of 1972, the accumulated value of private U.S. foreign investment was $135 billions. This total resulted from direct long-term and portfolio investments, plus reinvested earnings and net gains in market prices of foreign securities. Table 10-1 shows the volume of long- and short-term investment in selected years (as of December 31).

Table 10-1. FOREIGN PRIVATE INVESTMENT
          (in billions of dollars)

	1950	1955	1960	1965	1971
Long-term					
Direct	$11.8	$19.3	$31.9	$49.5	$ 86.1
Portfolio	5.7	7.4	12.7	21.9	29.9
	$17.5	$26.7	$44.5	$71.4	$116.0
Short-term	1.5	2.4	4.8	10.1	18.9
Total	$19.0	$29.1	$49.3	$81.5	$134.9

SOURCES: *Federal Reserve Bulletin*; *Survey of Current Business*.

The portfolio investments in Table 10-1 include purchases of foreign securities and other long-term instruments. The former have, however, diminished very substantially in recent years. In 1971, for example, they amounted to only $900 millions. Such purchases have been greatly inhibited by the interest equalization tax (see below).

Government Investment Abroad

At the beginning of 1972, U.S. Government credits and claims totalled about $3.4 billions. This foreign investment has increased, on the average, $15 billions for each year in the 1960s.[1] The Federal government was looked to for the bulk of exported American funds until recent years, because the general investment background of most foreign countries precluded substantial new private direct and portfolio investment from American sources. Although private investment burgeoned in the 1950s and 1960s the Federal government is still an important partner in the provision of American capital abroad.

The Appeal of Foreign Securities

Although most American investors are still reluctant to subject their funds to the risks of foreign commitment, the quantity of foreign securities placed on the American market is evidence of a strong appeal which stems from a combination of factors:

[1]*Federal Reserve Bulletin; Statistical Abstract of the United States.*

1. *Higher income.* Capital flows naturally toward the places where it is most highly valued. When foreign securities are offered to American investors at yields substantially in excess of those obtainable on domestic issues of apparently comparable quality, investors have a strong inducement to enjoy the extra returns. As indicated by the yields on foreign securities shown in Table 10-3, foreign government and corporate dollar bonds yield (early 1972) from 4 to 10 per cent, depending on quality and maturity. Not many high-grade issues are available. Such yields appealed to the more venturesome American investors until interest rates on American obligations moved up to record levels in 1966–1970. Under conditions prevailing in 1971–1973, the differential between domestic and foreign yields has become much less attractive.

2. *Desire for international diversification.* The spreading of risk through diversification is a time-honored protective measure that induced many American investors to enter into the purchase of foreign securities, until developments in the mid-1960s made these relatively less attractive.

3. *Trade factors.* Nations making diligent efforts to expand their foreign trade must make available adequate arrangements for financing such trade. American funds have "followed the flag" in the sense that exports have been encouraged by willingness to finance foreign government and corporate needs.

4. *Sentiment.* Many American nationals have been interested in foreign securities as a phase of their interest in world rehabilitation and the development of American leadership in a world of unrest.

5. *Profits for underwriters and distributors.* The underwriting margin on the sale of foreign securities has traditionally been substantially above the margin on domestic issues. Gross margins of as high as 10 per cent on foreign bonds have not been uncommon.

6. *Regulation of foreign issues.* New public offerings of foreign securities in the United States are subject to the registration and prospectus requirements of the Securities Act of 1933, and the stock of a foreign issuer listed on a U.S. exchange is nominally regulated under the Securities and Exchange Act of 1934. The disclosure provisions of the latter legislation have been, however, difficult to apply. And unlisted foreign securities have, until recently, escaped regulation. The amendments of the Securities Act in 1964 require that the same standards of disclosure applying to domestic companies must apply to foreign companies whose securities are traded in the United States, including those traded over-the-counter. (See Chapter 16.)

Special Factors in Foreign Security Analysis

The analysis of a foreign security requires the use of extra dimensions beyond the measurements employed in domestic analysis. A given set of conditions is accepted as applicable to all domestic securities. Uniformity of fundamental factors, such as law, currency, governmental stability, and commercial procedure, permits the analyst of a domestic issue to devote his entire time to an intensive study of the security itself. The almost complete lack of such uniformity in the world at large compels the analyst of foreign bonds or stocks to make an extensive study of numerous factors which are quickly passed over in the domestic field.

The world has no international code of laws, ethically speaking. The American investor in domestic securities has the uniform protection of the U.S. Constitution behind all of his commitments. He is reasonably sure to receive fair treatment in any court action under laws with which he is conversant and which he is obliged to respect. The investor in foreign securities does not have an equal measure of assurance. Not only are foreign laws different, but courts of jurisdiction naturally have a friendly bias to domestic debtors.

The currency problem is troublesome because of instability of the values of the respective units. The inability of most of the leading nations of the world to keep their currency on a firm basis has caused great monetary confusion. Depreciation in the value of the national currency directly harms the position of the securities of the country through the increase of the burden of debt service.

Governmental stability is a third additional factor of high importance. So unsettled have national governments become that a veritable epidemic of revolutions has occurred in recent years. The list of countries that changed their governments by force after the First and Second World Wars is both impressive and significant. In some cases, the new administrations have fully honored the debts of old regimes; in other cases, less fortunate developments ensued; but in all cases, investment values have been impaired. Certain countries have moved back into a more respectable investment status, including, interestingly enough, former enemies such as Japan and Germany.

Lack of the reliable information required for careful analysis is another special hazard that confronts the investor in foreign securities, both government and corporate. Information with respect to trade, resources, tax revenues, total debt, and other vital matters, although more readily available than heretofore for the analysis of foreign government obligations, is still not in convenient form for use by the typical investor. And he has difficulty adjusting the data on private foreign issues to American accounting and analytical standards.

Quality Tests of Public Issues

The tests of quality of the dollar obligations of foreign governmental bodies are the same as in the domestic field: ability to pay, willingness to pay, and legality of issue. Ability to pay is indicated by several factors discussed below, willingness to pay by the default record, and legality of issues by the pertinent legislation.

Ability to pay. The ability of a foreign government to service its debt abroad depends first upon the availability of revenues with which to purchase the necessary exchange. The sources of revenue of foreign states are similar to those previously discussed in connection with domestic public loans, with some noteworthy additions. In some countries, export taxes are levied upon the shipment of raw commodities, such as on coffee in Brazil, on tin in Bolivia, and on nitrates in Chile. In other countries, monopolies have been established on articles of popular use, such as salt, tobacco, and matches, whereby the government directly, or indirectly through franchise grant, controls the market and profits through the maintenance of artificially high prices. In numerous instances, countries with inferior credit have issued bonds secured by a prior claim upon revenues from such special sources. Experience has taught, unfortunately, that this priority is not always observed when other sources of revenue fail. Creditors cannot seize a specific security or pledged revenues.

The revenues available for foreign debt service depend not only on the gross tax income of the borrower, but on its total burden of debt, both internal and external. Where a choice has to be made, default on external debt is likely to be preferred to internal default. This is especially the case where unstable or uneconomic governments are unable to collect sufficient revenues or to control expenses. Default on external debt service is one of the easiest solutions for an unbalanced budget.

Equally important is the amount of dollar exchange available for the purpose of meeting interest, sinking funds, and principal. The supply of exchange depends, in turn, on exports and services rendered to foreign nationals. The conventional key to this supply is found in the balance of international payments.

Internal depreciation of the debtor country's currency magnifies the cost of such dollar exchange. The fluctuating exchange rates that have characterized the postwar period have exaggerated the difficulty of many foreign countries by making dollars very expensive, even though substantial sums of local funds could be raised. All factors contributing to a varying and declining foreign exchange position—both economic and political—thus have a bearing on a country's ability to pay obligations held abroad.

Willingness to pay. Willingness to pay is fully as important as ability to pay, for the foreign government cannot be sued, and the application of pressure by private holders of its bonds abroad is difficult. A government that wants to pay will tighten its belt and keep its credit good at all costs. Finland, Australia, France, the Netherlands, Switzerland, and Sweden provide examples of fully maintained payments on dollar bonds in the face of adversity. Norway and Denmark, although occupied by the enemy in World War II, managed by great efforts to find sufficient dollar exchange to pay the interest on dollar bonds.

The sense of moral obligation that moves some countries to fulfill their promises, and the lack of it that has been partially responsible for the dismal debt record of others, springs from a variety of sources: education, character, experience and ability in foreign transactions, political stability, and pride in reputation. There is no substitute for good faith in international finance.

The Record of Foreign Public Bond Issues

In contrast to conditions in the domestic field, where default means failure to pay interest or principal when due, default in the foreign field occurs in a variety of ways, many of which arise out of unwillingness to pay and are tantamount to repudiation. Foreign defaults may occur in any of the following ways:

  1. Interest
     (a) Postponement in full or part
     (b) Suspension
     (c) Reduction in coupon rate
  2. Principal
     (a) Postponement
     (b) Reduction in face value
     (c) Forced conversion
  3. Sinking Fund
     (a) Postponement
     (b) Suspension
     (c) Reduction in annual provision
  4. General
     (a) Divergence of pledged funds
     (b) Repudiation of debt

The adoption of any of these expedients by a nation is considered a default and should be seriously regarded. A minor infraction, such as postponement of the annual sinking fund provision, is significant in that it is often a precursor to a more serious default.

During the years 1920–1930, approximately $7.0 billions of foreign dollar bonds were issued, which together with bonds previously and subsequently issued, made a total of more than $9.0 billions floated in the United States. By 1950, there was a reduction through the years, by retirement or otherwise, of approximately 60 per cent. At the end of 1970, the net total amount of government dollar securities, of which some part of each issue remained outstanding, was $6.7 billions.[2] When appraising foreign bonds as a whole, one must note that many were first adjusted and then redeemed at or near par so that, with the passage of time, defaulted issues tend to constitute a smaller proportion of the remaining outstanding bonds.

Of the total foreign government dollar bonds outstanding at the end of 1970, 4 per cent were in default as to interest and sinking fund payments, and another 5 per cent were paying interest and sinking fund installments under the terms of debt-adjustment plans.[3] (See Table 10–2).

A few Canadian municipal bonds are being paid on an adjusted basis. The Dominion and its provinces have consistently continued full service on external obligations. Other countries enjoying a clean record as of 1971

[2] Foreign Bondholders Protective Council, Inc., *Report 1968 through 1970* (New York: The Council, 1971), p. 2.
[3] *Ibid.*

Table 10-2. STATUS OF FOREIGN GOVERNMENT DOLLAR BONDS, 1970
(in millions of dollars)

			Outstanding December 31, 1970			
					In Default	
Area	*Originally Issued*	*Amount Outstanding*	*Receiving Full Service*	*Adjusted Service Available*	*Amount*	*Per Cent of Out-standing*
North America						
Canada	$ 4,680.5	$4,142.2	$4,142.2	$ —	$ —	—
Mexico	296.0	115.4	102.0	10.1	3.2	2.9%
Central America						
and Carribbean	161.3	86.0	33.0	.9	52.1	6.0
South America	1,021.3	136.9	—	136.9	—	—
Europe	1,659.4	815.5	442.4	186.3	186.8	22.9
Near East	1,319.2	928.4	928.4	—	—	—
Africa	6.0	1.4	1.4	—	—	—
Asia	702.1	164.9	158.6	.8	5.5	3.3
Australia and						
New Zealand	475.0	295.6	295.6	—	—	—
Total	$10,320.8	$6,686.2	$6,103.6	$335.0	$247.6	3.7%

SOURCE: Foreign Bondholders' Protective Council, Inc., *Report 1968 through 1970* (New York: The Council, 1971), pp. 3–5.

include Argentina (all bonds redeemed), Australia, Belgium, Denmark, Finland, France, Israel, Jamaica, Netherlands, New Zealand, Norway, Panama, Rhodesia and Nyasaland, South Africa, and Switzerland (all bonds redeemed). South American government dollar bonds have been placed on an adjusted service basis after revision of interest and/or sinking fund obligations. Cuban bonds are all in default, as are those of Bulgaria, China, Congo, Czechoslovakia, Danzig, Estonia, Hungary, Poland, Rumania, and the USSR.

At the beginning of 1972, sixty foreign governments had 149 issues listed on the New York Stock Exchange, with a market value of $1.9 billions.[4]

Foreign Corporate Issues

At the end of 1971, twenty-three foreign companies had thirty-two bond issues, with a market value of $732 millions (par $840 millions), listed on the New York Stock Exchange. In addition, forty-one issues of international banks valued at $3.1 billions were also listed.

American investors have long been familiar with such Canadian stocks as International Nickel, Canadian Pacific, and Aluminium Ltd. At the end of 1971, thirty-four foreign corporate stock issues were listed on the New York Stock Exchange with a market value of $12 billions.[5] Names becoming

[4]New York Stock Exchange, *Fact Book* (New York: The Exchange, 1972), p. 27.
[5]*Ibid.*, p. 34.

increasingly familiar include: Roan Selection Trust, Hiram Walker Gooderham & Worts, and Royal Dutch Petroleum. The American Stock Exchange is the largest listed market for foreign stocks in the United States. Sixty-seven stocks representing eight foreign countries were traded on the "Amex" in 1971. Among the stock issues, Canada led with forty-eight. Examples included Avien, British American Tobacco, Canadian Javelin, Courtlauds (American depository receipts) Rico Argentine Mining. About 9 per cent of the volume of trading on the American Stock Exchange is in shares of foreign countries (7 per cent in Canadian shares).[6] A considerable number of foreign stocks are traded over-the-counter. *Barron's* carries a list of the more active issues.

American investors are also participating indirectly in foreign securities, chiefly stocks, through the purchase of shares in investment companies that hold stocks of companies domiciled abroad. A number of such funds hold Canadian securities, which enjoy the absence of capital gains taxation. Funds have also been formed to invest in Western European corporation stocks (for example, Eurofund). The appeal of international funds, however, has diminished very substantially since the great declines in stock prices on foreign exchanges in 1961, 1966, and 1970, and since the 1964 imposition of the interest equalization tax (see below).

The analysis of foreign corporate issues presents special difficulties. Financial information is not disclosed by foreign companies as frequently as by American companies. Also, the data published are usually much less complete. Accounting procedure often follows radically different lines. For illustration, European profit and loss statements often start with gross profits from operations ("trading profit"), sales not being revealed; earnings are shown as barely adequate to cover dividends, with surplus profits carried into reserve accounts; fixed assets are often carried at nominal values in the balance sheets. The computation of investment ratios generally requires a realignment of the items in the income account. Of course for those issues that are listed on American exchanges, the same accounting standards apply to foreign as to domestic issues.

A further difficulty in investment in foreign corporate issues is the foreign exchange problem. Even if obligations of private borrowers can be collected in the currency of the country, the creditor may be prevented from converting the currency into dollars and from bringing it home. And, of course, unless listed on an American or Canadian exchange, the marketability of most foreign corporate securities is decidedly limited. To facilitate trading in foreign corporate stocks and the conversion of dividends into dollars and their remittance to the United States, some foreign shares are deposited with an American bank, against which *American depository receipts* are issued. The stock of British Petroleum Co., Ltd., is traded on an unlisted basis on the American Stock Exchange in the form of depository receipts issued share for share for the original stock held by the Morgan Guaranty Trust Company of New York.[7]

---

[6] *Amex Databook*, 1971, p. 26.

[7] The depository receipts are bought and sold in New York on a *dollar* basis even though the deposited stock bears a stated value in *pounds*. The original stock would not be acceptable delivery for a sale on the American Stock Exchange, whereas the depository receipts would be unacceptable on the London market.

Barriers to Portfolio Investments

As Table 10-1 shows, direct private investment has increased greatly in recent years, in spite of unsettled political and economic conditions in some
countries, tariff barriers, exchange controls, and foreign expropriations (as
in Bolivia, Mexico, and Argentina). Portfolio investments have suffered
from two additional major handicaps: (1) the great volatility of foreign
stock prices on *foreign* exchanges, beginning with the drastic declines in
1961 that were suffered on the Japanese and British exchanges, and (2)
the interest equalization tax enacted in September 1964 as a part of the
Administration's effort to correct the American balance of payments and
the gold drain, through curbing the outflow of investment funds.

The interest equalization tax is levied on the purchase price of securities
bought from foreigners: 15 per cent on stocks, and from 1.05 per cent (one-
year maturity) graduating to 15 per cent (28½ years or more) on bonds.
The tax does *not* apply to direct investments, bonds of the World Bank, or
securities of the "less developed" countries, such as in Latin America and
Africa. *New* issues of Canadian securities are exempt, as are shares of
foreign corporations which are (1) more than 50 per cent owned by U.S.
citizens and whose principal market is in the United States or (2) more
than 65 per cent American owned. A considerable number of foreign stocks
listed on the New York and American Stock exchanges are, therefore,
exempt.[8]

Protective Agencies

The holder of a foreign bond is in a weak position to enforce payment from
a reluctant foreign debtor. In the case of private obligations, suit in the
domestic courts of the debtor country may be undertaken, but is rarely
effective. As for government securities, diplomatic pressure, reprisal such as
the Johnson Act of 1934,[9] and other official measures have been well-nigh
fruitless. Until a foreign government is willing to meet its obligations,
American securityholders must depend largely on their own efforts. This
was recognized in 1933 in a White House announcement which stated that
the making of satisfactory arrangements and protecting American interests
was

> ...a task primarily for private initiative and interests. The traditional policy
> of the American Government has been that such loan and investment transac-
> tions were primarily private actions, to be handled by the parties directly
> concerned. The Government realizes a duty, within the proper limits of inter-

[8]Up to $100 millions per year of new securities issued by or guaranteed by the Government of Japan
can be sold in the United States free of the tax.

[9]Under this Act nations in default on war-debt obligations to our Federal government were prohibited from negotiating any new loans in this country while the war loans were in default. It has
since been repealed.

national law and international amity, to defend American interests abroad. However, it would not be wise for the Government to undertake directly the settlement of private debt situations.[10]

As a consequence, in 1933 the Foreign Bondholders Protective Council, Inc., was organized with government sanction to represent American holders of foreign bonds in default. It is the sole nationally credited bargaining agency to represent American holders of foreign securities.

The Council has performed extremely valuable services to American investors over the years. Its work of approaching defaulting government debtors as the bondholders' representative and seeking to obtain resumption of payments, or at least an adjustment plan, has resulted in the salvaging of very substantial sums. Since its inception, the Council has concluded negotiations and made favorable recommendations to bondholders on thirty-nine adjustment plans for twenty-four countries, usually at a reduced rate of interest, involving obligations having a principal of $3.5 billions. As of the end of 1970, forty-one permanent and temporary settlements for countries and their political subdivisions had been arranged with respect to a principal amount of $3.5 billions.[11] Formal negotiations have been carried on with other countries, and several debtor nations have taken steps towards future negotiations with the Council concerning resumption of service on their defaulted debts.

The World Bank

The International Bank for Reconstruction and Development was formed in 1945 as a result of the Bretton Woods Agreement to promote the international flow of capital for productive purposes and to assist in the reconstruction and development of the member nations' economic facilities. Its major function is to promote private foreign investment by means of guarantees or participations in loans and other investments made by private investors and, when private capital is not available on reasonable terms, to provide funds from its own resources.

The subscribed capital of the Bank as of June 30, 1972 was $26,606,-625,000, of which the United States' share was $6,350,000,000. At that time $2,660,663,000 of the total subscription had been paid in. In addition to its own funds, the Bank is entitled to borrow in the capital markets, and as of June 30, 1972, $6,938 millions including dollar bonds and the dollar equivalent in Canadian dollars, Belgian francs, Deutsch marks, Italian lira, Netherlands guilders, pounds sterling, Swiss francs, and Japanese yen were outstanding.

---

[10]Foreign Bondholders Protective Council, Inc., *Report for Years 1946 Through 1949* (New York: The Council, 1950), p. xv.

[11]Foreign Bondholders Protective Council, *Report 1968 through 1970* (New York: The Council, 1971), p. 1. Dollar loans remaining unsettled are those of the countries listed earlier in this chapter as being in default.

As of June 30, 1972, outstanding loans granted by the Bank totalled almost $12 billions (expressed in U.S. currency).[12] These had been made in some sixty countries to other members of the Bank or to a political sub-division or a public or private enterprise with the member's guarantee.

Bonds issued by the World Bank were described in Chapter 5. Technically, they are not U.S. obligations. But as long as their total does not exceed the amount of Bank capital to which the United States has subscribed, for practical purposes they belong in the Federal category. Their yields are slightly above those of direct government obligations of the same maturity.

Prices and Yields of Foreign Bonds

The instability and varying quality of foreign dollar bonds is best indicated by a survey of their price action. Table 10-3 reveals the vagaries of the

Table 10-3. PRICES OF SELECTED FOREIGN DOLLAR BONDS
(nearest whole dollar)

	Year Issued	1936–1970		1971		Yield
		High	Low	High	Low	Dec. 1971
Antioquia (Colombia) 3's, 1978	Exch. '49	96	46	96	90	4.14%
Australia Ext. 5's, 1978	1958	105	85	97	84	6.53
Bell Telephone (Canada) 1st K 3³/₄'s, 1979	1954	102	64	81	72	7.06
Berlin Adj. B 4¹/₂'s, 1978	Exch. '57	110	70	90	90	7.45
Bolivia Ext. 3's, 1995	Exch. '68	22	7	17	9	Default
Canada Perpetual 3's	1936	102	70	43	37	7.32
Can. Pac. Ry. perpetual deb. stk 4's	1921	121	31	54	46	7.55
Chile S.F. 3's, 1993	Exch. '48	54	25	50	32	10.16
Copenhagen Telephone SF 5³/₈'s, 1978	1963	102	81	87	86	7.66
Cuba Ext. 4¹/₂'s, 1977	Exch. '38	118	10	15	11	Default
Czechoslovakia Ext. Stpd. 6's 1960	1946	91	8	11	7	Default
Denmark Ext. 5¹/₂'s, 1974	1959	105	93	96	96	7.61
Imperial Oil (Canada) Deb. 3⁵/₈'s, 1975	1955	93	76	94	82	7.90
Int. Bk. for Recon. & Devel. 4¹/₂'s, 1977	1957	106	78	97	89	6.15
Italian Rep. Ext. 3's, 1977	1947	96	14	98	89	4.23
Jamaica Ext. 5³/₄'s, 1974	1959	107	76	94	87	8.86
Japan Ext. 5¹/₂'s, 1974	1959	103	88	100	97	6.31
Mexico Ext. 6³/₄'s, 1978	1963	105	81	97	88	8.59
Norway Ext. 5/¹/₄'s, 1978	1963	102	82	86	84	8.17
Panama 4.8's, 1993	1958	102	48	54	48	10.06

Source: Standard & Poor's *Bond Guide.*

[12]International Bank for Reconstruction and Development, *Annual Report,* June 30, 1972.

market for selected foreign government obligations and the low esteem in which many of such bonds have at times been held in this country. The table also reveals the revival in investment standing of issues previously regarded as well-nigh worthless.

Investment Position of Foreign Bonds

Some foreign government bonds enjoy a respectable rating, but even these show market price fluctuations that indicate the special risks attendant to these obligations. The work of the Foreign Bondholders Protective Council, the influence of the World Bank (which will not lend to countries that have been indifferent to their previous obligations), and the reviving economic conditions in some areas have all had a salutary effect on the foreign bond market. But until general world conditions improve, and until some foreign governments and companies see fit to take their external debt commitments more seriously and make the sacrifices that are necessary to redeem their credit in the United States, only those investors who recognize the risks and are in a position to sacrifice safety for a possible high yield should have any interest in the majority of foreign bonds.

REFERENCES

AMERICAN MANAGEMENT ASSOCIATION, International Management Division, *Sources and Methods of International Financing*. New York: The Association, 1961.

AVRAMOVIC, DRAGOSLAV, *Debt Servicing Capacity and Postwar Growth in International Indebtedness*. Baltimore: The Johns Hopkins Press, 1958.

FOREIGN BONDHOLDERS PROTECTIVE COUNCIL, INC., *Reports, triennial.*

GILBERT, R. A., *International Investment*. New York: Simmons-Boardman Publishing Corp., 1963.

KALISH, R. H., and W. F. O'CONNOR, *Guide to Federal Restrictions on Investment Abroad*. New York: Peat, Marwick, Mitchell & Co., 1968.

INSTITUTE OF INTERNATIONAL FINANCE, *Statistical Analysis of Public Offered Foreign Dollar Bonds*. New York: New York University Press, 1958.

KREFETZ, GERALD, and RUTH MAROSSI, *Investing Abroad: A Guide to Financial Europe*. New York: Harper & Row, Publishers, 1965.

MIKESELL, R. F., ed., *United States Private and Government Investment Abroad*. Eugene, Ore: University of Oregon Books, 1962.

MINTZ, ILSE, *Deterioration in the Quality of Foreign Bonds Issued in the United States 1920–1930*. New York: National Bureau of Economic Research, Inc, 1951.

STANDARD & POOR'S, *Foreign Securities Survey*. New York (monthly).

WHITMAN, MARINA, *Government Risk-Sharing in Foreign Investment*. Princeton, N.J.: Princeton University Press, 1965.

11 | Real Estate and Real Estate Obligations

SCOPE: This chapter discusses the investment aspects of real estate and real estate mortgages.

To most individual investors, the growing equity in a home is the most important single investment in their program. Others have found that real estate bought for income and appreciation has much appeal. Real estate mortgages appeal principally to institutions, although not exclusively so. The whole field of mortgage investment is heavily affected by regulation; nevertheless, the forces of supply and demand in the capital market affect this category of "securities," so that the investor must temper his policy to changing market conditions.

The place of real estate and mortgages in investment programming will be indicated in later sections; the material in this present chapter is largely descriptive. Nevertheless, some suggestions as to the merits and disadvantages of these categories of investments are given here. The order of discussion is: (1) size of the real estate and mortgage markets, (2) types of real estate investments, (3) the appeal of real estate investments, (4) real estate held for income, (5) indirect investment in real estate, (6) home ownership, (7) real estate mortgages—general characteristics, (8) volume of mortgage debt, (9) FHA-insured mortgages, (10) VA-insured loans, (11) conventional home mortgage loans, (12) second mortgages, (13) institutional sources of residential mortgage credit, (14) home mortgages as investments for individuals, (15) real estate (mortgage) trusts, (16) government agencies involved in home financing, (17) ownership of mortgage debt, (18) mortgage companies, (19) the secondary mortgage market, (20) mortgage yields.

Size of the Real Estate and Mortgage Markets

At the end of 1971, $500 billions of real estate mortgages were outstanding in the United States. In the capital markets this figure was exceeded only by the values of corporate stocks and of governmental obligations (see Chapter 2).

The value of real estate held for occupancy and for income (and appreciation) as contrasted with that held for operating purposes is difficult to estimate. As of 1968, the value of nonfarm residential land and structures was estimated at $1,100 billions.[1] Extension to 1971 would produce a figure of approximately $1,300 billions. Against this, about $375 billions of residential mortgages were outstanding, leaving a net worth of $925 billions. The value of farm structures and land was $200 billions in 1968,[2] an estimate for 1971 is approximately $235 billions. Offsetting this, $33 billions of farm mortgages were outstanding.

On the income side, of total national nonagricultural personal income of $800 billions in 1971, $23 billions represented rental income of persons. This was almost equal to dividends received ($25 billions) and over one-third of personal interest income ($65 billions).[3]

Types of Real Estate Investments

Investors who are interested in real estate and obligations secured by it may choose from a wide variety of types. For purposes of clarity, the different types are classified here; their investment aspects will be discussed throughout the following pages, with the exception of the last category, which was treated in Chapter 5.

I. Real estate, by purpose of ownership
   A. Current income
      1. Residential
      2. Farm
      3. Commercial and industrial
   B. Capital appreciation
   C. Occupancy
      1. Residential
      2. Business
II. Real estate mortgages
   A. By type of property pledged
      1. Farms
      2. One- to four-family residences
      3. Multifamily dwellings (apartments)
      4. Commercial and industrial property
   B. By level of lien
      1. First mortgages
      2. Junior mortgages (second, third)
   C. By type of lien
      1. Conventional
      2. Government-supported
         (a) FHA-insured
         (b) VA-guaranteed
   D. By use of property
      1. Owner-occupied: residential, commercial
      2. Rental: residential, commercial, industrial

[1]U.S. Department of Commerce, Bureau of the Census, *Statistical Abstract of the United States*, 1971, p. 328.
[2]*Ibid.*
[3]*Federal Reserve Bulletin.*

      E. By type of borrower
         1. Consumers
         2. Corporations
         3. Small businesses
         4. Farmers
      F. By purpose
         1. New construction
         2. Acquisition of existing property
         3. General financing
      G. By type of lender
         1. Financial institutions
         2. Governmental agencies
         3. Individuals
   III. Real estate securities
      A. Bonds
      B. Shares in real estate investment trusts that own loans and mortgages
      C. Shares representing ownership
         1. Shares in real estate trusts that own properties
         2. Shares in real estate companies
         3. Participation in real estate syndicates and partnerships
   IV. Bonds of Federal agencies that invest in mortgages

The Appeal of Real Estate Investments

Much of the appeal of real estate and obligations secured by it lies in its tangibility and permanence. The home, the income property, the farm, and the mortgage appear to have a stability of value and dependability that are in sharp contrast with the less measurable qualities of many corporate securities. The fact that one can see and inspect the property, or live in it, lends an air of certainty that is lacking in some other types of investments. Furthermore, credit secured by real estate has usually been relatively easy to obtain; institutions and many individuals have had a continuing interest in real estate mortgages. The returns from direct ownership are often higher than those obtainable from other equities, and the yield on obligations secured by real estate is more generous than on most other fixed-income securities. And the prospect always exists of substantial increases in value of owned property or property securing mortgage debt. Interest in home ownership, in real estate as a hedge against inflation, and in the relative safety and generous yields on real estate obligations have combined to interest a growing list of individuals and institutions in real estate investments.

On the debit side lies the need for careful and competent appraisal and reappraisal of real estate values—a problem that the general investor is unable to attack alone. The nature of the community, the character of the immediate neighborhood, the use to which the site is put, and the estimate of replacement value of improvements, costs, and net income are factors that are beyond the abilities of most laymen. Another disturbing element is the sharpness and length of the real estate cycle, bringing distress and often disaster when properties bought or mortgaged near the peak are sold at lower levels.

Other characteristics will be developed in subsequent pages. However, to generalize about all real estate and real estate obligations would be as dangerous as in the case of any other group of investments.

Real Estate Held Directly for Income

Problems. We cannot undertake here a complete analysis of all the problems associated with direct investment in real estate for income—a highly specialized and complex subject, whether the property be used for farm, residential, commercial, or industrial purposes. However, certain problems may be outlined, and certain general advantages noted.

THE PROBLEM OF APPRAISAL. The appraisal of property, both for loan purposes and for purchase, is a highly technical process. Yet as accurate a valuation as possible is fundamental to both owner and lender. Without attempting a detailed discussion, three general methods of appraisal may be indicated: (1) comparison with the established market values of similar properties, (2) capitalization of income, (3) calculation of replacement cost less depreciation. The first method has the advantage of simplicity, but lends itself to much inaccuracy. The second method is the going-concern approach; either the expected gross revenues can be capitalized (say, at 20 per cent), or better, the net income after all valid expenses can be capitalized at a much lower rate (5 to 10 per cent). This method produces only approximate results, as it rests on estimates of future revenues and of future costs. The third method is widely used, especially by institutional lenders on residential property. The total value of the property is the value of the land (separately determined) plus the depreciated replacement cost of the improvements. Special factors involved are the suitability and appropriateness of the building, the type of neighborhood, and the trends of community growth.

The immediate value of a property may be fairly accurately determined by tested methods of appraisal and valuation, but its long-range value is indefinite. Too many uncertainties exist that are associated with the property and with the real estate cycle.

ESTIMATING REVENUES, COSTS, AND NET INCOME. Whether income property is a good buy at a given price depends on the estimate of expected revenues and costs. The estimate of revenues involves a careful check on possible changes in the character of the neighborhood, prevailing rents for similar buildings, and a realistic allowance for vacancies. The estimate of costs should include adequate provision for taxes, special assessments, insurance, maintenance and other operating costs, interest on any borrowed money, and depreciation.[4] The net income, after income taxes, should produce a return on the owner's investment that will compensate for the risks of the

---

[4]In the case of an apartment building, other operating costs would include electricity, water, heating, decorating, janitor's salary and living quarters, and possibly building management. If the apartment is furnished, additional costs are involved.

situation. And since the annual depreciation allowance (at, say, 2 to 3 per cent of the improvements) is less than principal payments on most mortgages, for some time at least the total cash outlay is likely to be higher than cash income. The owner must be prepared to devote part of his profit to the retirement of the debt. Thus, if debt of 50 per cent of the value of the property has been incurred, on a twenty-year basis, the annual principal payments would equal a 5 per cent return on the owner's equity. Funds representing depreciation would cover part of the payments.

TITLE INSURANCE. Clear title to property bought for investment (or used as security for a mortgage loan) is of the utmost importance. Title insurance should be obtained from a title insurance company guaranteeing to indemnify the owner (or lender) up to the cost of the property in the event of a loss arising from a defect in the title. The cost of the policy is based upon the value of the property and the risk involved in the condition of the title. In communities where title insurance is not obtainable, verification of title and opinion as to its validity should be obtained from a competent attorney or title specialist. Where the state law provides for a registration certificate to be issued by the registrar of the county in which the property is located, opinion and interpretation of the certificate should also be obtained from a competent attorney.

THE PROBLEM OF LARGE DENOMINATION. The ownership of property involves a concentration of risk for all investors except those of very substantial means. The "denomination" is large and the rate of return should be much more substantial than the income from an equivalent sum invested in diversified securities. Shares in real estate trusts that own income property, and shares in real estate companies or in partnerships and syndicates, enable the investment in property with possibly a small outlay and thus defeat the defect of large denominations. These indirect methods of investment are discussed below.

TAX RISKS. General property taxes are a fixed expense that must be met if control of the property is to be maintained. The possibilities of burdensome general property tax rates and special assessments, together with variations in income taxes, present an unusual problem to the owner of income-producing real estate. However, large cash flows representing mainly the noncash expense of depreciation may prove a tax boon, especially in the early life of the property.

SPECIAL GOVERNMENT POLICIES. Special government policies for the protection of tenants, such as the rent controls of World War II and immediate postwar years, interfere with the free rental market and may upset the normal balance between income and costs. While such controls are not permanent, they are likely to be imposed in some degree when an emergency shortage of housing cannot be met by unrestricted building, or when really drastic measures are undertaken to control inflation. In the present state of the world such possibilities are always present.

RELATIVELY POOR MARKETABILITY. The marketability of real estate varies with the activity of the real estate market as a whole, with the business cycle, and with the demand for the particular property offered for sale. Land and improvements thereon represent "sunk capital," and the appeal to a prospective buyer rests on the prospects for income or appreciation of the specific site. Real estate *per se* generally lacks good marketability as compared with securities, although in fairness we should state that the marketability varies with the type of property, location, and future prospects. However, shares representing equity in real estate may be readily transferred.

THE NEED FOR SPECIAL MANAGERIAL SKILL. All of these special problems associated with the direct ownership of income property require special managerial skill. The owner must be prepared to follow rentals and changes in property values, and to cope with the problems of collection, repairs and maintenance, taxes, insurance, and general operation. Such problems may be delegated to outside management, but at a fee. Real estate trusts and companies have the advantage of relieving the shareholder of direct involvement in management.

Advantages. Offsetting the peculiar problems associated with investment in real estate for income are certain advantages that may make it very attractive. The supply of real estate is relatively fixed, and the possible growth in its value over a period of years is very substantial. During periods of inflation, real estate offers a hedge against the depreciating value of the dollar, provided it is well selected and that the carrying costs are not exorbitant. Under ideal conditions, the yield from sound income property is very attractive. And while not high, the loan value of desirable real estate is ordinarily good. Using leverage may magnify profits and permit a steady build-up of equity as the debt is amortized.

Improved real estate offers certain income tax advantages that give it a special appeal to many investors. The chief of these is the ability to charge depreciation of the improvements at the accelerated rates that are available to business in general. (See Chapter 26.) Assuming the income covers all expenses including depreciation, rapid amortization of the investment in buildings and equipment, together with any profit, provides a large "spendable cash flow" that can be used to reduce debt and/or to provide funds for acquiring an equity in additional properties. Under some conditions the cash flow will contain no taxable income at all. There may even be a large cash flow and a tax loss if depreciable assets are extensive. In the event of sale of the property, the owner will, of course, pay a capital gains tax, based on the difference between depreciated cost and market value. Rates applying to long-term capital gains are, however, much lower than rates on ordinary income.

In summary, we may say that for those willing and able to undertake the risks and special problems attendant to the ownership of real property, real estate for income has much attraction. Aside from the investment in his home, however, the average investor is advised to utilize other media for the placement of funds that may appropriately be devoted to equities, at least insofar as investment for income is concerned, or rely on shares of companies and trusts.

Investment in Real Estate Shares

The large denominations, faulty marketability, and specialized nature of real estate make direct outright investment in income property undesirable for many individual investors. Three devices for sharing ownership in small units have been developed: (1) real estate corporations, (2) real estate equity trusts, and (3) partnerships or shares in syndicates. The first are business concerns engaged in either land development or in the leasing or operation of commercial properties, including office buildings, retail buildings, and standardized warehouse and industrial facilities. Their shares, like those of any company, differ in quality and appeal. Investors should understand the specialized nature of the business and the special risks that attend the operation and management of real property. Shares of some of the larger companies are listed on the organized exchanges and enjoy adequate marketability.

Land development companies offer speculative participation in land and in residential communities and recreational projects. Profits depend not only on the cost of the original land and the sales of ultimate parcels, but also on the terms under which land parcels are sold, improvements made, and receivables or contracts collected. Most investors should consider only the largest and most successful concerns, and understand fully whether their returns will be derived from income or from eventual capital gains, that is, from the operation or from the sale of properties. They should have some knowledge of real estate accounting and taxation.

A number of lumber, paper, railroad, and diversified companies own large acreages which offer possibilities of ultimately sharing in the secular rise in land values. In such cases the investor is not wholly dependent on land development.

In very recent years investors have been offered participation in (limited) real estate partnerships and in syndicates, on a unit basis. Formerly these opportunities had been limited to closed groups. In some cases a minimum investment of $5,000 or $10,000 is required. Units are usually offered only to state residents who meet stated net worth requirements. As limited partnerships, investors can have no voice in management. The property may consist of one development, say, a large office or apartment building, or a variety of projects.

The advantages of real estate ownership without management responsibility can be very real. However, the wise investor will check the reputation, financial standing, and experience of the general partner(s) with special care. He must also be careful not to be misled by promises of very high projected "rates of return," which may consist of a number of elements, perhaps overlapping, and which are dominated by depreciation payout and eventual capital appreciation. Such rates of return are not comparable to the earnings yields on other forms of investments.

In recent years the real estate investment trust ("REIT") has attained great prominence. Shares of beneficial interest are available in well over 125 publicly owned trusts, with assets aggregating close to $5 billions. These trusts are like mutual funds in that to avoid income taxation they must distribute at least 90 per cent of net income from properties or mortgages owned. Officers and shareholders must not engage directly in the management of the property, which is contracted out to professionals. The trust must have 100 or more shareholders, may not deal (trade) in real estate, and may not be owned more than 50 per cent by 5 or fewer individuals. Shares in a number of the larger trusts are listed on the organized securities exchanges. Yields are generous—6½ to 9½ per cent. Trusts that own property (equity trusts) are in the minority. Those that invest in mortgages are discussed below.

Home Ownership

The most important investment made by most families is in a home. Four primary factors should be considered when the investor takes this important step: (1) determination of the real costs of ownership, (2) forecasting the costs of operating the property, (3) selection of the location of the home, and (4) selection of the property.

Real costs of ownership. The homeowner enjoys the use of his property at actual cost, a cost which remains fairly stable through the years. But what is this actual cost? How much should be invested in a home in relation to the owner's income? Is it cheaper to own than to rent? Such questions can be answered only by analysis of each situation, but certain generalizations may be advanced and illustrated.

Assume that a single-family dwelling is bought for $40,000, of which $8,000 represents the value of the land. Assume that a 60 per cent conventional mortgage ($24,000) is used in the purchase, bearing interest at 7 per cent and amortized over a period of twenty years. The outstanding debt will be reduced to zero in the last year, and the owner's equity will increase from $16,000 to $40,000, or an average of $28,000. The real investment cost of housing will be approximately as follows:

Interest on mortgage (average)	$ 840
Property taxes (2%)	800
Repairs and maintenance (1½%)	600
Insurance (½%)	200
Depreciation (2½% of $32,000)	800
Return on average equity (6%)	1,680
Total annual cost	$4,920
Per month	$ 410

If the owner assumes that he could earn, without risk, 6 per cent on his average investment or equity, the total housing costs would be in the neighborhood of $4,920 annually, or $410 monthly. If comparable premises could be rented for less than this amount, ownership of the property would have to be justified on sociological and psychological grounds, or by the expectation that the property would increase in market value through the years.

Two relationships can be developed from the foregoing approach: (1) the actual annual cost of housing is roughly 12 per cent of the value of the property, and (2) cost of housing probably consumes an appropriate share of the family income. In the hypothetical illustration, the $410 per month represents 26 per cent of a family income totalling $16,000 after income taxes, and the cost of the house is 2½ times this income.

The above schedule does not represent the actual *cash* or budget outlay, as it includes two "noncash" expenses, depreciation and return on the owner's investment, and excludes payments on principal. On a cash-outlay basis, the out-of-pocket costs for the prospective owner would be

Interest on mortgage ⎱	$2,230
Principal payment on mortgage ⎰	
Property taxes (2%)	800
Maintenance (1½%)	600
Insurance (½%)	200
Total annual cost	$3,830
Per month	$ 320

Payments to amortize the mortgage principal are included, but the depreciation and return on equity are omitted, in order to illustrate what the prospective buyer will have to pay out of earnings each month. The monthly cash payment of $320 is the figure that most home lenders would compare with the borrower's salary.

The costs of housing, on either the investment or the cash basis, may differ considerably from the above example if depreciation is exaggerated by a greater loss at the time of sale or if it is offset by market appreciation, or if any item in the schedule costs more or less than in the illustrative situation. Some items that may increase are taxes, insurance, and maintenance. Depending on market conditions at the time of purchase and of possible later sale, home ownership may turn out to be a bargain. In any event, it provides an incentive to save, offers the possibility of some hedge against inflation, and effects a saving in income taxes, because any interest paid, together with general property taxes, may be deducted from taxable income. Under current levels of income tax, the savings in Federal taxes by deduction of interest and taxes on a $40,000 home may be as much as $350 to $450 per year. Such advantages may, however, be offset by the fixed character of the housing cost and the risk of loss of capital.

Costs of operating the property. After the initial costs of ownership have been calculated, the prospective homeowner must calculate the additional fixed overhead that will be incurred, such as

1. Additional taxes—for example, sewer assessments (usually in a new area), personal property levies (in addition to the real property taxes considered above), local sales taxes, and the trend of property taxes in the area.

2. Changes in physical aspects—that is, if the house will need changes or improvements before the owner is satisfied, the outlay for these must be included in the overall cost picture. Examples are a new bathroom, new plumbing, repair and sealing of basement, and new landscaping.

3. Utilities—the cost of heat, light, telephone, and water.

4. Transportation—the cost to get to work, whether the location of the home makes an automobile essential.

We should note that in comparing the costs of living in a rented house and in one's own home, the latter factors (utilities and transportation) would be borne in either case. In comparing the costs of living in a rented apartment and those of living in one's own home, the total monthly cost of ownership *and* occupancy should be compared with the rental rates.

Selection of location. After determining how much the property will cost and what the operating outlay will be, many factors of an environmental nature must be considered. These items will have a very strong influence on the present and future value of the home, not only to the outside prospective buyer if the owner wishes to sell, but to him and his family.

A study of the community should be made in order to determine the social and living standards of the residents, the convenience of transportation to work, to school, to church, and to shopping centers, the zoning requirements generally applicable to the area, and the general growth trend of the area.

Each of these factors must, in turn, be considered in relation to the immediate neighborhood in which the prospective property is located. Adequately paved and lighted streets, utilities, police and fire protection, and absence of serious nuisances in the neighborhood are also important.

Selection of the property. Assuming that the prospective home meets the requirements of financing and location, what are the final determinants of the property itself? Does the size of the lot fit the zoning requirements and does it have room for an addition to the house if one is needed? Are the soil and drainage proper, is the lot well landscaped, fenced and walled, and so forth? Is the design of the house itself suitable to the needs of the owner and his family? Is it too big or too small, does it have an adequate garage, and adequate storage space? Will it provide for the needs of a growing family? Will it soon become obsolete in style and materials?

All of these factors should be considered in advance before a decision to invest in a home is made.

Real Estate Mortgages—General Characteristics

Money directly invested in real estate is represented by *deeds,* or instruments that evidence the ownership of real property and by which title is transferred. Money indirectly invested is represented by *mortgages* or other evidences of debt such as real estate bonds. Without going into legal technicalities, a mortgage (or "deed of trust") may be defined as an instrument under which real property is pledged as security for a loan. The owner of the property, the mortgagor, is borrowing money from a lender, the mortgagee, under a contract whereby the property is pledged as security for payment of interest and principal. Title and possession remain with the mortgagor until default occurs, in which event the property is sold through foreclosure proceedings for the satisfaction of the debt.

The mortgage recites the terms of the loan and a description of the property pledged. Covenants are customarily inserted under which the mortgagor promises to pay taxes and assessments and to keep the property fully insured and in good condition. An "acceleration of maturity" clause makes the principal of the loan due immediately in the event of default in payment of interest or any failure with respect to the covenants. Mortgages are customarily recorded in the public records of the community to protect mortgagees against any claims of third parties against the property.

A *first mortgage* has a prior claim upon the pledged property, subject to operating expenses and taxes. First mortgages on properties in the course of construction are also subject to liens for unpaid materials and services. Subsequent mortgages have subordinate claims to the first mortgage claim.

A *second mortgage* is one that has a claim upon the pledged property after that of the first mortgage. As first mortgages are usually placed for the largest amount which conservative investors are willing to lend on the property, the position of the second mortgage (discussed below) is often too hazardous for safe investment.

An *amortized mortgage* is one that is repayable in regular installments for the duration of the loan; monthly payments include principal, interest, and usually taxes and insurance.

A *leasehold mortgage* is secured by a long-term lease of real property and, therefore, is subordinate to the rental contract between the leasor and the owner. Such a mortgage is often placed upon property erected on leased land and, consequently, is in effect a first mortgage on the building and on the lease of the land. Even under this interpretation, the instrument has a junior claim upon the earnings of the property subject to the ground rent.

Most modern mortgages are of the amortized type. Early impetus to this type came from its adoption by the Home Owners' Loan Corporation, by savings and loan associations, and from past experiences with the shortcomings of nonamortized loans in the depression of the 1930s. Further impetus was derived from the insurance of amortized home mortgages by the Federal Housing Administration, changes in legislation governing institutional investments, and the home mortgage guarantee provisions of the Servicemen's Readjustment Act of 1944. Under the amortized loan the borrower agrees to make regular payments on principal as well as interest, and his equity in the property grows steadily as payments are made. The amount of the regular payment depends on the size of the loan, the interest rate, and the term of the loan. To repay $20,000 at 7 per cent in fifteen years requires monthly payments of $179.89. A thirty-year maturity at the same interest rate requires $133.20. These figures are, of course, exclusive of taxes and insurance. Because of the long-term character of real estate credit, the value of the property pledged is stressed more than the personal credit of the borrower, although this is by no means neglected. The income of the borrower is, however, of paramount importance under the GI bill. The tendency toward high loans in relation to value (as high as 90 per cent) and long maturities (up to thirty-five or even forty years) has forced special attention on the property and on accurate appraisal of its value.

Volume of Mortgage Debt

Table 11-1 shows the total mortgage debt outstanding at the end of selected years 1950–1971, classified by major types of borrowers and by type of lien. The postwar growth reflects a number of factors: general economic expansion, volume of construction, flow of available funds, rising costs, and propensity to borrow.

At the end of 1971, the volume of outstanding mortgage loans secured by one- to four-family nonfarm homes was $308 billions. The 1945 figure was $19 billions. The enormous rise in this type of debt since the end of World War II is attributable to the great development of housing that was financed substantially by savings institutions of all kinds on an amortized basis. Consumer incomes, population, prices, and construction costs all rose during the postwar period. Funds flowing into mortgages likewise have risen steadily, save for the years 1956–1957, 1966–1967, and 1969–1970, periods of "tight money." The result has been a tremendous increase in home mortgage financing. The average annual increase in one- to four-family mortgage debt was $9.5 billions in 1950–1960, and $15 billions in 1961–1971. The figures for multifamily and commercial mortgage debt were $3

Table 11-1. MORTGAGE DEBT OUTSTANDING AT YEAR-END, 1950–1971

(in billions of dollars)

	1950	1955	1960	1965	1971
Farm	$ 6.1	$ 9.1	$ 12.8	$ 21.2	$ 32.9
Residential					
One- to four-family	45.2	88.2	141.3	212.9	307.8
Multifamily	10.0	14.3	20.3	37.2	66.9
	$55.2	$102.5	$161.6	$250.1	$374.7
Commercial and industrial	11.6	18.3	32.4	54.5	92.3
	$72.8	$129.9	$206.8	$325.8	499.9
Conventional	$50.7	$ 87.0	$144.5	$244.6	$379.2
FHA-insured	11.8	18.3	32.6	50.1	81.2
VA-guaranteed	10.3	24.6	29.7	31.1	39.5
	$72.8	$129.9	$206.8	$325.8	$499.9

SOURCES: 1950–1955: S. B. Klaman, *The Volume of Mortgage Debt in the Postwar Decade* (New York: National Bureau of Economic Research, Inc., 1958); 1960–1971: *Federal Reserve Bulletin; Annual Reports*, Housing and Home Finance Agency and Federal Home Loan Bank Board.

billions and $10 billions, respectively, for these two periods. The latter types now constitute about 32 per cent of total mortgages outstanding. Institutional lenders provided the bulk of this financing, and the balance was lent by individuals and others (trust funds, endowments, and mortgage companies); much of this latter volume later found its way into the hands of insurance companies, banks, and savings and loan associations. The importance of institutional lending is indicated by the data on ownership of mortgage debt in Tables 11-2 and 11-3.

Individuals originate a substantial proportion of the home mortgage debt. The practice of individual mortgage lending occurs largely in smaller communities, many of which lack immediate institutional facilities. However, a substantial portion of mortgages *originated* by individuals has later found its way into institutional portfolios. And virtually all loans originated by mortgage companies are transferred to institutional lenders (see Table 11-2).

The three basic types of home mortgage loans are (1) those insured by the Federal Housing Administration, (2) those guaranteed by the Veterans' Administration, and (3) conventional loans. Of the $308 billions of mortgage loans on one- to four-family homes outstanding at the end of 1971, $203 billions or 66 per cent were conventional type, $66 billions or 21 per cent were FHA loans, and $40 billions or 13 per cent were VA loans.

Table 11-1 shows how the relative importance of these three types has changed through the years. Although the bulk of FHA and VA loans are mortgages on one- to four-family homes, loans are also made for purposes such as projects and property improvement.

FHA-Insured Mortgages

FHA loans are insured under the terms of Title II of the National Housing Act of 1934 as amended. Only first mortgage amortized loans on approved properties are insurable. In early 1973 the maximum interest rate on mortgages secured by small family units was 7 per cent, with the mortgagor paying an additional $\frac{1}{2}$ per cent to the FHA mutual insurance fund as an insurance premium. On such mortgages, of which there are several classes, the maximum maturities ranged as high as thirty-five years with maximum loan-value ratios of 97 per cent of the first $15,000 of value. Other interest rates, maturities, and loan-value ratios are found in the case of multifamily units. Monthly payments to the lender to cover taxes and insurance charges are added to the regular installments of interest and principal. Equities in the properties, subject to the loans, are transferable.

The original fixed interest rate on FHA loans was $4\frac{1}{4}$ per cent. Successive changes, up and down, have followed variations in general long-term interest rates. FHA's have sold higher (at premiums) but usually lower (at discounts) from face value and so at lower and usually higher yields than the contractual rate. Changes in the nominal rate (presently made by the Department of Housing and Urban Development) have usually been made to encourage home financing. The nominal rate rose to a peak of 8 ½ per cent in early 1970 near the peak of the "credit crunch," then declined to 7 per cent by February 1971, after general interest rates had declined. At that time FHA's sold at discounts so as to yield about 7.7 per cent (not including the ½ per cent insurance charge). The main market is still largely institutional, although individuals have been permitted to buy these loans since 1961. An impetus to indirect ownership by individuals was given by the creation of Government National Mortgage Association mortgage-backed securities in 1970 (see p.72).

The influence of FHA insurance in the mortgage field has been reflected in sounder and more thorough appraisals and in greater standardization, and has, along with other factors mentioned previously, led to the virtual disappearance of the old straight five-year loan in favor of the amortized type and to loans of higher percentages of appraised values. The most recent change in the program concerns its administration. Under the Housing and Urban Development Act of 1966, the Assistant Secretary of the new Federal Department of Housing and Urban Development serves as Federal Housing Commissioner and directs the FHA mortgage insurance programs.

VA-Guaranteed Loans

The Serivceman's Readjustment Act of 1944, as amended, provides for the guarantee by the Veterans Administration of loans made to qualified veterans by lending institutions for the purposes of home, farm, or business financing. The maximum maturity of these loans is set by the amended law at thirty years for guaranteed home or business real estate loans and forty years for farm real estate loans, and the nominal interest rate is (1972) set at 7 per cent.

The law provides a maximum guarantee of $12,500 or 60 per cent of the loan, whichever is less, and lenders may make loans for 100 per cent of the purchase price of the property. Borrowers must, however, pay closing costs in cash since these may not be included in the price.

The interest rate of 7 per cent represents a substantial increase over the original 4 per cent rate. Like the nominal rate on FHA-insured mortgages, that of VA loans has been adjusted through the years to changes in long-term interest rates so as to make them competitive. It was as high as 8½ per cent in early 1970. VA loans have not been attractive to individual investors, and many institutional investors have preferred the FHA type. (See Chapter 4.)

Some of the recommendations of the President's Commission on Financial Structure and Regulation (Hunt Commission) field in December 1971 bear specifically on the provisions of and market for FHA and VA mortgages, which if enacted, should make these liens much more attractive to investors. In addition to the broadening of the lending powers of institutions (see p. 59), the major items are

1. Elimination of ceiling interest rates on Federally sponsored mortgages—

a change that has long been recommended by institutions and mortgage bankers.

2. Interest rates on these mortgages to vary with the price level, with limits on the degree of change within stated periods. Variable interest rates have been recommended by investors after being caught during periods of price and yield changes. Variable interest rates present many problems, especially the uncertain position of creditors with respect to income.

3. Other provisions for strengthening the mortgage credit system include authority of institutions to lend in any part of the country, and to make equity investments in real estate developments.

Conventional Home Mortgage Loans

The noninsured and nonguaranteed amortized loan has consistently been more important than the two other types. While generalization is difficult, we can probably be correct in saying that their maturities have seldom exceeded twenty years, with the most typical term being twelve to fifteen years, depending on the property and the borrower's credit standing. Interest rates now (1973) range between 7½ and 8 per cent, depending on the property, the credit of the borrower, the geographical location, and competitive conditions. The loan-market value ratio has run as high as 80 per cent during periods of noninflated real estate prices, but has tended to be lower—from 60 to 70 per cent—during periods when market values were greatly in excess of appraised values. The various lending institutions have different policies in respect to maturities and loan ratios, and, of course, the terms of a specific loan are determined by the circumstances of the case and the legal restrictions imposed by the laws under which the institution operates.

Originations of new conventional loans have risen steadily through the years. Like other types, they dropped off temporarily in 1966 and 1969–1970 with the decline in housing starts and the tight market for mortgage money.

Second Mortgages

Second mortgages were a feature of the 1920s and 1930s, but fell into disrepute as a result of the losses that foreclosures brought to their holders in the Great Depression. After World War II the demand for second mortgage money again began to show itself on the real estate scene. Young families and small businessmen lacked the substantial down payments required behind conventional first mortgage loans. In 1956–1957 the tightened provisions and shrunken volume of first mortgages gave another impetus to junior financing. As of 1960, $3.8 billions of junior mortgages were outstanding, representing 2.4 per cent of residential debt.[5] This figure was

---

[5]U.S. Department of Commerce, Bureau of the Census, *Census of Housing* (Washington, D.C.: U.S. Government Printing Office, 1960), Volume V, "Residential Finance," Part 2, page *xxiii*.

probably well in excess of $7 billions in 1972. Owners include mortgage companies, individual investors, and sellers of homes. (Institutions such as banks, insurance companies, and savings and loan associations are not permitted to hold them.) Net yields of 10 to 15 per cent (resulting from the discounting of the paper) are not uncommon. Fortunately, the modern second mortgage calls for rapid amortization of principal over a short period, often as low as five years. Thus, as the loan is retired (along with reduction of the first mortgage), second mortgages grow in strength in relation to the value of the property. Nevertheless, the owner of a second mortgage, such as a seller who has had to take a junior mortgage in order to make a sale, is always in a vulnerable position. And if he wants cash, he must sell the junior lien at a very substantial discount that may run 8 to 15 per cent. Although rising property values, rapid repayment of junior liens, and higher personal incomes may prevent another major wave of defaults of second mortgages, the investor intrigued by the high yields should understand the nature of the junior lien and all of the factors that can make for its individual strength or weakness.

Institutional Sources of Residential Mortgage Credit

As indicated previously, mortgage loans on residential property are largely institutional, although the holdings of individuals are substantial. Table 11-2 shows the distribution, by type of mortgages, of *outstanding* mortgage loans on one- to four-family nonfarm homes, as of the end of 1950, 1960, and 1971.

The savings and loan associations hold the largest amount of urban home mortgages (46 per cent at the end of 1971), and their lead has been steadily increasing. As indicated in Chapter 4, home mortgage financing is their chief function. Their investment policies and legal restrictions on lending will be discussed in Chapter 22. We should note here that the bulk of the home mortgages held by these associations are conventional liens. There are several reasons for this: (1) The rates of interest on conventional loans are more attractive than those available on FHA and VA loans; (2) being

Table 11-2. OWNERSHIP OF NONFARM HOME MORTGAGE DEBT — ONE- TO FOUR-FAMILY

(dollars in billions)

Held by	1950 Amount	1950 Per Cent	1960 Amount	1960 Per Cent	1971 Amount	1971 Per Cent
S&L associations	$13.1	29.0%	$ 55.4	39.2%	$142.9	46.4%
Individuals and others	8.3	18.4	16.3	11.5	32.8	10.7
Life insurance cos.	8.5	18.8	24.9	17.6	24.6	8.0
Commercial banks	9.5	21.0	19.2	13.6	48.0	15.6
Mutual savings banks	4.3	9.5	18.4	13.0	38.6	12.5
F.N.M.A. and other agencies	1.5	3.3	7.1	5.1	20.9	6.8
Total	$45.2	100.0%	$141.3	100.0%	$307.8	100.0%

SOURCES: United States Savings and Loan League, *Savings and Loan Fact Book*; Federal Home Loan Bank Board.

local institutions in touch with their own borrowers, the associations feel safe in relying on their own portfolio rather than on insurance or a guarantee; (3) they are permitted to lend a higher percentage of value on a conventional loan than other financial institutions are, and hence, they find these relatively more attractive.

Commercial bank investments and the restrictions thereon will be discussed in Chapter 22. Although the volume of home mortgage lending by these institutions is very substantial, banks also make other types of real estate loans, such as those secured by commercial and industrial properties. However, FHA and VA loans were emphasized; by 1955 such loans comprised 50 per cent of the home mortgage holdings of commercial banks. At that time commercial banks were generally limited by law to a loan ratio of 60 to 66⅔ per cent and to a maturity of ten years on conventional home loans; hence, the higher loan ratios and longer maturities of the nonconventional loans had great appeal. The insurance or guarantee features were particularly attractive to a banking institution. However, the relative appeal of nonconventional mortgages has fluctuated with changes in market yields on other investments and with changes in bank regulations. The current yields on Federally underwritten mortgages are still (1972) not competitively attractive. Also, banks may now lend to 80 per cent of appraised value on conventionals, with a limit of maturity to twenty years. At the end of 1971, only $11.3 billions of the mortgages held by banks were FHA and VA loans.

Life insurance companies have traditionally been large investors in urban mortgages, which bear higher yields than bonds and are appropriate for the investment of insurance reserves. This interest has been encouraged by the "legalizing" of approved real estate mortgages in all states. Mortgages comprise nearly 34 per cent of the assets of the life insurance industry (down from 40 per cent in the early 1960s), amounting to $75.6 billions at the end of 1971—an all-time high. Housing, including single- and multiple-family units, accounts for nearly 55 per cent of all mortgages owned. In the residential field, the life insurance companies have been particularly interested in FHA and VA loans. These permit higher loan ratios than even the conventional 75 to 80 per cent legal limit in some states and are particularly adaptable to the use of the mortgage correspondent system. However, their fixed contractual interest rates are not always attractive compared with high-grade corporate bonds and conventional mortgages. At the end of 1971, of the $76 billions of mortgages held, only $16 billions or 22 per cent consisted of Federally underwritten liens.

Although life companies make mortgage loans directly through their branch offices, the bulk are originated and serviced by their mortgage correspondents—local mortgage banking companies which arrange the original transaction and then place the loan with the insurance company, thereafter collecting a service fee as agent of the company.

Sound home mortgages are almost ideal investments for mutual savings banks. At the end of 1971, such liens (including multifamily), totalling $53 billions, comprised about 60 per cent of their combined assets. The great postwar demand for housing credit, the development of Federally underwritten liens, the liberalization of regulations (which permit a loan-value ratio as high as 75 to 80 per cent on conventionals) and the increase in out-of-state lending through mortgage correspondents have all contributed to the banks' emphasis on residential loans. Mutual savings banks are the largest single source of FHA and VA financing; they held $28 billions of such loans, or 23 per cent of the total outstanding, at the end of 1971.

Home Mortgages As Investments for Individuals

Other owners of home mortgages include Federal agencies (described later in this chapter and in Chapter 5), individuals, and, to a modest extent, trustees, corporate pension funds, and state and local government retirement funds. Such owners are steadily increasing the dollar amount of mortgages held, but their relative importance has declined substantially in the postwar period.

The disadvantages of home mortgages as investments for individuals may be summarized as follows:

1. *Large denomination.* Individual mortgages represent substantial sums that make diversification impossible except for the institution or the investor of considerable means.

2. *Inadequate marketability.* The individual investor does not have access to the Federal National Mortgage Association, which buys only FHA-insured or VA-guaranteed mortgages. The investor is dependent on institutional buyers and local mortgage brokers and mortgage companies. If he wishes to sell a mortgage, he usually does so on a negotiated basis. In recent years "mortgage exchanges" have been established in a few large cities, where mortgages are "traded" at prices reflecting the terms and risk of individual loans. However, the volume of such trading is relatively small, and consists largely of second liens. The secondary market for mortgages is discussed further later in the chapter.

3. *Reinvestment.* The amortized mortgage now almost universally used requires much record-keeping and the reinvestment of the small regular payments on principal.

4. *Unusual care and management.* Investment in mortgages is a specialized business requiring a knowledge of land values, community and neighborhood changes, and construction standards. Numerous problems, such as checking the title, currency of tax payments, insurance, proper maintenance and repairs, are involved.

5. *Foreclosure process.* Although the mortgagor is permitted to buy in the pledged property at the foreclosure sale, in case of default, the foreclosure process involves considerable time and expense. In addition, many states provide for a period after foreclosure, in some cases as long as eighteen months, during which the mortgagor may redeem his pledge.

These disadvantages suggest why institutions equipped with staff, technical knowledge, and large funds, have traditionally dominated the mortgage field.[6] However, certain very real advantages may be enjoyed:

1. *Yield.* The yield on sound mortgages is at times considerably in excess of that available on high-grade and even good-grade bonds. (See Chapter 7.) And where less-sound and second mortgages are bought at substantial discounts, there is the possibility of substantial appreciation as the debt is reduced or as the value of the security increases.

2. *Safety.* Where the margin of safety is adequate, the long-term amortized mortgage offers real safety features to the lender. The growing equity of the homeowner provides a strong incentive against default. And the longer term and amortized payments prevent the whole debt from falling due at the wrong time for the borrower and during periods of depressed real estate values.

3. *Secured Value.* The property securing sound residential mortgages offers the stability, durability, and ready identification that characterize investment in real estate itself.

Real Estate Investment (Mortgage) Trusts. The basic nature of REITs was indicated earlier in this chapter, where those investing in real estate were described. Most trusts, however, invest in debt instruments. Some specialize in construction and development loans of three to twenty-four months in maturity, others in long-term first mortgages. Trusts use leverage to a substantial extent, some borrowing as much as two times their net worth through bank loans and the sale of debentures. Profits are derived from the spread between the rates of interest received (as high as 10 to 14 per cent on construction loans and 8 to 10 per cent on mortgages) and the cost of capital. High spreads make possible high earnings and, because earnings must be distributed, high dividends. Dividend yields run between $6\frac{1}{2}$ and 10 per cent.

Shares in REITs of the mortgage type are very attractive to investors interested in current income. A large number of trusts have appeared in recent years. The investor should confine his purchases to established firms that have demonstrated good management. Playing the spread between borrowing and lending, in a world of shifting interest rates, requires experience and good judgment.

About 20 per cent of mortgage trust assets are owned by trusts sponsored by banks or bank-holding companies. Mortgage banking firms and insurance companies are other important affiliates of such trusts.

Government Agencies Involved in Home Financing

Through various agencies and policies, the Federal government is heavily involved in home financing, chiefly in an effort to relieve distress, to make

---

[6]These disadvantages have been substantially reduced to large investors by the availability of mortgage-backed securities issued under the guarantee of the Government National Mortgage Association, a Federal agency described later in this chapter and in Chapter 5. But the minimum denomination of $25,000 makes these securities unattractive to the small investor.

ample mortgage credit available, to lower interest rates, and to standardize mortgage procedures. Mention has already been made in this chapter of the Federal Housing Administration and the Veterans Administration. Other Federal agencies include the Federal Home Loan Bank System and the Federal National Mortgage Association.

The Federal Home Loan Bank System (described in Chapter 4) functions through eleven regional banks and is supervised by the Home Loan Bank Board. Its purpose is to provide rediscounting facilities to savings and loan members.

The Federal National Mortgage Association was established in 1938 to provide a secondary market for institutional holders of FHA-insured and VA-guaranteed mortgages. The chairman of its Board is the Secretary of Housing and Urban Development. "Fannie Mae" obtained the initial funds for mortgage purchases by borrowing from the U.S. Treasury.

As indicated in Chapter 5, the Federal National Mortgage Association is now publicly owned, with its shares traded on the New York Stock Exchange. Its major activity is providing a secondary market for FHA and VA mortgages. It does not originate mortgages, and those it acquires are serviced by the originators—banks, mortgage companies, and other institutions—at an annual servicing fee of $\frac{3}{8}$ per cent. It acquires its assets by offering forward commitments of announced amounts to purchase eligible mortgages, with the prices (and yields) determined by auction bidding. Net annual purchases have been large in recent years, exceeding $5 billions in 1970 and $3 billions in 1971 and 1972. At the end of 1972, the Association held $19.8 billions of Federally supported mortgages, or about 15 per cent of the total outstanding. This made it the world's largest mortgage bank, and about sixth in asset size among American corporations.

Under the Emergency Home Finance Act of 1970, Fannie Mae was authorized to serve as a secondary market for conventional residential mortgages, with prices and yields established at periodic auction. The first four-month commitments were made in February 1972, with an average yield of 7.7 per cent.

An additional new secondary market for conventional mortgages is provided by the new Federal Home Loan Mortgage Corporation ("Freddie Mac"). This agency will acquire multifamily as well as one- to four-family loans, and will make commitments for up to two years on the former. A controversial feature is that at the outset, "Freddie Mac" subjects commercial banks to a $\frac{1}{2}$ per cent discount below prices paid to savings and loan associations. This because the latter have invested over $100 millions in the new agency. It has not yet (1973) developed a portfolio of any significance.

As noted in Chapter 5, the Government National Mortgage Association ("Ginny Mae") was created in 1968 to take over Fannie Mae's special assistance and management and liquidation functions.[7] Its new activity is to guarantee the timely payment of principal and interest on securities backed by pools of FHA and VA mortgages. The originators of these mortgages—mainly mortgage companies—who issue the securities must meet

[7]The Special Assistance Program involves the purchase of or participation in mortgages where established home-financing facilities are inadequate. The management and liquidating function has to do with Federally owned mortgage portfolios. Ginny Mae held over $5 billions of mortgages at the end of 1972.

certain minimum net worth requirements. Three types of securities may be issued against the pooled loans: (1) bond-type securities with fixed interest and maturities, but without interim amortization of principal, (2) "straight pass-through" securities under which G.N.M.A. guarantees that the holder will receive timely payment of the amortized principal and of interest *as collected,* and (3) "modified pass-through" securities, under which G.N.M.A. guarantees the timely payment of a specific portion of principal installments and a fixed rate of interest, *whether collected or not.* The G.N.M.A. guarantee is backed by the full faith and credit of the Federal government.

The chief buyers of mortgage-backed securities have been savings and loan associations, savings banks, pension funds, and insurance companies. It is expected that individual investors of means will become large holders, because of the safety and marketability of the issues. But "small" investors will be discouraged by the minimum denomination of $25,000 (the minimum size of a securities offering is $2 millions).

Bond-type and modified pass-through securities have been the chief types of mortgage-backed securities issued thus far. During 1972, $3.4 billions were sold.

G.N.M.A.-guaranteed mortgage-backed securities offer a number of advantages to investors: good yield (6¾ per cent in early 1973), highest quality, regular cash flow (in the case of the pass-through variety), and good marketability. They open up possibilities of a large flow of capital into mortgages from institutional and individual investors who were previously unable or unwilling to acquire such instruments directly.

Ownership of Mortgage Debt

At the end of 1971, one- to four-family residential mortgages comprised 62 per cent of mortgage debt outstanding. A breakdown (Table 11-3) of the

Table 11-3. OWNERSHIP OF MORTGAGE DEBT, December 31, 1971
(in billions of dollars)

Type	Savings & Loan Ass'ns	Life Insurance Cos	Commercial Banks	Mutual Savings Banks	Individuals and Others	FLB and FNMA	Total
Farm	$ —	$ 5.6	$ 4.2	$ .1	$15.1	$ 7.9	$ 32.9
Residential							
One- to four-family	142.9	26.6	48.0	38.6	32.8	20.9	307.8
Multifamily	16.8	16.6	4.2	14.7	13.5	1.1	66.9
	$159.7	$41.2	$52.2	$53.3	$46.3	$22.0	$374.7
Commercial and other	14.7	28.8	26.1	8.6	14.1	—	92.3
	$174.4	$75.6	$82.5	$62.0	$75.5	$27.9	$499.9
Conventional and other	$149.7	$59.3	$71.2	$33.8	$65.2	$ —	$379.2
FHA-insured	13.8	11.3	8.3	16.1	10.3	$29.9	81.2
VA-guaranteed	10.9	5.0	9.0	12.1	—	—	39.5
	$174.4	$75.6	$82.5	$62.0	$75.5	$29.9	$499.9

Sources: *Federal Reserve Bulletin; Federal Home Loan Bank Board Journal.*

ownership of *all* mortgage debt outstanding shows the relative importance of other types of liens held by major institutions and individuals, government agencies, and minor institutions.

Multifamily (apartment) loans. Loans secured by multifamily dwellings comprise about 18 per cent of residential mortgages outstanding. The very substantial increase in the postwar period reflects the rise in land values, the shift back to apartment living, and relaxed regulations that permit greater institutional investment in this type of loan. Apartment loans are much in demand by savings banks and life insurance companies and to a lesser extent by savings and loan associations. Their higher yields also give them appeal to many individual investors.

Commercial and industrial mortgages. Loans secured by commercial property such as stores and office buildings represent a highly specialized business involving a knowledge of both real estate and business factors and so are made in the main by commercial banks and by life insurance companies and their correspondents. There is no arrangement for government insurance or guarantee.

Commercial mortgages for substantial amounts are almost always amortized and have maturities as long as thirty years. Many of these mortgages belong in the category of "term loans," as indicated in the section on bank investments. (See Chapter 22.) Amortized loans on hotels, apartments, and office buildings have largely replaced the real estate mortgage bond issues so common in the 1920s.

When industrial properties are financed by individual mortgages (as distinguished from corporate mortgage bonds), again the institution, especially the life insurance company, is the chief source of funds. Such mortgages are too large and the credit problems too specialized for the individual investor. These loans are frequently amortized in as short a period as ten years, to reflect the special risks attendant to business property. Institutional mortgage lending for industrial purposes is increasingly encroaching on the more traditional method of property financing through corporate bonds.

In recent years, especially during periods of very high interest rates (1968–1970), yields on mortgages secured by income property bumped into state usury ceilings (often 10 per cent). For this reason, and because they could demand almost any terms during the "credit crunches," life insurance companies required special "sweeteners" such as equity participation, rent sharing, and other features, in multifamily, industrial, and commercial mortgages.

Farm mortgages. The farm mortgage situation has shown vast improvement since the critical years of 1930–1935, when wholesale defaults and liquidation, special Government aid, and even moratoria on farm debts were the order of the day. In 1930, farm *mortgage* debt totalled $9.6 billions. At the end of 1945 the figure stood at $4.8 billions, and rose to $32.9 billions at the end of 1971.

Total farm debt includes a wide range of types and maturities. The volume of long-term mortgage loans, and the amounts held by the principal lender groups, are shown in Table 11-4. (The totals differ from those in Table 11-1 because of differences in dates.)

The twelve Federal Land Banks (described in Chapter 5) were established in 1916 to make long-term loans through National Farm Loan Associations. These loans are financed through the issuance of Federal Land Bank bonds. The volume of Land Bank lending reached its zenith in the 1930s. During the 1940s, improvement in farm prices and farm income substantially reduced the need for Federal credit. Between 1933 and 1947, the Federal Farm Mortgage Corporation made distress loans to prevent default or foreclosure, as an activity of the Land Bank Commissioner. Federal Land Banks and the Federal Farm Mortgage Corporation are part of the comprehensive administrative organization, the Farm Credit Administration.

Life insurance companies have always been important investors in farm mortgages. The 1971 (year-end) farm mortgage total of $5.6 billions was 17 per cent of the total volume of farm mortgages outstanding. However, this was less than 3 per cent of total life insurance company assets. Individuals are the most important category of ownership.

Table 11-4. OWNERSHIP OF FARM MORTGAGE DEBT, 1950–1971,
as of January 1

(in millions of dollars)

Lender group	1950	1955	1960	1965	1971
Federal Land Banks and Federal Farm Mortgage Corp.	$ 965	$1,280	$ 2,335	$ 3,687	$ 7,145
Life insurance companies	1,172	2,052	2,820	4,288	5,610
Banks	937	1,210	1,631	2,669	4,445
Farmers Home Administration	193	287	439	619	347
Individuals and others	2,312	3,416	4,857	7,631	11,986
Total	$5,579	$8,245	$12,082	$18,894	$29,533

SOURCE: U.S. Department of Agriculture, *Agricultural Statistics*, annually.

Commercial and savings banks lost much of their interest in farm mortgages in the 1930s as a result of the wave of failures and foreclosures of that decade. Beginning in 1947, however, a marked expansion of farm financing took place, reflecting the policy of banks to emphasize loans rather than investments.

The Farmers Home Administration was established in 1946 as an agency of the U.S. Department of Agriculture. It makes operating loans of from one to five years in maturity and farm-ownership loans of as long as forty years. It insures mortgage loans made by private lenders, and so is in a sense an organization similar to the FHA. It serves as an agency for applicants unable to obtain credit from other sources.

Individuals continued to play an important role in farm mortgage lending despite the rapid growth of Federal aid.[8] The inherent qualities of farm mortgages as an investment appeal to many local capitalists and former landowners. Private mortgage companies serve as middlemen between investors and farmers requiring long-term credit.

Such investments are recommended only to investors capable of keeping close watch on farm commodity prices, farm values, and the earning power of individual situations. The replacement of the old five-year loan by the amortized type has introduced many desirable features, but the inherent risks of instability of farm income still persist, along with the disadvantages of poor marketability, inadequate diversification, and others discussed earlier in connection with urban financing.

Mortgage Companies

Mortgage companies (sometimes called mortgage bankers) play an increasingly important role in the primary market for mortgages. These firms seek out and originate loans, secure interim bank financing, and resell the loans to financial institutions. Thereafter they service the loans at a typical fee of $\frac{1}{2}$ per cent per year, collecting and remitting the monthly payments of interest plus principal, and seeing that the tax and insurance payments are kept current. Over 2,000 such companies are in operation, with assets of $4\frac{1}{2}$ billions, and they service approximately $82 billions of mortgages, or 17 per cent of the national total, with emphasis on one- to four-family residential liens, both conventional and underwritten. In 1970, almost half of their servicing volume was for life insurance companies, who used their services for 45 per cent of their mortgages, and 19 per cent was for mutual savings banks (for 27 per cent of their holdings).[9] They also serve the F.N.M.A., G.N.M.A., commercial banks, and savings and loan associations.

Mortgage companies make an important contribution to a national mortgage market by originating and servicing loans in capital-starved areas such as the South and the Middle West and transferring them to owners in capital-surplus areas such as the East and California.

The Secondary Mortgage Market

Individual and institutional investors, mainly Federal agencies, use the secondary market to buy and sell mortgages—chiefly residential—either through their own contacts or through mortgage brokers, which are local concerns acting as middlemen at commissions of $\frac{1}{4}$ to $\frac{1}{2}$ per cent. Purchases are used to round out mortgage portfolios when new originations are not sufficient. Recent data on market volume are lacking. In 1971 F.N.M.A. and G.N.M.A.,

[8]The figures for "individuals and others" in Table 11-4 include bank trustees, minor institutions and miscellaneous Federal agencies.

[9]Mortgage Bankers Association of America, *Mortgage Banking 1970*. (Washington, D.C.: The Association, Research Committee Trends Report No. 9, 1971).

the major secondary buyers, purchased $4.0 billions of Federally supported mortgages. It is likely that, including conventional liens, over $7 billions in mortgages of all types changed hands during the year.

Mortgage Yields

Market yields on FHA and VA mortgages, all of which must meet similar standards, tend to be fairly uniform on a national basis. Those on conventional mortgages, however, reflect variations in risk and geographical influences, so that generalizations on a national basis must be made with caution. Table 11-5 provides information from 1955 through 1972. The crudities of annual averages should be recognized—some variation within the year is of course to be expected. For purposes of comparison, the yield on Moody's Aaa corporate bond series is also shown in the table.

The table reveals a rough relationship between mortgage yields and bond yields, as the general supply of and demand for long-term funds rise and fall. Mortgage yields in general appear to be less volatile than bond yields, owing to the lack of a fully national flow of mortgage funds. Yields on Federally underwritten mortgages follow the contract rate, but reflect the consistent discounts that have prevailed in recent years. Discounts persisted in 1966–1969 even after successive increases had brought the contract FHA

Table 11-5. MORTGAGE YIELDS, 1955–1972

| | *FHA-Mortgages* | | *Conventional Home Mortgages* | *Aaa Corporate Bonds* | |
| | *(sec. 203)* | | | | |
	Contract Rate	*Market Yield (1)*	*(National Average) (2)*	*(3)*	*Spread (1) over (3)*
1955	4.5%	4.6%	5.2%	3.1%	1.5%
1956	4. 5–5. 0	4.8	5.4	3.4	1.4
1957	5. 0–5.25	5.4	5.8	3.9	1.5
1958	5.25	5.5	5.7	3.8	1.7
1959	5.25–5.75	5.7	6.0	4.4	1.3
1960	5.75	6.2	6.2	4.4	1.8
1961	5.75–5.25	5.8	6.0	4.4	1.4
1962	5.25	5.6	5.9	4.3	1.3
1963	5.25	5.5	5.8	4.3	1.2
1964	5.25	5.4	5.8	4.4	1.0
1965	5.25	5.5	5.7	4.5	1.0
1966	5.25–6.00	6.3	6.1	5.1	1.2
1967	6.00	6.5	6.3	5.5	1.0
1968	6.00–6.75	7.1	6.8	6.2	.9
1969	6.75–7.50	8.0	7.7	7.0	1.0
1970	7.50–8.50	8.5	8.3	8.0	.5
1971	8.00–7.00	7.7	7.6	7.4	.3
1972	7.00	7.5	7.6	7.2	.3

SOURCE: FHA yields from Federal Housing Administration. Conventional yields from Federal Home Loan Bank Board and U.S. Department of Commerce, *Construction Review*. These latter yields refer to loans on *new* single-family homes.

rate to 8½ per cent in early 1970. The increases reflected the effort by the FHA commissioner to make mortgage yields competitive and thus counteract the reluctance of builders and sellers of homes to absorb deeper discounts in order to attract sellers.

As long-term capital yields in the capital market declined, the ceiling rate on Federally supported mortgages was lowered, reaching 7 per cent in 1971. But at this point, price discounts ran as high as 5 per cent, and pressure for a "free market rate" in place of the nominal rate continued. It is interesting to note that the yield on conventional mortgages, with their freedom from regulation, has usually been lower than that on Federally supported liens. And the latter require an additional ½ per cent insurance or guarantee charge.

The spread between the market yield on FHA-insured mortgages and high-grade bonds fell to 100 "basis points," on the average, in 1964–1969. Rising interest rates on alternative investments in 1969–1970 continued to put pressure on mortgage yields, so that even after the peak in early 1970, by the end of 1970 FHAs yielded 8.3 per cent, and yields on conventional mortgages produced 8.2 per cent on a national basis, and as much as 9 per cent in areas in the Southwest and the West. In addition to requiring higher yields, lenders tended to be more selective about types of properties and borrowers, and maturities became less liberal. Mortgage yields declined modestly through 1970 to May 1971 as the flow of funds into savings institutions increased, but rose mildly in the latter part of 1971 as a result of increased building construction. They fell off slightly in most of 1972.

The spread between market yields on FHA mortgages and Aaa corporate bonds was reduced substantially in 1970–1972, reflecting the increased supply of savings funds flowing into institutional hands, especially savings banks and savings and loan associations.

REFERENCES

AMERICAN INSTITUTE OF BANKING, *Home Mortgage Lending.* New York: The Institute, 1963.

AMERICAN INSTITUTE OF REAL ESTATE APPRAISERS, *The Appraisal of Real Estate,* 5th ed. Chicago: The Institute, 1967.

BABB, J. B., and B. F. DORDICK, *Real Estate Information Sources.* Detroit: Gale Research Co., 1963.

BEATON, W. R., *Real Estate Investment.* Englewood Cliffs, N.J.: Prentice-Hall, Inc., 1971.

BENENSON, L. A., *Making Money in Real Estate.* New York: Grosset & Dunlap, 1963.

BERMAN, D. S., *How to Reap Profits in Local Real Estate Syndicates.* Englewood Cliffs, N.J.: Prentice-Hall, Inc., 1968.

BROWN, R. K., *Essentials of Real Estate.* Englewood Cliffs, N.J.: Prentice-Hall, Inc., 1970.

BRYANT, W. R., *Mortgage Lending,* 2nd ed. New York: McGraw-Hill, Inc., 1962.

CAMPBELL, R. D., *Mortgage Trusts.* New York: Audit Publications, 1970.

CASE, F. E., *Cash Outlays and Economic Costs of Home Ownership*. Berkeley, Calif.: Bureau of Business and Economic Research, 1957.

———, *Real Estate*, rev. ed. Boston: Allyn and Bacon, Inc., 1962.

COLEAN, MILES T., *The Impact of Government on Real Estate Finance in the United States*. New York: National Bureau of Economic Research, Inc., 1950.

———, *Mortgage Companies: Their Place in the Financial Structure*, a monograph prepared for the Commission on Money and Credit. Englewood Cliffs, N.J.: Prentice-Hall, Inc., 1962.

CONWAY, L. V., *Mortgage Lending*, 2nd ed. Chicago: American Savings and Loan Institute Press, 1962.

DOUGALL, H. E., *Capital Markets and Institutions*, 2nd ed., Chapter 11. Englewood Cliffs, N.J.: Prentice-Hall, Inc., 1970.

FEDERAL NATIONAL MORTGAGE ASSOCIATION, *Background and History of FNMA*. Washington, D.C.: The Association, 1963.

FRESHMAN, S. K., *Principles of Real Estate Syndication*. Los Angeles: Parker & Sons, Inc., 1971.

FRIEDMAN, E. J., ed., *Real Estate Appraising*, rev. ed. Englewood Cliffs, N.J.: Prentice-Hall, Inc., 1968.

HOAGLAND, H. E., and L. D. STONE, *Real Estate Finance*, 4th ed. Homewood, Ill.: Richard D. Irwin, Inc., 1969.

JONES, OLIVER, and LEO GREBLER, *The Secondary Mortgage Market*. Los Angeles: University of California Graduate School of Business Administration, 1961.

KAHN, S. E., et al., *Real Estate Appraisal and Investment*. New York: The Ronald Press Company, 1963.

KETCHUM, M. D., and L. T. KENDALL, eds., *Readings in Financial Institutions*. Boston: Houghton-Mifflin Co., 1965.

KLAMAN, S. B., *The Postwar Residential Mortgage Market*. Princeton, N.J.: Princeton University Press, 1961.

———, *The Postwar Rise of Mortgage Companies*, Occasional Paper No. 60. New York: National Bureau of Economic Research, Inc., 1959.

LEWIS, BERTRAM, *Profits in Real Estate Syndication*. New York: Harper and Row, Publishers, 1962.

LUSK, H. F., *Law of Real Estate*, rev. ed. Homewood, Ill.: Richard D. Irwin, Inc., 1965.

MAIR, GEORGE, and A. R. CERF, *Real Estate Analysis and Taxation*. New York: McGraw-Hill, Inc., 1969.

MAISEL, S. J., *Financing Real Estate*. New York: McGraw-Hill, Inc., 1965.

PEASE, R. H., and L. O. KERWOOD, eds., *Mortgage Banking*, 2nd ed. New York: McGraw-Hill, Inc., 1965.

RATCLIFF, R. U., *Real Estate Analysis*. New York: McGraw-Hill, Inc., 1961.

RING, A. A., *The Valuation of Real Estate*, 2nd ed. Englewood Cliffs, N.J.: Prentice-Hall, Inc., 1970.

———, and N. L. NORTH, *Real Estate Principles and Practices*, 6th ed. Englewood Cliffs, N.J.: Prentice-Hall, Inc., 1967.

ROBINSON, R. I., *Money and Capital Markets*, Chapter 12. New York: McGraw-Hill, Inc., 1964.

UNGER, M. A., *Real Estate, Principles and Practices,* 4th ed., Part 4. Cincinnati: South-Western Publishing Co., 1969.

WEIMER, A. M., and HOMER HOYT, *Real Estate,* 5th ed. New York: The Ronald Press Company, 1966.

WENDT, P. F., and A. R. CERF, *Real Estate Analysis and Taxation.* New York: McGraw-Hill, Inc., 1969.

12 Mathematics of Investment

SCOPE: The purpose of this chapter is to discuss the mathematical problems which arise in investment practice. The order of discussion is (1) definition of terms, (2) accrued interest on bonds, (3) accrued dividend on stocks, (4) yields on stocks, (5) yields on bonds, (6) values of convertible securities, (7) values of stock subscription rights, and (8) values of stock-purchase option warrants.

Mathematical Terms

Many of the mathematical terms used in the field of investments have meanings which are not always applicable in other fields. The first group of terms are used in connection with the prices of securities:

1. *Market price* is the value shown in the last previous transaction or indicated by the prevailing bid quotation or by the best price that any prospective buyer is willing to pay.

Corporate bond prices are expressed as percentages of face value (a price of 103½ means 103½ per cent of $1,000, or $1,035), whereas stock prices are expressed in dollars per share (a price of 46¾ means $46.75 per share). Prices of U.S. Government bonds are expressed in dollars with fractions denoting 1/32's. A price of 101.1 means 101.03125 per cent of $1,000 or $1010.3125.

The difference between market price and face value of bonds is known as *discount* when the market price is lower and as *premium* when the market price is higher.

2. *Conversion price* is the fixed price (in terms of face value of convertible bonds or preferred stock) at which common stock will be issued to holders of convertible bonds or preferred stock in exchange for these securities. Thus if a bond is "convertible at $50," the investor may exchange a $100 (par) bond for two shares of common stock.

3. *Subscription price* is the price at which additional stock or bonds will be sold to present stockholders. Sometimes the term also applies to the price at which securities are offered to the public.

The second group of terms are used in connection with interest calculations:

1. *Maturity* is the number of years (or fractions thereof) that a bond has still to run. A thirty-year bond issued in 1965 has a maturity of only twenty-two years as of 1973.

2. *Accrued interest* is the amount of interest that has accumulated on a bond since the last preceding semiannual payment date. In the case of new issues, the date at which interest begins to accrue is stated in the announcement.

3. *Accumulation* is the appreciation in the value of a bond bought at a discount, between the purchase date and the maturity date when it is payable at face value.

4. *Amortization* is the depreciation in the value of a bond bought at a premium, between the purchase date and the maturity date when it is payable at face value.

5. *Nominal yield* is the annual income rate specified on bonds (coupon rate) and preferred stocks (dividend rate in dollars or per cent). The actual per cent yield to the investor will be higher or lower than the nominal yield if the cost price is less or more than the face value.

6. *Current yield* is the annual income rate determined by the cost price without regard to accumulation or amortization. (A 7 per cent bond bought at 105, and due in twenty years, provides a current yield of 6.67 per cent per annum.)

7. *Net yield* (or *yield to maturity*) is the annual income rate as adjusted to the cost price and the amount of annual accumulation or amortization. (A 7 per cent bond bought at 105, due in twenty years, provides a net yield of 6.50 per cent per annum.)

Accrued Interest on Bonds

The prices of most bonds are quoted on an "and-interest" basis. In addition to the agreed price, the buyer pays the seller the amount of interest accrued since the preceding interest date because interest for the full six months will be paid to the buyer on the next interest date.

Accrued interest on bonds is calculated on the 360-day-year basis, except in the case of certain U.S. Government bonds on which the 365-day-year basis is used. Under the 360-day basis, each month is considered to have thirty days irrespective of the calender. The seller is entitled to interest up to, but not including, the day of delivery. Thus, if a 5 per cent bond with interest payment dates on January 1 and July 1 (J-J) is sold on Monday, October 12, for regular four-day delivery on Thursday, October 16, the seller is entitled to interest for three months (July, August, and September) and fifteen days (up to, but not including, October 16) at 5 per cent, or $14.31. If a 3 per cent bond with interest payment dates on March 1 and

September 1 (M-S) is sold on Thursday, October 17, for delivery on Wednesday, October 22, the seller is entitled to interest for one month (September) and twenty-one days (up to, but not including, October 22) at 3 per cent, or $4.25.

If interest is not paid at the subsequent payment date, the buyer may not recover the amount advanced to the seller but must endeavor to collect from the issuer.

Some bonds are sold "flat"; that is, the quoted price includes accrued interest, if any. Such bonds are likely to be either in default, or income bonds whose income is uncertain.

Accrued Dividend on Stocks

The amount of dividend which accumulates on corporate stock from each payment date to the next is included in the quoted price of the stock. No calculation of dividend accrual is involved. (An exception is found in the case of new issues of preferred being offered to the public at a certain price "plus accrued dividends from the date of issue.") Dividend payments involve declaration dates (say, March 1), record dates (say, March 20), and payment dates (say, April 15). Persons buying the stock on or before the record date are entitled to receive the forthcoming dividend. Because buyers after the record date (March 20) are not entitled to the next dividend (on April 15), the market price is said to be "ex-dividend" and usually declines by the amount of the quarterly payment around the record date, unless other influences offset the effect of the dividend.[1]

Yields on Stocks

The rate of return, or yield, on investments in corporate stocks is determined by dividing the annual cash dividend payment (in dollars) by the market price. A stock which costs $150 per share and which is paying an annual dividend of $6 per share has a yield of 4 per cent. Subsequent changes in the market price do not affect the rate of return to holders who paid $150 but do change the yield to new buyers. Subsequent changes in the dividend rate may affect the rate of return to all holders.

During the year, the investor may not know the final amount of the annual dividend. He calculates the yield either by estimating the current twelve-month dividend or by using the previous year's dividend.

When dividends are paid in shares of stock rather than in cash, the yield is usually indicated as a percentage increase. Thus a "2 per cent stock dividend" means that the holder of 100 shares receives 2 new shares. The

---

[1]The rule on stocks listed on the New York Stock Exchange is that transactions shall be ex-dividend on the fourth full business day preceding the record date or on the day the stock transfer books are closed. Otherwise, shares are ex-dividend on the date of record.

investor may calculate the market value if he wishes to do so. Fractional stock dividends are often paid in cash at their market value.

Another yield concept in the case of common stocks is the "earnings yield," or relation between earnings per share and market price. Most investors reverse the relationship and think in terms of the price-earnings ratio or multiple. A common stock selling at 60 that is earning $3.00 per share and pays a cash dividend of $2.40 has an earnings yield of 5 per cent, a price-earnings ratio of 20, and a dividend yield of 4 per cent.

Dividend rates on most preferred stocks are fixed in time and amount and, therefore, provide a more dependable basis for the calculation of an estimated future rate of income return. Dividend payments on common stocks are more irregular. In many cases the yield on common stock is virtually meaningless; in others, where the dividends are regular and appear dependable, the yield is a significant factor to investors. Whereas in the case of preferred stocks and bonds, the yield reflects the general quality of the security at the time, it may not do so for common stocks, where both price and yield may reflect appreciation possibilities and anticipated increases in dividends.

Net Yields on Bonds

Mathematically, the yield to maturity of a bond is a function of (1) its price, (2) its coupon rate, and (3) the length of time to maturity. Actually, however, the yield determines the price, given the other two factors. Some obligations, such as U.S. Treasury certificates and bills, municipal securities, and equipment trust certificates, are quoted in terms of yield rather than price because of the various maturities that are available.

The *current yield* on bonds is determined by dividing the annual interest payment by the cost price. A 6½ per cent bond purchased at 90 would afford a current yield of 7.22 per cent.

Where the principal of a bond is in default or undergoing readjustment, or where the income is very uncertain, the current rather than the net yield is used to indicate the rate of return. This practice should also apply to bonds on which the continuation of interest payments or the payment of principal at maturity is so much in doubt that they sell at very substantial discounts. In addition, where bonds are bought for trading purposes rather than to hold, the current yield is usually figured.

As stated earlier, bonds that are in default of interest are sold "flat," that is, without the interest added to the price. The same is true of income bonds where the amount of interest is uncertain.

With the exception of the types noted above, the annual rate of income on bonds is customarily calculated on the basis of net yield to maturity. The *net yield* may be determined approximately by dividing the annual income (interest plus annual accumulation or minus annual amortization) by the average value to maturity (as adjusted by accumulation credits or amortization charges). A 7 per cent bond due in twenty-five years which was purchased at 80 would afford an approximate net yield (to maturity) of 8.66 per cent, as thus calculated:

Annual interest .... $70 (7 per cent of $1,000)
        plus
Annual accumulation .... $8 ($1,000 − $800 = $200 ÷ 25 yrs)
        equals
Annual income $78
        divided by
Average value .... $900 ($800 + $1,000 = $1,800 ÷ 2)
        equals
Net yield (to maturity) ..   .0866

An 8 per cent bond due in twenty years purchased at 110 would afford an approximate net yield (to maturity) of 7.14 per cent, calculated as follows:

Annual interest .... $80 (8 per cent of $1,000)
        minus
Annual amortization ..... $5 ($1,100 − $1,000 = $100 ÷ 20 yrs)
        equals
Annual income $75
        divided by
Average value .... $1,050 ($1,100 + $1,000 = $2,100 ÷ 2)
        equals
Net yield (to maturity) 0714

Present value concept. Money has a time value. Those with funds to lend or invest expect a return on their funds. At any rate of interest, a sum of money is worth more at the end of a period than at the beginning. And at any rate of interest, money promised in the future is worth less at the beginning than at the end. Thus $100 placed in a savings account at 5 per cent is worth $105 ($100 × 1.05) at the end of a year. At the same rate of interest, $105 a year hence is only worth $100 (105 ÷ 1.05) at the beginning.

If interest is withdrawn or not reinvested, at *simple interest* the $100 in our illustration above grows to $105 each year. If the interest is not withdrawn or is re-invested at the same rate, the basis for calculating the next year's interest is $105, so that at the end of the second year the principal has grown to $110.25 ($105 × 1.05). This illustrates the concept of *compound interest*. The concept can be applied to the calculation of present value. The value of $100 to be received one year hence, at 5 per cent, is $95.20 ($100 ÷ 1.05); the value to be received at the end of two years is $90.70 ($95.20 ÷ 1.05). Another way of expressing the concept would be to say that at the rate of 5 per cent, the *discounted present value* of $100 to be received two years from now is $90.70.

The net yield (to maturity) as calculated in the two preceding examples is an approximate, rather than an exact, figure. The method is accurate

Table 12-1. AMOUNT OF $1 AT COMPOUND INTEREST

Years	5%	5½%	6%	7%	8%	9%
1	1.050	1.056	1.060	1.070	1.080	1.090
2	1.103	1.115	1.124	1.145	1.166	1.188
3	1.158	1.178	1.191	1.225	1.260	1.295
4	1.216	1.244	1.262	1.311	1.360	1.411
5	1.276	1.314	1.338	1.402	1.469	1.539
6	1.340	1.388	1.419	1.501	1.587	1.677
7	1.407	1.466	1.504	1.606	1.714	1.828
8	1.477	1.548	1.593	1.718	1.851	1.992
9	1.551	1.635	1.689	1.838	1.999	2.172
10	1.629	1.727	1.791	1.967	2.159	2.367
11	1,710	1.824	1.898	2.105	2.332	2.580
12	1.796	1.926	2.012	2.252	2.518	2.812
13	1.886	2.034	2.133	2.410	2.720	3.066
14	1.980	2.148	2.261	2.578	2.937	3.346
15	2.079	2.269	2.397	2.759	3.172	3.642
16	2.183	2.396	2.540	2.952	3.426	3.970
17	2.292	2.531	2.693	3.159	3.700	4.328
18	2.407	2.673	2.854	3.380	3.996	4.717
19	2.527	2.823	3.026	3.616	4.316	5.142
20	2.653	2.982	3.207	3.869	4.661	5.604
25	3.386	3.918	4.292	5.427	6.848	8.623
30	4.322	5.149	5.743	7.612	10.063	13.268
40	7.040	8.891	10.286	14.974	21.724	31.409
50	11.467	15.352	18.420	29.457	46.902	74.357

enough for many purposes, especially for short- and medium-term bonds selling close to face value. But from a strictly mathematical viewpoint, the annual amortization or accumulation is not a uniform amount, and the average value would be somewhat higher or lower than the figures here shown. Therefore, one must use a more accurate method in order to determine the value of future payments of principal and interest compound-discounted to the present. Tables are available which permit the ready determination of accurate yields when prices are known, or of exact prices when yields are given.

Compound interest formula. The formula for determining the future value of money invested at compound interest is

$$(1 + N)^n$$

in which N is the interest rate per year and n is the number of years.

Assume that $1.00 is invested at compound interest credited annually for twenty years at 7 per cent. By consulting a compound interest table (Table 12-1) the value of $(1 + .07)^{20}$ is found to be 3.869.

The indicated value of $1.00 would, therefore, be $3.869, and that of $1,000 would be $3,869.

Present worth formulas. The formula for determining the value of a principal sum of money payable at a future time, compound-discounted to the present time, is the reciprocal of the compound interest formula

$$\frac{1}{(1 + N)^n}$$

in which N is the discount rate per year and n is the number of years. (See Table 12-2).

Assume that $1.00 payable in twenty years is to be compound-discounted at 7 per cent:

$$\frac{1}{(1 + N)^n} = \frac{1}{(1 + 1.07)^{20}} = \frac{1}{3.869} = \$0.258$$

The indicated present value of $1.00 is 25.8 cents. The present worth of the principal of a $1,000 bond payable in twenty years, compound-counted at 7 per cent per annum, is $258.

The formula for determining the value of the total annual interest payments on a bond payable over a period of years, compound-discounted to the present time, is

$$\frac{C}{1 + N} + \frac{C}{(1 + N)^2} + \frac{C}{(1 + N)^3} \cdots\cdots \frac{C}{(1 + N)^n}$$

$$= \frac{C}{N}\left[1 - \frac{1}{(1 + N)^n}\right]$$

in which C is the coupon interest rate, N is the net interest rate of yield, and n is the number of years. (See Table 12-3).[2]

Assume that a $1,000 bond payable in twenty years carries an 8 per cent coupon rate, and that the interest payments are to be compound-discounted at 7 per cent:

$$\frac{.08}{.07}(\$1,000 - \$258) = \frac{8}{7}(\$742) = \$848$$

The total present worth of both principal and coupons on a $1,000 bond bearing an 8 per cent interest rate payable in twenty years is, therefore, the sum of $258 (the present worth of the principal) plus $846 (the present worth of the coupons), or $1,106. (Note that the investor who pays $1,106 for this bond is paying much more for the future interest payments than for the principal at maturity.)

Bond value formula. The formula for determining the present worth of

[2]Using the summation symbol, the formula is

$$\sum_{t=1}^{n} \frac{1}{(1 + N)^n}$$

Table 12-2. VALUES OF $1

Years	5%	5½%	6%	7%	8%	9%
1	.952	.948	.943	.935	.926	.917
2	.907	.898	.890	.873	.857	.842
3	.864	.852	.840	.816	.794	.772
4	.823	.807	.792	.763	.735	.708
5	.783	.765	.747	.713	.681	.650
6	.746	.725	.705	.666	.630	.596
7	.711	.687	.665	.623	.583	.547
8	.677	.651	.627	.582	.540	.502
9	.645	.618	.592	.544	.500	.460
10	.614	.585	.558	.508	.463	.422
11	.585	.555	.527	.475	.429	.387
12	.557	.526	.497	.444	.397	.355
13	.530	.498	.469	.415	.368	.326
14	.505	.472	.442	.388	.340	.299
15	.481	.448	.417	.362	.315	.274
16	.458	.424	.394	.339	.292	.252
17	.436	.402	.371	.316	.270	.231
18	.415	.381	.350	.296	.250	.212
19	.396	.361	.331	.276	.232	.194
20	.377	.343	.312	.258	.215	.178
25	.295	.262	.233	.184	.146	.116
30	.231	.200	.174	.131	.099	.075
40	.142	.117	.079	.067	.046	.032
50	.087	.069	.054	.034	.021	.013

a bond payable at a future date is obtained by combining the respective formulas for present worth of principal and present worth of coupons as follows:

$$\frac{1}{(1+N)^n} + \frac{C}{N}\left[1 - \frac{1}{(1+N)^n}\right]$$

This formula may be reduced and expressed more simply as

$$\frac{N + C(1+N)^n - C}{N(1+N)^n}$$

The preceding case of the 8 per cent, $1,000 bond payable in twenty years may now be applied to the simplified combined formula in order to determine the present value of the bond on a 7 per cent yield basis:

$$\frac{.07 + .08(1 + .07)^{20} - .08}{.07(1 + .07)^{20}} = \frac{.07 + .08(3.869) - .08}{.07(3.869)}$$

$$= \frac{.07 + .30952 - .08}{.27083} = \frac{.29952}{.27083} = 1.106 = \$1,106$$

The total value of the bond in question would, therefore, be $1,106, which confirms the separate values of $258 by the principal formula and of $848 by the interest formula.

In the preceding cases, the problem was to determine the price of a bond when the yield is given. In other cases, the problem may be to determine the yield when the price is given.

Assume that a 7 per cent bond due in fifty years is purchased at 105. The net yield would thus be determined by solving the combined formula:

$$1.05 = \frac{N + .07(1 + N)^{50} - .07}{N(1 + N)^{50}}$$

$$1.05N(1 + N)^{50} = .07(1 + N)^{50} + N - .07$$

As a net yield (N) of .0665 brings the two sides of the equation in almost exact balance, the bond in question has been bought at a price which affords a yield of 6.65 per cent per annum.

Table 12-3. PRESENT VALUE OF $1 EACH YEAR

Years	5%	5½%	6%	7%	8%	9%
1	.952	.948	.943	.935	.926	.917
2	1.859	1.846	1.833	1.808	1.783	1.759
3	2.723	2.698	2.673	2.624	2.577	2.531
4	3.546	3.505	3.465	3.387	3.312	3.240
5	4.329	4.270	4.212	4.100	3.993	3.890
6	5.076	4.996	4.917	4.767	4.623	4.486
7	5.786	5.683	5.582	5.389	5.206	5.033
8	6.463	6.335	6.210	5.971	5.747	5.535
9	7.108	6.952	6.802	6.515	6.247	5.985
10	7.722	7.538	7.360	7.024	6.710	6.418
11	8.306	8.093	7.887	7.499	7.139	6.805
12	8.863	8.619	8.384	7.943	7.536	7.161
13	9.394	9.117	8.853	8.358	7.904	7.487
14	9.899	9.590	9.295	8.745	8.244	7.786
15	10.380	10.038	9.712	9.108	8.560	8.061
16	10.838	10.462	10.106	9.447	8.851	8.313
17	11.274	10.865	10.477	9.763	9.122	8.544
18	11.690	11.246	10.828	10.059	9.372	8.756
19	12.085	11.608	11.158	10.336	9.604	8.950
20	12.462	11.950	11.470	10.594	9.818	9.129
25	14.094	13.414	12.783	11.654	10.675	9.823
30	15.392	14.534	13.765	12.409	11.258	10.274
40	17.159	16.046	15.046	13.332	11.925	10.757
50	18.256	16.932	15.762	13.801	12.233	10.962

Bond tables. The mathematical problems that arise most frequently in connection with bond investment are, first, to determine the net yield of a bond when price, redemption value, and maturity are known, and second, to find the price at which a bond of known redemption value and maturity must be purchased to yield a certain desired return. In either case, the solution is simplified through the use of bond table books.

Bond tables are not complete. Complete tables would show the net yield on every amount invested at every possible rate of yield for every possible maturity. Such a compilation is, of course, out of the question. A large assortment of tables is available, with a wide range in coupon rates, maturities, and prices. The more modern tables reflect the use of low and fractional coupon rates and provide means by which prices and yields for maturities involving monthly periods can be determined with a minimum of interpolation.

The *Expanded Bond Values Tables*[3] show the value, to the nearest cent, of a $100 bond with coupon rates from 1 to 12 per cent at intervals of $\frac{1}{4}$ per cent from 1 to 3 per cent; intervals of $\frac{1}{8}$ per cent from $3\frac{1}{8}$ to 10 per cent, and intervals of $\frac{1}{4}$ per cent from $10\frac{1}{4}$ to 12 per cent. Maturities are shown monthly to five years, quarterly to ten years, semiannually to forty years, and also at forty-five, fifty, fifty-five, and 60 years.

A specimen page from the *Expanded Bond Values Tables* is shown in Table 12-4. The coupon rate, 7 per cent, appears at the top of the page. Assume that a bond maturing in twenty-one years and bearing 7 per cent interest, is purchased at $94\frac{3}{4}$ ($947.50), find the net yield. Since the top horizontal row shows the maturities, reference is made to the column headed twenty-one years. In this column, 94.75 appears opposite 7.50 per cent in the first vertical column, which shows the net yield. The required net yield is, therefore, 7.50 per cent.

The second assumption is that the bond has the same maturity, twenty-one years, and bears 7 per cent interest; find the purchase price to yield 7.80 per cent. Reference is made to the column headed twenty-one years, and directly opposite 7.80 per cent, the desired net yield, appears 91.80 which shows the required purchase price to be $918.00 for a $1,000 bond.

Rarely do the bond tables give the exact desired information directly, because either the exact cost of the bond or the desired net yield, as the case may be, does not appear therein. Interpolation becomes necessary. Interpolation is a matter of proportion, as it is based upon the assumption that the changes in the bond table values are proportionate. This assumption is not absolutely correct, but the degree of variance is too small to be serious.

Assume that a 7 per cent bond is to run twenty years and is purchased at 94.50; find the net yield. Using the table, the nearest prices that appear are 94.86 and 93.88, which give net yields of 7.50 per cent and 7.60 per cent, respectively. The required net yield is, therefore, between 7.50 per cent and 7.60 per cent. The difference between the prices that bracket the solution sought is .98 (94.86 − 93.88) ; the difference in yield is .10 per cent. The given price 94.50, being .36 less than 94.86, will therefore yield 36/98 of .10 per cent more than 7.50 per cent, or 62/98 of .10 per cent less than 7.60 per cent, making the net yield 7.5367 per cent.

Next assume that a 7 per cent bond is to run twenty years; at what price should it be purchased to yield 6.75 per cent? The nearest net yields that appear in the table are 6.70 per cent and 6.80 per cent, which require a cost of 103.28 and 102.17, respectively. The difference of .10 in rate represents a difference of 1.11 in price. The difference of .05 per cent be-

[3]*Expanded Bond Values Tables* (Boston: Financial Publishing Company, 1970).

Table 12-4. BOND VALUES TABLE, 7%

7% Yield	18-6	19-0	19-6	20-0	20-6	21-0	21-6	22-0
4.00	138.95	139.66	140.35	141.03	141.70	142.35	142.99	143.62
4.20	135.77	136.40	137.02	137.63	138.23	138.82	139.39	139.95
4.40	132.68	133.25	133.80	134.35	134.88	135.40	135.91	136.41
4.60	129.68	130.19	130.68	131.16	131.64	132.10	132.55	132.99
4.80	126.78	127.22	127.66	128.08	128.50	128.91	129.30	129.69
5.00	123.96	124.35	124.73	125.10	125.47	125.82	126.17	126.50
5.20	121.22	121.56	121.89	122.22	122.53	122.84	123.14	123.43
5.40	118.57	118.86	119.15	119.42	119.69	119.95	120.21	120.45
5.60	116.00	116.25	116.48	116.72	116.94	117.16	117.38	117.58
5.80	113.51	113.71	113.90	114.10	114.28	114.46	114.64	114.81
6.00	111.08	111.25	111.40	111.56	111.71	111.85	111.99	112.13
6.10	109.90	110.04	110.18	110.32	110.45	110.58	110.70	110.82
6.20	108.73	108.86	108.98	109.10	109.21	109.32	109.43	109.54
6.30	107.58	107.69	107.80	107.90	108.00	108.09	108.18	108.27
6.40	106.45	106.54	106.63	106.72	106.80	106.88	106.96	107.03
6.50	105.34	105.41	105.48	105.55	105.62	105.68	105.75	105.81
6.60	104.24	104.30	104.35	104.41	104.46	104.51	104.56	104.61
6.70	103.15	103.20	103.24	103.28	103.32	103.36	103.39	103.43
6.80	102.09	102.12	102.14	102.17	102.19	102.22	102.24	102.27
6.90	101.04	101.05	101.06	101.08	101.09	101.10	101.11	101.12
7.00	100.00	100.00	100.00	100.00	100.00	100.00	100.00	100.00
7.10	98.98	98.97	98.95	98.94	98.93	98.92	98.91	98.90
7.20	97.97	97.95	97.92	97.90	97.87	97.85	97.83	97.81
7.30	96.98	96.94	96.91	96.87	96.84	96.80	96.77	96.74
7.40	96.00	95.95	95.91	95.86	95.81	95.77	95.73	95.69
7.50	95.04	94.98	94.92	94.86	94.81	94.75	94.70	94.65
7.60	94.09	94.02	93.95	93.88	93.82	93.75	93.69	93.64
7.70	93.16	93.07	92.99	92.92	92.84	92.77	92.70	92.63
7.80	92.23	92.14	92.05	91.96	91.88	91.80	91.72	91.65
7.90	91.32	91.22	91.12	91.03	90.93	90.85	90.76	90.68
8.00	90.43	90.32	90.21	90.10	90.00	89.91	89.81	89.73
8.10	89.55	89.42	89.31	89.19	89.09	88.98	88.88	88.79
8.20	88.67	88.54	88.42	88.30	88.18	88.07	87.97	87.86
8.30	87.82	87.68	87.54	87.42	87.29	87.18	87.06	86.95
8.40	86.97	86.82	86.68	86.55	86.42	86.29	86.17	86.06
8.50	86.14	85.98	85.83	85.69	85.56	85.43	85.30	85.18
8.60	85.31	85.15	85.00	84.85	84.71	84.57	84.44	84.31
8.70	84.50	84.33	84.17	84.02	83.87	83.73	83.59	83.46
8.80	83.70	83.53	83.36	83.20	83.05	82.90	82.76	82.62
8.90	82.92	82.73	82.56	82.39	82.23	82.08	81.93	81.80
9.00	82.14	81.95	81.77	81.60	81.43	81.28	81.13	80.98
9.10	81.37	81.18	80.99	80.82	80.65	80.48	80.33	80.18
9.20	80.62	80.42	80.23	80.04	79.87	79.70	79.54	79.39
9.30	79.87	79.67	79.47	79.28	79.11	78.93	78.77	78.62
9.40	79.14	78.93	78.73	78.53	78.35	78.18	78.01	77.85
9.50	78.41	78.20	77.99	77.80	77.61	77.43	77.26	77.10
9.60	77.70	77.48	77.27	77.07	76.88	76.70	76.52	76.36
9.70	76.99	76.77	76.55	76.35	76.16	75.97	75.80	75.63
9.80	76.30	76.07	75.85	75.64	75.45	75.26	75.08	74.91
9.90	75.61	75.38	75.16	74.95	74.75	74.56	74.38	74.20
10.00	74.93	74.70	74.47	74.26	74.06	73.87	73.68	73.51
10.20	73.61	73.37	73.14	72.92	72.71	72.51	72.32	72.14
10.40	72.32	72.07	71.83	71.61	71.40	71.20	71.00	70.82
10.60	71.06	70.81	70.57	70.34	70.13	69.92	69.72	69.54
10.80	69.84	69.58	69.34	69.11	68.89	68.68	68.48	68.29
11.00	68.65	68.39	68.14	67.91	67.69	67.47	67.27	67.08
11.20	67.49	67.23	66.98	66.74	66.52	66.30	66.10	65.91
11.40	66.37	66.10	65.85	65.61	65.38	65.17	64.96	64.77
11.60	65.27	65.00	64.74	64.50	64.27	64.06	63.86	63.66
11.80	64.20	63.93	63.67	63.43	63.20	62.98	62.78	62.59
12.00	63.16	62.88	62.63	62.38	62.15	61.94	61.73	61.54

SOURCE: Reproduced from *Expanded Bond Values Tables* p. 736, with permission of Financial Publishing Company, Boston, Mass.

tween 6.70 per cent and 6.75 per cent must, therefore, cover a difference of .55 in price, making the required price 103.28 — .55 or 102.73.

Yields on callable bonds. Most modern bonds contain a provision whereby they may be redeemed by the issuer after a certain date and prior to maturity at a premium over offering price. The call premium usually declines toward maturity. (See Chapter 8.) The option is with the issuer, and redemption will be made only when it is to the issuer's advantage and, conversely, probably to the holder's disadvantage, as when a higher-interest issue is called and replaced by a lower-interest issue. This presents a problem in yield calculation. The holder of a redeemable bond should always take the most conservative position, that is, use the least favorable maturity option when calculating its yield: (1) If the bond is bought at a discount, and is redeemable either at par or above, he should assume principal payment at the final date of maturity; (2) if the bond is bought at par but is redeemable at a premium, or (3) if it has been bought above par but is redeemable at no less a premium, the same assumption should be made; (4) if the bond is bought above par but is redeemable at par, the yield is calculated on the basis of the nearest call date; (5) if the bond is bought above par but is redeemable at an even greater premium, the net yield should be computed at both optional maturity dates, and the least favorable yield should be selected.

Even if the above procedures are followed, there is still uncertainty as to what the actual yield will be. Suppose a twenty-year, 8 per cent bond, callable at 106, with the call price declining to par at the end of fifteen years, sells at par to yield 8 per cent. If and when interest rates decline, the issue will likely be called if, including the required premium, the company can refinance at a lower net cost. But if the bond is called, the owner will receive a lower return on the new investment. Therefore, he may now wish to estimate the odds of call, at what price (terminal value) and under what market rates of interest, so as to estimate his real possible yield over the years. The terminal or "maturity" value would be over 100, and special bond yield tables would be used.

Long-term U.S. Treasury bonds are not callable before maturity in the ordinary sense, but have optional maturities, for example, the $4\frac{1}{4}$'s of 1987–1992. In choosing the maturity date that will provide the lowest yield, the above rules are followed. In the case of the example just given, the yield on February 1, 1973, at 76 18/32 was 6.25 per cent computed to the last callable date.

Convertible Securities[4]

The conversion ratio is expressed either as so much (say, $50) par value of bond or preferred stock for each share of common (for example, "convertible at any time into common stock at $50 per share") or as the number of shares into which the bond or preferred stock is convertible (for exam-

---

[4]See Chapters 7 and 8 for a description of these securities.

ple,⁵ "each share of preferred stock is convertible until December 31, 1980, into two shares of common stock").

The conversion clause, as stated in the bond indenture, or in the corporation charter in the case of preferred stock, frequently provides for exchanges into a decreasing number of common shares at specified intervals. In some cases, a time limit to conversion is set. Occasionally some cash must be delivered with the senior security when it is exchanged for common stock. And the clause will contain an *antidilution* provision whereby, in the event of a stock dividend or split, the conversion ratio will be adjusted to the larger number of common shares.

Knowledge of the established conversion price or ratio and the prevailing market prices of both the convertible security and the common stock is necessary to determine (1) whether conversion of presently owned convertible securities into common stock would be feasible, (2) how much the common stcok would have to rise in order to make conversion feasible if the convertible security were bought at its present price, and (3) the influence of the conversion feature on the price of the convertible security.

If an investor had paid 104 for a bond "convertible at $50 per share" into common stock presently selling at 45, obviously the conversion feature has little or no value to him, and conversion would be unprofitable, regardless of the relative income or yields on the two securities. The value of the bond in terms of common stock is only 90. If he wanted the stock, he would sell his bond and buy the stock. The "conversion parity" would be a value of $52 per share for the stock in this case. Only when the stock rose above $52 in market price would conversion by this investor be likely to take place.

If the investor is interested in a convertible security selling at 96, which is convertible into common at $50 or in the ratio of 20 shares for each $1,000 bond, the common would have to sell at above 48 to make conversion attractive. The investor should calculate the necessary per cent appreciation in the price of the common stock to make conversion attractive. In this case it would be 20 per cent if the price of the common stock is 40.

It is important to remember that the investor should never convert at a loss, that is, take less in market value of common stock than the market value of the security that is turned in. Conversion is likely to take place (1) when the conversion privilege is going to expire, (2) when the conversion price is going to rise, (3) when the convertible security is called at a price that is lower than its conversion value, or (4) because the dividends on the common exceed the income from the bond or preferred stock. But to repeat, under none of these conditions is a market loss acceptable. Where a loss would be incurred, it would be better to sell the bond or preferred stock and buy the common stock.

The convertible feature may add considerably to the market price of a security. Suppose that the *investment* value of a bond convertible into common at $50 is 100; that is, it would sell at par on its own merits as a bond without the conversion feature. But if the common stock is rising rapidly, the price of the bond might be bid up. And if the common were to rise to 60, any unconverted bonds would sell at at least 120. They could sell for even more if buyers are willing to pay extra for the option privilege. Some convertible securities sell at such a premium over conversion value as to produce a negative yield to maturity. In the previous example, redemption of the bonds by the corporation at, say, 104 would of course, force conversion of any remaining bonds.

Additional discussion of convertible securities is found in Chapters 7 and 8.

Subscription Rights

When new stock is issued by a corporation, the shares are customarily offered to existing stockholders at a price below the prevailing market price for the old shares. Rights to subscribe are issued to stockholders in the form of negotiable warrants which must be exercised on or before a specified expiration date. A stockholder owning 100 shares of old stock would receive a transferable warrant representing 100 *rights,* and if the rate of increase is 25 per cent, four rights would be required to purchase one new share at the subscription price.

The issuance of these rights is usually announced in advance of a certain record date. All stockholders of record on that date are entitled to participate in the new issue. The market price of the "old" stock includes the right to participate in the new offering until the record date and is, therefore, said to be *cum-rights.* Because the market price of the old stock after the record date does not include the right to participate in the new offering, it has proportionately less value and is said to be *ex-rights.* As the market price of the old stock is the chief determining factor in the value of the rights, a slightly different method of calculation is required before the record date than thereafter.

Rights are often traded before they are issued. The value of a right on a "when-issued basis" *before* the record date is calculated by dividing the difference between the prevailing market price for the old stock and the subscription price for the new stock by *one more* than the number of old shares required for a subscription to one new share. To illustrate, if new stock is being offered to old stockholders in the ratio of one new share for four old shares at $30 a share, the value of one right, as calculated before the record date with the old stock selling at $40 a share, would be $2 ($40 − $30 = $10 ÷ 5 = $2). The price of the stock would be likely to decline to $38 on an ex-rights basis.

The value of a right as determined *after* the record date, and before it expires, is calculated by dividing the difference between the prevailing market price for the old stock and the subscription price for the new stock by the *exact* number of old shares required for a subscription to one new share. Using the above example, the value of one right, as calculated after the record date with the old stock selling at $38 a share, would be $2 (38 − $30 = $8 ÷ 4 = $2).[5]

---

[5] The following formulas may be used for calculating the value of a right, where M = market price, S = subscription price, and R = number of rights required to purchase one new share:

$$\text{Value before ex-rights} = \frac{M - S}{R + 1}$$

$$\text{Value after ex-rights} = \frac{M - S}{R}$$

If any dividends are payable prior to the expiration date of the rights, one must reduce the market price of the old stock by the amount of the dividend payment before calculating the value of the rights, inasmuch as the new stock will not be entitled to the dividend.

The problem is more complicated when rights to buy new convertible securities are issued to common stockholders. The convertible bonds or preferred have no record of past market price. Until they are issued, they will be traded (if at all) on a when-issued basis. After they are issued, their price will reflect the value, if any, of the conversion privilege. Their price can be quite volatile, as will be the price of any rights still outstanding before their expiration date.

An example of the offering of convertible securities through rights is found in the case of the American Telephone and Telegraph Company. On June 2, 1971, the company offered to shareholders of record as of June 3, 27.5 million shares ($1,375,000,000) of new convertible preferred stock ($1 par), on the basis of 1 new preferred share for each 20 shares of common plus $40 in cash. Each share of the preferred was to be convertible, on or after October 1, 1971, into 1.05 shares of common stock (that is, at a conversion price of $47.50). At the time, the common stock was selling at 45, so that the new preferred stock had no conversion value. After the date of record, and until June 18, the day the rights were issued, the common stock sold ex-rights. Based on the when-issued value of the preferred of $57, on June 4 the rights sold for 11/32. Subsequently, until they expired on July 12, their price ranged from $\frac{1}{4}$ to $\frac{3}{8}$. The variation reflected the range in price of the preferred of $55\frac{1}{8}$ to $57\frac{3}{8}$.

Stock-Purchase Option Warrants

Certain companies have followed the practice of issuing long-term option warrants for the purchase of their common stocks at prices specified in the instrument, usually considerably above the market value at the time of issue. These warrants are usually included with junior bonds or preferred stock in order to make the securities more attractive, or as part of the terms of exchange in a merger. The warrants have no mathematical value so long as the market price remains below the option price; they do, however, have a practical value in that they provide a "call" on the stock over a designated period. Warrants issued by the Alleghany Corporation in 1952 gave the holder the privilege of buying common stock from the company at the price of $3.75 per share. The warrants were perpetual. In September 1953, at a low in the market, these warrants had a market value of 1-7/16 ($1.4725), despite the fact that the market value of the stock was only $3.00 per share. Speculators were willing to buy the warrants on the chance that the future price of the stock would rise above $5.2225 ($3.75+$1.4725). On October 23, 1972, when the stock sold at 13¾, the warrants sold at 10⅝, slightly above their theoretical value of $10.00 ($13.75—$3.75).

In May 1970, American Telephone and Telegraph Company offered to existing shareholders a package of new debentures plus warrants, through rights. The offering of $1,569,000,000 was the largest single corporate financing on record. For each 35 shares held, shareholders of record April 10, 1970 received rights to buy, at $100 per unit, $100 in 8¾ per cent debentures plus two warrants to purchase one share of common stock each at $52 a share. The warrants expire May 15, 1975. At the time of the offering, the common stock was selling at 47, so the warrants had no mathematical value. The price of the common ranged from 40⅜ to 53⅞ during the rest of 1970 through 1972, and so the warrants' market price reflected their possible long-run rather than their immediate-term value as options to buy shares. The price of the warrants ranged from 5¾ to 13 in 1970–1972.

One of the chief appeals of warrants is that they offer a possibly high degree of price "leverage." Suppose a company's stock is quoted at 15, and warrants are outstanding that permit the holder to buy shares at $20. The warrants have no theoretical value. But let us suppose that the outlook for improvement in the company's earnings is such that the warrants have a market value of $5. If the stock subsequently goes to 45—a 200 per cent increase—the warrants will be worth 25—a 400 per cent increase. If the warrants sell at 30, a 500 per cent increase is enjoyed. Chrysler Corporation has (1973) outstanding warrants (which expire in 1976) to buy common stock at 34. On February 1, 1973 the stock was quoted at 36¼. But the warrants sold at 14½, although they had a theoretical value of only 2½.

REFERENCES

BELL, CLIFFORD, AND L. J. ADAMS, *Mathematics of Finance.* New York: Holt, Rinehart & Winston, 1960.

BOGEN, J. I., ed., *Financial Handbook,* 4th rev. ed., Section 27. New York: The Ronald Press Company, 1968.

CISSELL, ROBERT, AND HELEN CISSELL, *Mathematics of Finance,* 3rd ed., Chapter 6. Boston: Houghton-Mifflin Company, 1968.

HART, W. L., *Mathematics of Investment,* 4th ed. Boston: D. C. Heath & Company, 1958.

HUMMEL, P. M., AND C. L. SEEBECK, *Mathematics of Finance.* Englewood Cliffs, N.J.: Prentice-Hall, Inc., 1971.

SHAO, S. P., *Mathematics of Finance.* Cincinnati, Ohio: South-Western Publishing Co., 1962.

SIMPSON, T. M., et al., *Mathematics of Finance,* 4th ed. Englewood Cliffs, N.J.: Prentice-Hall, Inc., 1969.

WILLIAMSON, J. P., *Investments: New Analytic Techniques,* Chapter 9. New York: Praeger Publishers, Inc., 1971.

13 Sources of Investment Information and Advice

SCOPE: This chapter and the next will indicate the more important sources of information and advice necessary for intelligent decisions. The order of discussion in Chapter 13 is (1) tools of investment, (2) general handbooks of economic information, (3) sources on current economic and business conditions, (4) general information on industries, (5) transportation, (6) public utilities, (7) finance, (8) real estate, (9) information on governmental securities, and (10) foreign securities.

The Tools of Investment

Intelligent investment is to a considerable degree a matter of adequate knowledge. Although all investment commitments involve estimates of future developments, the greater the knowledge the investor has of facts, the more satisfactory his experience should be.

A growing fund of information is available in a wide variety of sources. Some of these deal with the general business situation and outlook; others provide material concerning specific industries, companies, and securities. Some of the information is from primary sources; often it is offered in digested or semidigested form in secondary sources.

All investors use the advice or opinion of others to a certain extent. Some use the opinions of others merely to confirm or challenge their own ideas. Others depend almost completely on others' advice and counsel. Therefore, sources of information and sources of advice may logically be discussed in the same chapters. Indeed, some sources do two things: Give the investor information, and accompany it with opinion.

General Handbooks of Economic Information

General sourcebooks of economic information are mines of facts covering a very wide range of topics.

1. *Economic Almanac,* published annually by the National Industrial Conference Board, is a comprehensive statistical handbook of economic information.

2. *Handbook of Basic Economic Statistics,* published monthly, quarterly, and annually by the Economic Statistics Bureau, Washington, D.C. Each issue contains more than 1,800 series relative to different aspects of the national economy, collected by government agencies.

3. *Trade and Securities Statistics,* published by Standard & Poor's. A wide range of statistics is covered by the "Basic Statistics" section and kept up to date monthly by the publication of "Current Statistics."

4. *Statistical Abstract of the United States,* published annually by the U.S. Department of Commerce, Bureau of the Census, includes summary statistics from public and nongovernmental sources on industrial, economic, social and political subjects. Supplemented by *Historical Statistics of the United States, Colonial Times to 1957,* and *Continuation to 1962 and Revisions.*

5. *Survey of Current Business,* published monthly by the Office of Business Economics, U.S. Department of Commerce, includes a wide variety of statistical series that indicate the trend of business; these are combined in a biennial supplement, *Business Statistics.* The July issue of the *Survey* is the *National Income* number summarizing business activity for the preceding year.

6. *Supplement to Economic Indicators: Historical and Descriptive Background,* 6th ed., U.S. Congress, Joint Economic Committee, 1964. Historical data and descriptions of the series in *Economic Indicators.*

7. *Economic Report of the President,* transmitted to the Congress annually (January), includes a variety of statistical tables on income, employment, and production.

8. *Banking and Monetary Statistics,* published by the Board of Governors of the Federal Reserve System in 1943, and supplemented by a series of pamphlets that update the sections of the original volume, for example, *Money Rates and Securities Markets,* Section 12, 1966.

9. *World Almanac,* published annually by the Newspaper Enterprise Association, Inc., contains comprehensive information of wide coverage.

Sources on Current Economic and Business Conditions

Of the many papers and periodicals devoted in whole or in part to economic and business conditions, only a relatively small selection can be indicated here. Topical coverage by a much larger number of publications is found in such general indexes (monthly and annual) as *Reader's Guide to Periodical Literature, Public Affairs Information Service, Business Periodicals Index,* and *Applied Science and Technology Index,* available in all good libraries. *Vertical File Index* is an annual and monthly index to selected pamphlet material on a wide variety of subjects. *I.E.P. Index* is a monthly publication listing articles in leading American and foreign business and professional journals. Funk and Scott's *Index of Corporations and Industries* (weekly, monthly, and annually) indexes articles on companies and industries that have appeared in financial publications and brokerage house reports.

Daily business and financial pages and special papers. The investor can follow current developments in the financial section of his daily newspaper. Of these, *The New York Times* has the best coverage. (Another advantage of this source is that it publishes a semimonthly and cumulative index of all important news items.) But the information in most dailies is usually very sketchy. Financial material is better obtained from special daily business and financial papers. *The Journal of Commerce and Commercial* (New York) emphasizes commodities and shipping and commercial news. *The Wall Street Journal* is published in five editions—New York, Washington, Chicago, San Francisco, and Dallas. In addition to general business news, it emphasizes notes on individual companies and industries and has a fairly complete quotation section. An index of the New York (national) edition is published monthly and annually.

The information contained in the financial sections of the large metropolitan papers, and in the special business papers, is either statistical or general. The statistical news comprises business and price indexes indicating the state of business, summarized annual and interim reports of corporations, price quotations on commodities and securities, dividend payments, foreign trade and exchange, volume of securities traded, security price averages, and money rates.

The state of business activity throughout the country is measured by a variety of series and index numbers compiled by both public and private agencies. The most widely quoted of these are the monthly figures on Gross National Product, or the value of all goods and services produced in the nation, and the Federal Reserve Board's index of industrial production. Other indexes reveal changes in the cost of living, wholesale and retail prices, employment, and a wide variety of business trends.

In addition to their annual reports of earnings, interim reports on a semiannual or quarterly basis are published by the great majority of important companies. This information, which is summarized in the newspapers, helps investors to act quickly if necessary for the protection of their interests.

Investors should make proper allowance for seasonal influences upon interim reports. Earnings for the first quarter of the year are rarely a dependable guide for the entire year. For example, because of increased volume of crop movements during the harvest months, earnings of certain railroad companies during the second half of the year are generally much better than during the first half.

Price quotations on securities are obtained by the papers, in the case of listed issues, from reporting services using the mechanical price "tickers" operated from the securities exchanges. Quotations on unlisted securities are obtained from investment firms which maintain markets in such issues and from the National Association of Securities Dealers. Explanations of price quotations and their sources are given in the next chapter.

The larger newspapers also give daily information concerning the volume of trading on the last day of trading—the volume of stocks in shares and of bonds in dollars—sometimes compared with those for the equivalent day of the previous year.

The day's leaders—the stocks with the most shares traded—are often itemized in a separate table. Also shown are the number of issues traded that day on the particular exchange, the number of advances and declines from the previous day, and the number of new highs and new lows for the year to date. Even on a day of a general rise in shares, some make their new lows for the year. Seldom if ever have all stocks or bonds moved in the same direction on the same day.

A number of indexes and averages have been constructed to represent large groups of securities on the market as a whole. The large metropolitan dailies and the special business newspapers quote one or more of these. Security price averages are discussed in the next chapter.

Of great interest to most investors is the course of interest rates on various categories of loans and investments. Those basic "bellwether" rates frequently indicated in the papers, either in a special section or derived from price quotations, are as follows (as of January, 1973):

BROKERS' CUSTOMERS LOANS—6 TO 6¼ PER CENT. This rate applies to loans arranged by brokers and dealers secured by bonds and stocks, payable on demand. In 1969–1970, at the peak of the "credit crunch," the rate was as high as 8½ per cent. Brokers' loans may be made only from member banks of the Federal Reserve System and margin requirements are regulated by the Board of Governors of the Federal Reserve System.

COMMERCIAL PAPER (PRIME NAMES, FOUR TO SIX MONTHS)—5½ TO 5¾ PER CENT. Rates on this "businessmen's paper," issued through commercial paper houses, are representative of the short-term money market. They were as high as 9 per cent in December 1969.

BANKERS' ACCEPTANCES—5¼ TO 5½ PER CENT, 120 DAYS. These rates on bankers' bills are normally the lowest nongovernmental rates in the short-term money market. They were as high as 8¾ per cent in January 1970.

DISCOUNT RATE—4½ PER CENT. This is the rate on advances by the Federal Reserve Banks to member banks, secured by U.S. Government securities. The discount rate, formerly a powerful tool of credit control, has lost some of its direct effectiveness in recent years. But it still has a potent influence as an indication of the Federal Reserve Board's attitude toward the credit situation. Successive reductions from the peak rate of 6 per cent in 1969–1970 to 4½ per cent in 1972 accompanied a large increase in the money supply.

THE PRIME RATE—6 PER CENT. This is the rate charged by metropolitan commercial banks on unsecured short-term loans to the strongest business customers. It is very sensitive to credit tightness or ease, and was as high as 8½ per cent in early 1970. In 1971 some New York banks began to charge "floating" prime rates based on the going rate on prime commercial paper plus about ½ per cent.

TREASURY BILLS—5.75 PER CENT. The rate on 90-day obligations is the most sensitive short-term rate in the money market. It was as high as 8 per cent in January 1970 at the peak of the credit squeeze. Treasury bills are issued up to one year in maturity (see p. 68).

TREASURY NOTES—6.40 PER CENT. This is the effective rate of return obtainable from the purchase of U.S. Treasury notes due in four years. (Notes are issued from one to seven years in maturity.) It was as high as 8.3 per cent in January 1970. (Treasury notes are described in Chapter 5.)

TREASURY BONDS—6.85 PER CENT. This is the effective rate of return obtainable from the purchase of U.S. Treasury bonds of twenty years' maturity. *It is the most important interest rate in the capital market from the investment viewpoint.* It provides a continuous standard representing the riskless rental value of long-term money. The spread between other yields and the yields on Treasury bonds of similar maturity represents a reward for risk. The investor must decide whether the spread is satisfactory. (Treasury bonds are issued with maturities of 5 to 40 years. They are described in Chapter 5.)

The general news consists of reports on economic, business, and political conditions, with a growing emphasis on government activity and its profound effect on corporate earnings. Depending on the scope of the particular financial page, a very wide variety of business and financial news is reported in the daily press. A glance at *The New York Times* or *The Wall Street Journal* reveals information on the outlook for various industries, banking and credit, Treasury and municipal financing, foreign business and economic developments, corporate developments, consumption, trade and transportation developments, new security offerings, shipping news, and notes on business personalities. Opinion and comment often accompany reports on Federal finance, money and credit, prices, production, housing starts, building contracts, carloadings, department store sales, electric power production, employment and payrolls, crop production and prices, business inventories, and business failures.

Regular reading of the financial pages will go far toward explaining the forces that bear upon the investment markets. At the same time, the investor must discriminate between the vital and the unimportant, the petty and the significant. Sole reliance should not be placed on the rather superficial material that comprises much of the daily financial and business news. Systematic study of the more specialized sources, such as those indicated below, is necessary for sound investment judgment.

Weekly business and financial periodicals. *Barron's* is a very readable source on business trends, industries, companies, and securities. Short analyses of individual situations are emphasized. The central section, "The Stock Market at a Glance," provides a convenient compendium of security prices, earnings, and dividends covering unlisted securities and investment funds as well as stocks listed on the New York, American, regional, and Canadian exchanges.

Business Week covers the changing business scene and has an interesting section devoted to financial developments.

The Commercial and Financial Chronicle is the most comprehensive financial publication. The Monday issue (Section I) contains corporate notes and complete quotations on all exchanges. Over-the-counter quotations on all types of securities are included. Section II (Thursday) contains contributed articles and discussions of developments in the financial, banking, industrial, and commodities fields. Coverage is encyclopedic.

The Economist, published in England, gives an excellent survey of British and international economic developments and contains statistics on commodity production and prices.

Financial World is devoted to investment advice and information on a wide variety of securities, companies, and industries; it also publishes *Stock Factographs* annually with data on over 2,000 companies.

Investment Dealers Digest is devoted mainly to reports, lists, and advertisements of new corporate and municipal securities offerings.

National Industrial Conference Board *Weekly Desk Sheet* tabulates changes in twenty-one weekly economic indicators. It is accompanied by a semiannual *Chartbook of Weekly Business Indicators.*

United States Investor emphasizes investment news and policy for banks and insurance companies.

U.S. News and World Report covers political and economic developments and trends, and reprints the official texts of important political speeches and government reports.

The Wall Street Transcript reprints the reports of investment firms on companies and industries, and provides the texts of speeches by corporate executives to financial analyst societies.

Two weekly news magazines, *Time* and *Newsweek,* contain good business sections, with emphasis on interesting developments in specific companies. *Kiplinger Washington Letter* is devoted to legislative and official activities related to the economic scene.

Monthly business and financial peiodicals. With the exception of the *Magazine of Wall Street, Forbes,* and *Investor's Reader,* issued biweekly, and *Financial Analysts Journal,* issued bimonthly, the following are monthly journals which cover a wide range of interests:

Bulletins of commercial banks, such as the First National City Bank (New York) *Monthly Economic Letter,* the Cleveland Trust Company *Business Bulletin,* the *Guaranty Survey,* and the Chase Manhattan *Business in Brief,* contain critical and descriptive material on economic and business trends and the capital markets. *Monthly reviews or bulletins* of the several Federal Reserve Banks cover monetary, fiscal, and business conditions.

Credit and Financial Management is devoted primarily to short-term financing.

Dun's, published by Dun & Bradstreet, emphasizes management techniques, trade indexes, and failure data. The Dun & Bradstreet fourteen financial ratios are published periodically.

Economic Indicators, published by the Council of Economic Advisors, contains charts and tables on basic economic data. An annual summary is also published.

The Exchange, published by the New York Stock Exchange, gives information concerning securities listed on the "Big Board." The *American Stock Exchange Investor* is a similar publication.

Federal Reserve Bulletin, published by the Board of Governors of the Federal Reserve System, reviews banking and financial developments and provides a wealth of statistical information, both domestic and foreign, on money, credit, banking, and business. This is a basic source. Also very useful is *Federal Reserve Charts* (monthly and annually) on bank credit, money rates, and business conditions.

Forbes (biweekly) covers business and financial developments and investments. Its annual survey of American industry rates the management performance of a large number of companies.

Fortune presents in a unique fashion the picture of American business enterprise. Its discussion of domestic and foreign business and economic problems and its articles on industries, businesses, and business executives are colorful and comprehensive.

Harvard Business Review contains scholarly and practical articles on all aspects of business management (bimonthly).

The Institutional Investor discusses the problems and policies of large fund management.

Investor's Reader, distributed biweekly by Merrill Lynch, Pierce, Fenner & Smith, covers investment developments and company reviews.

Magazine of Wall Street (biweekly) discusses industries and companies and makes specific investment recommendations.

Monthly Labor Review, published by the U.S. Department of Labor, Bureau of Labor Statistics, surveys trends in the labor market.

The Money Manager (formerly *Bond Buyer*) provides news, quotations, and discussion of the money, capital, and foreign financial markets.

National Industrial Conference Board Business Record surveys opinion on business trends and provides many business indexes of the direction of business activity.

Nation's Business, published by the U.S. Chamber of Commerce, contains articles on general business subjects from the standpoint of the business executive.

Stock Market Magazine emphasizes reports on growing industries and companies; it also provides current information on mutual funds, mergers, new security issues, and general economic conditions.

Survey of Current Business (see general handbooks above).

Quarterly investment and financial periodicals. *Financial Analysts Journal,* published (bimonthly) by the New York Society of Security Analysts, is devoted to analytical methodology and portfolio management.

The Journal of Finance, published by the American Finance Association, contains articles on investment, business finance, money and credit, and international finance, with emphasis on research material.

Pensions is devoted to the management and investment problems of private pension funds.

Annual government policy reports. Certain reports indicate the course of Federal public policy on the economic front. These are the *Midyear Economic Review* and the *Annual Economic Review* of the President's Council of Economic Advisors (the *Annual Review* accompanies the President's Economic Report to the Congress), and the report to Congress of the Joint Committee on the Economic Report.

Information on Industries—General

We cannot indicate here all of the many sources of information concerning industries. The following classifications should, however, prove useful. (More specific sources on special classifications of industries and companies are indicated later.)

Business and financial newspapers and periodicals. (see above).

Government publications and documents. A mass of information on many industries is available in government releases, especially information of a statistical character and on regulated groups. Special mention should be made of the U.S. Department of Commerce, Bureau of the Census, publications such as *Current Industrial Reports, Business Cycle Developments* (monthly), *Business Conditions Digest* (monthly), *Survey of Current Business, Survey of Manufacturers* (annual), *Monthly Retail Trade Report, Statistical Abstract of the United States, Census of Manufacturers* (latest 1967), *Census of Mineral Industries* (1967), and *Census of Business* (latest 1967); *Minerals Yearbook* is published by the U.S. Department of the Interior, Bureau of Mines. U.S. Business and Defense Services Administration issues (annually) *Industry Trend Series* showing recent trends and outlook for over fifty selected industries. Reports of regulatory commissions having to do with railroads, utilities, and banks will be indicated in the sections, below, which are devoted to these industries. Others include annual reports of the Federal Aviation Agency, Federal Communications Commission, Federal Trade Commission, the Maritime Administration, and the annual and special reports of the Securities and Exchange Commission. Of special interest are the S.E.C.'s quarterly reports on *Plant and Equipment Expenditures of United States Business, Net Working Capital of United States Corporations,* and *Quarterly Financial Report: U.S. Manufacturing Corporations.* Special governmental hearings and investigations are useful but irregular in appearance. The reader should consult the monthly and annual catalogs of the U.S. Superintendent of Documents for additional sources.

A valuable source of financial statement data on corporations by groups is *Statistics of Income,* issued annually by the Internal Revenue Service, U.S. Treasury Department.

The *Yearbook of International Trade Statistics* and the *Statistical Yearbook* (annual), published by the United Nations, provide valuable data on foreign business and finance. Other publications concerning foreign economic conditions include the Chase Manhattan Bank *Latin American Business Highlights* (quarterly) and *Europa Year Book* (annually); the First National City Bank (New York) *Foreign Information Service;* and the U.S. Department of Commerce *International Commerce* (weekly).

Trade association publications. Many trade associations publish statistical material that indicates the conditions and trends in various industries. Examples are the annual review or statistical issues of the American Iron and Steel Institute, the Manufacturing Chemists Association, the American Meat Institute, the National Lumber Manufacturers Association, the United States Copper Association, the American Petroleum Institute, and the Rubber Manufacturers Association.[1]

Trade journals. Magazines devoted to special industries are excellent sources of information in their respective fields. The following are representative: *American Gas Journal; Automotive Industries; Canner; Chemical Week; Coal Age; Electrical World; Electronics; Food Industries; Iron Age; National Petroleum News; Oil and Gas Journal; Public Utilities Fortnightly; Railway Age; Rayon Organon; Rubber Age; Textile World;* and *Steel.* A number of trade journals publish annual statistical or review bulletins.[2]

Reports of statistical and rating services. The two major statistical and financial services provide considerable information on industries, along with their other data on companies and securities. (See Chapter 14.) *Moody's Manual of Investments, Industrials* (annually) contains a central "blue section" that provides ratios and data on industrial groups; *Moody's Stock Survey* (weekly) reviews developments in various industries. Standard & Poor's *Industry Surveys,* divided into basic and current sections, indicates how various industries are performing. The same company's *Outlook for the Security Markets* (weekly) includes short industry reviews, as does its weekly *Highlights. Trade and Securities Statistics* provides a wealth of data and index numbers on every phase of business activity and on major industries.

Reports of private agencies. Certain private agencies specialize in statistical information concerning specific industries. Examples are the F. W. Dodge Corporation *Dodge Statistical Research Service, Construction,* the Ward *Automotive Reports and Automotive Yearbook,* and the Alfred M. Best & Co. *Best's Insurance Reports.* The *Industry Composites* prepared

---

[1]For lists of trade associations see: *Directory of National Trade and Professional Associations of the United States* (Washington, D.C.: Columbia Books, Inc., 1971); *Encyclopedia of Associations: National Organizations of the U.S.,* 6th ed. (Detroit: Gale Research Company, 1970).

[2]See *Statistical and Review Issues of Trade and Business Periodicals* (Boston: Baker Library, Harvard University Graduate School of Business Administration, 1964).

by Studley, Shupert, & Co. provide annual group balance sheet and income statement data on a number of industries. Standard & Poor's publishes annually composite corporate per share data, by industries. Stanford Research Institute publishes the *Chemical Economics Handbook* and *Industrial Economics Handbook* that provide data and charts on many important industries. Commodity Research Bureau, Inc., publishes annually the *Commodity Yearbook*. National Industrial Conference Board has issued a series of volumes on various industries, *Statistics of Manufacturing Industries*. Investors Management Sciences, Inc., publishes detailed quarterly and annual computerized data on all major companies in *Financial Dynamics*.

A large number of publications provide operating results and financial data of specific industries. For a complete list, see Robert Morris Associates, *Sources of Composite Financial Data: a Bibliography*, 2nd ed. (Philadelphia: Robert Morris Associates, 1971).

Reports of investments advisory services. In addition to reports and appraisals of specific companies, industries and their trends are appraised in many specific general investment and business services, such as *United Business Service, Babson's Investment and Barometer Letter, The Value Line Investment Survey*, and others.

Reports and brochures of brokerage and investment banking firms. As part of their service to clients, such firms frequently prepare special industry studies that are available at their offices or by mail.

A special service of great value is provided by the Funk & Scott *Index of Corporations and Industries* which lists (weekly and annually) periodical articles and published investment house brochures, classified by industries and companies. An allied publication is the Funk & Scott *Index, International* (annually).

Other industrial sources. *Electronic News Financial Fact Book and Directory*, published annually by Fairchild Publications, covers new developments in the electronics field.

Fairchild's Financial Manual of Retail Stores (annual) and *Textile and Apparel Financial Fact Book and Directory* examine the retail industry.

Information on the Transportation Industries

Railroads.   General sources include:

1. Annual reports of the Interstate Commerce Commission.

2. Monthly reports of earnings to the Interstate Commerce Commission, which usually appear in the newspaper and investment services in summary form.

3. Part I of *Transport Statistics in the United States*, published annually by the Interstate Commerce Commission. Contains complete statistical information on every phase of operation and finance.

4. Numerous other reports and releases of the Interstate Commerce Commission, including traffic statistics and monthly statements of revenue, expenses, earnings, and balance sheet items. Upon request, the Commission will send the investor a list of its various publications.

Secondary sources for the railroad industry include:

1. *Railway Age* (monthly).

2. *Railroad Review and Outlook,* an annual survey of railway operations prepared by the Bureau of Railway Economics of the Association of American Railroads (discontinued after 1969). The same source publishes a report on railway revenues and expenses (monthly), *Operating and Traffic Statistics* (an annual compilation), and *Railway Revenues and Expenses* (monthly).

3. *Railroad Data,* a periodical featuring current railway statistics, developments, and problems, published semimonthly by the Committee on Public Relations of the Eastern Railroads.

4. *A Yearbook of Railroad Information,* a statistical and graphic study of railroad operations prepared annually by the Eastern Railroad Presidents' Conference Committee on Public Relations. Also published as *Railroad Facts* by the Association of Western Railways.

5. *Moody's Manual of Investments, Transportation* (blue section) on the industry with data on traffic, revenues, expenses, securities, and finances. A weekly supplement provides current information.

6. Standard & Poor's *Transportation Securities,* eleven sections (some weekly) covering all aspects of railroad operations and earnings. Includes a general *Weekly Outlook Section.* See also this service's *Industry Surveys* (Railroads).

7. *Transport Economics,* published by the I.C.C., to review and analyze the statements and reports filed by carriers with the Commission.

Air transport. The growing importance of air transportation securities deserves investment attention. The more important sources of current information are:

PERIODICALS. *Air Transportation* (monthly) and *Journal of Air Law and Commerce* (quarterly).

REPORTS OF GOVERNMENT AGENCIES. U.S. Civil Aeronautics Board, *Handbook of Airline Statistics* (annually), *Monthly Report of Air Carrier Traffic Statistics,* and *Air Carrier Financial Data* (quarterly and annually); U.S. Department of Transportation, Federal Aviation Administration, *Air Traffic Activity* (annually), and *Statistical Handbook of Aviation* (annually). See also the annual reports of these agencies.

PRIVATE SOURCES. Aeronautical Chamber of Commerce of America, *Aircraft Yearbook* (annually); Air Transport Association of America, *Air Transport Statistics* and *Traffic Statistics* (quarterly and annually), *Facts and Figures* (various years); *Moody's Manual of Investments, Transportation* (blue section); Standard & Poor's *Transportation Securities;* CBWL-Hayden, Stone Inc., *The Air Transport Industry* (annually).

Motor carriers.

GOVERNMENT SOURCES. Interstate Commerce Commission, *Transport Statistics in the United States,* Part VII (annually) and *Motor Freight Commodity Statistics* (annually); U.S. Department of Commerce, Bureau of Public Roads, *Highway Statistics* (annually).

PRIVATE SOURCES. Automobile Manufacturers Association, *Automobile Facts and Figures* (annually) and *Motor Truck Facts* (annually); American Trucking Association, *Financial and Operating Statistics of Class I Motor Carriers of Property* (quarterly and annually), *Carrier Reports* (quarterly and annually), and *American Trucking Trends* (annually); American Transit Association, *Transit Fact Book* (annually); National Association of Motor Bus Operators, *Bus Facts* (annually); *Moody's Manual of Investments, Transportation* (blue section); Transport Association of America, *Transportation Facts and Figures* (annually).

Oil pipelines.

GOVERNMENT SOURCES. I.C.C., Bureau of Transport Economics and Statistics, *Transport Statistics in the United States,* Part VI (annually); U.S. Department of Interior, Bureau of Mines, *Minerals Yearbook,* Volume II (annually). Federal Power Commission, *Statistics of Interstate Natural Gas Pipeline Companies* (annually).

PRIVATE SOURCES. Association of Oil Pipe Lines, *Transport Revenue and Traffic of Large Oil Pipe Line Companies* (annually).

Information on the Public Utilities Industries

Government sources. Securities and Exchange Commission, annual and special reports; Federal Communications Commission, annual reports, *Statistics of Communications Common Carriers* (annually), *Statistics of Telephone Carriers* (annually), and *Operating Data from Monthly Reports of Telephone Carriers* (monthly); Federal Power Commission, annual reports, *Statistics of Electric Utilities in the United States, Class A and B* (annual volumes on private and publicly owned systems), *Statistics of Natural Gas Companies* (annually), and *Electric Power Statistics* (monthly and annually); U.S. Department of Interior, Bureau of Mines, *Minerals Yearbook* (section on natural gas); annual reports of the respective state public service commissions.

Private sources. Periodicals, including *American Gas Association Monthly, Electrical World; Gas Age; Oil and Gas Journal; Public Utilities* (fortnightly).

Annual report on the output and capacities of the principal electric power companies, compiled by *Electrical World.*

Weekly and monthly reports on the outputs of the larger electric power systems compiled by the Edison Electric Institute. See also the Institute's annual *Statistical Yearbook of the Electrical Utility Industry, Advance Release,* and *Historical Statistics* (data 1920–1960).

American Gas Association, *Gas Facts* (annually) and *Gas Data Book* (a summary of *Gas Facts*).

Bell Telephone Securities, an annual publication of the American Telephone and Telegraph Company covering all securities issued by the Bell System.

Annual *Proceedings* of the National Association of Railroad and Utilities Commissioners.

Moody's Manual of Investments, Public Utilities (blue section) devoted to output and services, earnings and expenses, financing and regulation.

Standard & Poor's *Industry Surveys* (electric utilities).

Information on the Financial Industries

Banks.

1. Periodicals, including *Federal Reserve Bulletin* and monthly bank bulletins mentioned above; bank activities, legislation, stock quotations in daily *American Banker; Banking* (the official magazine of the American Bankers Association); *Bankers Monthly; Burroughs Clearing House* (Burroughs Corporation, monthly); *Savings Bank Journal* (monthly); *Trusts and Estates* (monthly); *The Trust Bulletin* (monthly); *National Banking Review,* published quarterly by the U.S. Comptroller of the Currency (until June 1967).

2. Annual reports of the U.S. Comptroller of the Currency (U.S. Treasury Department), the Federal Deposit Insurance Corporation, and state banking departments.

3. Federal Reserve System annual reports and *Assets and Liabilities of All Banks in the United States* (monthly), *Member Bank Call Report,* and *Federal Reserve Chart Book on Financial and Business Statistics* (monthly, with annual *Historical Chart Book*).

4. National Association of Mutual Savings Banks, *National Fact Book* (annually).

5. *Savings Banks Fact Book* (Savings Banks Trust Co., New York).

6. *Moody's Manual of Investments, Bank and Finance,* and current supplements.

7. Brochures on bank stocks issued periodically by investment houses.

Insurance.

1. Periodicals: *Eastern Underwriter* (weekly) and *National Underwriter* (weekly).

2. Alfred M. Best & Co. *Insurance Reports* (annually), *Life–Health,*

Property–Liability, Digest of Insurance Stocks, Aggregates and Averages: Property–Liability, and *Insurance Guide with Key Ratings.*

3. *Insurance Facts* (annually), published by Insurance Information Institute, New York.

4. *Life Insurance Fact Book* (annually), published by the Institute of Life Insurance, New York.

5. *Moody's Manual of Investments, Bank and Finance* (annually and current). *Moody's Insurance Stocks* (semiweekly) covering insurance, bank, savings and loan, finance, and mutual management companies.

6. Standard & Poor's *Industry Survey, Insurance.*

7. Brochures and studies issued by investment dealers.

Investment companies.

1. *Barron's*—quarterly section on investment companies.

2. *Forbes*—annual report on comparative performance.

3. *Fund Scope*—a monthly magazine devoted to investment company data and performance.

4. *Investment Dealers Digest*—annual special section "Mutual Fund Directory" showing earnings, dividend, prices, performance, and other information.

5. *Open-End Company Monthly Statistics* and *Mutual Fund Fact Book* (annually) published by Investment Company Institute, New York.

6. *Johnson's Investment Company Charts* (annual) showing the performance of leading funds.

7. *Trusts and Estates*—regular comment on performance of funds.

8. *Investment Companies* annually with quarterly supplements, published by Arthur Wiesenberger Services, Inc., New York. This is the most comprehensive source of information on the industry and the performance of individual funds. The *Wiesenberger Investment Report* (bimonthly) contains quarterly sections on investment company investment policy. *Mutual Fund Performance Monthly* rates funds by modern methods.

9. *Vickers Guide to Investment Company Portfolios,* published by Vickers Associates, Huntington, N.Y.

10. *United Mutual Fund Selector* (biweekly) which provides data on performance results and makes specific recommendations, published by United Business Service Co., Boston.

11. Reports and prospectuses of investment companies showing portfolios in detail.

12. Releases and brochures of investment companies and dealers.

Savings and loan associations.

1. *Savings and Loan News* (monthly).

2. Annual reports, *Source Book* (annually), and *News* (monthly), published by the Federal Home Loan Bank Board.

3. Annual reports of the Federal Savings and Loan Insurance Corporation.

4. Annual reports of the state building and loan commissioners.

5. *Savings and Loan Fact Book*, published annually by the United States Savings and Loan League.

Credit unions.

1. Reports of the National Credit Union Administration, Social Security Administration.
2. *Credit Union Yearbook,* published annually by the Credit Union National Association, Madison, Wisconsin.

Information on Real Estate and Real Estate Mortgages and Securities

Real estate.

1. Periodicals: *American Builder* (monthly); *Construction Review* of the Bureau of Labor Statistics (monthly); *Engineering News-Record*, especially its "Annual Report and Forecast," February issue; *National Real Estate and Building Journal* (monthly); McGraw-Hill, Inc., *Construction Daily Newspaper;* Bureau of the Census, *Current Construction Reports* (monthly).
2. Reports of special agencies: *Dodge Construction Statistics Services; Real Estate Analyst*—a complete service on real estate in all its aspects (monthly and intermittent bulletins) by Roy Wenzlick & Co., St. Louis, Missouri.
3. Annual reports of the U.S. Department of Housing and Urban Development, Washington, including the Federal Home Loan Bank Board and the Federal Housing Administration. The former's *Savings and Home Finance Source Book* is also very useful.
4. Bureau of the Census, *U.S. Census of Housing.*

Real estate mortgages.

1. Periodicals: *Federal Reserve Bulletin;* Mortgage Bankers Association of America's *Mortgage Banking* (monthly) and its *Quarterly Economic Report of Trends in the Mortgage Industry.*
2. *Life Insurance Fact Book; Savings and Loan Fact Book* (above).
3. Federal Home Loan Bank Board, *Savings and Home Financing Source Book* (annually), *Annual Report,* and *News* (monthly); U.S. Department of Housing and Urban Development, *Statistical Yearbook.*
4. Mortgage Bankers Association of America, *Mortgage Banking: Trends, Financial Statements, and Operating Ratios* (annually).

Real estate securities. This is an "industry" in which there are no group data. Individual situations must be studied separately in annual reports and in the corporation manuals of Moody's and Standard & Poor's. Real estate investment trusts are reported on in the statistical services.

Information on Governments and Their Securities

U. S. Government. The primary sources of information on U.S. securities are the official reports of the Treasury Department:

    1. Circular giving specific information on each issue prepared at the time of issue.

    2. Daily and monthly statement of the Treasury showing revenue and disbursements for year to date and amount of the Federal debt.

    3. *Treasury Bulletin* (monthly) showing the composition and ownership of the Federal debt, market quotations and yields, and financial and fiscal data.

    4. Annual report of the Secretary of the Treasury, with statistical appendix, giving a comprehensive picture of Federal fiscal operations during the year.

    5. Annual reports of the various government corporations and credit agencies, such as the Farm Credit Administration (Farm Mortgage Corporation, Federal Land Banks, Federal Intermediate Credit Banks), Commodity Credit Corporation, and the Federal National Mortgage Association.

The secondary sources of information on U.S. Government securities include:

    1. *Federal Reserve Bulletin* and *Federal Reserve Chart Book.*

    2. *Governmental Finances,* published by the U.S. Department of Commerce, Bureau of the Census (annually).

    3. *Moody's Manual of Investments, Municipal and Government; Moody's Bond Survey.*

    4. *Securities of the United States Government and Federal Agencies,* published by the First Boston Corporation, New York (biennially).

    5. Standard & Poor's *U.S. Governments* (monthly) and *Government Bond Selector.*

State and local governments. The primary sources of information on state and local governments and their securities are the annual reports prepared by the financial offices of the units. These vary from a brief financial statement to a comprehensive booklet such as that issued by the Comptroller of New York State.

The secondary sources (other than the general sources mentioned elsewhere in this and the next chapter) include

    1. Annual publications of the U.S. Department of Commerce, Bureau of the Census: *State Government Finances; Summary of State Government Finances; City Government Finances; Governmental Finances; Summary of Governmental Finances; State Tax Collections;* and *Local Government Finances in Selected Metropolitan Areas.*

    2. *The Blue List of Current Municipal Offerings,* a daily compilation of offerings of the larger municipal bond houses.

3. *The Money Manager* (New York) devoted mainly to news concerning municipal securities (weekly); *Municipal Bond Sales* (annually).

4. Dun & Bradstreet's *Municipal Credit Surveys,* on obligors having a substantial amount of debt outstanding.

5. Investment Bankers Association of America, *IBA Statistical Bulletin* (quarterly).

6. *Moody's Bond Survey* and *Moody's Manual of Investments, Municipal and Government.*

7. Prospectuses and special releases of investment banking houses interested in state and municipal securities.

8. Standard & Poor's *Municipal Bond Selector, Government Bond Selector,* and *Bond Guide.*

9. The Tax Foundation, Inc. (New York) *Facts and Figures on Government Finance* (biennially). (Also includes data on Federal finance.)

Foreign Securities

This category is not regularly reported on as a group. Individual government issues are reported in *Moody's Manual of Investments, Municipal and Government.* Where publicly offered in the United States, prospectuses required by the S.E.C. are available. Some information is found in the statistical manuals and financial journals. The C. J. Devine Institute of Finance of New York University issues bulletins on the foreign debt situation. The Foreign Bondholders Protective Council is a private organization designed to help investors in foreign securities; its biennial reports are of considerable interest. Special sources on foreign corporate securities include Standard & Poor's *Foreign Securities Survey* (monthly) and *International Stock Report* (monthly); Moody's *Bond Survey* and *Stock Survey:* White, Weld & Co., Ltd. (London), *International Bonds* (descriptions and annual price ranges); Capital Group, Inc., Los Angeles, *Capital International Perspective* (quarterly charts showing prices, earnings and yields, major companies outside of North America). A variety of other sources cover fiscal and trade conditions abroad.

REFERENCES

See end of Chapter 14.

14 Sources of Investment Information and Advice (cont.)

SCOPE: The previous chapter indicated major sources of investment information starting with the general economic scene and progressing through industries and major categories of securities. The investor is now ready to examine the facts on individual companies. He will then frame his investment policy in the light of general investment and market conditions, and make his specific selections. He must, of course, first understand the way in which securities are priced and quoted, individually and by groups or averages.

The order of topics in Chapter 14 is (1) information on companies and their securities, (2) sources on general investment and market conditions, (3) security price indexes and averages, (4) security price quotations, (5) general investment advice, and (6) professional investment management.

Information on Companies and Their Securities

In addition to the general and specialized periodical publications listed in the preceding chapter, the major sources of information on individual companies are:

Annual and interim reports to stockholders. These vary in detail and value. Some are packed with facts; others meet only minimum standards of accounting and financial information. Interim income statements—quarterly or semiannually—are issued by companies with securities listed on an organized exchange. A few industrial concerns publish monthly earnings; railroads are required to do so. The financial press reproduces the latest figures as they are released.

Prospectuses issued under the Securities Act of 1933. These provide much more detail than annual reports, but appear only when new financing is undertaken. The more comprehensive registration statements required by the same statute are available for examination at the offices of the Securities and Exchange Commission. Prospectuses and registration statements are discussed further in Chapter 15.

Form 10-K. Each company with securities listed on an organized exchange, and unlisted companies which had issued securities under the Securities Act of 1933 in excess of $2 millions, must file with the Securities and Exchange Commission on Form 10-K an annual balance sheet and income statement. The data may be more comprehensive than the annual report to stockholders. Form 10-K is available for inspection at the Commission offices and at the securities exchanges where issues are listed.

Statistical services. The two large statistical services—Moody's and Standard & Poor's—are engaged primarily in the publication of statistical data concerning corporations of investment interest. As we shall see below, they also offer opinion and investment advice.

The more important offerings of each of these services, with respect to factual information on companies, are

Moody's:

1. Annual Manuals: *Municipal and Government; Bank and Finance; Industrial; OTC* (over-the-counter); *Public Utility; Transportation.* The history, statements, security prices, and dividend records of a very large number of concerns are presented. The central "blue sections" provide valuable data concerning these industrial groups as a whole. The manuals are kept current by weekly or semiweekly supplements.

2. *Bond Survey and Stock Survey,* information on market trends, industries, companies, and investment recommendations (weekly).

3. *Bond Record,* a guide (monthly) of prices and earnings, including ratings, of some 3,000 bonds.

4. *Dividend Record,* issued semiweekly with a yearly base book.

5. *Handbook of Common Stocks* (annually).

6. *Insurance Stocks* (weekly) covering stocks of insurance companies, banks, savings and loan holding companies, and mutual fund management companies.

Standard & Poor's:

1. *Analysts Handbook,* per-share data on eighty-six industry groups and Standard & Poor's 425 industrials (annually with quarterly supplements).

2. *Bond Guide* (monthly), data on 3,000 corporate bonds.

3. *Bond Investments Service,* including *Bond Outlook* (weekly), *Industry Bond Selector* (monthly), and *Municipal Bond Selector* (monthly).

4. *Called Bond Record,* current lists of dates and provisions of bond redemptions (semiweekly, weekly, and quarterly).

5. *Corporation Descriptions,* factual information on a wide variety of companies, in loose-leaf form. Latest developments are reported in *Daily News Section.*

6. *Dividend Record* (week days and annually), information on dividends and rights issued by nearly 10,000 companies.

7. *Facts and Forecasts,* daily investment advice and observations.

8. *Fitch Survey of Over-the-Counter Securities,* current reports and advice on unlisted stocks.

9. *Foreign Securities Survey* (monthly), discusses foreign government and corporate securities.

10. *Industry Surveys,* compilations of group data and opinion on leading industry groups and major companies in each (weekly).

11. *Listed Stock Reports,* two-page descriptions and financial data on listed securities, with recommendations.

12. *New Issues Service* (weekly), summaries of prospectuses in advance of offering.

13. *The Outlook,* comment on the market, with recommended industries and companies (weekly).

14. *Standard & Poor's Investment Advisory Survey,* a general service on industries and companies, with recommendations.

15. *Standard & Poor's Register of Corporations, Directors, and Executives* (annual with three supplements), lists the officers, directors, and products of over 30,000 companies classified by industry; geographical index.

16. *Security Owners' Stock Guide* (monthly), shows prices and earnings data and buy, hold, or switch ratings on nearly 5,000 common and preferred stocks; pocket-size.

17. *Standard Bond Reports,* two-page descriptions of corporate bonds; a special service deals with *Convertible Bonds.*

18. *Status of Bonds,* calls, coupon-paying agents, bonds in default (annually, with five supplements).

19. *Stock Summary* (monthly), a digest on over 2,400 widely traded stocks.

20. *Transportation Securities,* coverage of transportation operations and earnings (weekly).

21. *Trend Line Daily Basis Stock Charts* and *Current Market Perspectives,* chart services.

22. *Unlisted Stock Reports* (including stocks traded on regional exchanges), two-page reports, periodically revised covering about 1,500 stocks.

23. *Commercial Paper Reports* (intermittently), finances and ratings of companies which have issued commercial paper.

24. *Earnings Forecaster* (weekly), corporation earnings estimates by leading investment organizations.

Other services:

1. *Walker's Manual of Far Western Securities* (annually), kept current by a *Weekly News Letter* and monthly *Supplements.*

2. Robert D. Fisher, *Fisher Mining Manual.*

3. *Investment Companies,* published by Arthur Wiesenberger Services, Inc. (see information on financial industries in Chapter 13).

4. *Financial World, Independent Appraisals of Listed Stocks* (monthly), gives summary data and ratings.

5. *Financial World Stock Factographs* (annually), provides a summary of basic information on stocks listed on the New York and American exchanges.

6. Financial Stock Guide Service, *Directory of Obsolete Securities* (Jersey City, N.J., biennially).

7. Sheets of basic financial information and ratios on a wide variety of

important companies issued by Studley, Shupert & Co. (New York), *Analyses of Corporate Securities, Analyses of Utility Securities,* and *Common Stock Summary;* Herrick-Smith & Co. (New York), *Common Stock Analyses;* and Forbes (New York), *Investographs.*

8. Information on convertible securities and stock warrants is available in Standard & Poor's *Bond Outlook;* Moody's *Bond Survey;* Kalb, Voorhees & Co., *Convertible Fact Finder* (weekly), *Convertible Preferred Chart Book* (monthly), and *Convertible Bond Chart Book* (monthly); Richard H. Morris Associates, *Warrant & Stock Survey* (weekly); and *Value Line Convertible Survey* (monthly).

Advisory services. *United Business Service, The Value Line Investment Survey, Forbes Investor, Tillman Survey,* and many others analyze industries and companies and make recommendations.

Reports and brochures of brokerage firms, security dealers, and investment banks. These reports are issued regularly or intermittently to customers and potential clients. These range from one-page summaries to comprehensive analyses. The information is usually accompanied by investment advice. For an index of such reports, see Funk & Scott *Index of Corporations and Industries.*

Lists of information on companies, officers, directors, products, sales, and employees. Dun & Bradstreet's *Million Dollar Directory* (annually with two supplements) and *Standard & Poor's Register of Directors and Executives* (annually with three supplements) list this information.

Information on General Investment and Market Conditions

Many of the sources outlined above provide comment and opinion on the general investment and market outlook. Such opinion ranges from careless to exact, and from condensed to complete. What are the forces at work in the investment market? What is the outlook for the bond and stock markets? Where will the averages go? What is the outlook for general business, and how well are the securities markets reflecting this outlook? The investor can get much free advice on such matters, or he can subscribe to services that purport to give him more expert comment.

1. The daily financial press (metropolitan dailies and the special business and financial dailies) reports the opinion of newsworthy persons and summarizes the attitude of Wall Street houses.

2. Certain periodicals such as *Barron's, Commercial and Financial Chronicle, Financial World, Magazine of Wall Street,* and *Investor's Reader* keep up a running discussion of the outlook on the market.

3. The statistical or subscription services devote much of certain of their publications to descriptions of the current market situation and prognostications of the near-term and long-term outlook. The following are representa-

tive: Moody's *Bond* and *Stock Surveys;* Standard & Poor's *Outlook;* and *United Business Service.*

4. Special advisory services, as well as investment counsels, keep their clients in tune with the general investment situation.

5. Brokers, dealers, and the larger bond houses offer a running commentary, oral and written, on the market and its condition. Their brochures and "letters" show interesting but confusing dissimilarities.

6. Special mention should be made of the forecasts of market price action, either in general publications or in special letters, furnished to clients at a fee. These in the main tend to project the current condition or trend in the market. Some are daring enough to predict change. The usefulness of such advice is limited because different securities have a way of acting differently unless the whole market is in a drastic upward or downward surge.

Certain well-known forecasts are based on interpretations of the Dow theory. Such opinions may help the investor avoid the worst mistakes in the timing of purchases and sales. However, other methods also exist by which the investor can minimize or even avoid this problem. (See Chapter 20.)

Security Price Averages and Indexes

A number of price averages and indexes have been constructed to represent large groups of securities or the market as a whole. The most widely published are the Dow-Jones averages, and the Standard & Poor's indexes, and the New York Stock Exchange Index. Other stock averages are published *by Moody's, Barron's,* and *The New York Times.* Most good financial pages will show one or more of these.

In addition to five bond averages, Dow Jones & Co. publishes four stock price series at the opening and close and at each hour of the New York Stock Exchange day: 30 Industrials,[1] 15 Utilities, 20 Transportation, and the composite of the 65. Such averages enable the reader quickly to observe the trend in prices more reliably than observing the movement of a few leading issues.

The Dow Jones Industrial Average of 30 stocks was originally computed by dividing the unweighted total value of the stocks by 30. Due to stock dividends and split-ups, however, the current (1973) divisor has been reduced to 1.661. This explains the high level of the "average" price. Quarterly dividends, earnings, and price-earnings ratios are also calculated for the four averages, again involving the use of the divisor. These are published in *Barron's.*

The Dow Jones averages have often been criticized as not representative of the market as a whole. But they are still widely used and quoted. The Dow Jones Company publishes an annual volume, *Dow Jones Investors'*

[1]The companies included in this popular stock average are (1972): Allied Chemical, Aluminum Company of America, American Brands American Can, American Telephone & Telegraph, Anaconda, Bethlehem Steel, Chrysler, DuPont, Eastman Kodak, General Electric, General Foods, General Motors, Goodyear, International Harvester, International Nickel, International Paper, Johns-Manville, Owens-Illinois, Procter and Gamble, Sears Roebuck, Standard Oil of Calif., Standard Oil of N.J., Swift, Texaco, Union Carbide, United Aircraft, U.S. Steel, Westinghouse Electric, and Woolworth.

Handbook, containing historical price, earnings, dividend, and other information on the four stock averages.

Two indexes are more representative of the market as a whole. The present Standard & Poor's Composite 500 (with separate series for 25 rails, 50 utilities, and 425 industrials) was first issued in February 1957. This is a weighted index, rather than an average, that is, the price of each share is multiplied by the number of shares outstanding. The aggregate value is then expressed as a percentage of the average value in the base period 1941–1943, then divided by 10. The new Industrials index started in 1957 at 47, which was about the average price of "Big Board" listed common stocks at that time. (See Table 14-1.) Price changes are computed hourly, and daily at the close of the market. Dividends, earnings, dividend yields, and price-earnings ratios for the Standard & Poor's series are published in *The Outlook* (weekly).

Objections to the misleading high value of the Dow-Jones averages, and the need for measures of change in the value of all listed stocks in more realistic terms, led to the production in 1966, by both the New York and American Exchanges, of daily indexes of all common stocks listed on the respective exchanges. The new N.Y.S.E. Index covers all of its more than 1,330 common issues, and it is weighted to reflect the number of outstanding shares of the individual issues. The base index was arbitrarily set at 50 as of December 31, 1965. Hourly changes in the composite are also converted into changes in terms of dollars and cents per share. The Exchange also publishes four separate indexes: Finance, Transportation, Utility, and Industrial.

An index based on thirty-five over-the-counter stocks is prepared by the

Table 14-1. STANDARD & POOR'S INDEXES OF COMMON STOCK PRICES

(annual averages of weekly indexes)

	500 Composite	*425* Industrials	*55* Utilities	*20* Railroads
1957	44.38	47.63	32.19	28.11
1958	46.24	49.36	37.22	27.05
1959	57.38	61.45	44.15	35.09
1960	55.85	59.43	48.86	30.31
1961	66.27	69.93	60.20	32.56
1962	62.38	65.54	59.16	30.56
1963	69.87	73.39	64.99	37.58
1964	82.05	86.19	69.91	45.54
1965	88.17	93.48	76.08	46.78
1966	85.26	86.78	68.22	46.34
1967	91.93	99.18	68.10	46.72
1968	98.70	107.49	66.42	48.84
1969	97.84	107.13	62.64	45.95
1970	83.22	91.29	54.48	32.13
1971	98.29	108.35	59.33	41.94
1972	109.20	121.80	56.90	44.11

SOURCE: Standard & Poor's *Trade and Securities Statistics.*

National Quotation Bureau and is available at dealers' offices and in some financial publications.

Price averages also indicate the trend of the market by classes of securities. Some newspapers show separate averages for utility, oil, steel, food, motor, and other groups of stocks and thus enable their readers to compare the prices of any particular group with the general trend of the market. Standard & Poor's *Trade and Securities Statistics* and *Outlook* provide an unusually large number of industrial group price indexes. Bond and preferred stock yield averages by quality groups are published by Moody's *(Bond Survey)*, Standard & Poor's *(Outlook* and *Trade & Securities Statistics)*, and *Barron's.*

Security Price Quotations

United States Government obligations. United States Treasury bonds are listed on the organized exchanges, but the bulk of the trades are in large amounts and take place over-the-counter. These bonds are quoted in percentages of par value, with fractions in 1/32 of a point. The unit of trading on the New York Stock Exchange is $1,000 par value, but price quotations are in terms of $100 of principal. For example, the following information on a specified Treasury bond appeared in the financial section of *The New York Times* on July 19, 1972, reporting transactions as of July 18:

			Bid	Asked	Net Change in Bid	Yield
June	'83–'78	$3^1/_4$'s	78.4	79.4	—	5.87%

These bonds bore a 3¼ per cent interest rate and were payable in June 1983, but were redeemable by the Government at any time between June 1978 and 1983. The best bid at the close of trading was 78 4/32 or $781.25 and the best offer (lowest asked price) was 79 4/32 or $791.25. The bid was unchanged from the closing bid of the previous day. The yield to maturity (1983) was 5.87 per cent.

Treasury notes, which represent debt of from one to seven years in maturity, are also quoted in thirty-seconds, but certificates of indebtedness and Treasury bills, also traded exclusively over-the-counter, are quoted on a percentage-of-yield basis. For example, on the date referred to above, the following quotation on Treasury bills appeared:

	Bid (per cent)	Asked (per cent)	Yield
October 26, 1972	4.02	3.84	3.95%

Listed bond price quotations. Foreign bonds and domestic corporation bonds that are listed on the New York Stock Exchange and the

American Stock Exchange are quoted in percentages of par, in eighths of a point. For example, on the same date as above, the following appeared under the general heading of "New York Stock Exchange Bond Trading."

Corporation Bonds 1972			Sales in				Net
High	Low		$1,000	High	Low	Last	Change
113	**104**	Beth Stl **9's, 2000**	1	**110^1/$_2$**	**110^1/$_2$**	**110^1/$_2$**	**—^{1}/$_2$**

The price of Bethlehem Steel 9 per cent bonds due in 2000 ranged from a high of $1,130 ($1,000. principal value) to a low of $1,040 during the period January 3 to July 18, 1972. On July 18, transactions totalled $1,000. The highest price at which a trade took place during the day was at $1,105 per bond, the lowest at $1,105 also. The closing price of $1,105 represented a decrease of $50 over the closing price on July 17 ($1,155).

Numerous abbreviations are used in bond titles appearing on quotation pages and elsewhere, of which the following are most commonly found:

adj., aj.	adjustment
asd., asstd.	assented
clt., col., col. tr.	collateral trust
con., cons.	consolidated
c., cou., coup.	coupon
ct., cv., conv.	convertible
deb.	debenture
div.	divisional
eq., equip.	equipment
ext.	extension
f.	flat
g.	gold
gen.	general mortgage
gu., gtd.	guaranteed
imp.	improvement
inc.	income bonds
int. ctfs.	interim certificates
it.	joint
m., mtg.	mortgage
p.m.	purchase money
perp.	perpetual
pr. ln.	prior lien
re., real est.	real estate
ref., rfg.	refunding
r., reg.	registered
ser.	series
s.f.	sinking fund
st.	stamped
war.	warrants
w.w.	with warrants
x.w.	without warrants
Ist 4s'	first mortgage 4 per cent bonds
77	due in 1977
85–77	due in 1985, may be paid 1977 to 1985

Listed stock price quotations. Quotations of listed stocks are fairly well standardized, and about the same methods are used on all of the exchanges. The following information on a leading industrial common stock listed on the New York Stock Exchange is taken from *The New York Times* of July 19, 1972, covering transactions on July 18, 1972.

High	Low	Stocks and Div. (in dollars)	Sales (100's)	First	High	Low	Last	Net Change
$49^1/_8$	$38^1/_4$	Gillette 1.40	256	$46^1/_4$	$47^1/_2$	$46^1/_8$	$47^1/_4$	$+^5/_8$

The price of Gillette common stock from January 3, 1972 to July 18, 1972, ranged from a high of $49⅛ per share to a low of $38¼. The current annual dividend rate was $1.40 per share, based on the last quarterly or semiannual declaration. (Sometimes the dividend is the amount declared or paid thus far in the year and is so indicated by a footnote designation.) The total volume of sales on July 18 was 25,600 shares. The opening transaction was at $46.25 a share, the highest during the day was at $47.50, the lowest was at $46.125, and the last sale before the close of the trading day was at $47.25. This was $.625 higher than the closing price on the previous trading day.

Unless otherwise designated, the quotation refers to the common stock of the company. Quotations on preferred stocks are indicated by *pf.* Other abbreviations and symbols frequently used in stock quotations and elsewhere are as follows:

A.D.R.	American depository receipts
com.	common
ct., ctfs., vtc.	voting trust certificates
cv.	convertible
ex d., xd.	without dividend
ex r., xr.	ex-rights
gtd.	guaranteed
pf.	preferred
pr. pf.	prior preferred
w.i.	when, as, and if issued

Quotations on listed stocks (and bonds) not traded on the exchange on a given day are found in a separate section and are in terms of bid and asked prices. The major New York dailies also report closing prices on a selected list of stocks on "out-of-town" exchanges.

Beginning early in October, 1972, a number of leading papers, including the *Wall Street Journal* and *The New York Times,* began to carry a daily price-earnings ratio for each stock listed on the New York and American stock exchanges.

Over-the-Counter Quotations. A large number of securities are not listed but are traded over-the-counter. In addition to the Federal obligations previously mentioned, this group includes: bonds of U.S. Government agencies that are fully guaranteed by the Government; bonds of Federally sponsored agencies, such as the Federal Land Banks; state and municipal bonds; railroad guaranteed stocks and equipment obligations; bank, insurance company, and investment company stocks; real estate securities; foreign securities (other than those listed); and a host of industrial, utility, and railroad bonds and stocks.

Quotations of local over-the-counter securities are obtained from dealer-broker houses, and the National Association of Securities Dealers, Inc. makes available daily and supervises the quotations for a large number of securities. The number of quotations varies from a long list in the major dailies and special financial newspapers to a short list in smaller local dailies.

In early 1971, a national automated quotation system (NASDAQ) was inaugurated; desk-top equipment provides instant quotations on several thousand over-the-counter securities to subscribing brokers and dealers.

Over-the-counter quotations are confined to bid and asked prices, and may be accompanied by dividend information (in the case of stocks). The bid price on the previous day is sometimes shown. (The over-the-counter market is discussed in Chapter 16.)

Sources of published price quotations:

1. Daily range and close: metropolitan newspapers; *Wall Street Journal.*

2. Weekly range and close: *Barron's; Commercial and Financial Chronicle* (Section II).

3. Monthly range: *Bank and Quotation Record,* published monthly by Dana & Co., New York.

4. Annual range: some metropolitan newspapers; *Wall Street Journal; Barron's* (see first issue in January for twelve-month range); *Commercial and Financial Chronicle* (Section II); *Moody's Manuals* (also "blue sections"); Standard & Poor's *Corporation Descriptions, Listed Bond Reports, Listed Stock Reports, Over-the-Counter and Regional Exchange Stock Reports, Bond Guide.*

5. Quotations on unlisted securities: available at brokers' offices from National Quotation Bureau, Inc. lists. This firm also publishes *National Stock Summary* and *National Bond Summary* (semiannually and monthly) giving quantity of orders and offers, and prices, of unlisted stocks and bonds.

6. State and municipal bonds: *Blue List of Current Municipal Offerings; Bank and Quotation Record; Moody's Bond Survey; The Money Manager.*

General Investment Advice

The investor who is unwilling or unable to make his own investment selections has a number of sources of investment advice at his disposal. Some of this advice is aimed at all who read or subscribe; other advice is pointed at particular clients. But even if he relies somewhat on the opinions of others, the intelligent investor should be able to judge the reasonableness of the opinion he seeks.

Periodicals. Certain journals are devoted primarily to investment advice. These include *Financial World, Magazine of Wall Street,* and to a limited extent, *Forbes. The Commercial and Financial Chronicle* runs a regular column, "The Stock I Like Best," reporting opinion of Wall Street analysts. *Barron's* articles suggest the investment position of industries and companies. *Financial Analysts Journal* reports the impressions of professional analysts on industries and companies.

Statistical or subscription services. Such services offer advice on industries, companies, and investment policy in their general publications such as Moody's *Bond* and *Stock Surveys,* Standard & Poor's *Outlook, Bond,* and *Stock Reports,* and *Industry Surveys,* and Fitch's (now Standard & Poor's) *Survey of Over-the-Counter Securities.* Standard & Poor's issues a weekly *Investment Advisory Survey* that makes specific recommendations. Included in the pocket-sized manuals of all of these services are lists of companies suggested for investment. One weakness of such advice is that securities are often recommended on the basis of their earnings prospects without much regard to their prices.

Security ratings. The statistical or subscription services also rate the quality of the more important securities by symbols such as Aaa, Aa, and so forth. Ratings are useful guides in the selection of suitable securities, but investors should find them valuable chiefly in confirming or challenging their own appraisals. Moody's and Standard & Poor's bond ratings are found in Moody's *Manual* and *Bond Survey* and Standard & Poor's *Corporation Descriptions* and *Bond Guide,* respectively. Another organization, Babson's Business Service, rates bonds (and stocks) in its reports to clients.

Standard & Poor's rates stocks in the pocket manuals and in the weekly advisory service. Common stocks bear symbols of A+ to C, preferred stocks AAA to C. Moody's *Stock Survey* rates by buying advice rather than quality: Buy, Hold, or Switch.

Financial World issues *Independent Appraisals of Listed Stocks* (monthly), in which stocks are rated by symbols. Quality symbols are also used in the *Value Line Investment Survey.*

Investment services. The statistical and rating services not only provide advance in their general publications, but also sell investment advisory service to a more restricted group of clients. A large number of other firms are solely in the business of selling investment advice: Babson's, Forbes Investographs, Value Line, United Business Service, and many others. Such services cover general market forecasting, general investment advice, and specific recommendations. The value of such services is difficult to assess. The investor should make a sample test of previous recommendations and discover how well they turned out.

Brokers, dealers, and investment banking houses. Investors probably rely more on their security brokers and dealers for advice than on any other source. Some of these maintain research and analytical departments. Many of them publish research bulletins, brochures, and regular "market letters." Some are speculatively minded, and are mainly interested in producing appreciation in their clients' portfolios. And all of them live on commission volume. Nevertheless, the skilled and conscientious broker will strive to serve his customer well.

Personal Investment Advice

One difficulty with the above sources of advice is that their counsel is not often directed towards the special needs and conditions of investors. This is to be expected, since much advice is free or relatively inexpensive. More personal advice costs money—and it is worth it if it gets good results. Sources of such advice are of four main types: (1) brokers, dealers, and investment houses; (2) banks and trust companies; (3) subscription services; and (4) professional investment counsel.

Brokers, dealers, and investment houses. These sources offer personalized portfolio management of large accounts for a separate fee. Many of them are registered investment advisers (see below).

Banks and trust companies. Many investors rely on their commercial banking connections for investment advice. Such advice is likely to be cautious, in keeping with banking tradition. More specific service, at a fee, is available from the larger banks on "agency" accounts, ranging from limited to full management. The trust department will also manage securities on a trust basis, individually or pooled in a "common trust fund."

The subscription services. In addition to their general services, the investment and rating services offer portfolio reviews and management supervision of special accounts. The fee for thorough service for individuals, small banks, pension funds, and other investors may run from $\frac{1}{4}$ to $\frac{1}{2}$ per cent of the principal, per annum, with a minimum of $500 to $1,000.

Professional Investment Management

Scope of the industry. The investment advisory industry has achieved a position of major importance as a result of the growing interest in securities, the development of investment capital in more and more hands, the growth of institutional accumulations of funds, and the increasing complexity of the task of investment management. At the end of 1970, about 3,500 firms were engaged in supplying, at a fee, investment advice to a wide array of corporate, institutional, and individual clients. Assets under advisement totalled 130 billions, divided among 85,000 accounts.[2] (These figures do not include advisers whose sole service consists of the issuance of written reports; bank trust departments and life insurance companies are also excluded from the definition of "investment adviser").

The assets managed by 1,343 firms (constituting the great bulk of the industry's business) were distributed among major clients as shown in Table 14-2.

Table 14-2. ASSETS AND ACCOUNTS OF INVESTMENT ADVISERS

Type of Client	Assets ($ bill.)		No. of Accounts
	Total	Common Stock	
Registered investment companies	$59.1	$48.3	893
Individuals and personal trusts	25.5	20.2	69,623
Employee benefit plans	13.1	8.4	4,337
State and local government pensions	6.5	1.5	191
Corporations	6.5	2.3	2,166
Educational endowments	5.7	3.6	477
Other non-profit organizations	3.3	2.1	1,614
Insurance companies	4.1	1.3	439
Non-registered investment companies	2.4	1.7	1,386
Advisers' own portfolios	1.6	1.2	804
Foundations	1.4	1.0	200 (est.)
Other	.8	.6	2,841
	$130.0	$92.2	84,971

SOURCE: *Institutional Investor Study Report of the Securities and Exchange Commission*, Chapter IV, p. 150. 92nd Congress, 1st Session, House Document No. 92-64.

The average size of advisory accounts was highest for investment companies and lowest for individuals. In a sample of 158 advisory firms with 42,118 accounts, 75 per cent of individuals' and personal trust accounts had assets of less than $.5 millions.

Investment policy. Of the total assets managed, $92 billions or 71 per cent consisted of common stock. The highest ratio of common was found in non-registered investment companies (hedge funds, offshore funds) and the lowest in insurance companies. Individuals' and personal trust accounts averaged 79 per cent in common stocks, but within this group there was a wide range of from zero to 100 per cent.

Of the total funds managed, $78 billions or 60 per cent of assets and 61,000 or 66 per cent of accounts were "discretionary," that is, the advisers had full jurisdiction over the portfolios. This arrangement is most pronounced in the case of investment company and individual clients.

[2]The factual data in this section are derived from *Institutional Investor Study Report of the Securities and Exchange Commission*, Chapter IV. 92nd Congress, 1st Session, House Document No. 92-64, March 1971. This source provides a wealth of information on investment advisers that was never available before, including size measurements, securities holdings, organization, operations, management fees, expenses, revenues, and other facts. A good deal of the detail is derived from a study of a large sample of firms.

Management fees. The average advisory fee ran .46 per cent of assets. Individuals' accounts fees were concentrated between .40 and .60 per cent. Fees based on performance were charged in a number of cases.

Types and affiliations of advisory firms. The term "investment adviser" includes a variety of types of firms. As indicated above, many securities brokers and dealers manage portfolios on a fee basis. The term also includes publishers of advisory services such as bulletins, financial letters, forecasts, industry and company analyses, and investment advice. Our interest here is in a more restricted group, the *investment counsel* firms, whose function is to supply, for a fee, direct investment supervisory services to the types of clients listed in Table 14-2, and particularly those serving individuals.[3] Until recently, counsels have been interested only in fairly large accounts of individuals, but now firms are appearing which accept accounts as small as $5,000–$10,000, with typical fees of two per cent with a minimum of $200. The larger firms (about fifty) are members of the Investment Counsel Association of America and operate under strict rules that require the highest level of professional conduct.

Regulation. Investment advisers who use the mails or interstate commerce must register with the Securities and Exchange Commission and are subject to regulation under the Investment Advisers Act of 1940.[4] They must file information with the Commission covering details of organization and operation, affiliations and qualifications of principals, records and contracts, scope of authority over clients' funds, management fees, and other details. Advisory contracts must be in writing. Fraudulent, deceitful, and manipulative conduct is prohibited. There is no requirement to file financial statements or periodic reports of condition with the Commission. The composition of clients' portfolios and the investment performance achieved are not made public. The investor who is considering employing an investment counsel must get any information on its investment competence from the firm or from other clients.

REFERENCES

Ad Hoc Committee of Librarians, *Sources of Information on Transportation,* published for the Transportation Center at Northwestern University. Evanston, Ill.: Northwestern University Press, 1964.

Andriot, J. L., *Guide to Government Statistics.* McLean, Va.: Documents Index, 1971.

Coman, E. T., Jr., *Sources of Business Information,* rev. ed. Berkeley, Calif.: University of California Press, 1964.

[3]The subscription services qualify as "investment counsels" under the Investment Advisors Act if a "substantial" part of their income is derived from fee accounts.

[4]Investment advisers whose only clients are investment companies have been required to register since December 1971.

D'Arcy, G. M., *Investment Counsel: Profit and Peace of Mind for the Investor.*
New York: I. Oblensky, 1964.

The Dow Jones Average 1885–1970. Princeton, N.J.: Dow Jones Books, 1972.

Flumiani, C. M., *How to Read the Wall Street Journal for Pleasure and Profit.*
Springfield, Mass.: Library of Wall Street, 1967.

Forest, J. G., *Financial News: How to Read and Interpret It.* New York: The
New York Times, 1965.

Hazard, J. W., and Milton Christie, *The Investment Business,* Chapter 5. New
York: Harper & Row, Publishers, 1964.

How to Read and Understand Financial and Business News, 9th rev. ed. New York:
Doubleday & Co., Inc., 1963.

Institutional Investor Study Report of the Securities and Exchange Commission,
Chapter IV. 92nd Congress, 1st Session, House Document No. 94–64. Washington: U.S. Government Printing Office, 1971.

Johnson, H. W., *How to Use a Business Library,* 3rd ed. Cincinnati: South-
Western Publishing Co., 1964.

Manley, Marion C., *Business Information: How to Find and Use It.* New York:
Harper & Row, Publishers, 1955.

McNierney, Mary A., ed., *Directory of Business and Financial Services,* 6th ed.
New York: Special Libraries Association, 1963.

Schmeckebier, L. F., and R. B. Easton, *Government Publications and Their Use,*
2nd rev. ed. Washington, D.C.: The Brooking Institution, 1969.

Select Information Service, *1970 Guide to Business and Investment Services.*
New York: Geo. H. Wein, 1970.

Selected Business Reference Sources. Baker Library, Graduate School of Business
Administration, Harvard University, 1965.

Stabler, C. N., *How to Read the Financial News,* 10th ed. New York: Harper &
Row, Publishers, 1965.

U. S. Dept. of Commerce, Bureau of the Budget, *Statistical Services of the
United States Government.* Washington, D.C.: U.S. Government Printing
Office (irregular).

Walter, H. C., ed., *Investment Information and Advice,* 2nd ed. Rochester, N.Y.:
Fir Publishing Co., 1964.

Wasserman, Paul, et al., eds, *Statistics Sources,* 3rd rev. ed. Detroit: Gale Research
Company, 1971.

Way, J. B., *Investment Information: A Guide to Information Sources.* Detroit:
Gale Research Company, 1969.

15 New Securities; Investment Banking

SCOPE: This chapter discusses the origination and distribution of the new securities which are offered to the public. It is chiefly concerned with the work of investment banking houses and with the regulation of their activities in connection with the marketing of corporate issues. The order of discussion is (1) economic function of investment banking, (2) business functions of investment banks, (3) types of investment firms, (4) internal organization, (5) direct selling and private placement of securities, (6) private negotiation, (7) competitive bidding, (8) the buying function, (9) underwriting, (10) prices and commissions on securities, (11) "best-efforts" selling, (12) "stand-by" underwriting, (13) selling the securities, (14) other banking services, (15) Federal regulation, and (16) state regulation.

Economic Function of Investment Banking

The investment banker is a middleman, between the governmental or business issuer of securities and the investing public. Through him, new long-term capital is obtained in large volume. To a large degree he influences the channels into which savings are directed. His responsibilities extend to the issuer for advice, aid in financing, and determination of sound financial practices. To his investing clients he is responsible for thorough investigation of the issuer and its securities, selection of sound issues, formation of investment judgment, and aid in maintaining a market, that is, standing ready to buy the securities he has helped to sell. He thus plays an extremely important role in capital formation both by making available to business concerns and public bodies the funds required for the operation and growth of the economy and by obtaining these funds from the savings of many millions of investors, directly and through financial institutions. As of 1962 about 4,000 firms regularly or at times acted in some sort of investment banking capacity, of which the core was represented by the 800 members of the Investment Bankers Association of America.[1]

[1]Irwin Friend et al., *Investment Banking and the New Issues Market.* Cleveland: The World Publishing Company, 1967, p. 11.

In the past,[2] investment bankers have underwritten over 50 per cent of the securities sold in the United States, and aided in the placement of another 20 per cent.

Annual data are available on the gross proceeds of new corporate security issues (over $300,000 in size) offered for cash in the United States.[3] (See Table 15-1.) Most of the issues sold publicly involve some or all of the services of investment bankers; many of those sold *privately*, that is, directly from corporation to institutional investor, are also placed by investment bankers acting as agents.

Table 15-1. PUBLIC AND PRIVATE SECURITY OFFERINGS, 1971

Public offerings	
Registered under Securities Act of 1933	$35,613,501,000
Unregistered	1,796,841,000
Private offerings	7,679,982,000
Total	$45,090,324,000

Business Functions of Investment Banking

The chief function of the investment banker is the distribution of new issues of securities. He assists the issuer during the entire process of raising its required new capital, from the initial planning of the financing to the final placement of the securities with investors. He performs the same function as the merchant who buys goods on a wholesale basis and sells them at retail. In most transactions he also advises the corporation as to the form and timing of the sale, and plays an important part in the investment planning of his ultimate clients, the investors.

In acting as merchants engaged in the business of distributing securities, investment bankers differ from commercial bankers, who are primarily the custodians of funds deposited with them. The commercial banks, in loaning these funds, are, in effect, using capital which belongs to other people and which they must be prepared to return at short notice.[4] Investment bankers, who are not allowed to engage in deposit banking, must supply their own funds for use in purchasing securities, or use short-term bank credit for this purpose. As merchants, they place their capital in inventories which must be resold before additional securities may be purchased.

The investment banker should be distinguished from the *broker*, who is mostly concerned with executing transactions in securities that are already outstanding, for the account of others, and from the *dealer*, who buys and sells securities for his own account. Neither of these as such plays any part

---

[2]*United States* v. *Henry S. Morgan, Harold Stanley, et al., Defendants' Preliminary Memorandum*, U.S. District Court for the Southern District of New York (Civil No. 43–757, 1950), pp. 12, 24. See also Table 15-2 of this book.

[3]Securities and Exchange Commissions, *Statistical Bulletin*.

[4]During recent years, commercial banks have been making "term loans" for periods as long as ten years, in contrast to the traditional limit of one year for bank loans. This innovation has enlarged the scope of commercial banking and reduced the field of investment banking. (See Chapter 22.)

in the actual origination of new security issues, although they may be involved in the retail distribution of such issues.

Many brokerage houses maintain investment banking departments, and many investment banking firms have brokerage divisions and act as dealers in securities, both listed and unlisted, and in mutual funds. A number of investment houses act as managers of portfolios for investors, organize and manage investment companies, deal in government securities, and maintain facilities for trading in commodities.

Types of Investment Banking Houses

Investment banking houses may be classified as follows: national or local, depending upon their field of activity; partnerships or corporations, depending upon the form of organization; and underwriters or distributors, depending upon the relationship with the issuer. Many of the larger investment houses (such as Halsey, Stuart and First Boston) do a nationwide business with offices in the principal cities; some of the very largest have no out-of-town offices (such as Morgan Stanley and Kuhn, Loeb). Some conduct a purely wholesale business; others are both wholesalers and large retailers. These firms are able to distribute relatively large portions of new issues and usually join in the original underwriting. Others are known as distributors, although the underwriting firms also act as distributors.

Only about 300 firms regularly accept corporate underwriting commitments. Only about fifty firms manage the major issues of securities; these have their headquarters in New York, Chicago, and San Francisco.

Internal Organization

The internal organization of an investment banking house depends chiefly upon its size. The larger houses have three major departments: a buying department, which investigates new clients, originates new issues, and deals with institutional investors in private placements; a syndicate department, which deals primarily with other firms in organizing purchase groups to handle large issues; and a sales department. Large firms also maintain statistical and research organizations. The smaller houses necessarily combine many activities into a few operating departments. From a functional viewpoint, the work of an investment banking house, as distinguished from that of a securities brokerage firm, may be divided into five fields:

1. The buying function is that of purchasing, through underwriting or otherwise, new issues of securities to be offered for resale.

2. The selling function is that of distributing, either at wholesale through other dealers or at retail to the public, the securities previously purchased.

3. The advisory function is that of giving professional advice to issuers and buyers of securities, based on information compiled by the statistical or research department.

4. The protective function is that of protecting the interests of holders of securities through the provision of secondary markets and aid in the reorganization of companies in trouble.

5. The service function is that of performing a number of miscellaneous services for the convenience of the investor.

Investment banks participate in the following major types of transactions related to the raising of capital:

1. Private placement of securities with institutions, the investment bank acting as the agent of the issuer.

2. Underwritten negotiated public offerings, where the investment bank obtains the issue, for resale, by direct negotiation with the issuer.

3. Underwritten sealed-bidding public offerings, where the issue is obtained by a successful bid in competition with other bidders.

4. Agency or best-efforts issues, where the firm sells securities to the public as the issuer's agent, without any underwriting risk.

5. Privileged subscription offerings, where the firm guarantees the successful sale by the issuer to its own stockholders.

Direct and Private Sale of Securities

Not all securities are placed in the hands of investors through investment banking houses. Direct selling is employed by the Federal government in the issue of new obligations. Direct selling is also employed by new, weak, and speculative concerns that cannot obtain or cannot afford the services of an investment banker. Sale of securities to employees and executives is also direct, as is the sale of new stock or convertible bonds to present stockholders by privileged subscription. (The offer of stock by rights is described in Chapter 12.) In many cases, however, the issuing corporation may have the successful sale of securities through rights guaranteed or underwritten by investment bankers, under a "stand-by" agreement described later in this chapter.

Direct selling also takes the form of *private placements,* whereby a corporation sells securities in large blocks to large investing institutions, chiefly life insurance companies, without utilizing the underwriting services of the middleman. Investment bankers participate in such offerings by acting as the intermediary for their corporate clients. Their "finding fee" will range from $\frac{1}{4}$ to $1\frac{1}{2}$ per cent of the issue. An offering to not more than twenty-five potential buyers is generally considered to be a private sale and exempt from registration under the Securities Act of 1933. Most private sales are made to one or a very few buyers. Over 50 per cent of corporate bond offerings, consisting mainly of high-grade industrial securities, are now privately offered.

The growth of private placement is attributable in part to the requirements of the Securities Act of 1933 with respect to issues publicly offered. It avoids the time, work, expense, and possible liability incurred in registration of new issues and the uncertainty that accompanies the required waiting period that precedes the public offering. Private placement also eliminates the traditional underwriting commission of the investment bankers. But the chief reason for its growth in recent years is the opportunity to tap the great institutional market with "tailor-made" contracts that shape the debt to the needs of both corporation and investor. A technical disadvantage is found in the ineligibility of such securities for resale to the public at a later date until the proper registration procedure is then completed. The major disadvantage, however, is that the investing public not only is prevented from participating directly in the better new issues which are preempted by relatively few large institutions, but also is deprived, through refunding operations, of bonds that are redeemed with the proceeds of new issues privately placed.

Private Negotiation

The new securities bought by investment banking houses for resale are obtained either through privately negotiated sales, by the issuer to the bankers, or through competitive bidding. Under the former method, an investment banking house, or more frequently, a group of participating houses, acquires the issue from a corporation in a private deal. The sale may go to a particular banking house because of previous satisfactory services. Or the origination of the issue by a particular firm may result from the search for new issues, or from relations with other bankers. New financing proposals may also reach investment banking houses through the direct application of the corporation seeking funds. Choice of the banking house to handle an issue is very important because of the close and confidential relationship that will prevail between the investment banker and his client.

Negotiated underwriting is largely confined to the issues of industrial companies as contrasted with railroad and public utility securities, which are ordinarily acquired by competitive bidding. The lack of uniformity and comparability among industrial companies makes competitive bidding inappropriate for their securities.

Competitive Bidding

The traditional custom of investment bankers in buying new corporate securities through private negotiation has been considerably undermined by regulation requiring competitive bidding for certain types of securities. Approximately one-half of all corporate bonds, including nearly all railroad and most utility bonds, and virtually all state and municipal bonds, are now sold through this procedure.[5] Few industrial bonds are offered in this

---

[5]In 1963, 47.5 per cent of corporate bonds sold to the public for cash were acquired by competitive bidding, of which 44.4 per cent consisted of utility bonds; and 51.9 per cent of the bonds were acquired by negotiation, of which only 8.5 per cent were utility bonds. The remaining bonds were not underwritten. Irwin Friend, *op. cit.*, p. 390.

manner. In 1919 Massachusetts required electric and gas companies to offer their bonds through competitive bidding. Since 1926, the Interstate Commerce Commission has required this type of bidding for equipment trust issues of railroads and, since 1944, for other types of railroad debt securities. Certain state utility commissions, such as those of New Hampshire, Indiana, California, and New York, require competitive bidding for companies under their jurisdiction, as does the Federal Power Commission. The Securities and Exchange Commission requires competitive biddings for security issues of registered holding companies and their gas and electric subsidiaries. Issues of less than $1,000,000 are exempt, as are issues sold pursuant to preemptive rights.

Competitive bidding is necessary and appropriate in the case of municipal bonds. The main reason for its extension to the sale of corporate securities has been the desire to eliminate or lessen monopoly in securities underwriting. Advocates of the practice also maintain that securities will be better priced, commissions more reasonable, distribution wider, and unwise dominance of corporations by their bankers eliminated. The leading arguments (among many) against the practice are as follows:

1. The investment banker becomes a mere merchant and cannot provide the issuer with advice on the terms of the issue, the timing of the offering, and the appropriate price. However, in some cases the corporation employs an investment banking firm to assist it in designing an issue for public sealed bidding, at a fee for services as a financial expert. Such advisers may not participate as underwriters.

2. Issues may become overpriced and consequently run the risk of "stickiness" in anything but a very strong market.

3. Small dealers are discouraged from participating through the decline in their portion of the gross commission.

4. The investment banker cannot represent the interests of the investor as well as through private negotiations, because of the less complete investigation, lack of advice to the issuer, and possible overpricing of the issue.

The Buying Function

The buying department of a large investment banking firm is ordinarily organized into two divisions: corporate and municipal. Firms which act as distributors rather than underwriters do not have buying departments; the new securities they offer for sale are obtained from underwriting firms through sales agreements.

When a corporate bond issue is sold through competitive bidding, decisions concerning the amount and form of the financing are made by the company's management, which (if required) files a registration statement with the Securities and Exchange Commission and issues an invitation for public bidding after the customary twenty-day waiting period. In the case of larger issues, bidding groups are formed to enter joint offers. The bidders make an intensive study of the quality and terms of the issue and of the market for similar securities. A bond or preferred stock issue is awarded to the bid that provides the lowest cost of money; the highest net price per share wins the bid on a common stock issue.

As indicated previously, municipal securities are purchased through competitive bidding. The municipality advertises its issue in a daily newspaper or in *The Bond Buyer,* stating the terms of the issue and calling for sealed bids. Usually the bid showing the lowest net interest cost to the issuer is accepted. When the proposed issue is larger than single firms can handle, bids are placed for a designated part of the issue. Because the aggregate price obtainable from the best combination of partial bids is frequently less than the price offered by bidder for the entire issue on an "all-or-none" basis, buying firms usually offer group bids for the entire issue on joint account.

The work of the buying department in making a bid for a new issue of municipal bonds is chiefly mathematical. After estimating carefully the price which could be received from the sale of the bonds to the public, with due consideration for interest rate and maturity date, a profit differential is subtracted and a bid price is determined. If it is assumed that the bonds could be sold on a 4.65 per cent yield basis, which would indicate a sales price of 105.20 ($1,052 per bond) for 5 per cent bonds with a twenty-year maturity, a profit margin of .85 point ($8 per bond) might be subtracted, leaving an indicated bid price of 104.4 ($1,044 per bond). In a strong municipal bond market, the profit margin might be cut to $\frac{1}{2}$ of 1 per cent ($5.00 per bond), indicating a bid price of 104.70 ($1,047 per bond). As other bidders have probably calculated along the same lines, the actual bids are seldom in simple fractions but in involved decimals such as 104.735, which produces a lower net interest cost.

As indicated previously, most industrial securities are purchased through private negotiations between the investment house and the corporation. The usual procedure of an investment banking firm may be divided into three major steps. The first is the preliminary, or office, analysis that follows the first discussions. The second is the engineering, legal, and accounting examination. The third is the negotiation conference, at which the final decision is reached.

The office analysis is a preliminary survey which covers the financial statements and the general character of the company. Important factors to be considered are (1) the size of the company (larger underwriters do not care to handle issues of less than $500,000), (2) nature and stability of the industry to which the company belongs, (3) position of the company in the industry, with special reference to its earnings record, and (4) company management. Many proposals do not get beyond this initial survey.

If the preliminary analysis is favorable, representatives of the investment house conduct a searching inquiry into the internal affairs of the company. Appraisers value the buildings, equipment, and inventories. Auditors verify the financial records and inspect the accounting methods, with particular regard to such important practices as depreciation policy. Industrial engineers observe production methods. Marketing specialists analyze the distribution of the product and determine the position of the company in its field. Legal counsel passes upon franchises, leases, and contracts. If reports on all of these phases are favorable, the negotiation conference is arranged. Where the investment bank has previously aided in the financing of a company and is familiar with its operations, the new inquiry into the affairs of the client is less exhaustive.

At the negotiation conference an overall informal agreement is reached covering the amount of the issue and the provisions of the securities that are best suited to the issuer's needs and that will meet the requirements of the market for the particular type of issue. A tentative schedule of the steps required prior to actual public offering is drawn up. If the issue is to be offered under the terms of the Securities Act of 1933, a definite public offering price is not set until a day or two prior to actual sale, but a price range is agreed upon that may be subject to later change. The underwriting spread or total bankers' commission is also tentatively set at this point. If the purchasing function is properly performed, the issue is, to use a maxim in financial circles, "half sold."

The Underwriting of Securities

After the negotiations between the originating house and the corporation, an agreement is drawn up between the corporation and the purchaser. But large issues involve more risk than a single investment house is willing to assume. Wide and rapid distribution is necessary, and one house cannot afford to have a large portion of its capital in one issue. For these reasons, while the negotiations are nearing completion, the originating house, acting as group manager, invites a group of investment houses to share in the purchase. The number invited varies with the size and character of the issue and the current condition of the securities market. It may range from as few as 2 to over 200. The $200,000,000 issue of Communications Satellite Corporation common stock in June 1964 was underwritten by 385 houses. The financial responsibility of the participants, the particular markets in which they specialize, their past records, and their ability to distribute securities are the chief criteria for their selection. The managing or originating house determines the size of the individual participations.

Prior to the passage of the Securities Act of 1933, only the originating firm signed the purchase agreement with the corporation. Under the present practice, the agreement is signed by the originating firm as the representative of all members of the purchase group. Prior to the Act of 1933, the agreement was binding and guaranteed the issuer the entire net proceeds of the financing, except under extreme circumstances. The Securities Act requires a waiting period of twenty days between the filing of the registration statement and the effective date of public offering of the issue. The agreement to purchase is contingent on the registration statement's becoming effective, for without effective registration the purchasers cannot publicly offer the security, if the offering falls under the scope of the Securities Act. This is why the final agreement is not actually signed until just before public offering.

The purchase agreement between the underwriters (purchase group) and the corporation contains provisions covering the following: (1) title, amount, and complete description of the provisions of the security; (2) warranties by the issuer, including full compliance with the Securities Act, proper accounting certification, correct financial statements, absence of lawsuits against the issuer, and qualification of the issue under state blue-sky laws; (3) the agreement of the underwriters to purchase and of the issuer to sell the entire issue, usually with several liability on the part of the underwriters, and on the amount each underwriter agrees to purchase; (4) the price of the issue, the underwriting discounts or commissions, and the method of payment and delivery; (5) the agreement of the underwriters to make a public offering within a fixed period after the effective date of registration at a stipulated offering price; (6) the agreement of the issuer to pay all expenses in connection with the issuance and delivery of the securities to the purchasers; (7) the agreement of the issuer to deliver copies of the prospectus if required under the Securities Act; (8) the agreement of the issuer and underwriters to indemnify each other against any liabilities under the Securities Act, with certain reservations; (9) any limitation on obligations of the underwriters, such as those arising out of adverse changes in the condition of the issuer or in the market; (10) the furnishing of certified financial statements by the issuer.

The purchase group (also known as the *purchase syndicate* or *underwriting syndicate*) is tied together by an "agreement among underwriters" that is a temporary partnership agreement which sets forth the rights and liabilities of the underwriters among themselves. It authorizes the originating firm to act as agent and manager of the group (for which it is paid a specified sum), stipulates the terms of payment by each underwriter for his share of the issue, and contains provisions for stabilizing the market, disposition of unsold securities, termination of the contract, and the nature of the obligation or liability of the members. The liability of each member is limited to the amount of his participation.

Several days after the public offering the company delivers the securities to the underwriters, or to their representative, and the managing underwriter delivers to the company a check in payment of the agreed price for the entire issue. The firms participating in the purchase group "take down" only that part of their subscription which they plan to sell directly and leave the remainder for distribution to members of the selling group, from whom they will receive reimbursement through the underwriting managers.

Pricing and the Underwriters' Spread

An important and delicate task of the investment banker is to set the price at which the issue is to be sold to investors. He is guided by the prices and yields prevailing in the market on comparable issues. Underpricing deprives the issuer of funds that might otherwise have been raised. Overpricing may result in large losses for the underwriters.

The price must also reflect the underwriters' spread or commission.

Spreads vary with the size, type, and quality of the issue, with the anticipated case of distribution, and with market conditions. They may be as low as 1 per cent of face value or even less in the case of a very high-grade municipal bond that is readily marketable, from less than 1 per cent to 2 per cent on high-grade corporate bonds, and to as high as 20 per cent on unseasoned stocks that require intensive sales effort and greater risk. Each new flotation involves the reputation as well as the capital of the underwriters.

The cost of flotation, representing commissions and discounts to investment bankers, on various types of securities registered with the Securities and Exchange Commission for public distribution in 1963 (bonds) and 1963–1965 (stocks) shown in Table 15-2.

Table 15-2. UNDERWRITING SPREADS AS A PERCENTAGE OF PROCEEDS OF PUBLIC SALE OF CORPORATE SECURITIES

Size of Issue ($ millions)	Bonds 1963	Preferred 1963–1965	Common 1963–1965
Under .5	a	16.0	11.3
.5 – 1.00	4.7	11.1	9.7
1.00– 2.00	7.9	11.4	8.6
2.00– 5.00	5.9	6.1	7.4
5.0–10.0	a	1.6	6.7
10.00–20.00	0.9	1.8	6.2
20.00–50.00	0.8	3.1	4.9
50.00 and over	0.8	1.7	2.3

aNot available.

Sources: Irwin Friend et al., *Investment Banking and the New Issues Market*. (Cleveland: The World Publishing Company, 1967), pp. 408–409; Securities and Exchange Commission, *Cost of Flotation of Registered Equity Issues, 1963–1965.* (Washington, D.C.: U.S. Government Printing Office, 1970.)

The spread or commission consists of three elements: (1) the management fee of about 20 per cent in negotiated transactions and 5 per cent of the gross spread in most competitive transactions, (2) the compensation for underwriting of about 30 per cent of the gross spread after allowing for the management fee, and (3) the selling commission of about 50 per cent. Thus, in a negotiated deal with 2 per cent overall spread, management might receive ⅜ per cent, ⅝ per cent might be retained by the underwriters, and one per cent might be the compensation for selling. (Members of the National Association of Securities Dealers, Inc., are customarily allowed a "trade" concession of ⅛ per cent.) Where an underwriter sells all or part of his participation to his own clients, he receives both the underwriting and selling portions of the spread on all bonds taken up. Under the Securities Act of 1933 the amount of the commission or discount to be retained by the underwriters must be fully disclosed in the registration statement and in the final prospectus describing the offering.

Underwriting spreads as a percentage of gross proceeds of corporate securities offered for public sale (exclusive of rights issues) are shown in Table 15-2.

In addition to bankers' commissions and discounts, the corporation incurs other expenses of flotation including preparation of the registration statement and prospectus.

"Best-Efforts" or Agency Selling

A deviation from outright purchase by underwriters under a firm commitment is an arrangement whereby the investment house takes no risk but merely acts as agent for the company, agreeing to use its best efforts to distribute the securities at the public offering price. Such arrangements are found chiefly in the distribution of stocks, particularly unseasoned and speculative issues, although very occasionally a high-grade bond issue will be sold under these terms. The underwriting spread or commission in such cases chiefly represents payment for sales services rendered.

"Stand-by" Underwriting

In its strict sense, the term *underwriting* refers to an insurance function whereby underwriters agree to take up the unsold portion of an issue that is being offered by the corporation directly to the investor. The definition of an *underwriter* contained in the Securities Act of 1933 includes both this arrangement and outright purchase by investment banks. The term *stand-by* or *pure* underwriting is used to describe the former arrangement.

The most frequent use of the stand-by arrangement is found in the issuance of stock or convertible bonds to present stockholders under privileged subscription.[6] Where the issuer does not wish to incur the risk, an underwriting group is formed to stand by to take any securities not purchased by stockholders. A commission is paid consisting of a certain rate on the whole issue; an additional commission may be paid on all shares taken up by the banking group. If stockholders subscribe to the whole issue, the underwriters have been paid for their assurance that the funds will be available when required and for advisory services. The additional commission is in the nature of a real purchase-and-resale discount.

Typical minimum commissions for better-grade securities offered through rights will run (1) convertible debentures of industrial companies, 1.00–1.25 per cent; (2) preferred stocks of industrial companies, 1.50–3.50 per cent; (3) industrial common stocks, 1.00–4.00 per cent; and (4) utility common stocks, .50–3.00 per cent. Additional compensation is usually paid on any securities not subscribed and taken up by the underwriters.

Occasionally a corporation will offer securities to present owners, through rights, at a subscription price so far below market price or in such a strong stock market that it dispenses with stand-by underwriting. A spectacular example of this is found in the case of the offering of $713,313,000 con-

---

[6]See discussion of convertible securities in Chapters 7, 8 and 12.

vertible 4¼ per cent debentures of 1973 by the American Telephone & Telegraph Company in January 1958, at par ($100). Each $100 debenture was to be convertible into a share of common stock by delivery of the debenture and $42 in cash. The market price of the company's common stock at the time was $170 per share. This was the largest single piece of private corporation financing on record until the some company offered the largest bond issue on record in May 1970. The offering of $1,569,000,000 debentures, plus warrants, was made through rights. No underwriters were involved (see p.236). And in June 1971, the company sold, through rights, $1,375,000,000 of new convertible preferred stock. Again, no stand-by underwriting was used (see pp. 235 and 236.

Selling the Securities

Once an issue is underwritten, it must be sold as rapidly and as widely as possible in order to satisfy the issuer and limit the risk of the underwriters. In the case of large issues, the usual device for distributing the issue to the ultimate investor is the *selling group,* which sells that portion of the issue not sold by the underwriters directly to their own clients. The selling group, or "representative dealers," consists of many dealers (sometimes as many as several hundred), who are invited to enter into an agreement entitling them to share in retailing the issue; they are selected on the basis of their ability to obtain permanent placement of the securities. The members of the group receive the portion of the gross spread mentioned previously that is allotted to the selling function on all securities passed along to them. The members of the group are committed financially only for those securities for which they elect to subscribe.

Invitations to participate in a selling group are sent out early, but the actual formation of the group, in the case of securities whose offering is subject to the provisions of the Securities Act of 1933, is delayed until the effective date of the registration statement. In the interim, the dealers are acquainted with the details of the forthcoming issue by means of a preliminary or "red herring" prospectus which differs from the final one in omitting the price at which the issue will be offered to the public or the concession (share of the spread) that will be allowed the members of the selling group.[7]

The arrangements between the purchase and selling groups are set forth in an agreement in the form of a letter from the manager to the selling group members. It includes, among other matters, the offer of a specific amount of securities to the invited dealer, the public offering price, and the amount of the dealer's concession, together with provisions for terminating the group. The securities cannot be offered to the public below the public offering price during the life of the group, which, under present-day practice, seldom exceeds one month. Some offerings are not quickly absorbed, how-

[7]The term "red herring" is derived from the fact that each page of the prospectus contains a statement, printed in red, that information is subject to correction and that the document is not an offer to sell or a solicitation of an offer to buy the securities described.

ever, because of unforeseen market conditions or because they have been overpriced.

Underwriting groups make a practice of supporting the market while offering new securities. To avoid the harmful effect of reported transactions at prices lower than that set in the public offering, the underwriting manager places buying orders in the market for the purchase of the bonds at the public offering price. The market price of a new issue is not allowed to fall below the established price during the period of distribution. Such market stabilization has been approved as an essential part of security distribution. However, two rules must be observed: (1) Notice of the intention to support the market must be included in the prospectus, and (2) daily reports of stabilizing operations conducted to facilitate the distribution of a registered security must be made to the Securities and Exchange Commission.

New issues of securities are ordinarily sold through direct solicitation of salesmen employed by the investment dealers, who are compensated on a commission basis. Since salesmen seek a maximum volume of business, temptation is strong to induce clients to switch from old into new securities, or to buy securities that may not be suited to their investment needs. Investors should realize that all securities are not of uniform quality and are, therefore, not equally suitable for all buyers. While reputable investment houses naturally avoid poor securities, they do not confine themselves to those of the highest grade. The more conservative houses instruct their salesmen not to offer securities indiscriminately. Investors, in turn, should not assume that all securities offered by a house in which they have confidence are desirable commitments. They should seek advice but should also be prepared to make their own decisions.

Other Investment Banking Services

The advisory function. Investment houses provide advice to issuers of securities. A corporation that desires to raise capital through the sale of securities will consult with the investment house which usually handles its issues before determining the nature of the offering. The house is constantly in touch with market conditions and is in a position to recommend the type of security that will prove most attractive under existing conditions, the provisions it should include, and the price it should bring. Moreover, it may advise on future needs and market conditions. This advisory function has been explained as follows:

> What the issuer is normally interested in, when it selects an investment banker to assist it in raising capital, is getting the required amount of funds at a cost of money that is as low as is consistent with a number of vital considerations: these include the maintenance of a sound capital structure, its credit standing and its relationships with its securityholders, as well as the imposition of restrictions on its operating flexibility. A form of security which would result in the cheapest cost of money to the issuer at the particular time, for example, may in fact turn out to be far more expensive to the issuer because it is not

suited to its overall financial and operating requirements. There is an enormous variety of securities and provisions which can be designed to meet the needs of a particular issuer and the demands of particular markets. In the determination of the proper combination of provisions for the particular security, all the above-mentioned factors must be taken into account.[8]

Investment houses also advise investors. They are always willing to discuss the suitability of a particular security to the needs of the investor, either in personal consultation or by correspondence. Many houses invite their customers to submit investment lists for periodical examination, on the basis of which recommendations are made for changes they believe will be beneficial. Most houses will cheerfully prepare an analysis of any security in which a customer may be interested, even though the firm may have no interest in the issue. Charges are seldom made for these services beyond the profit obtained on securities bought through the house.

The protective function. Investment houses usually act to protect the interests of customers in securities issued by the house which later meet default. They form protective committees to represent the securityholders in the reorganization of the company so as to obtain the most equitable treatment.

As an additional method of protecting the interests of their customers, investment houses usually maintain trading departments. These provide what is called a *secondary market* for securities, originally sold by the firm, which customers desire to dispose of. The trading department usually "makes a market" in securities previously issued by the house by maintaining bid and asked prices. Orders for the purchase and sale of securities not issued by the house are handled through this department. Requests for price quotations from customers are likewise answered by this division. The work of the trading department is especially valuable in connection with unlisted securities, because of the lack of reliable quotations for many issues in this important group. Unlike the trading department of a brokerage house, which is operated for the prime purpose of direct profit, the trading department of an investment house is maintained principally to assist the sales department in the distribution of new issues. During the offering period, the house or selling syndicate operates a trading account through which the price of the securities is stabilized until the entire issue is sold. Such trading is legitimate if it is made known to prospective buyers in the offering prospectus (see below).

The service function. Investment houses perform many minor services of considerable benefit to their customers. They protect securities in their vaults in special safekeeping envelopes. They collect interest and dividend payments when so requested. They notify investors of called bonds and of opportunities to profit from sinking fund offers or conversion options.

---

[8]*U.S.A.* v. *Henry S. Morgan, Harold Stanley, et al., Brief on the Service Function of the Investment Banker* (September 28, 1951), p. 52.

They keep files of customer security holdings and stand ready to make suggestions for the improvement of portfolios. They maintain analytical departments that produce information available to customers. They advise customers on income and estate tax problems in connection with security holdings. Usually, no special charges are made for these services.

Federal Regulation of Security Selling

Legislation designed to protect the public in the purchase of securities made a decided advance in the passage of the Securities Act of 1933. This law marked the passing of an old order and the beginning of a new epoch in the business of security marketing. As aptly remarked by President Roosevelt in recommending such legislation, the old slogan of "let the buyer beware" has been amended to "let the seller also beware." The obligation of telling the whole truth in connection with new security offerings has been placed upon the issuing corporation and the distributing investment house.

The Securities Act does not eliminate statutes ("blue-sky" laws) governing intrastate sale of securities, or interfere in the security-approval functions of the Interstate Commerce Commission or the state public utility commissions. The Federal law supplements existing state laws which have not proved sufficiently rigorous in preventing severe losses to the investing public, and which lack uniformity. It applies only to securities offered through the mails or in interstate commerce.

The purpose of this discussion is to indicate the nature of the protection afforded by the statute. In general, the law requires that specific information on new security offerings be filed with the Securities and Exchange Commission prior to sale to the public and that the issuers be held responsible for the completeness and accuracy of such information.

Exempt securities. Certain classes of domestic securities are exempted from the provisions of the Securities Act:

1. United States Government obligations and bonds of territories and Federal instrumentalities;
2. State and municipal bonds;
3. Securities issued by railroads and other common carriers subject to Federal regulation;
4. Receiver's and trustee's certificates, issued with court approval;
5. Issues aggregating less than $500,000 in any one year if regulations of the Commission are complied with;
6. Securities of savings and loan associations and banks;
7. Securities issued in exchange for old securities in a reorganization or recapitalization;
8. Intrastate issues;
9. Securities sold by private placement.

Exempt transactions. Certain transactions are exempted from the Securities Act:

1. Transactions in new issues, not through an underwriter and not involving a public offering (that is, sold to 25 or less persons),
2. Transactions by persons who are not issuers, underwriters, and dealers,
3. Brokerage transactions, executed upon unsolicited customers' orders, and
4. Offerings limited to the residents of a state by an issuer in that state.

Registration statement. Before new securities may be offered to the public, a registration statement, which becomes effective twenty days later, or earlier—as the Commission may determine—must be filed with the Securities and Commerce Commission. This statement must be signed by designated officials of the company, and copies must be made available to the public. The Commission may issue a deficiency statement or serve a stop order if the statement is incomplete or inaccurate in any material respect. The registration statement must give specific information on a number of designated points, among which are the following:

1. General information on the issuer—location, products, and so forth;
2. Purposes of issue;
3. Price at which offered to the public;
4. Price at which offered to any special group;
5. Promoters' fees;
6. Underwriting fees;
7. Net proceeds to the company;
8. Remuneration of any officers receiving over $25,000 annually;
9. Disclosure of any unusual contracts, such as managerial profit-sharing;
10. Detailed capitalization statement;
11. Detailed balance sheet;
12. Detailed earnings statement for three preceding years;
13. Names and addresses of officers, directors, and underwriters;
14. Names and addresses of stockholders owning more than 10 per cent of any class of stock;
15. Pending litigation;
16. Copy of underwriting agreement;
17. Copy of legal opinions;
18. Copy of articles of incorporation or association;
19. Copies of indentures affecting new issues.

A separate group of requirements is provided in connection with new issues of foreign governments.

The prospectus. The prospectus is the document supplied to the investor which offers a security for sale. Its information must coincide with that in the registration statement, with the omission of certain technical features, as stated in the law and as determined by the Commission.

Injunctions and criminal proceedings. Willful violations of the Act are subject to injunction by the Commission, which may also institute criminal proceedings against the violators in the Federal courts, with possible fines and imprisonment.

Civil liability. If the registration statement contains any untrue statement of a material fact or omits any material fact, any purchaser unaware at the time of purchase of such situation may take legal action, within three years, for recovery of loss against the persons mentioned in the statement as officers or directors of the company, as professional advisers, or as underwriters. To escape liability such persons (other than the issuer) must prove that after reasonable investigation they had no reasonable ground for belief that the information was incomplete or inaccurate. Damages may not exceed the price at which the security was offered to the public.

Financial statements. In connection with the balance sheets and earnings statements required in the registration statement, the Securities and Exchange Commission is empowered to prescribe the forms in which the information is to be submitted, the items to be shown, and the methods to be followed in the preparation of accounts, in the appraisal of assets and liabilities, in the determination of depreciation and depletion, and in the differentiation between charges to capital accounts and to operating expense.

Speculative securities. The purpose of the Securities Act is not to prevent the sale of speculative issues, but rather to stop the sale of fraudulent securities and to place before the investor all the facts necessary for intelligent judgment. Investors must rely upon their own opinions in arriving at a decision to purchase.[9]

Appraisal of the Securities Act. The effectiveness of the disclosure provisions of the Securities Act of 1933 is difficult to evaluate. Many issues of securities never get through the registration procedure, being screened out by the inability or unwillingness of their promoters to disclose the required information. How many other questionable issues are never filed for registration because of inability or unwillingness to disclose the facts will never be known. How much reliance the average investor places on the

---

[9]The position of the Commission in this important respect has been officially stated as follows:

The public should thoroughly understand that the Commission is not authorized to pass in any sense upon the value or soundness of any security. Its sole function is to see that full and accurate information as to the security is made available to purchasers and the public, and that no fraud is practiced in connection with the sale of the security.

Speculative securities may still be offered and the public is as free to buy them as ever.

The Commission's duty is to see that the security is truthfully presented to prospective purchasers. The fact that a description of the security and of the concern issuing the security is filed with the Commission is in no sense and must not be regarded as an endorsement or approval of the security or the concern by the Commission.

copious information available in the prospectus cannot be measured. At least, it is there for him to use if he wishes to use it and can understand it. But, generally, most individual investors do not rely heavily upon it.

The effectiveness of the fraud sections of the Act is also difficult to appraise. An unknown number of persons have been deterred, by fear of possible indictment, from interstate sale of securities or use of the mails. But others have run the risk and paid the penalty. Up to June 30, 1971, the Commission had obtained convictions against 2394 defendants in the criminal cases developed by it.[10]

Special Federal Securities Regulation

The issuance of certain securities exempt from the provisions of the Securities Act, notably that of railroads and other interstate common carriers, is subject to special regulation. The purpose of issue, form of issue, and disposition of funds raised through the sale of securities (with certain exceptions) are subject to the control of the Interstate Commerce Commission. Such regulation, like that of the financing of utilities registered under the Public Utility Holding Company Act of 1935 and those affected by state utility commission control, is largely designed to assure conformity with sound principles of finance. Although railroads are not required to issue prospectuses in the form prescribed by the Securities Act, similar documents are often used to describe railroad issues.

State Securities Regulation

State statutes, popularly known as "blue-sky" laws, exist in all states except Nevada for the purpose of protecting investors from fraudulent security offerings. These laws lay down certain rules for the sale of securities within the state and impose penalties for their violation. About one-half of them require the registration or licensing of distributors; most require that securities be registered. In four states (Delaware, Maryland, New Jersey, and New York) the statutes include antifraud laws that enjoin and prosecute fraud when or after the issue has been sold. State blue-sky laws exempt many types of securities.

The lack of uniformity of the state securities laws and the fact that they applied only to issues within the state were among the reasons for the passage of the Federal law in 1933. In general, the Federal law is much stricter.

---

[10] *Thirty-seventh Annual Report of the S.E.C.* (Washington, D.C.: U.S. Government Printing Office, 1971), p. 230.

REFERENCES

BLACK, HILLEL, *The Watchdogs of Wall Street*. New York: William Morrow & Company, Inc., 1962.

BOGEN, J. I., ed., *Financial Handbook,* 4th rev. ed., Section 9. New York: The Ronald Press Company, 1968.

CAROSSO, V. P., *Investment Banking in America: A History.* Cambridge, Mass.: Harvard University Press, 1970.

CHILDS, J. F., *Long-Term Financing,* Chapter 7. Englewood Cliffs, N.J.: Prentice-Hall, Inc., 1961.

CHOKA, A. D., *An Introduction to Securities Regulation.* Chicago, Ill.: Twentieth Century Press Co., 1958.

CLARK, F. G., AND R. S. RIMANOCZY, *Where the Money Comes From.* New York: Van Nostrand Reinhold Company, 1961.

COHAN, A. B., *Cost of Flotation of Long-Term Corporate Debt Since 1935.* Chapel Hill, N.C.: School of Business Administration, University of North Carolina, 1961.

———, *Private Placements and Public Offerings: Market Shares Since 1935.* Chapel Hill, N.C.: School of Business Administration, University of North Carolina, 1961.

COREY, C. R., *Direct Placement of Corporate Securities.* Boston: Harvard University, Graduate School of Business Administration, 1951.

DEBEDTS, R. F., *The New Deal's S.E.C.: The Formative Years.* New York: Columbia University Press, 1964.

DOUGALL, H. E., *Capital Markets and Institutions,* 2nd ed., Chapters 9, 10. Englewood Cliffs, N.J.: Prentice-Hall, Inc., 1970.

FRIEND, IRWIN, et al., *Investment Banking and the New Issues Market.* Cleveland: The World Publishing Company, 1967.

GOLDBERG, S. E., *Private Placements and Restricted Securities.* New York: Clark Boardman Co., Ltd., 1971.

INVESTMENT ASSOCIATION OF NEW YORK, *Wall Street, 20th Century,* rev. ed. New York: The Association, 1960.

INVESTMENT BANKERS ASSOCIATION OF AMERICA, *The Role of the Investment Banker in Arranging Private Financing.* New York: The Association, 1961.

ISRAELS, C. L., ed., *S.E.C. Problems of Controlling Stockholders and in Underwriting.* New York: Practicing Law Institute, 1962.

KNAUSS, R. L., *Securities Regulation Sourcebook.* New York: Practicing Law Institute, 1970.

LEFFLER, G. L., AND L. C. FARWELL, *The Stock Market,* 3rd ed., Chapter 25. New York: The Ronald Press Company, 1963.

LOSS, LOUIS, *Securities Regulation,* 2nd ed. Boston: Little Brown & Company, 1961.

———, AND E. M. COWETT, *Blue Sky Law.* Boston: Little Brown & Company, 1958.

RAPPAPORT, L. H., *SEC Accounting Practice and Procedure,* 2nd ed. New York: The Ronald Press Company, 1966.

ROBINSON, G. J., *Going Public: Successful Securities Underwriting.* New York: Clark Boardman Company, 1962.

ROBBINS, SYDNEY, *The Securities Markets: Operations and Issues.* New York: The Free Press, 1966.

SECURITIES AND EXCHANGE COMMISSION, *Cost of Flotation of Corporate Securities, 1963–1965.* Washington, D.C.: U.S. Government Printing Office, 1970.

———, *General Rules and Regulations Under the Securities Act of 1933.* Washington, D.C.: U.S. Government Printing Office, 1965.

———, *The Securities and Exchange Commission: Its Functions and Activities.* Washington, D.C.: The Commission, 1964.

STEVENSON, H. W., *Common Stock Financing.* Ann Arbor, Mich.: School of Business Administration, Bureau of Business Research, 1957.

WATERMAN, M. W., *Investment Banking Functions.* Ann Arbor, Mich.: School of Business Administration, Bureau of Business Research, 1958.

WINTER, E. L., *A Complete Guide to Making a Public Stock Offering.* Englewood Cliffs, N.J.: Prentice-Hall, Inc., 1962.

16 Old Securities; Exchanges and Markets

SCOPE: This chapter discusses the operations of the "secondary" markets for outstanding securities and how they are regulated for the protection of investors. The order of topics is (1) functions and classes of security markets, (2) functions of the exchanges, (3) advantages of listing to the investor, (4) organization and operation of the exchanges, (5) the Securities Exchange Act, (6) the Securities and Exchange Commission, (7) regulation of exchanges and listed securities, (8) regulation of dealers and brokers, (9) report requirements, (10) trading by "insiders," (11) proxies and their solicitation, (12) credit control, (13) control of price manipulation, (14) buying and selling large orders, (15) unlisted trading privileges, (16) the over-the-counter market and its regulation, (17) the third market, and (18) the fourth market.

Functions and Classes of Securities Markets

Securities markets exist to assist buyers and sellers of securities in carrying on transactions in an orderly manner and at fair prices. The marketability that they give to securities, in varying degrees, facilitates the ready conversion of securities into cash at prices that reflect the consensus of investment judgment at any one time. It is important to investors, to industry, and to the public that securities markets provide breadth, continuity, and stability to security transactions.

Three main types of secondary securities markets are found in the United States: (1) the organized exchanges—central points where transactions are conducted in listed securities on an auction basis through brokers acting as agents for their customers; (2) the over-the-counter markets for unlisted securities, where prices are determined by negotiations between buyers and sellers of securities on the one hand and dealers on the other, or between dealers themselves; and (3) the over-the-counter "third market" for listed securities.

The organized exchanges have traditionally been thought to provide numerous advantages and closer prices than the unlisted market, but in recent years the distinction has become less unfavorable to the latter type. In the first place, the number of unlisted issues has grown tremendously during recent years with respect to both quality and quantity. In the second place, the investment firms which deal principally in unlisted issues provide trading facilities that are often comparable to the markets for listed issues. In the third place, certain issues of quality cannot, because of either small capitalization or limited distribution, meet the listing requirements of the exchanges. And, lastly, relatively reliable quotations on prices of many unlisted securities are now available without delay.

The preference of investors for listed issues has become somewhat outmoded by these developments. So extensive has become the unlisted market embracing issues of the highest quality, such as Treasury obligations, municipal bonds, and railroad equipment obligations, that many investors buy as freely from the unlisted group as from the listed issues. Nevertheless, listing does provide some advantages that are outlined below.

Functions of the Exchange

Securities exchanges are auction markets in that brokers for sellers deal directly with brokers for buyers in competitive bidding and offering. The broker for the buyer tries to obtain the lowest possible price, while the broker for the seller tries to obtain the highest possible price; consequently, prices change from sale to sale according to the volume of securities offered and sought.

Members of the securities exchanges generally act as brokers who execute orders sent to them by their respective clients. They may, however, act as principals or dealers in purchasing and selling for their own account. In the latter capacity, they are not permitted to take advantage of their position but must give precedence to orders held for others at the same price. Their principal advantages over nonmembers are the saving in time effected by their actual presence on the floor of the exchange and the saving in commission charges.

The primary purpose of a securities exchange is to provide a continuous and liquid market for the exchange of outstanding issues.[1] Indirectly, however, the exchanges aid corporations in raising new funds by providing advantages to both the corporation and the investor. To the corporation, the listing of its securities may add marketability, may result in wider distribution of the securities, and may provide some publicity that may be of value as long as the corporation is making a good record and the market is stable. And, the more precise valuation of its securities is an aid in determining the proper offering price of new issues and in fixing the terms of exchange of securities in a merger.

Listing is not without some disadvantages to the corporation. Compliance with the registration and reportings requirements for listed securities is time-consuming, expensive, and imposes potential liabilities that are avoided by

[1]Leffler and Farwell suggest three important functions of the exchanges: (a) to create a continuous market, (b) to provide a means for the determination of fair prices, and (c) to aid, indirectly, in financing industry. See G. L. Leffler and L. C. Farwell, *The Stock Market* (New York: The Ronald Press Company, 1963), pp. 71–78.

purely over-the-counter trading. The dangers of excessive speculative trading and possible manipulation are also greater where the securities are readily traded and subject to immediate pressure. A low valuation known to all may also prove a handicap when the company is planning additional financing.

Advantages of Listing to the Investor

Improved marketability is an advantage to the investor as well as to the issuing corporation. A listed security can be bought or sold where buyers and sellers meet, where the value of the security is best known, and where the most favorable price is obtainable. Moreover, if the investor is not immediately interested in buying or selling, he can keep in touch with the market by observing the prices at which the security is being sold. If he is an owner, a downward trend in the price may warn him that an exchange is desirable and an upward trend may enable him to realize a profit if he believes the movement is temporary. If he is not an owner, repeated publication of current prices acts as an invitation to buy, particularly if the price is attractive.

Mere listing on an exchange will not automatically guarantee good marketability, in the sense that the volume of trading will be large so that purchases and sales can be made with a minimum of price movement. A number of listed securities are relatively inactive. Other things being equal, however, the continuous market provided by an exchange is an important advantage.

The fact that a security is listed is no assurance that it is a quality investment. But the investor knows that the listed company (at least at the time of listing) is a substantial going concern with a considerable public following. Some of the guides used by the New York Stock Exchange for an initial listing are national interest in the company and its stock, at least 2,000 owners of 100 or more shares, 1 million common shares in the hands of the public, demonstrated net income before taxes of $2,500,000 at the time of listing, and both tangible assets and common stock outstanding with an aggregate value of at least $16,000,000.

Listing adds to the collateral value of a security. Banks generally prefer as collateral those securities that are readily marketable. The chief consideration is the relative convenience with which the collateral may be converted into cash if the loan is not paid. Bankers usually have neither the time nor the facilities for investigating the intrinsic value of each security offered as collateral and, therefore, accept the market quotation as their chief criterion.

The regulation of listed issues, the required publicity of the affairs of the issuers of listed issues, and knowledge of price and volume of trading add protection to the holdings in listed securities that may be very valuable to the investor.

Listing has greatest significance in the case of stock. Stocks of leading companies are customarily traded through the exchanges, whereas bonds are usually bought and sold over-the-counter. Although the larger part of the shares of stock traded in New York is handled through the exchanges, less than 10 per cent of bonds traded is covered in exchange transactions.

Organization of the Exchanges

A stock exchange exists for the purpose of providing a securities market open only to members, who act chiefly as brokers for the buyers and sellers of the securities traded in that market. The exchange itself does not buy or sell securities nor does it establish their prices. The exchange is an auction market in which the buying and selling of thousands of investors and traders produce a large volume of transactions at the prices established by those transactions. Each sale ends the auction of a certain lot of securities, and a new auction is then started. There are no secret transactions, and complete publicity is given to the bond and stock prices by means of the stock and bond ticker tapes.

The New York Stock Exchange, whose origin can be traced back to 1792, is the largest and most important of the exchanges and constitutes a national center for securities trading. It has set the standards by which the other exchanges operate. The second largest exchange, as measured by the number of listings and the volume of trading, is the American Stock Exchange, also in New York. Exchanges exist in other cities to serve mainly as trading places for securities with a more local interest.

Of the fourteen exchanges, twelve are classified as national, being subject to the regulations of the Securities Exchange Act of 1934, while two are exempted. (See Table 16-1.) The activity of the exchanges is indicated by

Table 16-1. DATA ON EXCHANGE ACTIVITIES
(dollars in millions)

	Number of Issues Registered June 30, 1971		Market Value of Trades During 1971	
	Stocks	*Bonds*	*Stocks*	*Bonds*
New York	1,915	1,827	$147,098	$8,009
American	1,226	177	17,664	710
Midwest	327	16	7,443	1
Pacific Coast	717	47	6,962	80
Philadelphia-Baltimore-Wash.	236	55	4,265	2
Boston	64	13	1,090	—
Detroit	76	—	351	—
Honolulu[a]	42	—	6	—
Cincinnati	28	8	93	—
Salt Lake	52	—	5	—
Richmond[a]	23	—	—	—
Spokane	31	—	3	—
National	146	7	57	1
Chicago Board of Trade	2	—	—	—

[a]Exempted exchanges.

SOURCES: Securities and Exchange Commission, *Annual Report*, 1971 and *Statistical Bulletin*.

certain data concerning listings and trade volume. The figures for the lesser exchanges omit the much larger number of issues admitted to unlisted trading.

The New York Stock Exchange is a voluntary association of 1,366 (as of 1972) individuals who are the exchange *members.* Members comprise three different classes: (1) partners or stockholders in about 570 commission houses devoted to the handling of orders on the exchange, conducting business in about 500 cities across the country; (2) registered traders operating for their own account; (3) capitalists or representatives of estates who maintain membership for the convenience of trading and for the savings on commissions resulting from the ownership of a "seat" or membership.

The first group of members represents what are called *member firms and member corporations.*[2] The 4,000 other partners or stockholders in these firms are known as *allied members*; they cannot go on the floor of the exchange, they have no voice in its management, and their allied memberships have no monetary value. The value of a seat or membership, however, has been as high as $625,000 (1929) and as low as $17,000 (1942). In 1968–1969, a seat sold as high as $515,000, and in 1973, as low as $92,000.

Operations on the New York Stock Exchange

The activities on the floor of the exchange are conducted by its members, whose functions can best be described by a classification of the types of brokers or dealers:

The *commission broker* executes orders for his firm on behalf of its customers, at the established commission rates.

The *floor broker* ("two-dollar" broker) transacts business on the floor of the exchange for other exchange members who have more orders in different stocks than they can handle alone or who wish aid in handling large orders. He shares the commission received by the member firm.

The *registered trader* buys and sells on the floor of the exchange for his own account. He does not represent outside customers or execute orders for other members of the exchange. He derives his profit (or loss) from trading on relatively small price fluctuations.

The *registered trader* succeeds the former "floor trader," and his activities are subject to strict regulation enacted in 1964 that stemmed from the Special Study of the Securities and Exchange Commission.[3] He must have adequate capital, and most of his trading must be at prices above (for purchases) or below (for sales) the last different price. He must relinquish priority preference and parity to off-floor dealers, so that his position on the trading floor will not give him an advantage over the investing public.

The *specialist* acts as both broker and dealer. As a broker, he executes

[2]Corporations were first admitted as member firms in 1953; they must be exclusively in the securities business.

[3]Report of the Special Study of Securities Markets of the Securities and Exchange Commission, 88th Cong., 1st Sess., House Document 95, (Washington, D.C.: U.S. Government Printing Office, 1965), Part II Chapter 6. Hereafter called *Special Study.*

orders in the stocks in which he is registered as a specialist; his work in this capacity is largely confined to limited orders (see Chapter 17). As a dealer, he buys and sells shares in his special stocks for his own account, subject to the rules of the exchange and of the Securities and Exchange Commission.

The *odd-lot dealer* buys from and sells to commission firms less than 100-share lots of stock at prices based on round lots plus or minus a differential of 12½ cents a share on shares selling below $55, and 25 cents on stocks priced at $55 or above.

The *bond broker* specializes in trading in bonds on a commission basis, although a few of them operate as dealers for their own account.

Only listed securities can be traded on the floor of the New York Stock Exchange, and under the Securities Exchange Act of 1934 all of these must be registered with the Securities and Exchange Commission. (On the American and the regional exchanges, trading in unlisted securities provides a substantial volume of business, under conditions explained later in this chapter.) The Department of Stock List restricts the privilege to seasoned issues of established, substantial going concerns in which there is sufficient distribution and trading interest to assure an adequate market. Securities of about 1,430 different companies are on the trading list, including 1,400 common (37 of which are foreign), 530 preferred, and 2,000 bond issues (including foreign and government bonds). The market value of all stocks and bonds listed on the Exchange is $871 billions.[4]

Recent Developments. Certain important developments affecting the members and operations of the New York Stock Exchange have taken place in very recent years:

1. The failure and/or merger of over 110 member firms that was caused by the bear market of 1968–1970, lack of capital, "back office" confusion and inefficiency, "fails" (failure of brokers to deliver sold stock or bond certificates to the buyers within the required five days), and very high operating expenses. Most of these problems are gradually being overcome.

2. Permission of the Board of Governors of the Exchange in 1969 for member firms to "go public," that is, sell shares to the general public. Several leading firms have done so.

3. The listing on the Exchange of the stock of several firms that had "gone public."

4. Federal chartering of the Securities Protection Corporation in 1970. The members of the Corporation, all of whom are registered broker-dealers and members of national securities exchanges, pay initial assessments of ⅛ per cent of gross receipts (going eventually to 1 per cent). The fund protects each customer-investor against losses of $50,000 (of which no more than $20,000 can be in cash) in the event of the failure of a member firm. The seven-man board of directors includes representatives of the general public, the securities industry, the U.S. Treasury, and the Federal Reserve Board.

---

[4]Data as of January 1972. Source: New York Stock Exchange, *1972 Fact Book.*

5. Reconstitution of the Board of Governors of the Exchange. In July 1972 a 20-member Board was elected, including 10 "public" directors.

6. In January 1973 institutions such as mutual funds and insurance companies were given permission to hold seats on the Exchange provided they do 80 per cent of their business with the public.

Other developments are indicated in Chapter 17.

American, National, and Regional Exchanges

Although the stocks of many large companies are listed on the American Stock Exchange (Amex), this "board" in the main provides a market for securities of companies not large enough or otherwise not qualified for the "Big Board." Its listing requirements are much less stringent, it encourages the registration of relatively young companies, and its list includes a considerable number of foreign stocks including American depository receipts. A special feature of its organization is the use of associate members who are not entitled to trade on the floor of the exchange but who may transmit orders through regular members at a reduced commission.

The National Stock Exchange, in New York, was opened in 1962. It is still relatively small, with no rigid listing requirements. Unlike the regional exchanges, it does not permit listing of stocks that are listed on other exchanges.

The regional exchanges were originally established to provide organized markets for local securities. But with the advent of rapid communications with New York, the growth in size of regional companies, and the expansion of the over-the-counter market, the importance of trading in regional stocks has declined to the point where over 90 per cent of the trading is in stocks either dually listed on the New York exchange or admitted to unlisted trading privileges (see the discussion below).

Securities Exchange Act

The securities exchanges of the United States were first brought under Federal control under the provisions of the Securities Exchange Act of 1934. This law created a Federal Securities and Exchange Commission appointed by the President. It provides for the registration with the Commission of any exchange as a National Securities Exchange. It forbids the operation of .any unregistered exchange except those which may be exempted by reason of a limited volume of transactions. It places the control of the credit used in the purchasing or carrying of securities with the Board of Governors of the Federal Reserve System. It prohibits the manipulation of security prices and the use of deceptive devices for such purpose. It requires all companies that have securities listed on the registered exchanges, and large companies whose securities are traded over-the-counter, to file comprehensive information of their affairs and to keep the information reasonably current. It imposes severe penalties for violations. In short, it aims to eradicate the more serious abuses in securities trading that characterized the period of the 1920s.

The Securities Exchange Act of 1934 may be regarded as a logical supplement to the Securities Act of 1933, whose purpose is to provide adequate protection to investors in the purchase of *new* issues. The objective of the Securities Exchange Act is to safeguard investors in brokerage transactions involving the purchase or sale of *outstanding* securities. Through such legislation, the Federal government has assumed far-reaching regulatory control of the investment markets.

The Securities and Exchange Commission

The Federal Securities and Exchange Commission was created for the purpose of administering the Securities Act of 1933 and the Securities Exchange Act of 1934.[5] This commission is comprised of five members appointed by the President and has wide discretionary powers in the administration of the laws. Registration statements, listing applications, and periodic reports must be prepared according to its requirements. Important exemption powers are granted to the Commission with respect to exchanges, securities, and reports.

Registration and Regulation of Exchanges

As one of the means toward the securing of fair and orderly markets for securities, the Securities Exchange Act requires that exchanges be registered with the Commission as national exchanges or be exempted from registration. At the present time (1973) there are twelve registered and two exempted exchanges specializing in a few local issues.

In the registration statement, the exchange must provide full information concerning its activities, organization, membership, and rules of procedure, and agree to comply with and enforce the provisions of the Act. Registration brings the trading rules of the exchange under the control of the Commission.

Registration of Securities

Transactions on national securities exchanges are restricted to those securities which have been officially registered with the exchange and with the Commission, or which are legally exempted under the provisions of the law. The exempted group comprises, in general, government bonds, and shares in mutual investment companies (separately regulated under other laws). Companies which desire to have their securities listed on a national securities

[5]The jurisdiction of the Commission under other statutes is described in various other sections of this book.

exchange must submit detailed information of their affairs at the time of application, and must agree to keep such information reasonably current thereafter. This information includes

1. The organization, financial structure, and nature of the business.

2. The terms, position, rights, and privileges of the different classes of securities outstanding.

3. The terms on which securities are to be and, during the preceding three years, have been offered to the public or otherwise.

4. The directors, officers, and underwriters, and each security-holder of record holding more than 10 per cent of any class of any equity security of the issuer, their remuneration, and their interests in the securities of and their material contracts with the issuer and with any person directly or indirectly controlling or controlled by the issuer.

5. Remuneration to others than directors and officers exceeding $25,000 a year.

6. Bonus and profit-sharing arrangements.

7. Management and service contracts.

8. Options existing or to be created in respect of their securities.

9. Balance sheets and profit and loss statements for not less than the three preceding fiscal years, certified by independent public accountants.

10. Trust indentures, underwriting contracts, articles of incorporation, and other documents and agreements as the Commission may require.

Under the 1964 amendments to the Securities Exchange Act, registration requirements were extended to companies engaged in interstate commerce or whose securities are traded over-the-counter by the use of the mails or in interstate commerce. Registration will be required of issuers with assets in excess of $1 million for each class of equity security which is held by at least 500 persons. Banks whose deposits are insured by the F.D.I.C. are included, but administration of the registration requirement is delegated to the appropriate Federal bank regulatory agency.

The registration statements referred to above should not be confused with those required under the Securities Act of 1933 described in the previous chapter. The latter describe the offerings of *new* securities that are affected by the regulation of security issuance.

Regulation of Dealers and Brokers

Broker-dealers in either listed or unlisted securities are required to register with the S.E.C. as a condition of dealing across state lines. The amended Act also empowers the Commission to prescribe rules with respect to floor trading by exchange members and to prevent excessive trading off the floor by members for their own account that would be detrimental to the maintenance of a fair and orderly market. One of the main problems has been to deal with the situation wherein the same individual acts as an agent for a customer and also trades for his own account as a dealer. Such a conflict of interest may abuse the fiduciary relationship inherent in the brokerage function. The Commission has promulgated no rules on this matter but has aided in an advisory capacity in the drawing up of trading rules by the exchanges themselves. The Act itself contains two rules that apply to brokers and dealers generally, whether or not they are exchange members: (1) A broker-dealer may not extend credit to a customer on any security which was part of a new issue in the distribution of which the broker participated within thirty days prior to the transaction, and (2) a broker-dealer must disclose to the customer the capacity in which he is acting.

Report Requirements

Issuers of securities registered under the Securities Exchange Act are required to keep the information filed with the Commission "reasonably current" and to submit such annual and quarterly reports as may be prescribed. These reports must be prepared in such detail and according to such accounting procedures as are required by the Commission. The Commission prescribes the methods to be followed in the preparation of the reports, in the appraisal or valuation of assets and liabilities, in the determination of depreciation and depletion, in the differentiation of investment and operating income and of recurring and nonrecurring income, and in the matter of separate and consolidated income statements and balance sheets. The rules governing the form and content of the financial statements filed with the Commission under the Securities Exchange Act of 1934 and the Securities Act of 1933 are found in the Commission's Regulation S-X. The registration statements are available for public inspection at the offices of the Commission.

More important to the average investor is the amount and quality of information supplied by the issuer in its financial reports. The amended Securities Act requires issuers of listed securities and those of larger publicly held unlisted securities to make adequate information available to shareholders in interim and annual reports. The information must be substantially the same as that required in 10-K registration statements.

Trading by "Insiders"

Many investors have always been afraid that officers and directors could exercise undue influence over the prices of the securities of their companies and could take advantage of inside information at the expense of the investing public. The Securities Exchange Act provides that each executive officer, each director, and each owner of more than 10 per cent of the equity securities of registered companies must report changes in his holdings monthly. These changes are in turn published by the Commission. And in order to prevent the unfair use of confidential information, such persons must, within six months, account to the corporation for profits realized from any transaction in their company's stock. These profits are recoverable by the company by suit within two years. Short sales by "insiders" are prohibited.

Proxies and Their Solicitation

To promote more democratic and informed action on the part of company stockholders, the Securities Exchange Act requires that any proxies sent out by registered companies must be accompanied by a proxy statement that discloses fully the matters to be voted upon, and that provision be made for voting either yes or no on all matters. Proxies may not be solicited until the material has been submitted to the Commission. The proxy statements that reach the hands of stockholders are often very revealing. They include remuneration paid to officers and directors, an annual report for the last fiscal year, and the stockholdings of the management.

Credit Control

One of the features of the capital markets prior to 1930 was the degree to which excessive speculation was encouraged by the flow of bank credit into securities transactions. Under the Securities Exchange Act, two provisions have greatly restricted the use of borrowed funds in the purchasing and carrying of securities: (1) The Board of Governors of the Federal Reserve System now fixes the margin requirements for both banks and brokers. Since November 24, 1972, the minimum margin (or equity) has been 65 per cent on registered common stock and 50 per cent on corporate bonds (margin trading is described in Chapter 17). (2) Exchange members, or brokers and dealers transacting business through them, may obtain brokers' loans only from member banks of the Federal Reserve System or nonmember banks that agree to comply with the restrictions on securities loans.

High margin requirements have been bitterly opposed by many brokers and dealers. Their precise effect is hard to evaluate, but obviously in a bull market the volume of business handled by brokers is curtailed by such limitations on margin accounts.

Manipulation of Prices

The reported prices of securities must be the result of legitimate and open trading. Whether the price of a security is high or low, fluctuating or stable, it should represent the consensus of buyers' and sellers' valuations without artificial influence. Pool operations and manipulative practices were frequent in the 1920s but, since the passage of the Securities Exchange Act, have largely disappeared from the scene. The Act specifically prohibits five types of manipulation:

1. *Matched orders,* or fictitious transactions by two or more persons that create a price without any actual change of ownership.

2. *Wash sales,* where one person "paints the tape" by fictitiously buying and selling a stock at the same time, thereby recording a price, but again without any change in ownership.

3. *Pool operations,* whose purpose is to raise the price of a security (or depress it by short sales) through the concerted activities of the members of the pool, followed by the unloading of the stock on the public at a price influenced by the manipulation and accompanying information concerning the security.

4. Dissemination of false information to the effect that the security's price will rise or fall as the result of manipulation.

5. The spread of false information concerning a security; for example, incorrect information concerning the earnings of a corporation, in order to induce its purchase or sale.

Short selling as such is not prohibited, except in the case of officers and directors. However, the price at which a short sale may be executed is regulated. (See Chapter 17.)

Buying and Selling Large Orders

Various procedures have been developed, with S.E.C. approval, to facilitate the purchase and sales of blocks of stock within a reasonable time and at a reasonable price. The customer who originates the large block order pays a special commission that may run three or four times the usual auction market rate. The more important of these procedures are

1. *Block transactions.* Transactions involving 10,000 shares or more are executed on the floor of the New York Stock Exchange. The market value of the 693 million shares of such transactions in 1971 was $24.2 billions, or 17.8 per cent of total reported volume.[6] These figures reflect the participation of institutions and other large investors.

2. *Exchange distribution (or acquisition).* The broker may accumulate orders for sale (or purchase) and then fill the original block order on the floor during regular trading hours, at prices between the current bid and ask quotations.

3. *Secondary distribution.* Under this method, which is used for extremely large sell orders, the member usually acts as a dealer, combining with other members and nonmembers to effect the sale of the large block after trading hours and at a fixed price.[7]

[6]New York Stock Exchange, *1972 Fact Book,* p. 12.

[7]In 1970, on all exchanges, only 16.6 million shares with a value of $504 millions were offered through secondary distributions, and only 2.1 million shares ($42 millions) through exchange distributions. *Annual Report* of the Securities and Exchange Commission, 1971, p. 224.

Unlisted Trading Privileges

The New York Stock Exchange does not admit to trading privileges any securities not formally listed with it. But other exchanges do a very considerable volume of trading in securities that have not been formally listed. On the American Stock Exchange the number of stocks of companies who have never formally applied for listing privileges but which have been of sufficient interest to warrant trading is diminishing. The regional exchanges, however, have relied to a very considerable extent on unlisted trading, especially in stocks not listed locally but already listed on the New York Stock Exchange. The American Stock Exchange does not permit trading in stocks listed on the New York Exchange.

An exchange may be authorized by the S.E.C. to continue unlisted trading in three groups of securities: (1) those that enjoyed such privileges prior to March 1, 1934; (2) those since listed on another exchange and for which there is adequate public distribution and sufficient trading activity in the vicinity of the applicant exchange to justify unlisted trading (this is the dynamic source of new issues for trading on regional exchanges); and (3) a few issues on which there is information substantially similar to that field for listed companies.[8]

A large portion of the unlisted trading on regional exchanges consists of trading in New York Stock Exchange-listed stocks, especially in odd-lot business. In addition to such trading in stocks listed elsewhere, *multiple listing*, whereby a stock is specifically listed on more than one exchange, has appeared in recent years. However, the practice does not appear to be as significant as that of obtaining unlisted trading privileges on regional exchanges for issues registered on some other exchange.

The Over-the-Counter Market

The majority of security issues are not listed on any of the securities exchanges. Although less important in aggregate value than the listed issues, the unlisted or "off-board" group is much larger, because of the inability or the unwillingness of corporations to gain listing privileges for their securities. In comparison with the approximately 4,100 securities of 2,500 issuers listed on the various national exchanges, there are about 50,000 additional issues in which a market is maintained throughout the country, of which about 14,000 stocks and 3,500 bonds are actively traded. Over-the-counter sales of active stocks (exclusive of mutual fund shares) grew from $4.9 millions or 31 per cent of all stock sales in 1949 to $38.9 billions or 37 per cent in 1961.[9] Estimates for 1971 would run $65 billions or about 40 per cent of all stock sales. Of the corporate bond business of the country, 80 per cent

---

[8]As of June 30, 1971, 2,397 stocks were admitted to unlisted trading on the exchanges (including duplications). *Ibid.*, p. 35.

[9]*Special Study, op. cit.*, Part II, p. 547.

is carried on over-the-counter. Although many of them are listed, the over-the-counter market accounts for nearly 100 per cent of the trading in U.S. Government issues. The following types of issues are usually in this classification:

1. United States direct and guaranteed issues;
2. State and local government bonds;
3. Railroad equipment trust certifications and guaranteed stocks;
4. Many railroad bonds and stocks;
5. Many public utility bonds and stocks;
6. Most industrial bonds and stocks;
7. Most bank and insurance stocks.

So extensive has the group of unlisted securities become that few intelligent investors now confine their commitments to the listed group. Listing, even on an important exchange, does not assure ready marketability. The activity of many dealers has resulted in the creation of a market in which many unlisted securities have marketability as adequate as that of the average listed issue. Furthermore, the achievement of a satisfactory diversification grouping almost necessitates the holding of some unlisted securities. Firms that provide markets in unlisted securities make no attempt to cover the entire field. One group will specialize in municipals, another in bank and insurance company stocks, and still another in Federal issues. The investor must ascertain the particular firms that "make a market" in issues in which he is interested. He must also appreciate that transactions in unlisted securities are handled differently from dealings in listed issues.

The market in unlisted securities is made by dealers at prices reached through *negotiation,* which means through bargaining bid and offered prices. In most, but not all, transactions, the dealer acts as a principal, not as an agent for his client as the broker does. His compensation is the spread between purchase and resale price. He may have a desired security in his own inventory, or he may acquire it from another dealer. In any event, in transactions with the public his spread may run as high as 5 and 10 per cent, and is typically about 3 per cent on common stocks.

The quotation by an unlisted dealer is generally *subject to confirmation* and represents the range in which he is willing to bargain. A quotation of "92–94" means that he is willing to pay at least 92 and does not expect to sell for more than 94. He is usually willing to *close the spread* to secure an order, and in the preceding case might bid 92½ for 100 shares or offer 100 shares at 93½ on a *firm* basis, generally subject to immediate acceptance.

The quotations on unlisted securities which appear in the newspapers are given in the form of bid and asked prices rather than those of actual transactions. They represent bid and asked prices as reported by representative dealers. The newspapers have space for the publication of only a limited number of quotations and usually give preference to local issues. Comprehensive lists of quotations on unlisted securities are available to all investment dealers, however, who are usually able to provide an immediate quotation on any important unlisted security from the daily sheets of the National

Quotation Bureau, Inc. This organization supplies subscribing houses with daily reports from all over the country of bid and asked prices on the more active securities and the names of dealers who are interested in the securities. On an average day, as many as 8,000 stocks and 2,000 bonds may be quoted.[10] In February 1971, the National Association of Securities Dealers, Inc., commenced public operation of the NASDAQ automated quotations system which provides instant bid and asked quotations on nearly 3,000 unlisted stocks, supplied by nearly 500 firms making markets in those securities.

Regulation of the Over-the-Counter Market

Regulation of the over-the-counter market is effected through the National Association of Securities Dealers, Inc. (NASD), an organization set up under the Maloney Act in 1938, which constituted an important amendment to the Securities Exchange Act. The association includes about 3,500 dealers and operates under strict rules designed to maintain fair practices among its members. It has the power to expel members guilty of unethical practices. Its rules are filed with the Commission and, in turn, it has adopted the rules of the Commission governing over-the-counter transactions. One of the interesting features of the Association's work has been its sponsorship of a maximum mark-up or spread of 5 per cent of asked over bid prices.

The membership of the Association includes nearly all of the brokers and investment banking houses, and most of the active over-the-counter dealers. One reason for the comprehensive membership is that, under the Maloney Act, registered members of the Association enjoy preferential treatment in a number of respects. For example, price concessions from underwriters or wholesalers to retailers can be given only to Association members.

Under the Securities Exchange Act of 1934, all over-the-counter brokers and dealers other than those whose business is exclusively intrastate, or who confine their activities to tax-exempt securities, must register with the Securities and Exchange Commission. Registration may be suspended or revoked if a broker or dealer or any member of his organization has been convicted of a crime or has been enjoined in connection with a securities transaction, has made a willful misstatement in the registration, or has willfully violated the securities laws and the rules of the Commission. Brokers and dealers are prohibited from engaging in manipulative, fraudulent, or deceptive practices in over-the-counter transactions and from inducing the purchase or sale of any security by willful omission or misstatement of a material fact.

The Third Market

Over-the-counter trading, by nonmembers, in common stocks listed on national exchanges, is known as the *third market*. Although most of the

---

[10]For sources of quotations on unlisted securities see Chapter 14.

transactions involve large institutional and securities dealers, individuals are increasingly turning to this market also. The chief reason for its use is the possible savings on commissions on large orders. Also, listed securities may be traded off-board without restrictions by broker-dealers who are not members of an exchange. About seventeen firms do the bulk of the business.

During the fiscal year ended June 30, 1965, as a result of the comprehensive study of the third market by the S.E.C.,[11] the Commission proposed rules that would produce more complete information on this market, including an identification of broker-dealers making off-board markets in listed securities, and the filing of data showing the volume of such trading in listed common stocks. Such reporting began in 1965. In 1971, the value of third-market dealings was $12.4 billions, equal to 8.4 per cent of the value of exchange transactions.[12]

The Fourth Market

Large institutions and, occasionally, large individual investors have, for a number of years, directly bought and sold securities, or exchanged securities, with each other. The principal reasons for the fourth market are to obtain a better price, to save commissions, and to make portfolio changes without registering with the S.E.C. The volume of such transactions is unknown.

Recent developments. In August 1971, William McChesney Martin, former president of the New York Stock Exchange, issued a report that commanded wide attention and that will probably lead to substantial changes in the securities markets. The important recommendations that bear on the material in this chapter were

1. The Exchange should be thoroughly reorganized, with increased capital requirements, member ownership of shares, and member control.

2. Institutional membership in the Exchange should be prohibited. (But see p. 295.)

3. Uniform commission rates should be effected on all securities transactions, on all exchanges, and in unlisted securities.

4. Commissions on large transactions should be negotiated. (This is already in effect).

5. A national public auction market should be created; all brokers would have access, with all trading subject to the same rules. This would eliminate the "third market."

6. The stock certificate should be eventually eliminated.

In early 1972 the Securities and Exchange Commission presented a series of recommendations for innovations in securities trading. The more important were

[11]*Special Study*, Part II, pp. 870–911.
[12]S.E.C. *Statistical Bulletin*, March 1972.

1. All national and regional exchanges should be tied into a single electronically united market with respect to publication of prices and trading volume. This would give all investors the same information and opportunity.

2. Institutions such as mutual funds should be permitted to own or be affiliated with stock exchange member firms, provided "significantly more than one-half" of the member's trading volume comes from the public rather than from the parent company. (For the actual rule, see p. 295.)

The intent of the first proposal is to enable the investor to get the best price and performance; the second proposal would permit the parent firm to save on commission expense and pass this saving on to investors (such as mutual fund shareholders), yet be subject to more rigid rules than now prevail on those regional exchanges that have admitted brokerage affiliates of funds to membership.

REFERENCES

BACKGROUND AND OPERATIONS OF THE SECURITIES INDUSTRY. *A Program of Self-Instruction.* New York: Association of Stock Exchange Firms and New York Institute of Finance, 1965.

BLACK, HILLEL, *The Watchdogs of Wall Street.* New York: William Morrow & Company, Inc., 1962.

BOGEN, J. I., ed., *Financial Handbook,* 4th rev. ed., Section 10. New York: The Ronald Press Company, 1968.

BOOZ, ALLEN & HAMILTON, INC., *Over-the-Counter Markets Study.* Prepared for the National Association of Securities Dealers, Inc. Washington, D.C., 1966.

CHOKA, A. D., *An Introduction to Securities Regulation.* Chicago: Twentieth Century Press, Inc., 1958.

COMMERCE CLEARING HOUSE, *Securities Act Amendments of 1964.* Chicago: Commerce Clearing House, Inc., 1964.

COOKE, G. W., *The Stock Markets,* rev. ed. Cambridge, Mass.: Schenkman Publishing Company, 1969.

EITEMAN, W. J., C. A. DICE, AND D. K. EITEMAN, *The Stock Market,* 4th ed. New York: McGraw-Hill, Inc., 1966.

———, AND D. K. EITEMAN, *Leading World Stock Exchanges.* Ann Arbor, Mich.: Bureau of Business Research, Graduate School of Business, University of Michigan, 1964.

FRIEND, IRWIN, et. al, *The Over-the-Counter Securities Markets.* New York: McGraw-Hill, Inc., 1958.

HAZARD, J. W., AND MILTON CHRISTIE, *The Investment Business. A Condensation of the SEC Report.* New York: Harper & Row, Publishers, 1964.

LEFFLER, G. L., AND L. C. FARWELL, *The Stock Market,* 3rd ed. New York: The Ronald Press Company, 1963.

LOLL, L. M., AND J. G. BUCKLEY, *The Over-the-Counter Securities Markets.* Englewood Cliffs, N.J.: Prentice-Hall, Inc., 1961.

LOSS, LOUIS, *Securities Regulation,* 2nd ed. Boston: Little, Brown & Company, 1961.

MERRILL LYNCH, PIERCE, FENNER & SMITH, *How Over-the-Counter Securities are Traded.* New York: Merrill Lynch, 1968.

MUNDHEIM, R. H., ed., *Conference on Securities Regulation,* Duke University School of Law, November 1964. New York: Commerce Clearing House, Inc., 1965.

NEW YORK STOCK EXCHANGE, *Understanding the New York Stock Exchange.* New York: The Exchange, 1970.

POLAKOFF, M. E., AND A. W. SAMETZ, *The Third Market—The Nature of Competition in the Market for Listed Securities Traded Off-Board.* Reprint Series No. 33. New York: New York University Schools of Business, 1966.

PRENTICE-HALL, INC., *Securities Regulations,* 2 vols. (loose leaf). Englewood Cliffs, N.J.: Prentice-Hall, Inc.

ROBBINS, SYDNEY, *The Securities Markets: Operations and Issues.* New York: The Free Press, 1966.

ROBERTS, EDWIN A., JR., *The Stock Market.* Silver Springs, Md.: The National Observer, 1965.

SECURITIES AND EXCHANGE COMMISSION, *Report of the Special Study of the Securities Markets of the S.E.C.,* 88th Congress, 1st Session, House Document No. 95. Washington, D.C.: U.S. Government Printing Office, 1963.

SHULTZ, B. E., *The Securities Market and How It Works,* rev. ed. New York Harper & Row, Publishers, 1963.

SOBEL, ROBERT, *The Big Board: A History of the New York Stock Exchange.* New York: The Free Press, 1965.

SOWARDS, H. L., *The Federal Securities Acts: Analysis, Procedures, Forms.* New York: Matthew Bender & Co., Inc., 1965.

SPRAY, D. E., ed., *The Principal Stock Exchanges of the World.* Washington, D.C.: International Economic Publishers, 1964.

TYLER, POYNTZ, ed., *Securities, Exchanges and the SEC.* New York: The H. W. Wilson Company, 1965.

WEST, R. R., AND S. M. TINIC, *The Economics of the Stock Market.* New York: Praeger Publishers, Inc., 1971.

ZARB, F. G., AND G. T. KERCKES, eds., *The Stock Market Handbook,* Section I. Homewood, Ill.: Dow Jones–Irwin, Inc., 1970.

17 Buying and Selling Securities

SCOPE: This chapter discusses the manner in which orders are placed for the purchase and sale of securities and some of the factors that the investor should keep in mind in connection with the transfer of securities. The order of discussion is (1) buying and selling orders, (2) buying new securities, (3) buying and selling unlisted securities, (4) market and limit orders, (5) day and open orders, (6) stop-loss orders, (7) the function of the specialist, (8) odd-lot orders, (9) short selling, (10) options, (11) buying on margin, (12) trading in rights and warrants, (13) ordering listed bonds, (14) delivery, (15) commission charges, transfer taxes, and fees, and (16) transfer of securities.

Buying and Selling Orders

The method used in the purchase or sale of a security is determined largely by the type of issue. Orders for the purchase or sale of listed issues are normally placed with brokerage firms that are members of the particular exchange involved. "Unlisted" issues are bought and sold through firms which act as dealers in such issues. Investors who do not have their own brokers often have their banks place their orders for them.

New issues of securities are ordinarily bought from investment bankers at a fixed price. Subsequent purchase and sales are usually handled by brokerage firms which charge a commission for their service. In the case of unlisted securities, investors are occasionally charged commissions but ordinarily the dealer's compensation is the spread between bid and asked price.

In addition to the listed and unlisted secondary markets, there is a growing third market (see Chapter 16) where listed securities are purchased from the inventories of dealers. Such transactions usually involve substantial blocks of securities.

Buying New Securities

Four arrangements for the purchase of new securities are of interest to individual investors: (1) purchase (and redemption) of U.S. Savings bonds, (2) purchase (and redemption) of shares of open-end investment companies, (3) purchase of new corporate and municipal securities from investment bankers and dealers, and (4) purchase of new securities direct from the issuing corporation.

United States Savings bonds, Series E, are purchased at the cost of $75.00 per $100 of maturity value at U.S. post offices, Federal Reserve Banks, savings and loan associations, commercial banks, or directly from the Treasurer of the United States, and are redeemable for cash at fixed redemption values at the same places. Bonds of Series H are purchased at Federal Reserve Banks or from the Treasurer of the United States.[1]

Shares of most open-end investment companies are purchased from investment dealers or the company's sales representative at their net asset value at the time of purchase plus a loading charge, the bulk of which goes to the dealer or representative as a commission; they are redeemable by the company at any time at their net asset value following receipt of the endorsed stock certificate and redemption request. The quotations of such shares found in the financial section of the leading papers are shown as bid and asked prices. The bid price is the asset or redemption value. The asked price is approximately the asset value plus the loading charge of up to 8¾ per cent.[2]

Shares in mutual funds offered by investment counsel firms, and other "no-load" funds, are priced at net asset value, without a "load" or commission. This is because little or no sales effort is undertaken by the firm or its distributor.

New offerings of corporation and municipal securities sold by the issuers through investment banks and commercial banks are purchased at the public offering price, which includes the underwriting discount. (The bankers' discount, or spread, as explained in Chapter 15, varies with the size and quality of the issue.)

Securities purchased directly from the issuing corporation, such as those of smaller new companies that do not obtain underwriting services, those offered under privileged subscriptions, and those acquired through the exercise of stock-purchase warrants are bought at the offering price without any commission as such.

Buying and Selling Unlisted Securities

As explained in the previous chapter, the market for unlisted securities, the over-the-counter market, is a trading market for thousands of issues of bonds

---

[1]See Chapter 4 for further information.

[2]See Chapter 9 for further details.

and stocks. Orders for purchase and sale are placed with dealers (including, in the case of U.S. Government securities and municipal obligations, commercial banks), who operate mainly as principals. The customer usually buys directly from the dealer, who fills the order by buying from another over-the-counter house or from his own "shelf" if he is "making a market" or has "a position" in the security. The difference between the price paid by the dealer for the security and the price at which he sells it to the investor is the spread or mark-up and represents the dealer's compensation. Bid and asked prices on unlisted issues are made available to dealers, for "inside" trading among themselves, on the daily quotation sheets of the National Quotation Bureau, Inc., and by using the new electronic desk-top quotation machine. The quotations found on the financial pages are supplied by the National Association of Securities Dealers. The investor should note that some lists of quotations (often "national" lists) are bids and offers quoted by over-the-counter dealers to each other; they do not include retail mark-up or commission. Other lists (often local) are interdealer prices on the bid side, but the asked prices have been adjusted upwards to include approximate markup. Some lists contain both quotation arrangements. In contrast with the organized exchanges, prices at which actual transactions have taken place in the over-the-counter markets are not available.

Market and Limit Orders

Orders for the purchase or sale of securities may be placed on a *market* (no price limit) or a *limit* basis. An order "at the market" means an immediate order "at the best price available" but without limitation as to price; on a quotation of 92 bid, 93 asked, an order to buy at the market would be executed at 93, and an order to sell at the market would be executed at 92. Although the broker will try to get better prices on such orders, he cannot afford to delay, because other orders may intervene. On limit orders, the investor places a price limit which the broker may not violate; on a selling order, the broker must not sell for less than the price limit but may accept more, whereas, on a buying order, the broker must not pay more but may pay less than the price limit.

Whether market or limit orders are the more advisable is debatable. The advantage of the market order is in immediate execution; the chief disadvantage is at times an unsatisfactory price. The advantage of the limit order is the avoidance of an unsatisfactory price; the chief disadvantage is delay in execution and the possibility that the order will never be executed.

Price quotations on securities represent bids and offers for limited quantities. Orders exceeding the established unit of trading (which is usually one $1,000 bond or 100 shares of stock) frequently cannot be filled at the prevailing quotation. An order to buy at the market 1,000 shares of a certain stock which is quoted $52\frac{1}{2}$–53 may be filled on a basis of 100 shares at 53, 200 at $53\frac{1}{8}$, 100 at $53\frac{1}{4}$, 200 at $53\frac{1}{2}$, and 400 at $53\frac{3}{4}$. An order to sell 1,000 shares under the same conditions might be filled on the basis of 200 at $52\frac{1}{2}$, 100 at $52\frac{1}{4}$, 300 at 52, and 400 at $51\frac{3}{4}$. An order to sell $10,000 of a certain bond issue quoted at 88–90 might be executed on a basis of $2,000 at 88, $2,000 at 87¾, $1,000 at 87½, and $5,000 at 87¼. So "thin" are the markets on some bonds that an offer of $10,000 in such bonds may cause the price to drop as much as one to two points.

Day and Open Orders

Limit orders for the purchase or sale of securities may be placed on an *open* or a *day* basis. The investor may state that the order is to be held until it is executed, which, in the case of price-limit orders, may require several months or longer. Such orders are known as G.T.C. orders, or "good until cancelled." Without specific instructions that the order is to remain open, however, it is understood to be a day order, and is regarded as automatically cancelled if not executed on the day it is placed.

Open orders world seem preferable to the investor who is in no hurry to act and who is not satisfied with prevailing prices. But this practice will not always work to his advantage. Frequently, open orders to buy at prices below the prevailing market are executed when adverse developments, which make the security much less attractive, come too quickly to allow the investor to cancel the order. Sometimes open orders are executed to the subsequent surprise of investors who had completely forgotten the commitment. The investor should be in constant touch with his broker if substantial orders are pending.

Stop-Loss Orders

Investors who wish to limit their losses sometimes place orders to be executed at prices below the prevailing market. An investor who has bought 100 shares of a certain stock at $50 a share, and who desires to limit his maximum loss to about $5 a share, places an order to sell at "45 stop." This order is not an instruction to sell now at $45, but rather an order to sell at the market "if and when" the price should decline to $45. This type of order is also to protect profits gained from price advances as well as to limit losses on short sales. In the preceding case, the investor holding stock quoted at $60 which cost $50 may place an order to sell at "55 stop," so as to assure a profit of $5 a share. A speculator who has sold "short" 100 shares at $50 per share may place an order to buy at "60 stop" in order to limit his loss to around $10 a share. In a very rapidly declining or rising market, however, such stop prices are by no means guaranteed.

The advisability of placing stop-loss orders is questioned by many. A market which has many stop-loss orders just below prevailing prices is technically weak, since a limited volume of selling would bring prices down to the stop limits. The automatic execution of these orders would further depress the price, thereby "setting off" stop orders at lower limits. After the cumulative effect has run its course, the price may rise, to the embarrassment of those who were sold out at lower levels. Investors should not place selling orders until they are ready to sell. It is usually wiser to place an immediate order to sell at the prevailing price than a deferred order to sell at a lower price.

Function of the Specialist

Orders which are placed for execution at prices which are "away" from the prevailing market customarily are turned over by brokers to other members who act as *specialists* in the particular stocks. Every stock on the New York Stock Exchange is assigned to a specialist. These specialists maintain records, known as books, in which these orders are entered in the sequence received.

Table 17-1. SPECIALIST'S BOOK

	Buy		*Sell*
50	1 Brown 2 McGill 1 Jones	**50**	
$^1/_8$		$^1/_8$	
$^1/_4$	2 Ewart	$^1/_4$	
$^3/_8$		$^3/_8$	
$^1/_2$		$^1/_2$	
$^5/_8$		$^5/_8$	1 Newton 1 Farmer
$^3/_4$		$^3/_4$	1 Starr 1 Tomkins
$^7/_8$		$^7/_8$	

Table 17-1 shows the specialist's book for orders in a certain stock at prices between 50 and 50¾. The highest (best) bid is for 200 shares at 50¼, and the lowest (best) offer is for 200 shares at 50⅝. The quotation would then be 50¼–50⅝. A new order to buy 400 shares *at the market* would be executed: 200 at 50⅝ and 200 at 50¾. An order to sell 600 shares *at the market* would be executed: 400 at 50, and 200 at 50¼. However, the specialist, acting as a dealer for his own account, may decide to close the spread between bid and asked by buying at 50½, making the quotation 50½–50⅝, or by selling at 50½ making the quotation 50–50½. He is more likely, however, to enter his own orders when the spread is much more substantial than in this example, so as to perform his function of maintaining a fair and orderly market.

The specialist provides a convenient concentration point for orders which otherwise could not be expediently handled by the regular brokers. In addition to acting as a brokers' broker, the specialist has the responsibility of maintaining an orderly market in the stocks assigned to him. He does this by buying and selling for his own account when a temporary disparity occurs between supply and demand. There are about 350 specialists on the New York Stock Exchange, or about one out of each four members.

Odd-Lot Orders

Orders for the purchase or sale of less than the established unit of trading on the various exchanges are handled through "odd-lot" dealers. For the great majority of stocks on the New York Stock Exchange, the unit of trading is 100 shares or a *round lot,* although ten-share markets have been established for a group of stocks in which activity is limited for various reasons, mainly their high price. Brokers who receive orders to buy or sell less than 100 shares place these orders with odd-lot dealers on the exchange, who fill them at prices slightly different from the prevailing round-lot prices. On odd-lot orders at the market, the price is set at $12\frac{1}{2}$ cents a share higher on buying orders and lower on selling orders than the round-lot price. On odd-lot limit orders, execution does not take place until the round-lot price reaches the $12\frac{1}{2}$-cent differential. An order to buy twenty-five shares at 37 is not filled until the regular price reaches $36\frac{7}{8}$; an order to sell twenty-five shares at 27 is not filled until the regular price reaches $27\frac{1}{8}$.

The ordinary differential for odd-lot orders on the New York Stock Exchange is $12\frac{1}{2}$ cents a share, or $\frac{1}{8}$ point. The odd-lot price differential represents the compensation of the odd-lot dealer that goes to him for his risk. In addition, the buyer or seller must also pay the established commission.

Odd-lot trading permits the investor of limited means to buy modest numbers of shares in several corporations and thus obtain some diversification. The big disadvantage is the fact that the odd-lot price differential plus the minimum commission (see discussion of commissions, below) comprise a significant percentage of the purchase and sale price on small orders, especially on low-priced stocks. Such a disadvantage is maximized if the shares are held for a short time.

Short Selling

A *short sale* is the sale of stock which the seller does not own but which he expects to acquire in the future. The short seller, anticipating a decline in the price of the stock, hopes to make a profit from selling the stock now and buying it back later at a lower price. The broker to whom the order is given arranges to borrow it—either from his own stock or from stock of customers who have allowed their securities to be used for this purpose, or from some other broker who has stock available for lending.

Where stock is borrowed by the broker from a customer, the latter turns it over without security but continues to receive any dividends paid during the transaction. The customer who lends the stock relies on the broker to return the same number of shares of stock on demand. Where stock is borrowed from another broker, the borrowing broker deposits with the lender of the stock the full market price of the borrowed shares, the money having been obtained by their sale. Thus the lender has the use of cash during the period the stock is lent, and when stocks are freely available for lending, he may pay interest, at the "loaning rate" of, say, 1 per cent. Where not much stock is available for borrowing, it is usually loaned "flat," with no payment for its use. When stock is in much demand for short selling, the lender may even receive a premium for the use of the stock, stated in terms of $1 or a multiple thereof for each day on each 100 shares borrowed. As the price of loaned stock rises and falls, the amount of cash held as security is increased or decreased as either party requests that it be made equal to market price. Any dividends on loaned stock go to the lender.

Loans of stock may be called by either party on three days' notice. The short seller continues his "short position" until he decides to "cover" his short sale by buying an equivalent number of shares and delivering them to the lender in return for the cash.

An order for a short sale must be so designated when placed, and cannot be executed at a price lower than that established in the last preceding regular (as distinguished from short) sale.[3] It can be executed at a higher price, or at the last price, provided this in turn is higher than the next preceding different price. The purpose of these rules is to prevent the use of short sales to depress the market price of the issue.

Some short sales are made "against the box." The short seller owns the security being sold short, but makes delivery by borrowing it, and later covers either by using his own stock or buying in the market. Such operations are usually made for income tax and hedging purposes.

Some persons believe that short selling should be outlawed as detrimental to investment values. Others claim that it provides a corrective check to abnormally high prices as well as a protective cushion to declining prices. Short selling is much more prevalent in periods of market weakness or uncertainty than in periods of great strength, and buying orders to cover short positions rarely change the trend of the market. Instead of acting as a brake on an advancing market, short selling may actually result in higher prices as short sellers place buying orders to cover their positions when prices advance.

The *short position* in individual listed stocks, that is, the number of shares sold short and not covered as of a particular date, is regularly computed by the New York Stock Exchange and published monthly in the financial sections of the leading newspapers.

Options

An *option* is a contract which involves the right to buy or sell securities (usually 100 shares) at specified prices within a stated time. There are

---

[3]On regional exchanges (outside of New York), the price can be equal to the last sale prevailing on the New York Stock Exchange.

various types of such contracts, of which *puts* and *calls* are the most important. A *put* is a negotiable contract which gives the holder the right to sell
a certain number of shares (usually 100) at a designated price within a
limited time. An investor holding 100 shares of a certain stock selling at $50
a share who fears that the price may decline substantially because of an
impending development, but who otherwise desires to keep his stock, may
purchase a put giving him the right to sell his stock at, say, $45 a share
to the seller of the option.

A *call* is a negotiable contract which gives the holder the right to buy a
certain number of shares (usually 100) at a designated price within a limited
time. An investor considering the purchase of 100 shares of a certain stock
selling at $50 who feels that the time is not opportune, but who fears that
the price might rise suddenly while he is waiting, may purchase a call giving
him the right to buy the stock at, say, $55 a share from the seller of the
option.

There are two types of puts and calls. *Wide-price options* are thirty-day
options at prices away from the market. Their use has declined considerably
in recent years. The trend is more toward the so-called *market option,*
ranging from sixty days to over six months in maturity. The six-month option
(six months plus ten days) has the advantage of bringing any profits into
the long-term capital gains period for income tax purposes.

Option prices are set by the option dealers and are determined by the
condition of the market. The cost of these contracts depends on the value
of the stock and is currently $137.50 per hundred shares on a thirty-day
wide-price option on stock selling in the 20–30 range, where the option
price is a number of points away from the market. Options at the market
are usually much dearer; on a three-month option, prices range from $137.50
to several hundred dollars, per hundred shares.

Although the contracts are used chiefly by speculators, they are occasionally used by investors as insurance against contingencies.

Buying on Margin

The two main types of accounts with brokers are cash accounts and margin
accounts. In a cash account, purchases are made outright for full ownership
and sales are made against immediate delivery of securities. To open a
margin account, the buyer deposits with his broker cash or securities equal
to a portion of the price of the security (the margin) and his broker
advances the balance. To finance this balance, the broker uses his own capital or obtains funds by pledging the securities purchased with a bank as
collateral for a loan. If the price of the stock declines, the buyer must keep
the margin good by depositing additional cash or securities so that at all
times the margin will meet the required minimum percentage of the market
price. If the margin falls below this percentage, a margin call is sent to the
customer. If the customer fails to provide the additional margin, the broker
sells out the account.

The volume and origin of the brokers' loans that arise out of securities transactions are now subject to regulations under the Securities Exchange Act of 1934. The *initial* margins which members of security exchanges registered under the Act shall require from their customers are laid down by the Board of Governors of the Federal Reserve System. A margin of 100 per cent (no loanable value) was in force from January 1946 to February 1947; since that date the percentage has varied between 50 and 90, and since November 24, 1973, has been 65.[4] The Securities Exchange Act also provides that members of registered securities exchanges and brokers and dealers who do a security business through such members may borrow (for securities transactions) only from member banks of the Federal Reserve System and nonmember banks that agree to comply with the regulations as regards securities loans.

In addition to the Federal Reserve regulation of *initial* margins, the New York Stock Exchange also has certain credit requirements. No person may open a margin account with a member firm without depositing at least $2,000 or its equivalent in securities. And generally speaking, a customer's equity may at no time be less than 25 per cent of the market value of securities carried. Some firms require 40 per cent.

To illustrate the combined effects of the Federal Reserve minimum initial margin requirements and a 25 per cent minimum *maintenance* requirement, suppose a customer of a member firm buys on margin 200 shares of stock at 100. His initial equity or margin is $13,000 and his debt or debit balance is $7,000. The stock could fall to $60 per share before he would be required to deposit additional margin. At $60 the market value of his 200 shares would be $12,000 and his margin one-quarter of that amount or $3,000 ($12,000—$9,000).

Trading in Rights and Warrants

Rights to subscribe to stock under privileged subscriptions are sometimes very actively traded, and examples of listed rights are usually found in the stock quotations. After the official announcement of their issue, the Committee on Stock List of the New York Stock Exchange announces a date on which the rights may be traded on a "when-issued" basis. Under this arrangement, buyers (and sellers) of rights receive delivery of (or deliver) the rights and make the appropriate settlement after the rights are actually issued. Thereafter, the rights are bought and sold in the regular way until the date of expiration, after which they have no value.

Many companies provide facilities or retain a bank or trust company to assist stockholders in disposing of their rights or in acquiring additional rights so as to round out the number needed to purchase an even number of shares of new stock.

Stock-purchase warrants are attached to bonds or preferred stock at the time of issue or are issued in mergers as payment for services. They entitle

[4]The minimum margin on Federal obligations is 5 per cent of principal, on state and local government bonds, 15 per cent of principal or 25 per cent of market value, whichever is lower, and on registered corporate bonds, 50 per cent.

the holder to purchase common stock from the issuer at a specified price within a definite period of time or indefinitely. When the warrant is detachable, it may have a separate listing and enjoy an active market. The most actively traded warrants are listed on the American Stock Exchange, but in 1970 the New York Stock Exchange first admitted them to listing.

The methods of determining the value of rights and warrants are explained in Chapter 12.

Buying and Selling Listed Bonds

Although the bulk of bonds are traded over-the-counter, some 1,900 bonds are listed on the New York Stock Exchange, and the other leading exchanges also quote bonds although they have much smaller lists. (See Chapter 16.) The ordinary unit of trading on the exchanges is one $1,000 bond, and quotations are shown as a percentage of face value. Thus, the price of a $1,000 bond quoted at 98 is $980. As explained in Chapter 12, three types of quotations are used: (1) *and interest,* with accrued interest from the last coupon date added to the price; (2) *flat,* with no addition of accrued interest, in the case of bonds whose income is not assured or is in default; and (3) on a *yield basis,* the bid and asked values being expressed in terms of yield rather than price.

Bid and offering prices of bonds are usually in ⅛'s except in U.S. Government securities, where the values are expressed in 1/32's. Quotations on the New York Stock Exchange and the American Stock Exchange are sent out over ticker service; the bonds are designated by their coupon rates—and by their maturities if the same company has two or more issues with the same coupon rate. The price of a registered bond, the transfer of which involves time and expense, is usually slightly lower than that of an identical bond in coupon form.

Time of Delivery

Securities bought and sold on the securities exchanges must be delivered within the time specified by the exchange. Under the rules of the New York Stock Exchange, regular delivery is required on the fifth full business day (excluding Saturdays, Sundays, and holidays) following the day of sale.[5] Sales not made in the regular way may be made for *cash,* which means for delivery and payment on the day of sale. Sales may also be made for *delayed delivery,* which gives sellers up to seven days in which to arrange delivery. (Short sellers are not allowed to use the delayed delivery option, which is restricted to actual owners of securities.) Or the seller may have his broker offer the stock *seller's option* and specify the number of days, from five to sixty, for delivery. The prices at which stocks are sold on other than *regular-way* delivery are usually slightly lower because these other arrangements operate more to the benefit of the seller than that of the buyer.

[5]An exception is found in the case of Government bonds, for which regular delivery is the next day.

In the hectic days of 1967–1969, many brokerage houses suffered from "back-office log jam"; that is, they were unable to manage the massive amounts of securities being bought and sold. "Fails" to deliver reached a peak of over $4 billions in December 1968. Although some share volume was higher in 1970–1972 than in 1968, the volume of "fails" has declined to less than 1 billion, due to improved operations techniques, the larger size of transactions on the Exchange, and the installation of the Central Certificate Service. This service centralizes and applies modern clearing-house methods to interhouse transfers of stock certificates. In 1971 and 1972, much thought and research was being devoted to the possibilities of doing away with stock certificates altogether, substituting electronic bookkeeping and transfer of ownership units.

When unlisted issues are bought or sold through dealers, the time of delivery is set more by informal agreement than by formal rules. In general, however, the practice closely conforms to that of the listed group.

Commission Charges

When listed securities are purchased or sold directly from or to investment dealers, ordinarily no commission charge is made, since both parties usually act as principals in the transaction. When securities are bought or sold through brokerage houses, a commission charge is paid by both the buyer and the seller. Minimum commission rates are established under the rules of the exchanges where the securities are sold. Graduated scales are in vogue varying, in the case of bonds, with issuer, price, and maturity and, in the case of stocks, with market price.

The following schedule shows the minimum commission rates per $1,000 of principal on long-term corporate bonds traded on the New York Stock Exchange in 1972:

Price per $1,000 of Principal	Commission per $1,000 Bond
Less than $10	$ .75
$10 but under $100	1.25
$100 and over	2.50

The total purchase price (exclusive of taxes, fees, insurance, and postage) for buying, on March 15, $5,000 in par value of a 7 per cent bond with interest payable April 1 and October 1, at 105, is computed as follows:

Principal: $5,000 at 105%	$5,250.00
Interest: $5,000 at 7% for 5 mo. and 19 days	164.30
Commission: 5 bonds at $2.50	12.50
Total cost	$5,426.80

In the foregoing illustration, the accrued interest is computed up to but not including the day of delivery, which would be March 20. The entire payment of $164.30 for accrued interest would be recovered on April 1, when interest amounting to $175.00 would be collected for the six months thus ending. The net cost to the buyer would, therefore, be $5,262.50.

Revised commission charges for stocks were applied beginning March 24, 1972, and represented a drastic change from the previous system. Under the older schedule, fees were based on the charge for one "round lot" (100 shares) multiplied by the number of round lots involved in the transaction. In addition, a surcharge of one-third of the standard commission (to a maximum of $15.00) was collected on each order of 1,000 shares or fewer. Thus the commission was the same percentage of value for 1,000 shares as for 100. In the case of "odd lots" (less than 100 shares) a differential was added: 12½ cents per share on stock selling below $55, and 25 cents on stock selling at $55 or more. (The odd-lot differential was standardized at 12½ cents a share in July, 1972).

The new schedule abolished the surcharge, and fees are based largely on the dollar amounts involved in each trade. Single round lot orders and multiple round lot orders have different rates:

Single Round Lot Orders		*Multiple Round Lot Orders*	
Money Involved In the Order	*Minimum Commission*	*Money Involved In the Order*	*Minimum Commission*
$ 100-$ 799	2.0% + $ 6.40	$ 100-$ 2,499	1.3% + $ 12.00
800- 2,499	1.3 + 12.00	2,500- 19,999	0.9 + 22.00
2,500- And Above	0.9 + 22.00	20,000- 29,999	0.6 + 82.00
		30,000- 500,000	0.4 + 142.00

Subject to the provision that the minimum commission on single round lot orders is not to exceed $65.00.

Plus

First to tenth round lot	$6.00 per round lot
Eleventh round lot and over	$4.00 per round lot

But in no case shall the minimum commission per round lot exceed the single round lot commission. Also, in no case shall the minimum commission for a round lot plus an odd lot exceed the commission on the next larger round lot.

Odd Lot Orders. Same as single round lot rate less $2.00, subject to the provision that the minimum commission on an odd lot order is not to exceed $65.00.

On low-priced issues the commissions are smaller than previously. On more typically priced issues—say those selling at $40—fees are lower on odd-lot orders, and on large orders—say 800 shares. But on trades in the range of about 80 to 700 shares, commissions have been increased. On stocks carrying larger prices—for example, $100—fees are higher on trades of virtually all sizes except the very largest.

Table 17-2 selects three prices—$10, $40, and $100 a share—and compares the old and the new commissions.

The total purchase price (exclusive of taxes, fees, insurance, and postage) for buying 100 shares of a common stock at $40 is computed as follows:

		Former	*Present*
Principal: 100 shares at $40		$4,000.00	$4,000.00
Commission	$20 + $19 + $15	54.00	58.00
		$4,054.00	$4,058.00

Table 17-2. COMPARISON OF COMMISSIONS ON STOCKS BEFORE AND AFTER MARCH 24, 1972

Number of Shares Bought Or Sold	At $10 a Share		At $40 a Share		At $100 a Share	
	Former Charge	Fee Starting March 24, 1972	Former Charge	Fee Starting March 24, 1972	Former Charge	Fee Starting March 24, 1972
10	$ 10.25	$ 7.65	$ 14.75	$ 13.65	$ 25.00	$ 25.50
20	11.50	10.90	22.00	22.90	42.50	41.00
30	14.25	14.15	29.25	29.35	54.50	54.50
40	18.50	17.40	36.50	35.80	62.00	66.00
50	21.25	20.65	43.75	42.25	69.50	77.50
70	26.75	27.15	54.75	53.95	76.50	82.50
90	32.25	32.95	61.25	63.65	83.50	87.50
100	25.50	25.00	54.00	58.00	64.00	65.00
200	49.00	50.00	93.00	106.00	113.00	130.00
500	100.00	97.00	210.00	232.00	260.00	325.00
700	134.00	127.00	288.00	292.00	358.00	455.00
1,000	185.00	172.00	405.00	362.00	505.00	602.00
2,000	260.00	302.00	620.00	562.00	980.00	1,042.00
5,000	530.00	562.00	1,310.00	1,162.00	2,450.00	2,362.00
10,000	980.00	962.00	2,460.00	2,162.00	a	a

[a] On transactions of more than $500,000, commissions on the portion over $300,000 will continue to be negotiated, not fixed.

SOURCE: New York Stock Exchange.

The total purchase price (exclusive of taxes, fees, insurance, and postage) for buying 700 shares of a common stock at $10 is computed as follows:

		Former	Present
Principal: 700 shares at $10		$7,000.00	$7,000.00
Commission	$119 + $15	134.00	127.00
		$7,134.00	$7,127.00

The total purchase price (exclusive of taxes, fees, insurance, and postage) for buying fifty shares of a common stock at $100 plus the odd-lot differential of $\frac{1}{8}$) would be computed as follows:

		Former	Present
Principal: 50 shares at $100		$5,000.00	$5,000.00
Commission and differential	$25 + $17 + $15 + $12.50	69.50	71.25
		$5,069.50	$5,071.25

In the preceding illustrations, the respective proceeds to the *seller* would be less than the amounts shown, as the commission charges would be deducted rather than added. Furthermore, transfer taxes and registration fee would be paid by the seller.

Transfer Taxes and Federal Registration Fees

The purchase or sale of securities involves the payment of a broker's commission by both buyer and seller. In addition, the *seller* has deducted from the proceeds of the sale (1) the Securities and Exchange Commission's registration fee, (2) a state transfer tax levied in some states (including New York) on stock transactions made within the state, and (3) insurance and postage. The S.E.C. registration fee is imposed on the exchange and is collected from its members, who in turn charge the seller of the security, at the rate of 1 cent for each $500 or fraction thereof. New York State imposes an excise tax on transfer of stocks within the state on a graduated scale ranging from $1\frac{1}{4}$ cents a share on stocks selling under $5 a share to 5 cents on stocks selling above $20. There is no New York tax on bond transfers. Insurance and postage runs about 40 cents per $1,000 of value.

The seller of the stock in the first round-lot illustration above would now receive $3,936.90 (less insurance and postage), computed as follows:

100 shares at $40		**$4,000.00**
Less:		
Brokerage commission	**$58.00**	
N.Y. State tax	5.00	
Registration fee	.10	63.10
		$3,936.90

The innovation, in April 1971, of negotiated commissions for transactions exceeding $500,000 was the subject of much debate. Such fees are an application of competition in the securities service price structure. The negotiated feature has created problems for institutional investors who are expected to obtain the best net buying or selling price for their investors and, at the same time, execute orders promptly and efficiently. Nevertheless, in April 1972, by order of the Securities and Exchange Commission, the ceiling was lowered to $300,000. And legislation lowering it to $100,000 was being sponsored in Congress. It was argued that the resulting savings would be passed along to the ultimate investors in mutual fund shares, pension plans, and other institutional portfolios.

Transfer of Securities

Bonds are negotiable instruments, and stocks are in effect negotiable under modern stock transfer laws. Title may be transferred by simple delivery, in the case of coupon bonds which are payable to bearer, or by endorsement or assignment and delivery, in the case of registered bonds and all classes of corporate stock. Endorsement in blank converts an instrument payable to a specified party into an instrument payable to the holder. The law generally upholds the title of an innocent purchaser to a negotiable instrument, so that buyers and sellers of securities should be most careful in arranging transfers. Because dividend payments are made only to stockholders of record, new owners should arrange for immediate transfer to ensure the receipt of future payments. In the event of loss through delay, such owners may recover only from the former owners.

Each seller of a negotiable instrument gives three implied promises in the transfer to a buyer: (1) that the instrument is genuine, (2) that the seller is not aware of any defect in its validity, and (3) that the seller is the legal owner with full power to sell.

Stock certificates are registered in the names of the owners or their brokers ("street names"). Sometimes, owners prefer to have their stocks registered in the names of nominees, who have the right of transfer. The certificates may be transferred by endorsement or through an attached written assignment.

Each certificate is numbered, states the total number of authorized shares and the number of shares represented by the certificate, and bears the name of the registered owner, the signature of two properly designated officers of the company, and the respective authentications of the registrar and transfer agent. On the reverse side of each certificate appears a transfer order which represents a combination of a bill of sale and a power of attorney with authority to transfer.

The signature on the assignment must correspond in every way with the name written on the face of the certificate. The endorsement must be guaranteed by a responsible financial institution. The actual transfer on the books of the company is usually arranged by the new owner or his broker, but the seller sometimes makes the transfer to be assured that his name no longer appears as a stockholder.

The transfer of stock held by a corporation, or in the name of a decedent or an estate, or in the name of a trustee or guardian, or by an alien or nonresident requires additional documents of a nature too technical for discussion in this volume.

REFERENCES

BOGEN, J. I., ed. *Financial Handbook,* rev. ed. New York: The Ronald Press Company, 1968.

COOKE, G. W., *The Stock Markets,* rev. ed. Cambridge, Mass.: Schenkman Publishing Company, 1969.

DADEKIAN, Z. A., *The Strategy of Puts and Calls.* New York: Corinthian Editions, 1968.

EITEMAN, W. J., C. A. DICE, AND D. K. EITEMAN, *The Stock Market,* 4th ed. New York: McGraw-Hill, Inc., 1966.

Encyclopedia of Stock Market Techniques, rev. 2nd ed. Larchmont, N.Y.: Investors Intelligence, Inc., 1965.

ENGEL, LOUIS, *How to Buy Stocks,* 5th rev. ed. Boston: Little, Brown & Company, 1971.

FINLEY, H. M., *Everybody's Guide to the Stock Market,* rev. ed. Chicago: Henry Regnery Co., 1968.

LEFFLER, G. L., AND L. C. FARWELL, *The Stock Market*, 3rd ed. New York: The Ronald Press Company, 1963.

NEW YORK STOCK EXCHANGE, *Understanding the New York Stock Exchange*. New York: The Exchange, 1970.

REINACH, A. M., *The Nature of Puts and Calls*. New York: The Bookmailer, 1961.

SARNOFF, PAUL, *The Wall Street Thesaurus*. New York: I. Obolinsky, 1963.

SCHULTZ, B. E., *The Securities Market and How It Works*, rev. ed., A. P. Squier, ed. New York: Harper & Row, Publishers, 1963.

Understanding the Modern Securities Market. New York: Securities Publishing Division, Commodity Research Publications, Inc., 1960.

WEAVER, MARK, *The Technique of Short Selling*. Palisades Park, N.J.: Investors' Library, 1963.

WYCKOFF, PETER, *Dictionary of Stock Market Terms*. Englewood Cliffs., N.J.: Prentice-Hall, Inc., 1964.

18 Taxation of Investments

SCOPE: This chapter discusses the degree to which investments and investment income are taxed and the influence of taxation on investment policy. The emphasis is on income from securities, but other types of investments are not overlooked. The order of discussion is (1) taxation and investment policy, (2) Federal personal income taxes, (3) yields on tax-free bonds, (4) capital gains and losses, (5) Federal personal income taxes on dividends, (6) corporate income taxes, (7) state and municipal income taxes, (8) Federal estate taxes, (9) Federal gift taxes, (10) state estate and inheritance taxes, (11) estate planning, (12) personal property taxes, (13) transfer taxes, (14) taxation of insurance, pensions, and annuities, and (15) taxes on real property and income.

Taxation and Investment Policy

Protection against taxation, especially that imposed on income, is becoming a major requirement in the investment programs of individuals and taxed institutions. Indeed, for many investors, it is the dominating influence.

A wide variety of tax levies must be given careful consideration. The Federal government imposes income, gift, and estate taxes; state governments impose income, estate or inheritance, and (in a few cases) property taxes; local county and municipal bodies impose property taxes.[1] The incidence of these taxes does not apply uniformly to all investment media, or to all investors, individual or corporate, or in all localities. The importance of taxation to the individual investor varies with his income, the size of his estate, the place of his residence, the number of his dependents, the location of his commitments, and any special tax advantages or disadvantages that apply to him. The small investor has little or no interest in tax factors; the large wealthy investor has a major interest. To the large middle group they supplement other more important factors. To corporations and institutions the significance of taxes varies from none at all to being a major investment consideration.

[1] In addition, a few states levy gift taxes, and a few municipalities (for example, Philadelphia) levy income taxes. But these are of minor significance.

The term *tax-exempt,* frequently used in connection with securities, usually refers only to income taxes and generally to Federal income taxes. The bonds of many states and municipalities are known as tax-exempt issues. Thus, if bonds of Boston are owned by an investor in Albany, New York, no Federal tax is imposed upon the interest, but the New York State income tax applies, as well as the Federal and New York State estate taxes in the event of the death of the holder. Tax-exemption, therefore, applies primarily to income taxes and not to estate, gift, and property taxes.

The tax position of the investor is complicated by overlapping taxes. The income available for dividend payments by a corporation is substantially reduced by corporate income taxes, which in 1972 were imposed at rates as high as 48 per cent. The dividend income of the stockholder is further reduced by personal incomes taxes, which were imposed at rates as high as 70 per cent.[2] The estates of investors are subject to death taxes by both the Federal and state governments (at rates as high as 77 per cent in 1972).

Federal Personal Income Taxes

Federal incomes taxes comprise the heaviest tax burden for most investors. Currently, the Revenue Code imposes a personal income tax computed for single tax payers (unless a special tax table for incomes up to $10,000 is used) at 14 per cent on the first $500 of taxed net income (after deductions and personal exemptions) and rising by graduated brackets to 70 per cent on taxed net income in excess of $100,000. The maximum rate on total taxable income is 60 per cent. Married persons filing separate returns, heads of households, and married persons filing joint returns are subject to different rates than the above. Using the rates applicable to income for the calendar year 1972; an investor with a gross income of $18,500, with a wife and two children, would calculate his tax as follows (assuming a joint return):

Gross income	$18,500
Deductions (standard deduction assumed)	2,000
Net income after deductions	$16,500
Exemptions ($750 for each spouse and dependent)	3,000
Taxable income after exemptions	$13,500
Tax thereon	$ 2,635

The total Federal income tax of $2,635 is about 20 per cent of the taxable income. The tax rate on the highest income bracket in this case is 25 per cent, which is the lowest effective rate on any new investment income of the taxpaying couple that files a joint return.

The Federal income tax levy increases rapidly with the size of the annual income. To investors in the higher tax brackets, securities that are exempt

[2]Less the $100 dividend exclusion described later in this chapter.

from ordinary Federal income taxes naturally make a strong appeal. These now (1972) include the following issues:

1. Bonds of Puerto Rico;
2. Bonds of states and political subdivisions (municipalities);
3. Revenue bonds issued by authorities that operate public facilities under the egis of a municipality or state, and other nonguaranteed municipal bonds such as those issued to finance municipal utility operations.[3]

The income from all obligations of the United States and its instrumentalities, issued after March 31, 1941, is fully taxable by the Federal government, but not by state or local governments.

Some securities bear tax-free covenants under which the issuing corporation pays part of the state or Federal income tax imposed on the holder. As the amount paid is usually "up to 2 per cent," the advantage to the holder is almost insignificant. Federal laws do not recognize such covenants for obligations issued since 1934.

Yields on Tax-Free Bonds

An investor subject to a tax rate of 30 per cent pays a $21 tax on the $70 received annually from a 7 per cent taxable bond; this payment reduces his income to $49. The purchase of a tax-exempt 4.9 per cent bond at par produces the same net return to that individual. The purchase of a tax-exempt 5 per cent municipal bond at par affords the same return as a taxable 10 per cent corporate bond bought at par to the investor subject to a tax rate of 50 per cent on the income from the additional investment.

Investment policy with respect to Federal income taxes depends on the

Table 18-1. EQUIVALENT YIELDS ON TAX-FREE AND TAXABLE SECURITIES

(rates applying in 1972)

Individuals Married (Separate Return)

Selected Taxable Income Brackets	Highest Bracket Rate	Tax-Free Yields					
		3.5%	4.0%	4.50%	5.00%	5.50%	6.00%
$ 8,000–10,000	28%	4.86%	5.56%	6.25%	6.94%	7.64%	8.33%
16,000–18,000	42	6.03	6.90	7.76	8.62	9.48	10.34
22,000–26,000	50	7.00	8.00	9.00	10.00	11.00	12.00
38,000–44,000	58	8.33	9.52	10.71	11.90	13.10	14.29
60,000–70,000	64	9.72	11.11	12.50	13.89	15.28	16.67
90,000–100,000	69	11.29	12.90	14.52	16.13	17.74	19.35
Over 100,000	70	11.67	13.33	15.00	16.67	18.33	20.00
Corporations (on income over $25,000)	48	6.73	7.69	8.65	9.62	10.58	11.54

[3] See Chapter 6.

size of the annual personal net income. The total tax rate of investors of limited means is small, and they should buy taxable securities and pay the tax. Investors with very substantial incomes find the purchase of tax-exempt securities more advantageous. As shown in Table 18-1, a married investor with a taxable income of $44,000 (separate return) would have to receive a yield of 11.90 per cent on a taxable bond to equal a yield of 5.00 per cent on a tax-free bond.

The effective tax rate to an investor is the one that applies to his highest income bracket, inasmuch as income from investments is reported in addition to income from other sources. The highest bracket of an investor with a taxable income of $90,000 (married and filing a separate return) is 69 per cent. Hence, he must receive 16.13 per cent from a taxable bond in order to have 5.00 per cent remaining after the 69 per cent tax.

The appeal of tax-exempt bonds to investors in the higher tax brackets is reflected in their yields in relation to those on taxable bonds. The yields in the various Moody's bond groups, in January 1973, are shown in Table 18-2.

Table 18-2. YIELDS BY BOND GROUP

	January 1973
Corporate bonds (composite)	
Aaa	7.15%
Aa	7.35
A	7.50
Baa	7.90
Long-term municipals	
Aaa	4.90
Aa	5.10
A	5.25
Baa	5.40
U.S. Treasury, long-term	5.90

SOURCE: Moody's *Bond Survey*.

To obtain an after-tax yield on corporate bonds equal to the tax-free yield on municipals, the investor in the upper brackets would have to take considerable risk. In January 1973 he could get a return of 4.90 per cent on the best municipals, and 5.40 on good-grade municipals. If he were to purchase a corporate bond, and its interest fell into the 50 per cent bracket, such a bond could have only very poor quality.

The advantage to be gained from the purchase of tax-exempt bonds varies from time to time with the changing spreads between yields on different securities. (Comparative yields are discussed further in Chapter 6.)

The investor should also consider the alternative yields on common stocks. In the postwar period until 1959, the yield on representative stock averages consistently exceeded that on high-grade municipal bonds. Whether the after-tax yield was relatively attractive depended on the effective tax rate that applied to particular investors. In 1950, when the dividend yield on the Dow Jones 30 industrial stocks averaged 7.5 per cent, the average yield on

Moody's Aaa municipals was 1.56 per cent. Only investors in the very highest brackets would have preferred the latter for income. However, as stock yields declined in subsequent years, accompanied by a rise in state and local government bond yields, the advantage of stocks, with respect to current income, first disappeared and then became negative. In 1964 the yield on Moody's Aaa municipal bond series averaged 3.09 per cent, while that of the industrial stocks was 3.00 per cent. In January 1970, at the peak of interest rates, the municipals series yielded 6.4 per cent, while the industrial stock average yielded 3.60 per cent. In January 1973, the rates were 4.95 and 2.55 per cent, respectively.

Such figures suggest that stocks have been preferable to tax-free bonds for price appreciation rather than for income. Certainly the investor of means who held good stocks through the great postwar bull market that reached its peaks in 1966 and 1973 would have been much further ahead from the combination of income plus appreciation on stocks than by holding municipal bonds, especially when the lower income tax rates on capital gains are considered. In the latter half of the 1960s and in 1970–1971, stocks failed to regain the high level set in 1966, and the risks of holding equities became very evident in the falling markets of 1966 and 1970. The high yields on municipal bonds that characterized the more recent period mean that such investments would have outperformed common stocks in total rate of return, especially on an after-tax basis.

Generalizations concerning the appeal of stocks versus tax-exempt bonds must be tempered with the reminder that different investors bear different tax rates, and that yields change through time. Under rates applying to 1972 income, the first $10,000 of taxable income (separate return) was taxed at as high as 27 per cent. To equal a tax-free yield of 5 per cent, the investor whose income hit the 27 per cent bracket would have to receive nearly 8 per cent current income from stocks. To do this with equivalent safety is impossible. A good case can be made for stocks as a component of many portfolios along with municipal bonds. But the investor must realize that his return from most stocks must come mainly from appreciation rather than from dividends and that substantial risks must be assumed. And he must recognize that the differential between gross yields on tax-free bonds and on stocks will continue to change.

There are other methods of reducing Federal income taxes on family income from investments, in addition to the purchase of tax-free bonds (or of shares in unit trusts whose portfolios consist of tax-free bonds) : (1) the use of the joint return (mentioned above) whereby a married couple can split its combined income and thus move each half of the income into a lower tax bracket; (2) irrevocable gifts of securities to members of the family (but subject to gift taxes) and to trusts with a minimum duration of ten years; (3) the use of family partnerships and corporations (under certain conditions) ; (4) postponement of some income until retirement through participation in pension plans whose income is accumulated tax-free; rates applying after retirement will presumably be lower; (5) purchase of bonds at a discount (see below) ; (6) the acquisition of securities whose income is taxed as capital gains or is a return of capital and so not taxed (see below) ; (7) investment for appreciation so as to enjoy a possibly reduced rate on capital gains (discussed below). This includes appreciation in bonds bought at substantial discounts.

Capital Gains and Losses

The fact that capital gains receive special treatment is of considerable interest to many investors in the upper brackets. Profits and losses on the sale or exchange of capital assets held for more than six months are long-term capital gains and losses, those on the sale or exchange of capital assets held for not more than six months are short-term capital gains and losses. In calculating taxes, capital gains and losses are offset against each other. First, short-term gains are applied against short-term losses, and long-term gains against long-term losses. Then the results are combined. If a net short-term gain remains after deducting a net long-term loss, it is added to ordinary income and taxed at regular rates. If a net long-term gain remains after deducting long-term losses and any net short-term loss, it is taxable at a maximum rate of 25 per cent on the first $50,000 of such gains ($25,000 in the case of a married individual filing a separate return) and 35 per cent on any gains in excess of such an amount (in 1972 and thereafter). The taxpayer then calculates the tax by adding to ordinary taxable income one-half of the net long-term gain and applying the appropriate rate.[4]

A net short-term capital loss (with no long-term loss) is applied against any net long-term gain, and the balance may be used as a deduction, of up to $1,000, from the year's ordinary income. Any loss still remaining can be carried forward. A net short-term loss in excess of any long-term capital gain, or a net long-term loss, may be applied, up to $1,000 in a joint return, against the year's ordinary income, but taken into account at only 50 per cent. That is, it takes $2,000 of net long-term loss to obtain a $1,000 deduction. Any remaining net short-term or net long-term losses that are carried forward to a future year retain their original character.

The 25 to 35 per cent limitation on the tax on net long-term capital gains provides a special impetus to investors in the higher tax brackets to seek appreciation rather than regular income, and may thus greatly influence the composition of the portfolio. The purchase of low-yield growth stocks that offer promising appreciation, emphasis on oil, mining, natural gas, and other natural resource investments, and the purchase of real estate for appreciation, are all encouraged by the capital gains provisions.

Investors should be acquainted with some of the special measures by which the capital gains tax can be used to advantage (apart from the timing factors discussed below). The more important of these are as follows:

1. Purchase (in the market) of corporate and Federal bonds at a discount. Upon later resale or call, any appreciation is taxed as a capital gain.

---

[4]Or he may use an alternative method by calculating the tax without including the long-term gain, and adding 25 per cent of the amount (up to $50,000) by which net long-term gains exceed net short-term losses, and 35 per cent of the amount in excess of $50,000. However, unless the unmarried or head-of-household taxpayer's income is over $38,000 (or $26,000 if married and filing a separate return, or $52,000 in the case of a joint return) the alternative computation is not feasible.

The greatest advantage is derived from bonds where most of the yield is represented by a deep discount rather than by the income on low-coupon bonds. (An exception is found in the case of U.S. Savings bonds, Series E, whose entire yield is represented by the discount and is taxed as ordinary income.)

2. The purchase of state and local government bonds at a discount. Any realized appreciation is taxed at the capital gains rate. But because their coupon income is tax-free, the preferable municipal bond is the one whose yield, or most of it, is represented by coupon income.[5]

3. Depending on the investor's tax bracket and the sums involved, selling one security at a capital loss may be preferable to disposing of another at a gain, since the tax saving from the loss, plus the net proceeds of the sale, may exceed the after-tax proceeds from the profitable security. This is especially true if excess net capital losses are used to offset ordinary income.

4. Investment in certain categories of stocks where dividends consist in whole or in part of distributed capital gains or of a return of capital rather than ordinary investment income (see below).

The timing of purchases and sales of securities is also affected by this special influence. Without discussing the subject in detail, the following practices should be considered, especially by those benefiting by the 25 to 35 per cent top tax rate on net long-term gains:

1. Hold appreciating capital assets over six months so as to gain the reduction applying to long-term gains.

2. Use capital losses to offset short-term gains or ordinary income, rather than long-term gains. (In 1972, short-term loss can be used 100 per cent as an offset to ordinary income, but long-term loss only 50 per cent. The unused portion of loss can be carried over and applied against ordinary income until exhausted.)

3. Take long-term gains before unused loss carryovers expire.

4. Take losses and profits in different years so as to obtain the best results from matching gains and losses attributable to different years.

5. Realize on reinvested earnings by sale before large dividend payments are made; the latter enter the stream of ordinary income that may be taxed at a higher rate.

6. Use short sales to postpone realized gains, by selling short those stocks showing long-term paper gains and closing out such sales by delivering the holdings in the following year.

7. Record capital gains that can be offset by capital losses, by buying back the same or a similar security at once (at the cost of the brokerage commission). Also, record capital losses now and repurchase thirty-one days

---

[5]When municipal bonds are bought at a premium, the premium must be amortized against the coupon income and deducted from the cost basis in computing any subsequent capital gain or loss. It may be to the advantage of the investor to handle corporate bonds in the same way; his taxable income is reduced, but although the cost basis is likewise reduced, any later realized gain will be taxed at the capital gains rate.

or more later, or buy a similar security now. (Or double up on the original shares so as to have the same securities after the sale.)

Additional suggestions on timing purchase and sales, offsetting gains and losses, and using the carryover provisions to take full advantage of the special treatment of capital gains and losses are available from security dealers and brokers and from tax services and tax consultants.

Federal Personal Income Taxes on Dividends

Cash and property dividends are fully taxed (with certain exceptions noted below) as income. The corporation also pays a tax on the net income from which the dividends are derived, and the result is, of course, double taxation on the original corporate profits.

There is, however, partial relief from the double taxation of corporate profits. The first $100 of "qualified" dividend income received during the year ($200 in a joint return where both husband and wife received $100 dividend income) is excluded.

Some "dividends" are, in whole or in part, a return of capital, representing liquidation rather than earnings. The chief examples are found in the case of "wasting assets" companies whose distributions exceed earnings after depletion. In the calculation of any later realized capital gain or loss, the cost basis of the stock is reduced accordingly.

All or part of some dividends represent capital gains distributions rather than ordinary income. The chief examples of this type are the realized capital gains distributions of regulated investment companies. (See Chapter 9.)

Dividends in the form of stock have special treatment. Where the stockholder has periodic choice between cash or stock dividends, he pays a tax on receipt of either type. He also pays a tax on stock dividends that discharge dividend arrearages of the current or preceding year. But if the dividend is an ordinary common stock dividend paid on common stock, it is not taxed on receipt. Upon subsequent sale, only the gain is taxed, and at the capital gains rate that applies to the taxpayer. In calculating the amount of gain (or loss) on sale of the shares, the cost basis of the original shares is adjusted to reflect the increased number of shares. Thus, if the investor had bought 100 shares of common stock for $1,000, and subsequently received 25 additional common shares as a stock dividend, the cost basis of the 125 shares would become $8 per share. Subsequent purchases, sales, stock dividends, and stock splits present problems of identification. A careful record of the specific blocks of shares bought and sold, and of shares to which the dividends have applied, is necessary to calculate the cost basis of each share sold in order to determine any capital gain or loss. Invoices of all purchases and sales should be retained, otherwise the "first-in, first-out" rule may be applied, to the possible detriment of the investor.

Stock rights also receive special Federal income tax treatment. They are not taxable on receipt. Unless the market value of the rights is more than

15 per cent of the value of the outstanding stock at the time of distribution (an unlikely event), the cost basis of stock acquired through rights is the subscription price, and that of the original stock remains unchanged. If the rights are subsequently sold, the cost basis is zero and the entire net proceeds are considered capital gains, either short- or long-term. The holding period of the new stock begins on the date the rights are exercised; that of the rights begins at the time the underlying stock was acquired.

Corporate Income Taxes

The investor is, of course, considerably affected by the corporate income taxes that reduce his earnings and dividends, and by the influence of taxation on the prices and yields of corporate securities. Under rates applying to 1972 income the ordinary corporation is subject to the following rates:

On all taxable income	22%
On taxable income over $25,000	26%

This means that for larger companies, the effective rate is virtually 48 per cent.[6]

High corporate tax rates, followed by even higher rates on dividends as personal income, provide a strong motive for retention rather than distribution of profits by many corporations. To prevent undue retention, a tax on the improper accumulation of surplus of from 27.5 per cent to 38.5 per cent is imposed on that portion of the earnings (over $100,000) retained but not necessary for the reasonably anticipated needs of the business. Use of earnings for expansion, or to provide for reasonable contingencies or to retire prior obligations, is not penalized. This section of the Internal Revenue Code applies mainly to closely held corporations.

Corporations are subject to taxation of capital gains. For virtually all corporations the effective rate is 30 per cent on net long-term gains. Ordinary corporations pay a tax on dividends received on common and preferred stock investments, but after an 85 per cent deduction. This gives stocks a special appeal to business corporations holding stocks as general investments and to certain taxed institutional investors for which stocks are eligible assets. The special tax advantage of investment in high-grade preferred stocks to business firms, insurance companies, and other taxed institutions accounts in part for the fact that the yields have been as low as, and in some cases, lower than those on high-grade bonds.[7] Institutional investors, such as approved pension funds and college endowments, whose income is tax-exempt, find no particular advantage in purchasing preferred stocks (unless convertible) rather than bonds, and of course, such funds avoid investment in state and local government bonds whose yields are unattractive.

[6]To prevent splitting businesses into two or more companies to reduce the individual corporation's net income below $25,000, there are special regulations governing multiple-corporate operations.
[7]See Chapter 8, Table 8-2.

Taxed corporations, such as banks and insurance companies, find a major advantage in investing in tax-free state and local government bonds, whose yields greatly exceed the yields on Federal and on high-grade corporate bonds after the application of a high tax rate.

Certain types of corporations are subject to special income tax rates or provisions. Life insurance companies, under legislation passed in 1959, are taxed under a special formula that reduces the effective tax rate on investment income to between 25 and 30 per cent.[8] Other insurance companies are taxed at the regular corporate rate less allowed reserves against losses, as are savings banks, savings and loan associations, and commercial banks. Public utility companies are allowed a special deduction from taxable income for dividends paid on nonparticipating cumulative preferred stock issued before October 1942. Investment companies may obtain tax-exemption by complying with the provisions of the Investment Companies Act of 1940 and the Internal Revenue Code that qualify them as "regulated investment companies," including the important requirement that they distribute in dividends at least 90 per cent of each year's net investment income.[9]

Ordinary corporations find many ways to reduce the impact of income taxation. Among these are the use of carrybacks and carryforwards; the application of special depletion rates for tax purposes by "wasting asset" companies; the use of accelerated depreciation and amortization which reduces and postpones (possibly indefinitely) part of the tax bill because of increased depreciation expense, the use of the investment credit for equipment purchased, and the use of debt financing to take advantage of the deductibility of interest as an expense for income tax purposes. These and other devices are fully described in works dealing with business finance and accounting.

State and Municipal Income Taxes

Some forty-one states now levy personal income taxes. The exemption limits are generally higher than those permitted by the Federal returns, and the rates, while graduated, run much lower. Thus, in California (1972 returns) the rates on taxable net income after exemptions and deductions, single person, graduate from 1 per cent on the first $2,000 to 10 per cent on taxable income over $14,000. The state income tax is deductible in computing the Federal income tax.

State and higher Federal rates in the upper brackets combine to impose a very substantial levy on investment income. Some relief is found in those states that permit the splitting of income (and exemptions) to bring the respective portions of a joint state return into the lower brackets. In fourteen states the Federal income tax is a partly or wholly deductible expense.

State tax regulations differ considerably in the treatment of such items as capital gains, dividend and tax deductions, medical expenses, and many

[8]See Chapter 30.
[9]See Chapter 9.

other items. The trend, however, is towards more similarity with the Federal rules in respect to such details.

Where taxable income is derived in more than one state, duplicate taxation is avoided in the case of states which have entered into reciprocal agreements. For example, California has (1972) such agreements with twenty-eight other states.

About forty-six states now impose income taxes on corporations, with the rates typically 5 to 6 per cent. In addition, some hundreds of municipalities, mainly in Pennsylvania and Ohio, impose income taxes on wages, salaries, and business profits; investment income is ordinarily exempted, however.

Interest on Federal obligations is exempt from income taxes in all states. The interest on state and local government bonds of the state of issue is exempt "at home." Further discussion of this subject is found in Chapters 5 and 6.

Federal Estate Taxes

The Federal estate tax is based on the right of the Federal government to tax the transfer of property, not the property itself.

All estates, above certain exemptions, are subject to a graduated tax, increasing in rate with the size of the estate. Under legislation applying in 1971–1972, the net taxable estate is determined by reducing the gross estate by administration expenses, debts, charitable bequests, and other deductions including a marital deduction not in excess of 50 per cent of the value of the estate after debts and expenses, and a specific exemption of $60,000. The first $5,000 of the net estate is taxed at 3 per cent and the next $5,000 at 7 per cent, the rate continuing to advance to a maximum of 77 per cent on the net estate over $10,000,000. The ultimate tax is the sum thus computed less a credit equal to 80 per cent of a special "gross basic estate tax" or the amount of state inheritance taxes paid, whichever is the smaller.

No securities are exempt. The estate tax may be reduced, however, through outright lifetime gifts, as is shown in the subsequent paragraph. Another device is to buy certain issues of Treasury bonds whose face value is acceptable in payment of estate taxes. The advantage of buying such bonds at a discount is obvious. Their appeal for estate tax purposes is attractive enough to cause them to sell at higher prices and lower yields than other Treasury bonds with the same maturities.

Federal Gift Taxes

A graduated tax is placed upon all gifts between living persons after a cumulative lifetime exemption of $30,000 plus $3,000 to any person in any year. The gift tax rates are uniformly three-fourths of the corresponding estate tax rates. They range from 2¼ per cent on the first $5,000 after exemptions to maximum of 57¾ per cent on amounts in excess of $10,000,000.

State Estate and Inheritance Taxes

With the exception of Nevada, all states in the United States now impose some form of death tax. The *estate tax* is levied directly against the net estate as an entirety, generally on a graduated scale. Such a tax is used alone by a dozen states, including New York. The *inheritance tax* is levied on the individual shares of the beneficiaries after the net estate has been divided. Most states levy this type of tax. In all states except Nevada, an additional estate tax is levied to take advantage of the credit for state death taxes that is allowed against the Federal estate tax.

To avoid tax duplication, the Federal law allows a credit for state death taxes based on a special table. No credit is allowed on the first $40,000 of the taxable estate. The *maximum* credit graduates from .8 per cent on $40,000 to $90,000 to 16 per cent on any excess over $10,400,000. For example, on a $240,000 net taxable estate, the maximum credit is $3,600. If the state tax were $1,500, the credit would be $1,500, and the states have increased their taxes to at least equal the Federal credit. Most states also set smaller deductions and exemptions from the gross estate and so tax many estates which are not subject to the Federal tax.

Some fifteen states levy gift taxes patterned after the Federal legislation.

Estate Planning

Estate planning involves the planning of investments, life insurance, and the terms of wills so as best to serve the needs of the investor and his family and to minimize current and future taxes. It involves the judicious use of insurance arrangements, *inter vivos* gifts, life estates, short-term and testamentary trusts, the marital deduction, and charitable beneficiaries. A major goal in many cases is to prevent death taxes from depleting capital in each generation to which the estate may pass.

Heavy Federal and state taxes of the estate or inheritance type prove a special problem for investors of large means who have been able, in spite of high income taxes, to accumulate a substantial estate. A very substantial portion of the estate must be held in cash or highly marketable securities lest the sudden need for cash for the payment of levies coincide with a period of depressed security prices. Or, where the estate consists of assets that are not readily marketable, special insurance is often taken to provide tax funds and preserve the estate for the heirs.

The whole subject of estate planning is complex and generalizations are dangerous. Each situation requires its own solution. The reader is advised to consult special works on the subject, such as those listed in the references to this chapter, and to make no important moves without competent legal advice.

Personal Property Taxes

Taxes on real and personal, tangible and intangible properties are imposed by some 12 states and by virtually all municipal governments. Investors are especially interested in those taxes that apply against securities which are regarded as personal intangible property. Some states impose taxes specifically against security holdings. For example, the Pennsylvania tax is .4 per cent annually (the 4-mill tax) on the value of securities (other than stocks of corporations domiciled in the state) held by residents of that state. The more general practice is to impose on securities the same tax rate as that levied on tangible real property such as land and buildings.

The levy and collection of taxes on personal property of either a tangible or an intangible nature are much more difficult than in the case of real property. In New York City, for example, personal property tax revenues were so small as to cause the abolition of this tax in 1933. The significance of such taxes to the investor depends upon the seriousness with which they are regarded in the community in which he is a resident. The location of the issuer of the securities and the domicile of the security instruments are also factors to be considered in the assessment of these taxes.

Although some states impose personal property (as well as income and estate) taxes on securities held within those states for the account of non-residents, the general practice is to the contrary. The constitution of New York State guarantees that the state will not impose any property, income, or estate tax on any securities held within the state for non-residents of the state, in safe-deposit boxes or in safe-keeping, custodian, or trust accounts.

Transfer Taxes on Securities[10]

The New York State transfer tax applies only on sales of stock. In 1973 it was 5 cents per share on stock selling at or over $20, 3¾ cents per share on stock selling between $10 and $20, 2½ cents on stock selling between $5 and $10, and 1¼ cents on stock selling at less than $5. The tax can be avoided by trading on regional exchanges. The tax is reduced by 80 per cent for nonresidents.

Taxation of Insurance Proceeds, Annuities, and Pensions

The proceeds from life insurance policies received by a beneficiary or by the insured when "cashed" are subject to special Federal income tax treatment. The proceeds of a lump-sum payment of the full face value of a policy are generally free from income tax. Installment payments spread over the expected life of the beneficiary or over a fixed number of years are taxed only if they exceed the installment period's portion of the principal plus a spouse's

[10]See also Chapter 17.

exclusion of $1,000. In the case of installment payments when there is no lump-sum option, the discounted value of the policy at the date of the insured's death is used as the principal amount. However, when proceeds of policies are left on deposit, the interest on the proceeds is fully taxed, as is the interest on retained "dividends" from participating policies during the life of the insured.

The income tax status of annuities is quite complex. The taxability of the proceeds depends on the life expectancy of the beneficiary or beneficiaries, whether there are any refund features in the policy, and the period over which benefits are to be received. The Internal Revenue Service provides life expectancy tables that apply to refund annuities and joint life and survivor annuities, for calculating the share of each year's payments that is a return of the original investment. The tax regulations or Master Tax Guides provide the details of the procedure.

The growing importance of pension and retirement plans, including deferred profit-sharing plans, was indicated in Chapter 3. Company contributions while the investor's account is being accumulated are tax-free provided the plan meets the requirements of the Internal Revenue Code. The tax treatment of the retirement income depends on how the benefits are distributed, the proportion of the investor's own previous contributions, and other factors. The tax status of pensions is complex and difficult to summarize.

Deferred salary and profit-sharing plans have the general advantage of reducing income until after retirement when the investor's total income is presumably lower and taxed at lower rates. Social Security retirement income is tax-free.

Taxes on Real Property and Income

Real estate property taxes, for the most part levied by municipal jurisdictions, vary with the value and location of the property and the tax rates applied by particular local governments. Their burden is of special interest to the investor in income-producing property. They are a legitimate deduction in determining taxable net income. But since income tax rates never reach 100 per cent, rising property taxes are, in effect, shared by the owner. The same is true of taxes on property held for occupancy, which are also deductible in calculating personal income taxes. This is a factor in determining the feasibility of home ownership. (See Chapter 11.)

More important in a work on investments are the methods available to individuals, real estate companies, and real estate trusts to minimize taxes on income from productive property by the judicious use of accelerated depreciation and of the capital gains provisions of the income tax regulations. Such influences on real estate investment are discussed in Chapter 11.

Another aspect of property taxation of interest to the homeowner at or before retirement is the treatment of capital gains on houses sold. Prior to 1964, any tax on capital gain was postponed only if, within twelve months, the owner replaced his home with another costing at least as much. When these conditions were not fulfilled, realized capital gain was taxable. Under the 1964 Amendment the profit from the sale of a house for $20,000 or less, sold after 1963 by a person aged sixty-five or over, is exempt. If the selling price is higher, one half of the gain attributable to the first $20,000 of sale price is exempt, and the other half is taxable at the capital gains rate. Certain age and timing factors must, however, be applicable.

REFERENCES

APPLEMAN, J. A., ed., *Basic Estate Planning.* New York: Matthew Bender & Co., Inc., 1961.

BOWE, W. J., *Tax Savings through Estate Planning.* Nashville, Tenn.: Vanderbilt University Press, 1963.

BROSTERMAN, ROBERT, *The Complete Estate Planning Guide.* New York: McGraw-Hill, Inc., 1964.

CASEY, W. J., *Estate Planning.* Larchmont, N.Y.: Institute for Business Planning, Inc., loose-leaf.

————, *Tax Planning.* Larchmont, N.Y.: Institute for Business Planning, Inc., loose-leaf.

COMMERCE CLEARING HOUSE, INC., *Federal Tax Course.* New York: Commerce Clearing House, Inc., annual.

FARR, J. F., *An Estate Planner's Handbook,* 3rd ed. Boston: Little, Brown and Co., 1966.

Federal Tax Revision: A Summary of the 1969 Act. New York: Tax Foundation, Inc., 1970.

GOLDBERG, P. J., *Tax Planning for Today and Tomorrow.* New York: Oceana Publications, 1961.

INSTITUTE FOR BUSINESS PLANNING, INC., *Hidden Gold and Pitfalls in the New Tax Law.* Larchmont, N.Y.: The Institute, 1970.

KAPLAN, PHILIP, *Tax Savings to Increase Your Income the Year Round.* Larchmont, N.Y.: American Research Council, 1962.

LASSER (J. K.) Tax Institute, *Fifty-three New Plans for Saving Estate and Gift Taxes,* New York: The Institute, 1965.

————, *J. K. Lasser's Successful Tax Planning for Real Estate,* rev. ed. Garden City, N.Y.: Doubleday & Co., 1972.

————, *J. K. Lasser's Your Income Tax.* New York: Simon & Schuster, Inc., annual.

————, AND J. D. CUNNION, *Lasser's Treasury of Tax Savings Ideas,* 2nd ed. Larchmont, N.Y.: Business Reports, Inc., 1960.

PRENTICE-HALL EDITORIAL STAFF, *Federal Tax Course.* Englewood Cliffs, N.J.: Prentice-Hall, Inc., annual.

SNEE, T. J., AND L. T. CUSAK, *Principles and Practice of Estate Planning.* Englewood Cliffs, N.J.: Prentice-Hall, Inc., 1960.

U.S. TREASURY DEPARTMENT, INTERNAL REVENUE SERVICE, *A Guide to Federal Estate and Gift Taxation.* Washington, D.C.: U.S. Government Printing Office, 1971.

————, *Your Federal Income Tax.* Washington, D.C.: U.S. Government Printing Office, annual.

WHITE, E. H., ed., *Fundamentals of Federal Income, Estate and Gift Taxes,* 8th ed. Indianapolis, Ind.: The Research & Review Service of America, Inc., 1962.

19 Investment Principles

SCOPE: Up to this point the material in this book has provided the background and information needed by the investor to design an intelligent investment program. Following a discussion of the general economic setting of the subject (Part I), the major general types of investment media were described (Part II). Then came a series of chapters (Part III) dealing with the mechanics of investment: the financial language, the sources of investment information and advice, the origin of new securities, the market for outstanding securities, the techniques of purchase and sale, and the tax treatment of various types of investments. We are now ready in Part IV to consider the development of the investment program. Chapters 19 and 20 outline the general principles that govern investment policy. The more specific application of the principles to individual investment programs is found in Chapter 21 and to institutions in Chapters 22 and 23.

The order of discussion in Chapter 19 is (1) steps in framing an investment program, (2) budgeting for investment, (3) determination of the investor's objectives, (4) investment requirements, and (5) types of investment risk.

Steps in Investment Planning

Investing is a serious business. It should be based on a well-considered plan that takes into account the needs of the investor and the degree of risk he is able to assume. The development of a plan involves six steps: (1) budgeting and allocation of funds for investment; (2) determination of the investment goals in the order of their priority; (3) analysis of the risks involved in the use of the various types of investments; (4) allocation of the available funds to the general types of investment media so as to meet the objectives and avoid or minimize the risks; (5) selection and timing of the specific investments; and (6) continuous reappraisal and revision of the program in the light of changing circumstances and market conditions. This approach appears complicated, but it is better to err on the side of careful planning than to hazard the hard-earned savings of a family or the funds entrusted to institutions.

This chapter deals with the first two of these steps, Chapter 20 with the third, and Chapters 21 to 23 with the fourth. General types of investments are discussed in Part II with some suggestions as to the risks involved, and the whole of Part V is devoted to the important problems of analysis and valuation of corporate securities.

Budgeting for Investment

People have available to invest in securities and other media what they save after consumption needs and debt repayments have been met. However, a certain amount of savings should be included in the budget, possibly at the expense of consumption, so as to recognize the importance of future needs along with present needs. Some saving is forced through expenditures—for example, regular payments on a mortgage, premiums paid to keep insurance and annuities in force, payroll deductions for Social Security, and, with less obligation, voluntary retirement plans and payroll purchase of Savings bonds. These are all the savings (and investment) some families can produce. However, in many others, additional voluntary savings can be planned, although some fortitude may be necessary to stay with the plan. To make such savings more vital, definite goals for their ultimate use should provide the proper incentive.

To suggest any general rules concerning the portion of the total family income that should be saved, and invested in various types of media, would be folly. The circumstances of each situation must govern.

Institutions that collect and invest the savings of depositors or contract-holders do not need as much moral compulsion to put these savings to work. They must do so if their contracts are to be fulfilled.

Determination of Investment Objectives

No investment, however "safe' it may be with respect to income and principal, is a "good' investment unless it fits the purposes of the investor and helps to achieve his appropriate goals. For example, a very wealthy individual whose whole estate consists of Treasury bonds would be making a "safe" investment if he purchased additional Treasury bonds with new funds. Such a policy might not be "good," however, because this investor can take advantage of the tax-exempt features of municipal bonds, take the risks involved in owning equities, and direct at least a portion of his funds toward the goals of capital appreciation and preservation of purchasing power. The purchase of additional Treasury bonds would be intelligent only if he needed high liquidity and was satisfied with a relatively low rate of return. At the opposite extreme, the investor of limited means with dependents to provide for, and whose funds are already wholly invested in common stocks, might make a relatively safe investment (as stocks go) if he purchased additional shares of strong, prosperous industrial corporations enjoying regular earnings and paying regular dividends; but such a policy might hazard his need for recovery of principal and for highly dependable income, and he would be incurring risks that he is in no position to take.

Whether a certain investment is "good" depends, then, on the circumstances of the investor or investing institution, on the goals toward which savings or institutional funds should be applied, and on the risks that can be assumed. A discussion of the various goals of individual investors is contained in Chapter 21, while the investment objectives of institutions are set forth in Chapters 22 and 23.

Investment Requirements

Investment objectives may be viewed in one of two ways. The first is to consider the specific *personal* or institutional goals to which savings will be devoted, such as purchase of a home, education of a family, provision for retirement income, or, for an institution, the production of a regular income to meet a contract. A second approach is to consider the general *financial* requirements that have to be met if these goals are to be achieved. The first approach will be considered in the chapters dealing with individual and institutional investment policy. At this stage we shall consider the *general* requirements that have to be considered by investors, noting how their relative importance differs with the needs and purposes of the investor. The following list is not necessarily arranged in order of relative importance, although the first factors mentioned are probably more important to most investors than are the last.

Immediate recovery of principal. For the majority of investors the protection of the dollar value of investments is of prime importance. Savings accounts involve no risk of immediate loss provided the savings institution remains solvent and financially liquid. The principal of securities may be recovered through resale only if the instrument is readily marketable and enjoys price stability; those with a fixed maturity provide eventual recovery of principal at maturity, except in case of default. But recovery in the short term is assured only through the purchase of very short maturities. Temporary recovery of at least part of the principal may be obtained through loans.

Emergency funds require complete liquidity, and this is achieved only at some sacrifice of income. The same is true of the investments of institutions such as banks that must meet payments on demand or on very short notice. Immediate recovery of funds held as protection against the death of the income-producer is likely to be necessary for only part of the estate. Funds accumulated for an immediate equity in a home must also be protected against shrinkage.

Investments made for purposes such as education of dependents require considerable safety and possibly complete availability, depending on when the funds are needed. In most situations, the investor should be unwilling to risk the dollars saved for such an objective if the need is immediate. Funds earmarked to produce supplemental income for the individual investor before retirement can be invested by some families so as to risk change in market value, provided the income produced is satisfactory. The importance of preservation of immediate dollar value for this purpose varies widely, since the dependence on savings and income differs so greatly. The same is true of investing for retirement.

The creation of an eventual estate (other than through insurance) is impelled by a wide variety of reasons. The estate may have to provide for dependents, or it may be planned as a gift to endowed or charitable institutions or for many other purposes. In many cases, however, immediate recovery of principal is not required, save for the payment of estate taxes, other expenses, and debts of the deceased.

Eventual recovery of principal. Although funds may not be immediately required, safety of principal, or more accurately, ultimate recovery of principal, may be an important requirement. Funds held for emergencies must be available, without shrinkage, five or ten years from the present. Funds provided against the death of the income-producer are assured mainly through life insurance. Deposit types of investments and Savings bonds will provide full recovery, but marketable securities and real estate investments will rise and fall in value. The importance of avoiding loss of principal varies greatly from case to case. Purchase of a home on a long-term amortized mortgage plan avoids the problem of investment in instruments with fluctuating values, as payments on principal are made from current income.

Generalizing about provision for urgent family needs, such as education, is difficult. In many cases, the family can assume considerable risk if it has confidence in the eventual payout of its portfolio. The steadily rising costs of education suggest that well-selected common stocks or mutual fund shares are appropriate in many plans to offset inflation and participate in a growing economy. Whether the family will wish to guarantee future dollars, as through the accumulation of Savings bonds, or will accept the inevitable fluctuations in the value of stocks, is an important decision.

Funds accumulated to produce supplemental income before retirement can be invested at some risk unless other sources of income are inadequate. The degree of risk is again a matter of individual choice. The creation of a substantial estate imposes the least pressure on eventual recovery of principal.

The above sketchy account suggests that the need of immediate or ultimate recovery of principal depends on (1) the objectives of the investor and (2) the degree of risk that can be assumed.

Assurance of current income. For many investors this requirement has even greater importance than recovery of principal. Except in the cases where total income is already very large in relation to need, or where income from sources other than investments is very substantial, or where capital appreciation and tax considerations are important, current income is likely to take a senior place in the priority of investment considerations.

Whether the dollars of income will be assured depends on the solvency and earning power of the user to whom the funds are committed and, in the case of corporate stocks, on the dividend policy of the corporate management. Methods of determining these factors comprise much of the material in Part V of this book. But the need of assured income is determined prior to the selection of the investments that are expected to produce it. The use of a few of the same general situations that were discussed in connection with the factor of safety of principal will illustrate this point. Emergency funds that must be available on short notice have historically produced a relatively low rate of income, as in the case of savings deposits or Savings bonds cashed well before maturity. In 1966–1973 however, savings deposits yielded substantial rates. If loans are based on the cash-surrender value of insurance, the income is likely to be negative in that the rate charged will exceed the return produced on the insurance company's reserves. Many investors need income at a minimum of risk immediately and continuously; in other cases, such as for retirement purposes, it will be needed in the possibly remote future, but funds to produce it must be built up on the basis of a certain rate of return. Generally speaking, the smaller the fund and the greater the importance of each dollar of income, the less the risk that can be assumed and the lower the rate of income that can be obtained with required safety. The small investor cannot have immediate recovery of principal, assurance of income, generous returns, and capital appreciation through the same investments. If assurance of income is paramount, other features must be sacrificed. The same is true for most institutional investors. In other situations, however, regularity and certainty of income may be much less important than capital preservation and appreciation, tax savings, or protection against inflation.

In the preceding discussion, *current income* means regularly received income in the form of interest or dividends. The concept of income can also include capital appreciation derived from the increase in market value of equities. Some rapidly growing corporations distribute only a very modest proportion of their earnings, and the bulk of such earnings can be obtained only by resale, if the price reflects such reinvestment. And in comparing the returns on bonds and common stocks, it is necessary to include both current income and change in price, because only a portion of profits is declared in dividends, and yields on stocks are typically lower than those on bonds (see p. 142). Such a concept of income is perfectly legitimate provided the source of appreciation is growth in real value and not merely a temporary rise in market values owing to temporary changes in the outlook for the corporation or a cyclical rise in the price of its stock. Much impetus to the choice of capital gains as against income in the traditional sense has also been given by the special tax treatment of such gains. Such a transfer of emphasis from present income to future income and hence to future appreciation is appropriate only for investors who do not need assured *current* income and who can afford the risks of price change that buying and holding for appreciation involve. The important thing is that the risks be recognized and that the selection and timing of the purchases and sales be made intelligently and at prices that do not overvalue present assets and income and future prospects.

In recent years the term income or "total return" has come to mean interest or dividends plus price appreciation, whatever the reasons for the latter may be—real growth in value or cyclical, seasonal, or speculative rise. The danger in such a concept is that the gain will be relied upon as certain. Indeed, some pension funds assume a compounded rate of return of this type, as if it were an actuarial certainty. The events of the years 1965–1971 should have disillusioned most investors in this respect. It is better clearly to distinguish income from price appreciation (if any), however important the latter may be, and however preferable it may be from the standpoint of income taxation.

Freedom from management. Many investors must be as carefree as possible, either in the sense that safety of principal and stable income are assured or in the sense that only limited management can be assumed. Or the same investor may need freedom from management for part of his fund and be willing to undertake the tasks of selection, timing, and supervision of the balance.

Freedom from care through safety can be obtained by making investments that are subject to little or no shrinkage in dollar value and income, but such freedom, while important for some investors, is obtained only at the sacrifice of income. The holder of an insured passbook deposit in a strong bank or savings and loan association has freedom from care—and (at the time of writing) 4 to 5 per cent interest. The holder of a Series E Savings bond has freedom from care—and $5\frac{1}{2}$ per cent return if the bond is held to maturity. To obtain assurance of a steady small income or to obtain a higher income and still enjoy release from responsibilities of investment management requires the transfer of such responsibilities to others—either investing institutions which operate a portfolio of investments, or investment advisors.

The importance of freedom from care depends on the size of the fund, the need of assurance of income and recovery of principal, and the amount of attention and skill that the investor is able to devote to his investment affairs. All investments in savings institutions, including deposits, insurance, and annuities, involve delegation of authority to others. Investments in very high-grade securities may be made directly with a minimum of effort and supervision. Investments of all other types require either delegation of responsibility or the ability on the part of the investor himself to select, appraise, time, and supervise the funds. It is impossible to generalize on the degree to which this may be done in a skillful fashion. But in many cases the investment of funds for emergencies, for home ownership, for essential goals such as education, and for retirement should be as carefree as possible, in both the senses in which we use the term.

Satisfactory denominations. The small investor with limited funds finds a special advantage in savings accounts and Savings bonds, in which the sums invested in any one medium may be small indeed. Denominations of common stocks are similarly small, but purchase and sale of odd lots is expensive. Shares in mutual funds are ordinarily low priced. But marketable corporate and government bonds are usually available in only $500 or $1,000 denominations, and the size of individual real estate mortgages is much greater. Participation in real estate proper has the same objection, unless shares in real estate companies or trusts are acquired.

The importance of denomination lies in its relation to diversification in direct investments. Large investing institutions have no problem in this connection. The small investor, however, must emphasize liquidable small units, and has great difficulty achieving substantial diversification in corporate issues unless he emphasizes the purchase of mutual fund shares or stocks in banks and insurance companies, which provide diversification through indirect investment.

Diversification as a risk-avoiding device is discussed in more detail in the following chapter.

Tax considerations. Tax considerations do not influence the policy of the investor in the low tax brackets. But the higher the investor's income, the more such matters will determine the character of his commitments. Indeed, for investors of means and some institutions, it may be the dominating influence. The subject of taxation of investments is treated in Chapter 18 and in various other chapters where such material is pertinent. At this point we need only suggest that the prospects for continued high personal and corporate taxes and for substantial estate and inheritance taxes will continue to have a major influence on many portfolios. Two devices for minimizing income taxes—the purchase of tax-exempt state and municipal bonds and the use of the special capital gain provision—are especially significant.

Protection against inflation. Inflation has followed all of the wars in which the United States has been involved and is again a dominating and disconcerting feature of our economy. The actual decline in the value of the dollar to date, and the prospects for its continuation, mean that to a greater degree than ever, investment policy will be influenced by attempts to offset declining real income. The means by which such attempts may or may not be feasible and successful are given full treatment at various points in this volume. At this time it is necessary to suggest four problems in connection with the matter of hedging against inflation, each of which will be further developed elsewhere: (1) Cash and savings deposits provide no hedge at all; (2) fixed-income obligations have rarely provided protection save in 1966–1972 when the rate of interest exceeded the rate of price inflation; (3) the small investor, in making his choice between the safety of *dollars* of principal and income and the preservation of the *purchasing power* of those dollars, must select the first alternative, for he cannot afford the risk that equities (with the possible exception of home and business properties) inevitably involve. One of the tragedies of life is that the investor who most needs protection against rising prices can least afford it; (4) common stocks and real estate offer an inflation hedge only in varying degrees, depending on the timing of purchase and sale and the selection of the particular securities or property.

The need for and ability to hedge varies among different types of investors. And the degree to which the value and income of a particular investment are themselves affected by changing prices is a matter of serious importance. As has been indicated, the investment plans of some investors, especially those of institutions with fixed-dollar obligations, can ignore inflation; some investors are affected by inflation but can do little or nothing about it; some investors and institutions make the problem of offsetting the decline in the value of the dollar a dominating influence in their investment planning. This latter point of view is based on the assumption of continued inflation.

Two cautions should be indicated. The first is that the postwar rate of inflation may not continue indefinitely. One of the major goals of the Nixon Administration's wage-and-price "freeze" policy of 1971–1972 was to reduce the annual rate of general price rise to the neighborhood of 2½ to 3 per cent. Second, equities protect against inflation only in the long run. As indicated elsewhere, for months and even years, consumer prices and common stock prices may go in different directions (see p. 358). It is entirely possible that for many extended periods, the investment in common stocks as an inflation hedge may be neither necessary nor desirable.

Legality. The final requirement that must be considered, at least by institutional investors, is the matter of legality. These investors, especially those in a fiduciary position, must arrange their programs within the framework of the legal restrictions laid down by Federal and state governments. These restrictions change through the years. They apply with special strictness in some situations, for example, in the investment of savings bank funds, and allow very considerable latitude in others, as in the case of fire insurance companies and investment companies. But in all cases, the question of what the institution would *prefer* to do is dominated by the legal controls over what it is *permitted* to do.

Legality is important to individuals as well as to institutions. In the first place, indirect investment through the medium of a savings or investment institution is *ipso facto* affected by the legal requirements bearing on that institution. Thus, the participant in a pension plan which does not permit the company to purchase common stocks might find the rate at which his reserve is accumulated lower but less volatile than it might be if such investments were made. In the second place, the investor in certain securities, notably those issued by states and municipalities, must not only investigate the matters of willingness and ability to pay but must be satisfied that the security conforms to the legal restrictions on the borrowing government.

The preceding discussion suggests that a wide variety of investment objectives exist, expressed in either explicit or general terms, and that these will differ in relative importance from case to case. Furthermore, in seeking to meet these objectives a number of types of risks must be confronted. Before a definite program can be constructed, the nature of these risks, and the methods of minimizing or avoiding them, should be well understood.

Types of Investment Risk

Once the investor has determined his objectives, but before he selects the general types of investments, he should become thoroughly acquainted with the hazards he may confront, and make his later selections with these in mind. Some investors can incur considerable risk. But others cannot. The important thing is to relate the objectives and the risk-taking in a rational way. This involves recognition of the risks and devising means of minimizing them to the extent necessary, or at least of insuring that the greater the risk, the higher the possible returns.

Whatever the investor does, some kind of risk will be present. The central problem of investment is to work out a program that will meet his objectives without incurring more risk than can be afforded, and that will produce a return that will compensate for this risk. Too often investors ask themselves, "What return would I like?" and then frame their investment program accordingly. The more sensible approach would be, "What are my objectives, what financial requirements must be considered in order to achieve these goals, and what return can I expect to get or afford to get if these objectives and requirements are fulfilled?" One of the great temptations of investment is to incur substantially greater risk, say, through the purchase of second-grade securities, in order to obtain an increased return that often does not compensate for the increase in risk involved. For example, at the time of writing the spread between the per cent yield on a very high-grade bond and a medium-grade corporate bond is less than 1.0 per cent. The difference is not substantial enough to warrant a switch on the part of those investors to whom safety of capital and assurance of income are of primary importance. The spread between the yield on high-grade bonds and common stocks is actually negative in most cases. At the time of writing, (1972–1973), investment-grade stocks were yielding much less than high-grade bonds. Why should the investor be attracted by a 4 or 5 per cent current return on an industrial common stock when he can get over 7 per cent on a high-grade bond? He would select the stock only if he is primarily interested in appreciation rather than current income, and can afford to take the risks involved, or if he is convinced that *eventual* dividends will provide a satisfactory return on today's price. Of course, where a second-rate stock yields 8 or 9 per cent, the higher current income, plus some chance of appreciation, may be attractive enough to compensate for the additional risk.

The two major types of investment risk are (1) possible loss of dollars of income or principal of the fund and (2) possible loss of its purchasing power. These can be further classified as follows:

1. Loss of dollars of income or principal owing to
    (a) Decline in investment quality
        (1) Faulty initial selection
        (2) Deterioration of once-sound securities
    (b) Cyclical change
        (1) In the economy as a whole
        (2) In the profitability of a particular industry or company
        (3) In security prices
    (c) Changing interest rates (money-rate risk)
        (1) Bonds
        (2) Preferred stock
        (3) Common stock
    (d) Faulty valuation
2. Loss of purchasing power of principal and income owing to the changing value of money (purchasing power risk)

Risks of loss of income or principal. The risks that threaten the value of the principal or income may be encountered separately or in combination. For example, the dividend income from a stock may decline because the company is basically poorly managed or unproductive, or it may decline temporarily in a recession period not because of any inherent weakness in the company (except its vulnerability to the cycle), but because it is caught in cyclical forces largely beyond its control. Or the price of the stock may decline even though its earnings and dividends hold up, because of the drop in stock prices in general, or because investors demand a higher price-earnings ratio. The worst losses are encountered when several risks have their effect simultaneously. Thus, an inherently weak stock, in a cyclical industry, in a period of recession in security prices, will suffer the worst price decline. On the other hand, a high-grade high-profit concern, with earnings and dividends strong even in a recession period, may have a price decline in a real bear market but will recover fast and pay dividends in the meantime.

Quality of investment.

SELECTION OF HIGHLY HAZARDOUS SECURITIES. The first risk often encountered by investors derives from the improper selection of highly hazardous securities. The argument against such securities is not that they present hazards. Some investors can assume great risks in the hope of obtaining high return or appreciation. The chief objection is that the information provided and the appeals made may not only be misleading but may play on the avarice of the investor and tempt him beyond the boundaries of sensible risk-taking. Fortunately the application of the Federal securities' legislation of 1933 and 1934 and the stricter enforcement of state securities legislation have weeded out a number of highly questionable promotions and offers of securities that could not stand the light of day. Nevertheless, within the borders of states that do not require accurate disclosure of facts, the earmarks of a questionable security are still noticeable. They include vague projections of "extremely rapid growth"; new technological "breakthroughs;" "the next IBM;" "superindustries of the future;" and so on.

Very few securities of companies in the development or promotional stages deserve investment consideration. Only those persons who are able and willing to assume large risk of loss should place their funds in such enterprises. Admittedly, the rewards obtainable from an early commitment in a successful undertaking may greatly exceed those that come to investors who wait until earning power has been clearly demonstrated. But there are enough established companies with promising futures to intrigue even the investor interested mainly in capital appreciation. Intelligent analysis and valuation, together with diversification, are the investor's protection against imprudent commitments.

To many investors, shares in firms "going public" have a special allure. It is true that some of these have developed good records as closely held firms. But a public offering of stock is usually made under conditions favorable to the sellers, and after the initial enthusiasm a substantial price decline is often suffered by even the most respectable newcomers in the market.

DETERIORATION OF ONCE-SOUND SECURITIES. A problem which the investor faces in the selection of particular industries involves the avoidance of "over-age" as well as "under-age" companies. Industries have life cycles through sequential stages of experimentation, development, saturation, and decline. This is well illustrated in the loss of investment status suffered by many railway bonds and stocks, and those of technical and conglomerate firms. The investor's main protection against industrial senility is a thorough analysis of both past record and future prospects of the industry, as described in Part V of this book.

Within an industry, the fortunes of individual companies wax and wane. Here again, intelligent analysis and valuation, together with diversification, may be used to avoid concentration of loss.

Risk of cyclical changes. The cyclical ebb and flow of business affects investments in three ways. (1) Corporate earnings and financial strength rise and fall with general business conditions. (2) Some industries (the "prince-or-pauper" group) are heavily affected by the cycle; others are only mildly cyclical; still others seem to escape it altogether; thus, ability to meet interest and dividend payments is tied to cyclical experience in varying degrees. (3) Security prices rise and fall in varying degrees in anticipation or in reflection of the cyclical changes in earnings, with equities tending to magnify the fluctuations because of their relatively inferior position.

Ideally, to relate investment policy to the business cycle, the investor should make four types of forecasts: (1) of economic conditions as a whole; (2) of security price movements in general, both of stocks and of bonds; (3) of the movement of earnings for a particular industry and the probable price action of securities in that industry; and (4) of the movement of earnings, dividends, and security prices for a particular company.

The trend of business conditions traces an irregular line, now advancing, now receding. At times, the advances become so pronounced that they are apparent to everyone in the form of greater activity and increased earnings. At other times, the recessions become equally pronounced and are apparent in the form of unemployment and decreased earnings. However, such fluctuations in business activity rarely follow a curve of regular ascent and descent. The absence of uniformity in the extent and duration of business movements makes economic forecasting a most difficult problem.

Most investors should not attempt the difficult if not impossible task of forecasting the general business cycle. The most they can hope to accomplish is to recognize the current phase, whether it be recession, recovery, boom, or panic, and govern themselves accordingly.[1] The aim of the Federal government to maintain full employment and to take many courses of action to prevent excesses either of inflationary booms or deflationary recessions appeared, in the period following World War II, to make the obligation to

---

[1] A number of economic indicators help to reveal the current phase of the business cycle, including such well-known series as Gross National Product, personal income, business capital expenditures, unemployment, industrial production, construction, carloadings, manufacturers' inventories, commercial bank loans, corporate profits, and interest rates. Wholesale and consumer prices are no longer reliable in this connection.

forecast much less incumbent than was once the case. But the recessions of 1957–1958, 1960–1961, 1967, and 1969–1970 proved otherwise, and the potential for such excesses in the future still remains. The defense economy in which the United States has lived for some years and will continue to live, and the antirecession and antiinflation activities of the government and the monetary authorities, will go far toward preventing the recurrence of a drastic depression such as occurred in 1929–1933. The problem of the business cycle has not been solved, although the length and slope of its phases are much less extreme than in the past.

If security prices followed the same cyclical pattern that is apparent for business as a whole, the investor's problem would be greatly simplified. He would determine the phase in which business in general appears to be operating, and act courageously and somewhat contrary to his natural inclinations. He would buy sound securities in periods of recession and sell them when he felt that the boom period was nearly at an end. Such a policy would be based on the assumption that the investor can intelligently interpret the trend of business activity, and that he can distinguish clearly those industries and companies that will recover first and most. It also assumes that he has the patience to await the opportune times to buy and sell. Such qualities could not be expected of many investors.

Regardless of ability or willingness to interpret business trends and to act somewhat unnaturally from a psychological aspect, such an approach would be faulty for three reasons. The first is that stock prices and earnings in general do not always move in the same direction, as a study of the periods 1956–1958, 1962, 1968, and 1969–1970 reveals. The second is that different industries have different cycles. The amplitude of the variations in their profits (and of the prices of their stocks) is considerable. In fact, some industries are depressed in times of general prosperity (for example, coal and cement in the 1960s). Others prosper in times of recession, either because they benefit from lower costs of operation and a relatively fixed demand for their products (as in gold mining) or because their secular growth more than offsets a temporary cyclical influence.

The third and more important reason is that the movements of common and high-grade preferred stocks and of bonds do not coincide cyclically. When business is recovering from an inactive stage, prices of both bonds and stocks advance, the increased earning power of business enhancing the safety position of bonds and improving the earnings prospects for stocks. In a period of business activity, bond prices decline somewhat, owing in part to higher interest rates and in part to the increased popularity of stocks; during this same period, stock prices continue to advance practically to the peak of the boom, reflecting continued expected increases in corporate earnings. When business is declining or during severe credit strain, prices of stocks fall more rapidly than prices of bonds, owing chiefly to the realization that earning power was too liberally estimated in prosperous times. In a period of business recession, prices of bonds strengthen, because of their safety and because of falling interest rates, whereas prices of stocks reach low levels. Bond prices tend to move ahead of stock prices, rather than conversely. In periods of prosperity, stock prices are high and bond prices are low; in periods of recession, bond prices are strong and stock prices weak.

The movement of high-grade bond prices in relation to stock prices in the prosperity period of the late 1940s did not conform to this pattern, largely because of the great institutional demand for bonds and the special support of government bond prices (and hence of prices of all high-grade bonds), both of which kept interest rates low and bond prices high. In 1960 stock prices showed substantial weakness, reflecting general economic deterioration, while bond prices rose and yields declined. In 1961 stock prices rose to their then highest level, while bond prices declined and yields rose. In 1962 came the steepest decline in stock prices since 1929–1932, ending in June; bond price movements were irregular, but closed higher. The year 1963 saw increasing stock prices, accompanied by declining bond prices and rising yields. The course of stocks in 1964–1966 was dramatically upward to their (then) all-time peak in early 1966; bond prices were fairly level in 1964, but declined steadily in 1964–1966 as interest rates reached the highest levels since 1929. The sharp decline in stock prices after their peak in 1966 was accompanied by a similar decline in bond prices, although the short-term outlook for the economy was still favorable. In the latter months of 1966, bond prices rose modestly as yields declined; stock prices showed a greater recovery until weakness developed in the spring of 1967 in recognition of the uncertain outlook for the economy.

When bond yields reached their historical highs in late 1969 and early 1970, bond prices were, of course, correspondingly low. When safe yields of 8 or 9 per cent were available on high-grade bonds, stocks with modest earnings and growth prospects had little appeal. The long-term "rate of return" on stocks, which had historically been 8 to 9 per cent (including dividends and price appreciation), was no longer appealing. Stocks rallied in early 1971, declined in the autumn, and were strong in early 1972. One, but certainly not the only, reason for the failure of many "blue-chips" to reach former levels until very early in 1973 was that bond yields were attractive, and low prices on low-coupon bonds offered the prospects of substantial capital gains.

Insofar as high-grade bonds are concerned, as long as they remain high-grade, the long-term investor can safely ignore those cyclical price changes that arise (as we shall see in more detail later) mainly from changes in interest rates and not from changes in the issuer's earnings or financial condition. Furthermore, since the investor's main interest lies in acquiring and holding suitable securities at suitable prices (in contrast to the speculator's main interest in profiting from short-term price fluctuations), he can ignore price declines in stocks unless they are very substantial or reflect a deterioration in inherent *quality* apart from general market changes. Insofar as price rises are concerned, he should sell stocks if he is convinced that they are overvalued in terms of long-run prospects, and not merely because he believes the peak of a stock market boom is approaching. The reason for this position is that, if the investor attempts the task of selection and sale of stocks (and low-grade bonds) on the basis of his judgment concerning the phase of the security-price cycle, he is likely to be wrong a good deal of the time. If he concentrates on *values* rather than on mere price movements as such, he is likely to keep his money more fully employed and produce a better long-run result. That is to say, if he purchases a stock because it is undervalued in terms of its own merits and not because the general market is low, or sells it because it is overvalued and not merely because he feels the general market it too high, in the long run he is likely to benefit more from price fluctuations than from setting himself up as smarter than the trading public. He does not ignore market price fluctuations —he uses them as a basis of judgment concerning the value of his securities and not as the basis of a speculative game. Part V of this book is devoted to the subject of quality evaluation.

As was indicated previously, industries, and the prices of their stocks, do not act alike with respect to cyclical variations. A disadvantage of using the earnings or price record of any average or group of securities, especially of stocks, as indicative of the general trend is that within the group certain industries go counter to the group. Thus in 1971, the profits of 2319 manu-facturing corporations rose 13 per cent as compared with 1970.[2] Noting a few examples, profits of auto and trucks rose 159 per cent, sugar 44 per cent, and aerospace 39 per cent. But profits of nonferrous metals declined 49 per cent and those of paper declined 23 per cent. In the financial field, earnings of property-casualty insurance companies rose 77 per cent while those of bank holding companies rose only 11 per cent.

"Growth" industries offer a special appeal over the long run. But even these have to be selected carefully, and much patience may be required over a considerable period. Companies with aggressive management, that follow a program of research to develop new products and markets and enjoy steady increases in sales, strong finances, and a continued high or increasing return on invested capital, fit best into the growth pattern. One difficulty with "growth stocks" is that the investor may have to pay too high a price for the growth factor. Their valuation is discussed in Chapter 25.

The prospects for an individual company, like those for an industry, can best be determined by analytical methods. The investor can take advantage of the cyclical swings in the general market by purchasing securities, notably equities, when they appear undervalued, except when the whole general market is in an extreme range and even the most promising situations are vulnerable to a general collapse in market price. And he can use the market level for determining the points at which to sell securities when they are overvalued marketwise. One must realize, however, that companies in gen-eral or even all companies in a given industry do not act alike with respect to prospects and price. In both 1967 and 1970 (depression years in the steel industry), with only one or two exceptions profits of all ten major steel companies declined. But in 1969, an average year, profits of three companies increased, those of two were unchanged, and those of five declined. In 1970, on the average, the prices of the stock of the ten companies declined 26 per cent. But three stocks enjoyed increases in price.

As for stocks in general, the Dow Jones Industrial Average of 30 stocks declined 22 per cent in price from the high to the low in 1970. But within this group, Allied Chemical lost 14 per cent and Chrysler, 55 per cent. From the end of 1970 to the end of 1971, the DJIA rose 6 per cent. But within

[2]First National City Bank of New York, *Monthly Economic Letter*, April 1972.

the group, the range was from a rise of 35 per cent (Proctor & Gamble) to a decline of 29 per cent (International Nickel).

Risk of changing money rates.

BONDS. The prices of bonds rise and fall because of changes in interest rates as well as because of changes in quality as measured by earnings and assets protection. The prices of the most riskless of marketable long-term issues, namely, Treasury bonds, are effected solely by the former factor, aside from the influence of Federal support. In the postwar period they have sold, on average, to yield as high as 6.85 per cent (1970) and as low as 2.12 per cent (1946). Yields on other bonds reflect both changing interest rates and changing estimates of quality.

Interest rates on long-term investments follow trends which are somewhat independent of cyclical influences. Rates (on high-grade corporate bonds) fluctuated mildly in the 1940s, and in 1950 they were only slightly different from those of 1940. They rose somewhat in early 1951 as a result of changed Federal Reserve policy with respect to the support of Government bond prices. The yield on high-grade corporates was 3.0 per cent at the close of the year. In subsequent years the average yield was as low as 2.8 per cent (1954) and as high as 7.9 per cent (1970).

Experience has demonstrated the futility of attempting to predict the turning points in long-term interest rates and hence in high-grade bond prices. If economic history is to provide a reliable guide, however, a reasonably sound statement in early 1973 appears to be that yields on high-grade long-term bonds should not long continue above 7 per cent or under 5 per cent. Nevertheless, this range still permits a very substantial variation in bond prices. A 5 per cent bond due in thirty years is worth par in a 5 per cent market; a rise in interest rates to 7 per cent would cause a decline to $74.93 or 25 per cent in market value. Investors interested in minimizing the risk of price change in bonds should follow a policy of staggering the maturities in the bond portfolio so as to keep a substantial portion of the fund in shorter-term instruments. The closer the maturity date of a bond, the greater is its price stability. In contrast to the thirty-year bond mentioned above, a rise from 5 to 7 per cent in yield will reduce a fifteen-year 5 per cent bond from par to $81.61, a ten-year bond to $85.79, and a five-year bond to $91.68.

To obtain the greater price stability found in shorter-term bonds the investor will ordinarily have to accept a lower yield than on longer-term loans. When interest rates are generally low, as in 1950, differences in maturity were reflected in a wide variation in yields. The prevailing rates on high-grade corporate bonds were ½ to 1 per cent on two-year bonds, 1¼ per cent on five-year bonds, 1¾ per cent on ten-year bonds, 2½ per cent on twenty-year bonds, and 2¾ per cent on thirty-year bonds. However, in times of "tight" money (1957, 1959, 1966, and 1969–1970), short-term rates rise to a point where they equal or even exceed those on longer-term instruments. Table 19-1 shows the fluctuations in yields on U.S. obligations in recent years, the greater volatility of short-term than long-term rates, and

Table 19-1. YIELDS ON U.S. TREASURY OBLIGATIONS

	3-*Month* Bills	3- *to* 5-*Year* Issues	*Long-Term* Bonds
December 1959	4.57%	4.95%	4.27%
December 1960	2.27	3.51	3.88
February 1965	3.93	4.08	4.16
June 1965	3.81	4.09	4.14
February 1966	4.65	5.02	4.61
September 1966	5.36	5.62	4.79
March 1967	4.31	4.50	4.42
January 1970	7.87	8.14	6.85
March 1971	3.38	4.72	5.75
July 1971	5.39	6.77	5.91
February 1972	3.18	5.51	5.67
December 1972	4.88	6.04	5.65

the higher yield on three- to five-year issues than on long-term bonds in "tight money" situations.

The desire of investors to obtain a favorable rate of return frequently results in the assumption of risk beyond a reasonable limit. The highest-grade issues afford the lowest yields because they are exceptionally well secured and have the greatest price stability. The lower-grade issues afford higher yields because they are less secure and are more subject to fluctuations in market value. The purchase of the lower-grade bonds in 1955 would have afforded rates of return only about ½ per cent higher than the higher-grade issues; the additional compensation was not commensurate with the greater hazard involved. The average yield on Moody's Aaa corporate bonds was 3.06 per cent and on Baa bonds 3.53 per cent. Even in January 1970, at the peak of interest rates, the medium-grade bonds provided only a modest additional yield over high-grade obligations—Moody's Aaa bond series yielding 8.04 per cent and Baa bonds yielding 9.11 per cent. Such a small differential is attractive only to large institutional investors to whom every "basis point" (.10 per cent yield) is important.

Second-grade bonds should be bought only by persons who can afford to assume the commensurate high degree of risk. An axiom of the investment business holds that the higher grade the securities the smaller will be the potential market depreciation, so that while high-grade bonds sometimes prove to be weak investments, seldom indeed do low-grade bonds prove to be safe investments.

PREFERRED STOCKS. Changes in money rates also affect the prices of preferred stocks. The very highest-grade preferreds, with their fixed dividend income virtually assured, rise and fall like bonds. The yields on lesser-grade preferred stocks reflect not only changes in money rates, but changing prospects of earnings and thus of dividend payment. Low-grade preferreds act like common stocks with respect to price. The highest-grade preferreds, whose dividends are earned many times over, should provide a higher yield than high-grade, long-term bonds because they represent ownership, not debt.

Their income is a distribution of profit, not interest. However, in January 1973, the yield on Moody's Aaa industrial corporate bond series was 6.95 per cent, whereas the yield on the same service's high-grade industrial preferred series was only 6.45 per cent. This anomaly is explained by the fact that taxed corporate investors find preferred stock advantageous (85 per cent of the dividend being tax-exempt) and so drive down their market yields. (See Chapter 8.)

COMMON STOCKS. Prices of common stocks are also affected by changing interest rates, although their effect is usually overshadowed by the even more important influence of earnings and dividend prospects. The rate at which the market capitalizes the earnings on a common stock includes the basic interest rate plus an additional increment that reflects the risk in the situation. Stated in an oversimplified fashion, the value of a share of common stock reflects principally the expected future earnings capitalized at a rate that is commensurate with the risk involved, adjusted for the actual dividend prospects. The value, therefore, changes when either or both of the two components (earnings and capitalization rate) change, and the most drastic change in value, of course, occurs when the two components change in opposite directions—that is, when expected earnings decline (or increase) and the rate of capitalization increases (or declines). A simple hypothetical example will serve to illustrate this point. If the anticipated earnings on a share of common stock are $5 and the rate of capitalization demanded by the market is 10 per cent, the value of the stock is $50. If the earnings remain the same, but the rate is reduced to 5 per cent, the value is $100. The value of a share of stock may thus change through the influence of the going rate for the risk in the particular situation even though the outlook for earnings remains the same. Moreover, if the earnings are increased to $10 and the rate reduced to 5 per cent, the value is $200.

The custom in financial circles is to express the relationship between earnings and price in terms of a price-earnings ratio, or the reciprocal of the rate of capitalization. Thus, where the market capitalizes $5 of earnings at 10 per cent to produce a value of $50, the stock sells at 10 times earnings; capitalization of $5 of earnings at 20 per cent means that the stock sells at 5 times earnings. The actual record of the thirty stocks making up the Dow Jones Industrial Average shows how market price may be influenced principally by the rate of capitalization or its reciprocal, the multiple of earnings. In December 1961, the average stood at 739, which was 23 times estimated earnings for 1961. In September 1963, the average stood at 740, an almost identical figure, but this was only 18 times expected 1963 earnings. Between the two dates, the ratio, or multiple, that satisfied traders in these common stocks as a group had changed so materially that even the very substantially higher earnings on the group of stocks produced only the same average value. In February 1966, the average was 996, a figure that capitalized expected 1966 earnings at almost seventeen times. The high price level reflected a combination of higher dollar earnings, and a lower multiple, than had prevailed five years earlier.

The effect of changing earnings and price-earnings ratios is well illustrated in more recent years. In early January 1970, the DJIA was earning at an annual rate of $57 and selling at 810 for a price-earnings ratio of 14. By late May, the price had fallen to 640, to a ratio of 11. In January 1973, at a price of 1,052, the average sold at 14 times estimated 1973 earnings.

This explanation of the forces affecting the prices of common stock is, of course, greatly oversimplified in that it gives no attention to the influence of *stability* of earnings, dividend record, or asset values—factors that have considerable influence on stock prices. But it does indicate that the investor in common stocks must be prepared to see the market values of his securities decline even though earnings remain stable or even increase; it also suggests the possibility of substantial appreciation in price even in the face of declining earnings. A more complete discussion of the problem of valuation of common stocks is found in Chapter 25.

Risk of faulty valuation.   At any stage in the market price cycle, the prices of securities reflect the voting consensus of value. The stock market is often said to be right in the long run, but wrong in the short run. That is, actual price movements are exaggerated above and below true value by temporary pessimism or optimism. This imposes on the investor the responsibility of calculating (or adopting) a value for each stock and incorporating it in his buying and selling decisions, if he is to manage his portfolio on a valuation basis. Paying too much even for a sound stock may involve more loss than poor timing of transactions. Losses owing to faulty valuation can be very substantial in the case of stocks. Differences of opinion with respect to the value of bonds are much less extreme. The usefulness of the valuation approach is discussed further in the following chapter and in Chapter 25.

Risk of changes in purchasing power.   Even though the dollars of principal and income may remain the same, their value in terms of purchasing power rises and falls with changes in the price level. This fact is becoming increasingly important as the prospects for rising prices are confirmed. The dollar has lost over half of its purchasing power in the period of inflation since World War II. Protection against the purchasing-power risk, or inflation hedging, thus becomes an increasingly important consideration for investors who can assume the risks that such protection inevitably involves. It is the basis for much of the current discussion concerning the position of an investment fund that should be placed in "aggressive" securities or other investments of the equity type.

The loss of value of both principal and income that results from rising prices and a rising cost of living is easily illustrated by referring to the changes that took place in the period 1945–1972. As Table 19-2 shows, the Bureau of Labor Statistics Consumer Price Index stood at 53.9 for the year 1945 (1967 = 100). In December 1972, the index was 127.3. Thus, the buying power of $1.00 cash or principal in securities was reduced to 42 cents in the 27 year period. An investor who had bought a $100 Series E Savings bond for $75 in mid-1945 and retained it for twenty-six and a half years could redeem it for $191.64 in December 1972, but he was repaid only $81.00 in 1945 purchasing power, including 27 years' accrued interest.

Table 19-2. PRICE INDEXES AND COMMON STOCKS

	BLS Consumer Price Index	BLS Wholesale Commodity Price Index	Moody's 125 Industrials		
			Price	Earnings	Dividends
1945	53.9	57.9	$ 43.94	$ 2.72	$1.75
1950	72.1	81.8	57.83	8.45	3.77
1951	77.8	81.9	70.72	7.37	4.44
1952	79.5	88.6	75.63	7.18	4.20
1953	80.1	87.4	76.05	7.71	4.19
1954	80.5	87.6	95.81	8.38	4.46
1955	80.2	87.8	130.66	10.51	5.13
1956	81.4	90.7	149.41	10.35	5.81
1957	84.3	91.3	143.65	10.27	5.91
1958	86.6	94.6	149.81	8.31	5.75
1959	87.3	94.3	186.26	9.85	5.91
1960	88.7	94.9	173.18	9.62	6.03
1961	89.6	94.5	199.90	9.61	6.07
1962	90.6	94.8	189.25	11.10	6.43
1963	91.7	94.6	218.24	12.43	6.98
1964	92.9	94.7	258.55	14.35	7.70
1965	94.5	96.6	284.32	16.42	8.48
1966	97.2	99.8	266.77	16.78	9.17
1967	100.0	100.0	290.05	15.76	9.03
1968	104.2	102.5	315.86	17.58	9.24
1969	109.8	106.5	313.15	17.53	9.89
1970	116.3	110.4	270.83	15.34	9.76
1971	121.3	113.9	318.75	17.40	9.50
1972	125.2	119.0	362.44	20.40[a]	9.61

[a]Estimated annual rate.

Similarly, any fixed income had been reduced 58 per cent in effective value over this period.

In view of the decline in the purchasing power of each dollar of income and principal, one is not surprised that a growing number of investors are seeking a means of protection against inflation. Only those institutional investors whose obligations are in terms of dollars are oblivious to the buying value of their portfolios, and even these are confronted with rising costs of operation that indirectly influence their need for higher investment income. Unfortunately, the individual investor whose holdings consist primarily of fixed-income securities, or who is otherwise in the position of a creditor, say, as the recipient of a fixed annuity or pension, is hit the hardest by inflation. And, unfortunately, the smaller the fund and the more important each dollar of it, the greater is the impact of reduced purchasing power and the greater is the temptation to sacrifice the certainty of dollars for the possibility of greater buying value. Conversion of a substantial portion of the fund to common stocks and to real estate, in the hope of obtaining (1) a greater dollar income and (2) an appreciation of principal becomes very tempting when the prospects for continued inflation are strong.

Investments in real estate and common stocks offer the best possibilities of an inflation hedge. But the former represents a highly specialized type of commitment and one that requires considerable management, knowledge of land values and knowledge of community development. It also has the disadvantage of inadequate diversification.[3] Common stocks, on the other hand, are easily bought and sold, and in large or small amounts. Much has been written and said about the practicability of common stocks as protection against rising prices. And this protection is, in fact, afforded over long periods of time, but subject to decided limitations. The 27 year period 1945–1972 again provides an illustration of the fact that over a considerable period commodity prices and the cost of living, on the one hand, and common stock prices, on the other, do move in the same general direction. Table 19-2 shows (1) the Consumer Price Index (1967 = 100), (2) the Index of Wholesale Prices (1967 = 100), and (3) the price, earnings, and dividends of Moody's Index of 125 Industrial Stocks. In each case, the average for the year is shown.

Over the whole period the increase in stock prices and dividends far outran the increase in the cost of living. Stocks rose 700 per cent, dividends 450 per cent, and consumer prices 130 per cent. But within the period, marked discrepancies appeared. In six periods—1956–1957, 1959–1960, 1961–1962, 1965–1966, 1969–1970, and during much of 1971, while the cost of living continued to rise, stocks declined. From the middle of 1965 to December 1970, while consumer prices rose 12 per cent, industrial common stocks in general, as measured by Moody's Industrial Average, began and ended at the same level.[4] Certainly investors in such a period became disillusioned about the efficacy of stocks in general as a counterinfluence to inflation. Of course, individual stocks showed a wide range of price change.

The limitations of common stocks as an inflation hedge may be summarized as follows:

1. The hedge works only over a considerable period of time.

2. To enjoy the greatest advantage, the stocks must be purchased at depressed levels within this period.

3. All stocks are not equally good for inflation protection. Various industries, and hence their common stocks, act differently with respect to earnings. Subgroups of stocks go in different directions even during a period of general rise. The problem of *selection* still persists.

REFERENCES

Babson, R. W., *Business Barometers for Profit, Security, Income,* 10th ed. New York: Harper & Row, Publishers, 1961.

[3]See Chapter 11 for a more extensive discussion of real estate as an investment.

[4]With its emphasis on manufacturing concerns, even the 30-stock Dow Jones Industrial Average is not the best representative of stocks as a whole. For example, this average reached 1052 in January 1973. But both the Standard & Poor's 425 Industrials and the New York Stock Exchange composite average had attained new record highs before that time.

BUTLER, W. F., AND B. A. KAVESH, eds., *How Business Economists Forecast*. Englewood Cliffs, N.J.: Prentice-Hall, Inc., 1966.

CHAMBERS, E. J., *Economic Fluctuations and Forecasting*. Englewood Cliffs, N.J.: Prentice-Hall, Inc., 1961.

COOPER, R. U., *Investments for Professional People*, rev. ed. New York: The Macmillan Co., 1959.

COTTLE, SIDNEY, AND W. T. WHITMAN, *Corporate Earning Power and Market Valuation*. Durham, N.C.: Duke University Press, 1959.

EITEMAN, W. J., AND D. S. EITEMAN, *Common Stock Values and Yields, 1950–61*. Ann Arbor, Mich.: Graduate School of Business Administration, 1962.

GRAHAM, BENJAMIN, *The Intelligent Investor*, 3rd rev. ed. New York: Harper & Row, Publishers, 1965.

HICKMAN, WALTER B., *Corporate Bond Quality and Investor Experience*. Princeton, N.J.: Princeton University Press, 1958.

HOMER, SIDNEY, *A History of Interest Rates*. New Brunswick, N.J.: Rutgers University Press, 1963.

MEISELMAN, DAVID, *The Term Structure of Interest Rates*. Englewood Cliffs, N.J.: Prentice-Hall, Inc., 1962.

MOORE, G. H., ed., *Business Cycle Indicators*. Princeton, N.J.: Princeton University Press, 1961.

SMITH, E. L., *Common Stocks and Business Cycles*. New York: William-Frederick Press, 1959.

SPRINKEL, B. W., *Money and Stock Prices*. Homewood, Ill.: Richard D. Irwin, Inc., 1964.

TURNER, J. P., AND R. C. TURNER, *Business Conditions Analysis*, 2nd ed. New York: McGraw-Hill, Inc., 1967.

20 Investment Principles (cont.)

SCOPE: This chapter continues the discussion of investment principles begun in Chapter 19. The order of discussion is (1) methods of minimizing risk, (2) management of investments by others, and (3) safeguarding of securities.

Methods of Minimizing Risk

While it is difficult to fulfill all of the requirements called for in a given situation, and impossible to eliminate all of the risks that were outlined in the previous chapter, certain investment policies will at least go far toward minimizing those risks.

Intelligent and dispassionate analysis and selection of media. Much of the latter part of this book will be devoted to the analytical methods used in the appraisal and selection of industries and individual companies when the purchase of securities is to comprise an element in the investment program. Underlying the choice of individual industries and securities is the more fundamental problem of selection of the appropriate *general* investment media that will best serve the needs of the particular investment situation. Possibly neither corporate stocks nor bonds are necessary or desirable to achieve a certain goal. If so, the investor avoids the whole problem of analysis of corporate securities. As we have seen in the previous chapter, before individual selections are made, the order of investment planning is (1) budgeting for savings and investment, (2) determination of investment objectives, (3) appraisal of the various types of risk, and (4) choice of the *general* types of media that are most feasible in the investment situation. In many cases, corporate stocks will not be reached at all in this order of thinking.

Intelligent selection and analysis helps to avoid the selection of high-risk investments to begin with, if these are not appropriate in the investor's portfolio. It helps to recognize the deterioration of investments that were once sound but have since lost ground. It can help to offset the risk of cyclical changes in individual investments whether caused by factors affecting those securities alone or by general market factors. It is valuable in minimizing the money-rate risk in two respects: (1) in aiding the investor to determine whether the premium over the riskless interest rate offered by the yield on the investment (either bonds or preferred stocks) is adequate and (2) in suggesting a program of staggered maturities in a bond portfolio that will go far to offset the fluctuations in interest rates and will aid in profiting from favorable trends. And we have seen that proper selection is vital to take advantage of investment in equities as a means of inflation hedging.

The importance of analysis varies with different types of investments. In general, the savings types discussed in Chapters 3, 4, and 5 require little work on the part of the investor, save for an understanding of their characteristics. Mortgages and real estate are highly specialized and should be avoided by individual investors who lack training and experience in this field; institutional investors are better equipped to deal with this category. Very high-grade bonds, including government issues, pose few difficulties if they are held to maturity, save for an understanding of their characteristics and the influence of money rates on their prices and yields. Of course, even high-grade corporate and municipal bonds may not remain high grade, so that continual inspection of quality is necessary. It is in the selection of lesser-grade bonds and preferred stocks, and of common stocks, that very careful analysis becomes vital. And the investor must decide whether to undertake this task himself or rely on the judgment of others.

Intelligent valuation. When securities are to form a part of the investment program, *the price at which a security is to be bought (or sold) is as important a decision as the selection of the security itself.* As suggested earlier, the investor may be able to recognize only the most violent cyclical swings in the market as a whole, but this does not eliminate the necessity of recognizing when a particular instrument is over- or underpriced. One of the disadvantages of concentrating purchases of stocks in the "growth" group is that these stocks often sell at a premium resulting from their popularity; furthermore, the unwary investor may fail to recognize that they have lost their quality of growth until after that condition has become evident. Possibly the most difficult task in the field of investments is that of determining what a security, especially a common stock, is really worth. Aids to this task are suggested in Part V of this volume. In passing we should note, however, that valuation of securities, especially of equities, can be made only within a considerable range. Since such securities are ordinarily purchased and sold on the basis of going-concern value, no man can tell precisely what they are worth. The common stock of the General Electric Company may be undervalued at 60 and overvalued at 70. To decide that it is worth precisely 65, and not 64 or 66, however, leaves no room for all of the uncertainties of the present and the future which confront any stock.

Intelligent valuation of investments will aid in minimizing all of the risks that have been previously discussed. All of these risks are magnified if the investment is overpriced when purchased or underpriced when sold.

Proper timing. Equally important and difficult is the problem of timing purchases and sales. As was suggested previously, this problem involves four types of forecasts that for the great majority of investors are either difficult or impossible. As was also suggested, however, advantage can be taken of the fluctuations in security prices in the selection of securities on their own merits. This requires patience and the ability to ignore the crowd psychology of the moment.

Three types of devices aid the investor in either determining the direction of the stock market or eliminating the need to do so: (1) technical devices, (2) dollar-cost averaging, and (3) formula plans.

TECHNICAL DEVICES: DOW THEORY. The many technical devices that look at the action of the market itself as the indicator of its direction and of the direction of business can first be illustrated by one device that has had considerable use, the Dow theory.

Stated in its simplest form, the Dow theory is a mechanism designed to indicate the major trend of the market without forecasting the extent of the movement in time or degree. It is based on the premise that the stock price averages, reflecting the activities of thousands of investors, discount all important economic and financial factors that could affect the supply and demand for stocks.

According to the theory, stock prices have three basic movements: (1) the major or primary trends lasting for a year or more in which a general change of more than 20 per cent occurs, (2) secondary trends (within the primary) which may last from three weeks to three months and which may retrace as much as one-third to two-thirds of the preceding primary movement, and (3) daily fluctuations. A comparison of the successive high and low points reached in the secondary fluctuations of the stock market enables an observer who notices that the successive high and low points are advancing to determine the primary trend of the market. If the price average should rise from a low point of 820 to a high point of 860, then fall to 840 and advance to 865, an upward primary trend was indicated when the decline stopped at 840 and was confirmed when the new advance went above 860. If the upward trend continues until the price average reaches 875, a subsequent change in the direction of the market trend would not be indicated until a recession from that level was followed by a recovery to *less* than 875 and a subsequent recession to a lower point than on the preceding decline. In an advancing market, a change in the direction of the trend is indicated when an advance fails to carry higher than the preceding advance and when a decline goes lower than the preceding decline. In a declining market, a change in the direction of the trend is indicated when an advance goes higher than the preceding advance and when a decline does not go as low as the preceding decline.

The Dow theory is based on the use of both the Dow Jones industrial and transportation averages and is valid only when the movements of both averages are confirmatory. When all of the fundamental forces in the market are bullish, both averages will advance, and new high points will be made by both averages, each confirming the other. If either average consistently refuses to confirm the other, a major movement is probably near its end.

The Dow theory does not pretend to forecast the duration and degree of price movements, and often it does not indicate a change in the direction of the primary trend until sometime after the change has taken place. Thus, in the summer of 1959, the industrial average reached its peak in July (678) and the (then) rail average in August (174). Confirming bear signals were not given until the industrials declined to 609 in February 1960, and the rails to 147 in March. Again, the rail average peaked at 153 in October 1961, and the industrial average at 735 in December. But it was not until March–April that confirming signals (672 and 139) indicated the course of the 1962 break that was one of the severest in history.

In February 1966, a major uptrend ended with the industrial stock price average at 996. The Dow theory did not confirm the downtrend until May, when the average stood at 898. The downtrend ended in October with the average at 744, but the uptrend was not confirmed until January 1967.

The Dow theory is also faulty because it places too much faith in the particular stock averages used. Common stock prices in general do not discount all economic factors, the Dow Jones averages are not truly representative of the market, and, finally, no one "buys the averages." All common stocks do not rise and fall together. The typical investor is more interested in his own portfolio than in the securities that comprise a particular average or index.

Such "mechanical" devices as the Dow theory may serve the investor by offering warnings that may prevent disaster.[1] To the extent that the opinion of general market movements induces the investor to review the composition and values of his own portfolio, such approaches as the Dow theory have much merit.

TECHNICAL DEVICES: CHARTING. The Dow theory is used to identify trends *after* they have begun. Other technical approaches attempt to *predict* changes in trends of price averages or of individual stocks. Charting involves (1) bar-charting the daily (or other interval) price as a vertical line showing the the range from high to low, with the closing price indicated as a crossline on the bar, or (2) point-and-figure charting of price change, using "x's" for price increases and "o's" for declines, on paper that is marked off into square blocks. In each type the left-hand or vertical scale indicates price. In the bar-chart the horizontal scale indicates time, and below the bar-chart is a separate scale showing volume of trading. Prediction for both types involves the recognition of formations that are similar to previous patterns and that, therefore, signal price change.

Charting can be highly technical, and the interested reader is advised to consult special works on the subject such as those listed in the references for this chapter. A major criticism of the validity of charting is found in the

---

[1] For a study of the indicated results from the Dow theory applied to the Dow Jones Industrial Average, 1897–1963, see Benjamin Graham, *The Intelligent Investor*, 3rd rev. ed. (New York: Harper & Row, Publishers, 1965), pp. 32–34. Other studies are as follows: for 1897–1967, with a chart of all signals 1917–1967, William Gordon, *The Stock Market Indicators*, Chapter 2 (Palisades Park, N.J.: Investors Press, Inc., 1968); for 1896–1938 and 1938–1967, P. H. Greiner and H. C. Whitcomb, *The Dow Theory and the Seventy-Year Forecast Record* (Larchmont, N.Y.: Investors Intelligence, Inc., 1969); for 1923–1964, H. M. Finley, *Everybody's Guide to the Stock Market*, rev. ed., Chapter 8 (Chicago: Henry Regnery Company, 1968).

"random walk" theory, which holds that stock markets are efficient so that prices respond to all new information at any point in time. Analysis of past price action data is invalid. In other words, stock prices have no memory, and the actual prices are good estimates of value. Successive price changes are statistically independent.

It is possible that when accompanied by the study of other information such as trading volume, charting can aid in the detection of short-run price movements. But indicators of longer-run movements must still depend on "fundamental" analysis of earnings, dividends, interest rates, economic and political conditions, and all the other factors examined in the analytical section of this book.

DOLLAR-COST AVERAGING. Another method of dealing with the timing problem—in fact, of avoiding it—is known as *dollar-cost averaging*. This is useful to investors who are accumulating capital and who wish to avoid always buying common stocks when they are too high and to benefit from the expected variations in market price. Stated in its simplest terms, this involves regular purchase of securities in equal dollar amounts, regardless of their unit price. As the price of the security or securities bought declines and rises, a greater or smaller number of shares can be bought with the same amount of money. Over a long period of time, as long as the market price rises and falls, the average *cost* of shares purchased will be lower than the average *price* at which the shares are bought. These elements may be illustrated by a simple example (Table 20-1). Suppose that $1,000 is invested in the shares of a company at regular intervals, beginning at 50 per share, with a subsequent decline to 20 and recovery to 50.

Table 20-1. DOLLAR-COST AVERAGING

Purchase	Price	Shares Purchased Each Interval	Total Shares Purchased	Total Amount Invested	Value of Total Investment
1	$50	20	20	$1,000	$ 1,000
2	40	25	45	2,000	1,800
3	30	33.3	78.3	3,000	2,350
4	20	50	128.3	4,000	2,567
5	30	33.3	161.6	5,000	4,850
6	40	25	186.6	6,000	7,467
7	50	20	206.6	7,000	10,334

At the end of the period, the average cost of all shares purchased is $33.88, whereas the average price is $37.14. The reason is, of course, that more shares have been bought at the lower prices. While the example is extreme in that it is based on a very sharp decline and recovery in a short period, three points are worth noting: (1) While the loss at the low point is 36 per cent, the stock had only to advance to a little over 30 to recover the entire loss, and from then on profits mounted rapidly; (2) as long as prices eventually recover from their lows, a wide fluctuation in price is advantageous; (3) the ending rather than the starting prices are important. Even better results would, of course, be obtained if there had been a secular rise in the stock.

If followed regularly and courageously, dollar averaging is likely to produce far better results than attempts to "buy low and sell high." The investor must, of course, be prepared to commit funds regularly over a considerable period of time, say, ten to twenty years, so as to include several market cycles. He must have the nerve (and the capital) to keep buying as the market declines, and at relatively short intervals, at least several times a year. He must choose his stocks with great care, preferably those with volatile price action but long-term growth. And he must be prepared to change his portfolio—the favorite stocks of today may be poor choices ten years from now. The program of many investors should consist of the regular purchase of shares of well-managed investment companies. Some of these offer plans whereby dividends are automatically reinvested in new shares.[2] The compounding of dividends, coupled with the regular investment of new principal, produces a very substantial accumulation over a period of years, provided the period is long enough and provided the investor has the fortitude, funds, and emotional poise to continue buying through all phases of the price cycle.[3]

FORMULA PLANS. Another method of attacking the timing problem is by the use of a formula plan by investors who have already accumulated a substantial fund and who wish to preserve and increase their capital over the years and at the same time avoid the use of judgment concerning the course of the market. The formula plan substitutes an automatic device for emotional and erroneous decisions concerning the best buying and selling points. It offers a compromise by which the investor can take some advantage of the swings in the market. Formula plans differ considerably, but they all have in common the use of two funds—the *aggressive fund,* consisting of common stocks, and the *defensive fund,* consisting of high-grade bonds and/or cash. Under the constant-ratio type of plan, the investor determines in advance the proportions of aggressive and defensive securities that he wishes to maintain. When the market moves up and down sufficiently to alter this ratio by a predetermined amount, he switches funds from one to the other of the type of securities to restore the original ratio. Thus, a plan could start with a "normal" ratio of 50 per cent in common stocks and 50 per cent in bonds. In a rising market for common stocks, the common stock portion is permitted to rise until it reaches 60 per cent of the value of the fund; it is then cut back to 50 per cent. In a falling market, after the common stock portion reaches 40 per cent, stocks are bought to raise this portion to 50 per cent.

---

[2] See Chapter 9.

[3] Using the Standard & Poor's Index of 500 Stocks, an annual investment of $2,000 a year started on January 1, 1962, including all dividends and after brokerage fees and taxes, would have produced a market value of $27,930 in January 1971 from an investment of $20,000, despite the fact (or owing to the fact) that several reactions were experienced in the market, including the very severe last six months of the 1968–70 bear market. Individual stocks would, of course, have shown widely different results.

Under the variable-ratio type of plan, the proportion of stocks is reduced in a rising market and increased in a declining market, the decisions being based on predetermined levels in a selected market index. When the market reaches a predetermined point on the up-side, stocks are gradually sold and all or part of the proceeds are placed in cash or bonds. When the stock market reaches a certain point on the downward cycle, bonds are sold or cash is used to purchase stocks on a gradual basis. Such a procedure is a compromise application of the "buy-low-sell-high" principle. To produce satisfactory results, the following conditions must be met: (1) A satisfactory formula must be devised; (2) stock prices must have moved up and down sufficiently to bring the plan into action; (3) the common stocks must be carefully selected (shares in well-managed investment trusts are recommended); (4) the price action of the particular securities selected must not deviate substantially from that of the market as a whole; (5) the market for stocks must not remain on a permanently high or low level; (6) when either bonds or stocks are sold, the other type of security must be expected to remain level or to rise. (The plan will not work if, as in 1969–1970, prices of both bonds and stocks decline at the same time, and subsequently rise together. Under these conditions cash rather than bonds is the best medium for the defensive fund); (7) the investor must exercise patience and fortitude by selling when stocks are rising, buying when they are falling, *waiting out* the greater peaks and valleys that may appear after his action has been taken. The average individual is not likely to possess sufficient skill to observe all of these conditions. And it is also necessary for him to forecast the longer-term trend of stock prices. ·Most individuals would be advised to have a formula approach managed by the adviser to an investment company group that offers this service through different types of funds.

Adequate diversification. To the protection afforded by the careful selection of commitments, all but the most aggressive investors will add the safeguard of diversification. Through distribution over a number of issues, he does not lessen the risk attendant to any one security, but he does limit the loss that would be encountered if a substantial part of his fund were concentrated in an issue which depreciated in value.

Diversification is accepted as sound practice by all large investors and has been officially recognized by legislative bodies and courts. The New York State law definitely limits the proportion of funds that savings banks may invest in real estate mortgages (65 per cent, not including FHA-insured mortgages), in railroad bonds (as a group: 25 per cent; as single companies: 10 per cent), in electric and gas bonds (as a group: 10 per cent; as single companies: 2 per cent), in telephone bonds (as a group: 10 per cent; as single companies: 2 per cent), in housing projects (5 per cent), and in modernization loans (1 per cent).[4] The courts have held that trustees should diversify trust funds, and they have, in at least one case, surcharged a trustee for a substantial loss sustained from an unduly large investment in a single issue.[5] Moreover, as will be shown, commercial banks, insurance com-

[4]See Chapter 22 for greater detail.
[5]183 Massachusetts 499 (1903).

panies, investment companies, and other large investors almost universally practice diversification methods.

The more popular applications of diversification, from the aspect of safety, are limitations of the amounts which may be invested in (1) any one security or company, (2) any one kind of enterprise, (3) any one grade of securities with respect to (a) yield and (b) marketability, and (4) any one geographical district. From the viewpoint of convenience, restrictions apply less rigidly to (1) income payment dates, (2) maturity dates, and (3) maximum and minimum commitment amounts.

The investor should not go so far in diversifying by industries and general categories of securities that he obtains only mediocre results. The investment companies that have made the best performances are not those that have spread their funds over hundreds of separate issues. Moreover, as more and more individual companies diversify their own activities, a smaller number of securities provides a greater amount of economic diversification. The investor in Goodyear is investing in tires, tubes, individual rubber products, chemicals, and plastics. The owner of Philips Petroleum stock has a stake in oil, natural gas, petrochemicals, and nuclear energy. Adequate diversification still requires intelligent selection of industries and companies and a willingness to change proportions as conditions change.

In recent years a new approach to industrial portfolio diversification has been widely adopted, namely, to classify companies and "industries" by their major markets rather than by specific products. For example, the portfolio might include groups of "housing" stocks, "consumer service" stocks, "finance" stocks, "international" stocks, "natural resource" stocks, "energy" stocks, and so on. Different industries are found within each of these securities groups. The housing group could include cement companies, appliances, mobile home manufacturers. The finance group could include banks, savings and loan holding companies, and commercial credit companies. "Leisure time" and "antipollution" stocks are examples of very modern groups within which a diverse selection of traditional industries may be included, but which enjoy a common economic demand.

The proportions of the fund to be invested in relatively high-, medium-, and low-yielding securities depend upon the position of the investor and his ability to assume risk. Similarly, the proportion to be invested in securities of limited marketability will depend upon the individual situation. A substantial part of the fund must necessarily be invested in marketable securities if the fund may have to be converted into cash at short notice.

The diversification of an investment fund according to geographical boundaries affords more theoretical than actual advantages. The investor who practices national distribution finds the task complicated because of limited opportunities in certain sections and because of the nationwide activities of the more important companies. Only in the cases of investors with extremely large funds, such as life insurance companies, is geographical diversification of practical value. Securities of the American Telephone & Telegraph Company represent national diversification in themselves, just as securities of the General Electric Company represent international diversification.

Diversification according to income payment dates is based upon the fact that bond interest is generally paid semiannually and stock dividends quarterly. A fund can be arranged to produce an approximately equal amount of income monthly or quarterly.

Diversification of a bond fund by maturity dates endeavors to minimize the losses which may be involved in reinvestment. Large maturities are uneconomical in years of low interest rates, since the new securities bought with the proceeds of maturing obligations produce a lower rate of return. Large investors distribute maturity dates in order to avoid concentration in any particular years and generally refer to their *maturity calendars* before buying new issues. The average investor will usually find it more convenient to distribute his holdings of bonds into the three chronological groups of short-term (up to five years), medium-term (five to ten years), and long-term (over ten years). He can limit his commitment in any group to, say, 40 per cent of his bond fund, or better still, he can buy long-term bonds when yields are high, and when interest rates are low, he can put any new money into short-term maturities. As interest rates decline, the prices of long maturities increase, and the risk of price loss in the event of an increase in rates is minimized with the purchase of short maturities. This means that the concept of dollar-cost averaging can be applied to the accumulation of a bond portfolio.

Assuming the necessity of diversification as a risk-avoiding device, the question of the optimum-size portfolio is receiving considerable attention from the quantitative point of view, by the use of models and computer simulation. The goal is to produce the highest rate of return with the least risk from the least number of securities. Approaches to this problem are found in a growing body of literature that deserves close attention by serious investors and portfolio managers. (See Chapter 23.)

The achievement of satisfactory diversification by direct investment of a relatively small fund is practically impossible. Fortunately, several media exist for indirect investment of small funds, such as the investment company and the common trust fund, that enable the investor of limited means to obtain diversification that he could not obtain alone.

Continuous management. The management of an investment fund that includes securities requires a degree of care equal to, if not exceeding, that required in the original selection of investments. Conditions are always changing, with material influence upon investment values. Securities that appear to be in an impregnable position at the time of purchase may become highly speculative in a few years. Events, such as wars, earthquakes, political upheavals, crop disasters, and many others, may adversely affect security values overnight. Such factors are uncontrollable and unpredictable. Investment policy must be sufficiently flexible to permit ready adjustment to the unexpected. The experience of recent years has taught the lesson that a rigid investment policy is unwise. No policy should assume that occasional losses are avoidable or that the intrinsic value of any security is not subject to change. Various elements of risk are present in all investments; they are magnified in the case of securities and especially formidable in the case of equities. Continuous scrutiny should be applied, not only to guard against loss and to take advantage of favorable exchange opportunities, but to keep the investor's fund in line with his changing needs and goals and with conditions which affect his status but over which he has little or no control.

Circumstances continually arise that change investment values collectively and separately. Some industries enter the stage of expansion as others fall into decline. One company prospers at a time when other firms in the same field are operating under deficits. Investment popularity swings from one type of security or enterprise to another. Market prices, price-earnings ratios, and interest rates rise and fall. Values in the less popular fields decline as prices in the more interesting groups advance. While diversification tends to minimize the losses often sustained in these changes, the sale of securities which face unpromising prospects is even more effective as a safeguard against decline in value.

Security exchanging is an important phase of investment management. The theory that some securities were safe for investors to "buy and forget" has been invalidated in the experience of recent years. Neglect of a regular scrutiny of investment holdings results in the loss of favorable exchange opportunities; it may also lead to a serious decline in the aggregate value of the fund. As with diversification, however, exchanging may be overdone, when it develops into promiscuous trading. An exchange of securities is justifiable only when the position of the investor is improved. The conditions under which such betterment is possible are

1. Greater safety at the same yield;
2. Higher yield with equal safety;
3. Better marketability at the same yield;
4. Improved tax position;
5. Improved diversification;
6. Greater appreciation opportunity.

As securities change in quality and appeal, exchange opportunities are constantly afforded to the vigilant investor. If all security buyers were purely investors, such opportunities would be fewer, but since prices are also influenced by speculators, prices and yields are driven into and out of the value range, and opportunities for profitable switching are magnified. As yield does not always vary with quality, because of the presence of such technical factors as seasoning, convertibility, marketability, taxability, legal status, and redemption option, investors cognizant of these features are frequently in a position to make advantageous exchanges resulting in an enhanced rate of return on their securities.

Regardless of the degree to which the investor may be determined to manage his own financial affairs, using the information described in Chapters 13 and 14, he should take advantage of the advice and services of others in whom he has confidence. But he should always review any suggestions for change in the light of his own requirements.

Management of Investments by Others

The problems of selection (and diversification), timing, and supervision may be passed along to others, at a cost, of course. Freedom from care and a high degree of safety are provided by institutions of the savings type, as described in Chapters 3 and 4. These institutions also provide diversification to their creditors, although the type and degree of diversification depend on the institution selected for savings. No protection against inflation is obtained.

Insofar as investment in securities is concerned, the common trust fund (Chapter 22), the investment company (Chapter 9), and the insurance company (Chapter 30) relieve the investor of management, except that in the case of the last two, decisions concerning the selection of the fund and the timing of the purchase or sale of its shares must still be made. The natural inclination of most trustees to operate a common trust fund conservatively gives the beneficiary lower income and less appreciation than he might possibly obtain alone. But diversification, superior stability, and some protection against inflation, together with freedom from care, give the common trust fund a strong appeal to many investors seeking these requirements. The portfolios of these funds are seldom published and the results of their management can be obtained only by direct inquiry. On the other hand, the portfolio and record of insurance companies and investment companies are always available. As indicated in Chapter 9, investment companies differ widely with respect to investment goals and policy. Some seek reasonable income and considerable stability. Others are operated for capital appreciation. The goals of the investor, the investment requirements that should be fulfilled, and the risks that can be undertaken are factors that must be considered, together with the record of its management, in the choice of any fund. The great growth of investment funds until very recently attests to the desire of many investors to transfer their investment problems to others.

The investment counsel also stands ready to take the responsibility for investment management, but at fees which are likely to make his services prohibitive for the small investor. For those who can afford their advice, the investment advisers are prepared to tailor the investment programs of their clients to their individual needs, balancing the several factors of income, recovery of principal, appreciation, tax protection, diversification, and inflation hedging (and the possibility of subsequent deflation) in one coordinated pattern. For the most part, the well-established counsel firms are careful not to promise too much and lean toward long-run results rather than toward spectacular performance. (See Chapter 14.)

Other methods of transferring managerial responsibility on a fee basis include the investment departments of large banks and the supervisory services of some of the larger stock exchange firms. In any case, the investor should know his own needs and risks thoroughly so that he can understand and approve the decisions of the experts to whom he transfers the main responsibility for investment management.

Safekeeping of Securities

Security instruments should be carefully guarded through deposit in a protected place. Most banks offer safe-deposit-box service at a low annual rental. A duplicate list of the securities should be prepared (one to remain in the box) showing the number of each security, the amount, the name, the maturity date, and the rate and dates of income payments. Stock certificates should be transferred to the name of the new owner. Bonds bought for long-term holding should be registered in full, or at least as to principal. If a security is lost, notice with full description should be sent immediately to the issuing corporation and also to the firm through which it was purchased. Bond coupons should not be detached prior to due dates.

Investors who desire to be relieved of the detail involved in the care of securities may establish *custodian accounts* with banking institutions. The services provided by the bank (for a fee) include

1. Collection of interest, dividends, and principal;
2. Purchase and sale of securities at the investor's request;
3. Rendition of periodical statements of the account;
4. Provision of income tax information;
5. Special reports on securities held;
6. Information on called bonds, stock rights, and sinking fund offers.

These services should not be confused with the bank *trust* arrangement in which the bank takes title in trust for the investor and makes the investment decisions.

REFERENCES

ALLEN, L. B., *A Method for Stock Profits Without Price Forecasting.* Garden City, N.Y.: Doubleday & Company, 1962.

BISHOP, G. W., JR., *Charles H. Dow and the Dow Theory.* New York: Appleton-Century-Crofts, 1960.

COHEN, A. W., *Technical Indicator Analysis by Point and Figure Technique.* Larchmont, N.Y.: Chartcraft, Inc., 1970.

COOTNER, P. H., ed., *The Random Character of Stock Market Prices.* Cambridge, Mass.: MIT Press, 1964.

COTTLE, C. S., AND W. T. WHITMAN, *Investment Timing: The Formula Plan Approach.* New York: McGraw-Hill, Inc., 1953.

EDWARDS, R. D., AND JOHN MAGEE, *Technical Analysis of Stock Trends,* 5th ed. Springfield, Mass.: John Magee, Inc., 1966.

FEYLOR, S. F., *Income Growth with Security: The Formula Plan Solution.* New York: The Macmillan Co., 1958.

FINLEY, H. M., *Everybody's Guide to the Stock Market,* rev. ed. Chicago: Henry Regnery Company, 1968.

GORDON, WILLIAM, *The Stock Market Indicators*. Palisades Park, N.J.: Investors Press, 1968.

GRANVILLE, J. E., *Granville's New Key to Stock Market Profits*. Englewood Cliffs, N.J.: Prentice-Hall, Inc., 1963.

GREINER, P.H., AND H. C. WHITCOMB, *The Dow Theory and the Seventy-year Forecast Record*. Larchmont, N.Y.: Investors Intelligence, Inc., 1969.

JENKINS, DAVID, *Continous Profits Through Formula Investing*. Larchmont, N.Y.: American Education Council, 1960.

MARKOWITZ, H. M., *Portfolio Selection: Efficient Diversification of Investments*. New York: John Wiley & Sons, Inc., 1959.

RUSSELL, RICHARD, *The Dow Theory Today*. New York: Russell Associates, 1961.

SMILEN, K. B., AND K. SAFIAN, *Investment Profits Through Market Timing: A Professional Approach*, 2nd ed. New York: Smilen & Safian, 1961.

WESSMAN, LUCILE, *Practical Formulas for Successful Investing*. New York: Willard Funk, 1955.

WIESENBERGER, ARTHUR, *Investment Companies*, 1972 ed., Part II. New York: Wiesenberger Services, Inc., 1972.

WILLIAMSON, J. P., *Investments: New Analytic Techniques*, Chapter 7. New York: Praeger Publishers, Inc., 1971.

21 Individual Investors

SCOPE: This chapter applies the material in earlier chapters concerning investment media and principles to the problems of investment by individuals. The order of discussion is (1) review of investment media, (2) individual differences, (3) application of investment principles, (4) illustrative situations, and (5) explanation.

Review of Investment Media

The media of investment were classified in Chapter 1 and described in Chapters 3–11. Two types of media were omitted from the discussion: (1) bank stocks and (2) shares in insurance companies. The general description of these types should be combined with the techniques of analysis applied to them, and thus, they are discussed later in the chapters devoted to these groups. (See Chapters 29 and 30.)

The description of investment media shows the surprising variety of types available. No one type is likely to suit the needs and purposes of the investor, but various combinations may satisfy his requirements. The investor owes it to himself to be acquainted with all possibilities. With a few exceptions, such as insured deposit accounts and Federal obligations, it is difficult if not impossible to generalize about the investment merits of any class of media, because of the range of quality within each class. The investor's problem is not solved unless he is able to choose discriminately *within* the group that in general seems most feasible for his program.

Individual Differences

Individuals and their needs are affected by such a wide variety of factors that one cannot generalize concerning their investment objectives or the means by which these may be accomplished. Variations occur with respect to annual income, amount of funds available for investment, the total resources of the investing individual or unit, his or their age, health, training, temperament and ability to manage their own affairs, the number of dependents, the amount of time and attention that can be devoted to financial affairs, social and personal ambitions, and many others. All of these will cause each investor's problem to be different in some degree from that of all other investors. However, an approach may be made toward itemizing commonly found objectives and the principles that should govern investment for the attainment of these goals.

Application of Investment Principles

The following discussion is based on certain widely held investment objectives and the application to these aims of the general principles of investment management discussed in previous chapters. The order of priority and the portion of the savings to be devoted to each objective will vary from case to case. Obviously, the amount of funds available for investment restricts or widens the objectives that can reasonably be attained. In budgets allowing for very modest savings, the only objectives that can be obtained are those at the top of the suggested list. As annual savings increase or are accumulated, the objectives can be widened and more risk can be taken. And the objectives themselves will change through the years with the changing circumstances of the investing individual or family.

Reserve funds. A reserve of from three to six months' after-tax income to take care of sudden hazards or drains that confront many investors is high on the priority list. Together with life insurance, it enjoys first place in most programs. The possibility of sudden stoppage of income (other than through the death of the income-producer), sudden expenditures not provided for by casualty and property insurance, unexpected personal expenses, and many other items suggests that some savings be maintained in highly liquid form. The inherent conservativeness of the investor will also affect his feeling concerning the need for resources that are available on very short notice.

The main requirement for emergency funds is recovery of dollars when needed, and only modest income can be expected. This portion of the fund is held in the form of bank savings deposits, accounts in savings and loan associations, and Savings bonds. The cash-surrender value of life insurance policies should never be relied on as a regular segment of the emergency fund; it may have to be withdrawn or borrowed in case of dire need, but this threatens the continuation of the protection.

The investment attributes of the cash reserve are (1) recovery of principal on short notice, (2) modest income, (3) freedom from care, and (4) satisfactory denomination. Tax status is not considered, and there is no attempt to hedge against inflation.

Protection against death of the income-producer. For the majority of investors, the death of the income-producer constitutes a threat that can be met only by adequate life insurance. Insurance provides an estate that would be difficult for most investors to provide through any other means.

The investment attributes of life insurance and the main types of policies were discussed in Chapter 3. The amount of protection that is needed depends on circumstances that vary from case to case: the number and age of dependents, the funds available for premiums at the age of the insured, the living standards desired for dependents, and the size of the estate exclusive of insurance. An insurance plan providing for maximum protection when most needed and retirement income when the need of death benefits has been reduced can be worked out for each individual family.

The investment requirements fulfilled by insurance are as follows: recovery of principal (in the event of death); income for the beneficiaries through any one of several methods of distributing the face of the policy, and possible retirement income for the assured; complete freedom from care and management; satisfactory denomination and diversification; and favorable income tax status (insofar as proceeds are concerned). No protection is provided against rising prices, because the obligation of the insurance company is to pay a contractual dollar sum. Because insurance promises to pay in terms of dollars rather than in purchasing power, the insured must increase his insurance protection against the prospect of cheapened dollars at the time of death or retirement. Some argue that if the life insurance company were permitted to invest heavily in common stocks, the higher return obtained would permit lower premiums (more insurance) and more generous "dividends" or rebates that would help to offset rising prices. To obtain such results at the expense of safety would, however, threaten the basic purpose of insurance. It would be sounder for the insured to supplement his insurance estate by his own purchase of equities if he can assume the risks of such commitments.

Over and above minimum protection provided by insurance, pensions, and Social Security, funds accumulated for the support of dependents in the event of death of the insured can be invested in a variety of forms, depending on the risks that can be assumed. A wide range, from income-producing high-grade bonds to common stocks, can be utilized. Such factors as the degree of management required, tax status, and inflation hedging will bulk large or small depending on the individual circumstances. For wealthy investors, estate and inheritance tax considerations are a major consideration.

Since protection of dependents is high on the list of priorities, most investors should begin to build this portion of the fund at a minimum of risk, through the use of insurance, even in the face of continued decline in the purchasing power of the fund. Regardless of how astute the investor may be in the management of funds, to rely on market appreciation of securities to provide the minimum essentials for dependents is to flirt with disaster.

Home ownership. The purchase of a home is probably the largest single investment made by the majority of families. The financial aspects of the commitment were discussed elsewhere. (See Chapter 11.) At this point we need only suggest that funds accumulated for eventual home ownership should be relatively risk-free. The investment requirements are recovery

of principal, possibly modest income until the home is acquired, considerable
if not total freedom from care, and diversification until the home is acquired. If the purchase is considerably in the future, and if the family can
afford the risk of equities, the growth of a fund invested in stocks, directly
or indirectly, may offset the rising costs of real estate. But relatively few
investors should hazard the sum being accumulated for such an important
purpose. And the time of the purchase might coincide with depressed stock
prices.

The modern method of amortizing the purchase of a home through a
long-term mortgage solves many of the problems in investing for this purpose
and relieves the home buyer of the responsibilities of management of the
funds in the meantime. The required payments of interest plus principal are
a budget item that ranks in importance only second to food and clothing.
The hazard of loss of savings being held by the investor against eventual
purchase of property is eliminated, at least as long as he is able to meet the
terms of the loan.

Once a substantial equity has been acquired, the investor has a considerable sum tied up in fixed property. This portion of his savings is subject to
the risks of changing land values, obsolescence, neighborhood decline, and
the swings in the real estate market. The denomination is large and diversification is sacrificed. To offset these perils, the owner of well-selected, well-
maintained property may derive a considerable imputed income from this
part of his funds, achieves an income tax expense in the property taxes paid,
and may enjoy a valuable hedge against the decline in the buying power of
the dollar. The ownership of such property provides the most important
opportunity for hedging that many investors are in a position to enjoy.[1]

Education and other family needs. A variety of specialized objectives are found in every family's investment plan. Among these the education of children frequently plays a prominent part. Funds saved for this
purpose should be invested so as to accumulate a certain definite sum when
needed. For such a purpose regular investment in Savings bonds is almost
ideal. These can be bought in large or small denominations to mature during
the period when the funds are needed, and, if the plan is begun early
enough, the compounding of the $5\frac{1}{2}$ per cent yield to maturity will add
considerably to the size of the fund. A certain portion of life insurance
should also be earmarked for education and similar vital purposes so that
these goals may be fulfilled whether the head of the family survives or not.

The previous paragraph suggests that little or no risk should be assumed
in the investment of funds for education. Conservative investors would agree.
However, the constantly rising costs of education pose a serious problem to
young families. When the fund is begun many years before need, the
purchase of sound common stocks will, over the years, provide a hedge
against rising costs and permit the young family to participate in the growth
of the economy. To avoid decisions with respect to timing and selection,
many young families would be advised to dollar-average in well-managed
mutual fund shares.

[1] The investment aspects of home ownership are discussed further in Chapter 11.

Retirement income. In many cases the next investment objective is the provision of income at retirement. The importance of this goal will also vary from case to case. For young families it will be given little attention during the early years when other needs are more pressing. But with the passage of the years, the need for taking care of retirement begins to loom large. Some investors will rely substantially on Federal Social Security benefits, on other public retirement arrangements, or on private pension plans. Others can supplement these plans with accumulations under their own control.

For investors to whom a minimum of risk and complete freedom of management is important, the fixed-dollar annuity is likely to produce the best long-run results. Modern annuity contracts are written at very modest "guaranteed" rates of accumulation—some as low as $2\frac{1}{2}$ to 3 per cent—and this in the face of a secular rise in the cost of living, so that a much larger outlay for annuity protection is required to produce the same real income at retirement. The investor who is in no position to assume risk or to assume the responsibilities of managing an investment fund must rely heavily on the fixed annuity for an assured stipend in later years. But he pays a penalty in a low rate of return.

Now that variable annuties (described in Chapter 3) are commercially available in some states, the investor has access to a type of retirement income contract that will reflect the changes in common stock values so as to provide a possible hedge against the rising cost of living. This assumes that the stocks held by the variable annuity company increase over the years as much as the value of the dollar declines.

Other investors may prepare for retirement through a long-range program of direct security purchases, using a balanced fund of bonds and stocks or the regular purchase (possibly dollar-averaging) of carefully selected investment company shares. The value of such a fund will rise and fall with the course of the security markets, but over the long run the result should be an accumulation considerably in excess of the value of a fixed-dollar annuity. This is especially the case if current income is reinvested and compounded over a considerable period of time, at the generous yields available in 1973. Investors with sufficient time and skill to manage their own funds may emphasize the direct purchase of sound growth stocks; others would be well advised to rely on good-grade corporate bonds and Savings bonds and the shares of investment companies which have produced a better-than-average record. The proportions of the retirement fund to be devoted to bonds and to equities depend on the size of the fund and the skill and knowledge of the investor. The character of the fund will also be influenced by the relative importance of suitable denomination, tax status, and the need for offsetting the declining value of the dollar.

To an increasing extent, corporate and public pension funds, with their growing emphasis on equity investments, are relied upon for retirement income and hedging against inflation. Such funds provide freedom from care and management, tax relief, and the benefits of compounding of interest and of economic growth. Their investment aspects are discussed in Chapter 3, and their investment policies in Chapter 23.

Supplementary income before retirement. When the primary objectives outlined above have been fulfilled or funds are being regularly set aside for their eventual fulfillment, the remainder of the investment program can involve more risk-taking. Recovery of principal can be given less importance and current income can be stressed. Investors who have achieved their early and important goals may consider a balanced fund of bonds and stocks (or other equities) to supplement their regular income, and in the selection of these securities they may use the sources of information and the analytical methods described elsewhere in this volume.

The need for a "second income" derived from investments grows as the price level rises. Such an income can be obtained in a haphazard fashion by the occasional purchase, at opportune times, of income-producing securities. Here the investor faces the problems of selection, valuation, and timing that require considerable skill and experience. He must decide either to direct his own investment buying and selling, with the aid of services and other sources of advice and information, or to turn his affairs over to others. Even if the latter decision is made, the investor should be well acquainted with investment principles so that he can understand and review the decisions made on his behalf.

The types of investments for supplementary income will vary with the individual case. Where modest but secure income is the goal, a balanced fund at their present generous yields, and stocks with unusual dividend records, is indicated. Complete freedom from management can be obtained through the establishment of a living trust or the purchase of an immediate annuity. The business or professional man may take advantage of the higher average yields on liberal-dividend common stocks and on fairly good bonds by the acquisition of a diversified list of such securities, or by the purchase of shares of investment companies that invest primarily for income. The investor of means may take advantage of the tax-exemption feature of state and municipal bonds for a substantial section of his fund. Such an investor is, of course, likely to place more importance on preservation of capital and on estate planning than on current income.

A major problem in the early 1970s is to obtain a respectable income from common stocks. Dividend yields on high-quality stocks are low in relation to the rates on alternative investments. The investor in quality equities must sacrifice current for potentially higher future returns, by selecting good stocks with increasing dividend payouts.

Creation of an estate. The final goal of some investors is the creation of an estate for dependents (over and above minimum insurance and Social Security), charities, and other beneficiaries. Estate planning is a complex problem involving income and estate tax considerations, drafting of an adequate will, selection of executors and trustees, gift planning, insurance, and general investment policy. The investor who has provided for the more important needs can retain the services of firms making a specialty of estate planning. These firms employ or retain attorneys, tax experts, insurance advisers, and investment counsel. The investor should, however, be well acquainted himself with everything that is done for him.

The investment requirements in planning for a substantial eventual estate are (1) tax relief on current income; (2) a substantial degree of liquidity for estate and inheritance tax purposes, through either insurance or a liquid segment of the portfolio; (3) minimizing the estate and inheritance tax burden; (4) the growth of the fund over the years by compounding the returns derived from the portfolio; and (5) provision against dissipation of the fund by loss of dollars and of purchasing power. Practically all of the media of investment described previously might be involved in such a program, the amounts and proportions of each being determined by the individual circumstances.

Illustrative Situations

INVESTMENTS OF THE YOUNG FAMILY. The young family consisting, say, of husband, wife, and two small children, with an annual income of $15,000 before taxes, is likely to be unable to do more than make a start on the more fundamental investment objectives outlined previously. Under present-day conditions provision for an emergency fund, a modest amount of low-cost insurance (say, three times annual income), and payments on a home are likely to absorb most available savings. Funds for education and other family needs may be accumulated through the purchase of Savings bonds as the income increases, and a start toward retirement income may be provided through Social Security payments and company or public pension plans. For many young families, emphasis on investment for appreciation, although desirable in a period of rising prices, is highly questionable. For some years deposit-type investments, U.S. Savings bonds, and other safe and liquid sources with modest income, such as high-grade corporate bonds, will probably dominate the program. Only when first things have been taken care of will common stocks predominate, and even then many young families would be advised to use shares in investment companies for diversification and professional management.

Since the young family's need of funds for education and similar requirements will not be felt for a number of years, it should include in its initial investment program a segment of common stocks or investment company shares and continue their purchase over the years on a dollar-averaging basis, and thus take advantage of the secular increase in common stock values and enjoy compounding of those values through reinvestment of dividends. However, the rewards of successful investment in common stocks are available—or should be—only to those able to assume their risks and possibly their management. Unless the young family is temperamentally and economically equipped to try its hand at risk-taking, it had better follow a conservative policy. But if it is, and when extra savings are available, regular purchase of high-grade stocks or investment company shares on an averaging basis can produce good results over the long run. The goal should be annual income plus appreciation of at least 10 per cent. Less than this does not reward adequately for the risks of price fluctuation; good-grade bonds with much lower price risk can be had (early 1973) to yield 7 to 8 per cent.

The New York Stock Exchange's Monthly Investment Plan, providing for the purchase through Exchange members of any "Big Board" stock or stocks (by payment of from $40 quarterly to $999 monthly) is a convenient device for dollar-cost-averaging by the small investor.[2]

Many young businessmen participate in stock-purchase and stock-option plans that may prove very valuable over the years. Eventual retirement income of substantial proportions can be obtained through participation in company profit-sharing plans.

The established professional man. The professional man well launched on a prosperous career is likely to have made provision for the prime essentials at the top of the list of investment priorities and may assume considerable risk, depending, of course, on his individual circumstances. Such an investor would put major emphasis on (1) additional current income, (2) provision for eventual retirement, and (3) the creation of a substantial estate over and above that provided by insurance. Investing for capital appreciation is involved in the last two of these goals. The investment program should include a fund of seasoned bonds to provide a backlog of less volatile securities, and a steady accumulation of common stocks over the years, preferably through the use of the dollar-cost-averaging technique. If his fund is very substantial, he can afford to employ the services of an investment counsel; otherwise, he should consider investing in the shares of carefully selected investment companies. His absorption in professional activities is likely to leave little time and provide little opportunity for training in security analysis and the management of his own funds. He may be a shrewd direct investor, but he is ordinarily out of touch with business and financial affairs and may be tempted to make sudden and possibly ill-advised investment decisions.

Depending on the size of the accumulated fund and the annual savings available for investment, the age and health of the investor, the number of dependents, and numerous other considerations, the degree of risk that can be undertaken will vary greatly. In the majority of cases the professional man had better lean to the conservative side lest his time and attention be diverted from his main line of activities. However, he can commit a substantial portion of his savings toward retirement to growth and inflation-protection stocks or to shares of investment companies that emphasize these qualities.

Under conditions prevailing in the early 1970s, good-grade corporate bonds should not be ignored. For many years these securities had little or no appeal for the individual investor. But the attractive yields available in 1970–1973 have caused many persons to turn to bonds. Compounding the interest in 7 to 8 per cent bonds can double the principal of a fund in ten years, with modest price risk. A compromise position could be taken with the purchase of convertible bonds at prices at or not much above their conversion values. In many cases these produce higher current income than

---

[2]Local "investment clubs," in which individuals pool and manage small monthly purchases of common stocks, provide experience in investing as well as possible diversification. There are some 60,000 of these organizations.

the common stocks of the same companies, and yet have the "downside" protection of bonds.

Depending on the tax bracket in which any new income would fall, this investor may be interested in tax-exempt municipals for that portion of his retirement fund devoted to high-grade securities.

The established businessman.

The frequently used expression "businessman's risk" or "businessman's investment" implies two things: (1) that this type of person can assume considerable risk and (2) that his business training and experience fit him to keep a close eye on economic and financial conditions and to exercise unusual acumen in the selection and management of securities. These qualities may or may not exist. Furthermore, preoccupation with his own affairs may not leave enough time for adequate investment management; on the other hand, he may be in close contact with and be able to interpret and use sources of investment information that will produce better-than-average results.

Many businessmen have fulfilled the important initial objectives and so their investment policy can be directed to supplementary income before retirement, a retirement fund, and estate creation. More risky securities both for higher income and for appreciation are appropriate in their plans. Investment counsel can be obtained (the fee is an expense for tax purposes) or emphasis placed on investment company shares.

If our successful businessman is in no need of large current income from his portfolio, and if he is in the upper tax brackets, he should pay particular attention to the production of long-term capital gains. He is also likely to be interested in short-run or speculative activity and in investment bargains.

This type of investor can devote some portion of his stock fund to securities whose appeal is temporary, as in the case of war beneficiaries; the balance of his equities should consist of stocks or convertible securities selected for their long-run merits. An honest appraisal of past experience will suggest his real ability to make sound decisions concerning the selection and timing of purchases and sales; a disappointing record in this respect would suggest that at least a portion of his aggressive portfolio should be placed in the hands of others with more experience and more facilities for appraisal of the market and of individual securities.

The "businessman type" includes such a variety of investment situations as to make dangerous any generalizations concerning ability to assume risk, to gauge market trends, or to select and manage a securities portfolio. Tax considerations will vary in importance with each case. The need for liquidity will also vary, depending especially on the type of business in which he is engaged and whether his own business is stable or uncertain. If a substantial portion of his savings are tied up in his own enterprise at considerable risk, his investment portfolio should lean toward the conservative. The established businessman, if he is a corporate officer, can likely participate in a company stock-option plan and in a program of deferred compensation based on company contributions. Such programs provide tax relief and may result in a very substantial accumulation of equities.

The widow or retired couple.   A growing number of persons, both in absolute terms and as a percentage of the population, depend on a fixed-dollar income after the working years have passed. The extension of Social Security and pension benefits to an enlarged list of the elderly, plus the increase in their dollar amount, has made a substantial provision against actual want after retirement. But the *maximum* Social Security retirement income (mid-1972) is $4,045 a year for an individual and $8,490 a year for a widow with two children.[3] To supplement these benefits, and to be independent of relatives and charity, retired persons need supplemental income from private pensions and investments.

For purposes of this discussion, we assume that the retired investors we have in mind no longer need to provide for dependents and that other objectives, such as home ownership, have been reached. The main problem is the maintenance of an income for their own needs. Once the sum of $100,000, or even $50,000, invested in high-grade securities could provide for reasonable living standards. Just prior to World War I, for example, an investment of $100,000 in high-grade bonds provided $5,000 tax-free income. After World War II, allowing for the decline in interest rates (to 2¾ per cent), for income taxes, and for the lowered buying power of the dollar (45 per cent of 1913), it took $500,000 to provide the same real income.[4] In 1972, much higher interest rates were available, but the dollar had less than 28 per cent of its 1913 buying power. Using the postwar period, the buying power of the dollar declined nearly 48 per cent from 1945 to 1972. Thus, a real dilemma is posed for the *rentier* class—whether to live on modest income, or to take greater risk and try to magnify income through investment in equities, or to consume principal.

Table 21-1 shows the pretax dollar return from a $100,000 fund invested in various media, under conditions prevailing in January 1973. At that time interest rates were still historically very high, and a fund of $100,000 invested then would produce $8,000 annually from good-grade corporate bonds and $7,200 from very high-grade bonds. Preferred stock yields also outranked deposit-type yields by an ample margin. The latter brought a lower return than on Treasury bonds but involved no price risk. Savings bonds were relatively more attractive than they had been for some time. Common stock yields in general stood at the bottom of the yield scale. But within the common stock group, the actual range was from zero to perhaps 9 per cent. The general stock averages are heavily influenced by stocks that are more attractive for growth than for current income.

To the majority of retired investors, the avoidance of loss must be the major consideration. The dilemma involved in this choice between good income with low risk and possibly high income with high risk can best be solved by utilizing *both* income and principal to maximize annual cash

---

[3]These benefits will not be payable for several years. To receive these benefits, the average salary of the worker, excluding the lowest five years, would have to be $10,800. Benefits were increased 20 per cent in September 1972.

[4]Benjamin Graham, *The Intelligent Investor*, 3rd ed. (New York: Harper & Row, Publishers, 1965), p. 6.

**Table 21-1. YIELDS FROM SELECTED INVESTMENT MEDIA
January 1973**

Medium of Investment	*Representative Yield—Per Cent*	*Dollar Income*
"Blue-chip" industrial common stocks	3.00%	$3,000
Commercial bank passbook account	4.00	4,000
Certificates of deposit (6 months)	4.00	4,000
Mutual savings bank passbook account	4.50	4,500
Savings and loan association passbook account	5.00	5,000
"Income" mutual funds	5.00	5,000
U.S. Savings bonds, Series H	5.50	5,500
Long-term U.S. Treasury bonds	5.65	5,650
High-grade utility preferred stocks	7.00	7,000
High-grade corporate bonds	7.20	7,200
Medium-grade corporate bonds	8.00	8,000

returns (1) through annuities established as such or based on the proceeds of life insurance policies, (2) through gradual liquidation of high-grade securities not subject to material market fluctuation, or (3) through the establishment of a living trust providing for regular payments of interest and principal.

The wealthy investor. The wealthy investor enjoys several distinct advantages with respect to investment policy: (1) He can afford the risks that equities inevitably involve; (2) he can obtain ample diversification in his own portfolio; (3) he can take advantage of the tax-exemption feature of state and municipal bonds and should substitute these for other high-grade corporate and Federal obligations in the bond section of his portfolio; (4) he can make full use of the capital gains provisions of the Federal income tax law; (5) he can afford the services of competent investment counsel to "tailor" a program that will combine his needs for income, capital appreciation, and estate tax protection; (6) he can employ the formula-planning device to avoid timing the swings in the securities market; (7) he can use some of his principal if he wishes to do so.

For such investors, matters of income and estate tax planning bulk even larger than purely investment considerations. Apart from a substantial fund in high-grade short-term securities held for the purpose of meeting estate and inheritance taxes, together with any specific investments that represent business commitments, the wealthy investor's portfolio will consist substantially of tax-exempts, a varying defensive balance in cash or high-grade bonds, and common stocks. Whether he manages such a portfolio himself, utilizes an investment company, or employs professional management, will depend on his investment competence and confidence and on the complexities of the particular situation.

The wealthy investor can achieve a considerable degree of freedom from care through the medium of a personal trust fund, through holding investment company shares, or through the use of counsel. However, he should always review and check the decisions of others.

A Word of Explanation

In the preceding suggestions for different types of investors, recommendations of specific lists of securities have been avoided. This is because investment portfolios have a way of becoming inappropriate or even obsolete. The circumstances of the investor, the appeal of industries and companies, and rates and prices in the investment market all change through time. Investment is a dynamic art and no program can remain static. Nor can any itemized array of securities or plan involving certain proportions of different types of investments be applicable to any large number of situations even within a general type. Constant vigilance and willingness to change are required of the investor or of those to whom he entrusts his investment problems.

REFERENCES

BABSON, T. E., AND D. L. BABSON, *Investing for a Successful Future.* New York: The Macmillan Co., 1961.

BARNES, LEO, *Your Investments.* Larchmont, N.Y.: American Research Council, 1967.

BELLEMORE, D. H., *The Strategic Investor: Individual Portfolio Management.* New York: Simmons-Boardman Publishing Corp., 1963.

COBLEIGH, I. U., *All About Stocks.* New York: Weybright and Talley, 1970.

COOPER, R. U., *Investments for Professional People,* rev. ed. New York: The Macmillan Co., 1959.

CRANE, BURTON, *The Sophisticated Investor: A Guide to Stock Market Profits,* rev. ed. New York: Simon and Schuster, Inc., 1964.

EDITORS OF FORTUNE, *Fortune's Guide to Personal Investing.* New York: McGraw-Hill, Inc., 1969.

ENGEL, LOUIS, *How to Buy Stocks: A Guide to Making More Money in the Market,* 5th rev. ed. Boston: Little, Brown & Company, 1972.

FINLEY, H. M., *Everybody's Guide to the Stock Market,* rev. ed. Chicago: Henry Ragnery Company, 1968.

FISHER, P. A., *Common Stocks and Uncommon Profits,* rev. ed. New York: Harper & Row, Publishers, 1960.

————, *Paths to Wealth Through Common Stocks.* Englewood Cliffs, N.J.: Prentice-Hall, Inc., 1960.

GRAHAM, BENJAMIN, *The Intelligent Investor,* 3rd rev. ed. New York: Harper & Row, Publishers, 1965.

HAZARD, J. W., AND L. C. COIT, *The Kiplinger Book on Investing for Years Ahead.* Garden City, N.Y.: Doubleday & Co., 1962.

LASSER, J. K., AND SYLVIA PORTER, *Managing Your Money,* rev. ed. New York: Doubleday & Co., 1963.

LASSER (J. K.) INSTITUTE AND S. SHULSKY, *Investing for Retirement.* Larchmont, N.Y.: Business Reports, Inc., 1963.

LOEB, G. M., *The Battle for Stock Market Profits.* New York: Simon and Schuster, Inc., 1971.

MARION, L. F., *Understanding Investment: A Primer for Wives, Widows and Other Capitalists.* Seattle, Wash.: University of Washington Press, 1964.

ROSENBERG, CLAUDE, JR., *Stock Market Primer.* Cleveland: The World Publishing Company, 1970.

SCHEINMAN, W. X., *Why Most Investors are Mostly Wrong Most of the Time.* New York: Weybright and Talley, 1970.

SHULSKY, SAM, *Investing for Financially Successful Retirement.* Larchmont, N.Y.: American Research Council, 1961.

SMITH, ADAM, *The Money Game.* New York: Random House, Inc., 1968.

STILLMAN, R. J., *Guide to Personal Finance.* Englewood Cliffs, N.J.: Prentice-Hall, Inc., 1972.

UNTERMAN, ISRAEL, *Creative Money Management for the Executive.* Garden City, N.Y.: Doubleday & Co., 1962.

WEST, D. A., *The Investor in a Changing Economy.* Englewood Cliffs, N.J.: Prentice-Hall, Inc., 1968.

22 Institutional Investors

SCOPE: This and the following chapter discuss the investment policies of the more important financial institutions through which the savings of individuals are put to work. The order of discussion in Chapter 22 is (1) magnitude of institutional investment, (2) restrictions on institutional investment, (3) commercial banks, (4) mutual savings banks, and (5) savings and loan associations. In Chapter 23 the order is (4) trusts, (5) endowments and foundations, (6) life insurance companies, (7) uninsured private pension funds, (8) measuring investment performance, (9) state and local government retirement funds, and (10) federal retirement funds. Discussion of the investment policies of two other types of financial institutions—investment companies and fire insurance companies—is found in Chapters 9 and 30. They lack the trust characteristics of the other institutions, they have much more leeway in the selection of their investments, and their own investment policies determine to a large extent the investment appeal of the securities they themselves have issued. Thus, the management of the funds of these institutions is more appropriately discussed in connection with the analysis of their shares.

Commercial banks, savings banks, and savings and loan associations as locations for savings have already been discussed in Chapter 4. The material in the present chapter is, therefore, confined to the management of their investment portfolios.

Magnitude of Institutional Investment

Savings flow into the capital market through a variety of institutions that play a constantly increasing role as owners of investment instruments. Individuals are, therefore, concerned with institutional investment policy for two main reasons: (1) Institutional supply and demand is a major influence on the market prices and yields of investments; (2) individuals depend on the portfolio managers of the savings institutions to protect and increase the value and income of their savings. The importance of the institutions we have or will discuss is indicated in Table 22-1.

Bank trustees are included in the table, although they do not own the securities they manage, nor do they issue securities obligations against such assets. The policies that determine the distribution of the investment assets of the above institutions are discussed in this and the following chapter and in Chapters 3, 4, 9, and 30.

**Table 22-1. INSTITUTIONAL OWNERSHIP OF SECURITIES
AND MORTGAGES, DECEMBER 31, 1971**

(in billions of dollars)

	U.S. Govt. and Agency Securities	State and Municipal Bonds	Corporate Bonds	Corporate Stocks	Mortgages
Commercial banks[a]	$82.9	$82.4	$ 4.3	$ .2	$ 82.5
Mutual savings banks	5.5	.4	12.8	3.0	62.0
Savings and loan associations	17.5	[d]	—	—	174.4
Life insurance companies	4.4	3.4	79.2	108.4	2.4
Noninsured private pension funds[c]	3.0	—	25.9	86.8	3.2
Bank administered trusts[b]	8.8	14.0	11.9	108.4	2.4
State and local govt. retirement funds[c]	7.5	1.9	36.2	11.2	7.1
Federal trust funds	82.0	—	—	—	—
Investment companies (mutual)	.6	[d]	4.9	47.1	—
Non-life insurance companies	3.9	19.3	9.3	15.5	.3

[a]Includes trading-account securities.
[b]Exclusive of pension trusts and agency accounts.
[c]Book value.
[d]Less than $100 millions.
SOURCES: See citations in Chapters 3, 4, 9, 22, 23, 29, 30.

Restrictions on Institutional Investment

The common characteristics of the institutions discussed in this and the following chapter is that they act in a position of trust, investing not their own money, but the funds of others entrusted to their care. Such a position requires a greater degree of prudence and caution than the individuals might employ in the selection of their own commitments.

The latitude within which such institutions may exercise investment discretion depends upon the nature of the contract or trust, the powers granted by the contract or by the maker of a trust, and the Federal and state laws governing the investment policy of fiduciary and similar institutions. Commercial banks, savings banks, savings and loan associations, trustees, and life insurance companies are obliged to observe strict regulations concerning their investments, although in the case of trustees, the individual trust arrangements may provide considerable latitude. On the other hand, educational and other endowments are governed mainly by their own investment policies or self-imposed conditions. And a particular security which may be a legal investment for one class of institution may be ineligible for another.

Commercial Bank Investments

Commercial banks as investors. Commercial banks form a very important segment of the investment market. As of December 31, 1971, commercial banks in the United States owned $65 billions of direct and guaranteed Federal debt, or 15 per cent of the total then outstanding, $18 billions or 42 per cent of Federal agency debt outstanding, and $82 billions of state and municipal obligations or about 56 per cent of the total outstanding. They held $82 billions, or 16 per cent of total mortgage debt outstanding.[1] Bank management bears a particularly grave responsibility in investing depositors' funds so as to provide safety, adequate liquidity, and earnings, and at the same time protect the solvency and flexibility of the bank credit system.

Types of bank assets. The assets of commercial banks consist of three major types: (1) primary reserves of cash and balances with other banks, including legal reserves, (2) earning assets, consisting of loans and investments, and (3) fixed assets. The earning assets can be divided into four other categories: (1) secondary reserves, consisting of highly liquid loans, such as bankers' acceptances, prime commercial paper, and short-term Treasury obligations; (2) the bond investment account; (3) securities held for trading; (4) other earning assets, consisting of commercial, consumer, and real estate loans. The secondary reserve should be of such high quality and liquidity that it can be converted into cash at any time without material loss.

In determining the relative proportion of assets in each group, the bank faces the difficult problem of maintaining liquidity and at the same time deriving a reasonable income. The primary reserves are completely liquid but produce no income. The secondary reserves are extremely liquid but at times pay a low rate of return. Ordinarily, they yield a low rate of return, but in times of credit stress, their rates of interest exceed those of long-term securities. The investment account consists mainly of Federal, Federal agency, municipal, and corporate obligations. The municipals group yields the highest after-tax return, but lacks the liquidity and marketability of the Federal obligations. Corporate bonds are relatively unattractive for after-tax income. Commercial loans produce higher yields but are not dependable sources of funds on short notice. Real estate and consumer loans provide favorable yields but are the least liquid of the entire portfolio.

Investment Restrictions. The investment policies of the commercial banks that are members of the Federal Reserve System are governed by Federal statute and the rulings of the Comptroller of the Currency. Nonmember state banks are governed by the banking laws of the state where they are located. The member banks comprise 40 per cent of all commercial banks in the country but hold 80 per cent of the total commercial bank deposits; the following discussion emphasizes their policies.

Commercial banks are not permitted to participate as principals in the underwriting of corporate securities, although they may do so with respect to Federal and general obligation municipal bonds. They are not permitted to purchase stocks, with the exception of certain specific types.[2] They may

---

[1] *Federal Reserve Bulletin*; Federal Deposit Insurance Corporation, annual reports.

[2] Up to 15 per cent of capital and surplus may be invested in the stock of a company engaged in the safe-deposit business. Stock of a company holding property necessary for banking purposes or

buy no convertible bonds at a price above their value without the conversion feature.[3] They may buy no securities which are in default. They are prohibited from purchasing securities in which the investment characteristics are predominantly speculative.

All securities held by a bank which are not specifically exempted from regulation (such as Federal, Federal agency, state, and local bonds—except revenue bonds) or which are not prohibited must qualify as *investment* securities and must be readily marketable, that is, have such a market as to render sales at fair values readily available. Evidence of marketability must be either (1) public distribution of the particular issue or (2) public distribution of other issues of the obligor. If there has been no public offering, eligible bonds are limited to ten-year (or shorter) obligations of established enterprises, having sound values, with an acceptable sinking fund. Where the above tests are met, not more than 10 per cent of the unimpaired capital and surplus of the bank may be invested in the securities of any one obligor. If the purchase price is above par, the premium must be regularly amortized. Profits from the sale of securities must not be considered as earnings until adequate reserves for actual or estimated losses have been provided.

Bank examiners divide securities into four groups according to quality. All eligible securities are placed in Group I and are valued on the basis of cost, less amortization of any premium. Securities of investment quality include general market obligations rated in the first four groups by the recognized investment services: Aaa, Aa, A, and Baa or A1+, A1, A, and B1+. (While such ratings are valuable, they should not be a complete substitution for a bank's own judgment concerning quality.) Securities in Group II are predominantly speculative in character and are valued at the average market price for the eighteen months preceding the examination. At least 50 per cent of the net depreciation, if any, must be deducted from the capital of the bank in determining its solvency. Group III consists of securities in default; these must be immediately written down to market value. Group IV consists of stocks and similar holdings. All depreciation on them is considered a loss and must be written off against capital immediately (a bank may have acquired stock through foreclosure of a collateral loan).

Significance of investments as assets. The role of bank investments has changed greatly in the past two decades, as indicated by the figures in Table 22-2. In examining the figures, note not only the changes in absolute amounts, but also the changes in the relative importance of the various categories. Observe that the classification of earning assets referred to above is not used in the official reports.

During the 1930s the dearth of commercial loans and the banks' desire

---

providing accounting services may be acquired, as well as stock in small business investment companies. Under certain circumstances, up to 10 per cent of capital and surplus may be invested in the stock of corporations engaged in foreign banking. In addition, all member banks must subscribe to Federal Reserve Bank stock.

[3] As explained in Chapter 12, the holder of a convertible bond may exchange it for common stock at a ratio fixed in advance. When the common stock rises sharply in value, the bond will also rise, often above its value as a bond alone.

for liquidity following the banking crisis led to a market shift from loans to investments, especially U.S. Government obligations. During World War II, in spite of an increase in business loans, the trend toward Government secu-

Table 22-2. EARNING ASSETS OF COMMERCIAL BANKS
AS OF DECEMBER 31
(in billions of dollars)

	1950	1955	1960	1965	1971
Loans					
Commercial and industrial*a*	$ 21.9	$ 33.2	$ 43.4	$ 71.9	$118.5
Agricultural	2.9	4.5	5.7	8.2	12.5
For purchasing and carrying securities	2.9	5.0	5.1	8.6	10.9
Real estate	13.5	20.8	28.8	49.7	81.6
Individual, consumer, and other	11.6	20.3	37.1	68.5	104.2
Total loans*b*	$ 52.2	$ 82.6	$118.1	$202.8	$321.2
Investments*c*					
U.S. Govt. obligations	$ 62.0	$ 61.6	$ 61.0	$ 59.7	$ 64.9
Bonds of Federal agencies	1.7	1.9	1.8	4.6	17.9
Municipal obligations	8.1	12.7	17.6	38.7	82.4
Corporate bonds	2.2	1.6	.9	.9	4.3
Other	.4	.5	.6	.8	.1
Total investments	$ 74.4	$ 78.3	$ 81.9	$104.7	$169.6
Total loans and investments	$126.6	$160.9	$200.0	$307.5	$490.8

*a*Includes open-market paper purchased.
*b*Totals show net of reserves.
*c*Includes trading-account securities.
SOURCES: *Federal Reserve Bulletin*; Federal Deposit Insurance Corporation, Annual Reports.

rities was accentuated by the role of the banks in financing the war effort. By the end of 1945, total investments were 79 per cent, and Federal obligations 73 per cent, of commercial banks' earning assets. Since World War II, bank lending to business and real estate has grown at the expense of investments; at the end of 1971, bonds had fallen to 34 per cent of total loans and investments, and direct Federal obligations to 13 per cent.

Factors determining investment policy. The investment policy of a commercial bank is governed by regulation and by considerations of income and risk. In the purchase of securities other than U.S. Government obligations, the main objective is to obtain a' higher after-tax return than that available in the comparable maturities in the Government market. But such an increased return carries increased risk from possible unwise selection and subsequent market declines. The factors that help to shape investment policy may be outlined as follows.

THE NATURE OF DEPOSIT LIABILITIES. Banks which normally carry large demand deposits, especially those which act as depositories for other banks, must maintain a higher degree of liquidity than those whose time deposits predominate or whose demand deposits are unusually stable. Liquidity is reflected in the proportion of short-term Government securities among the earning assets.

THE RELATIONSHIP BETWEEN DEPOSITS AND CAPITAL FUNDS. Banks normally have a very small net worth in relation to assets, as compared with business firms. The capital (stock), surplus, undivided profits, and contingency reserves that comprise the net worth represent the protection afforded by the owners to the depositors. The lower the ratio of net worth to deposits, the greater the risk and hence the greater the need for liquidity through high quality and short maturity. The appropriate capital funds-to-deposits ratio was formerly considered to be in the neighborhood of 10 per cent. At the end of 1971, the ratio stood at 9 per cent for all commercial banks in the United States. National banks showed a ratio of 8 per cent. Because of their importance as correspondent banks, member banks in New York City showed a ratio of 10 per cent.[4] Such ratios are justifiable only as long as commercial banks remain very liquid.

THE PATTERN OF ASSETS. Closely allied to the previous factor is the amount and character of the bank's assets other than its highly liquid investments. If assets *at risk*—that is, loans and discounts exclusive of open-market paper, and longer-term investments—bulk large among the earning assets, the risk element in the investment program must be kept at a minimum through emphasis on higher quality and shorter maturities in the bond account. Assets, deposits, and net worth are related by the supervisory authorities and by bank management. The less liquid the assets, the greater proportion net worth must bear to deposits. The bank with a maximum of loans and a minimum of liquid investments must have a higher cushion of owners' equity.

THE BANK'S EARNINGS REQUIREMENTS. This factor is placed last because a bank's investment policy must always be based more on considerations of safety than of income. A bank has the objective of earning an attractive rate on the investment of its stockholders, but its first responsibility is to its depositors. High risk and high earnings go hand in hand (at least until disaster strikes); low risk-taking produces low returns. To strike the proper medium between these extremes is the central investment problem of banking. The relation of capital funds to deposits, the character of the deposits, and the types of services rendered by the bank all affect the degree of risk it assumes; the same factors also determine its earning power. When, in order to produce satisfactory earnings, the cash position of a bank is reduced, or loans and investments of longer maturity or of lower quality are acquired, or deposits are greatly increased, the interests of the stockholders and those of the depositors must be balanced with unusual ingenuity.

The market value of the bonds—even those of "money bonds" of the highest quality—in a bank's investment account may decline, either through

---

[4]Complied from group data in *Federal Reserve Bulletin*.

a decline in their investment standing or through a rise in prevailing money rates that is reflected in declining prices.[5] Banks guard against the first of these risks by purchasing and holding bonds of obligors of the highest credit standing. But they have no control over the second influence. They can offset it, however, by a system of staggered maturities or the proper distribution of their holdings in short-, medium-, and long-term obligations. As time passes, securities move steadily into the short-term category. A maturity program requires prediction of the course of interest rates. If a rise is expected, banks prefer shorter maturities to avoid the expected depreciation; if interest rates are expected to decline, longer-term bonds are preferred. However, in recent years banks have made a practice of concentrating on relatively short maturities (up to ten years) so as to be able to shift funds into their growing loan portfolios without material market loss. The shape of the yield curve, with attractive yields on short- and medium-term issues, has also encouraged such concentration.

Types of securities investments. The bank's investment portfolio includes securities not classed as secondary reserves, and consists of obligations with medium and long maturities. Investments provide a residual account that varies with the demand for the higher-yielding loans.

U.S. GOVERNMENT OBLIGATIONS. Commercial banks are the largest institutional owners of Federal debt. At the end of 1971, their holdings of $64.9 billions comprised 15 per cent of direct Treasury debt. Their holdings of $51.4 billions of marketable Government debt comprised 20 per cent of the amount outstanding.

Federal obligations bulk large in bank portfolios because they possess several attractive features: (1) They involve the least credit risk; (2) they involve the least risk of substantial market price fluctuation; (3) with the exception of certain types, they have perfect marketability; (4) they may be used for bank borrowing at the Federal Reserve banks without payment of penalty rates; (5) they are preferred over other investments by bank examiners and other supervisory authorities. Within its Government bond portfolio, of course, a bank has the problem of distributing maturities. Its policy in this respect will affect its liquidity and its income. In recent years the great bulk of Government holdings has been in maturities of five years or less.

STATE AND LOCAL GOVERNMENT BONDS. Commercial banks are also the largest institutional owners of municipal securities. At the end of 1971, their holdings of $82 billions comprised about 56 per cent of total state and local debt. (See Chapter 6.) Investment in such securities has increased so substantially that at the end of 1971, they represented nearly 50 per cent of total bank investments. Banks are permitted to underwrite municipal securities (other than revenue bands), whose tax-exempt yield is very attractive in relation to the yield on corporate bonds. Holdings of municipals are adjusted with changing demand for loans, the banks' reserve position, and yields on alternative investments.

[5]See Chapters 5, 6, and 7 for discussions of changing bond yields.

CORPORATE BONDS. Banks' interest in corporate bonds had declined steadily in recent years. The after-tax yields of the bonds of required quality are not attractive compared to those on high-grade tax-exempt municipals, and they lack the price stability and liquidity of Federal obligations. Direct term loans to corporations, with their higher yields, are the modern substitute. Convertible bonds are not attractive; banks are not allowed to pay more than the investment or "straight" value for such securities.

Profits and losses on securities.

Bonds should be bought by banks for income, not for capital gain. This does not mean that banks hold all bonds to maturity. Constant reappraisal of bond holdings and the need to diversify maturities, as well as the use of bonds to feed the secondary and primary reserves when necessary, create a certain turnover in the bond account. Banks thus incur profits and losses in securities even though short-term trading is ordinarily avoided.

The regulations of the Comptroller of the Currency require banks to use any profits realized in the sale of securities to offset actual losses before such profits may be included as income.[6]

Other bank investments.

Discussion of the loaning activities of commercial banks would involve a digression into commercial bank management too extensive for our purposes. However, two types of loans, because of their longer maturity, properly belong in a discussion of bank investments, namely, term loans and real estate mortgages.

Term loans are business loans running from one year to ten years in maturity and amortized by regular installments. The typical term loan is expected to be repaid out of future cash flow. It contains written covenants on the part of the borrower to conduct his financial affairs in a manner agreed upon by the borrower and the lender, such as restrictions on other debt and on dividend distributions. It is usually secured, although the larger term loan is less likely to be secured than is the small one.

Studies of term loans reveal that these credits, which first appeared in the latter 1930s, have become a very important factor in the credit supply. At the end of 1971, they totalled $32 billions, or nearly 40 per cent of the aggregate industrial and commercial loans of the large banks that hold 70 per cent of all bank business loans.[7] This means that for the banking system, the total was between $45 and $50 billions—equal to about one-third of total securities investments and many times the holdings of corporate bonds. The larger loans are used most frequently by businesses such as metals and metal products, petroleum, coal, chemicals, rubber, transportation, and communication, which have a heavy fixed investment with a relatively long service life. The smaller loans, for working capital purposes, are used mostly by retail trade and service concerns.

Term loans are a substitute for two other types of bank earning assets that have declined in importance (for banks) in recent years. One is the short-term loan that was almost automatically renewed if the borrower's credit

---

[6]See Chapter 29 for a discussion of bank earnings derived from investments.
[7]*Federal Reserve Bulletin*, monthly tables.

standing remained satisfactory. The other, as indicated previously, is the corporate bond. While loans with maturity of from one to ten years violate the traditional theory of bank liquidity, experience has shown their usefulness provided they are made wisely, they are followed and collected carefully, and the bank is otherwise liquid.

Real estate loans, along with term loans, are appropriate investments for saving deposits which have much less volatility than those in the demand category. They have played an increasingly important role in commercial bank portfolios. At the end of 1971, commercial banks held a total (before reserves) of $82.5 billions in mortgages, or 16 per cent of mortgage debt outstanding, consisting of $4.2 billions in farm mortgages, $48.0 billions in one- to four-family residential (of which $8.3 billions were FHA-insured and $3.0 billions VA-guaranteed), and $30.3 billions in multifamily, commercial, and industrial mortgages.

The experience of banks with real estate mortgage loans in the 1930s was not a happy one, especially for smaller banks. Since that time, practices have been greatly improved by experience and by regulation. National banks may buy any FHA-insured or VA-guaranteed mortgage. In addition, they may acquire conventional first mortgages on improved real estate not exceeding 66⅔ per cent of appraised value, in the case of ten- to twenty-year amortized loans, and 90 per cent for a term of thirty years if the entire principal will be amortized within that period. Single-maturity loans are limited to 50 per cent of appraised value and a maturity of five years. A national bank may make aggregate mortgage loans up to either the amount of its unimpaired capital and surplus or 70 per cent of its time and savings deposits, whichever is the greater.

The amortization features of modern real estate loans, together with the insurance or guarantee by Federal agencies of loans qualified for such insurance, have done much to put mortgages back into the class of respectable bank assets. Their lack of liquidity is mitigated by the fact that banks can obtain special four-month advances against mortgages from the Federal Reserve Banks, and by the fact that FHA-insured mortgages may be sold to the Federal National Mortgage Association. In case of default, insured mortgages are exchanged for Government-guaranteed debentures of the Federal Housing Administration.[8]

Consumer loans have increased greatly in recent years. This category includes personal loans and loans made for financing automobiles and other durable consumer goods. For the most part this type of loan is repayable in installments and so offers little liquidity, but if made soundly and with adequate diversification is an appropriate investment of savings deposits.

Summary of investment requirements. Recovery of principal through safety and marketability of investments are the foremost considerations in bank investment policy. Second in importance is assurance of income; the high-grade and relatively short-term bank investments produce a modest but certain yield. Other important requirements are legality (the bank's investments must conform to legal and regulatory requirements), diversifica-

---

[8]A more complete discussion of mortgage loans is found in Chapter 11.

tion (especially for smaller banks), freedom from management in the case of banks without specialized investment managers, and tax status (the bank is taxed at corporate tax rates and finds municipal bonds attractive). Although the bank's expenses rise in periods of rising wages and prices, its obligations are dollar obligations, and it is, therefore, not concerned about protecting its depositors against inflation.

Savings Bank Investments

General factors determining Investments.

The general characteristics of savings banks described in Chapter 4 help to explain why these institutions need less liquidity than commercial banks, and therefore, why their cash and reserve requirements are lower and why their investments include a greater proportion of longer-maturity instruments. The savings bank can invest savings funds in securities of limited marketability and in home mortgages that are adequately safe and pay a higher rate of income than do the more marketable and short-term securities.

But safety in the investment of savings bank funds should not be compromised. The purposes for which these banks have been established have led to restrictions on their investment powers. They may hold high-grade investments only, including real estate mortgages, government bonds, and prime corporate issues. Such a selection may provide safety but lack flexibility. State legislatures have been slow to liberalize savings bank investment laws, on the ground that to do so might jeopardize the savings of the low-income classes.

Legal investments in New York State.

No two states have identical laws regarding the eligibility of securities for savings banks. Because the New York law is representative of fairly conservative legislation and has served as a model for a number of other states, the present *legal list* in New York is set forth below. While this list has not provided complete protection against investment losses, the solvency record of New York savings banks is testimony to the efficiency of the law. No savings bank has failed in New York in over sixty years, and no depositor in a New York State savings bank has lost money by reason of the failure of the bank during the present century.

An official list of the specific eligible securities is issued by the State Banking Department at the beginning of July in each year.[9] The following is a summary of major types, without spelling out the specific requirements to be met in the case of corporate and municipal bonds:

1. Direct and guaranteed obligations of the United States;
2. Bonds of New York and other states based on full faith and credit;
3. Direct obligations of New York State municipalities;

---

[9]A convenient reference on New York and other states is provided in *Encyclopedia of Banking Laws.* Boston: The Banking Law Journal, 1964, with Supplements.

4. Obligations of municipalities in other states meeting certain population and debt-to-property standards;

5. Obligations of the Dominion of Canada and Canadian provincial and municipal bonds meeting specified tests of debt-to-property value;

6. World Bank bonds;

7. Mortgages on improved real property in New York State up to 75 per cent of the appraised value of residential and business property, up to $25,000 or 90 per cent of the appraised value of one- or two-family owner-occupied residences, to a maturity of thirty years on an amortized basis;

8. Mortgages on unimproved real property in New York to 50 per cent of appraised value, with certain limitations;

9. Conventional mortgages meeting New York requirements secured by property outside of New York State, to 20 per cent of the bank's assets;

10. Insured FHA mortgages and VA-guaranteed mortgages, if $20,000 is guaranteed;

11. Bonds of railroad, electric, gas, and telephone companies that meet specified tests of interest coverage and of debt in relation to net worth;

12. Consolidated debenture bonds of the Federal Land Banks, Federal Home Loan Banks, and Federal Intermediate Credit Banks, and bonds of the Federal National Mortgage Association;

13. Stock in a Federal Reserve Bank and a Federal Home Loan Bank in the amount required for membership;

14. Stock of New York State housing corporations under certain conditions;

15. Obligations of various New York State revenue authorities;

16. Preferred stocks showing specified coverage of fixed charges plus preferred dividends;

17. Common stocks listed on registered exchanges that have ten-year dividend records.

The maximum proportion of total assets that may be invested in certain of the preceding groups is as follows: real estate mortgages, 75 per cent (exclusive of FHA-insured and VA-guaranteed mortgages) ; railroad obligations, 25 per cent; electric and gas bonds, 25 per cent; telephone bonds, 25 per cent; real estate (for transaction of business), 25 per cent of surplus; housing projects, 15 per cent (or 50 per cent of surplus). The limitations on investment in stocks are indicated below.

In two states (Maryland and Delaware), the "prudent man" investment rule applies. Theoretically, this permits broad discretion away from a legal list. In fact, however, even in these states strict policies still apply.

Actual investment policy. During World War II Federal obligations became the banks' most important investment; at the end of 1945, these comprised 63 per cent of total assets. With the expansion of residential building in the 1950s, 1960s, and early 1970s, a great move out of Government securities and into the higher-yielding mortgages took place, so that at the end of 1971 the banks held only $3.3 billions of Treasury obligations, or less than 4 per cent of their total assets. The emphasis has been on short and medium maturities to provide the liquidity needed to offset the growing emphasis on mortgages.

Although mutual savings banks pay the same Federal income tax rate as other corporations (on income after approved reserves for losses), tax-free state and local government bonds have played a minor role as investments. At the end of 1971, their total was only $390 millions or 4 per cent of combined total assets. Holdings of corporate bonds have increased moderately in the postwar period, comprising about $13 billions or about 14 per cent of total assets at the end of 1971. The banks vary their investment in these securities with the demand for mortgage loans.

At the end of 1971 savings banks held $62 billions of mortgages (net after reserves), comprising 69 per cent of their total assets. This reflects the great demand for housing credit, the relatively attractive yields on mortgages, the liberalization of rules governing mortgage investments such as increases in loan-to-value ratios, the growth of out-of-state lending, and the appeal of FHA-insured and VA-guaranteed liens, of which the banks are the largest owners. At the end of 1971 they held $28 billions of Federally supported mortgages, or nearly one quarter of the combined total of these types outstanding. Such liens comprised 30 per cent of the total assets.

A startling change in the principles of savings bank investment policy took place in 1952 when banks domiciled in New York were permitted to purchase common stocks. The holdings of stocks must be kept to a very modest level (one-third of surplus and undivided profits or 3 per cent of assets, whichever is less) and must meet high qualifications of marketability and earnings.[10] The purpose of this change was to increase the earnings of the banks at a time when interest rates were low and dividend yields were high. It is highly questionable, however, whether the savings of small income-earners should be risked in stocks, however carefully selected—especially at yields prevailing in 1970–1973. The purchase of common stock by mutual savings banks was also given impetus in 1951 by the imposition of income taxation. Dividends (with their 85 per cent exemption) took on special appeal. Despite this advantage and the liberalization of state laws, at the end of 1971 corporate stocks totalled only $3 billions or 3.3 per cent of total assets.

The limited liquidity required of savings banks is obtained through modest cash balances and holdings of high-grade marketable bonds. Safety is also fostered by deposit insurance. As of June 30, 1971, 327 of the 490 banks were members of the Federal Deposit Insurance Corporation, and all but one of the others participated in special state deposit insurance systems.

Summary of investment requirements. The savings bank's liabilities are longer-term and less volatile than those of the commercial bank; hence less emphasis is placed on liquidity and more on income. Their portfolio emphasizes longer-term bond issues, along with amortized real estate loans. Like commercial banks, they are taxed at corporate rates. Nevertheless, municipal bonds have played an unimportant role in their investment policy.

[10]Including preferred stocks, the restrictions become one-half of surplus and undivided profits or 5 per cent of assets, whichever is lower. Investments in the stock of one corporation are limited to 2 per cent of the outstanding shares of the company and to 1 per cent of the assets of the bank.

The larger banks are able to manage their own investment affairs. Smaller organizations obtain freedom from care by more emphasis on Government bonds and by using investment services. Like commercial banks, protection of depositors against inflation is unnecessary, so that regardless of legal limitations, substantial investment in equities is not required.

Investments of Savings and Loan Associations

General investment characteristics. The general nature of savings and loan associations was indicated in Chapter 4. We saw that their major functions are to act as a location for savings, and to lend on home mortgages. The association is the only specialized homeowner credit institution in the American financial system. At the end of 1971, funds aggregating $174 billions were "deposited" in the 5,540 savings and loan associations throughout the United States. While these institutions are technically not depositories, they are so regarded by their accountholders. Their assets must be sound and reasonable liquidity must be maintained. However, because the association does not accept demand deposits, the need for liquidity is not so urgent as in the case of commercial banks. Loans from regional Federal Home Loan Banks are available to take up variations in cash flow.

Actual investment policy. The combined statement of all associations, showing the breakdown of assets by major classes of investments at the end of 1971 is given in Chapter 4. Mortgages comprised 85 per cent of total assets. The bulk of these, 60 per cent of assets, were amortized conventional loans on one- to four-family housing units, resulting from the associations emphasis or local lending at high loan-to-value ratios. Their interest in FHA-insured loans has been increasing in recent years ($13.8 billions held at the end of 1971), and they have been substantial buyers of VA-guaranteed loans, holding $10.9 billions as of December 31, 1971. The associations' share of the national total of home loans reached 47 per cent at the end of 1971.

Principal and interest on conventional loans to finance new single-family properties are paid in monthly installments, with maturities ranging from fifteen to thirty years, at interest rates of from $7\frac{1}{4}$ to 8 per cent. The loan-to-value ratio now runs as high as 95 per cent—substantially higher than is allowed on most conventional loans banks and life insurance companies. Although the maturities of individual home mortgages are long, the turnover of the mortgage portfolio is relatively fast—about 15 per cent a year—arising from the steady amortization of loans. Loans to finance existing homes, and to provide interim construction financing, usually bear a lower loan-to-value ratio (up to 80 per cent) with maturities of fifteen to twenty years.

In recent years the mortgage lending powers of savings and loan associations have been expanded to include loans on multifamily and commercial properties, loans for home repair and modernization, and loans for acquisition and development of residential land. As of the end of 1971, $31 billions or 18 per cent of mortgages held were for multifamily and commercial purposes. The lending powers of associations have also been extended beyond their immediate areas through use of correspondents and through participations in first mortgage loans held by other institutions. Of the $39.4 billions of mortgage loans made in 1971, $6.8 billions or 17 per cent were for one- to four-family home construction, $18.8 billions or 48 per cent for home purchases, and $13.8 billions or 35 per cent for all other purposes.[11]

In addition to qualified mortgages, associations can invest in Government obligations and those of certain Federal agencies, and (since 1964) Federally chartered firms may acquire the four top grades of state and municipal bonds. Treasury bonds are held for liquidity; their proportion of total assets has run around 5 to 6 per cent in recent years, with emphasis on short and intermediate maturities to offset the long maturities of the mortgage portfolio. At the end of 1971, cash and U.S. Government bonds totalled $19.7 billions or 9 per cent of total assets.

Secondary markets. The concentration of investments in mortgages might appear to be dangerous to the solvency of savings and loan associations. But the type of loans made, the amortization feature, and the availability of a secondary market all contribute to soundness. This secondary market exists in insurance companies and in the Federal agencies which stand ready, as in the case of the Federal Home Loan Banks, to lend on mortgages or, as in the case of the Federal National Mortgage Association, to buy them. The latter organization, privately owned, was formed for the purpose of establishing and maintaining a market for mortgage on homes, including large-size housing projects, insured by the Federal Housing Administration and the Veterans' Administration. Total purchases in 1971 were $3.5 billions. "Fannie Mae" is now also empowered to provide a secondary market for conventional mortgages, although its activity in this area has not yet been developed. The Government National Mortgage Association ("Ginnie Mae") is an instrumentality of the U.S. Government operating within the U.S. Department of Housing and Urban Development. It buys mortgages and also provides an indirect secondary market by guaranteeing securities backed by FHA and VA mortgage loans. At the end of 1971 it held $5.3 billions of such assets.[12]

Summary of investment requirements. Savings and loan associations need less liquidity than savings banks. The legal and economic character of their "deposit" accounts permits a very heavy concentration in mortgages. Normal cash requirements are light, and need for adequate and stable income predominates. Loans from the Federal Home Loan Banks help to fill the seasonal and cyclical cash requirements. Security investments are almost exclusively Federal obligations, which are generally short- and medium-term maturities to support the small cash balance. Legal regulations are liberal, and income taxation presents no problem because, after "dividends," earnings go largely into authorized reserves and make taxes nominal. No inflation hedge is required for the protection of creditors.

The chief problem of the associations in very recent times has been to attract a sufficient supply of deposits to service the home mortgage market. To do so, rates on passbook savings as high as 5 per cent were being offered

[11]United States Savings and Loan League, *Fact Book, 1971*, Table 71.
[12]See Chapter 11 for further discussion of F.N.M.A. and G.N.M.A.

in 1972; rates as high as 6 per cent were paid on term deposits. To pay such rates, high yields on mortgage investments are necessary. Under such conditions, maintenance of quality in the mortgage portfolio places severe demands on management.

REFERENCES

AMERICAN BANKERS ASSOCIATION, *The Commercial Banking Industry,* a monograph prepared for the Commission on Money and Credit. Englewood Cliffs, N.J.: Prentice-Hall, Inc., 1962.

———, *Utilization of Bank Funds.* New York: The Association, 1964.

AMERICAN SAVINGS AND LOAN INSTITUTE, *Lending Principles and Practices.* Chicago: American Savings and Loan Institute Press, 1971.

———, *The Role of Investments in Bank Asset Management.* New York: The Association, 1965.

BECKHART, B. H., ed., *Business Loans of American Commercial Banks.* New York: The Ronald Press Company, 1959.

CROSSE, H. D., *Management Policies for Commercial Banks.* Englewood Cliffs, N.J.: Prentice-Hall, Inc., 1962.

DOUGALL, H. E., *Capital Markets and Institutions,* 2nd ed., Chapters 2, 3. Englewood Cliffs, N.J.: Prentice-Hall, Inc., 1970.

HAYES, D. A., *Bank Lending Policies.* Ann Arbor, Mich.: Graduate School of Business Administration, University of Michigan, 1971.

HODGMAN, D. R., *Commercial Bank Loan and Investment Policy.* Champaign, Ill.: University of Illinois Bureau of Business Research, 1963.

Institutional Investor Study Report of the Securities and Exchange Commission, Supplementary Volume I, Chapter 5. 92nd Congress, 1st Session, House Document No. 92–64. Washington: U.S. Govt. Printing Office, 1971.

KENDALL, L. T., *The Savings and Loan Business: Its Purpose, Functions, and Economic Justification,* a monograph prepared for the Commission on Money and Credit. Englewood Cliffs, N.J.: Prentice-Hall, Inc., 1962.

KLAMAN, S. B., *The Postwar Residential Mortgage Market.* Princeton, N.J.: Princeton University Press, 1961.

LYON, R. A., *Investment Portfolio Management in the Commercial Bank.* New Brunswick, N.J.: Butgers University Press, 1960.

NATIONAL ASSOCIATION OF MUTUAL SAVINGS BANKS, *Mutual Savings Banking: Basic Characteristics and Role in the National Economy,* a monograph prepared for the Commission on Money and Credit. Englewood Cliffs, N.J.: Prentice-Hall, Inc., 1962.

PROCHNOW, H. V. AND R. A. FOULKE, *Practical Bank Credit,* rev. ed. New York: Harper & Row, Publishers, 1963.

REED, E. W., *Commercial Bank Management.* New York: Harper & Row, Publishers, 1963.

ROBINSON, R. I., *Money and Capital Markets.* New York: McGraw-Hill, Inc., 1964.

———, *The Management of Bank Funds,* 2nd ed. New York: McGraw-Hill, Inc., 1962.

WELFING, WELDON, *Bank Investments.* New York: American Bankers Association, American Institute of Banking, 1963.

23 Institutional Investors (cont.)

Trustee Investments

Nature of a trust. A *trust* involves the passing of title to property by deed or will (the estate) from an owner (the settlor—or testator, in the case of a trust created by will) who creates the trust, to a trustee who is to hold the property for the benefit of another, the beneficiary. The trust principle has many applications. We are concerned here with the creation and administration of trusts designed to produce income for the beneficiary, who may be the trustor or another person or persons. The relationship between the trustee and the beneficiaries is strictly fiduciary, and involves the highest degree of good faith and fidelity on the part of the trustee and of confidence on the part of the creator and the beneficiary.

Trusts are created for a wide variety of purposes—to support dependents, to educate children, to support educational or charitable organizations, to manage pension and profit-sharing plans, to relieve the creator of the burden of management of funds, and many others. Any legally competent person may set up a trust by an agreement setting forth the identity of the trustee or trustees, the manner in which the funds shall be invested, the distribution of the income from the estate, and the disposition of any principal to the remainderman when the trust terminates.

Types of personal trusts. A trust created by will and which becomes effective upon the death of the testator is a *testamentary* trust or trust *under will.* A *living* or *inter vivos* trust is created by deed or declaration and becomes effective during the life of the maker, who may even designate himself as the beneficiary. The trust may be revocable or irrevocable. In a *life insurance trust,* the body of the trust consists of life insurance policies on the life of the creator, the proceeds of which are payable to a trustee when due. The purpose is to provide flexible arrangements that will relieve the dependents of the responsibility of investing and possibly mismanaging substantial sums of money. As an alternative, the funds may be left with the insurance company and distributed under various settlement options, or the proceeds may be made payable to the estate of the insured and pass into a testamentary trust created under his will.

Corporate trustees. Although individuals may be named as trustees, the responsibilities of the trust function and the growing complexity of security and property management have influenced a trend toward the appointment of banks or trust companies as trustees. State banks have long been permitted under special state laws to act as trustees and to engage in other fiduciary activities. National banks received this right in 1918, but not until they were given perpetual existence in 1972 was it practical for them to engage in trust activities. Most large state and national commercial banks now have trust departments that perform a wide variety of functions for individuals and corporations. Trust companies as such were originally formed to act as incorporated trustees, but in most states they are now permitted by law to perform all the functions of a bank. Today, few trust companies are without banking powers.

In the rendering of trust service, the corporate trustee offers a number of advantages over the individual trustee:

1. *Perpetual existence.* Continuous administration of a trust is important not only because the trust may extend over a long period of years, but also because the interruption of the performance of trust duties, say by the death of an individual trustee, involves legal and accounting complications, as well as possible changes in investment policy.

2. *Financial responsibility.* The corporate trustee, with its substantial resources, strict regulation, and segregation of trust assets, provides financial assurance that most individual trustees could not offer.

3. *Business responsibility.* A trust institution prospers only if it provides satisfactory service, and so it has a compelling incentive to efficiency and aggressiveness in caring for the trust that may not exist in the case of an individual trustee.

4. *Specialization.* The bank or trust company is experienced in the handling of trust business. It also offers the services of specialists in a large department as well as the ancillary facilities of the banking department.

For some years the Comptroller of the Currency has revealed the size and composition of the assets for which the trust departments of national banks have investment responsibility, both as trustees and agents. Since 1968 the Comptroller had joined in measuring the trust department assets of all commercial banks. As of the end of 1971, these totalled $343 billions, of which $270 billions were in trust. The composition of the aggregate figures in shown in Table 23-1.

Legal restrictions on trust investments. The investment policy of the trustee is governed by the instructions, if any, in the trust instrument. If investment powers are not specified, the trustee is restricted to investments permitted by the laws of the state of domicile. The instrument itself may designate the types of securities to be purchased or may impose restrictions.

Or it may provide for discretionary powers authorizing the trustee to buy any securities he wishes, subject only to the exercise of prudent judgment. A fourth alternative is the restriction to specific securities turned over at the inception of the trust or to be purchased by the trustee. Testamentary trusts must provide the greatest flexibility in investment policy so that the trustee may fit the trust to the needs of the beneficiaries and under changing conditions obtain reasonable income commensurate with safety. A trust must also provide the trustee with adequate power of sale and purchase.

State laws governing trust investment are far from uniform. In some the legal list is strictly defined by a state board or commission. In others only the general qualifications of legals are set forth. In most states, however, the laws have been liberalized or court decisions have been rendered to permit the trustee to buy any securities, subject only to the prudent man rule first set forth in Massachusetts over a century ago:

> All that can be required of a trustee to invest is that he shall conduct himself faithfully and exercise a sound discretion. He is to observe how men of prudence, discretion, and intelligence manage their own affairs, not in regard to speculation, but in regard to the permanent disposition of their funds, considering the probable income, as well as the probable safety of the capital to be invested.[1]

Prior to 1950, New York State represented an example of the "legal list" type of statute. Trust investment was limited, with certain minor exceptions, to the same kinds of securities and mortgages in which savings banks of New York State were authorized to invest, unless other forms of investments were specifically sanctioned by the trustor. When, in 1950, New York followed the lead of twenty-four other states, including Illinois, California, and Massachusetts, in adopting, in part at least, the "prudent man" rule, a considerable impetus to the use of common stocks for trust investment was felt. As of 1971, the rule had been adopted in some forty-five states. Today, large banks are rarely restricted by "legal lists."[2]

Distribution of trust investments. The traditional attitude of trustees toward common stocks, with the exception of Massachusetts and a few other states where equities have been looked upon with favor for many years, was that they lacked the stability of income and market value required in a trust fund. Investment in stocks and in real estate was regarded as equivalent to partnership in business ventures with the risks that such a position inevitably involved.

The trend toward the prudent man rule and greater holdings of stocks is explained by three factors: (1) the low yields traditionally derived from high-grade bonds and other legals, (2) the rise in the cost of living and the need for protecting the principal and income of the fund from the effects of inflation, and (3) the assumption that in the long run a well-selected list

---

[1]*Harvard College* v *Armory*, 9 Pickering 446 (1830).

[2]For detailed information on the size, growth, operations, legal environment, and compensation of bank trustees see *Institutional Investors Study Report of the Securities and Exchange Commission*, Chapter V. 92nd. Congress, 1st Session, House Document No. 92–64, March 1971.

of common stocks will provide greater income than high-grade bonds, where both cash income from dividends and change in market value are included in the concept of "total return." None of these influences has had much validity since 1965. Bond yields have been much higher—at times phenomenally higher—yields on stocks in general have remained low, and stock prices in early 1973 were only modestly above the 1966 peak. A substantial improvement in stock prices will be necessary to restore faith in the "total return" concept.

The New York State law permits fiduciaries to invest up to 35 per cent of restricted trust funds in "such securities as would be acquired by prudent men of discretion and intelligence in such matters who are seeking a reasonable income and the preservation of their capital." Subject to the interpretation of prudence, funds may be placed in bonds not on the legal list, as well as in preferred and common stocks of domestic corporations. Except for bank and insurance company stocks, only those common stocks fully listed on a national securities exchange may be considered.

The distribution of the market value of assets of trust departments of insured commercial banks over which investment responsibility is exercised is shown in Table 23-1. Employee benefit funds, being free from income taxes, include no state and local government bonds, so that they account for the bulk of the corporate bonds held. The very large proportion of trust assets represented by common stocks reflects (1) a changing attitude toward the appropriateness of such assets by trustees and by their clients, and (2) the rise in the market values of stocks during recent years.

Table 23-1. DISTRIBUTION OF ASSETS OF INSURED COMMERCIAL BANK TRUST DEPARTMENTS, DECEMBER 31, 1971

(in billions of dollars)

	Amount	*Per Cent*
Cash assets	$ 7.4	2.2%
U.S. Govt. and agency securities	17.2	5.0
Municipal securities	19.5	5.7
Other bonds	46.4	13.5
Common stocks	223.9	65.2
Preferred stock	7.0	2.0
Mortgages	6.5	1.9
Other assets	15.4	4.5
	$343.3	100.0%

SOURCE: Board of Governors of the Federal Reserve System, Federal Deposit Insurance Corporation, and Office of the Comptroller of the Currency, *Trust Assets of Insured Commercial Banks—1971.* (Washington, D.C.: U.S. Government Printing Office, 1972). Agency and advisory accounts ($73 billions) are included.

Such aggregate figures are, however, quite misleading. There is a wide diversity of trust investment policy, ranging from the very conservative to the aggressive. Some trust accounts are wholly invested in common stocks. The new concept of "prudence" is not so much risk avoidance as the construction of an investment account that will meet the necessary objectives, assume as much risk as it is appropriate to assume, and as a result of expert planning and analysis, achieve a risk-reward relationship that is suitable for the particular situation.

Fiduciaries are still limited by a long line of court decisions, precedents, and experience that cause them to select mainly seasoned high-grade stocks with long dividend records and above-average market stability. Trustees are still obliged to exercise "prudent" care; but their ability to keep their funds productive has been enhanced by the expansion of the legal list and by increased powers of discretion. Some banks have gone so far as to allocate specific proportions of certain trust funds to "glamorous" common stocks that are speculative in the traditional sense. Such securities are, however, usually found in pension trusts rather than in individuals' accounts. Another recent development is the investment in shares of small business investment companies so as to allocate trust funds for "venture capital" purposes.

Common trusts. The handling of small trusts on a profitable basis while obtaining safety and diversification has long been a problem for trustees. Safety and liquidity may be obtained by restricting such funds to high-grade bonds, with emphasis on U.S. Government obligations. But such a policy sacrifices income and protection against inflation. Another alternative that is growing in favor is the use of the *common trust,* in which a number of trust funds are combined for purposes of economy and efficiency of administration. Such consolidated funds are permitted by legislation or court decision in fifty states. State banking institutions must operate common trusts in accordance with the law of the state in which the bank is located; national banks must follow a uniform plan as laid down by the Board of Governors of the Federal Reserve System. Formerly, the maximum participation of any one fund was restricted to $100,000 in order to limit the trust to small funds whose administration expenses are relatively high and in which adequate diversification of risk is difficult to obtain. This limit was lifted in 1963. The trust may not invest more than 10 per cent of its assets in any single enterprise other than U.S. Government securities. Cash and readily marketable securities, defined as subject to frequent dealings in ready markets, should comprise about 40 per cent of the trust. Participations and withdrawals are permitted only on quarterly valuation dates. Funds may not participate in a common trust if any assets in the trust are illegal for the fund to hold or if the trust agreement does not expressly sanction the arrangement.[3]

The common trust fund provides diversification and flexibility not otherwise obtainable in small trusts, as well as the possibility of a larger income. A survey of 773 funds, holding $7.3 billions in assets as of 1971, showed that

---

[3]For regulatory history, legal background, and management practices of common trust funds see *Institutional Investor Study Report of the S.E.C., op. cit.,* Chapter V, pp. 444–450. This source also reveals the investment performance of a large sample of pooled employee benefit trusts and common trust funds in the period 1960–1969. In the aggregate, the trusts showed a lower rate of return than the rate that would have been obtained by a hypothetical unmanaged portfolio having the same volatility. But many of them individually showed lower volatility.

$3.9 billions or 54 per cent was invested in common stocks and convertible securities, $1.5 billions or 20 per cent in straight corporate bonds, $1.2 billions or 17 per cent in municipal securities, $.2 billions or 3 per cent in U.S. Government and agency securities, and $.5 billions or 6 per cent in cash assets, mortgages, and other assets. But the proportions varied among the four main types of funds: (1) 278 common stock funds with $2.5 billion in assets, almost all common stocks and convertibles; (2) 174 diversified (balanced) funds with $2.1 billions in assets, of which 63 per cent was common stock and convertibles and 21 per cent straight corporate bonds; (3) 234 income funds with $1.4 billions in assets of which only 9 per cent was in "equity securities"; and (4) 87 tax-exempt funds whose assets of $1.2 billions were almost all municipal bonds.[4]

The combined investments of all common trust funds, as the end of 1968, totalled 9.5 billions.[5]

Investment procedure. The investment policy of a trustee is complicated by the fact that the wishes of two and often three parties must be respected—the trustor, the present beneficiaries (life tenants) entitled to the income, and the ultimate beneficiaries (remaindermen) who will receive the principal at the expiration of the trust. The present beneficiaries desire as high a rate of income as might reasonably be expected, and their best interests may not be served if the trustees buy only the very safest securities, with a relatively low rate of return. On the other hand, the trustee must be mindful of the ultimate beneficiaries who are entitled to the principal of the fund as nearly intact as conservative stewardship can preserve it, plus protection against inflation. Between the opposing viewpoints, the trustee must steer a middle course, concentrating neither in the highest-grade issues with low yields nor in the low-grade issues with high yields. Because ultimate safety of principal is paramount, however, he must go below medium-grade issues only rarely and should prefer the higher-grade issues. In a market where the yield on the best grade of long-term corporate bonds is about $7\frac{1}{2}$ per cent, an average current rate of return of over $8\frac{1}{2}$ per cent would be an unreasonable expectation from a conscientious trustee. But appreciation of principal value could still be enjoyed.

Trustors often make restrictions that hamper the trustee. In some cases, he is required to hold certain securities which might better be sold. In other cases, he is not given the power to purchase securities which in his judgment would be appropriate.

Traditionally, the trustee was regarded as a conserver of capital, with little or no obligation to increase the value of a fund. The argument in favor of common stocks for trust accounts, at least until recent years, was twofold: (1) the eventual higher income that stocks often (but not always) produce in comparison with bonds, and (2) their inflation hedge possibilities. Under conditions prevailing in the latter 1960s and early 1970s, these arguments have lost a good deal of their force. We still recognize that, where the risk-taking permits, the duty of the trustee is to preserve purchasing power as well

[4] *Trusts and Estates*, May 1972, pp. 362–367.
[5] *The National Banking Review*, June 1969, pp. 435–447.

as dollars, but this responsibility must always be secondary to that of maintenance of dollar safety.

Summary of investment requirements.   Generalizations concerning the investment policy of trustees are difficult because of differences in size and requirements. The emphasis is on production of reasonable income and preservation of principal, but within these general limitations many variations in investment policy must be expected. Trust officers, by the very nature of their fiduciary position, must always lean to the conservative side.

The importance of diversification depends on the size of the fund and the requirements of the case. As we have seen, the common trust fund has been developed to provide this factor for smaller estates. Tax status may be very important for larger funds, and particularly in large discretionary accounts, protection against inflation is sought through investment in equities including common stocks, convertible securities, and real estate. Legality must always be strictly observed, but the spread of the prudent man doctrine has released trustees from strict adherence to the specific legal lists.

Bank agency accounts.   Although banks are not permitted to operate mutual funds as such, they have become increasingly active in the management of agency and advisory accounts. In the case of agency accounts, the trust department holds the clients' securities and has an agreed amount of responsibility for investment decisions. In the case of advisory accounts, the bank has the status of an investment counsel. Both types of accounts can be terminated by the investor.

In neither of these accounts does the bank serve as trustee. Title to the assets remains with the investor. And the bank is not restricted by regulations governing trust investments. Because individual portfolios vary widely depending on the investors' preferences, there are highly aggressive common stock portfolios, balanced portfolios, and accounts invested in high-grade bonds, and generalizations on investment policy are not possible. Performance results are similarly varied.

Investment of Endowments and Foundations

The endowed funds of charitable, religious, and educational institutions are administered by trustees who are limited by their fiduciary responsibility and by the provisions of specific grants. But "fiduciary responsibility" is an elastic concept. The trustees generally enjoy considerable flexibility in managing the portfolio, and their policies range from strict preservation of principal with a safe return to maximization of income.

The typical endowment fund needs little liquidity. The traditional investment policy of most college and university endowment trustees or managers emphasized bonds, preferred stocks, and mortgages, to achieve safety of income and principal. And income included only current cash interest, dividends, and rents. But in recent years, there has been a decided shift toward common stocks, so that stocks now comprise as much as 80 per cent of some portfolios; other portfolio managers still adhere to the more historically orthodox investment ratios.[6]

The rising costs of college operation, the decline in the ratio of endowment income to total income, and the threat of continued inflation have led the trustees of a number of institutions to a more aggressive investment policy. This trend was stimulated by a very critical report from the Ford Foundation in 1969.[7] The report discussed the typical attitudes of college trustees with respect to endowment management, and concluded, in general, that (1) the investment record of endowment management had been poor; (2) the time-honored distinction between income and capital appreciation should be abandoned, and trustees should seek, within clearly defined risk limits, to maximize *total* return; (3) total return should be figured as mutual funds measure their total performance, namely, by calculating the percentage of income plus appreciation to beginning market value; (4) the portfolios should be put on a unit basis; that is, the total should be divided into a number of units and the value of each unit calculated at regular intervals, and as new funds are received. This would enable a comparison with other endowments and with the performance of mutual funds; (5) trustees should set the general investment policy, including a desired rate of total return and the risk to be assumed, but employ professional investment management to operate the fund (a practice already followed by some institutions); (6) monies that may have to be used within, say, five years should be invested in short-term obligations; (7) the bulk of the list should consist of growth stocks, save for some bonds held as a reserve against periods of distress; (8) a certain percentage of market value should be moved over to income each year.

The high yields on bonds, especially in 1969–1971, and the 1964–1971 generally flat secular price record of common stocks have, however, cast considerable doubt on the feasibility of the growth stock approach, except over the very long run. The 1960s and early 1970s have not produced the eight or nine per cent overall return from stock that had been achieved in previous long periods, and early 1973, with Aa corporate bonds yielding 7½ per cent, and income stocks from 5 to 7 per cent, aggressive portfolio management that emphasized growth stocks had, at least temporarily, lost some of its validity.

An interesting development in college and university finance has been the growing investment of endowment funds in income-producing real estate, including property leased on long terms. This reflects efforts to increase the rate of return in the face of rising costs. Another development in very recent years is the establishment of common pools in which endowments of small size are commingled, under the management of professionals, to achieve better performance.

---

[6]The last comprehensive study of college endowment funds showed, for 1969, that of a total of $7.6 billions (market value) held by seventy-one institutions, common stocks comprised 60 per cent and bonds 21 per cent. But within the group, the percentage of funds allocated for common stocks ranged from 33 to 80 per cent. The cash yield ranged from 2.44 to 5.85 per cent. See *A Study of College and University Endowment Funds, 1969* (Boston: Boston Fund, 1970).

[7]The Ford Foundation Advisory Committee on Endowment Management, *Managing Educational Endowments* (New York: The Foundation, 1969).

In the administration of their security portfolios, some institutions or their advisors use formula-timing plans as guides for switching from defensive to offensive securities in falling and rising markets.[8]

Very recent figures on the total market value of college and university endowment funds are not available. The estimate for 1969 was $12.8 billions, of which $5.7 billions was administered by investment advisors, $2.4 billions by banks, and the balance mainly by the institutions themselves. Of the total, common stock comprised $7.7 billions or 60 per cent.[9] This supports the figure for the larger institutions given in footnote 6.

In addition to college endowments, many thousands of nonprofit foundations are established for a variety of social, educational, and charitable activities. The assets of 5,454 funds totalled $25.2 billions in 1970.[10] The Securities and Exchange Commission found that for a sample of 29 large foundations with total assets of $8.7 billions in 1969, the ratio of common stocks to total portfolio at market value was 79 per cent—unchanged from 1964. Eighty-five per cent of the stocks were listed on the New York Stock Exchange.[11]

Investment requirements of foundations differ widely. In some cases, only the income is spent, and as this (including capital appreciation) varies through time, so does the payout in support of beneficiaries. In other cases, steady income is essential to meet commitments. In some instances, liquidity is important; in others, immediate recovery of principal is not required. The degree of risk assumed depends on purpose and management philosophy.

Life Insurance Company Investments

Scope of the industry. The life insurance company is the most important single type of savings institution. At the end of 1971, the domestic legal-reserve life companies had combined assets of $222 billions. The growth of the life insurance company group is indicated in Table 23-2.

At the end of 1971, life insurance companies owned .9 per cent of the Federal debt, 2.3 per cent of domestic state and municipal bonds, 35 per cent of the corporate bonds outstanding, and 15 per cent of all mortgages outstanding. Their assets are currently growing at the rate of $15 billions per year.

At the beginning of 1972, 51 per cent of the life insurance in force was accounted for by mutual companies, companies owned by the policyholders and managed by directors elected by them. The balance is outstanding from

[8]See Lucile Wessman, *Practical Formulas for Successful Investing* (New York: Willard Funk, Inc., 1955).

[9]*Institutional Investor Study Report of the S.E.C.*, op. cit., Chapter VIII. The New York Stock Exchange estimates that in 1971 endowments held $7.1 billions of stocks listed on the Exchange. New York Stock Exchange, *1971 Fact Book*, p. 50.

The National Bureau of Economic Research has estimated that endowment portfolios grew from $3.3 billions in 1953 to $11.1 billions in 1966, with common stocks growing from $1.5 to $6.1 billions. *Institutional Investor Study Report of the S.E.C.*, Supplementary Volume I, p. 372.

[10]The Foundation Center, *The Foundation Directory*, 4th ed. (New York: Russell Sage Foundation, 1971), p. 15.

[11]*Institutional Investor Study Report of the S.E.C.*, op. cit., Chapter VIII. See this source (pp. 1246–1284) for a detailed study of the investment practices of the sample foundations.

Table 23-2. SELECTED DATA ON LIFE INSURANCE COMPANIES
(in millions of dollars)

Year Ending	Total Assets	Policy Reserves	Total Income	Life Insurance in Force in U.S.
1940	$ 30,802	$ 27,238	$ 5,658	$ 115,530
1945	44,797	38,667	7,674	151,762
1950	64,020	54,946	11,337	234,168
1955	90,432	75,359	16,544	372,332
1960	119,576	98,473	23,007	586,448
1965	158,884	127,620	33,167	900,554
1971	222,102	179,250	54,202	1,621,768

SOURCE: Institute of Life Insurance, *Fact Book* (annual).

stock companies operated for their owners like other corporations. Most of the insurance sold by mutuals is of the participating type in which the policyholders share in the net earnings of the company through rebates or "dividends."

Sources of funds for investment. The funds available for investment by life insurance companies are derived from three principal sources: (1) premium income over and above that portion allocated to cover expenses and current payments on policies, (2) net income from the existing investment portfolio, and (3) maturing principal of mortgages, term loans, and bonds. Total cash flow for investment purposes runs over $20 billions annually.

As indicated in Chapter 3, most life insurance policies require an annual premium that is more than sufficient in the earlier years to meet death losses, and the excess is represented by a policy reserve to cover claims in later years when the annual premium is insufficient. This reserve is accumulated at a rate of interest specified in the insurance contract. The investment problem is to earn this rate, maintain sufficient liquidity to meet death claims and withdrawal or borrowing of the reserve, and produce a surplus. If the actual rate earned falls below the assumed or guaranteed rate, the company must make up the difference by savings in operating costs or mortality experience, or else increase the premium rates on new contracts. If the premium payments plus the income on investments exceeds death claims and expenses and the necessary additions to reserves, a surplus arises which may be distributed to the holders of participating policies or to the stockholders, in the case of stock companies.

Factors determining investment policy. The nature of the life insurance business permits a conservative yet somewhat flexible investment policy determined by the following factors: (1) The liabilities are essentially long-term, thus permitting investment in longer-term, less marketable issues with attractive rates of return; (2) steady cash flow from premium payments based on actuarial calculations, investment income, and redemption of securities and mortgages provides liquidity adequate for death claims and for emergency needs arising from a sudden demand for policy loans; (3) the premium rates assume a moderate rate of return on investments, so any pressure to obtain yields higher than those provided by high-grade securities is eliminated; (4) the ultimate safety required for the protection of policyholders requires investments that meet high standards; diversification is also a means of protecting against losses of principal; (5) actuarial commitments require the companies to remain fully invested save for working cash balances; (6) since contracts are in terms of dollars, inflation hedging through investments is unnecessary, save to offset higher operating costs; (7) strict rules of valuation of assets and regulation of permitted assets must be observed.

Investment restrictions. The public interest with which life insurance companies are vested, arising from their commitments to millions of policyholders and their role as savings institutions, requires strict regulation of operations in general and of investment policies in particular. The companies operate under fifty state charters and are regulated by the insurance commissioners of the various states in which they do business. In addition, the character of their investments is set forth by state statute. Companies that operate on a national scale must comply, to some extent, with the investment laws of all states in which they operate. Thus, the requirements of the most stringent of these states determines the level of investment quality for the particular company. State regulation varies considerably, but the general pattern runs as follows: (1) Federal and state government obligations are approved without limit as to the proportion of total assets that may be so invested; (2) bonds of municipalities in the state of domicile, and bonds of subdivisions in other states, must meet certain qualifications; (3) corporate bonds, debentures, and direct business loans are restricted to the higher-grade issues—limitations are imposed with respect to the percentage of total assets so invested, as well as requirements for adequate earnings in relation to fixed charges; (4) first mortgages are generally approved, subject to certain limitations on the amount lent in relation to the value of the real estate mortgaged (from 60 to 80 per cent); (5) common and preferred stocks are prohibited in a few states, and where permitted, are restricted to a small percentage of total assets, and strict asset and earnings standards are required; (6) investment in real estate, other than company-used property, is generally restricted, although in recent years most states have permitted investment in rental housing and redevelopment projects and certain types of commercial and industrial property up to a modest percentage of total assets; (7) loans to policyholders equal to the reserve value of their respective policies are authorized in every jurisdiction.

Return on investments. Such provisions would appear to give life insurance companies sufficient flexibility and scope in their investment policy without any need to depart from the traditional forms of securities and other investment media. Although in recent years the earnings rate produced on investments has tended to increase, following closely the interest rates on U.S. Government securities and high-grade corporate bonds, it is still modest. The net rate of return earned by U.S. life insurance investments on their

Table 23-3. NET RATE OF RETURN ON ASSETS INVESTED BY LIFE INSURANCE COMPANIES

1930	5.05%	1955	3.51%
1935	3.70	1960	4.11
1940	3.45	1965	4.61
1945	3.11	1970	5.30
1950	3.13	1971	5.44

SOURCE: Institute of Life Insurance, *Life Insurance Fact Book*. Beginning in 1940, the rates are before Federal income taxes.

aggregate mean ledger assets is shown in Table 23-3. To bolster their net investment earnings that fell below 3 per cent (after taxes) in 1946–1948, the companies reduced the interest rate "guaranteed" in new policies, in some cases to as low as 2½ to 3 per cent, and sought new forms of investment within the framework of changing regulations. In more recent years the assumed interest rates in new policies have increased modestly. But they are still considerably below the average rate of return actually earned on operating assets, with resulting benefit to policyholders receiving "dividends" and to stockholders in stock companies, and as an offset to higher operating costs.

Investment policy. An examination of the assets of domestic life insurance companies indicates some significant changes in investment policy. Table 23-4 shows the percentage breakdown of the assets of legal-reserve companies at the end of 1950, 1960, and 1971.

Table 23-4. ASSETS OF LEGAL-RESERVE COMPANIES
(in billions of dollars)

Assets	1950 Amt.	Per Cent	1960 Amt.	Per Cent	1971 Amt.	Per Cent
Bonds						
U.S. Govt. and agency	$13.5	21.0%	$ 6.5	5.4%	$ 4.4	2.0%
Domestic municipal	1.2	1.8	3.6	3.0	3.4	1.5
Foreign government	1.4	2.3	1.4	1.2	3.2	1.4
Corporate						
Railroad	3.2	5.0	3.7	3.1	} 79.2	35.7
Utility	10.6	16.5	16.7	14.0		
Industrial and misc.	9.5	14.9	26.6	22.3		
Total bonds	$39.4	61.5%	$ 58.5	48.9%	$ 90.2	40.6%
Mortgages						
Farm	1.3	2.0	3.0	2.4	5.6	2.5
Residential	11.1	17.3	28.8	24.2	41.2	18.5
Commercial and other	3.7	5.8	10.0	8.4	28.8	13.0
Total mortgages	$16.1	25.1%	$ 41.8	35.0%	$ 75.6	34.0%
Preferred stocks	1.5	2.2	1.8	1.5	3.8	1.7
Common stocks	.6	1.0	3.2	2.7	16.8	7.6
Real estate	1.4	2.3	3.8	3.1	6.9	3.1
Policy loans	2.4	3.8	5.2	4.3	17.1	7.7
Cash and misc.	2.6	4.1	5.3	4.4	11.7	5.3
Total assets	$64.0	100.0%	$119.6	100.0%	$222.1	100.0%

SOURCE: Institute of Life Insurance, *Life Insurance Fact Book* (annual).

At the end of 1945, the investment in Federal securities totalled over $20 billions or nearly 46 per cent of total assets. Life insurance companies subsequently reduced their holdings very substantially in order to provide more funds for business capital and mortgage financing and to improve their rate of earnings. At the end of 1971, the holdings of direct and agencies securities totalling $4.4 billions represented only 2.0 per cent of life insurance company assets. The emphasis is on intermediate- and long-term maturities.

Holdings of domestic state and local government bonds have actually declined since 1960, and at the end of 1971 comprised only 1.5 per cent of total assets. With the increase in taxable bond yields, tax-free municipals have become less attractive to the insurance companies paying income taxes at only about a 25 per cent rate. Nearly three-fourths of the domestic municipals held by life insurance companies are revenue bonds; these offer very attractive yields and generally long maturities. Canadian local and provincial bonds have become very attractive in recent years, owing to their high yields.

Railroad bonds form a smaller portion of life insurance company investments than at any time since the 1880s. Around 1900, they were the largest single type of investments held, and in the mid-1920s, they amounted to one-fifth of total assets. The depression of the 1930s, with its cruel effects on the railroad industry, caused a shift away from the rail group; the holdings of rail bonds increased somewhat through 1955, but have since declined to $3.6 billions in 1969, when they represented only 1.8 per cent of total assets.[12] However, because railroads have been systematically reducing their funded debt, the insurance companies' share of this debt has actually increased.

Holdings of public utility bonds grew to $1.8 billions or over 9 per cent of total assets at the end of 1969, of which about one-half were electric light and power, about one-quarter gas and gas pipeline, and one-fifth communications. The large investment in utility bonds reflects the postwar expansion of the utilities industries, and the high investment status of utility bonds. This group has, however, declined in relative importance owing to even greater emphasis on industrial securities. Furthermore, most high-grade utility bonds · are sold through competitive bidding in which insurance companies seldom participate.

The industrial bond group has shown a great absolute and relative increase; at the end of 1969, $50 billions in this category represented 2.5 per cent of total assets. This reflects the great postwar industrial expansion and the substantial upgrading of investment quality enjoyed by manufacturing and commercial companies, and expansion of legal lists to include debts of industrial concerns that meet rather stringent earnings requirements. Life insurance companies acquire the bulk of such securities by direct placement. (See Chapter 15.)

The industrial bond category includes instruments that are not bonds in the technical sense. These are long-term notes representing direct lending, similar to, but with longer maturities than, bank term loans. Such financing permits the "tailoring" of loan arrangements to suit each particular situation, and provides a vehicle for financing smaller concerns who do not have access to the bond market.

Real estate mortgages have always formed a significant segment of life

[12]The recent *Life Insurance Fact Books* do not show the major categories of corporate bonds.

insurance company investments, but their relative importance has changed greatly over the years. The experience in the depression years of the 1930s and the lack of marketability of mortgages, together with the appeal of corporate bonds, reduced mortgages from the most important single type of investment to one of only substantial proportions. The low point was reached in 1946, when they accounted for less than 15 per cent of total assets. Since that year, the great expansion in housing and the more attractive yields on mortgages brought these investments to a record high in 1971. At the end of that year, life insurance companies were second only to savings and loan associations and commercial banks in their holdings of mortgages on one- to four-family residences ($24.6 billions or 8 per cent of the national total), and they held $5.6 billions or 17 per cent of total farm mortgages. The $75.6-billions total of all mortgages represented 34.0 per cent of their total assets. High-grade mortgages are attractive to insurance companies because of their relatively attractive yields, their general ultimate safety, their long maturities, the constant of turnover of principal through regular amortization, the variety of types available, and the use of mortgage company correspondents to effect geographical diversification.[13]

Real estate investments include property used in operations, and, with rather strict legal limits, property held for income. Of particular interest is the ownership of commercial and industrial properties leased back to their users. The net return on such investments may run as high as 10 per cent. Life companies have also pioneered in construction and operation of large-scale housing projects.

Policy loans reach their highest levels during depressions, when they serve a useful purpose in helping to tide policyholders over periods of stress. They reached a peak of $3.8 billions, or 18.2 per cent of total assets, at the end of 1932, and fell to $2.0 billions in 1945. That they do not vanish entirely in good times is indicated by the $17.1 billions outstanding at the end of 1971, reflecting the need for funds by policyholders in periods of tight money and high interest rates.

Preferred stocks, which totalled $3.8 billions or 1.7 per cent of total assets at the end of 1971, are attractive for their high tax-free yields. (See Chapter 8.)

A notable development in recent years has been the increase in life company holdings of common stocks, which totalled $16.8 billions or 7.6 per cent of industry assets at the end of 1971. Most states now permit the purchase of common stock by life insurance companies, up to as high as 10 per cent of total assets. But even in those states such as New York and Pennsylvania, where common stock purchase is permitted, management has been somewhat reluctant to change from its conservative attitude to take the greater risks involved in equities.

In 1951 and 1957, the New York State insurance law was amended to permit insurance companies domiciled in that state to make limited investments in common stocks. New York companies are allowed common stock investments up to 10 per cent of admitted assets, or 100 per cent of surplus, whichever is the smaller. Since surplus is usually less than 10 per cent of

---

[13]See Chapter 11 for additional discussion of mortgage loans by insurance companies.

assets, the legal limit is provided by the surplus for most companies. Holdings of the common stock of any one corporation are limited to one per cent of the life insurance company's assets and 5 per cent of the issuing corporation's outstanding stock. To be eligible for insurance company investment, the stock must meet the following requirements: (1) The stock—except bank and insurance company shares—must be listed on an exchange registered with the Securities and Exchange Commission; (2) dividends must have been paid for seven years prior to acquisition, and the company must have earned during such period an average annual rate of 4 per cent of par or of the issue price; (3) all of the bonds and preferred stock, if any, of the issuer must be eligible for insurance company investment.

The change in the New York law opened up a large potential market for qualified securities for New York companies and for out-of-state companies doing business in New York. The increase in common stock investments has been substantial, although some companies are unwilling to expend very for into the common stock field.

Much of the original appeal of common stocks grew from the need for a higher rate of return than bonds could earn, rather than for an inflation hedge. Modern stock yields are now, however, lower than those on bonds. An even greater problem is the need for adequate outlets for the vast sums being accumulated by the insurance companies. In each year, between $10 and $11 billions of new money needs to be invested, together with $10 to $11 billions of funds from maturing assets. What shall be done with this money? High-grade corporate bonds are appropriate in character, and now yield a return substantially above that on Federal obligations. There are not always enough of these obligations, however, together with mortgages, to soak up the insurance funds seeking investment. Loans to business and investment in housing projects and commercial income-producing real estate offer high yields, but the managerial costs are high. The vast supply of common stocks appears to offer additional intriguing possibilities for insurance investment.

Against this point of view are the arguments that (1) the amount and timing of dividends are uncertain, whereas the companies must accumulate their policy reserves on the assumption of a "guaranteed" rate of interest; (2) common stocks are subject to wide price swings that would impair the reserves of the companies in depressed markets,[14] (3) the obligations of insurance companies are in fixed-dollar amounts and so they do not need to invest in common stocks as an inflation-hedging device; (4) current dividend yields on good stocks are low. Such arguments will probably continue to be debatable. Net acquisitions of common stocks are now (1972) running at about $2 billions per year.

A special influence that led to increases in commercial and industrial mortgages, and to substantial investments in common stocks, was the high

---

[14]Common stocks are valued for reporting purposes at market price as of December 31. Government securities, as well as corporate bonds (if they are not in default), are carried on an amortized basis (adjusted each year so as to produce face value at maturity). For a detailed study of investment organization and portfolio management practices of life insurance companies with emphasis on their holdings of common stock, see *Institutional Investor Study Report of the S.E.C., op cit.*, Chapter VI.

level of yields on residential mortgages in 1969–1970; such yields bumped into state usury limits. To earn, say, 9 to 10 per cent, special "kickers," such as a share of profits, warrants, and others, were attached to commercial and industrial liens.

Summary of investment requirements. Eventual recovery of principal, adequate yield, and only moderate liquidity are the keynotes of life insurance investment policy. Skilled management can be employed, and wide diversification enjoyed. Tax savings are important, but state and municipal bonds are bought for their own merits as well as for their tax-exempt income. Legality is of prime importance. But since the obligations of the life insurance company are in terms of a definite number of dollars, a hedge against inflation is not necessary, save in the attempt to offset higher operating costs with higher income.

Uninsured Private Pension Funds

Investment policy.   The great growth of corporate and other private pension funds, now at a rate of $9 to $10 billions a year, was discussed in Chapter 3. At the end of 1971, $125 billions in market value of assets or reserves had been accumulated, in contrast to the $7 billions in 1950.

The investments of insured funds are commingled with those of insurance company resources in general. The assets of uninsured private funds (including profit-sharing plans) were distributed in the postwar period as shown in Table 23-5. The figures are for all private funds including multiemployer plans and those of nonprofit organizations.

The group figures hide differences in investment policy among individual funds. But taking the group as a whole, the shift into common stocks has been marked. At the end of 1971, these comprised 68 per cent at market value, of total assets. Liquidity, as represented by cash and Government

Table 23-5. ASSETS OF UNINSURED PRIVATE PENSION FUNDS[a]
(in billions of dollars, at market value)

	1950	1960		1965	1971	
	Amt.	Amt.	Per Cent	Amt.	Amt.	Per Cent
Cash	$ .3	$ .5	1.4%	$ .9	$ 1.6	1.3
U.S. Govt. and agency securities	2.0	3.1	8.4	3.6	3.0	2.4
Corporate bonds	2.8	14.2	38.3	21.2	25.9	20.7
Preferred stocks	.3	.7	1.9	.8	2.0	1.6
Common stocks	.8	15.8	42.6	40.0	84.8	67.9
(Own company)		(2.0)	(5.4)	(4.4)	(7.6)	(6.1)
(Other companies)		(13.8)	(37.2)	(35.6)	(77.2)	(61.8)
Mortgages	.1	1.3	3.5	3.4	3.2	2.5
Other assets	.4	1.4	3.8	3.0	4.5	3.6
Total	$6.7	$37.1	100.0%	$72.9	$125.0	100.0%

[a]Data may not add due to rounding.

SOURCES: *Federal Reserve Bulletin;* S.E.C. *Statistical Bulletin.*

securities, has declined in relative importance, as have corporate bonds, although the latter remain important. Mortgages are becoming attractive for their higher yields.

The return earned on the assets of a pension fund is of prime importance. In 1971 the average rate of return on uninsured funds in total was 3.6 per cent. But after realized profits on sale of assets, the return became 4.4 per cent. Certainly, change in market value of the portfolio has become much more important than current income insofar as eventual contribution to employee benefits is concerned. The generally upward trend of interest rates on corporate bonds has been offset by an increasing investment in the lower-yielding common stocks.

Investment principles. Uninsured (trusteed) corporate and other private pension funds differ in size, type of management, whether they produce a fixed actuarial benefit, the proportions of company and employee contributions, whether they include profit-sharing benefits, and in many other respects. Thus it is difficult to generalize concerning their investment policies. But the following discussion of investment requirements will apply to a majority of the funds. The funds are usually in the hands of trustees and are invested within the framework of trust investment regulation; however, since the trust agreements usually provide for discretion, and since the prudent man rule is in effect in the more important states, a wide latitude in policy is permitted. Many pension portfolios are managed by investment counsel firms, which sometimes share the fund and compete for the best performance.

1. Assurance of income is of paramount importance. The reserves accumulated over the years are expected to grow through the compounding of income as well as through increased contributions. Where the benefits are computed actuarially as definite liabilities, certainty of income is especially vital. At the same time, yield should be maximized within the boundaries of sensible investments. A difference of one percentage point in average yield (say, an increase from 3 to 4 per cent) can mean a difference of 25 per cent in the size of the eventual accumulation or a reduction in corporate contributions. With the greater emphasis on common stocks in recent years, even a 4 per cent return requires the inclusion of gain in market value in the concept of total return. Thus, benefits that are based on an actuarial rate of return on assets are vulnerable to short-run declines in the market value of portfolio assets.

2. Preservation of principal, or the avoidance of dollar loss, is of course important in the long run. But temporary variations in the market value of the portfolio are not. And even these can be minimized through regular dollar-cost-averaging with the new receipts into the fund.

3. Immediate recovery of principal is unimportant for most funds; in most cases the payments into the fund, together with earnings and proceeds of maturing bond issues, will exceed withdrawals for many years to come. Both retirement benefits and payments are subject to forecast. There is little compulsion to liquidate sound securities in unfavorable markets. Nevertheless, estimates of retirements are required to determine those periods when some

liquidation of pension fund assets may be required, and investment policy adjusted accordingly, especially during periods of low market prices of securities.

4. Skilled management can be hired if it is not available at the company or through the trustee, in the person of investment counsel. For smaller funds, investment in mutual investment company shares can provide management for the major portion of the fund.[15]

5. Diversification is available in all but the smallest funds, and these can obtain it individually through investment company shares or even in common trust funds. In this connection a good general principle is to stay out of the stock of the company itself. The employee has enough at stake in his job in the company without tying his retirement income to the fortunes of the same firm.

6. Tax considerations are unimportant. A properly drawn pension trust, in which the employer's contribution are irrevocably beyond company ownership and are to be distributed in a nondiscriminatory manner, qualifies as a tax-exempt organization. Hence tax-exempt municipal bonds have no appeal as pension fund investments.

7. Protection against inflation is very important. This is a recognized goal of many funds, and explains much of the growing emphasis on common stocks as investments. However, such protection is not automatic and requires proper selection of growth stocks. A substantial rate of return, compounded through the years, is a better way of offsetting the rising cost of living than a haphazard investment in equities.

8. Legality is most important, both from the standpoint of conformance with state trust law and with the Internal Revenue Code.

Insured pension funds. As indicated in Chapter 3, there has been a substantial increase in pension funds placed with insurance companies. This has been the result of several factors, notably the use of "deposit administration" group contracts, including those represented by separate accounts. Investment of the latter is not restricted by the rules applying to life insurance company "general accounts," and so these reserves can be, and often are, invested 100 per cent in equities. The same is true of accounts representing "Keogh plan" and other "tax-sheltered" arrangements for individuals and small groups.

Measuring Investment Performance

Rates of return. Traditionally, corporate pension fund managers—company committees, trustees, or investment advisers—viewed investment performance over the longer term. The objectives were to compound a modest but assured rate of return, and where stocks were held, to equal and hopefully exceed the appreciation of the general market averages.

[15]For a detailed study of the investment management of a large sample of uninsured pension funds see *Institutional Investor Study Report of the S.E.C.*, op. cit., Chapter VIII.

Increasing emphasis on investment in common stocks, together with the desire to compare performance with other funds and with investment companies, however, has led to new emphasis on performance and more sophisticated methods of measuring it. These involve (1) a rate-of-return concept that includes market value change as well as current income, (2) consideration of risk as is measured by the volatility of the (total) return, and (3) the risk-reward relationship.

Calculation of the rate of return can be simple or sophisticated. Where the fund is static, a crude "internal" rate of return can be measured by the difference between ending asset value plus interest and dividends received, and beginning value, taken as a percentage of beginning value:

$$R = \frac{(V_{t+1} + I_t) - V_t}{V_t}$$

This is the same technique used in calculating the performance of mutual funds (see page 168). This method is sufficiently precise for mutual funds because per-share values are used, and any inflow (sales) or outflow (redemptions) influence per-share value throughout the period. But in endowment and pension funds that are not managed on a unit basis, the problem of intermittent and possibly large and varying contributions to the fund must be dealt with. Also, the concept of compound interest should be incorporated into the method. That is, at what rate of discount will the ending values (asset value plus income) equal the beginning value? And how does one account for the fact that new funds have been acquired at irregular intervals during the period? (New funds consist of contributions plus investment income less distributions and expenses.)

The model that denotes the "internal" or "dollar-weighted" rate of return, and incorporates money flows and the amount of assets at work during each period, is as follows:

$$V_e = V_b(1+r) + C(1+r)^j$$

That is, the value of the fund at the end of the measuring period (V_e) equals the value at the beginning of the measuring period (V_b) plus the value of net contributions (C) during the period, compounded at the rate of return. The symbol j is that fraction of the measuring period during which each portion of the net contributions is available to the fund. The measurement of rate of return can be applied to individual periods (normally quarters, half-years, and years) and to cumulative results over several years. A feasible arrangement is to assume that contributions are received quarterly.

The "internal" or "dollar-weighted" rate of return shows the average or overall growth of a fund due to investment returns, given the fund's peculiar cash flow. Since this cash flow is beyond the control of the actual manager of the fund, unless he is permitted to invest or to withhold cash, another measure of performance—that of the manager—must be used.

To derive this rate of return, the fund is valued whenever new money is received by the manager, and the return in each period that begins with the new valuation is calculated. The amount of new money and the length of the periods may be large or small. The rate of return for a given arbitrary period, say, for the fund's fiscal year or for calendar years, is then calculated by taking the geometric mean of the intermediate-period rates of return. The result is called the "time-weighted" rate of return. Only when the cash flows tend to be small in relation to the value of the fund, or where they are uniform in size and periodicity, are the "dollar-weighted" and the "time-weighted" rates of return the same. Use of the "time-weighted" rate is, of course, necessary where different funds are being compared.[16]

Risk and its measurement. Investors and professional investment managers have always been concerned with the several kinds of risks that affect values and income, and which must be appraised and dealt with in investment policy. Methods of minimizing these risks, or of obtaining satisfactory rewards for the risks that are deemed appropriate for a given program, play an important role in investment policy and management. (See Chapter 20).

The various types of investment risk—business and financial risk, money rate risk, and purchasing power risk—are reflected in the amount and stability of corporate earnings, which in turn are capitalized in the market place. Changes in market value, plus income, are combined in the total rate of return. Variation in the rate of return, then, becomes the specific definition of risk. This concept has been especially useful in pension fund management after the refined measurements of rate of return, discussed previously, were developed. Pension fund committees and fund managers turn to the variation in the time-weighted rate of return to measure risk and to appraise and compare investment results.

The degree of variability in the rate of return may be measured in different ways. One of these is to calculate the average deviation of quarterly time-weighted rates of return from the mean, or, in other words, the absolute value of the deviations from the average return, whether these be positive or negative. The following example is illustrative.

	1971 Quarterly Rates of Return		*Deviation of Quarterly Rates from Mean*
	Actual	*Annualized*	
First quarter	+6.5%	+26%	26 − 4 = 22
2nd quarter	−5.0	−20	20 − 4 = 16
3rd quarter	0	0	0 − 4 = 4
4th quarter	+2.5	+10	10 − 4 = 6
Sum		+16%	48
Mean		+ 4%	12

In the above illustration the fund had an average quarterly return of 4 per cent in 1971 and an average variation of 12 per cent about that average. Another fund with a 4 per cent rate of return but with a mean absolute deviation of 24 per cent would be considered as having shown twice the risk. The goal of fund management is to maximize the return from a port-

---

[16]The pioneer work that emphasized these refined rates of return was done by the Bank Administration Institute. See References, end of this chapter.

folio that is permitted a certain level of risk, or, conversely, to minimize the risk that is permitted a portfolio designed to produce a certain rate of return. It is widely accepted that, over the long run, risk and return are positively correlated.

Relative performance. Committees in charge of pension fund management like to make regular comparisons of the performance of their fund(s) with that of other funds, taking into account the general differences in the funds and the degree of risk assumed. There are services that provide such information. But the question almost always arises (rightly or wrongly) "how have we done in comparison with the market as a whole?" Fund managers are expected to outperform the market regardless of the objectives of the fund, and regardless of the fact that they all cannot do so.

The "beta" concept (shown on next page) is used to determine the action of a particular fund (and of individual securities). "Beta" is the average rate of change in rate of return relative to that of the general market. It is obtained by plotting the rates of return in a series of periods for a fund (or for individual securities) on the vertical axis Y, in relation to the rates of return for stocks representing the market (ordinarily the Standard & Poor's 500) for the same periods, on the horizontal axis X. Then a line of best fit is drawn to indicate the relationship of the two variables. The slope of this line is the "beta volatility coefficient." The line can be drawn by sight but for greater precision a regression line is used, based on the equation $Y = \alpha + \beta X$. Y is the dependent variable.

Beta quantifies the change in the fund's rate of return that was experienced in the past, and can be expected in the future, from a series of general market changes. A beta of 1.00 is assigned to the general market movements. The closer the individual stock or fund moves in relation to the market, the closer its "beta" is to 1.00. The further away, the greater the degree of variation of its rate of return from that of the general market. For example, a beta of 1.50 would mean a (past) movement one and a half times as great, on average, as that of the general market. Translated into expectations for the future, the portfolio with a beta of 1.50 will be expected, for example, to increase or decrease $7\frac{1}{2}$ per cent, on average, with a 5 per cent change in the general market. A beta of .50 should show a variation of only one-half (and therefore, risk of only one-half) that of the general market. If beta is 1.0, market and fund return are expected to be equally volatile.

This approach enables a pension committee to first decide in quantitative terms what risk it is willing to take, then to select investments accordingly, to measure the actual results, and to make comparisons with other funds where the data is available. Certain investment services provide "betas" for a wide list of stocks.[17]

"Beta" does not represent *total* risk, but only the market-related portion. If beta is 1.0, market return and fund return are equally volatile, and any

[17] A refinement of the beta technique is to calculate how much variation from its average change during a period a stock (or a portfolio) may have, using the standard deviation as the measure. Two securities or two portfolios may, for example, both have a beta of 2.0 and an average change in value of say plus ten per cent, during a series of periods. But if one stock has a 5 per cent standard deviation and the other an 8 per cent, the former is less likely to vary from its average performance.

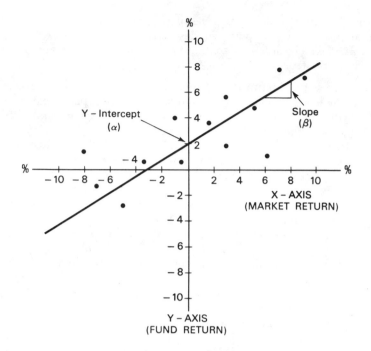

difference in return is attributable to the fund's own characteristics, that is, to the fund management. The difference between the fund's return (Y) and the risk-adjusted market return (β times X) is alpha ($\alpha = Y - \beta X$). On the preceding diagram, alpha is the point at which the sloped line intercepts the Y axis. Alpha represents the extra influence exerted by the fund management over and above mere co-movement with the market.

Another method of comparing fund management with the market uses "excess return" as a measure of performance. It is computed by mixing appropriate portions of "risk-free" assets (such as Treasury bills) and assets presumed to be invested in the general market (say as measured by the Standard & Poor's 500 stock index). The proportions are selected so as to produce the same beta coefficient as historically shown by the actual portfolio being measured. For each subsequent time period, comparison of the real and the imaginary ("standard") portfolios shows whether actual management performance, after adjustment for volatility, was better or worse, on average, than that of the unmanaged portfolios. For example, if the average period change for the real portfolio were .10 per cent and the imaginary portfolio with equivalent volatility (beta) had an average of .42 per cent, the "alpha", as calculated in the manner described, would be minus .32 per cent.[18]

---

[18]In its recent study the Securities and Exchange Commission recommends the use of such a measure of performance, and suggests that the results of institutional managers be disclosed. The Commission actually applied it to mutual investment companies, separate pension accounts of life insurance companies, and bank commingled trust funds. *Institutional Investor Study Report of the S.E.C., op. cit.,* Chapters IV, V, and VI.

The use of the alpha-beta approach forces pension committees, as well as portfolio managers having discretion, to adopt a specific standard of risk and return, and to run the fund accordingly. It can be a useful tool in after-the-fact analysis and in policymaking. But the approach has its limitations. It is based on past performance, and future performance is not likely to be the same. Many funds would be advised to aim for something short of the maximum return so as to avoid vulnerability to larger variations in the future value of the fund than have occurred in selected periods in the past. A more basic criticism is that the approach overemphasizes the importance of market value change. In a growing pension fund considerable variation in market values can be absorbed. Possibly more important than temporary changes in value are the risks of changes in the basic quality and in the marketability of the securities that comprise the portfolio. In any event, the pension committee must have a clear concept of the purpose of the fund; the need for safety of principal; the importance of current income; the projected growth of the fund; the timing and size of contributions and withdrawals; the degree of liquidity required; the level of risk that should be assumed; the need to meet actuarial requirements; and other features that are peculiar to a particular fund.

Many pension fund committees employ securities houses to provide information on the comparative performance of funds classified by size and portfolio mix. Some of these services use simple, others use sophisticated measurements. The houses are compensated with brokerage business. A criticism of the use of such services is that they emphasize short-run results. This in turn leads to the temptation to invest in high-flying investments. The managers of most pension funds should, theoretically at least, take a long-run point of view. The real basic test of portfolio management is whether the management meets its *own* investment objectives within the degree of risk deemed appropriate to the situation.

"Efficient" portfolios. In recent years much attention has been given to portfolio diversification on a quantitative basis. That is to say, how can the portfolio mix be so selected as to produce the most "efficient" portfolio? The efficient portfolio either (1) maximizes the expected return at a given (and acceptable) level of expected risk or (2) minimizes the expected risk at any acceptable rate of expected return. The concept involves *expected* return and risk because the portfolio manager makes his decisions on the basis of estimates of the future.

The concepts of rate of return and risk discussed in the previous sections are basic in constructing the efficient portfolio. As we have seen, rate of return is measured by change in value, plus any distributions in a particular period, and risk is measured by the volatility of rate of return. The degree of risk is the extent to which the actual (weighted average) rate of return is likely to differ from its expected level; the variance is measured by the standard deviation of expected variations around the expected return. The higher the standard deviation, the greater are the probabilities that the rate of return will in fact not be achieved. The risk on a Treasury bill is very low. That of a speculative stock can be very high. The efficient portfolio combines selected assets so as to produce the desired combination of risk and return.

In the case of stocks, variations in the rate of return are, under present conditions, chiefly the result of changes in market value. There are two types of change: (1) "systematic" variations in general market prices; (2) "unsystematic" or independent changes associated with the portfolio itself. If a portfolio were to consist of all stocks in the market, the second type of risk would be zero. A very widely diversified portfolio would have almost the same result. If a portfolio consisted of a few stocks, the independent risk could be very high, but rate of return could likewise be high.

Wide diversification lowers the "unsystematic" risk. But diversification can be over done, even when low risk is desired. A relatively small list can involve relatively low risk and produce an acceptable rate of return if the components are carefully selected. The problem here is to avoid "correlated" securities—those that can be expected to act alike, such as those in the same industry, or those which have the same characteristics, such as the same cyclical pattern. Under a cautious policy, risk could be reduced below the systematic level, but the manager would wish not to reduce the return in the same proportion. Under an aggressive policy, the manager would be willing to assume possibly high risk, but would wish to be compensated with a return that is even higher in proportion.

All this means that each portfolio manager has a very wide array of possible portfolios, from which he is to select the one expected to bear an acceptable rate of return but which has the least risk exposure at that rate. Consider the following attainable portfolios.

Portfolio	Expected Rate of Return Percentage	Expected Risk (Standard Deviation)
A	12	5
B	16	14
C	6	3
D	9	4
E	5	4
F	6	10
G	12	14
H	12	10
I	16	15
J	9	7

A, B, C, and D are the efficient portfolios because they offer the highest expected returns at particular levels of risk. No one would consider E. A is better than H and G. B is better than I. C is better than F. D is better than J. The choice among A, B, C, and D would depend on a number of factors in the particular fund situation.

Markowitz pioneered in developing the "efficient portfolio" concept.[19] Others have refined the technique. A number of decisions are necessary, not the least of which is the choice of the period during which past risk and return are deemed to be portents of the future. Few individual investors have access to the mass of statistics relating to hundreds of securities, the computer equipment, or the skill in programming, that are necessary to produce the most efficient funds. Institutional investors have these resources, and may adopt the approach if they approve its basic assumptions.

State and Local Government Retirement Plans

The emphasis that has been placed, in investment circles, on corporate and other private pension plans should not obscure the importance of those operated for the employees of state and local governments. At the end of 1970, about 2,100 such plans were in effect, covering some 8½ million persons.[20] The recent annual rate of growth of assets is $4 to $7 billions, so that total assets at the end of 1971 were about $65 billions (at book value).[21] Table 23-6 shows the composition of the assets of state and local funds for selected recent years, at book value.

The relative investment in Federal government securities has steadily declined, as has that in state and local government bonds. The latter are inappropriate in funds whose income is free from both Federal and state income taxes; they are owned presumably to meet archaic statutory requirements. Corporate bonds have become the biggest single assets, accounting for 56 per cent at the end of 1971. In over twenty states, common stocks are now eligible, in recognition of the need for inflation hedging and for long-term growth. Mortgage investments are growing rapidly with the search for higher yields and the increase in available funds.

The investment requirements of such funds are similar to those of corporate pension funds, except that statutory restrictions curtail somewhat the

Table 23-6. ASSETS OF STATE AND LOCAL GOVERNMENT RETIREMENT PLANS

(in billions of dollars)

	1950	1960	1965	1971	
	Amt.	*Amt.*	*Amt.*	*Amt.*	*Per Cent*
Cash	$ .1	$ .2	$ .3	$ .5	.8%
U.S. Govt. and agency securities	2.5	5.9	7.8	6.0	9.3
State and local government bonds	1.5	4.4	2.6	1.9	3.0
Corporate bonds	.6	6.7	16.3	36.2	55.8
Corporate stocks	—	.4	1.6	11.2	17.1
Mortgages	.1	1.5	3.7	7.1	11.0
Other assets	.2	.5	.8	2.0	3.0
Total	$5.0	$19.6	$33.1	$64.8	100.0%

SOURCES: U.S. Department of Commerce, Bureau of the Census, *Finances of Employee-Retirement Systems of State and Local Governments* (annual); *Federal Reserve Bulletin; S.E.C. Statistical Bulletin.*

[19]H. M. Markovitz, *Portfolio Selection: Efficient Diversification of Investments.* New York: John Wiley & Sons, Inc., 1959.

[20]See Chapter 3.

[21]S.E.C. *Statistical Bulletin,* July 1972, p. 24.

purchase of equities and encourage government and corporate bond holdings. But there are signs that equities will play an increasingly important role. The share of annual cash flows devoted to stocks has been rising steadily as equities are made legal in an increasing number of states and as previous limits on common stock investment, now usually 30 per cent of portfolio when permitted at all, are raised. In 1969, Oregon pioneered in allowing outside professional managers to handle a portion of the equity funds.

Federal Retirement Funds

The Federal government collects receipts and disburses payments from a variety of trust funds which support Federal pension plans. The most important of these are the Railroad Retirement Fund (administered by the Treasury), Federal Employees' Retirement Fund (Civil Service), and Disability Trust Fund. The income of the funds is derived from taxes (including individual and employer contributions), premiums, and investment income. Net receipts after payments are entirely invested in Federal securities, with emphasis on special nonmarketable issues. At the end of 1971, the funds held $37 billions of Government bonds, or about 9 per cent of total Government debt then outstanding (see also Chapter 3). In addition, the Federal Old Age and Survivors Insurance Fund (Social Security) had reserves totalling $34 billions.

REFERENCES

AMERICAN BANKERS ASSOCIATION, *Proceedings, Seminar on Fiduciary Responsibility.* Washington, D. C.: The Association, 1970.

BANKERS TRUST COMPANY, *1971 Study of Industrial Retirement Plans.* New York: Bankers Trust Company, 1971.

BOSTON FUND, *The 1969 Study of College and University Endowment Funds.* Boston: The Fund, 1970.

BREALEY, R. A., *An Introduction to Risk and Return for Common Stocks.* Cambridge, Mass.: M.I.T. Press, 1969.

BRIMMER, A. F., *Life Insurance Companies in the Capital Market.* East Lansing, Mich.: Bureau of Business and Economic Research, Graduate School of Business Administration, Michigan State University, 1962.

CARY, W. L., AND C. B. BRIGHT, *The Law and the Lore of Endowment Funds.* New York: The Ford Foundation, 1969.

COHEN, K. J., et al., *Measuring the Performance of Pension Funds for the Purpose of Inter-Fund Comparison.* Park Ridge, Ill.: Bank Administration Institute, 1968.

COOKE, G. W., et al., *Financial Institutions: Their Role in the American Economy.* New York: Simmons-Boardman Publishing Corp., 1962.

DIETZ, P. O., *Pension Funds: Measuring Investment Performance.* New York: The Free Press, 1966.

DOUGALL, H. E., *Capital Markets and Institutions*, 2nd ed. Englewood Cliffs, N.J.: Prentice-Hall, Inc., 1970.

ELLIS, C. D., *Institutional Investing*. Homewood, Ill.: Dow Jones-Irwin, 1971.

FEDERAL TRUST FUNDS, *Budgetary and Other Implications*. New York: Tax Foundation, Inc., 1970.

FRANCIS, J. C., *Investments: Analysis and Management*. New York: McGraw-Hill, Inc., 1972.

FRIEND, IRWIN, et al., *Private Capital Markets*, research studies prepared for the Commission on Money and Credit. Englewood Cliffs, N.J.: Prentice-Hall, Inc., 1964.

GARDNER, E. B., ed., *Pension Fund Investment Management*. Proceedings, CFA Research Seminar, 1968. CFA Monograph Series, No. 3. Homewood, Ill.: Richard A. Irwin, Inc., 1969.

GOLDSMITH, R. W., *Financial Institutions*. New York: Random House, Inc., 1968.

HORVITZ, P. M., et. al., *Private Financial Institutions*, research studies prepared for the Commission on Money and Credit. Englewood Cliffs, N.J.: Prentice-Hall, Inc., 1963.

INSTITUTIONAL INVESTOR STUDY REPORT of the Securities and Exchange Commission, Chapters V, VI, VIII, and Supplementary Volume No. 1, Chapters 2, 5. 92nd Congress, 1st Session, House Document No. 92–64. Washington, D.C.: U.S. Government Printing Office, 1971.

JACOBS, D. P., et al., *Financial Institutions*, 5th ed. Homewood, Ill.: Richard D. Irwin, Inc., 1972.

JONES, L. D., *Investment Policies of Life Insurance Companies*. Boston: Division of Research, Graduate School of Business, Harvard University, 1968.

LIFE INSURANCE ASSOCIATION OF AMERICA, *Life Insurance Companies as Financial Institutions*, a monograph prepared for the Commission on Money and Credit. Englewood Cliffs, N.J.: Prentice-Hall, Inc., 1962.

LORING, A. P., *A Trustee's Handbook*, J. F. Farr, rev., 6th ed., Chapter 8. Boston: Little, Brown & Company, 1962.

LUDTKE, J. B., *The American Financial System; Markets and Institutions*, 2nd ed. Boston: Allyn and Bacon, Inc., 1967.

McDIARMID, F. J., *Investing for a Financial Institution*. New York: Life Office Management Association, 1961.

McGILL, D. M., *Fundamentals of Private Pensions*, 2nd ed. Homewood, Ill.: Richard D. Irwin, Inc., 1964.

Measuring and Reporting Investment Performance of Pension Funds. National Foundation of Health, Welfare, and Pension Plans, Inc., Milwaukee, Wisc.: 1966 and 1967.

METZGER, B. L., *Investment Practices, Performance and Management of Profit Sharing Trust Funds*. Evanston, Ill.: Profit Sharing Research Foundation, 1969.

NELSON, R. L., *The Investment Policies of Foundations*. New York: Russell Sage Foundation, 1967.

Personal Trust Investment Management. Proceedings, CFA Research Seminar, 1967. CFA Monograph Series No. 2. Homewood, Ill.: Richard D. Irwin, Inc., 1968.

Proceedings, The Endowment Conference, sponsored by Donaldson, Lufkin & Jenrette, Inc. New York, 1969, 1970, 1971.

SHARPE, W. F., *Portfolio Theory and Capital Markets*. New York: McGraw-Hill, Inc., 1970.

SILBER, W. L., *Portfolio Behavior of Financial Institutions*. New York: Holt, Rinehart and Winston, 1969.

STEPHENSON, G. T., *Estates and Trusts,* 4th ed. New York: Appleton-Century-Crofts, Inc., 1965.

THE FORD FOUNDATION ADVISORY COMMITTEE ON ENDOWMENT MANAGEMENT, *Managing Educational Endowments*. New York: The Foundation, 1969.

WALTER, J. E. *The Investment Process, As Characterized by Leading Life Insurance Companies*. Boston: Graduate School of Business Administration, Harvard University, 1962.

WILLIAMSON, J. P., *Investments: New Analytic Techniques,* Chapters 2, 3. New York: Praeger Publishers, Inc., 1970.

WOOD, N. R., *Measuring the Investment Yield of Pension Funds*. New York: Alexander and Alexander, Inc., 1964.

24 General Tests of Quality: Corporate Securities

SCOPE: This chapter provides an introduction to the problems of analysis of corporate securities. The specific applications are reserved for subsequent chapters. The order of discussion is (1) quality of investments, (2) tests of internal risk, (3) other factors affecting recovery of principal, (4) other factors affecting income and yield, and (5) the factor of marketability.

The Quality of Investments

The traditional meaning of quality. In the traditional sense, investment "quality" has been synonymous with investment "safety." A "good investment" has been said to offer safety of principal and safety of income, or the assurance of a reasonable return. And because a "good investment" is usually thought to involve little risk of principal or income, it would, therefore, produce a relatively low rate of return while a poor investment would involve high risk and require the possibility of a high return or capital appreciation to compensate for lack of safety. A good or safe investment would also command excellent marketability—that is, ready convertibility into cash without sacrifice of value owing to lack of access to buyers.

Defects of the traditional concept of quality. This traditional concept creates several difficulties. In the first place, a safe investment is not necessarily wise; that is, it may not fit the needs of a particular investor at a particular time. Moreover, other considerations, such as tax status, denomination, degree of management required, and protection against inflation, may be just as important as safety in a given situation. Nevertheless, so fundamental is the matter of safety to many investors that it must be given primary emphasis. And even though a particular investment situation can afford a considerable degree of risk, the degree of that risk must be measured as accurately as possible to determine whether the current income and/or appreciation adequately compensates for risk in comparison with alternative investment commitments.

The second defect of the traditional concept of quality is that the degree of safety can be measured only approximately. Accurate analysis of all of the forces—economic, political, and managerial—that play upon investment values is impossible. Especially difficult is the task of predicting future events and weighing a myriad of factors that effect investment results such as technical change, accounting practices, and market psychology. And even the known facts can be variously interpreted. To a considerable extent, investment analysis remains an art, that is, involving qualitative factors, rather than a science. The task of the analyst is to apply such tests as indicate *relatively* rather than absolutely the degree of risk involved in the purchase of any corporate security.

A third difficulty of the traditional concept of quality is that the longer the maturity of the investment, the more difficult it is to estimate how assured are the principal and the income. The future always holds a number of uncertainties. Examination of the past record and prevailing condition of the issuer is helpful; knowledge of prevailing business and economic conditions and estimates of the future are essential. But these can never be infallible guides to the future. Who can say how "safe" is the principal of a bond due in fifty years? How "safe" are the dividends of a corporation ten years from now? How can the "safety" of preferred or common stocks, redeemable only in the market or in liquidation, be measured?

Finally, the return of principal and the amount and rate of income are affected by factors other than those associated with the issuer and with the inherent quality of the instrument. Even if one were satisfied that the issuer of a bond would not fail to pay full principal and interest when due, the market value of the bond will be influenced by factors, such as the trend of interest rates (and others that will be discussed below), that may profoundly affect the recoverable value before maturity. Investors who paid par for long-term marketable U.S. Government securities saw their prices decline to the 80's in 1920, in 1932, and in 1956–1966, and to the 60's in 1969–1970, not through any change in quality but because of changes in capital market conditions.

A revised concept of investment quality. The defects in the traditional concept of quality or safety suggest that *recovery of principal* would be a better term. The principal is relatively safe when good evidence exists that it can be recovered at maturity, or recovered through resale, which implies relative price stability and marketability. Similarly, the term *assurance of income* should be substituted for the traditional *safety of income*. The assurance of bond interest is determined by the future willingness and ability of the issuer to earn and pay interest, insofar as these can be measured. The assurance of dividends is determined—and with far less accuracy—by one's estimate of future earnings and of the equally important matter of dividend policy. A corporation may earn a substantial dividend but decide to retain the bulk of its earnings. The real return on its common stock may have to be measured by price appreciation.

Quality, therefore, is redefined to mean relative assurance of recovery of principal by any means, relative assurance of stable or growing income, and adequate marketability.

Although payment of income and recovery of principal would appear to be distinctly different operations requiring separate analysis, the two are inextricably woven. Where income is assured, the recovery of principal is assured, save for intermediate market fluctuations owing to changing maturity, interest rates, and other influences. Inability to pay income seriously impairs the value of the principal, as is invariably shown in the decline of security prices when default is threatened. The two factors must be measured together.

The measurement of quality. The degree of quality or amount of risk contained in any investment security is indicated—sometimes exactly, sometimes only approximately—by the examination of certain important factors. We should emphasize that such examination does not constitute the whole of investment analysis; it pertains solely to the quality of the issue being examined. As we have seen, of equal importance are an understanding of the investor's objectives, the proper timing of purchase and sale, and the important matter of valuation. A particular security may demonstrate quality, but for some reason it may not be appropriate in a particular portfolio. Or the purchase of this security may not be feasible at a particular time. Or the investor might like everything about a security but its price. Procedures for valuing securities are discussed in the next chapter.

In the analysis of the quality of a corporate security to determine as accurately as possible the degree of recovery of principal and assurance of income, much of the emphasis must be placed on those factors of risk that are associated with the issuer's ability to pay. In additions, there are other factors affecting principal or income that do not pertain to the strength or prospects of the particular company. And finally, the important matter of marketability should be investigated.

Tests of Internal Risk

In examining an investment security for those internal risk elements that in the main determine its strength and the adequacy of the income that should compensate for that risk, a logical approach is to proceed from the general—the industry of which the company is a part—to the specific—the particular security that is being examined. The order will run (1) the nature of the enterprise, (2) the financial tests of quality revealed by an examination of the issuer's statements, (3) the provisions of the particular security, and (4) the degree of seasoning. While few investment tests may be uniformly applied to all securities, some are sufficiently broad in scope to be applied to the general list. More specific tests are reserved for the chapters that follow.

Nature of the enterprise. The quality of securities is affected by the risks that prevail in the industry to which the issuer belongs. The loans of government bodies dependent upon taxes rather than profits are generally more secure than the bonds of corporate borrowers. (This is not to say, of course, that all government bonds have high quality—those of some municipalities, and of many foreign states leave much to be desired.) The securities of operating public utility companies, by reason of greater stability of revenues, present less risk *as a class* than those of competitive industrial companies. (Here, again, such a sweeping statement must be qualified: Not all utility securities are high grade, and many industrial securities possess very high quality.) Railroad securities run the whole gamut from high grade to very weak, but all railway issues reflect, to a greater or lesser extent, the fundamental characteristics and trends in the industry.

Succeeding chapters will indicate some of the special risks or uncertainties that pertain to various classes of enterprise. At this point, the relationship of the general class of business enterprise to the stability of corporate earning power may be indicated by reference to the earninge record of large groups of companies in selected years.

The years selected for Table 24-1 include the years of peaks and lows in corporate profits 1950–1970. Although the figures are not adjusted for secular growth or for price changes, one can see that the mining, transportation, and services groups show the greatest instability in net income available for dividends, and the utility and finance groups the greatest stability. The industrial group is large and includes many diverse types. But the marked cyclical pattern is apparent. Railway securities as a class have lost caste, because of their fluctuating record and their failure to reach a decent earnings level, and securities of operating gas and electric utilities have replaced them as prime corporate issues. We should point out, however, that the securities of a number of industrial companies which exhibit extraordinary growth and earnings command as much, or more, respect as the utility group. The variations within the industrial group will be discussed in Chapter 26.

Issuer's financial strength. The financial tests in the analysis of the issuer are explained in considerable detail in subsequent chapters, with emphasis upon the features pertinent to the respective fields. At this point, the more important general tests are discussed.

The *balance sheet* is the statement of resources and liabilities on a given date, the difference between the two (the balance) being the net worth or owners' equity in the enterprise. The asset items may be classified into two main groups: (1) fixed assets, consisting of plant and equipment, long-term investments in other companies, and intangibles such as patents and goodwill, and (2) current assets, the more liquid resources including cash, accounts and notes receivable, inventories, and temporary investments. Similarly, the liabilities may be classified as (1) long-term, or due after twelve months, and (2) current, or due within twelve months. The former would include such items as bonds, mortgages, and intermediate-term loans, and the latter accounts and notes payable, the current portion of maturing long-term debt, accrued wages, interest, taxes, and cash dividends payable.

The assets are carried at *book* values, ordinarily cost (less depreciation or other reserves) for fixed assets and cost or market value for current assets. Book value seldom indicates liquidating value and, especially in the case of

Table 24-1. CORPORATE PROFITS AFTER INCOME TAXES

(in millions of dollars)

Group	1950	1952	1955	1958	1959	1960	1961	1966	1967	1970
Mining	$ 1,115	$ 846	$ 1,046	$ 778	$ 607	$ 755	$ 842	$ 822	$ 579	$ 339
Contract construction	325	305	266	395	343	224	292	1,096	1,187	1,006
Manufacturing	13,290	9,566	14,453	10,299	13,986	12,631	12,046	24,670	22,275	16,911
Transportation	1,107	846	704	316	452	295	314	1,393	732	−761
Communication	406	465	810	1,073	1,308	1,366	1,496	2,539	2,464	2,330
Electric, gas, and sanitary services	884	999	1,280	1,336	1,583	1,859	1,864	2,826	2,691	2,461
Wholesale and retail trade	3,743	2,267	2,802	2,414	3,160	2,531	2,882	5,571	6,047	7,044
Finance, insurance, and real estate	2,597	2,854	3,711	3,653	4,791	4,722	4,851	6,302	5,816	6,269
Services	326	297	336	318	433	405	322	1,154	1,227	776

SOURCE: U.S. Department of Commerce, Office of Business Economics.

fixed assets, is often arbitrary. Hence, measurement of the real asset protection behind securities has distinct limitations.

The *test of fixed assets* measures the relationship between the value of the fixed assets (less any reserves) and the face value of the securities outstanding. Even assuming that the properties have been properly maintained and adequately depreciated, the value of the fixed assets should substantially exceed the long-term debt. The relationship between fixed assets and net worth should also be noted, to determine whether the owner's investment is represented by illiquid assets. The conservative analyst usually ignores the intangible assets in such tests, as these are likely to shrink in value with any decline in earning power, and their balance sheet value is usually arbitrary.

The *tests of working capital position* indicate the short-term liquidity of the business. The importance of liquidity depends on the nature of the business, the rate at which assets are converted into cash through operations, and the need of the company for working funds. The (net) *working capital* is the difference between current assets and current liabilities. The relationship of current assets to current liabilities, and the turnover and valuation of individual current asset items, should be examined carefully. These tests are discussed in more detail in Chapter 26.

In addition to these general tests, the relation of working capital to long-term debt and to capital stock indicates the liquid protection behind each layer of securities.

The *tests of total asset value* show the protection that is provided the various issues of outstanding securities. Bonds and preferred stock should be supported by ample total assets of tangible character. The value of common stock, which represents the residual equity in the business, often reflects superior or inferior earning power, and hence its *tangible book value* (total tangible assets less all liabilities and preferred stock) seldom coincides with its market value. This phenomenon is also attributable in part to the arbitrary fashion in which assets are carried on the balance sheet.

The *tests of capital structure* show the amounts and relative importance of the various sources of long-term funds. *Capital structure* (sometimes called invested capital or long-term investment) includes the *capitalization* (or securities outstanding) plus the surplus accounts.[1] The most conservative capital structure includes only common stock and surplus; no "senior capital" has been issued. Where substantial amounts of bonds, preferred stock, or both are included, the company has committed itself to fixed or contingent charges through the issuance of senior securities. Such a practice may or may not be dangerous, depending on the assets and earnings support to such securities. The nature of the enterprise is a governing factor in this regard; companies with relatively stable earnings may safely issue a larger proportion of bonds. Conservative investors seeking high quality in securities should favor those companies with the smaller percentages in bonds and preferred stock. (Standards of capital structure will be suggested in succeeding chapters.) But others may prefer companies with high leverage, which will result in earnings being magnified in good times; by the same token, such investors

---

[1]In many discussions, the term "capital structure" is omitted and "capitalization" is used to denote total securities plus surplus.

must be willing to accept the risk that in periods of low earnings leverage may severely reduce the earnings on common stock.

Earning power. The *income,* or *profit and loss statement,* shows the earnings of the company for the period indicated—annual or interim, as disclosed in the revenue and expense figures. The amount of each major item of revenue and expense, and the relationships between them, and between investment and earnings, must be given very close scrutiny. The final figure of net income, or the earnings produced for the owners of the business, is the addition to the net worth (before any cash dividends) produced during the period.

The income statement is more "reliable" than the balance sheet in that most of the items shown thereon are statements of fact. Nevertheless, the reported earnings figures are subject to considerable control, that is, are affected by accounting decisions. The expenses of depreciation and depletion may not reflect the actual rate of decline in the physical value of fixed assets, especially when tax considerations dominate the calculations. Nonrecurring items of both income and expense, the treatment of charges representing a variety of special reserves, policy with respect to charging deferred income taxes, and a number of other factors make the earnings figures reported for a particular year or interim period somewhat arbitrary. For these reasons long-term rather than short-run information should be emphasized.

Reported earnings, of course, reflect trends and relationships of revenues and expenses, whose analysis is discussed in later chapters. Such analysis uncovers the *reasons* for the size and rate of change of the earnings figures.

The *tests of earning power* are possibly the most important financial tests used in investment analysis. These include the trend, volatility, and size of the return on capital investment, the coverage of interest on bonds and other long-term debt, coverage of preferred stock dividends, and capacity to pay current and future dividends on the common stock. These are basic criteria of investment quality.

The overall rate earned on the *total* long-term investment or capital structure is computed by dividing income before any bond interest, but after income taxes (or, net income with interest added back) by the average total capital structure. This shows the productivity of the business without regard to the methods of long-term financing employed, save for the influence of interest on the income tax bill.

The earnings protection to bondholders is revealed by the comparison of the annual interest charges (and other fixed charges such as fixed rent) to the total income available for their payment (times charges earned). The computation of this "times earned" figure can use either earnings before fixed charges, or before fixed charges and after income taxes. Both are valid —the first because interest and rent are expenses in determining taxable income, the second because, once the tax bill is computed, it has a prior claim over payments to creditors and lessors.

The rate of return on total net worth or owners' investment is calculated by dividing the average net worth (at book value) into net income after taxes. The figure is, of course, influenced by any leverage resulting from the use of debt.

The protection to the preferred stock dividends is revealed by comparing the total income and the preferred dividend requirements (plus bond interest, if any). The *coverage* may also be calculated by dividing income (before interest) by interest plus two times the preferred dividend. The reasoning is that, assuming a 50 per cent rate of income taxes, the company will have to earn the interest plus twice its preferred dividends to cover the latter once. The appropriate margin of safety required to assure the payment of bond interest and preferred dividends will, of course, vary with the nature of the enterprise, the character of its assets, and the stability of its earnings.

The coverage of preferred stock dividends is often indicated by dividing the net income by the number of shares outstanding. Thus, if a company reports net income of $12.00 per preferred share, and if the dividend is $4.00, preferred dividends are said to have been earned three times in the given period. A similar result is obtained by dividing net income by the annual preferred dividends. These methods are misleading for companies with both bonds and preferred stock outstanding because they hide the existence of prior deductions in the form of fixed charges that do not vary with changes in total income. For this reason, as indicated above, the better method of indicating preferred dividend coverage is to calculate the number of times total fixed charges *plus* dividends have been earned in the period. Otherwise, the preferred stock might, under certain conditions, show higher coverage than bonds senior to it! Table 24-2 shows the various methods of calculating the coverage of charges mentioned above.

Table 24-2. COVERAGE OF CHARGES

	Year A	Year B
Available for fixed charges	$200	$60
Fixed charges (interest and fixed rent)	40	40
Income before income taxes	$160	$20
Income taxes (at 50 per cent)	80	10
Net income	$ 80	$10
Preferred dividends	10	10
Times fixed charges earned (before taxes)	5	1.5
Times fixed charges earned (after taxes)	3	1.25
Times interest plus preferred dividends earned	2.4	1
Times interest plus twice preferred dividends earned	3.3	1
Times preferred dividends earned	8	1

The past earnings and the estimated future earnings on the common stock are the most important factors of concern to the owners or potential owners of that stock, and the most important determinants of its value. The potential earnings should be commensurate with the risks of the enterprise. Their amount and stability primarily determine the dividends to be received as well as the growth from retained earnings that will enhance the investment quality of the stock through the years. The productivity of the common stockholder's stake in the business, in terms of the size and trend of the rate earned on common equity (net income after preferred dividends divided by average common stock plus surplus), is a basic factor in choosing among alternative equity investments, and is the chief influence on the value placed by the market on each dollar of profits (the price-earnings ratio or multiplier).

The *dividend payment test* involves an examination of the common stock dividend record of the company over a period of years: the amount of earnings available for dividends, and the proportion of earnings that has been and may in the future be distributed in dividends. Investors must realize that such dividends are contingent not only on earnings but on the management's policy as to the portion of those earnings that are to be distributed. In many growth situations, retained earnings are more valuable to the stockholder than are dividends, because they add to investment that earns a higher rate than the investor could earn, after income taxes, on alternative commitments. Indeed, in a market such as in the 1960s–1970s, investors have been willing to pay more, in the case of growing companies, per dollar of earnings that are retained than are paid out.

Traditionally, earnings on common stock have been reported as so much per outstanding share, based either on the average number of shares for the period, or on the shares at the end of the period. In recent years, however, the accounting profession has recognized that where a company has issued convertible securities and/or warrants, the number of shares will be increased when and if the options are exercized. So the "fully diluted" earnings are computed by adding to the present shares the number that may be issued for conversion or for sale through warrants, and dividing this number into the adjusted earnings.

In recent years investors have paid increasing attention to *cash* earnings per share. This is derived by using earnings before depreciation and other noncash expenses, and after income taxes. "Cash flow per share" would be a better term, because the exempted expenses are indeed real. The cash flow figure reveals the total internally generated funds that are available for expansion if needed; in burgeoning situations such funds, invested at a high rate, can compound to the advantage of the stockholders. The investor is cautioned, however, not to substitute cash earnings for real earnings in appraising the value of a stock. Such a practice has too often been used to rationalize a very high market price.

Athough unbroken dividend records extending for decades do not assure future payments, many companies have compiled an impressive record in this respect. Their ability to maintain disbursements under all manner of conditions in the past is evidence of financial stability and underlying strength.

The particular security. The type of security and its peculiar terms and characteristics obviously have an important bearing on its quality. We saw in the earlier chapters describing the various classes of securities that these may range from prior-lien bonds with very wide safety margins of both assets and earnings to common stocks representing a very thin equity in the corporate property and income. One cannot generalize about whole groups of securities; many exceptions make it impossible to say that all senior mortgage bonds are safer than junior mortgages, all secured bonds safer than debentures, all debentures safer than preferred stocks, or all preferred stocks safer than common stocks. The quality of an issue depends not only upon its relative rank but on the resources and earnings of the issuer.

The preferred stock of one company may exhibit more real strength than the first mortgage bonds of another company. The strength of the issuer, the support given its various security issues, and the particular provisions of those issues must be closely inspected. Only within the financial structure of an *individual* company can one safely expect the type and ranking of an issue to determine its relative quality.

Notwithstanding the above comments, the inherent differences between debt and equity, between senior and junior debt, and between preferred and common stocks require that the junior issues present a wider margin of protection if they are to be considered as having real investment quality.

Degree of seasoning. Seasoning applies to the industry and company as well as to a particular issue. New securities are issued at arbitrary prices that may or may not be accepted by the market. The price tends to fluctuate over a seasoning period of a few weeks to several months. Often new securities decline in price after the primary distribution has been completed, owing to the removal of artificial support. And time is needed for the issue to "settle down" in strong investment hands. The industry and company likewise require consideration with respect to seasoning. Most investors should avoid new enterprises in the experimental stage. If newer companies are chosen, they should be sufficiently seasoned to have revealed definite earning power.

Other Factors Affecting Recovery of Principal

The ability of the issuer to pay principal at maturity and the ability of the investor to recover principal through resale are determined primarily by the strength of the company and the issue as revealed by the general tests outlined previously and the more specific tests described in later chapters. But other influences unrelated to quality are also important, insofar as recovery by resale is concerned. These include the maturity (if any) of the security, the course of money rates, and the vagaries of the capital markets.

Maturity of the issue. The shorter the maturity of a bond, the less it will fluctuate in market value. This is because the short maturity presents less risk and is affected less by future contingencies. In addition, a change in money rates results in a very minor shift in price in the case of a short maturity, whereas the same change would require a considerable shift in the case of a long maturity. Consider two 7 per cent bonds each selling at par to yield 7 per cent, one maturing in three years and the other in fifty years. To produce a yield of 8 per cent, the three-year maturity would fall to 97.38 whereas the fifty-year maturity would fall to 87.75.

Another influence of maturity is found in the steady rise (or decline) of a bond bought at a discount (or premium) as maturity approaches.

Interest rates. As we saw in Chapter 19, changing interest rates affect the values of fixed-income obligations and, to a certain extent, of common stocks, entirely apart from any change in their inherent quality. An illustration of this effect is found in the softening of prices on long-term U.S. Government bonds in 1960–1970. For example, in mid-July 1961, the Treasury 4¼'s due in May 1975–1985 sold at 103²%₃₂ to yield 3.94 per cent. In January 1970, at the peak of interest rates, they were bid at 72²⁰%₃₆ to yield 7.16 per cent.

Uncertainties of the market. The value of all securities, but especially of stocks, reflects the waves of optimism and pessimism concerning future economic conditions and corporate earning power. As we have seen earlier, not even the strongest securities are exempt from such influences. But those lower down in the echelons of rank are particularly vulnerable to the ebb and flow of market evaluations. A stock may shrink 50 per cent and then rise 100 per cent in market value, and all the while represent virtually the same intrinsic values. Was the stock of International Business Machines that sold at the low of 141 in 1961 vastly different from the stock that sold as high as 400 in 1972?[2]

A bond or stock may be "safe" in the traditional sense yet present a varying market value that makes recovery of the original price impossible under the worst conditions of timing of purchase and sale, due to drastic increases in interest rates. In the case of a great many securities, then, market action becomes as important as the inherent quality of the issue.

Emphasis on changing market prices of securities is central to the definitions of risk that are being used in the more sophisticated analyses of securities and of portfolio performance. Here, risk is measured by the variation in price or in total rate of return, defined for this purpose as income plus price change during a period. The use of this concept in analysing pension fund management is discussed in Chapter 22.

Other Factors Affecting Income and Yield

The relative size of the income, as related to the amount invested, usually indicates the degree of risk assumed. A high rate of return is evidence of uncertainty with respect to future payments. Investors who are willing to purchase securities with relatively uncertain future returns naturally demand compensation in the form of a higher rate of return as a premium for risk. Investors who will buy only securities with relatively assured futures must accept lower rates of return. (An important exception is found in the case of those common stocks whose value reflects reinvestment of earnings rather than distribution of generous dividends.)

Thus, quality is the main determinant of investment return. This return, expressed in percentage relationship between the annual income and the

[2]Adjusted retroactively for stock dividends and splits through 1972.

amount invested, is called, the *yield*.[3] It is much less reliable in the case of stocks than in the case of bonds because of the contingent nature of dividends and the influence of speculation as a motivating force in stock purchasing. It is not always reliable even in the case of bonds and investment-grade preferred stocks because of certain market and technical features that affect the price (and, hence, the yield) and that are extraneous to the main factor of quality. The more important of these qualifying factors are here listed.

The trend of interest rates. Changing interest rates produce changing yields, which as we have seen, force changes in price. As fundamental conditions change in the capital and money markets, money rates also change. (See Chapter 2.) Furthermore, because the investment market is divided into credits of varying durations, there is no such thing as a single interest rate prevailing at any one time. Short-term rates are subject to more rapid percentage variations and wider swings, while the long-term, or investment, rates change less rapidly and within narrower limits.

Marketability. Securities issued by large enterprises are better known than those of smaller companies. Listed and active over-the-counter issues provide a better opportunity for purchase and sale at a known price than do lesser issues and, as a consequence, command a higher price and afford a lower rate of return.

Redemption option. Most corporate obligations are subject to redemption at the option of the issuer at a fixed price prior to the date of final payment. The market price will rarely exceed the redemption option price, so the redemption feature keeps the market price down to the call price when it might otherwise go higher. A noncallable 8 per cent bond may be selling at around 111, giving a yield of 7 per cent; at the same time, an equally good 8 per cent bond, redeemable at 105, will be selling at around 105 and giving a yield of nearly 7.5 per cent.

Tax position. The income from certain securities is not subject to income taxes, and so these issues command relatively high prices and afford correspondingly low yields. Because of tax-exemption, high-grade municipal bonds afford lower yields than the bonds of the Federal government, although the Federal bonds are definitely superior on a quality basis. The influence of taxation on other yields is discussed in Chapter 18.

Maturity. Traditionally, short-term interest rates have been lower than long-term rates, so that short-term bonds have borne lower yields than long-term bonds of equal quality. This is seen in the list of prices and yields of U.S. Government obligations, all of which are equal insofar as safety is concerned. Exceptions to the general pattern of yields as influenced by maturities were found in 1956–1957, 1959, 1966, and 1969–1970, when

---

[3]"Rate of return" on securities, especially stocks, is also used in some contexts to signify income plus price appreciation (see p. 419). And the term has a special meaning in the utilities industries. (See Chapter 27.)

"tight money" forced some short-term rates up to and above long-term rates. (See Chapter 2.)

Institutional market. The growing demand for portfolio investments by bank trustees, life insurance companies, savings banks, and other institutional buyers puts pressure on securities eligible for purchase by such regulated buyers, detracts from their floating supply, and places an artificial premium on price so as to lower yield.

Conversion privilege. Securities which may be converted into common stock at the option of the investor tend to rise in market price when the second security advances. Especially during bull markets, some convertible bonds and preferred stocks have sold at very low and even minus yields. (See Chapter 7.)

The Factor of Marketability

The term *marketability* connotes access to a large volume of trading without substantial loss of value because of a poor market. The holder of a security should realize that, under the worst conditions, he might find himself with a security for which there may be no demand at all when he desires to sell.

Apart from developments which affect whole groups of securities, the marketability of individual security issues is determined largely by the following factors.

Listing. Securities which are listed on any of the national securities exchanges have a centralized market where buyers and sellers may conveniently place orders. Very active issues traded over-the-counter, on which there are constant quotations, afford a similar opportunity to sell on short notice. Mere listing does not guarantee marketability, however. Many listed securities are traded only occasionally.

Size. A large issue of securities attracts more attention and is usually held by more investors than a smaller issue. Price quotations which appear regularly in the daily newspapers generally include only the larger issues.

Reputation of issuer. The securities issued by companies which are well and favorably known usually have good marketability. It is difficult to believe that securities of companies such as General Electric or General Motors would ever lack buyers.

Institutional ownership. Securities eligible for purchase by financial institutions have a special market appeal. At the same time, where an issue is largely in institutional hands, the regular volume of trading may be small.

Seasoning. Securities which have been outstanding a year or more are regarded as "seasoned" issues with greater price stability than new issues. Such issues are preferred by many investors.

The marketability of a security may be determined at any time by seeking a price quotation. If the quotation is easily secured, either in the daily newspaper or immediately through a broker, if the "spread" between the price asked and the price offered is close, and if the volume of trading is substantial, good marketability is indicated.

Marketability is important to all investors. While it is especially significant in temporary investments, it should not be overlooked by permanent investors. Emergencies may arise that would require immediate liquidation of security holdings. Since marketability "costs money" in the sense that the more marketable security gives a lower yield, the average investor should seek a reasonable rather than a maximum degree.

A noteworthy feature of marketability is its close relationship to collateral value. When securities are offered as collateral for a bank loan, the bank is as much interested in the marketability of the issue as in its quality. Banks greatly prefer listed securities as collateral.

REFERENCES

BADGER, R. E., *The Complete Guide to Investment Analysis.* New York: McGraw-Hill, Inc., 1967.

BOGEN, J. I., ed., *Financial Handbook,* 4th rev. ed., Sec. 8. New York: The Ronald Press Company, 1968.

FOULKE, R. A., *Practical Financial Statement Analysis,* 6th ed., Part I. New York: McGraw-Hill, Inc., 1968.

GRAHAM, BENJAMIN, D. L. DODD, AND SIDNEY COTTLE, *Security Analysis,* 4th ed., Chapters 2, 7. New York: McGraw-Hill, Inc., 1962.

————, AND CHARLES MCGOLRICK, *The Interpretation of Financial Statements,* rev. ed. New York: Harper & Row, Publishers, 1964.

GUTHMANN, H. G., *Analysis of Financial Statements,* 4th ed., Part I. Englewood Cliffs, N.J.: Prentice-Hall, Inc., 1953.

KENNEDY, R. D., AND S. Y. MCMULLEN, *Financial Statements,* 5th ed., Part I. Homewood, Ill.: Richard D. Irwin, Inc., 1968.

MAURIELLO, J. A., *Accounting for the Financial Analyst.* Homewood Ill.: Richard D. Irwin, Inc., 1967.

MYER, J. N., *Financial Statement Analysis,* 4th ed. Englewood Cliffs, N.J.: Prentice-Hall, Inc., 1969.

————, *What the Investor Should Know About Corporate Financial Statements,* 2nd ed. Larchmont, N.Y.: American Education Council, 1965.

WIXON, RUFUS, ed., *Accountants Handbook,* 5th ed., Sec. 3. New York: The Ronald Press Company, 1970.

25 Valuation of Corporate Securities

SCOPE: In this chapter we are concerned with the important problem of valuation of securities. The subjects discussed are (1) significance of valuation, (2) general problems, (3) valuation of corporate bonds, (4) valuation of convertible securities, (5) valuation of preferred stocks, and (6) common stock valuation.

The discussion emphasizes the corporate securities group of investments. Regarding other investments, marketable Federal government obligations bear no risk of default of interest or principal. Their value depends on the interest rate applying to a particular maturity at a particular time. Price rises and falls conversely with this rate, but always equals investment value. Decisions with respect to the purchase and sale of Federal obligations, therefore, are made on considerations other than value. Obligations of state and local governments are valued on the basis of risk, adjusted for the influence of exemption from income taxation. (See Chapter 6.) Because the importance of tax-exemption varies among different investors, these securities are worth different amounts to different investors. Yet there is only one market price for a particular issue. The valuation of investment company shares was discussed in Chapter 9. Real estate presents peculiar problems, as indicated in Chapter 11.

Significance of Valuation

In contrast to that of the trader, whose chief interest lies in short-term price changes, the portfolio of the investor in corporate securities for income or long-term price appreciation should consist of the best values chosen from the large number of available bonds and stocks. Why pay too much? Why hold a security if others offer more value for the money? But the answers to these questions present difficult problems, especially in the case of common stocks. The investor may avoid these problems by seeking out those securities that may perform the best in the *market,* regardless of value. But here he is relegating the·performance of his portfolio to the market, that is, to the decisions of others. And outguessing the market is a difficult game.

The investor can also avoid the valuation problem by turning it over to others. He may buy investment company shares, place funds in a common trust fund, or use some other means of indirect investment. Or he may

443

simply rely on the advice of others in the direct purchase or sale of securities. But even if he elects to emphasize value in his own operations, he can ease his task in two ways: (1) by dollar-cost-averaging, counting on the swings in the market above or below value to produce good long-run results; (2) by diversification, so that, within a total list, too much paid for one security may be offset by underpayment for another. Many funds, individual and institutional, combine these approaches.

The following discussion is based on the assumption that value is important and that the investor will use swings in market prices to his advantage. Sharp changes in market price may bring a security into or out of its value range as determined by the methods discussed below. Although acute bull or bear markets drive most securities, especially stocks, up or down together, some are always over-, under-, or correctly valued at any level in the market. The task of the investor or his adviser is to recognize when price and value coincide or differ.

General Problems

One may like everything about a security but its price. Indeed, to buy (or sell) a security at too high (or too low) a price is almost as bad as to buy (or sell) the wrong security. While this may be an exaggeration, it suggests that within the host of alternatives, the investor may always find some securities that are suitably priced. Or if the ones in which he is interested are overpriced, later market corrections may bring some or all of them into proper buying range.

All securities have one thing in common: they are worth the present value of their expected future income or, in the case of bonds, the present value of future interest plus the present value of the principal at or before maturity. (See Chapter 12.) Save in sale or liquidation, corporate assets in general are worth what their future earnings are worth. Very liquid assets, of course, are a special factor because they may be used to fill the gap between temporarily low earnings and interest or dividends.

The basic problem of valuation, therefore, is to estimate future income and to pay a price for it that properly reflects the degree of uncertainty of that income. Even a careful analysis cannot predict the future with accuracy. But it can diminish uncertainty and prevent some purchases at grossly excessive prices, and some sales at the very worst time.

The discussion in the previous chapter and in those that follow reveals that all security analysis is pointed either directly or indirectly at future income. The financial strength (current and long-term) of a company, its asset values, its management, and the other elements involved in security investigation, in the end, relate to the size and regularity of earnings and of income.

Certain problems arise from this approach. The income of ordinary bonds and preferred stocks is cash income consisting of interest or dividends. In common stocks, however, only part of the company's earnings—

or perhaps none—may be distributed in dividends, at least in the foreseeable future. But in the *long run,* dividends must be received if the stock is to have value. Retained earnings, even if put to work at a high rate (and reflected in price appreciation) can be realized (short of liquidation or sale of the business) only in dividends or in realized market profit that capitalizes future dividends. For *shorter-run* purposes, however, earnings (the source of dividends) are the basic criterion of value.

Many securities do not lend themselves to valuation because future earnings and dividends cannot be estimated. These include securities of small, new companies, those with unusually large earnings fluctuations, those affected by special factors such as a drastic change in management, product lines, or public policy, and those whose prospects depend mainly on foreign operations. These are some of many *qualitative* factors that may so outweigh the quantitative or measurable factors as to make any attempt at valuation a mere guessing game.

A second problem is to determine the usefulness of *past* earnings (and interest or dividend payments) and past price history as the basis for estimates of the future. The past record is the only *known* clue to the future. It reveals past earnings, asset values, and quality and intentions of management, as well as relationships between earnings and price. To this record must be added an appraisal of any changes that can be anticipated. At worst, the future is unknown to any man. At best, a study of the past record can aid in diminishing the uncertainty of future prospects.

A third problem is to weigh those forces affecting value that are external to the particular company or security, such as changes in interest rates in the capital market, features of the tax structure, institutional demand, and market efficiency. Security values change not only because of estimated changes in the basic qualities of the issuer, but sometimes more importantly, because of such factors that affect all securities or specific groups such as bonds or stocks.

A final general problem of valuation is to account for those characteristics that are not associated with inherent risk or quality, such as special features of bonds and preferred stocks (call prices and convertible clauses), marketability, and tax status, as discussed in the previous chapter. The valuation should first be made on the basis of quality; then, the bearing of the other factors is taken into account.

Valuation of Corporate Bonds

A (straight) bond is worth the present value of future coupons plus the present value of principal at maturity, discounted at a yield rate that compensates for risk. "The price goes where the yield sends it." The methods of price calculation, given the yield requirement, are presented in Chapter 12.

The value of high-grade and good-grade corporate bonds is determined by the yield that properly reflects the difference between certainty of income and the risk involved. The analysis seeks to answer this question: "Is the yield sufficiently above the riskless rate (for an equivalent maturity) to reward the buyer properly for the risk of nonpayment of interest (and principal), as determined by analysis?" If a twenty-year Treasury bond yields 5½ per cent, does a corporate bond yield of 7 (or 7½, or 8) per cent provide a sufficient spread (1½, 2, or 2½ per cent) to compensate for the risk? The decision is made after the analysis of the industry, company, and security, along the lines outlined in succeeding chapters, has been completed.

The investor should also compare the yield on a corporate bond with those on high-grade bonds *of the same maturity,* in the same category. Yields on various high-grade bond series are published regularly by Moody's and Standard & Poor's.

Suppose, for example, that the average yield on long-term high-grade industrial bonds is 7 per cent. Such bonds have been rated twice—by the rating agency and by the market. But the careful investor should satisfy himself that the yield properly reflects the risk. Is the bond really high-grade? Care must be taken to compare similar maturities and to recognize the special factors, apart from quality, that may influence yield.

The valuation of high-grade bonds presents few difficulties. The chief problem is to detect later deterioration in quality, and this requires watching. Medium-grade bonds take more care, because the spread between the riskless rate and their yields is wider and more variable, and they may move both up and down in quality.

A low-grade bond, where payment of interest and/or principal is in doubt, should be analyzed like a common stock. Where only a very rough estimate of future earnings can be made, future interest payments are a matter of conjecture, and these should be considered in the category of dividends (unless liquidation, sale, or reorganization is in prospect). Yield *to maturity* is almost meaningless, and current yield must be used, and possibly compared with the dividend yields on common stocks. Where no current income is available, the bond sells flat. (See Chapter 12).

Valuation of Convertible Securities

The value of convertible securities (described in Chapters 7, 8 and 12) is based on two elements: (1) the "investment" value of their future interest coupons or dividends, and principal (bonds) at maturity, at an appropriate yield rate determined by analysis, plus (2) the value (if any) of the conversion feature. The latter may send the price of a convertible security above, and the yield below, that which it should bear as a "straight" security. After conversion point is reached, the price will continue to rise (and the yield at market price to fall) with the rise in the value of the shares into which each bond or preferred shares is convertible. After this point, their analysis involves that of the stock itself.

Valuation of Preferred Stocks

The valuation of sound preferred stocks is similar to that of bonds. The price should produce a yield that is sufficiently above either the riskless rate, or the rate on the very highest-grade preferreds of the same industry, to compensate for the risks as analyzed. Two factors that differentiate preferred stocks from most bonds should be reemphasized: (1) Their income is not a fixed charge; it is *dividend* income—dependent on earnings and dividend policy; (2) they have no maturity (save for possible call or redemption by the issuer). Because preferred stocks are *equity* securities in the legal sense, the yields of even the strongest ones should exceed those of high-grade bonds. However, as we have seen, the income tax appeal of preferred stocks, to taxed corporate investors, has a special influence on their prices and yields.

Very weak preferred stocks are valued like common stocks, plus the possible additional value of any accumulated preferred dividends. With respect to the latter, the investor must estimate the chances of (1) full cash payment, sooner or later, (2) part cash payment, (3) payment in securities rather than cash, by a "recapitalization," and (4) complete default.

Common Stock Valuation

Principles. The basic criteria of common stock values are the amount, reliability, and stability of future earnings and, therefore, dividends. Tests of financial condition, operating efficiency, asset values, and management, as suggested in the previous chapter and in succeeding chapters, all bear on these fundamental factors. The main problem of common stock analysis is twofold: (1) to estimate future earnings (and dividends) and (2) to apply a rate of capitalization (or its counterpart, a price-earnings or price-dividends ratio) that will satisfy for the risks as analyzed. With the necessity of combining the two variables—earnings and multiple—the resulting valuation can be approximate at best and is subject to regular reassessment and possible correction.

A common stockholder may obtain the earnings of his company in only two ways (other than through liquidation): (1) by receipt of cash dividends and (2) by *realized* appreciation in market value that reflects the retention of earnings. Where the bulk of earnings is distributed in dividends, and where such dividends have been and are expected to be regular, the chief basis of valuation is the estimated stream of future cash dividends. The investor demands a dividend yield sufficiently above the bond rate to reflect the uncertainty in the amount and stability of the future dividend stream. Under normal conditions for the average stock, an appropriate yield on current market price should be about 50 per cent above the bond rate, say, 8 per cent if the bond rate is 5½ per cent. A lower yield is justified, for "income" stocks, only if the same dividend is certain or if the rate of dividends is expected to increase. As of 1972–1973, few common stocks provide yields that equal or exceed 150 per cent of the bond rate. This is because the basic test of value is *future* returns.

But what if earnings are not distributed? Retained in the company, they may do little more than temporarily strengthen a weak situation. On the other hand, they may compound at such a good rate (as in the case of attractive "growth" stocks) as to increase the net worth rapidly. Under these conditions the anomaly appears: the lower the cash dividends, the higher the value. This is the case where the company can earn a much more attractive rate than the investor could find in a sound income-producing investment, net after taxes. The tax treatment of capital gains adds additional worth to retained earnings under these circumstances, so that the valuation of current earnings is high (the price-earnings ratio is high) and any modest cash dividends produce a very low yield on market price.

In the long run, then, the high appraisal of "growth" stocks stems from the possibility of *ultimately* high dividend distributions. In the shorter run, undistributed earnings may be worth much more than earnings paid out.

What about asset values? The book or "net asset" value of common stock should be given only modest consideration in the valuation of stocks other than those of utilities (where, through regulation, earnings stem from investment), financial companies (where book values represent realizable liquid values), and real estate companies or trusts with realizable properties. In other cases a share of stock is worth what it can earn, not what was spent for the assets it represents. However, two uses may be made of the book value figure. First, where it is much lower than appraised value based on earnings, reflecting a high intangible element, the investor must be confident that the current high rate of earnings on book investment will continue. Second, where it is much higher than appraised value, a bargain is suggested provided: (1) Analysis reveals that earnings—and dividends—may be expected to increase in a "turnaround", or (2) complete or partial liquidation is a possibility. Stocks that sell at or near the net *current* asset value per share (which means that the buyer is paying little or nothing for plant and equipment) offer a low base price that should be considerably enhanced by even a modest increase in earnings. Otherwise, the company is "worth more dead than alive."

With the above general concepts in mind, more specific approaches to common stock valuation can now be outlined. We should recognize, however, that only a *range* of value, not a precise figure, can be developed, and that this range will be wide or narrow depending on the uncertainties of the particular situation. A stock with such regularity of earnings and dividends as to resemble a bond can be valued fairly precisely. A stock presenting great uncertainties can be valued, if at all, only very crudely.

Use of relative values. Individual common stocks are often considered under- or overvalued in relation to the market as a whole, or to other securities of the same industry. Thus, if the Dow Jones 30 industrial stocks were selling at 15 times current earnings, and at a 3.25 per cent yield from current dividends, a particular industrial stock selling at 10 times earnings and producing a 5 per cent yield, might at first sight be deemed undervalued. But the sophisticated investor should compare the projected rate of growth of earnings and/or dividends on "the Dow" with that of the individual stock, if a comparison is to have any merit.

Another use of the relative approach is to compare the price-earnings ratio and the dividend yield of a particular stock with those of other firms in the same industry or with the industry average. This may reveal differences that deserve an explanation and may suggest interesting investment possibilities.

Such approaches are not, however, real valuation. At any particular time the market may over- or undervalue most of the leading stocks. Nevertheless, a comparison within the general market may provide a clue to an over- or undervalued situation, that can be confirmed by analysis, as well as by a check on the investor's valuation after he has completed his analysis. The same is true of comparisons within an industry. The relative approach may also be useful in that, over the long run, the market is usually right (though often wrong on the short run). The relationships in the market as a whole, that is, how investment-grade common stocks in general and in specific groups are valued by the consensus of investment opinion, provide benchmarks that have considerable validity and usefulness, when followed by real investigation of the particular situation.

Determining intrinsic value. Where investment policy is to be based on real valuation, however, the investor is faced with the problem of choosing among several approaches. Valuation can be based on

1. Short-run dividend prospects (income stocks);
2. Current or short-run earnings;
3. Discounted projected dividends, or dividends plus terminal value;
4. Discounted projected earnings;
5. Projected five- to seven-year earnings or rate of growth, without formal discounting;
6. The bond rate.

Each of these methods and certain variations will now be described, with comment on their merits and limitations. More extensive discussion of these and other methods is found in works cited in the references at the end of the chapter.

NONGROWTH INCOME STOCKS. Common stocks that offer the prospect of only very modest growth of earnings and which are expected to distribute all or most of their earnings in dividends, are attractive for income rather than for price appreciation. Their value is determined by capitalizing their expected short-run (three- to five-year) dividends at a rate that compensates for risk. This rate is constructed by adding to the *bond rate,* or rate on "riskless" money as represented by the return on long-term Treasury bonds, a premium reflecting the "quality" of the dividends, or assurance of payment, as determined by analysis. As an illustration, consider a sound company whose dividends grew from $1.20 to $1.60 per share in the past ten years, and for which a reasonable expectation of average dividends for the next five years is $1.75, reflecting modest growth of earnings and a high payout ratio. Using a bond rate of 5½ per cent, plus 2 per cent for risk, a capitalization rate of 7½ per cent is derived which, applied to $1.75, produces a value range of 22 to 25. Such a valuation, involving a low premium over the bond rate, reflects an appraisal that the stock has high general quality and that dividends will likely continue to grow at the same modest rate *after* the five-year period. Otherwise a high-grade bond yielding 7½ per cent would be preferable.

Instead of using the "riskless" rate as a base, some recommend the yield on high-grade corporate bonds or the dividend yield on sound income-producing public utility stocks. The flaw here is that other people's opinions of value must be accepted. In addition, in the case of the utility stocks, stock market prices are involved, so that the investor is using the market to determine intrinsic value. Neither of these defects is involved when the Treasury bond rate is used.[1]

In many cases the dividend cannot be projected beyond one year, and even the income for the current year may be questionable. In such cases the current dividend should be capitalized at a high rate to reflect the uncertainty. Under these conditions it would be better, however, not to attempt a valuation at all.

Where substantial increases in dividends can be expected in the future, and if, based on past and current policy, the company can be expected to pay out most of its earnings, the valuation of income stocks becomes similar to that of other stocks as discussed below.

VALUATION BASED ON CURRENT OR SHORT-RUN EARNINGS. Where dividend payments are erratic, and where a projection of earnings is not feasible, the stock can only be valued, if at all, on the basis of *current* earnings. The choice of the appropriate multiplier of earnings presents a problem, because real value still depends on the course of future events. In such case any attempt at intrinsic valuation had better be abandoned, and the appeal of the stock on a *relative* basis should be used to indicate a trading situation or a candidate for later valuation when a valid projection becomes possible.

VALUATION BASED ON DISCOUNTED FUTURE DIVIDENDS. In theory, the intrinsic value of a share of stock (and of the going concern as a whole) is the present value of *all* future dividend payments. Future price appreciation will represent the value of future dividends from any point in time. Such an approach applies to stocks the same valuation concept as would be applied to a perpetual bond, except that future dividends are not expected to remain unchanged, in contrast to the fixed-interest return on

---

[1]In any use of the yield on Treasury bonds, the investor must be careful to employ an average yield on long-term issues that are not affected by "deep-discount" prices. Both Moody's and Standard & Poor's publish acceptable representative yield figures, as does the *Federal Reserve Bulletin*.

the bond.[2] Where dividends are not expected to increase at all (in a no-growth situation), the value (V) is D/K, where the rate K is the required rate as contrasted with the bond rate. Where the future dividends (based on an assumed payout of projected earnings) are expected to change, the value is shown by

$$V_0 = D_0 + \frac{D_1}{(1+K)^1} + \frac{D_2}{(1+K)^2} + \frac{D_3}{(1+K)^3} \cdots$$

$$= \sum_{t=1}^{\infty} \frac{D_t}{(1+K)^t}$$

or where g represents the expected (constant) rate of growth of dividends:

$$V_0 = \sum_{t=1}^{\infty} \frac{D_0(1+g)^t}{(1+K)^t} = \frac{D_0}{K-g}$$

Again, K is the rate of capitalization, based on risk, or the investor's desired rate of return. This can be derived either by adding a premium to the bond rate or (less acceptably) by using a "normal" rate reflecting the company's growth and stability in relation to that of the economy. The premium added to the bond rate would reflect primarily the expected stability of earnings and dividends. This in turn requires a careful analysis of all pertinent factors.

Another approach to deriving the appropriate rate at which dividends are discounted is to start with the "historical" long-term rate of dividend return on stocks and add a premium for expected growth in dividends that exceeds the normal rate, or deduct a penalty for lesser expected performance. The difficulty with this approach is that the historical rate is a function of the period selected. Some use a twenty-, thirty-, or even fifty-year rate. In a world of change, what rate is "normal"?

More complicated applications of this approach assume that there will be various rates of growth through different future periods, such as a transitional period, a period of stability, and then possibly a period of decline. And to reflect the increased risk of the future, the discount rate applied to future dividends is increased at either a fixed or variable rate.[3] Growth-rate tables are used to locate the factors in the individual case.

Such complexity is unrealistic in a changing economic world. It is impossible to make a reliable projection of dividends over a long period of years based on the projected rates, levels, and duration of earnings growth. In addition, the choice of the multiplier at which projected dividends are capitalized is very much a matter of opinion. Writers using this approach who suggest multipliers based on the historical average dividend yields for

---

[2] The pioneering work in this field is J. B. Williams, *The Theory of Investment Value* (Cambridge, Mass.: Harvard University Press, 1938). The derivations of models using different dividend assumptions are found in M. J. Gordon, *The Investment, Financing, and Valuation of the Corporation*. Homewood, Ill.: Richard D. Irwin, Inc., 1962.

[3] See citations to Clendenin, Bauman, and Soldofsky, in the reference list at the end of this chapter.

high-grade stocks, adjusted for risk, are in part turning to the stock market to determine intrinsic value.

A variation of this method, using a shorter-range dividend projection, may appear to have more practical validity. The value of a stock is the discounted value of future dividends plus the discounted value of estimated sales proceeds (terminal price) at a given future time.[4] Here, the dividend projection, say, for three or four years in the future, may not be difficult, but the sales price of the stock requires a guess at market conditions and the company's prospects three or four years from now. And the problem of the appropriate discounting rate remains.

VALUATION OF DISCOUNTED (LONG-TERM) PROJECTED EARNING. A more refined application of the dividend-valuation approach pays specific attention to retained earnings and their effect on dividends. Corporate earnings can either be distributed or reinvested, and the payout is a function of earnings growth. The valuation process then becomes one of capitalizing projected *earnings* per share as they are affected by the retention of profits. Historically, for common stocks in general, the combination of dividends and price appreciation owing to earnings growth has been 8 to 9 per cent. Tables have been constructed to show the multipliers of $1 to be applied to "normal" earnings. The multipliers are a function of the estimated trend of earnings growth for a constant growth period followed, say, by a diminishing growth period, and of the investor's desired rate of return. The latter will have been chosen by considering alternative investments or by using the historical average return as a guide. As an example, suppose the "normal earnings" of a company, derived from past and current earnings, are $6.00 a share, that its projected rate of earnings growth is 6 per cent (from a constant growth period of seven years, followed by a diminishing growth period of ten years), and that the investor's desired rate of return is 8 per cent. The tables show that the appropriate multiplier is 14.5. Applying this multiplier to $6.00 produces a value of $87.

VALUATION OF PROJECTED EARNINGS, WITHOUT DISCOUNTING. Some of the approaches just described assume that making long-range earnings and/or dividend projections is feasible. But in a world of change, projecting earnings for even a few years in the future becomes difficult if not impossible. This situation can be met by basing the valuation on a projection of *average* future earnings for a *limited* number of years. The price-earnings multiplier, or the rate of capitalization, is adjusted for the likelihood of continued earnings growth beyond that period.

One commonly used application of this simpler approach involves estimating average future earnings for, say, five to seven years, and applying to such earnings the multipliers that have been typical of the stock in the past. The past relation between price and earnings reflects the judgment of many buyers and sellers. If a stock has always sold at a high multiple, this is because, in actual transactions, a high opinion of the com-

[4] The present value of the terminal price (P), $P_n/(1 + K)^n$, would be added to the first equation above.

pany has been registered. Where this opinion has not always been borne out by the actual record, the price will have been readjusted to the facts of the case. Granted that the market-earnings relationship may have often been in error, and that the *future* of the company may not resemble the past, such past opinion should not be overlooked. The average multiple based on several years of record can thus be applied to estimated earnings to produce a current valuation. In using this approach, the investor must realize that past price-earnings relationships in the market *as a whole* may not recur for some months or even years. New conditions, especially large changes in interest rates, require new price-earnings relationships that may prevail for some time. Similarly, substantial changes in interest rates may affect the rates at which stock earnings are capitalized and hence produce new price-earnings multiples for *all* grades of stocks, as illustrated by the decline in the prices of most stocks in 1966 and 1969–1970, when interest rates on fixed-income obligations rose to record heights.

Applying *past* price-earnings multipliers to *future* earnings also has a technical defect. The past multipliers were based on the then *current* earnings, but reflected future earnings growth. To apply these to *future* increased earnings in order to derive a current valuation involves a double counting of growth. Such earnings should be discounted to the present if this approach is used. Or this method should be used to estimate *future* rather than current value.[5]

Another approach is to estimate the rate of growth of future earnings per share, and to apply to the average of say seven years' future earnings a multiplier that is itself a *function of the rate of growth of earnings*. The multiplier is based on a modification of the historical norm for the market as a whole, adjusted for the individual situation. Thus, if the average rate of growth of earnings over the next seven years (fourth-year earnings) is estimated at 3.5 per cent (the very long-run rate of the Dow Jones 30 industrial stocks), a multiplier of 13.5 is applied. If the annual rate of growth is estimated at 5 per cent or 7.2 per cent, the multiplier becomes 14 times and 15 times, respectively, and so forth, to a top limit of 20 where earnings will grow 20 per cent annually.[6]

In such an approach, because *both* the projected earnings per share and the multiplier are a function of growth of earnings, the problem of double counting again occurs. This is dealt with by the assumption that the growth will continue *after* the seventh year, and that the multiplier incorporates this factor. We should also note that the system assumes that the stocks being valued are all of investment grade. Lower multipliers would have to be applied to stocks falling below this standard.

VALUATION BASED ON THE BOND RATE. Some of the valuation methods previously described rely, at least in part, on the record in the market itself

---

[5]A sophisticated method of determining *future* value based on projected three- to five-year earnings (and dividends) by applying past "normal" price/*cash*-earnings relationships and past "normal" dividend yields is found in the Value Line investment service. The method is explained in Arnold Bernhard, *The Evaluation of Common Stocks* (New York: Simon and Schuster, Inc., 1959).

[6]See Benjamin Graham, D. L. Dodd, and Sidney Cottle, *Security Analysis: Principles and Techniques*, 4th ed., Chapter 29 (New York: McGraw-Hill, Inc., 1962).

to help establish the value of a share of stock. What is needed is an approach that is *independent* of the stock market. The purpose of valuation is to establish an intrinsic value, so that this value can be compared with market price, as a basis of buy or sell decisions. The *bond-rate method* is suggested as a means to this end.

The investor always has the alternative of buying riskless bonds and enjoying the "pure" rate of interest available at the time of purchase. Equities present more risk than Treasury bonds. Thus, in the long run the *earnings yield* on common stocks should be substantially higher than the bond rate. How much higher? This depends on the risks in the situation.

With a long-term riskless rate of, say, $5\frac{1}{2}$ per cent, the average stock should sell at an earnings yield of at least $8\frac{1}{4}$ per cent, that is, at about 12 times average *future* earnings. Assuming an 8 per cent rate of growth of earnings (or 7 per cent compounded), about equal to the long-term growth of the Gross National Product, this would mean a price of about 14.5 times *current* earnings. If 60 per cent of the earnings were distributed in dividends, this price would produce an average five-year dividend yield of $5\frac{1}{2}$ per cent on the original price. A lower dividend payout would have to be compensated by a higher rate of growth. As an example, suppose an average-grade stock were currently earning $6 per share, and that the price were 90, or 15 times current earnings. This is equivalent to about 12 times average five-year future earnings of $7.35 (assuming a 7 per cent compounded rate of growth). A 60 per cent payout would produce a $3.60 dividend in the first year and $5.00 in the fifth year.

The investor would be willing to pay more than 15 times current earnings only if future earnings were expected to rise at an above-average rate. He would be willing to pay 20 to 30 times current earnings if future earnings growth were expected to be exceptionally high.

A given stock should be classified as to quality as belonging to one of five categories, based on analysis of earnings growth and stability, short- and long-term financial strength, dividend record and prospects, asset values, and management. (See Table 25-1.) An earnings yield based on expected average five-year *future* earnings, ranging from 1 to 2 times the bond rate, is appropriate for a given category. The average stock belongs in category 3. The Dow Jones industrial stocks, being above average, would belong a little above category 3. They should sell (when the bond rate is $5\frac{1}{2}$ per cent) at about an earnings yield of 8 per cent of average *future*

Table 25-1. VALUATION BASED ON BOND RATE

| Quality Category | Bond Rate | *Using Five-Year Average Future Earnings* | | |
		Earnings Yield X Bond Rate	Earnings Yield	Price-Earnings Multiple
1	$5\frac{1}{2}\%$	1	5.5 %	18
2	$5\frac{1}{2}$	$1\frac{1}{4}$	6.75	15
3	$5\frac{1}{2}$	$1\frac{1}{2}$	8.25	12
4	$5\frac{1}{2}$	$1\frac{3}{4}$	9.5	$10\frac{1}{2}$
5	$5\frac{1}{2}$	2	11.0	9

five-year earnings (or at a price-earnings multiple of future earnings of a little over 12, if one assumes a 7½ per cent rate of growth.

By using average projected five-year earnings as the basis of valuation, a growth stock of great strength could be worth 40 times current earnings, but only if it will *double* its *average* annual earnings in the next five years. A stock of lesser quality is worth 23 times present earnings only if its *average* earnings are expected to increase 50 per cent over the next five years, and so forth.

Let us take three or four hypothetical examples. Suppose a company is presently earning $4.00 per share. The company "has everything." An extraordinarily high rate of growth is expected, that will send the annual earnings to $12.00 a share five years hence, or to an average of $8.00. It has great financial strength and superlative management. It is placed in category 1. (See Table 25-1.) With the bond rate of 5½ per cent, this stock would be worth $8 × 18 = $144 or 36 times present earnings. Very few companies belong in such a category. Or take a company with high but less stable earnings growth prospects, good financial strength, steadily increasing dividends, and good management. Earnings per share *may* grow from $2.00 to $4.00 in five years (average $3.00), but some uncertainty exists. It is placed in category 2. A rough valuation becomes 45 a share. This is over 22 times *current* earnings. Or take a public utility company that has prospects for only modest growth. The current earnings are $4.00 per share, and may grow to $5.00 in five years. Dividends are currently $3.00. The stock is valued largely on an income basis, and is placed between categories 3 and 4. A rough valuation is 45, or about 11 times *current* earnings, to yield 6.7 per cent from the current dividend. Or take a growing but highly cyclical industrial company whose current earnings are $5 per share. Depending on economic conditions, the company will earn between $3 and $8 per share during the next five years. The stock is placed in category 4, and valued at 50. A non-growth utility company would also belong in this category. Or lastly, take a mediocre situation. The current earnings per share are $2.00. But these are not expected to increase. Indeed, they may well decrease. Financial strength is only fair. Management is only so-so. It is placed below category 5. A rough valuation is 12 or less.

In recognition of the inability to read the future with accuracy, we might better cite *ranges* of value for the above situations such as 140 to 150, 42 to 48, 42 to 47, 47 to 52 and 10 to 14. This would allow for the fact that both variables—earnings and multiplier—are subject to error.

Note that in the rough method of valuation used above, earnings five years from now are not being bought at face value. In effect, they are discounted, as they should be. (A dollar five years from now is not worth a dollar today.) Yet credit *is* given for any expected growth. Likewise, if a company's earnings are on the decline, such decline would produce a still lower valuation.

The method just described might appear deceptively simple. Actually, the category in which the company is placed—that is, the quality rating that determines the appropriate multiplier of future earnings—is chosen only after thorough analysis. The estimate of future earnings is also based on the analysis and projection of all of the factors that will affect earnings. For these reasons the number of quality categories is limited to five. Where one or both of these analyses cannot be made with reasonable assurance, a valuation should not be attempted.

The above valuations are based on an assumed riskless bond rate of 5½ per cent. As interest rates fall or rise, this rate would change, producing different value results. The relationship between interest rates and stock prices was dramatically illustrated in 1966, when much of the decline in stock prices could be attributed to rising interest rates, and later in 1967, when stock prices rose as interest rates declined. In 1969–1971 the general stock averages fell nearly 35 per cent as bond yields rose to unprecedented heights. Much of the subsequent recovery can be attributed to declining bond yields. Events of recent years have shown conclusively that stock prices and bond yields are competitive, and therefore interrelated. This is why analysts of general stock price movements pay so much attention to the money supply, the flow of institutional savings, and other factors affecting interest rates.

Methods of projecting earnings.   Most of the above methods of valuation involve a projection of per-share earnings. One approach is to project the earnings-per-share figure itself, using past trends and future growth expectations. However, the net income figure is the result of all previous items on the income statement, and a projection of net income may overlook very important changes in items that have a powerful influence on the final earnings-per-share figure. A sounder approach is to project the sales, and apply to this basic figure the gross and net profit margins, estimated nonoperating income, fixed charges, and income taxes that analysis suggests will apply in the future. Care should be taken to eliminate nonrecurring items that may have disguised the real past earnings and so interfere with a valid projejction of future results.

The following chapters indicate the analytical approaches that will aid the investor to size up the rate, stability and prospects of earnings, the long- and short-term financial strength, the value of the assets, and the quality of management, in various types of industries. Such approaches provide the basis for intelligent investment decisions.

REFERENCES

BAUMAN, W. S., *Estimating the Present Value of Common Stocks by the Variable Rate Method.* Ann Arbor, Mich.: Bureau of Business Research, University of Michigan, 1963.

BELLMORE, D. M., AND JOHN RICHIE, JR., *Investments: Principles, Practices, Analysis,* 3rd ed., Chapters 13, 14. Cincinnati: South-Western Publishing Company, 1969.

BERNHARD, ARNOLD, *The Evaluation of Common Stocks.* New York: Simon and Schuster, Inc., 1959.

CLENDENIN, J. C., *Theory and Techniques of Growth Stock Valuation.* Los Angeles: Bureau of Business and Economic Research, University of California, 1957.

COHEN, J. B., AND E. D. ZINBARG, *Investment Analysis and Portfolio Management,* Part II. Homewood, Ill.: Richard D. Irwin, Inc., 1967.

COTTLE, SIDNEY, AND TATE WHITMAN, *Corporate Earning Power and Market Valuation, 1935–1955.* Durham, N.C.: Duke University Press, 1959.

FRANCIS, J. C., *Investments: Analysis and Management.* New York: McGraw-Hill, Inc., 1972.

GORDON, M. J., *The Investment, Financing and Valuation of the Corporation.* Homewood, Ill.: Richard D. Irwin, Inc., 1962.

GRAHAM, BENJAMIN, *The Intelligent Investor,* 3rd rev. ed., Chapter 10. New York: Harper & Row, Publishers, 1965.

————, D. L. DODD, AND SIDNEY COTTLE, *Security Analysis,* 4th ed., Part IV. New York: McGraw-Hill, Inc., 1962.

HAYES, D. A., *Investments: Analysis and Management,* 2nd ed., Chapters 13, 14. New York: The Macmillan Co., 1966.

McCARTHY, C. D., AND R. E. HEALY, *Valuing a Company: Practices and Procedures.* New York: The Ronald Press Company, 1971.

MERRILL, A. C., *Investing in the Scientific Revolution.* Garden City, N.Y.: Doubleday & Company, 1962.

O'CONNOR, W. P., JR., *Techniques for Maximum Market Profits: A Guide to Preselecting Growth Stocks.* Englewood Cliffs, N.J.: Prentice-Hall, Inc., 1964.

SOLDOFSKY, R. M., AND J. T. MURPHY, *Growth Yields on Common Stocks; Theory and Tables,* rev. ed. Iowa City: Bureau of Business and Economic Research, State University of Iowa, 1963.

WILLIAMS, J. B., *The Theory of Investment Value.* Cambridge, Mass.: Harvard University Press, 1938.

WILLIAMSON, J. P., *Investments: New Analytic Techniques,* Chapter 6. New York: Praeger Publishers, Inc., 1971.

A number of excellent articles on common stock valuation have appeared in *The Financial Analysts Journal* over the years. Convenient selections of the more useful of these articles from this and other publications are found in the following collections of readings:

BALL, R. E., ed., *Readings in Investments,* Part II. Boston: Allyn & Bacon, Inc., 1965.

FREDERICKSON, E. B., ed., *Frontiers of Investment Analysis,* rev. ed., Part IV. Scranton, Pa.: International Textbook Company, 1971.

LERNER, E. M., ed., *Readings in Financial Analysis and Investment Management,* Publication of the Institute of Chartered Financial Analysts, Inc., Sections V, VI. Homewood, Ill.: Richard D. Irwin, Inc., 1963.

THE INSTITUTE OF CHARTERED FINANCIAL ANALYSTS, *C.F.A. Readings in Financial Analysis,* 2nd ed., Part V. Homewood, Ill.: Richard D. Irwin, Inc., 1970.

WEST, D. A., *Readings in Investment Analysis,* Part IV. Scranton, Pa.: International Textbook Company, 1969.

WU, H. K., AND A. J. ZAKON, eds., *Elements of Investments: Selected Readings,* rev. ed., Part III. New York: Holt, Rinehart and Winston, Inc, 1972.

26 Industrial Securities

SCOPE: This chapter discusses the investment position of securities issued by industrial enterprises. The order of discussion is (1) field of industry, (2) accounting problems, (3) industrial characteristics, (4) economic analysis of the industry and company, (5) income statements, (6) balance sheets, (7) working capital changes and flow of funds, (8) analysis of industrial statements, (9) consolidated statements, (10) industrial bonds, (11) preferred stocks, and (12) common stocks.

The Field of Industry

Industrial companies are engaged in the production and sale of commodities and services under competitive conditions. They comprise the great extractive, manufacturing, and distributive agencies of the nation. The extractive industries include mines, oil, timber, and fisheries.[1] The manufacturing industries cover all phases of manufacture, from automobiles and airplanes to textiles and typewriters. The distributive industries include merchandising operations of all kinds, wholesale, retail, and direct selling by mail. The term *industrials* also includes construction and service concerns, and a host of special types. The industrials group includes all forms of private industry not formally classified as transportation, public utilities, financial, or real estate companies.

As a group, the industrials provide in large measure the economic life of the country. Important as the railroad, utility, and financial enterprises are, they serve subordinately as facilitating agencies for the industrial companies.

Accounting Problems

In contrast with the comparability of financial statements of railroad and public utility companies, analysis of industrial companies is complicated by

[1]Natural gas companies, which also belong in the extractive group but which are regulated public utilities, are discussed in Chapter 27.

a lack of uniform accounting procedures. Within the boundaries of acceptable accounting practice room still exists for variations with respect to (1) annual depreciation and depletion allowances, especially the differences between calculations for book and for tax purposes (such variations affect both the reported net income and the balance sheet valuation of assets); (2) valuation of investments in securities held as assets; (3) inventory valuation, as reflected in the balance sheet and in the calculation of cost of sales on the income statement; (4) balance sheet valuation and income statement amortization of intangible assets; (5) capitalization, or setting up as an asset to be amortized over the years, versus charging to annual expense, such items as organization and financing costs, promotion and research expenditures, and intangible items such as drilling costs in the oil industry; (6) location and classification of reserves as current liabilities, long-term liabilities, or net worth, and the charging of expenses (that are credited to reserves) to net income or to retained earnings; (7) accounting for deferred income taxes ("flow-through" versus "normalizing") that affects the reported net income and the handling of deferred tax credits as liabilities or as net worth; (8) treatment of nonrecurring gains or losses either as influences on reported earnings or on the surplus account; (9) revision of earnings per share to account for possible dilution resulting from the conversion of bonds and preferred stock; and (10) consolidation of assets and earnings of subsidiaries and affiliates.

Lack of uniformity is also found in annual financial reports to stockholders. Some companies present detailed and fully explained balance sheet and income statements; they also provide useful comparative annual figures for a number of years. Others are miserly with facts. They present only the minimum information required by their auditors. Investors are compelled to base their decisions more upon the reputation of the company and confidence in the product and the management, than on reported information. Fortunately, the trend is toward more complete and uniform information as a result of corporate policies to "open up" their affairs to stockholders, investment analysts, and the public. Regulation such as that imposed by the Securities Act of 1933 and the Securities Exchange Act of 1934 is also responsible for improvement of reports, as are progress in accounting and auditing standards and the influence of professional security analysts.

Another important factor in the industrial field is the growing tendency on the part of companies to diversify their activities. This is apparent in various forms, such as (1) the manufacture of a more diversified list of products, (2) integration of operations from extraction of raw materials to sale to consumers, and (3) the purchase of control of other companies in a variety of fields. Agricultural implements no longer comprise the major part of the sales of International Harvester; this company has become one of the largest makers of motor trucks in the country. American Brake Shoe (now Abex Corp.) derives less than 40 per cent of its sales from railroad equipment, and Textron, with an aggressive diversification program, now depends on textile products for less than 25 per cent of total sales. Eastman Kodak has engaged in textile manufacturing. General Electric has built up an enormous domestic appliance business in addition to its manufacture of industrial apparatus. Thus, many companies with diversified activities are difficult to compare.

Industrial Characteristics

Industrial enterprise has certain characteristics whose analysis is important to interested investors. In contrast to the characteristics of public service companies, these may be stated concisely. *Economic* features include (1) greater cyclical variation in prices, sales, and profit, (2) competition for the business available, (3) lack of special regulation, (4) a greater variety of lines produced or sold, (5) greater emphasis on new product development and research, (6) greater dependence on foreign markets, and (7) greater dependence on management. *Financial* characteristics (in addition to instability of earnings) include (1) greater investment in current assets and working capital, (2) faster turnover of operating assets, (3) higher operating ratios and lower profit margins, (4) higher average rates of return on investment, (5) greater importance of intangible assets, (6) special hazards of inventory and credit losses, and (7) more conservative methods of financing.

Just as the whole industrial group and the diverse types of business included vary widely, so also do the characteristics just noted vary greatly from company to company. Yet the group has sufficient homogeneity to warrant some generalizations.

Industrial operations are notoriously unstable, being affected not only by changing conditions in each industry but also by swings in the general business cycle. A variation of from 10 to 20 per cent in annual revenues is unusual in utility operations; in contrast, annual sales of industrial companies may move in a much wider range. Such variation has a magnified effect upon earnings through both operating and financial leverage. Bondholders should realize that an impressive margin of safety in prosperous times may dwindle or even disappear in times of recession. Stockholders, especially, should be as well prepared for deficits in poor years as for surpluses in good years. Industrial earnings in prosperous years can be very misleading.

The yearly variation in industrial earnings is indicated by the data in Table 26-1 showing the results of operations of leading manufacturing corporations on the stockholders' book investment (net worth) and net income after taxes. While the dollar figures are not strictly comparable because of the variation in the number of companies, the annual financial results indicate the general pattern and trends. One should note, however, that in such aggregate data the extremes—high or low—experienced by the best and poorest companies and industries in the group are not revealed. These figures show some important relationships. In general, falling sales were accompanied by declining net income margins and declining return on owners' investment (1949, 1958). The leverage of rising sales accompanied by a rising margin produced a sharp rise in rate of return (1959, 1963–1966,

Table 26-1. NET EARNINGS OF LEADING MANUFACTURING COMPANIES
(dollars in millions)

	No. of Cos.	Net Income	Net Worth Jan. 1	Return on Net Worth	Sales	Net Income as a Percentage of Sales
1946	1,511	$ 4,091	$ 33,674	12.1%	$ 68,180	6.0%
1947	1,571	6,317	37,062	17.0	88,970	7.1
1948	1,680	8,063	42,607	18.9	107,510	7.5
1949	1,710	6,998	50,656	13.8	103,220	6.8
1950	1,693	9,288	54,403	17.1	120,620	7.7
1951	1,763	8,711	60,617	14.4	140,500	6.2
1952	1,788	8,093	65,990	12.3	149,870	5.4
1953	1,781	8,781	70,218	12.5	165,680	5.3
1954	1,778	9,280	74,825	12.4	157,290	5.9
1955	1,765	12,373	82,599	15.0	184,670	6.7
1956	1,843	12,724	91,659	13.9	212,070	6.0
1957	1,835	12,903	100,545	12.8	218,690	5.9
1958	1,852	10,643	108,140	9.9	204,670	5.2
1959	1,944	13,327	114,446	11.6	229,770	5.8
1960	2,034	12,810	121,720	10.5	237,220	5.4
1961	2,138	12,891	128,002	10.1	238,720	5.4
1962	2,316	14,681	134,145	10.9	267,000	5.5
1963	2,280	16,261	141,922	11.5	285,280	5.7
1964	2,328	18,774	148,385	12.7	307,770	6.1
1965	2,298	22,001	158,061	13.9	343,760	6.4
1966	2,279	24,074	170,405	13.0	381,120	6.3
1967	2,292	23,307	186,380	12.5	408,900	5.7
1968	2,250	26,066	198,730	13.1	457,300	5.7
1969	2,068	26,650	212,793	12.5	493,520	5.4
1970	2,127	23,413	232,025	10.1	508,980	4.6
1971	2,319	26,971	248,584	10.8	573,830	4.7

Source: First National City Bank of New York, *Monthly Economic Letter, April* issues.

1968). But a rise in sales accompanied by a level margin increased the return on owners' equity only modestly (1962), and in 1969–1971 the lower margin produced a lower rate of return in spite of increased sales. Any general statement concerning the variations in sales and profits must be qualified by recognition that some groups—notably those supplying low-priced consumer necessities—have fared much better than the average in periods of recession, while others—notably the capital goods industries—have fared much worse. Certain industrial groups have shown stability equal to that enjoyed by the utilities.

The industrial field is characterized by a high degree of competition in a wide number of forms influencing product prices, volume of business, and operating costs. Competition within industries is often limited by integration, control of raw materials, patents, trademarks, brand names, tariffs, and other advantages such as product monopoly through research and development. Yet actual or potential competition always stands as a threat to the sales and *earnings* of industrial enterprises.

Industrials are not subject to the *special* regulation that is imposed on public service companies with respect to prices, wages, service, financing, and other activities, except when national policy dictates, such as during the price-and-wage "freeze" of 1971–1972. The absence of such regulation in normal times permits a high rate of earnings under conditions of brisk business. But industrials lack the protection that regulation affords railroads and utilities. This is one of the many factors that contribute to the general instability of industrial sales and rates of profit.

In the industrials group, the production of a very wide variety of goods and services, combined with sales at changing prices, makes for a lack of uniformity in methods of operation and accounting. It thus becomes extremely difficult to make comparisons of operating performance. Even the statements of two steel corporations may reflect the difference in output between heavy and light or specialty steels. This problem is further aggravated when the same corporation or a parent and its subsidiaries are engaged in a number of different lines of business. Application of the basic tests of financial condition and earning power are about the only practical approach to the analysis of such "conglomerates."

The changing economic and technical scene in which business operates requires a constant program of research and new product development. The heavy expenses of such effort are capital expenditures (whether charged to the period or capitalized), and they are mandatory for progress in a competitive age. Farsighted firms are also developing foreign markets either through foreign subsidiaries or affiliates or by direct sales effort from home.

All of the above factors combine to give the *management* factor unusual importance in industrial analysis. Unlike the public utility companies, where the range of decision-making is limited by regulation, in the industrial field management policies have wide scope. These policies are evolved out of the experience of the company applied with sufficient flexibility to meet changing conditions. Efficiency of management is shown in a variety of ways, such as quality of the product, improvements in production and marketing methods, rate of growth, development of new products, and strong finances. But the outstanding test is the rate and growth of earning power.

In addition to their economic characteristics, industrials as a group display certain common financial traits, although here again the reader must be cautioned not to expect any marked degree of uniformity. In general, current assets and short-term sources of funds as represented by current liabilities play a much more important role in the industrial than in the public service balance sheet. Merchandising concerns may show as high as 70 to 80 per cent of assets in current form; heavy goods manufacturers and mining companies may show a predominance of fixed assets, but not to the same extent as the typical utility or railroad. This condition reflects the large investment in inventories and receivables of the industrial corporation and its greater need of a substantial cash balance. This emphasis on current assets in part explains why many industrial companies rely heavily on bank loans, trade credit, and other current sources of funds.

Another financial feature of industrials is their generally more rapid turnover of investment, as indicated by the relation of sales to operating assets. A public utility may have from $3 to $5 invested for every dollar of sales; a manufacturing company, however, may turn its investment once or twice a year, and a merchant as many as seven or eight times a year, taking all operating assets into account. Accompanying the faster turnover of investment is a higher operating ratio and lower margin of operating earnings and net income (earnings in relation to sales). But even a low ratio of profit to sales may produce a high rate of return on investment (see below). Such a return is necessary to attract capital in the face of the greater variation in earnings.

A special feature of the competitive industrials is the frequent importance of patents, brand names, goodwill, and other intangible assets, including expenditures on research, trade position, and the like. In fact, the common stocks of many industrials are supported primarily by such intangible values. The practice of carrying valuable intangible assets on the balance sheet at a conservative figure—often as low as $1—produces a low book value for the common stock, but recognizes the fleeting value of this type of property, which depends, in the last analysis, on the *earning power* of the enterprise.

The industrial company, with its large investment in inventories and receivables, is subject to the special risk of loss in the value of these assets as a result of declining prices and depressed business conditions. This risk may be diminished by conservative methods of valuation and adequate reserves.

All of the special hazards to which industrial companies are exposed require a conservative capital structure in which senior securities play a much less important role than in the utilities. Although few prominent companies now avoid long-term debt financing altogether, in most cases the burden of interest is modest. While such a policy overlooks the possible advantages of greater leverage, it produces much greater stability in net income and in dividend payments.

The preceding description of financial features is illustrated in Table 26-2 by reference to 1970 figures of some selected groups of industrial corporations as compared with those of electric and telephone utilities and railroads.[2] Note that these are aggregate figures and that within their respective groups individual companies may differ considerably. Group data, however, provide a point of reference.

[2]The Robert Morris Associates wishes the following disclaimer statement to accompany the data in Table 26-2:

RMA cannot emphasize too strongly that their composite figures for each industry may *not* be representative of that entire industry (except by coincidence), for the following reasons:

1. The only companies with a chance of being included in their study in the first place are those for whom their submitting banks have recent figures.

2. Even from this restricted group of potentially includable companies, those which are chosen, and the total number chosen, are not determined in any random or otherwise statistically reliable manner.

3. Many companies in their study have *varied* product lines; they are "mini-conglomerates," if you will. All they can do in these cases is categorize them by their *primary* product line, and be willing to tolerate any "impurity" thereby introduced.

In a word, don't automatically consider their figures as representative norms and don't attach any more or less significance to them than is indicated by the unique aspects of the data collection.

Table 26-2. FINANCIAL CHARACTERISTICS, SELECTED INDUSTRY GROUPS, 1970

Industry Group (and no. of companies)	As a Percentage of Total Assets					Long-term Debt as a Percentage of Cap. Structure	As a Percentage of Sales	
	Plant (Net)	Current Assets	Inventories	Current Liabilities	Net Sales (Revenues)		Cost of Sales	Net Income before Income Taxes
92 Bread and bakery products	53%	40%	13%	23%	285%	18%	62%	4%
49 Brick and clay tile	50	41	18	19	90	33	77	—
49 Drugs and medicines	32	58	25	29	150	23	59	-.2
197 Electronic components	27	66	31	31	146	26	74	15
28 Electronic computers	28	58	30	27	109	36	69	12
93 Farm machinery equipment	21	72	41	33	144	20	75	4
226 Gen'l industrial machinery	25	68	33	32	156	18	73	6
98 Industrial chemicals	38	55	23	28	155	23	74	7
89 Iron and steel foundries	41	52	22	26	165	20	83	5
146 Meat packing	37	58	21	33	688	23	92	1
61 Motor vehicles	21	69	39	34	179	20	82	5
125 Motor vehicle parts	29	66	35	28	177	20	79	5
58 Pulp and paper	48	46	19	20	154	24	83	3
113 Wholesale jewellers	6	89	46	39	203	10	73	6
167 Department stores	22	72	41	35	227	23	69	4
187 Groceries and meat stores	38	57	37	36	598	27	83	2
All private light and power companies	91	6	2	8	28	55	71	24
71 Class I railroads	77	11	2	10	35	40	89	1

SOURCES: For all groups except light and power and railroad companies, data derived from The Robert Morris Associates, *Annual Statement Studies*, 1971 edition. Copyright, the Robert Morris Associates, 1971; reproduced by permission (see footnote 2); Federal Power Commission, *Statistics of Electric Utilities in the United States*, 1970; Interstate Commerce Commission, *Transport Statistics in the United States*, 1970, Part I, *Railroad Companies*.

Economic Analysis of the Industry and Company

The first step in the study of a company is to describe the industry to which it belongs, that is, its market structure or major divisions and products, its size in terms of sales and possibly number of employees, the location of its operations, and the degree of concentration or number of major companies involved. This information provides the setting for identifying a company within its group and noting its relative importance.

The next step is to examine the economic characteristics of the industry and compare the company with the group to which it belongs. Among the more important economic factors to be considered are (1) the rate of growth or stage in the life cycle, (2) the stability or cyclical performance of sales and earnings, and (3) the special factors that characterize the industry.

Industries pass through life-cycle stages from infancy to senility, although wars have a way of giving some of the older groups (such as steam railroads and coal) a new lease on life. The investor should be satisfied that the long-term trend of the industry, as measured by production and sales, at least keeps pace with the rate of growth of the economy as measured by GNP, disposable consumer income, and other indicators. But he should note that rapid growth alone does not necessarily produce immediate high earnings, and that a long period of maturity, after the stage of early growth, may bring its reward in terms of stability, as in the case of the tobacco companies. Examples of growth industries are found in the chemicals, electronics, office machines, ethical drugs, and containers industries, to name only a few. An exact definition of a "growth industry" or a "growth company" is difficult. Growth in the investment sense is not mere growth in size (assets, sales, employees), but rather growth in the rate of earnings on invested capital that is in turn reflected in growth in market value of shares. The leading characteristics of a *growth stock* are (1) continuing increase in sales that produces a continuing increase in earnings and a high rate of return on invested capital, (2) reinvestment and compounding of the bulk of profits, and (3) high earnings attributable chiefly to research, product development, and forward-looking management. These characteristics cause the price of growth company shares to rise much faster than the average, and to sell at higher-than-average multiples of earnings. We should also note that some growth industries are highly vulnerable to the business cycle (paper, for example). Their secular or long-run expansion makes them interesting for investment, but not necessarily stable. They could be called "cyclical growth" situations.

Some of the basic indicators of growth and the stage in the life cycle of an industry, and of the companies within it, that explain the growth of earnings are growth of markets in terms of geography and products; increased labor productivity as measured by labor costs in relation to product prices; development of patents, processes, and products or services that preserve the competitive position; gains in efficiency as represented by per-unit production and sales costs; preservation and expansion of raw material resources; continuous expansion of capital expenditures without a sacrifice of earnings; and attraction of farsighted and aggressive management personnel. Sales, production (in units of product), and earnings of the industry and of individual companies can be related to the basic indicators of the progress of the economy as a whole.

The stability of an industry, and of its constituent companies, is important to most investors. The more important indicators of stability are (1) degree of cyclical variation in sales and earnings, (2) rate of growth or stage in the life cycle, (3) degree of competition within the industry and between the industry and its rivals, (4) labor relations and wage policy, (5) prices and inventory value, (6) tariff and other political influences, and (7) availability of managerial skills. Cyclical variations in sales, production, and earnings are studied in relation to the general economy. Among the chief causes of such fluctuations are dependence on sales to the capital goods market, vulnerability of prices in relation to operating costs, and dependence on other industries which themselves are cyclical.

Among the many special factors affecting industry (and company) results and prospects are the following: (1) degree of inter- and intraindustry competition, (2) labor relations and wage policy, (3) special inventory risks, (4) dependence on tariffs, (5) "political" risks, (6) reliance on foreign markets, (7) dependence on new product development, and (8) dependence on defense contracts.

As was mentioned previously, industrial companies are characterized as a group by a high degree of competition. The extent to which different types of industrials are subject to competition from within or without, and whether the competition is cutthroat or healthy varies widely. Competition is, of course, important in respect to its effect on the rate and stability of earning power. Healthy competition, as seen in the automobile industry, may actually tend to stabilize earning power. Extreme competition, as in the meat-packing group, may so reduce the margin of profit as to prevent any member from producing a satisfactory return, or may eliminate earnings entirely for some firms. Efforts to limit or minimize competition, and so produce an advantage at least within the group, are found in the use of valuable patents and processes, brand names, favorable channels of distribution, progressive research, successful advertising, control or ownership of raw material sources, tariff protection, and control of unusual managerial and technical talent. However, the more successful a particular company or group of companies becomes in dominating the field by any of these methods, the more exposed it becomes to government antitrust action, as is illustrated by developments in motion pictures (divorce of production and distribution through exclusive dealer contracts), aluminum (compulsory separation of stock ownership interests in the major American and Canadian companies), and automobiles (divestment of General Motors stock by du Pont).

Labor relations and wage policy have become increasingly important in recent years because of the growing ability of organized labor to introduce pressure on costs and profits, especially in such industries as steel and automobiles, where wages constitute a large proportion of the cost of the product. The investor should be satisfied that labor relations are amicable and that the industry has a good strike record.

As was noted earlier, as a class, industrial concerns are characterized by a relatively large investment in inventories. The data previously presented indicate that, as a percentage of total assets and of current assets, inventories vary in importance from one industrial subgroup to another. The greater the investment in inventory, the greater is the special risk from sudden declines in price, and the greater the "artificial" profit achieved as a result of price increases. Efforts to eliminate inventory risks are illustrated by the hedging operations of milling companies, which carry inventory for which there is a constant market at published prices. Other concerns minimize the effects of fluctuations in the value of both raw materials and finished goods by using the "last-in, first-out" (LIFO) method of inventory accounting in calculating cost of goods sold.[3] Others set up special reserves against inventory fluctuations. A rapid turnover is, of course, the best protection of all.

Some industries derive special protection from foreign competition by tariffs, as in the case of nonferrous metals and wool. Such protection is not a dependable assurance of profits in a world that may become increasingly free-trade minded. The automobile industry provides an example of a stronger situation, namely, such a level of large-scale production as to compete successfully with low-cost foreign producers. The same ability to achieve the economies of mass production permits this industry to compete abroad with producers having low wage scales. (The increase in the sale of foreign cars in the United States has made this illustration less valid than formerly.)

A host of special political factors are faced during periods of national emergency, such as excess profits taxes, price controls, materials allocation, and the like. Such factors affect the short-run outlook for an industry but (one hopes) do not disturb its long-run earning power.

Many industries and companies are expanding their foreign markets, which offer great potential, but are fraught with unusual political, economic, and exchange market risks. Investment in securities of foreign affiliates, and loans by American banks to foreign-based firms are likewise discouraged by the equalization tax and the Administration's voluntary program to curtail the export of American capital. (See Chapter 10.)

The astounding march of technical progress in the postwar period is reflected in the great emphasis on research and new product development on the part of industrial firms. To keep up in the competitive race such expenditures must not only be ample, but ultimately productive. The mere allocation of large sums to research and development is not enough. New product sales and earnings must be forthcoming.

The defense activities of the Federal government constitute the biggest economic activity in the nation, with an annual budget of about $80 billions. Whole industries are primarily dependent on their share of this total, and the fate of thousands of companies hangs on their participation as successful contractors.

[3]Under the LIFO method, cost of goods sold is charged with the cost of the latest additions to inventory, so that in a period of rising prices, gross profits from operations are reduced over those that would have been reported under FIFO (first-in, first-out).

All these risks and changing conditions in industry place a premium on management. While good management is important to the success of every business, the greater the special hazards to which it is subjected, the greater the emphasis that should be placed on analysis of management in the investment appraisal.

One method of testing management competency is to compare the relative status of the company in its field—whether it is improving its trade position or share of the available market and of the total industry earnings over a period of years. More specific tests are indicated in the discussion that follows.

After the examination of economic factors, attention is next given to tests of financial strength and earnings as revealed by analysis of the company's statements.

Income Statements

The income statement (Table 26-3) shows the earnings of the company for the given period. Revenues and expenses for the period are matched to

Table 26-3.   INDUSTRIAL COMPANY INCOME STATEMENT

		Percentage of Sales
Statement of Profit and Loss		
Net sales (gross sales less returns, discounts, and allowances)	$150,000,000	100.0%
Cost of goods sold	$120,500,000	80.3
Depreciation, depletion, and amortization	2,500,000	1.7
Selling, general, and administrative expenses	14,500,000	9.7
Net operating profit	$ 12,500,000	8.3
Other income	1,500,000	1.0
Gross income	$ 14,000,000	9.3
Deductions from income		
Interest on funded debt	1,800,000	1.2
Other deductions	200,000	.1
Net income before income taxes	$ 12,000,000	8.0
Provision for Federal income taxes	6,000,000	4.0
Net income before special items	$ 6,000,000	4.0
Special items (adjusted for related income taxes)	$ 150,000	.1
Net income transferred to retained earnings	$ 5,850,000	3.9%
Statement of Retained Earnings		
Balance, end of previous year	$ 25,000,000	
Net income for year	5,850,000	
	$ 30,850,000	
Cash dividends paid		
Preferred stock, $3.25 per share	800,000	
Common stock, $4.00 per share	2,000,000	
Balance, end of year	$ 28,050,000	

reveal the net profit from operations. Interest, income taxes, and any special losses in asset values attributable to the period are then deducted to determine the net income transferred to retained earnings (earned surplus). The illustrative tables are designed to show the most useful and representative presentations of items, and suggest the form in which the actual statements of an industrial company may be rearranged for analytical purposes.

Net sales. Net sales represents the revenue received from the aggregate invoices of the company. The almost universal practice is to show only one figure and not to disclose departmental results. The amount shown should be compared with sales in previous years for a study of the growth and stability of the company. The trend over a series of years is as important as the variations from year to year.

Cost of goods sold. For merchandising concerns, the cost of goods sold is found by adding purchases to the beginning inventory and deducting the inventory at the end of the period. For manufacturing concerns, the figure is the total of direct labor, materials, and manufacturing expenses, including depreciation. Inventories are ordinarily valued at cost, figured by average cost; first-in, first-out; last-in, first-out; or some other recognized method. Cost of ending inventory is then compared with market value, and the lower of the two is used on the balance sheet. The use of the LIFO method has the result of minimizing the effect of price changes on profits. (See footnote 2.)

On some statements, the deduction of the cost of goods sold from net sales is shown as gross profit on sales or gross profit from operations. Taken as a percentage of sales, it is also referred to as the gross profit margin. This is a particularly useful ratio, as it enables one to compare the actual cost of purchase or production of one company with that of other concerns or with the performance of a group of companies serving as a standard.

Depreciation. This expense, representing the estimated wear and tear of physical property during the period, is one over which management has considerable discretion. Its over- or understatement can substantially affect the end-profit results. The adequacy of depreciation is measured by comparing the depreciation expense as a percentage of gross plant with similar figures for other companies and for the industry. As permitted by the Internal Revenue Code, accelerated depreciation has tended to increase the current rates of most companies so that the basis of charging this expense must be examined. The growing practice is either to segregate depreciation and show operating profit before and after this item, or to indicate by a footnote the amount charged to cost of sales. In either case, comparisons of operating results with the industry and with other companies is facilitated, because of the differences in policies of accounting for noncash expenses.

Depletion. Depletion, or the allowance for actual loss of assets, as in mining and oil companies, is a major item on many statements. For *book* (annual report) purposes, it is usually calculated at the investment cost of the units sold. Higher depletion for income tax purposes may (temporarily, at least) reduce the current income tax, helping to make this figure appear small in relation to earnings before taxes.

Amortization. Amortization of intangible assets whose value is used up in production, such as the write-off of intangible drilling costs by oil companies, is affected by policy with respect to the expensing of such costs. Some companies capitalize the outlays and amortize them over a period of years; others charge them as incurred. Comparisons of this item must be made with care.

Selling, general, and administrative expenses. These expenses are sometimes itemized but, regrettably, are more frequently combined. Their importance differs considerably among various types of industrial concerns. They include sales commissions and salaries, selling expenses such as advertising, storage and delivery costs, officers' salaries, general office expenses, and many miscellaneous items that constitute the overhead of the business. Financial expenses such as interest on short-term bank loans and on factored receivables are usually included in the general expense category. Interest on funded debt is sometimes included, but this is more properly itemized later in the statement to facilitate comparison with income available for interest.

Net operating profit. This is the sum available before interest on long-term debt, income taxes, and any extraordinary debits or credits. It measures the operating skill of the management and, related to the investment in operating assets, shows the rate of return on the assets devoted to the business proper. The ratio of net operating profit to net sales, or *net operating profit margin,* is the complement of the operating ratio. An operating ratio of 91.7 per cent (as in Table 26-3) produces a net operating profit margin of 8.3 per cent. This is a highly useful ratio in comparing operating efficiency of different companies.

Other income. Other income or income credits represent earnings derived outside of the regular operations of the business, such as rentals, royalties, interest, and dividends (from affiliates and investments). This is at times a very substantial figure.

Gross or total income. This figure is the total of net operating profit and other income. It is then reduced by *deductions from income,* or *income charges,* chiefly interest on funded (and sometimes unfunded) debt and amortization of bond discount and expense.[4]

---

[4]The treatment of leases and rental expense presents special problems. Annual short-term lease rentals are ordinarily included in either cost of sales or general expenses, depending on the nature and use of the facilities. Long-term leases, however, represent the use of other people's capital and the rent is akin to interest on a mortgage. Rents payable on such leases should be shown, along with interest on long-term debt, among the deductions from gross income. Too often, however, they are buried in operating costs. Recent accounting literature strongly suggests that annual lease commitments be itemized, at least in footnote form.

The relation of gross income to regularly recurring income deductions indicates the coverage of *fixed charges,* although as stated elsewhere, it is more conservative to calculate this coverage after deduction of income taxes.

Provision for Federal (and state) income taxes. Income taxes are the estimated levy to be paid on profits. In case of a net operating loss, the tax refundable through carryback to a prior year, or the carryforward against profits in a future year, reduces the tax expense for the period.

The tax expense shown on the income statement is associated with the financial income reported on that statement but is derived from the income on the company's tax return. The two income figures may be very different. For example, suppose a company computes depreciation for income tax purposes on an accelerated basis (the fixed-percentage-of-declining-balance method or the sum-of-the-digits method) but, in its reports to stockholders, charges ordinary straight-line depreciation. It now has two choices. On the assumption that in later years depreciation will decline and taxable income will rise, it may "normalize" its current reported net income by charging deferred tax expense and crediting (on the balance sheet) a deferred liability for taxes payable in the future. Or it may allow the temporarily higher pretax net income to "flow through" to final net income. The former system has been widely accepted.

Net income. This is the amount earned for the stockholders of the corporation and is the final measure of success or failure. Unfortunately, the figure is never accurate. This is because the actual gain or loss of a business over a period can be determined precisely only when the business is liquidated. For a going concern, the reported net income is the result not only of actual receipts and payments but of a variety of estimates. The degree to which reported net income is affected by policy is well illustrated by the treatment of special nonrecurring items such as loss or gain on sale of capital assets, legal judgments, write-downs of land or other assets below book value, tax assessments attributable to prior years, and adjustments for depreciation and for uncollectable accounts set up in prior years. Where such items affect the net income, the *clean surplus* theory is being followed, that is, all gains and losses are reflected in profits (net of taxes involved). Otherwise, all or part of them may be charged to the retained earnings (earned surplus) account.

The net income figure is used to determine the rate of return earned on net worth (and on common stock, after deduction of preferred dividends), as well as the percentage of sales "brought down" to the owners.

Retained earnings. The retained earnings (surplus) section shows the beginning surplus (in many cases, both capital and earned), profits for the year, and the deductions—chiefly dividends and any special charges run through the surplus account, such as special reserves and nonrecurring losses or gains adjusted for related income taxes. The final figure coincides with that found on the balance sheet as of the end of the period.

Balance Sheets

The balance sheet (see Table 26-4) shows the total assets or resources of the company, carried at values that reflect the methods of accounting used. The total *book value* of the assets will not coincide with their liquidating value, cost of reproduction, or sales value as a going concern. Offsetting the assets are the sources from which the resources have been derived, in two main categories—liabilities or debts, and the net worth section showing the owners' investment.

Current assets. Current assets are the items that are generally realizable within one year, chiefly cash, receivables (balances owed by customers), inventories, marketable securities held as a temporary investment of idle cash, and prepaid expenses.

CASH. Cash includes the funds on hand and on deposit in banks that are available for general corporate use. Special funds earmarked for particular long-term purposes are not included among the current assets.

MARKETABLE SECURITIES. These are temporary investments, chiefly U.S. Government securities, that are held pending the need of more cash for operations. The preferred method of valuation is at cost, unless market value is substantially lower. Some industrial companies have very large holdings of such securities. Where large sums are being held for specific purchases or investments at a later date (after one year), such amounts are ordinarily not classified as current assets.

Sometimes, U.S. Government securities held for meeting income tax liability are offset against the liability. The net working capital remains the same but the current ratio is increased (if above one to start with).

RECEIVABLES. These include trade notes and accounts receivable, less an estimated allowance for bad debts that is based on collection experience. Other receivables, as from officers, directors, and affiliates, may be included among the current assets if they are to be realized within a year. The more conservative practice, however, is to show these as miscellaneous assets.

INVENTORIES. Inventories represent the value of merchandise on hand. In manufacturing companies, the item is divided into finished goods, work in process, and raw materials. Supplies are sometimes included. In merchandising concerns, the inventories consist of goods for resale.

The basis of valuation of inventories is very important. The most widely used method is *cost or market, whichever is lower.* The basis of cost is usually indicated—last-in first-out, average cost, or some other method. Since inventories bulk very large on industrial statements, their balance sheet valuation should meet reasonable standards, as revealed by tests that will be explained later in this chapter.

Table 26-4. INDUSTRIAL COMPANY BALANCE SHEET

Assets		*Liabilities and Stockholders' Equity*	
Current assets		Current liabilities	
Cash	$15,000,000	Accounts and notes payable, trade	$ 9,500,000
Marketable securities	1,000,000	Notes payable, bank	700,000
Receivables (net)	28,000,000	Accrued salaries and wages	1,200,000
Inventories	27,000,000	Accrued interest	250,000
Prepaid expenses	500,000	Provision for income taxes	5,000,000
		Accrued other taxes	1,250,000
		Cash dividends payable	2,000,000
		Long-term debt due within one year	100,000
Total current assets	$71,500,000	Total current liabilities	$20,000,000
Long-term investments and receivables	5,500,000	Deferred credits to income	200,000
Property, plant, and equipment	29,000,000	Long-term liabilities	
Less depreciation	7,000,000	Mortgage bonds	20,000,000
	$22,000,000	Term loan	900,000
		Reserves	1,500,000
Deferred charges	700,000	Deferred Federal income taxes	500,000
Intangible assets	100,000	Stockholders' equity	
Other assets	200,000	Preferred stock $15,000,000	
		Common stock 4,000,000	
		Capital surplus 3,000,000	
		Earnings reinvested 34,900,000	$ 56,900,000
Total	$100,000,000	Total	$100,000,000

PREPAID EXPENSES. These expenditures are those for benefits and services to be enjoyed in the next fiscal year, such as for supplies, rent, insurance, and commissions. They qualify as current assets because they obviate cash payment in the near future. They are valued at cost. Many firms, however, show them under miscellaneous assets at the bottom of the balance sheets, or lump them with deferred charges.

Permanent investments.

These include holdings of securities that are not readily marketable, and investments in subsidiaries and affiliates. The item may bulk very large if the company is a parent or has substantial control of other corporations. The basis of valuation (ordinarily cost) should be clearly indicated. A clue to the real value of investments is found in the amount reported as "other income" on the income statement. If other income is 25 per cent of the book value of investments, undervaluation is suspected.

The property account.

Fixed assets include land, buildings, and equipment, and occasionally improvements to leased property. The customary method of valuation is cost less (except in the case of land) the accumulated allowance for depreciation (and sometimes depletion). The book value of such assets may be far removed from their real value to the business. Reserves may be inadequate or overstated, and periodic appraisals may distort the comparability of successive balance sheet figures.

Depreciation is calculated by various methods, of which the most important are:

1. *Straight-line.* Cost, less estimated salvage value, is divided by the estimated years of life, producing (for each type of fixed asset) a uniform depreciation expense each year—for example, 10 per cent each year for ten years—as long as the asset remains unretired.

2. *Declining-balance.* The cost value is reduced by a constant rate to produce a successively lower depreciation expense each year. For tax purposes, this rate may be as high as twice the straight-line rate. At a rate of 20 per cent, assets with a cost of 100 would be valued at 80, 64, 51.2, and so on.

3. *Sum-of-the-digits.* Asset cost is multiplied by reducing fractions whose denominator is the sum of the digits of the years and whose numerator is the digit for each year of life in reverse order. Thus, for an asset with a five-year life, the denominator is 15 $(1 + 2 + 3 + 4 + 5)$ and the numerators are 5, 4, 3, 2, and 1 for each year, in that order. The result is a progressively lower depreciation expense (5/15, 4/15, 3/15, 2/15, and 1/15 of cost).

4. *Unit-of-production or service.* The asset cost is divided by a rate per unit of output or service (tons, miles, flying hours) multiplied by the units for a particular year. This produces a varying annual depreciation expense.

Accumulated depletion represents the amount of original cost of "wasting" assets that have been sold off through inventory. Successive book values are divided by successive estimates of remaining units of oil, minerals, or timber to arrive at the remaining capacity.

The *accumulated depreciation* shows the total amount by which the original cost of the fixed assets has been reduced by annual charges to depreciation expense. The amount may be quite different from the actual sum that would be necessary to replace the assets.

Deferred charges. These charges represent outlays for the benefit of the long-run future such as costs of organization and of bond financing. The former may be amortized over a five-year period, and the latter over the life of the bond issue. Such assets belong in the intangible category and, along with the other intangible assets noted below, are usually deducted in calculating the "tangible book value" of common stock.

Intangible assets. These include such items as patents, trademarks, copyrights, franchises, and goodwill. These are often carried at purely arbitrary values, not infrequently at some nominal sum such as $1, even though they may be very valuable. With the exception of goodwill, they may properly be amortized against income over their legal lives. Conservatism is to be desired in valuing such items, as they would depreciate greatly in case of liquidation resulting from failure, and would be worth very little in the case of prolonged deficits.

Other assets. This is a catch-all account which includes all items not important enough for separate itemizing. The amount is usually relatively small.

Current liabilities. These are obligations due within one year. Deducting their total from the total current assets produces the figure of (net) *working capital*. The items shown in the illustrative balance sheet are self-explanatory; others sometimes found in this category are deposits made with the company (say, to bind a purchase, or on containers or equipment) and advance payments made by customers.

The ratio of current assets to current liabilities is the familiar current or working capital ratio that is widely used in statement analysis. This test will be discussed later.

Deferred credits to income. These credits represent income which has been credited on the books as received but which will not be earned until a year after the date of the balance sheet, for example, prepayments for finance charges. Amounts to be earned in the next twelve months may appear as current liabilities.

Long-term liabilities. These liabilities include all obligations due in more than twelve months. They include corporate bonds, term loans from banks and insurance companies, and, occasionally, individual long-term mortgages. The good industrial statement will indicate the maturity of each major item of long-term liabilities. Any portion of a bond issue or a term loan that is due within a year should appear in the current liability section of the statement.

Reserves. Reserves represent either provisions for specific claims or losses, or appropriations of retained earnings. The former ordinarily appear just above the net worth section, and include such items as provision for foreign investment and exchange losses, pending lawsuits, self-insurance, employee benefits, and workmen's compensation. General *reserves for contingencies* that relate to nebulous or undetermined hazards should be found in the net worth section as "earmarked" earned surplus.

Deferred Federal income taxes. As explained previously, when a company charges accelerated depreciation for tax purposes but uses straight-line depreciation in its report, it may charge tax expense on the income statement and credit deferred income taxes on the balance sheet, in the amount of current tax saving. The accumulated deferred income tax item on the balance sheet represents a type of reserve to be used in later years when depreciation charges for tax purposes may be lower than the straight-line charges made on the books. Considerable argument occurs on whether this item is a true liability or part of the net worth. The conservative position favors the former treatment, although in an expanding company that continues to add to its fixed assets the item is likely to become permanent.

Net worth. The net worth section of the balance sheet contains the capital stock and surplus accounts and reserves of the surplus variety, unless the latter have been segregated elsewhere.

PREFERRED STOCK. This represents the value at which this class of stock is carried on the balance sheet—at par value or, in the case of no-par preferred, at a stated value that may be quite arbitrary. The standard practice is to indicate the number of shares authorized, the number outstanding, and the preference over the common in involuntary liquidation, together with the annual dividend rate.

COMMON STOCK. This represents the value at which this class of stock is carried on the balance sheet. An arbitrary value is employed for no-par issues. The number of shares outstanding, with par or any stated value, should be indicated.

SURPLUS. Surplus is of two main kinds, earned and capital. Earned surplus (retained earnings) represents the reinvested profits of the business. This account shows the maximum that could be distributed in dividends. In actual fact, the surplus is not represented by actual cash or any other particular asset.

Capital surplus is derived from all other sources, as from amounts paid in by stockholders in excess of par or stated value, from write-up of assets, from donations, or from reduction of par or stated value by formal action of the stockholders. It is not ordinarily available for dividends.

The total surplus account represents the difference between the total assets at their balance sheet value, and the total liabilities plus capital stock. A large surplus is to be desired as a cushion or buffer to take up any shrinkage in asset values. But it is no guarantee of dividends, especially of cash dividends.

Where a company has reacquired a part of its capital stock by purchase or donation, such *treasury stock* is ordinarily deducted from total net worth at its cost to the company.

Working Capital Changes and Flow of Funds

Neither the balance sheet nor the income statement directly reveals the factors causing change in particular categories of assets. Two special statements are often employed in industrial annual reports to explain changes in liquidity: the statement of working capital changes, and the cash flow statement. The latter is actually an extension or refinement of the former.

Table 26-5. STATEMENT OF WORKING CAPITAL CHANGES

Period _____

Increases:		*Decreases:*	
Net income	$ 840,000	Purchase of fixed assets	$ 480,000
Depreciation	320,000	Retirement of term loan	80,000
Sale of fixed assets	80,000	Purchase of treasury stock	40,000
Sale of bonds	1,000,000	Cash dividends	1,440,000
Sale of common stock	1,000,000		
Total	$3,240,000	Total	$2,040,000

Net increase in working capital: **$1,200,000**

The working capital statement in Table 26-5 shows that in the fiscal period the firm distributed more dividends than it earned (presumably dipping into retained earnings), that it acquired new plant in excess of the depreciation charges, and that it raised funds by new long-term securities financing in excess of debt and stock retired. But it does not show the changes in the individual *components* of working capital. This can be done by comparing the balance sheets at the beginning and the end of the given period. Or, as is often the case, a report may do the work for the investor, as in Table 26-6.

As Table 26-6 shows, the company increased its working capital but at the expense of cash position and investment in inventories. The growth of plant and of receivables was the culprit. A check on the collection period or turnover of receivables, and of the turnover of plant, would be in order. The notes payable have also increased, suggesting a "freezing" of the open accounts owed to suppliers, even though the firm may have reported a profit and paid substantial income taxes. Long-term debt (bonds) has increased, but the stockholders have also made a substantial new investment in com-

Table 26-6. CHANGES IN COMPONENTS OF WORKING CAPITAL

	Increase (Decrease)
Changes in current assets	
Cash	$ (250,000)
Marketable securities	(180,000)
Receivables	2,260,000
Inventories	(460,000)
Prepaid expenses	30,000
Total	$1,400,000
Changes in current liabilities	
Notes payable	$ 200,000
Accounts payable	(240,000)
Federal income taxes payable	240,000
	$ 200,000
Change in working capital	$1,200,000

mon stock. The decrease in cash of $250,000 is the result of all the other items noted above. (See Table 26-7.)

Table 26-7. CASH FLOW STATEMENT

Increases in Cash		*Decreases in Cash*	
Item	*Amount*	*Items*	*Amount*
Net income	$ 840,000	Purchase of fixed assets	$ 480,000
Depreciation	320,000	Retirement of term loan	80,000
Sale of fixed assets	80,000	Retirement of treasury stock	40,000
Sale of bonds	1,000,000	Cash dividends paid	1,440,000
Sale of common stock	1,000,000	Increase in receivables	2,260,000
Decrease in marketable		Increase in prepaid expenses	30,000
securities	180,000	Decrease in accounts payable	240,000
Decrease in inventories	460,000		
Increase in notes payable	200,000		
Increase in income			
taxes payable	240,000		
	$4,320,000		$4,570,000
		Decrease in cash—	$250,000

The *net internal cash flow* from operations is the sum of net income and depreciation, or $1,160,000. This could be used to calculate the cash flow per share. However, we note that such funds were more than offset by drains on cash. Cash flow per share should never be used as a substitute for earnings per share.

Analysis of Industrial Statements

Short-term creditors, such as banks and trade suppliers, long-term investors in bonds and stocks, and corporate management are all interested in the financial health and earnings of the company, but each group emphasizes different aspects of analysis. The current creditors are primarily concerned with liquidity, or the ability of the firm to meet its current obligations promptly. The long-term investors do not neglect working capital position but emphasize ultimate solvency and earning power. Management is interested in all aspects of the company's performance, but operating performance and earnings receive primary emphasis. In our discussion of industrial statement analysis, the investor's point of view will be kept in mind.

Statement analysis is not solely a matter of calculating and comparing ratios, although these are useful tools provided their limitations are kept in mind. A ratio may have considerable value in its own right, but it is most revealing (1) where it is compared with similar ratios of other companies *in the same industry* and (2) where it is computed for a period of years to reveal the trend.[5] Furthermore, a ratio is the relationship between two variables, and it disguises the actual dollar amounts involved. Thus, two companies may show the same current ratio (see below), say, 2:1 or 200 per cent, but one may have ten times as much working capital.

Ratios of working capital position or liquidity. The time-honored test of current position is the *current* or *working capital ratio* of current assets to current liabilities. A relationship of 2:1 is often offered as a standard, but no ideal ratio is applicable to all industries. A 2:1 ratio simply indicates that the current assets could shrink 50 per cent in value before the current creditors would be in jeopardy.[6] Some industries require a much higher degree of protection. Furthermore, the adequacy of this ratio depends on the types of the current assets, the liquidity of those other than cash, and seasonal requirements.

A company may show a favorable current ratio but be in a weak position because assets other than cash either form a large portion of current assets or are not liquid. One must, then, examine the quality of these other current assets. The *collection ratio* is a crude test of the quality of the receivables. It is found by dividing annual credit sales (when such information is available) by 360 to obtain credit sales per day; this figure is divided into the receivables on the books (less reserve for bad debts) to give the collection period or number of day's sales uncollected. If terms of thirty days are allowed customers, the ratio should be not much more than 30.[7]

The liquidity of the remaining important current assets is roughly measured by calculating the *inventory turnover*: cost of goods sold divided by average inventory at cost. This figure varies greatly among different indus-

---

[5]A convenient table of average ratios for a variety of manufacturing, wholesaling, and retailing groups is found in R. A. Foulke, *Practical Financial Statement Analysis*, 6th ed. (New York: McGraw-Hill, Inc., 1968).

[6]The *acid test* ratio, computed by dividing current assets less inventories by current liabilities, shows the ability of the company to meet current debts without relying on the least liquid of the current assets. A ratio of 1:1 is often considered a minimum standard.

[7]A similar ratio is the *turnover of receivables*, found by dividing net credit sales by average receivables. A turnover of 12 would be expected if terms of thirty days are allowed.

tries. Its trend is perhaps more important than its amount. Another test of inventory is its relationship to net working capital. The higher this ratio, the greater the dependence on inventory for solvency and the greater the risk from a sudden decline in its value.

Tests of fixed assets and capital structures. The investor in securities is specially interested in the long-term financial health of the business as represented by the support offered by fixed assets and the character of the capital structure. The ratio of *total liabilities to tangible net worth* reveals the burden of debt, both fixed and current, in relation to the owners' equity—exclusive of intangible assets, which are subject to uncertain valuation and rapid shrinkage. Rarely, if ever, should the ratio exceed 100 per cent, to avoid excessive maturities and interest charges. A similar test is the ratio of *net worth to total assets.*

The relationship of *net fixed assets to (tangible) net worth* measures the degree to which the owners' investment is "tied up" in a permanent form. Fixed assets require large maintenance and depreciation allowances and possibly large interest charges on borrowed money; in addition, funds are not available in liquid form to take advantage of cash discounts and other current needs. A maximum of 75 per cent is suggested for most manufacturing companies; the ratio would be considerably less for merchandising concerns.

The capital structure proportions. Ratios of bonds and other long-term debt, preferred stock, and common stock plus surplus, to total capital structure, vary greatly in the industrial field. Some companies have no senior securities outstanding and rely solely on common stock and reinvested earnings as long-term sources of funds. Others use substantial leverage and incur heavy interest charges and large preferred dividend requirements. Generally speaking, the investor will favor those industrial concerns that have a modest amount of bonds and preferred stock outstanding in relation to tangible net worth. In few cases would the 40 to 50 per cent debt ratios of utilities be acceptable in the industrial field.[8] Where funded debt and preferred stock each exceeds one-third of capital structure, unusual *stability* of earnings and of asset values would be required for these securities to enjoy a respectable investment status.

A supplementary test of the quality of industrial bonds and preferred stocks is to use the *market* value of the common stock in lieu of stated common stock and surplus on the balance sheet. This test indicates the market's valuation of the common equity as a cushion for senior capital, and is often a more realistic basis of comparison in the case of companies whose earnings bear only small relation to balance sheet figures of fixed or current assets. Examples can be found in chemicals, drugs, electronics, and other growth industries where the book value of the common stock is typically very low compared to average market price.

More specific asset tests of the burden of funded debt are found in the ratio of such debt to net (depreciated) fixed assets and to net working

[8]See Table 26-2.

capital. The long-term debt should be adequately supported by plant and equipment; a maximum ratio of debt to net plant of 50 per cent is sugested for manufacturing concerns; merchandising companies with smaller fixed assets may show a higher proportion, but the debt must be supported by a greater amount of working capital. The long-term debt should also be supported by liquid assets to ensure continuation of interest payments; long-term debt in excess of (net) working capital is not recommended for industrial concerns.

The asset support behind the preferred stock is measured by the ratio of preferred stock to tangible net worth, which should not exceed 50 per cent. A similar approach is to compute the book value of the preferred on a per-share basis. If this is $400, each share of preferred is protected by net tangible assets (after all liabilities) considerably in excess of its preference in liquidation over the common stock.[9]

The *book value* of the common stock is found by subtracting from total assets (or, preferably, from total tangible assets) all liabilities and the liquidating preferences of the preferred stock, including any accumulated preferred dividends. The net tangible assets applicable to the common stock, divided by the number of shares of common stock outstanding, gives the tangible book value per share. While not nearly so important as earnings per share, the figure indicates the investment in tangible properties that may, under proper conditions, produce a reasonable return on the common stock. Common stock may sell at several times book value, either because the assets are carried at very conservative figures or because of unusual earnings; they may sell at a fraction of book value where the opposite conditions prevail. (See Table 8-1.) Indeed, some common stocks even sell at a price below the per-share equivalent of *current* assets less all liabilities and preferred stock. Here, the investor is paying nothing for the fixed assets, but these have little investment value as long as the company is not producing satisfactory earnings, or is not going to liquidate.

Tests of operations or performance. The effectiveness of management is revealed by ratios of various income and expense items to net sales, taking the latter figure as 100 per cent. The use of such "common-size" statements enables the comparison of annual figures that differ in dollar amounts, and of the statements of different companies within the same industrial group. Among the more important relationships are the *gross profit margin* (gross profit from operations as a per cent of sales), the *net profit margin* (net profit from operations as a per cent of sales), the *operating ratio* (cost of sales plus expenses as a per cent of sales), and the *net income ratio* (net income either before or after taxes, as a per cent of sales), together with the ratios of important single expense items, such as depreciation, to sales. Illustrative figures of the last two of these main relationships are found in Table 26-2. Standard or average percentage costs for particular industrial groups have been compiled by trade associa-

[9]Note that the book value of preferred stock indicates the assets that support each share, not, as in the case of common stock, what each share would receive on liquidation of assets at their book value.

tions and by Dun & Bradstreet, Inc., for many line of trade, and certain financial services, such as Standard & Poor's and Robert Morris Associates, issue group data which can be used in studying the comparative performance of individual companies within each industry from year to year.

The net income ratio is especially significant in comparative analysis. It reveals the proportion of sales brought down to net income to provide the return on the owners' investment. But a high net income ratio alone is not the final measure of profitability. It is the rate earned on the investment that is important. A low net income ratio may provide a high return if net worth is small. Or, a concern that turns its investment many times during the year may produce the same per cent return on that investment by operating at a low net income ratio as another firm that requires a high investment and operates at a high ratio. The following hypothetical figures illustrate this situation:

	Company X	Company Y
Sales	$100	$100
Net worth	$ 50	$ 10
Net income ratio	5%	1%
Return on net worth	10%	10%

Depreciation expense deserves special attention, because the amount of this item affects both the reported earnings and the balance sheet valuation of the fixed assets and, hence, the reported assets' support to securities outstanding. In addition to studying the depreciation expense as a percentage of sales, its size in relation to gross property account, and the size of the accumulated reserve in relation to the cost of property, merit close scrutiny. Comparisons should be made with other similar companies, and the basis of depreciation for tax purposes should be taken into account. One should note that where a portion of the plant is leased, the depreciation expense as a percentage of sales will be reduced.

Ratios of operating profits and of net income to sales should be accompanied by others that reveal whether the assets, and the investment of various classes of creditors and of the owners, have been effectively used. The _turnover of operating assets_ is calculated by dividing net sales by assets exclusive of long-term investments and intangibles. This reveals the comparative efficiency of the resources devoted to producing sales. The _turnover of working capital_ (sales to net working capital) suggests the productivity of the funds supplied by short-term creditors. A fast turnover contributes to both liquidity and earning power, and may logically offset an otherwise weak current position. The utilization of plant investment is shown by _plant turnover,_ or gross plant divided into net sales. The effectiveness of the total long-term investment in producing revenues is measured by the _turnover of capital structure,_ and that of the owners by the _turnover of net worth_ (net sales to average stockholders' equity).

Tests of earning power. The profitability of the _total_ long-term funds is measured by the rate of return on invested capital, or the ratio of income before interest (and after income taxes) to the total capital structure. The trend of this "overall" rate of return through a period of years, and comparisons among different companies, is very revealing. A chronically low ratio indicates overinvestment, poor competitive position, or generally poor management. A high return is, of course, to be desired, but stability is of equal importance.

The overall rate of return is affected by the degree of leverage in the capital structure, because interest is a cost in determining taxable net income. To compare companies *without considering the effect of their financial policy,* the rate of return should be calculated on a pretax basis.

Tests of earnings in relation to the senior elements in the capital structure are as follows: (1) For bonds it is *times interest charges earned.* To achieve a high-grade status, industrial bonds should show a regular coverage of between 5 and 6 times, and the figure should not drop below 3 times in the poorest year (after taxes). An accompanying test is the *factor of safety,* or percentage of sales earned after bond interest and before taxes. This shows how much sales could decline and still leave interest charges covered once. (2) For preferred stock, it is *times interest charges plus preferred dividends earned.* High-grade industrial preferred dividends should show a regular coverage of at least 4 times.[10]

For common stock, net income is shown as so much per share. *Cash earnings per share* is increasingly used to reveal the internal funds generated for expansion and general corporate use. *Sales per share* relates the output of the business to a possibly changing number of shares outstanding. In the analysis of oil companies, barrels of reserves per share is a useful comparative figure. But the fundamental figure that reveals how effectively the business is being run for its owners is the rate of return on common equity, found by dividing the average common stock plus surplus by net income after preferred dividends. A company can show increasing earnings per share, but a declining rate of return, if earnings are not growing at the same rate as shares are increased.

The investor in common stock is interested in three other relationships involving earnings: (1) the *price-earnings ratio,* or ratio of net income per share to market price, (2) the *payout ratio,* or ratio of dividends to net income, and (3) the *dividend yield.* The latter is, of course, the result not only of price and earnings but also of dividend policy. In January 1973, the 125 companies comprising Moody's industrial stock average produced a dividend yield of 2.60 per cent, from expected 1973 dividends of $10.00 or 49 per cent of $20.40 earnings. These stocks, as a composite average, were selling at 19.0 times earnings (or at an earnings yield of 5.3 per cent). The price-earnings ratio of individual stocks varies widely, being influenced by many factors, including (1) the trend and stability of earnings, (2) dividend record and prospects, (3) the market's appraisal of management and the future prospects of the company, (4) financial strength, (5) the level of interest rates, and (6) the general psychology of investors and speculators at any given time.[11]

---

[10]See Chapter 24 for a discussion of the methods of calculating interest and preferred dividend coverage.
[11]Further discussion of the price-earnings ratio is found in Chapter 25.

Use of Consolidated Statements

A growing number of companies are becoming holding or parent companies through the control of voting stock of other corporations This is a favorite method of external expansion, as a substitute for extension of operating divisions. Where more than 50 per cent of the voting stock is held, the annual report usually includes consolidated statements of the group treated as one company, with intercompany items eliminated. Such statements should nearly always be used by the investor rather than those of the parent company alone. Certain unique features and ratios should be noted:

1. On the balance sheet, the assets of fully consolidated subsidiaries are commingled with those of the parent. The cost of shares of affiliates or of nonconsolidated subsidiaries is shown as a long-term investment.

2. Where the parent owns less than 100 per cent of the controlling stock of subsidiaries, the minority interest, consisting of the book value (stock plus its share of surplus) of the subsidiary's stock held by outsiders, is shown separately.

3. The consolidated capital structure of a parent and subsidiaries consists of (a) bonds of the subsidiaries, (b) bonds of the parent, (c) preferred stock of subsidiaries, (d) preferred stock of parent, (e) minority interest in subsidiaries, (g) common stock of parent, and (h) consolidated surplus. The last five items comprise the consolidated net worth.

4. On the consolidated income statement, the net income of parent and consolidated subsidiaries is combined. The dividends received from nonconsolidated subsidiaries and affiliates appear as nonoperating income.

5. In calculating earnings per share, the figure derived from the consolidated statements should be increased by the parent's share of undistributed subsidiary profits.

Industrial Bonds

Industrial companies are subject to a variety of risks suggested earlier in this chapter, and thus, as a class, would not be expected to rely on bonds as a means of financing to the same extent as would public service companies. However, few large corporations are now without funded debt of some sort.

The reasons for avoidance of publicly offered bond issues by concerns that could meet all tests adequately are (1) a conservative attitude toward long-term debt financing, (2) the adequacy of internal funds, that is, retained earnings and depreciation, to finance expansion, (3) the growing use of intermediate-term loans from banks and insurance companies, and (4) the growing practice of private placement of high-grade bonds directly with insurance companies and other institutional investors. Those industrial concerns that have issued bonds, in spite of the risk of debt, have seized the opportunity to finance at low cost and gain a tax advantage, or have been reluctant to rely on stock issues during periods when stocks have sold at relatively low multiples of earnings. Or sometimes when a concern needs money badly, it may have to offer its premier security.

The most common type of industrial bond is the unsecured debenture. Sinking fund or other repayment provisions have become almost universal in the modern longer-term industrial issues, and, because of the possibilities of high returns in common stock, the convertible feature is found much more frequently than in the case of utility and rail bond issues.

Bonds of industrial companies include a wide range of quality. At one extreme, issues of very strong companies supported by very large asset values and demonstrated earning power under a variety of business conditions command great investment respect; when the highest standards are met, such bonds sell at yields as low as those on high-grade utility issues. In January 1973, the yield on Moody's high-grade industrial bond series was 7.00 per cent, as compared with 7.35 per cent for public utilities. The very top-grade industrial bonds are the prime corporate obligations in the market. Where the highest standards can be met, industrial bonds are eligible for investment by trustees and other fiduciaries in a large number of states (in New York since 1939).

But the number of very high-grade industrial issues is relatively small, and from this peak the group extends over a wide number of issues that lack, in general, the safety of operating utility bonds. While generalizations are dangerous, we may probably say that, as a *class,* industrial bonds do not enjoy as high an investment standing as the utility group as a whole.

A good industrial bond should meet the following tests:

1. The industry should exhibit characteristics of stability and growth and freedom from unusual cyclical and other risks. Where such a condition is not found, as in the case of steel, the debt should be modest.

2. The company should be a demonstrated leader in its field, with superior management and prospects as revealed by careful analysis.

3. The working capital position should be very strong, to permit interest payments during possible periods of low earnings and to allow management flexibility in uncertain times.

4. The total long-term debt should ordinarily not exceed one-third of the capital structure. This limit may be exceeded only when interest coverage is more than ample.

5. The total bonds should not exceed 50 per cent of depreciated fixed assets or, where the latter are small, should more than meet the working capital test next indicated.

6. In any case, total bonds should not exceed net working capital.

7. Where not secured by a lien on valuable assets, the issue should contain the protective provisions outlined in Chapter 7.

8. The average total income for the five preceding years and for the previous year available (after taxes) for the payment of interest charges should be 5 to 6 times the fixed charges.

9. The maturity of the issue should not exceed thirty years, and a sinking fund or repurchase provision should be provided adequate to retire a substantial portion of the bonds before maturity.

10. The issue should be at least $10,000,000, well seasoned, and should preferably be listed to assure reasonable marketability.

Preferred Stocks

Preferred stocks of industrial companies are entitled to investment recognition only on the basis of demonstrated earning power of the issuing company. As with industrial bonds, the group includes a wide range, from high-grade to those little better than weak common stocks. In January 1973, when high-grade industrial bonds were yielding 7.00 per cent, high-grade industrial preferreds were yielding 6.45 per cent and medium-grade issues 6.65 per cent. These yields were lower than those of high-grade rail and utility preferred issues; but again we should note that the number of very strong industrial preferred stocks is limited, and that the standards for a high-grade rating are higher than for rail and utility preferreds.

The low yield on high-grade industrial preferreds is, however, chiefly explained by their appeal to taxed corporate investors such as insurance companies, because to corporations 85 per cent of dividend income is tax-free. This demand, together with a shrinking supply, has forced the yield on strong preferred issues below that of high-grade bonds. Under these conditions, the best preferred stocks have little appeal to individual investors.

At the opposite extreme are stocks that are preferred in name but that in reality are supported by little or no common stock equity, and so are in fact similar to common stocks in quality but (unless convertible) without the potentialities of common stocks with respect to income and price appreciation.

Where relative stability of price and assurance of income are required, an industrial preferred stock should meet the following tests:

1. See test 1 for industrial bonds.

2. See test 2 for industrial bonds.

3. See test 3 for industrial bonds.

4. The preferred stock should not exceed one-third of the total capital structure.

5. The preferred stock should not exceed 50 per cent of the tangible net worth.

6. The issue should contain the protective provisions described in Chapter 8 designed to prevent the deterioration of its position from the issuance of prior securities and debt or from the excessive payment of dividends on common stock.

7. The average income before interest (and after taxes) for the five preceding years and for the previous year should be at least 5 times the preferred dividend requirement plus bond interest, if any bonds are out-

standing, and 4 times preferred dividend requirement if no bonds are out-standing.

8. Where the issue is convertible into common stock, it should either be strong in its own right without such a feature or an excessive premium for this feature should be avoided.

9. The issue should be large, well seasoned, and preferably listed on an organized exchange, if ready marketability is important.

The investor should never lose sight of the fact that a preferred stock represents ownership in the corporation, that dividend payments are optional (even if cumulative), and that neither a larger corporate surplus nor a long dividend record assures the continuation of dividends in years of poor earnings.

Common Stocks

It is extremely difficult to generalize about the investment position of industrial common stocks. The group includes the widest range of issues— from those that have a long and honorable earnings and dividend record and relatively good price stability, to the wildest speculations. Few if any carry absolute assurance of income, but a well-diversified list of industrials is likely to produce a modest return even in times of adversity. No industrial common stocks offer price stability, and their price action is likely to be much less stable than that of operating utility issues. Yet through adequate diversification and wise selection and timing, the worst effects of the stock price cycles may be avoided. The most that the investor can hope to obtain is reasonable stability, unless he is prepared to risk the chance of no income at all and wide variation in price for the possibility of unusual capital gain. If income is the primary goal, the investor may achieve it through a list of sound dividend-payers, but he cannot avoid considerable variation in market value.

For these reasons, no summary list of specific tests of an industrial common stock is included in this final discussion. The investor must be satisfied that the price, return, and appreciation prospects from a given stock or group of stocks adequately compensate for the risks of the issues as measured by careful analysis. He must also be satisfied that such risks are appropriate in his own investment policy and program. As indicated previously in this volume, many methods exist by which, through careful selection and timing, or through the use of indirect means of investment, the common stock investor may reduce the risks involved and gain the real advantages that sound common stocks may offer in a balanced program. But the investor must never forget that common stock is the residual ownership of a business, subject to all of the vicissitudes of the corporation's affairs, of the industry to which it belongs, and of the economy as a whole. Industrial common stocks offer the prospect of the greatest rewards to the discriminating investor in whose portfolio they are appropriate; they also harbor the possibility of the greatest losses.

REFERENCES

ADAMS, WALTER, ed., *The Structure of American Industry,* 4th ed. New York: The Macmillan Company, 1971.

ALDERFER, E. B., AND H. E. MICHL, *Economics of American Industry,* 3rd ed. New York: McGraw-Hill, Inc., 1957.

BELLEMORE, D. H., *The Strategic Investor,* Part V. New York: Simmons-Boardman Publishing Corporation, 1963.

BOWYER, J. W., JR., *Investment Analysis and Management,* 3rd ed., Chapters 11, 12, 13. Homewood, Ill.: Richard D. Irwin, Inc., 1966.

FOULKE, R. A., *Practical Financial Statement Analysis,* 6th ed. New York: McGraw-Hill, Inc., 1968.

FREDRICKSON, E. B., ed., *Frontiers of Investment Analysis,* rev. ed., Part III. Scraton, Pa.: International Textbook Company, 1971.

GLOVER, J. G., AND R. A. LAGAI, *The Development of American Industries,* 4th ed. New York: Simmons-Boardman Publishing Corp., 1959.

GRAHAM, BENJAMIN, D. L. DODD, AND SIDNEY COTTLE, *Security Analysis,* 4th ed., Chapters 9–18. New York: McGraw-Hill, Inc., 1962.

——, AND CHARLES MCGOLRICK, *The Interpretation of Financial Statements,* 2nd. ed. New York: Harper & Row, Publishers, 1964.

GUTHMANN, H. G., *Analysis of Financial Statements,* 4th ed., Chapters 14, 15. Englewood Cliffs, N.J.: Prentice-Hall, Inc., 1953.

PLUM, L. V., ed., *Investing in American Industries.* New York: Harper & Row, Publishers, 1960.

VANCE, STANLEY, *Industrial Structure and Policy.* Englewood Cliffs, N.J.: Prentice-Hall, Inc., 1961.

See also references, Chapter 24.

27 Public Utility Securities

SCOPE: This chapter discusses the investment position of the securities issued by privately owned public utility companies. The order of discussion is (1) the utility industries—characteristics and importance, (2) franchise, (3) regulation, (4) significance of territory served, (5) significance of management, (6) public ownership, (7) balance sheet analysis, (8) types of securities, (9) income statement analysis, (10) electric light and power, (11) gas industry, (12) telephone industry, (13) telegraph industry, (14) water companies, (15) the holding company and its regulation, and (16) investment outlook.

The Utility Industries

Public utility companies are engaged in a business (1) affected with a public interest, that is, supplying services regarded as indispensable to the consuming public; (2) requiring a large capital investment so that duplication of competing facilities is not feasible; (3) operating under a franchise from a political authority that provides exclusive right to perform the service in the territory served; and (4) as a result of these characteristics, subject to regulation of rates, service, and other functions.

Financial characteristics of utilities include (with some exceptions) a preponderance of investment in fixed assets, large investment in plant in relation to revenues, relatively stable earnings, heavy use of bonds and preferred stocks as sources of funds, and rapid growth.

The utilities group includes electric light and power, gas distribution and transmission, telephone, telegraph, and water. (Utilities and railroads together constitute what is often called the "public service" group.) A distinction should be made between the *operating* utilities that provide the actual service and holding companies that control groups of operating companies serving several territories.

The importance of public utility companies in the investment field is clearly indicated by Table 27-1. The progress of the utilities stands in sharp contrast to the more static condition of the railroads. Whereas the development of the carriers has been chiefly in betterment of existing facilities, the

489

**Table 27-1. INVESTED ASSETS AND REVENUES OF PRIVATELY
OWNED PUBLIC UTILITIES, 1970**

(in millions of dollars)

Group	Assets	Revenues
Electric light and power	$87,500	$22,300
Gas		
Manufactured and mixed	300	130
Natural (distributing)	25,500	10,150
Natural (transmission)	19,800	5,900
Telephone	52,800	18,200
Telegraph (domestic)	1,850	400
Water (private)	1,100 (est.)	240 (est.)

SOURCES: American Gas Association; Federal Power Commission; Federal Communications Commission; *Statistical Abstract of the United States*.

growth of the utilities continues in extensive expansion into new fields of operation. But utility progress has not been uniform. As will be shown later, signs of retrogression have appeared in some divisions of the group.

The Franchise

The public utility company operates under a franchise, which is a contract between the company and the area served. From the standpoint of the investor, the more important agreements relate to type of service rendered, competition, territory, duration, and rates. Franchises may be *nonexclusive* or *exclusive*. The older type of award that allowed private competition has been largely replaced by the more satisfactory noncompetitive form; regulated monopoly has proved superior to competition and wasteful duplication of facilities.[1] The chief threat of competition is from municipal operation. The territorial limits in the franchise may prevent an operating company from extending its service to rapidly growing contiguous territory.[2]

Franchises may be *perpetual, limited, or indeterminate.* Originally, franchises were granted on a perpetual basis, but public sentiment later favored the limited duration basis (ten to fifty years); more recently the indeterminate, or indefinite, type, under which the franchise remains in effect as long as service is satisfactory, has come into favor. Usually in the event the municipality purchases the property, provision is made for the company to be compensated by a valuation set by an independent board of appraisal. It is important that any bonds of the company mature before the franchise expires.[3]

[1]In many large cities, the utility companies operate under a group of franchises, granted at various times to separate companies which are eventually merged into a single group. Where a utility serves a number of communities, it will operate under a number of separate franchises.

[2]Originally, the franchise of Commonwealth Edison Company confined it to the corporate limits of Chicago. In 1953, by a merger with a subsidiary, Public Service Company of Northern Illinois, the company acquired franchises in a number of communities to the north and west of Chicago.

[3]Utility bonds maturing beyond the expiration date of the franchise are not legal investments for fiduciaries in New York State.

Rate restriction clauses, under which a maximum charge per unit of service is stated, appear in many older franchises. Unfortunate experience with such clauses in recent years has led, in newer franchises, to the substituting of flexible rates based on cost of service; in most cases, however, rates are set by the state utility commission rather than by the franchise.

The franchise position is important. Vague statements to the effect that "the franchise situation is satisfactory" should not satisfy the investor. The most favorable type of franchise is exclusive and indeterminate with a flexible rate provision; the least satisfactory is the short-term, limited type with a maximum rate restriction.

Regulation

Utilities are regulated by Federal, municipal, and state authorities. Federal regulation is based on the interstate commerce section of the U.S. Constitution and the right to control the use of navigable waters. Its scope may be summarized as follows:

The *Federal Power Commission* (established in 1920) licenses power projects in navigable waters and regulates utility companies transmitting electric power and gas across state lines. Its jurisdiction extends to wholesale power and gas rates, cost of natural gas, accounting systems, and financial transactions. It prescribes a uniform system of accounts for all companies engaged in interstate power and gas operations.

The *Securities and Exchange Commission* (established in 1934) has jurisdiction under the Public Utility Holding Company Act of 1935 over electric and gas holding companies controlling subsidiaries in more than one state (see discussion at the end of this chapter). Regulation covers the security offerings, capital structures, accounts, control, recapitalization, and reorganization of registered holding companies and their subsidiaries. Competitive bidding for their bonds is required.

The *Interstate Commerce Commission* (established in 1887) has broad powers over the rates, service, financing, and accounts of electric railway and bus companies operating in interstate commerce.

The *Federal Communications Commission* (established in 1934) prescribes the rates and practices of telephone and telegraph companies engaged in interstate and foreign communications. It has developed a uniform system of accounts for telephone companies.

Local regulation is generally restricted to powers delegated by the states. Such powers may be limited or very far reaching, extending to "home rule" over certain utility activities, as in Minnesota, Nebraska, South Dakota, and Texas with respect to electric light and power. The franchise is the vehicle for such regulation.

State regulation of companies conducting an intrastate business is the most comprehensive. All the states now have a public service commission with broad and varying powers.[4] While these powers are by no means uniform, certain leading principles and practices apply in the majority of cases.

Rate regulation. The traditional theory of rate regulation has been to approve rate schedules that provide a "fair return" on the rate base or "fair value" of property used in the public service (value of the plant plus an allowance for working capital). Regulation is designed, on the one hand, to protect consumers from exploitation and, on the other, to permit a return to the company that will support the investment and attract necessary new capital. Historically, original cost (less depreciation) constituted the rate base or "fair value," although cost of reproduction new (less depreciation) has been argued by utility companies during periods of increasing costs of construction. But no consistent and universal agreement existed on what "fair value" meant. More recently, the *prudent investment theory,* which uses original cost plus cost of permanent improvements as the base (after depreciation, and plus working capital) has been adopted in a number of states. Finally, in the *Hope Natural Gas case,*[5] the "fair value" principle was virtually abandoned in favor of a widening of the discretion of the commission so as to permit earnings sufficient to attract capital, that is, cover the cost of capital adequately. At present, a few states still use original cost as the base; some have adopted prudent investment; still others consider all elements or follow the principal of "fair value" without defining it specifically.

In any case, the state commissions have in mind the earnings (after operating expenses and taxes, but before interest and dividends) that will support the investment and attract capital in the light of prevailing conditions in the capital market. Recently the prevailing range has been 6 to 8 per cent for electric and 7 to 8 per cent for natural gas companies.[6]

The investor in utility securities is deeply concerned with the attitude of the commissions concerning such matters as valuation and fair return. Except in four or five very liberal states, a utility that consistently earns in excess of 8 per cent on valuation is likely to have its rates reduced. One earning less than 6 per cent has reason to expect a favorable response to a request for rate increases. However, even if a company earns a modest rate on its total investment, by using senior securities (leverage), it may

---

[4]See *Moodys' Manual of Investments, Public Utilities,* for a chart of the regulatory powers of the various state commissions.

[5]*Federal Power Commission* v. *Hope Natural Gas Co.,* 370 U.S. 591 (1944).

[6]A fairly close approximation of the rate of earnings as calculated for rate-making purposes may be had by dividing net operating income by depreciated property plus about 3 per cent for working capital. A more detailed procedure is described in Federal Power Commission, *Statistics of Privately Owned Electric Utilities in the United States,* 1970 (Washington, D.C.: U.S. Government Printing Office, 1971, p. 751. This source shows the following range of rates of return for 193 companies in 1970:

Less than 5 per cent	5.2 per cent of companies
5 to 5.99 per cent	6.2 per cent of companies
6 to 6.99 per cent	30.6 per cent of companies
7 to 7.99 per cent	34.7 per cent of companies
8 per cent and more	23.3 per cent of companies

Flow-through accounting was used for liberalized depreciation.

produce a respectable return and adequate dividends for the common stock. The earnings on the common stock of a well-managed utility under fair regulation can be very substantial, but the theoretically unlimited opportunity that exists for industrial company earnings is not to be expected. Stability of earnings may, however, compensate for such limitation.

Competition. The commissions protect the interests of investors in utility securities by refusing *certificates of convenience* (which must be obtained by any new companies entering the field) to undeserving applicants. On the other hand, they may require forfeiture of franchise grants for nonuse. Certificates are issued only when the operations of the new company will not infringe upon the vested rights of any company already in the area, when the new company has capital adequate to carry out its plans, and when the organizers of the new company evidence successful experience as utility operators.

Securities regulation. In most states new securities may be issued only with the approval of the commission. A limited number of purposes are acceptable: (1) to construct new property, (2) to buy existing property, (3) to better existing property, or (4) to refund existing debt. The amount issued must be reasonable for the purpose. The form of issue, whether bonds or stock, must be in harmony with a balanced capitalization. The terms of the underwriting (the cost of distribution) must not be excessive. While such control does not assure complete investment protection, it undoubtedly does reduce the risk of loss. Some states, such as Massachusetts and California, require competitive bidding for new utility bond issues.

Accounts and reports. In most states, the commissions require a uniform procedure. Standard classifications for the more important branches of the industry have been adopted by large groups of states.[7] This results in a more accurate portrayal of financial condition and also facilitates the comparison of companies. The commissions also require detailed reports, which are submitted annually and are open to public inspection. The information forms the basis for the summary sent to the securityholders in the form of the annual report.

Territorial Analysis

One of the most important factors in the selection of public utility securities is the nature of the territory served. Unlike the railroads, which cover wide areas, and industrial enterprises, which may seek markets anywhere, a public utility company may operate only in a prescribed territory. The opportunity to prosper is definitely limited to a restricted area. Careful attention should, therefore, be given to features such as geographical location, population, and resources.

---

[7]Through adoption of the classifications developed by the Federal Power Commission or the National Association of Railway and Utility Commissioners.

Geographical location has economic as well as physical influence. The harbors of New York, Boston, Los Angeles, and San Francisco, among others, give those cities a natural advantage. With excellent water and rail facilities, Chicago, Cleveland, and Detroit are splendidly located. Proximity to established channels of trade is an economic advantage from a market viewpoint, just as nearness to natural waterfalls is helpful from a production standpoint. Cities in northern latitudes, which have a more rigorous climate, offer a somewhat more favorable residential market than do those in southern latitudes. Companies located in certain sections of the country encounter public sentiment generally hostile to private utility operation.

The population of the territory served greatly affects the size and the importance of the company. Investors should prefer the securities of companies located in large communities that show a favorable rate of growth.

The economics of the territory should also be carefully considered. Some areas are primarily industrial; others are commercial, agricultural, or residential. The great advantage of the large community lies in the diversity of resources, which makes for stability of demand for utility service. Industrial and commercial territories offer better markets than do agricultural and residential districts, but industrial and commercial demand is subject to greater instability than is residential demand.

The Factor of Management

The regulation of such important matters as rates, service, accounts, and financing has restricted the scope within which the management of the utility company exercises decision-making powers, and operating techniques have become fairly standardized within the various branches of the utility group. Such considerations might suggest that quality of management has only minor importance in this field. Although the utility company is not faced with all the problems of the competitive industrial business, nevertheless management is still important. Such matters as operating economies, new fuel sources, engineering of new plants, forecasting of demand, and provision of adequate plant and equipment at the proper time require considerable managerial skill.

Public relations are also important. Investors prefer the securities of those companies whose rate schedules are liberal and whose public relations are favorable. To adopt a maxim, utility companies must live with their customers. Companies with high rate schedules and indifferent public policies do not make good neighbors. The securities of such companies are especially vulnerable in periods of economic recession or political change.

Public Ownership

Gas and telephone properties are seldom publicly operated, but most waterworks are owned and operated by municipalities rather than by private companies. The relatively large amount of capital required, the routine nature of the operations, and the ability of the municipality to borrow at low rates are the chief factors explaining this situation. In the local transit field, inadequate returns or failure of private companies have forced municipal operation in many communities.[8] In the electric field, municipal ownership has been adopted by choice in some communities, such as Palo Alto and Seattle; in others, municipal plants have been constructed to provide service where profitable operation by private capital was questionable. In many communities public ownership has been a political issue not always settled by financial and economic considerations. The investor should examine the political climate and the attitude toward public ownership in the territory served, and insist on clauses that would provide adequate compensation in the event of recapture. Good public relations between the utility and the community are the best protection against the threat of municipal purchase.

Another development of major interest has been the rise of Federal power projects, such as the Tennessee Valley Authority, Bonneville Power Administration, Boulder Canyon Project of the Bureau of Reclamation, and many others. The effects of such projects have included the purchase by the authority of many private companies in the neighboring territory, the sale of public power to existing companies instead of the expansion of their generating facilities, and pressure for lower rates by applying the "yardstick" of public power costs.

Balance Sheet Analysis

The condensed corporate balance sheet of all Class A and B privately owned electric companies with annual electric revenue of $250,000 or more (see Table 27-2) illustrates the characteristics of the utility balance sheet. The bulk of the utility assets is in the form of fixed plant. Current assets play a relatively minor role, in the absence of a large cash balance and of inventories. Similarly, the sources of funds are long term, as represented by stocks, bonds, and surplus; current liabilities have relatively minor importance.

Gross electric plant per dollar of revenue is about $4.7, indicating an annual gross plant turnover of about 21 per cent. Gross plant rather than net plant after depreciation is used in an efficiency test because the volume of service rendered is related to the plant in use rather than to its valuation. From the financial standpoint, the productivity of the investment may be measured by using the net plant figure, to produce a turnover of about 33 per cent. The investment in gross assets per dollar of revenues is higher, possibly $6 in the case of an all-hydroelectric company, and lower, around $2.5 for natural gas distributing companies. The relationship between plant

[8]For many years the street railway service in Cleveland, Detroit, and Seattle has been publicly owned. In 1940, New York City "recaptured" the rapid transit facilities leased to the Interborough and Brooklyn–Manhattan companies. In 1947, Chicago set up a Transit Authority to operate a coordinated system of elevated, street car, and bus lines.

Table 27-2. CONDENSED BALANCE SHEET OF CLASS A AND B
         PRIVATELY OWNED ELECTRIC COMPANIES,
         DECEMBER 31, 1970
         (in millions of dollars)

Assets		
Electric utility plant	$93,303	
Other utility plant	8,974	$102,277
Less reserves for dep'n and amort.		22,349
Net plant		$ 79,928
Other property and investments		1,743
Current assets		5,321
Deferred debits		425
Total assets		$ 87,417
Liabilities		
Common stock		$ 13,282
Preferred stock		7,499
Capital surplus		4,401
Retained earnings		9,363
Long-term debt		41,937
Current liabilities		7,309
Deferred federal income taxes		2,198
Reserves (operating)		146
Deferred credits		799
Contributions in aid of construction		483
Total liabilities		$ 87,417

SOURCE: Federal Power Commission, *Statistics of Privately Owned Electric Utilities in the United States,*
1970 (Washington, D.C.: U.S. Government Printing Office, 1971), Table 1.

and revenues provides a rough check on the validity of the important figure
of investment in plant and the adequacy of the depreciation reserve.

The ratio of long-term debt to net property is very important. It shows
the assets support to the utility's bonds, and is also related to earnings support. If the utility earns a reasonable return on its property as valued for
rate-making purposes, this return will provide adequate support to funded
debt of, say, 50 per cent of net plant. A return of 7 per cent on total investment would provide interest coverage of 2.8 times on bonds equal to 50
per cent of property, at an average interest cost of 5 per cent. For the combined electric utilities whose statement is given above, the ratio of long-term
debt to net plant was 52 per cent as of 1970. The Securities and Exchange
Commission, in its regulation of holding companies and their subsidiaries
under the Act of 1935, has established 50 per cent of net plant as a debt
standard. Certainly, 60 per cent should be considered a maximum for
electric companies.

The pattern of long-term financing is revealed by the capital structure
proportions. For the electric industry, long-term debt comprises 54.8 per
cent, preferred stock 9.8 per cent, and common stock plus surplus 35.4 per
cent of total bonds, stock, and surplus. Utilities of all types rely heavily on
senior securities for two reasons: (1) The relative stability of earnings

makes feasible the use of such sources without undue risk; (2) by using bonds and preferred stock whose interest and dividend rates are substantially less than the overall rate earned on total investment, the return on the common stock can be magnified sufficiently to attract junior equity capital. This is important, since unlike the competitive industrial company, the public utility cannot rely on reinvested earnings as a major source of funds. In 1970 the net operating income of the electric utilities referred to above produced a return of 6.8 per cent on average capital structure. Deducting interest and preferred dividends, earnings available to common stock were 13.2 per cent on the average book value of the common stock.

A final balance sheet test is found in the relation of current assets to current liabilities. This familiar ratio is much less important for the public utility company than for the industrial concern, because its current items are relatively unimportant and because maturing current liabilities can be met with the steady cash income or funded into long-term obligations. For a strong and growing company, a ratio of less than one is not alarming; where earnings are weak, the ratio should be one or higher to permit the continued payment of bond interest.

Types of Securities

The capitalization of most utilities is relatively simple, consisting of a single large, open-end mortgage bond issue with perhaps several series outstanding, preferred stock, and common stock. Variations from this pattern are, however, frequently observed. Some have never issued preferred stock; others, especially in the telephone and natural gas groups, have relied on debenture bond financing because of the lack of mortgageable assets. The open-end mortgage bonds contain the protective provisions described in Chapter 7 that are designed to prevent dilution of assets and earnings from excessive new series.

Provision for rapid retirement of bonds through generous sinking fund or serial redemption requirements is still somewhat unusual, although modest sinking funds of 1 to 2 per cent are found in modern bond issues. The typical utility company assumes that it will always be in debt.[9] The conversion feature often used in industrial financing is not used frequently, though the practice is growing; the call or redemption feature is, however, customarily included in bonds and preferred stock.

Income Statement Analysis

The main items found on the utility statement are illustrated by reference to the combined income statement in Table 27-3. The operating revenues

---

[9]An exception is found in the large sinking funds of natural gas companies made necessary by the wasting character of their assets.

are the product of the number of units sold (kilowatt-hours, cubic feet of gas, and so forth) and the rates charged. The customers are classified, in the case of private electric companies, into the categories shown in Table 27-4.

Table 27-3. COMBINED INCOME STATEMENT OF CLASS A AND B PRIVATELY OWNED ELECTRIC COMPANIES—DECEMBER 31, 1970

(in millions of dollars)

Electric operating revenues	$19,791
Operating expenses	8,288
Maintenance	1,372
Depreciation and amortization	2,194
Income taxes (including deferred)	1,331
Other taxes	2,125
	$15,310
Electric utility operating income	4,481
Other utility operating income	404
Total utility operating income	$ 4,885
Other income, net	758
Total income before interest	$ 5,643
Interest changes	2,236
Net income	$ 3,407
Dividends declared	
Preferred stock	$ 362
Common stock	$ 2,159

SOURCE: See Table 27-2.

Table 27-4. SOURCES OF REVENUES OF PRIVATELY OWNED ELECTRIC POWER COMPANIES

(based on 1970 data)

	Sales		Revenues	
Class of Service	*Kilowatt-hours (millions)*	*Per Cent*	*Amount (millions)*	*Per Cent*
Residential	333,396	25.8%	$ 7,411	37.9%
Commerical	256,923	19.9	5,347	27.4
Industrial	450,893	34.8	4,588	23.4
Others	41,821	3.2	753	3.9
For resale	206,421	16.3	1,434	7.4
Total	1,289,454	100.0%	$19,533	100.0%
Other electric revenues			258	
Total operating revenues			$19,791	

SOURCE: See Table 27-2.

The regulatory authorities establish the general level of the utility's net operating revenues; the company determines the rate or rates charged different classes of customers that will produce the permitted income.

The investor should compare the level of a company's rates with national, state, or local average figures (in 1971, the average residential electric bill in the United States was $163.84, at an average rate of 2.32 cents per kilowatt-hour). Comparatively high rates are profitable, but may render the company vulnerable to rate reductions, or at least to slower rate increases. Comparatively low rates suggest a miserly attitude on the part of the commission but may also reflect types of fuel used and operating conditions.

Stability and growth of revenues are extremely important. Stability stems from the degree of diversification of the sources of revenue. In 1971, for the electric power industry as a whole, residential consumers accounted for 42 per cent of revenues, but their consumption of kilowatt-hours was only 32 per cent. Conversely, sale of kilowatt-hours to commercial and industrial customers was 63 per cent but because of the low average rate (1.57 cents per killowatt-hour) accounted for only 50 per cent of revenues. Utility companies relying primarily on industrial customers are vulnerable to changes in both volume of sales and of revenues. Growth stems from increased population and industrial activity, but may be unbalanced because of overdependence on one industry or a few major industrial consumers.

The residential load is ordinarily more stable than that of the commercial and industrial users, whose demands tend to vary more with business conditions. Furthermore, while industrial and commercial loads may be very large, their average rates are considerably lower. But such demand can contribute to a higher *load factor* (average consumption to peak consumption) by building up demand in off-peak hours or seasons, and thus produce lower unit costs and higher profits. The higher the load, the less the idle plant capacity. The load factor can be determined for any period—a day, a month, or a year. Consider an electric light and power company with a peak load of 100,000 kilowatts. If its annual output is 525,600,000 kilowatt-hours or 60,000 kilowatts per hour, its annual load factor is 60 per cent or about average for the industry.

In examining the operating revenues of a company, one should note the extent to which they are derived from the main activity of the company, such as electric light and power, and the extent from collateral services such as gas. Good results from one type of service may be offset by the greater risks of another. Furthermore, a mixture of revenues distorts the comparability of the ratios with those of other companies.

A basic test of operating efficiency is the familiar operating ratio, or ratio of total operating deductions, including all taxes, to operating revenues. Even more useful as a clue to control of everyday operations is the ratio of direct operating expenses (all expenses less depreciation and all taxes) to operating revenues. Typical ratios for various categories of utilities, on both bases, are shown in Table 27-5.

In addition to being affected by the type of industry, type of consumer, load factor, cost of fuel, and other factors, the operating ratio is greatly influenced by the depreciation and maintenance expense, over which management has some control from year to year. A low operating ratio may be the result of undermaintenance. Maintenance and depreciation *combined*

Table 27-5. UTILITY OPERATING RATIOS

	All Expenses and Taxes	Direct Operating Expenses
Hydroelectric	70%	40%
Steam electric	80	45
Natural gas distribution	87	71
Gas transmission	86	70
Telephone	83	52
Telegraph	90	80
Water	70	46

should not be less than 17 per cent of gross revenues for steam electric companies and 13 per cent for hydroelectric. Annual depreciation expense as a percentage of gross plant (exclusive of land) should run about 2½ per cent for gas distribution, 3½ per cent for gas pipeline companies, 2½ per cent for electric companies, and 4 per cent for telephone companies.

The net operating revenues plus the income from investments and other sources comprise the total income available for interest and is used to compute the coverage of fixed charges and of fixed charges plus preferred dividends. In 1970, for all private electric companies combined, interest was earned 2.5 times (after taxes)[10] and 3.1 times before income taxes. This is in contrast to an after-tax ratio of 3.8 times in 1965, and reflects the substantial rise in interest rates and outstanding debt since that year. Within the whole group, wide variations appear; nevertheless, the relative stability of utility earnings (save electric railway and telegraph companies) and their general ability to earn their fixed charges adequately have put their bonds in a relatively preferred investment position. The investor is satisfied with a lower record of interest coverage for a sound utility than for a railroad or an industrial company.

Another method of testing the ability of the company to earn its fixed charges is to compute these as a percentage of operating revenues. For a very efficient and conservatively financed steam electric light and power company, the ratio should not exceed 7½ per cent. Thus, if a company had net plant of $75,000,000, operating revenues of $27,000,000, and $37,000,000 in outstanding bonds with an average interest rate of 5.5 per cent, its interest charges would be about $2,000,000 or 7.6 per cent of revenues. And if operating expenses, taxes, and depreciation consumed 77 per cent of revenues, interest would be covered 3 times.

The 1965–1970 rise in interest rates sent the cost of new long-term borrowing to as high as 9 per cent for some companies, and raised the average cost on all outstanding debt substantially. As older debt bearing lower coupons has been retired or refinanced, coverage of total interest has declined.

---

[10]In these calculations, interest on short-term as well as long-term debt in included. "Interest charged to construction" is added back to net operating revenue to produce the amount of total income available for interest coverage. Although most income statements show this item as a reduction of fixed charges, the treatment explained is preferable.

The relatively stable earnings of utilities enable them to declare the bulk of their net income in dividends. Indeed, this is necessary if the capital stock, limited as it is in earning power, is to be attractive to investors. The typical dividend payout by a conservatively financed utility is about 70 per cent of net income.

Electric Light and Power

The electric light and power companies comprise the largest as well as the most popular utility group from the investment viewpoint. In the ninety years of its history, the electrical industry has grown from the small local station of 1,000 kilowatt capacity to the modern power plant of 200,000 kilowatt capacity serving thousands of customers over a wide area through an elaborate transmission and distribution system. At first, the electricity produced was used only for lighting, so that the plant was idle a good part of the time. So successful have the companies been in building up a day-time load, however, that the hours of darkness now represent the *valley* rather than the *peak* of demand. The growth of the industry has been the result of more extensive, as well as intensive, use of electrical energy.

Electricity now occupies a monopoly in the field of illumination, and new uses of power, including appliances and air conditioning, are improving the load factor. In the heating field, it has so far proved advantageous only in special applications. But the growth of space heating, especially through the use of the heat pump, offers prospects of more vigorous competition with coal, oil, and gas.

Electric power output has more than doubled about every ten years since the early 1900s. The spectacular growth of the industry is indicated by the data in Table 27-6.

The stability of earnings of the electric utilities is indicated by the fact that in 1933, when operating revenues were at the lowest level, the fixed

Table 27-6. POSTWAR GROWTH OF THE PRIVATE ELECTRIC LIGHT AND POWER INDUSTRY

	Installed Capacity (millions of kilowatts)	Production (billions of kilowatt-hours)	No. of Customers (millions)	Revenues (billions)	Net Income (millions)
1945	40.3	180.9	28.1	a	$ 545
1950	55.2	266.9	35.1	a	831
1955	86.9	420.9	41.5	$ 6.9	1,257
1960	128.5	578.6	46.5	9.7	1,747
1965	177.7	809.5	51.5	12.9	2,556
1971	286.9	1,250.0	58.2	24.7	3,774

aNot available

SOURCE: Edison Electric Institute, *Statistical Year Book of the Electric Utility Industry.* (New York: The Institute, annual).

charges (of the industry) were earned more than twice. In the early and middle 1960s, the coverage exceeded 3.5 times, but has declined for the reasons explained above.

The past rate of growth of over 10 per cent annually is likely to be maintained, and the burgeoning power needs of the country, stemming from population growth, industrial expansion, and increased per capita residential use, will sustain the industry's earning power for an indefinite period. The trend of rates is declining, and a lag still exists between rising costs (including costs of capital) and rate revisions. The industry faces increased competition from the aggressive natural gas business. Although atomic power poses a potential threat, numerous electric power companies are participating in a broad industry program aimed at bringing about economical nuclear power; as of June 1971, ninety nuclear power projects were in operation or construction. Securities of electric companies will, as always, continue to include some of mediocre quality. But, on the whole, the quality status of electric bonds and stocks should be maintained, although substantial variation in the market prices of common stocks will probably continue as price-earnings ratios and yields move up and down in reflection of changing interest rates. (The data on p. 515 show how these have changed in the period 1965–1972.)

Summary of power company tests. The balance sheets and income statements of an electric power company should be carefully analyzed. The better-managed companies report financial operations within recognized ranges, as indicated in the following comments. All of the following suggested tests will not be met at the same time. Each is a suggested maximum or minimum and should be considered separately.

With respect to the balance sheet

1. The value of the fixed assets (land, bulidngs, and equpiment before depreciation) should not exceed 4 times the operating revenue in the case of a team plant and 6 times in the case of a hydroelectric plant. (Using net plant, the suggested relationships are 3 times and 4.75 times, respectively.)

2. The amount of bonds outstanding should not exceed 50 to 55 per cent of the net value of the fixed assets or 50 to 55 per cent of total capital structure.[11]

3. The depreciation reserve should be at least 25 per cent of the value of the gross fixed assets for steam electric, 15 per cent for hydroelectric.

4. The preferred stock outstanding should not exceed 10 to 15 per cent of capital structure.

5. The common stock and surplus should represent at least 35 per cent of capital structure.

---

[11]Depending on preferred stock proportion. Debt of 50 per cent and preferred stock of 15 per cent of capital structure total 65 per cent. If a company has no preferred stock outstanding, a higher debt ratio is appropriate, say to a maximum of 60 per cent.

6. Unless the company is growing rapidly, the working capital ratio should be at least 100 per cent.

With respect to the income statement

1. The ratio of total expenses, including provisions for maintenance, depreciation, and taxes, to operating revenues should not exceed 80 per cent for a steam plant and 70 per cent for a hydroelectric plant.

2. The ratio of depreciation plus maintenance to operating revenues should not be less than 17 per cent for steam, 13 per cent for hydro.

3. The ratio of operating income, before the payment of interest charges, and after income taxes, to the net investment in plant and equipment should be between 7 and 8 per cent to show a fair return earned on the rate base.

4. The ratio of interest charges to the operating revenues should not exceed 7½ per cent. The total income (after all taxes) available for the payment of these charges should average at least 2.5 times the requirement over a representative period of years.

5. The ratio of the sum of the interest charges and the preferred dividend to operating revenues should not exceed 9 per cent. The total income available for the payment of these charges should be at least 2 times the "overall" requirement over a representative period of years.[12]

6. The balance available for dividends on the common stock should be at least 12 per cent of the operating revenues.

The Gas Industry

The production and distribution of gas on a commercial scale has been a major public utility enterprise in the United States for considerably more than a full century. From the first manufactured-gas plant in Baltimore in 1816, with a capacity of a few hundred cubic feet daily, to the modern Hunts Point plant of the Consolidated Edison Company in New York, with a daily capacity of several hundred thousand cubic feet, the industry has shown continued progress despite almost constant competition of alternative services. Prior to the development, about 1880, of the electrical lamp, gas was used almost exclusively for illumination. As electricity gradually gained supremacy in the lighting field, the gas companies turned to the heating field, with most successful results. The physical characteristics of gas make it an ideal fuel for heating purposes. As a result, the output of the industry has continued to grow faster than the general economy.

The great bulk of the gas sold by the American companies was once produced by the destructive distillation of coal. Although natural gas was used extensively in certain districts, for the main part it was available only

---

[12]If the preferred stock is to be considered high grade, the coverage of bond interest plus preferred dividends should be as high as the required coverage of bond interest. This means that for a given company, if the preferred is high grade, the bonds more than meet the standard.

to customers located near the producing wells. Extensive petroleum prospecting brought in many rich natural gas wells, especially in the Southwest. To find a market for this gas, companies built pipelines, extending hundreds of miles, bringing natural gas to metropolitan areas including Chicago, Cleveland, Detroit, St. Louis, Washington, Atlanta, New Orleans, Los Angeles, San Francisco, and, more recently, New England industrial centers.

Investors are interested in three types of gas companies: natural gas distributing companies, natural gas pipeline or transmission companies, and integrated companies performing both functions. The use of manufactured gas has almost disappeared. As shown in Table 27-7, by the end of 1970

Table 27-7. GROWTH OF GAS INDUSTRY, 1950–1970

Type	Number of Customers (millions)		Sales (billions of therms)		Revenues (millions)		Miles of Main (thousands)	
	1950	1970	1950	1970	1950	1970	1950	1970
Manufactured	7.6	.1	2.2	.1	$ 455	$ 12	55	1
Natural	14.3	40.9	38.5	158.9	1,361	10,145	314	906
Mixed	1.8	.5	1.3	1.4	111	120	12	7
Liquified petroleum	.3	a	.1	a	21	5	6	1
Total	24.0	41.5	42.1	160.4	$1,948	$10,282	387	915

aLess than 50 millions.

SOURCE: American Gas Association, Inc., *Gas Facts* (New York: The Association, annual).

natural gas accounted for the great bulk of both sales and revenues. Many companies selling manufactured gas were hard pressed by competition from the increasingly efficient electric power industry and by increasing costs, and most have converted to straight natural gas.

Only about 31 per cent of the consumption (but about 50 per cent of the revenues) of gas distributing companies is residential (cooking and heating). The commercial and industrial demand introduces an element of instability which has to a large extent been offset by continued growth, at least insofar as natural gas is concerned. (See Table 27-8.)

Table 27-8. GAS UTILITY REVENUES
       (based on 1970 data)

Class of Service	Sales		Revenues	
	Therms (billions)	Per Cent	Amount (millions)	Per Cent
Residential	49.2	30.7%	$ 5,207	50.6%
Commercial	20.1	12.5	1,620	15.8
Industrial	84.4	52.6	3,181	30.9
Other	6.7	4.2	274	2.7
Total	160.4	100.0%	$10,282	100.0%

SOURCE: American Gas Association, Inc., *Gas Facts* (New York: The Association, annual).

Gas company analysis: distributing. Analysis of the financial condition of a gas company involves the application of recognized standards of acceptability to the figures shown in the published financial statements.

With respect to the balance sheet

1. The value of the fixed assets (before depreciation) should not exceed twice the operating revenue (1.6 times after depreciation).

2. The amount of bonds outstanding should not exceed 50 per cent of net plant or capital structure.

3. The depreciation reserve should be at least 20 per cent of gross plant.

4. The preferred stock should not exceed 10 per cent of the capital structure.

5. The common stock and retained earnings should represent at least 40 per cent of the capital structure.

6. The ratio of current assets to current liabilities should be at least 100 per cent.

With respect to the income statement

1. Total operating revenue deductions, including depreciation and taxes, should not exceed 86 per cent of operating revenues.

2. Operating revenue deductions exclusive of depreciation and taxes should not exceed 70 per cent of operating revenues.

3. The ratio of depreciation plus maintenance to operating revenues should not be less than 9 per cent.

4. Gross income before interest charges should be at least 8 per cent of the net fixed assets or capital structure.

5. The ratio of interest charges and other deductions from gross income to operating revenues should not exceed 5 per cent. The interest charges should be earned 3 times (after taxes) over a representative period of years.

6. The ratio of the sum of fixed charges and preferred dividends to operating revenues should not exceed 6 per cent. Fixed charges plus preferred dividends combined should be earned 2.5 times over a representative period of years.

7. The balance available for common stock should be at least 7 per cent of operating revenues.

Gas pipeline company analysis. Rapid though its growth has been, the gas transmission industry presents special elelments of risk due to (1) the uncertain regulatory status of the industry and (2) the unusually large use of debt as a source of funds. The latter risk would be negligible if the former were removed, because the producing and transmission companies (who produce or buy gas in the field and sell it to retail distributing companies) enjoy resale contracts with large retailing utilities that justify a heavier debt financing than would be appropriate for a local company.

Regulation of natural gas in interstate commerce was given to the Federal Power Commission by the Natural Gas Act of 1938. The Commission's policy was to allow the average field price to be the guide in setting the value of a pipeline's own production. This encouraged the exploration and production of owned reserves. In 1954 the Supreme Court ruled that the Commission had jurisdiction over all sales of natural gas for resale in interstate commerce.[13] The control of the Commission over the cost of gas in the field is accomplished through area pricing procedures, under which ceilings on prices at which new gas can be sold are established in twenty-two separate areas.

The Commission has established standard accounting procedures for interstate companies. Of special interest is the rule that accelerated depreciation be utilized and that the resulting tax deferrals be passed through to the consumer in the form of lower rates.

With respect to the balance sheet

1. The value of the gross fixed assets should not exceed 3 times the operating revenue (2 times after depreciation).

2. The amount of bonds and other long-term debt outstanding should not exceed 65 per cent of the net plant or 60 per cent of the capital structure.

3. The depreciation reserve should be at least 30 per cent of the gross plant.

4. The preferred stock should not exceed 10 per cent of the capital structure.

5. The common stock and surplus should represent at least 30 per cent of the capital structure.

With respect to the income statement

1. The ratio of total operating deductions, including depreciation and taxes, should not exceed 87 per cent of operating revenues.

2. The ratio of operating expenses exclusive of depreciation and taxes should not exceed 70 per cent of operating revenues.

3. The ratio of depreciation plus maintenance to operating revenues should be not less than 10 per cent.

4. Gross income before interest charges should be at least 8 per cent of the capital structure or 8½ per cent of the net plant.

5. The ratio of interest charges and other income deductions to operating revenues should not exceed 7 per cent. Fixed charges should be covered by gross income at least 2.25 times over a representative period of years, after taxes.

6. The ratio of the sum of fixed charges and preferred dividends to operating revenues should not exceed 7 per cent. Interest plus preferred

[13]*Phillips Petroleum Co.* v *Wisconsin,* 374 U.S. 672.

dividends should be earned at least 2 times over a representative period of years.[14]

7. The balance available for common stock should be at least 8 per cent of operating revenues.

The Telephone Industry

The telephone industry has become an integral factor in the everyday life of the nation. In any age which puts a premium upon speed, instantaneous communication has inestimable value. Progressive policies on the part of operating management in the form of quicker service (automatic dials), promotional rates (at off-peak hours), universal connections (long-distance lines), and teletype service have caused an extraordinary growth in this field.

Although there are over 1,800 telephone companies in the United States, the Bell System, consisting of the parent American Telephone & Telegraph Company and its subsidiaries and affiliates, operates 83 per cent of the nation's telephones, does 80 per cent of the business in terms of number of calls, and controls over 85 per cent of the industry's assets. General Telephone & Electronics Corporation is the leading domestic independent, operating 40 per cent of the independent telephones, and International Telephone & Telegraph Corporation is important in the foreign field.

American Telephone & Telegraph Company owns and operates the connecting long-distance lines. It controls, through stock ownership, nineteen regional operating "Bell" companies and has a minority interest in two others; it also owns Western Electric Company, manufacturer of telephone equipment for the system, and Bell Telephone Laboratories, Inc., a research subsidiary. Its income is derived from toll-service revenues, license-contract revenues received for services furnished to the companies of the system, and dividends and interest on securities of subsidiaries. The postwar growth of the Bell System is indicated in Table 27-9.

Investment interest in Bell System securities is centered in the bonds and preferred stocks of the regional Bell companies, and the bonds, preferred stock, and common stock of the parent company. In general, the associated companies provide examples of able business management. The senior securities of the regional companies command high investment respect. The volume of debentures of the parent company has increased greatly in recent years. In 1970, $1,569,000,000 of debentures (with warrants) were sold. This was the largest single piece of corporate financing on record (see pp. 235–36.) Although the debt ratio has become less conservative, the company's debentures (including the convertibles) command the highest investment rating.

For the first time in its history, in 1971 the parent company sold preferred stock, issuing 27,500,000 convertible shares with par value of

[14]These figures assume that the company has some "other income" in addition to net operating income.

$1,375,000,000. The ratio of "senior capital"—bonds and preferred stock—to total capital structure stood at 46 per cent at the end of 1971. (See Table 27-10).

Table 27-9. GROWTH OF BELL TELEPHONE SYSTEM
YEAR-END 1950–1971

Items	1950	1955	1960	1965	1971
Telephones (1,000)	35,343	46,218	60,735	75,866	100,281
Average daily conversations (1,000)	140,782	168,936	219,093	279,686	388,000
Plant, before depreciation (millions)	$10,102	$15,340	$24,072	$35,334	$60,568
Operating revenues (millions)	$3,262	$5,297	$7,920	$11,062	$18,511
Employees (1,000)	602	745	736	795	1,001
Stockholders, parent (1,000)	986	1,409	1,911	2,841	3,010
Net income, parent (millions)	$346	$664	$1,213	$1,796	$2,240
Earnings per share, parent	$1.96	$2.18	$2.77	$3.41	$3.99

SOURCE: American Telephone & Telegraph Company, annual reports.

Table 27-10. CONSOLIDATED CAPITAL STRUCTURE, BELL SYSTEM
(in millions of dollars)

Items	1950 Amt.	1950 Per Cent	1960 Amt.	1960 Per Cent	1971 Amt.	1971 Per Cent
Funded debt						
Subsidiaries	$1,748.0	22%	$4,370.0	21%	} $21,228.3	43%
AT&T	1,885.0	24	2,962.2	15		
AT&T Preferred stock	—	—	—	—	1,373.2	3
Minority interest in subsidiaries	137.1	2	418.4	2	846.8	2
AT&T capital stock	3,611.7	46	9,920.8	48	14,455.9	30
Retained earnings	461.9	6	2,841.5	14	10,615.1	22
Total	$7,843.7	100%	$20,512.9	100%	$48,519.3	100%

Includes premium on shares.

SOURCES: American Telephone & Telegraph Company, annual reports and *Statistical Report*.

For many years, the common stock of American Telephone & Telegraph was regarded as a premier equity. Its unbroken dividend record partially explains why it is held by over 3 million investors as of 1973. Its appeal (and its market price) was increased considerably by a 3-for-one split in 1959 and a 2-for-1 split in 1964. Earnings per share rose to $3.99 a share in 1971 and 1972, and dividends rose from $2.00 in 1965 to $2.60 a share. But the lag of rates behind costs and the pending rate investigation (see below), together with the great increase in senior financing, have given the stock a more uncertain outlook and a volatile price record in recent years. In 1965 the stock sold as high as 70, and in 1970 as low as 41. The company's rate of return has remained below 7.5 per cent and has lagged behind the earning power of "growth" companies in the electric power industry.

Recent developments. On the whole, independent telephone companies have fared better than Bell companies during the postwar years, largely because of the greater importance of suburban and rural areas in their operations. The formation of Communications Satellite Corporation in 1963, which is owned 49 per cent by communications companies, opened up possibilities of potential earnings from both international and domestic messages. In October 1965, the Federal Communications Commission ordered a general investigation of interstate A.T.&T. rates that will take some years to complete.

Telephone company analysis. Analysis of the financial condition of a telephone company requires the application of standards of acceptability differing somewhat from those used for electric power and gas companies.

With respect to the balance sheet

1. The value of the fixed assets before depreciation should not exceed 3.5 times the operating revenue (2.75 times after depreciation).

2. The amount of bonds outstanding should not exceed 45 per cent of the capital structure.

3. The retirement (depreciation) reserve should be not less than 22 per cent of the gross fixed assets.

4. The comments with respect to preferred stock, common stock, capital structure, and surplus previously made in connection with power company balance sheets are applicable to telephone company statements except that smaller proportions of debt and of preferred stock are appropriate, to recognize the greater volatility of telephone company earnings.

5. Current assets should be at least equal 1.10 times current liabilities.

With respect to the income statement

1. The ratio of operating expense (including income taxes) to operating revenues should not exceed 83 per cent (70 per cent exclusive of income taxes).

2. The ratio of depreciation plus maintenance to gross revenues should be at least 35 per cent.

3. The ratio of income available for fixed charges (after income taxes) to capital structure should be at least 7.5 per cent.

4. The ratio of interest charges to operating revenues should not be more than 5 per cent, and total income should be at least 3.75 times the interest charges for a representative period of years.

5. The comments with respect to preferred dividends and balance of earnings remaining for the common stock previously made in connection

with power company income reports are equally applicable to telephone company statements ,except that interest plus preferred dividends should be earned more generously in the latter group.

The Telegraph Industry

The domestic telegraph industry of the United States is controlled by a single company, Western Union. Telegraphy is one of the oldest of the utility group, dating back over a full century to the Morse experiments, and it enjoyed remarkable prosperity until the depression of the 1930s. Western Union had a mild recovery, but in the 1940s the increase in costs outstripped the increase in revenues, and deficits were reported in 1946, 1948, and 1949. A modest profit was produced in 1950, and save for the strike year of 1952, revenues and profits stabilized at a respectable level in 1953–1958, and reached a then all-time high in 1959. Net income declined in 1960–1962, but by 1965 was again setting new levels. But the future of the company, and of its securities, is still ·open to conjecture. The radio, the teletypewriter, the long-distance telephone, and air mail have diverted a substantial part of the business which formerly went by telegraph and cable. The future lies in the development of other forms of electrical communication. One should not conclude, however, that the telegraph industry has reached the stage of senility. Handling the communication business means more than the transmission of messages. The early 1960s saw a substantial revival of earning power for Western Union, but they have since declined sharply.

In 1969 the Western Union Corporation was formed to acquire, by exchange of shares, all of the outstanding stock of the Western Union Telegraph Company. The parent company has acquired or formed a number of other subsidiaries for the transmission and processing of data and for high-speed communication. In Table 27-11 the data are drawn from the consolidated financial statements of the group.

Telegraph company analysis. Table 27-11 shows pertinent financial data for Western Union in 1960 and 1971. The high operating ratio, the vulnerability to economic recession, and the relatively low return on total investment suggest the necessity of caution with respect to long-term debt, the maintenance of adequate working capital, and a conservative dividend policy.

The Water Industry

Investment interest in the securities of water companies is quite limited, owing to the prevalence of municipal ownership in this field. The supply

Table 27-11. WESTERN UNION FINANCIAL ANALYSIS

	1960	1971
(Gross) plant turnover	63 %	31 %
Capital structure proportions		
Long-term debt	14 %	46 %
Preferred stock	—	11 %
Common stock and surplus	86 %	43 %
Reserve for depreciation as a percentage		
of gross plant	44 %	31 %
Current ratio	1.7	1.8
Operating ratio (including taxes)	94 %	91 %
Depreciation and maintenance as a percentage		
of revenues	22 %	29 %
Return on total capital structure	4 %	3 %
Times overall charges earned (after taxes)	4.3	1.2%
Percentage earned on common equity	4 %	2.6%
Earnings per common share	$4.96	$1.09
Dividends per common share	$1.40	$1.40

SOURCE: Western Union Corporation, annual reports.

of private water company securities is limited. Others are available in the municipal "revenue bond" category.

Relatively few large communities, notably Indianapolis, Indiana, Birmingham, Alabama, and San Jose, California are served by private companies. A number of smaller cities, such as New Haven, Connecticut and New Rochelle, New York have private service. Certain companies serve rather wide groups of communities. One—American Water Works—is the parent of seventy-four companies operating in fifteen states. The industry is the oldest of the utilities and for centuries has retained its essential simplicity of a "pump and a pipe." However, to reach adequate sources, the "pipe" has had to be lengthened in many cases.

Historically, water has almost always been obtainable in unlimited quantity at little or no cost, and its use has quite invariably been proportionate to population. Population growth in the United States is a little over one per cent yearly, and so the growth of water companies is equally slow. If, however, the water companies are handicapped by slow growth, they enjoy a compensating advantage in stability of revenue. The use of water, at least for domestic purposes, is seldom contingent upon cost; consequently, the output of water companies is remarkably steady. Stability of earnings is the outstanding advantage of water securities as investments and justifies a relatively high proportion of bonds in the capital structure.

Certain operating characteristics of water companies are worth noting. The investment in fixed assets is large in relation to revenues; in other words, the plant turnover is slow. However, this disadvantage is offset by a correspondingly low operating ratio.

Water company analysis. With respect to the balance sheet

1. The value of the fixed assets (before depreciation) should not exceed 6 times the operating revenues.

2. The amount of bonds outstanding should not exceed 65 per cent of the depreciated value of the fixed assets or of the capital structure.

3. The retirement (depreciation) reserve should be at least 15 per cent of the value of the fixed assets.

4. The preferred stock outstanding, when added to the bonds outstanding, should not exceed 75 per cent of the capital structure.

5. The common stock and surplus should be at least 25 per cent of the capital structure.

With respect to the income statement

1. The ratio of operating expenses, including all taxes, to operating revenues should not exceed 70 per cent. Direct expenses should not consume more than 45 per cent of revenues.

2. The ratio of depreciation plus maintenance to operating revenues should be at least 15 per cent.

3. Operating income after taxes should be at least 5 per cent of the capital structure.

4. The ratio of interest charges to operating revenues should not exceed 10 per cent. The total income after taxes should be at least 2.5 times the interest charges.

5. The preferred dividend requirement, plus the interest charges, should be earned at least 1.75 times on an overall basis.

6. The balance available for the common stock should be at least 10 per cent of the operating revenues.

The Holding Company and Its Regulation

Reference has previously been made to the importance of the holding company in the public utility field, especially in the electric, gas, telephone, and water services. The "pure" holding company's chief asset is the common stock of subsidiary operating companies. The "holding-operating" company owns and operates property in its own right and also controls subsidiaries through stock ownership.

The holding company was widely used in the utility field in order to give to the subsidiaries the advantages of combined management of operations, construction, public relations, and financing which they might not enjoy as separate local concerns. The use of the device also made possible the control of very large properties with small investment, and also made possible (under favorable conditions) a large return to the owners of the holding company common stock. The operating companies typically issued substantial nonvoting senior securities bearing fixed rates of interest and preferred dividends. Thus, they could be controlled by the purpose of common stock only. This application of the "trading on equity" or leverage principal magnified the earnings on the subsidiaries' common stock and, thus, the earnings of the parent.

The benefits of this system to the holding company's owners could be increased by carrying the leverage through an additional step, namely, the use of senior securities by the parent itself. A hypothetical example may serve to illustrate these ideas. Suppose two operating utilities are each financed with 7 per cent funded debt equal to 50 per cent of assets, and $6\frac{1}{2}$ per cent nonvoting preferred stock equal to 25 per cent of assets. The ownership of all or of a substantial portion of the common stock of each operating company gives the holding company control with a minor investment. If each operating company earns 8 per cent on total investment, after payment of bond interest and preferred dividends, 11.5 per cent is earned on the common stock equity. Now, if the holding company has obtained its own funds partly through the issuance of its own bonds and preferred stock, the return on its common stock, which represents a still smaller fraction of the assets of the group, is further magnified. But, in times of depression, of course, if the subsidiaries' earnings shrink even modestly, the return on the common stock is reduced in even greater proportion, if not eliminated. In the worst overpyramided situations, holding companies found themselves without revenues in the early 1930s and many failed as a result.

The senior securities of the holding company are actually junior securities within the consolidated group, and the common stock has a very thin equity in the earning power of the operating subsidiaries. This condition is even more attenuated when several intermediate holding companies intervene, each of which issues bonds and preferred stocks.

All holding company securities are not weak. Some companies are conservatively capitalized. Some control very valuable subsidiaries. Some enjoy advantages from control of contiguous properties. By and large, however, investors should realize that, as a class, holding company securities are fundamentally weaker than operating company obligations.

Analysis. Holding companies issue two different types of financial statements. The *corporate* statements refer to the holding company only. *Consolidated* statements include the combined finances of parent company and subsidiaries, eliminating intercompany transactions. For analytical purposes, the consolidated statements are used because they provide a comprehensive picture of the performance of the entire group.

The tests previously outlined should be applied to the consolidated statements of the group. However, two important refinements are necessary in recognition of the junior position of the (pure) holding company's securities:

1. The components of the *consolidated* capital structure of the holding company and subsidiaries should be arrayed in order of priority, and the

percentage of each item to total should then be calculated. The order is as follows:

> Subsidiaries' funded debt
> Subsidiaries' preferred stock
> Minority interest in subsidiaries' common stock and surplus
> Holding company funded debt
> Holding company preferred stock
> Holding company stock
> Consolidated surplus

2. Interest coverage is calculated by dividing consolidated gross or total income before interest and after taxes by interest on subsidiary debt plus dividends on subsidiary preferred plus interest on holding company bonds; preferred dividend coverage is calculated by adding to the above the holding company's preferred dividend requirements.

Where the corporate group includes companies providing more than one utility service, say, both gas and electricity, the analysis of the consolidated statements must adjust for the varying tests indicated previously. This is also the case where a single company is engaged in more than one type of business.

Public Utility Holding Company Act of 1935. The abuses that appeared in the management and financing of operating and holding companies led to the passage of an important Federal statute in 1935. Its major provisions may be summarized as follows:

1. Holding companies (and their subsidiaries) controlling gas and electric companies in more than one state are subject to the jurisdiction of the Securities and Exchange Commission.

2. The Commission must approve all security issues of the registrants, including new financing, refinancing, reorganizations, readjustments, and mergers; holding companies were to be confined to secured bonds and common stock. In passing on new financing, the Commission considers the appropriateness of the security to the earnings, asset values, and capital structure to the issuer; a general limit of bonds to 50 per cent and preferred stock to between 20 and 25 per cent of net plant is imposed. This requires a review of the values paid for assets and the adequacy of depreciation reserves.

3. All intercompany transactions must have Commission approval, including dividends, accounting, intercompany loans (with "upstream" loans prohibited), service charges (which must be at cost), and purchase and sale contracts. Registered companies may not acquire any securities or utility assets or any other interest in a business unless the transaction would work toward a more integrated utility system.

4. Proposals to alter the preferences or voting rights of securityholders

are subject to Commission review; unfair or inequitable distribution of voting is prohibited.

5. Competitive bidding is requred for the purchase of obligations of companies subject to S.E.C. jurisdiction.

Investment Outlook

The relative stability of earnings produced by public utility companies, their strong growth tendencies (telegraph excepted), and their established place in the American economy have created a firm position for utility securities in the investment field. The sounder utility bonds find a ready market in the portfolios of institutions. Utility preferred stocks are in demand on the part of investors (especially taxed institutions) seeking relative safety and generous yield. Utility common stocks, while lacking the possibilities of spectacular earnings and market appreciation of some industrial equities, provide a respectable income that is relatively stable through the vicissitudes of the business cycle. The fast-growing companies located in states such as Florida and Texas, where a high rate of return is permitted, have taken on the characteristics of "growth" companies, that is, high price-earnings multiples and low dividend yields. Some utility common stocks have a special tax appeal in that all or part of their dividends are exempt from income taxes, as a result of higher depreciation charges for tax than for report purposes.

Not withstanding these general comments, it is important that the investor recognize the changing investment position of utility common stocks in recent years. This is indicated by the record of their prices, price-earnings ratios, and dividend yields in comparison with those of industrial concerns. The following data are Moody's weighted averages. The reader is reminded that the record of individual companies may differ widely from that of the average, depending largely on whether the stock is characterized by growth or by stability of income and dividends. And the data do not reveal higher or lower figures within the annual periods.

	1965	1966	1967	1968	1969	1970	1971	1972
				Utilities				
Earnings per share ($)	5.92	6.30	6.67	6.67	6.92	6.89	7.20	7.70[a]
Market price per share ($)	117	103	102	98	94	79	84	80
Price-earnings ratio	19.8	16.3	15.3	14.7	13.7	11.5	11.7	10.4
Dividend per share ($)	3.86	4.11	4.34	4.50	4.61	4.70	4.77	4.87
Dividend yield (%)	3.3	4.0	4.3	4.6	4.9	5.9	5.7	6.1
				Industrials				
Earnings per share ($)	16.42	16.78	15.76	17.58	17.53	15.30	17.54	20.40[a]
Market price per share ($)	284	267	290	316	313	271	319	362
Price-earnings ratio	17.3	15.9	18.4	18.0	19.0	17.7	18.2	17.7
Dividend per share ($)	8.48	9.17	9.03	9.24	9.83	9.76	9.50	9.61
Dividend yield (%)	3.0	3.4	3.1	2.9	3.1	3.6	3.0	2.7

[a]Estimated.

The declining price-earnings ratios for the utilities have more than offset their increasing earnings and dividends. Because the chief appeal of most utility companies is income rather than growth, the "competition" of high yields on bonds has hurt their relative position. Even in the case of strong companies, the investor must not relax from a continuous analysis of all of the factors that affect their position.

REFERENCES

AMERICAN GAS ASSOCIATION RATE COMMITTEE, *Gas Rate Fundamentals*. New York: The Association, 1960.

BARY, C. W., *Operational Economics of Electric Utilities*. New York: Columbia University Press, 1963.

BONBRIGHT, J. C., *Principles of Public Utility Rates*. New York: Columbia University Press, 1961.

COUGHLAN, J. W., *What the Businessman Should Know about the Regulation of Public Utilities*. Washington, D.C.: Public Affairs Press, 1958.

FOSTER, J. R., AND B. A. BODEY, *Public Utility Accounting*. Englewood Cliffs, N.J.: Prentice-Hall, Inc., 1951.

GARFIELD, P. J., AND W. F. LOVEJOY, *Public Utility Economics*. Englewood Cliffs, N.J.: Prentice-Hall, Inc., 1964.

GRAHAM, BENJAMIN, D. L. DODD, AND SIDNEY COTTLE, *Security Analysis*, 4th ed., Chapters 20, 21. New York: McGraw-Hill, Inc., 1962.

GUTHMANN, H. G., *Analysis of Financial Statements*, 4th ed., Chapter 14. Englewood Cliffs, N.J.: Prentice-Hall, Inc., 1953.

————, AND H. E. DOUGALL, *Corporate Financial Policy*, 4th ed., Chapter 16. Englewood Cliffs, N.J.: Prentice-Hall, Inc., 1962.

HAWKINS, C. A., *The Field Price Regulation of Natural Gas*. Tallahassee, Fla.: Florida State University Press, 1969.

HOOLEY, R. W., *Financing the Natural Gas Industry*. New York: Columbia University Press, 1961.

HUNT, F. E., *Public Utilities: Information Sources*. Detroit: Gale Research Co., 1965.

KENNEDY, R. D., AND S. Y. McMULLEN, *Financial Statements*, 5th ed., Chapters 28, 29. Homewood, Ill.: Richard D. Irwin Inc., 1968.

McCRACKEN, P. W., *Economic Progress and the Utility Industry*. Ann Arbor, Mich.: Bureau of Business Research, Graduate School of Business Administration, University of Michigan, 1964.

PHILLIPS, C. F., *The Economics of Regulation*, rev. ed. Homewood, Ill.: Richard D. Irwin, Inc., 1969.

VENNARD, EDWIN, *The Electric Power Business*, 2nd ed. New York: McGraw-Hill, Inc., 1970.

YOUNG, H. H., *Forty Years of Public Utility Finance*. Charlottesville, Va.: The University Press of Virginia, 1965.

28 Railroad Securities

SCOPE: This chapter discusses the investment position of the securities of railroad companies. The order of discussion is (1) development, (2) regulation, (3) systems, (4) geographical influences, (5) operating data, (6) income statement analysis, (7) balance sheet analysis, (8) railroad bonds, (9) railroad stocks, (10) consolidations, (11) recent legislation, and (12) future prospects.

Development of the Industry

The development of the steam railroad industry during the past 140 years has closely followed the pattern of economic growth. The experimental stage began about 1830, with the construction of the short Mohawk and Hudson trackage from Albany to Schenectady, and ended in 1869, with the opening of the first transcontinental road, the Union Pacific. During this period, many short lines were placed in operation and were financed chiefly by local capital. The development stage, which began at the close of the Civil War and continued until the turn of the century, brought wide expansion of new lines to all parts of the country and many consolidations of small roads into large systems. The saturation stage began about 1910, attaining an apparent peak in 1926. During this third period, capital expenditure became intensive rather than extensive, as shown in track rehabilitation, equipment of greater capacity, increased terminal facilities, shop betterments, and power electrification. By 1926, the industry was, for all intents and purposes, completed. No part of the country lacked adequate railway facilities; in fact, in certain sections of the country, notably the Northwest, the facilities were beyond the economic needs of the territory served. The problem of railroad management became primarily one of operating efficiency—that of procuring a satisfactory volume of traffic and of moving it at a reasonable cost.

By the end of the 1920s, the industry had apparently reached the stage of maturity and even the beginning of economic senility. Passenger revenues in 1929 were lower by one-third than in 1920, reflecting the competition of the private automobile. Highway, intercoastal and inland waterway, and pipeline carriers were becoming more prominent as competitors for freight traffic, and their competition was fostered by continued railway rate increases. Railway gross revenues fluctuated wildly from their peak of over $6 billions in the late 1920s to half of that figure in the early 1930s. The loss of its monopoly position and its growing susceptibility to economic fluctuations, together with reliance on funded debt as a source of funds, brought the industry to a state of financial collapse and a wave of failures in the depression of the early 1930s. And although a modest recovery was made in postdepression years, permanent damage had been done to the investment position of the industry's securities.

World War II brought enormous demands for transportation, and the railroad industry responded with a magnificent record. Restrictions on the use of the private automobile returned passenger traffic to the rails. Heavy demands for shipping brought the industry's per cent of total freight tonnage of the country to approximately 85 per cent during the war production boom, as compared with 70 per cent in the middle 1930s, and this influence, coupled with increased rates, brought railroad gross revenues to their then all-time peak in 1943–1944. Revenues declined modestly in 1945. The rate of return on total investment, which had reached an all-time peak of 6.36 per cent in 1942, declined to 3.70 per cent in 1945 as a result of relatively high operating expenses.

Postwar years have not treated the industry very kindly. Railroads now carry only 40 per cent of the nation's intercity freight tonnage, and their share of intercity passenger traffic is now only 7 per cent.

Operating revenues reached $10.7 billions in 1953, but declined to $9.2 billions in 1961, and reached only $12.7 billions in 1971. In the postwar period the rate of return on net property investment never reached 4.5 per cent, fell below 2 per cent in 1961 and 1970, and reached only 2.5 per cent in 1971. The industry is still sharply affected by the business cycle and by increasing competition from other types of carriers.

Some of the shifts that have taken place in the industry in the past forty years are indicated in Table 28-1. Railway mileage has been gradually shrinking, although the property investment has increased, reflecting the greater investment per mile.[1] The industry has succeeded in keeping its long-term debt fairly stable, in spite of increases in equipment obligations. In terms of asset protection, the real weight of debt burden is measured by its relationship to total stockholders' investment, including retained earnings. This latter greatly exceeds the formal investment represented by capital stock. Equipment has decreased numerically, but product per unit has increased with more efficient assets, fuel, and operations. Freight traffic has been maintained, and at progressively higher rates, but the loss of passenger traffic has not been offset by higher rates. The rate of earnings on total investment is extremely low (the table does not reveal the peak rate of return of 6.36 per cent in 1942 and the low rate of 1.37 per cent in

---

[1]At the end of 1970, total investment of Class I railways in road and equipment, including cash, materials, and supplies, before depreciation, was $35.1 billions, or about $170,000 per mile of line of main track.

Table 28-1. DEVELOPMENT OF CLASS I RAILWAYS, 1930–1971[a]

Items	1930	1940	1950	1960	1971
Miles of first main track	242,391	232,524	226,101	217,552	205,000[d]
Property investment, after depreciation[b]	$24,176	$23,168	$24,952	$27,474	$28,127
Capitalization (net):					
Capital stock[b]	$ 7,185	$ 7,020	$ 6,980	$ 5,761	e
Long-term debt[b]	$11,880	$10,609	$ 8,638	$ 8,389	e
Total[b]	$19,065	$17,629	$15,618	$14,150	e
Passenger-train cars in service	52,130	37,817	37,146	28,305	6,842
Freight cars in service[c]	2,276	1,654	1,721	1,658	1,422
Locomotives in service	56,582	41,721	40,036	28,278	27,164
Revenue ton-miles[b]	383,450	373,253	588,578	572,309	739,404
Av. revenue per ton-mile	1.063¢	.945¢	1.329¢	1.403¢	1.594¢
Revenue passenger miles	26,815	23,762	31,760	21,258	6,908
Av. revenue per pass.-mile	2.72¢	1.75¢	2.56¢	3.01¢	4.25¢
Operating revenues	$ 5,281	$ 4,296	$ 9,473	$ 9,514	$12,689
Operating ratio	74.34%	71.90%	74.52%	79.52%	79.24%
Rate of return earned	3.59%	2.94%	4.23%	2.13%	2.47%
Net income, ordinary[b]	$ 524	$ 189	$ 784	$ 445	347
Average employees[c]	1,511	1,027	1,221	780	544
Payroll[b]	$ 2,590	$ 1,964	$ 4,594	$ 4,894	$ 5,893
Capital expenditures[b]	$ 873	$ 429	$ 1,066	$ 919	$ 1,177

[a]Class I companies are those whose operating revenues exceed $5,000,000 annually. The seventy one roads operate 94 per cent of total railroad mileage (1971).
[b]Millions
[c]Thousands
[d]Estimated
[e]Not available
SOURCES: Association of American Railroads, Economics and Finance Department; I.C.C., *Statistics of Railways in the United States*, and *Transport Statistics in the United States, Part I.*

1932). Railways are no longer major employers of labor. Their annual capital expenditures, together with the huge volume of securities outstanding, suggest their continuing economic and financial importance. Of interest in this connection is the decline over the period in the number of employees in relation to payroll.

Regulation

Through a process of evolution, railroading has become probably the most regulated of all private enterprises in the United States. Legislation enacted by state and local authorities, as well as by the Federal government, has severely restricted the powers of management. As most important railroads carry both interstate and intrastate traffic, they are subject to the regulations of the Interstate Commerce Commission and the public service commissions of the various states. While railroad management resents the constant encroachment of public regulation, investors have probably been helped by the development. The evils of unregulated competition, as shown in the railroad history of several decades ago, were immeasurably more harmful to holders of railroad securities than the disadvantages that currently arise in rate, wage, and financial controversies.

The principal regulatory body affecting the railroads is the Interstate Commerce Commission. The powers of the Commission, which were merely observatory when it was first organized in 1887, have been gradually increased, until they now comprise a wide scope of regulatory authority over all railroad operations. Many of these powers directly affect the investment position of railroad securities.

The outstanding power of the Interstate Commerce Commission is that with respect to rate regulation. The Commission is no longer required to give the companies a fair return upon a fair value, but approves rates sufficient to provide adequate and efficient service at the lowest reasonable cost.

The Commission has broad regulatory powers with respect to new financing. New securities may be issued only with the approval of the Commission after investigation of the purpose of the issue, the amount required, the nature of the security, and the cost of distribution. Investors are protected through this function, insofar as conditions then prevailing are concerned. The effect of changing economic conditions on the market values of railway securities over a period of time is another matter.

The authority of the Commission with respect to accounting procedure and periodical earnings statements is also helpful to the investor. All railroad companies are required to keep accounts in accordance with a standard uniform system that assures reliable statements and permits ready comparison of result. Moreover, all carriers must submit monthly statements of earnings, which are published in the newspapers and keep investors in close touch with the operations of the companies. Such figures permit a constant review of earnings that is most desirable.

New railroad mileage may be constructed and existing mileage abandoned only with permission of the Commission. Holders of securities in existing properties, as well as prospective investors in new lines, are thus protected against loss from uneconomic competition of facilities provided in excess of the demand. Conversely, holders of securities in unprofitable lines are not protected against continued losses incurred in the operation of such properties, save for rare cases of subsidization of passenger traffic.

Competing railroad companies are not allowed to consolidate without the approval of the Commission. As such approval is far from perfunctory and is based chiefly upon public advantage, this veto power of the Commission has become a potent factor in recent years, although numerous important consolidations have been approved in the 1950s, 1960s, and early 1970s.

Much criticism has been levied against the Commission (or rather, against Congressional failure to change its powers) with respect to a more liberal attitude towards competitive rates and service, abandonment of unnecessary properties, failure to encourage passenger transportation, and entrance into nonrailroad activities. Some of these problems are again under study and new legislation may result (see pp. 539–40).

Railroad systems and diversification. By a slow process of approved mergers, railway mileage has become increasingly concentrated in fewer major systems. And the original strictly railroad activities have been expanded by the formation of a number of holding company-subsidiary groups of which the railroad is only one, although ordinarily the chief, member.[2] Nonrailroad activities include manufacturing, oil production, land development, and truck and bus transportation. As a result, the consolidated financial statements of such groups become increasingly unlike railroad statements and so are difficult to compare and analyze by the application of traditional tests of operations and earnings. Fortunately, the parent companies must still report separately on railroad operations so that the major rail subsidiaries can be analyzed as railway concerns.

Geographical Influences

Geography plays an important part in railroad prosperity. The size of the territory served, its growth, physical features, density of population, natural resources, manufacturing plants, and commercial activities directly affect earning power. The investor seeks a favorable combination rather than a maximum of advantage in these respects.

The size of the territory limits the distance over which traffic may be carried. Because freight traffic contributes the bulk of railroad earnings, because freight rates vary with the distance carried, and because the transportation cost varies more with terminal expense than with distance, long-haul traffic is relatively more profitable than short-haul shipments. Companies serving extended areas, such as the Union Pacific and the Atchison, have an operating advantage over those serving smaller districts, such as the Western Pacific.

The topography of the territory has a distinct influence of operating conditions. Companies serving relatively level areas, such as the Mississippi Valley region, operate more economically than those serving mountainous districts. Rugged terrain means additional capital expenditures for bridges, cuts, tunnels, snowsheds, and extra locomotives, as well as greater expenditure for fuel and for repairing slides and washouts. Lighter trainloads are run at slower speed in a district of poor traffic density. On the other hand, flood conditions are always a potential danger in low, flat areas. Proximity of terminals to port is helpful in providing a source of traffic but harmful in offering a low-cost competitor.

The density of the population also has a bearing upon earnings. In a thickly populated region, passenger traffic is large—a negative factor in most instances, since passenger traffic is relatively unprofitable, requiring expensive terminals and careful train operation.[3] In such a region, property

[2]Burlington Northern, Illinois Central Industries, Kansas City Southern Industries, Rio Grande Industries, Santa Fe Industries, Seaboard Coast Line Industries, Union Pacific Corporation, and Western Pacific Industries are leading examples.

[3]According to the Interstate Commerce Commission computations, the passenger-operating expense ratio for Class I railroads in 1970 was 142 per cent. This is the main explanation for the creation of "Amtrak" in 1970 (See pp. 540–41).

values are high, making for high taxes, and expensive safety devices are necessary to prevent accidents. Concentration of population, however, usually means a higher-than-average rate of commercial and industrial activity, both of which bring lucrative freight traffic.

In many districts the prosperity of the entire region, including, of course, the carriers, depends heavily upon a few commodities. Cotton in the South, petroleum and wheat in the Southwest, wheat in the Northwest, corn in the Central West, coal in the Appalachian section, lumber in the South and the West, copper in the Rocky Mountain section, iron in the Great Lakes section, and citrus fruits in Florida, California, and Texas formerly dominated the traffic in these regions. Shipments of these commodities are usually carried profitably in bulk over long distances. Economic distress in any commodity, however, seriously harms the earning power of the railroad companies dependent upon it. The railroads have, of course, shared in the postwar tendency of industries to diversify their locations. The industrialization of the South and West has made the companies serving these regions less dependent on a few important commodities.

Manufacturing and commercial activity in any area bears directly upon the prosperity of the serving carriers. A high degree of activity and a broad diversification of enterprise make a satisfactory background for railroad traffic. Such areas provide a more profitable and a more reliable source of shipments than do districts rich in natural resources.

As railroad companies must compete for traffic, at fixed uniform rates, with one another, and with other means of transportation, the investor in railroad securities in any particular territory should carefully consider the competitive situation in a particular region and select those companies that are operating most efficiently, other things being equal.

Operating Data

The annual reports of railroad companies contain a vast amount of statistical and financial data, most of which are useful only to those intimately acquainted with railway operations. In addition, detailed elaborations are published by the Bureau of Transport Economics and Statistics of the Interstate Commerce Commission and in the statistical publications of the Association of American Railroads. Although all of this information directly or indirectly bears upon the investment position of railroad securities, the average investor should concentrate attention on a relatively small group of items among the operating data.

Miles of line operated. This indicates the size and the importance of the road and serves as a common denominator for comparison of roads of unequal size. As stated before, the longer-haul roads are regarded as the better. Important exceptions are found in the case of certain short-haul roads in Pocahontas territory.

Traffic density. This is the major indicator of volume of traffic and so is very important in measuring earning power. Freight traffic density is measured most simply by the revenue ton-miles carried per mile of line, and passenger traffic density by the number of revenue passenger-miles carried per mile of line. In normal times, a freight density of between 3 and 4 million ton-miles per annum would be average. However, since this figure is a measure of volume only, its significance depends on the character of the traffic and the rates charged. A road with relatively light freight traffic density derived from high-rate traffic may be as productive as one with heavier density consisting of low-grade traffic.

Commodity tonnage. These figures show the nature of the traffic handled and are usually shown on a percentage basis. Each company reports commodity statistics in major groups, as well as in separate detail. As freight rates are based upon the general principle of charging *what the traffic will bear*—that is, proportionate to the value of the shipment— valuable commodities produce higher . gross revenues, and the companies favored by shipments of higher value have an advantageous position. The more profitable traffic comprises (1) shipments in less than carload lots, (2) animal products, (3) manufactured products, and (4) forest products. The two least productive are (1) mineral products and (2) agricultural products. Profits are not directly proportionate to revenues, however, as the low-grade commodities can be moved more economically. That road is in the more favorable position which shows a fair percentage of the high-grade commodities (to gain a better average revenue per ton) and reasonable diversification over the group (to derive stability of earnings and to avoid uneconomical returning of empty cars from destination points).

Average length of haul. This is a significant figure. Although lower rates per mile are received, long hauls are made at a relatively lower cost, since terminal costs can be spread out over a longer distance. Further- more, long-haul traffic is less vulnerable to truck competition. For the year 1971 the average haul of revenue freight was 505 miles for all roads as a system.

Performance ratios. Various performance ratios are available for the railroad systems and (in the investment services) for individual carriers. Of these, only a few will be mentioned here. *Gross* or *net ton-miles per freight train-hour* is the best single measure of freight transportation effi- ciency since it combines the speed factor with the weight of the load (total and freight) behind the locomotive and tender and reflects the average performance for each hour of transportation. The figures were 77,017 and 35,722 ton-miles for all Class I railways in 1971. *Car-miles per car-day* measures the extent to which cars are kept moving and so contributing to revenue. The figure for freight-cars in 1971 for all Class I carriers was 53.4 miles, an increase from 45.7 in 1960. *Average speed of freight trains* has increased to 20.4 miles per hour in 1970 as compared with 18.5 miles in 1950–1960. See Table 28-2 for other measures of efficiency.

Table 28-2. MEASURES OF EFFICIENCY

	1950	1960	1971
Load per carload (freight) (tons)	42.0	44.4	54.9
Net ton-miles per freight train-mile	1,224	1,463	1,750
Net ton-miles per servicable freight car-day	972	954	1,376
Miles per freigh t car-day	46.5	45.7	53.3

Income Statement Analysis

The profit and loss report of a steam railroad company is prepared along lines peculiar to the conditions in the industry and differs materially from

Table 28-3. CONDENSED INCOME ACCOUNTS—CLASS I RAILWAYS FOR SELECTED YEARS
(in millions of dollars)

	1930	1940	1950	1960	1965	1971
Total operating revenues	$5,281	$4,296	$9,473	$9,514	$10,208	$12,689
Freight	4,083	3,537	7,817	8,025	8,836	11,786
Passenger	729	417	813	640	553	294
Mail, express, and other	469	342	843	849	819	609
Total operating expenses	$3,931	$3,089	$7,059	$7,565	$ 7,850	$10,055
Maintenance of way and str.	705	497	1,287	1,192	1,236	1,813
Maintenance of equipment	1,019	819	1,708	1,760	1,775	2,351
Traffic	128	108	192	258	262	282
Transportation	1,848	1,501	3,491	3,833	4,020	4,889
General and miscellaneous	231	164	381	522	557	720
Net operating revenue	$1,350	$1,207	$2,414	$1,949	$ 2,358	$ 2,634
Railway tax accruals	348	396	1,195	999	916	1,090
Railway operating income	$1,002	$ 811	$1,219	$ 950	$ 1,442	$ 1,544
Hire of equipment (Debit) ⎤			140	321	443 ⎫	848
Joint facility rents (Debit) ⎦	132	129	39	45	37 ⎬	
Net railway operating income	$ 869	$ 682	$1,040	$ 584	$ 962	$ 696
Other income	359	169	265	346	365	422
Total income	1,228	851	$1,305	$ 930	$ 1,327	$ 1,118
Miscellaneous deductions	$ 1	$ 28	$ 48	$ 63	$ 71	141
Income available for fixed charges	1,207	823	1,257	867	1,256	977
Fixed charges ⎤			$ 427	373	401	601
Contingent charges and ⎬	683	634				
other deductions ⎦			46	50	41	29
Net income (ordinary)	524	189	$ 784	$ 445	814	347[a]
Cash dividends	$ 497	$ 159	$ 312	$ 385	$ 471	$ 386

[a]Excludes extraordinary and prior period items.

Sources: Interstate Commerce Commission; Association of American Railroads.

that of an industrial company in the way in which revenue and expense items are presented. The combined income statement for all Class I railways, 1930–1971, (Table 28-3) is used as a reference.

Total operating revenues. These include all receipts from railroad operations as such. For all railroads, freight traffic contributes about 93 per cent of the total; passenger traffic, about 2 per cent (excluding Amtrak operations); and miscellaneous services, such as mail and express, about 5 per cent. The percentages for many individual roads differ considerably from the group aggregates. In 1971 the Long Island Railroad showed operating revenues of about 85 per cent from passengers, and Missouri Pacific 95 per cent from freight and less than .5 per cent from passengers.

Study of railway data shows the relation of freight revenues to general business conditions. Volume of freight traffic, or, more specifically, traffic density, is heavily influenced by the volume of production of heavy industry. Freight revenues diminished 50 per cent between 1929 and 1932; fair recovery took place in the middle 1930s, but 1938–1939 brought another substantial decline. During World War II both freight and passenger revenues soared to record heights; the immediate postwar years saw substantial declines, especially in passenger revenues. As a result of substantial rate increases, freight revenues increased substantially in 1948–1950; in the latter year, they fell just short of matching the record 1948 figure of approximately $8 billions. Save for declines in the recession years of 1954 and 1958, freight revenues levelled off at $9 billions in the middle 1950s, declining to $7.7 billions in 1961 and breaking through $10 billions in 1969. In 1971 there was a record level of $11.8 billions. Passenger revenues, however, have continued to decline. In 1971 they were less than 2.5 per cent of total operating revenues, and are now substantially exceeded by mail, express, and miscellaneous revenue.

Volume of traffic is one determinant of revenues; the other is the rate level. The price of railway service is best measured by *average revenue per ton-mile* and *per passenger-mile*. For Class I railways as a whole, the former figure was 1.59 cents and the letter 4.25 cents in 1971, as compared with .95 cents and 1.75 cents, respectively, in 1940. Such figures, especially for freight traffic, vary considerably among districts and companies, depending on the type of commodities hauled. Carriers handicapped by a low average revenue on a ton-mile basis (caused largely by low-grade shipments) face a formidable obstacle unless they enjoy unusually high traffic density or unusually long hauls.

In using such factors as traffic density, revenues per ton-mile, and other indicators, care must be taken to compare companies in the same geographical area and operating under substantially the same conditions, including vulnerability to competition from other carriers. Otherwise, wrong conclusions concerning differences in operating management might be drawn.

Total operating expenses. These include all the direct and indirect expenses, such as wages of employees, cost of materials purchased, and administrative overhead, incurred in operating expenses are not classified in the usual corporate manner of labor, materials, and overhead, but more in harmony with the major operating divisions. Hence, wages are included in several items rather than shown as a single expense. In 1971 salaries, wages and health and welfare benefits of all Class I railroads consumed 51 per cent of operating revenues, contrasted with a previous high of 52 per cent in 1958. Average number of employees has declined steadily and in 1971 was only 544,000, or 25 per cent of the peak number in 1920.

Maintenance of way and structures. This includes the cost of materials (rails, ties, ballast, and so forth) and wages consumed in the maintaining of the roadbed and structures (bridges, depots, shops, and so forth) used in operations. For the average Class I railroad, this item (including depreciation) requires about $8,800 per mile operated per year and represents about 14 per cent of operating revenues.

Since maintenance expenditure is controllable to a considerable degree, reports should be carefully scrutinized to ascertain its adequacy. Managements have been known to "skimp" on maintenance to show favorable earnings, obviously a short-sighted policy. On the other hand, the expenditure may be excessive, resulting in an understatement of earnings. Companies serving mountainous districts naturally must spend more for maintenance of way and structures.

Maintenance of equipment. This includes principally the cost of material and the wages consumed in repairing engines and cars owned. It also includes the amounts set aside for depreciation and retirement of equipment. For the average railroad, this item requires (1971) about $11,500 per mile operated per year and represents about 18 per cent of operating revenues. Failure to maintain rolling stock in good condition is a serious matter, since this equipment provides the direct source of revenues.[4]

Total maintenance expense ratio. This ratio, which is the ratio of maintenance of way and structures plus maintenance of equipment to operating revenues, is a comprehensive criterion of maintenance policy. A reasonable standard would be between 30 and 35 per cent of revenues.

In railroad accounting, depreciation expense is a subcategory of maintenance expense, so that rapid depreciation and write-off may be partly offset by lower repairs. Depreciation of equipment consumes about 5 per cent of operating revenues.

---

[4]The advanced student will find many elaborate statistics indicating relative adequacy of maintenance expense in the annual reports of the companies, in the I.C.C. annual volumes of transportation data, and in the reports of the Association of American Railroads, Economics and Finance Department.

Traffic expense. This is a comparatively small item which indicates the expense incurred in soliciting traffic. The amount seldom exceeds 2½ per cent of revenues.

Transportation expense. This is the largest item of operating expenses, comprising chiefly the wages of stationmen and trainmen and the cost of fuel. For the average railroad, this item runs about $24,000 per year per mile operated and represents about 38 per cent of operating revenues. Management has little control over this item, as wages are fixed largely by Federal authority and fuel prices depend upon economic conditions and the type used. A low transportation expense ratio is an excellent commendation. Proximity to the leading coal-mining regions benefits roads in the Pocahontas district in this regard. For this reason, Norfolk & Western normally reports transportation expense ratios between 34 and 36 per cent.

General expense. This includes chiefly administrative overhead, such as salaries of officers and clerks, legal fees, and pension benefits. The amount is usually 4 to 5 per cent of revenues.

Miscellaneous items. These seldom aggregate 1 per cent of revenues.

Total operating expenses. These are the sum of the separate expense items. For the average railroad, they run about $50,000 per year per mile operated and now represent 80 per cent of revenues.

The relation of operating expense to operating revenues, or *operating ratio,* is a time-honored financial measure of operating efficiency. In the 1920s and 1930s, the standard was 70 per cent, but increases in costs of materials, fuel, and labor, and the lag of rates behind costs, have resulted in a higher ratio for nearly all carriers in recent years. For Class I railways as a whole, the ratio fell as low as 62 per cent in 1942, before increased revenues were offset by increased costs, but rose to 83 per cent in 1946. Increases were not offset by increased revenues in subsequent years. In the 1950s the typical ratio was 78 per cent; it rose gradually to 80.5 per cent in 1970, and declined to 79.24 per cent in 1971. Under present conditions even a mild reduction in operating revenues will increase the ratio substantially, since costs cannot be reduced in proportion. And even if they are, the *dollars* of net revenue after expenses may drop to an unprofitable level.

In judging the operating ratio of an individual carrier, the maintenance and transportation expense must be considered. A low ratio may be the result of skimping on maintenance. High maintenance ratios accompanied by a low transportation ratio that combine to produce a low operating ratio in comparison with carriers operating under similar conditions indicate superior performance.

Net operating revenue. This is the balance remaining after operating expenses have been deducted from operating revenues. This is the gross profit from operations available for taxes and fixed charges.

Railway tax accruals. These represent the first charge against net revenue. The proportion (40 per cent) going to local governments is relatively stable from year to year. Federal payroll taxes have increased steadily in the 1960s, while Federal income taxes have dropped substantially. In 1971 they were only $108 millions, compared with $600 millions in 1950. The investment importance of total taxes is revealed by the fact that in 1971 they comprised 8.6 per cent of operating revenues.

The location of Federal income taxes on the railway income statement is unusual; technically, they should show as deductions from net income. However, to the railroad they represent expenses that should be covered by revenues so as to leave a fair return, and so are placed in the operating section of the statement. The analyst should keep in mind that in calculating coverage of fixed charges, he is using after-tax income.

Railway operating income. This is the balance remaining after deduction of the preceding expense and tax items. It is subject to adjustment in all individual cases (largely eliminated in the consolidated figure for all roads) for *hire of equipment,* under which one company pays another for the use of equipment loaned on through traffic, and for *joint facility rents,* which cover payments for the use of consolidated services, such as bridges and union passenger terminals. The amounts of these two items differ considerably among individual companies. Most railroads report net debit balances for these two items, but certain roads (Norfolk & Western, for example) obtain large credit balances from equipment and joint facility rents; this factor places these roads in a relatively favorable position.

Net railway operating income. This is the balance produced from operations for the securityholders. It is the return received from the capital invested in the operating property. The net railway operating income stated as a percentage of net property investment (after depreciation, plus cash, materials, and supplies) is the "rate of return" referred to by the railroads as indicating their overall earning power, and its unsatisfactory level in most years is the chief argument against "unfair" regulatory conditions and subsidization of competing forms of transport. A review of the rate earned by railroads as a group in the past five decades suggests the inadequate earning power of the industry. In only one of the years from 1921 to 1971 inclusive (1942) did the rate exceed 6 per cent. In only six of these years was it 5 per cent or above. In 21 of the years the rate was less than 3 per cent. A return of 5 per cent on investment is adequate to cover all fixed charges and leave a reasonable balance for dividends, but a return under 3 per cent provides inadequate coverage of fixed charges. Since 1960 the return has averaged about 2.75 per cent, and was only 1.73 per cent in 1970 and 2.47 per cent in 1971. The failure of the roads in the aggregate to show a good rate of return does not mean, however, that no individual companies have done so. As in other respects, a wide range exists within the whole group in this measure of earning power.

Other income. This income, also called *nonoperating income,* includes all revenues from sources other than direct operations, chiefly income from securities of other railroad companies and from nontransportation operations. The importance of this item is not uniform. It means a great deal, for example, to Union Pacific, which usually derives 40 to 50 per cent of its total income (see below) from this source. It is important also to the lines that are large holders of securities. However, other income is not always a reliable source of revenue when it is derived from dividends on stocks of other companies.

Interestingly enough, "other income" was only $273 millions less than operating income in 1971, reflecting the erosion of railroad earning power and the growing importance of nonrail sources as a means of meeting fixed charges and paying dividends.

Total income. This is the sum of net railway operating income and other income. *Miscellaneous deductions* consist of expenses incurred with the earning of nonoperating income, and are deducted from total income.

Fixed charges. These charges represent those financial expenses that must be paid as they fall due. They include (1) rent for leased road, usually in the form of guaranteed interest or dividends, (2) rent for miscellaneous properties, (3) interest on funded (long-term) debt, (4) interest on unfunded (short-term) debt, and (5) amortization of discount on funded debt. Where fixed charges exceed 4 per cent of operating revenues and are not earned (that is, covered by total income) at least 2.5 over a representative period of years, investment weakness is indicated, even for the senior securities of a company.

Until the mid-1960s the fixed charges of the railroads as a whole were materially reduced mainly as the result of three influences: (1) the reorganization of weaker roads after the depression of the early 1930s; (2) the refunding of outstanding debt at lower interest rates; and (3) the retirement of debt from earnings since 1940. In 1971 railways as a group earned their total fixed charges 1.8 times before income taxes and 1.6 after income taxes. But within the industry performance varies widely. Table 28-4 shows the 1970 coverage of fixed charges of selected railroads or systems.

Another method of showing the earnings protection of bondholders is the *factor of safety,* that is, the percentage of operating revenues earned after fixed charges but before income taxes. This is the "cushion" of earnings underlying the fixed charges—the proportion by which the revenues could decline without reducing the interest coverage to less than one.[5] In

---

[5]The factor of safety may also be computed by using the percentage earned after fixed charges and twice preferred dividends, and before income taxes, to show the margin of safety for preferred dividends. Doubling the preferred dividend recognizes a 50 per cent corporate rate.

**Table 28-4. TIMES FIXED CHARGES EARNED BEFORE FEDERAL
INCOME TAXES, SELECTED COMPANIES, 1970**

Bessemer & Lake Erie	111.4	Texas & Pacific	2.6
St. Louis Southwestern	46.7	Kansas City Southern	2.5
Denver & Rio Grande Western	8.9	St. Louis—San Francisco	2.4
Pittsburgh & Lake Erie	8.6	Gulf, Mobile & Ohio	2.2
Union Pacific	5.8	Louisville & Nashville	2.1
Atch., Topeka & Sante Fe	4.7	Western Maryland	1.9
Central of Georgia	4.3	Burlington Northern	1.8
Southern	3.3	Baltimore & Ohio	1.7
Chesapeake & Ohio	3.1	Delaware & Hudson	1.4
Seaboard Coast Line	3.1	Chicago & North Western	1.0
Illinois Central	3.0	Chgo., Milw., St. Paul & Pac.	.3
Southern Pacific	2.9	Central of New Jersey	a
Norfolk & Western	2.7	Penn Central	a
Missouri Pacific	2.7	Rock Island	a

aDeficit before fixed charges.

Source: *Moody's Transportation Manual.*

1971, the average railroad factor of safety was only 3.6 per cent, but the range was from 28 per cent (St. Louis Southwestern) to a deficit (for example, Penn Central). For ample protection, a factor of at least 8 is desirable.

Contingent charges. These are mainly interest on income bonds issued as a result of reorganization, on which interest is payable only if earned.

Net income. This is the balance remaining for dividends and surplus. The figure for Class I railways since 1929 has ranged from a deficit of $139 millions in 1932 to the peak of $927 millions in 1955. The 1970 figure was $227 millions of "ordinary income." After deducting "extraordinary and prior-year stems," the profit figure was even lower—$76 millions. But 1971 showed improvement, with "ordinary" net income rising to $347 millions. Such instability is the result of two main influences: (1) the fluctuations in net railway operating income, aggravated by (2) the presence of large fixed charges. Net results for individual carriers may differ greatly from those of the industry as a whole.

In recent years railroads have been allowed to accelerate depreciation for income tax purposes, but Interstate Commerce Commission regulations do not permit the higher allowances to be recorded in the income statement; straight-line depreciation is the rule. Nor can the railroads "normalize" their net income by charging deferred tax expense and setting up a reserve for deferred income taxes. The result is that the income tax bill looks low and net income may well be overstated. Some individual carriers (Union Pacific, for example) adjust the reported net income figure downward to one that would have been reported had the tax "relief" not been available.

The overall rate earned on the stockholders' investment is measured by the relationship between net income and average net worth. The range has been from a deficit (1932, 1938) to 7.8 per cent (1943). The figure for 1971 was 2.0 per cent. Again, performance of individual carriers varies widely.

Dividends. The dividends distributed in recent years have been relatively stable, considering the fluctuations in earnings. Since 1950 the payout ratio on common stock has varied between 37 per cent (1953) and 187 per cent (1970). The steady retirement of preferred stock has been partly responsible for maintenance of distributions on the common in years of low profits. Aggregate figures are, however, somewhat deceiving. Policy with respect to dividends varies widely among individual companies. Some have ploughed back most of their earnings or have reduced funded debt and fixed charges. Others have distributed virtually all of their profits. In 1970–1971, the low-earning carriers greatly outnumbered those that earned and paid dividends.

Balance Sheet Analysis (Assets)

Railroad balance sheets differ from those of other corporations in the terms used, the order of the items, and the relative importance of various items. Table 28-5 is a summarized statement for all Class I line-haul steam railways for 1970.

Fixed assets. Net assets, including investments in affiliated companies, dominate the balance sheet, comprising nearly 88 per cent of total assets. Using the gross figures of total physical property in relation to operating revenue, the gross plant turnover is 35 per cent. Net after depreciation, the physical plant turns 48 per cent year. In other words, for the industry as a whole, an investment of about $3\frac{1}{3}$ in gross plant and $2 in net plant is needed to produce $1 of revenue. Operating costs and taxes require approximately 94 per cent of gross revenues, so the remaining income produces a return of about 3 per cent on net property valued at 2 times operating revenues.

From the investor's viewpoint, however, the condition of the property is more important than the book value. Since personal examination is usually impossible, one must rely upon a careful analysis of the maintenance figures.

Depreciation is accrued by all companies on road and equipment. The annual expense charge is included in the maintenance account. The need to provide for ultimate retirement of equipment is greater than in the case of road. Accordingly, one is not entirely surprised to find that the consolidated balance sheet of Chesapeake & Ohio on December 31, 1970 showed a depreciation reserve of 47 per cent against equipment in service, in contrast to a reserve of only 14 per cent against road in use.

Investments in affiliated companies. These consist of holdings of stocks, bonds, and notes of associated companies. Although the investment

**Table 28-5. COMBINED BALANCE SHEET, CLASS I RAILWAYS
DECEMBER 31, 1970**
(in millions of dollars)

Assets		
Road and equipment property		$34,000.0
Improvements on leased property		533.6
		$34,533.6
Less depreciation and amortization		9,362.8
		$25,170.8
Miscellaneous physical property, net		629.7
Investments—affiliated companies and other, net		3,522.6
Current assets		3,582.5
Special funds		207.9
Deferred charges		201.9
		165.7
Other assets		
Total assets		$33,481.1
Liabilities and Stockholders' Equity		
Capital stock		
Preferred	$ 605.0	
Common	4,738.8	$ 5,343.8
Long-term debt after one year		
Funded debt*a*	6,934.5	
Equipment obligations	3,913.3	10,847.8
Current liabilities*b*		3,523.9
Reserves		528.3
Deferred credits		1,257.8
Surplus		
Capital	$2,306.8	
Retained income	9,672.7	11,979.5
Total liabilities and stockholders' equity		$33,481.1

*a*Includes amounts payable to affiliated companies and long-term debt in default ($441.8 millions).
*b*Includes long-term debt due within one year, $601.2 millions.

Source: Interstate Commerce Commission, *Transport Statistics in the United States, Part I, Railroad Companies.*

is represented by securities, one may assume that the amount represents investment almost as fixed and permanent as road and equipment. The amount involved is usually not large, but in some cases it is of major importance. The Southern Pacific reported $79 millions in such securities in 1971.

The investments in affiliated and other companies in the balance sheet are usually carried at cost, which may or may not reflect prevailing value. Union Pacific reported, for 1970, a $35.5-million investment in stocks of twenty-eight affiliated companies and a dividend income from these affiliates (only one of the twenty-eight companies paid dividends) of $125,000. The low rate of return in this situation suggests that some stock holdings are carried at quite liberal valuations. In addition to securities investments in other companies, there is often a substantial direct investment in nonoperating properties such as hotels, oil lands, and mining properties that produce important income. Such income appears as *nonoperating* or *other income* on the income statement.

Current assets. These comprise principally cash, temporary investments, accounts receivable, and materials and supplies on hand. These items have much less significance in the railroad field than in the industrial field. The regularity with which cash revenues are received assures a steady inflow of funds for current bills. In addition, most roads are able, in normal times, to correct an adverse current ratio by funding short-term debt from the proceeds of the sale of long-term bonds.

For these reasons, and because both the current asset and current liability totals are relatively small on the typical railway statement, a current ratio of less than 2:1 is not alarming. A higher ratio and a generally healthy working capital position, however, is needed by companies operating at a deficit or facing substantial bond maturities. The maintenance of stable dividends also requires that working capital be built up in times of good earnings. A disturbing sign of the declining liquidity of the industry as a whole was the steady reduction of net working capital from over $750 millions in the early 1960s to $90 millions in 1971.

Special sinking funds and deferred charges. These are generally small items having only minor significance.

Balance Sheet Analysis (Liabilities)

The items which appear on the liabilities side of the railroad balance sheet include capital stock, long-term debt, current liabilities, reserves, deferred credits, and surplus.

Capital stock. This represents the stated value of the stock outstanding. The stock, as in the case of the Atchison, may comprise both preferred and common shares or, as in the case of Penn Central, may represent only common shares. The value shown is usually par value, although some companies, as a result of reorganizations, have issued stock with no par value. Such companies, including the Erie-Lackawana and the Missouri-Kansas-Texas, place an arbitrary value on the capital stock account. Despite the large amount of debt retirements during the war years, most railroad companies still have a relatively heavy capitalization in debt. Bonded debt has been reduced in recent years, but equipment obligations have increased. At the end of 1970, total long-term debt composed 38 per cent of the combined capital structure of Class I railways. (See Table 28-6.) Debt levelled out in the 1950s and early 1960s but has since increased to offset the decline in retained earnings as a source of funds. Debt incurred in 1966–1972 bears high interest rates. The increase in fixed charges in the face of lower earnings available to pay them has seriously reduced the coverage of fixed charges for all but a few carriers, although 1972 showed some improvement. And many individual roads are even less conservatively financed than the whole group.

Railroads as a group have been gradually retiring their preferred stock, which now (1972) represents only 2 per cent of book capital structure. Preferred dividends declined from $87 millions in 1951 to $11 millions in 1970. But much of this decline represents default in preferred dividend payments. Common stock has been reduced by purchases for treasury and by merger. No new railroad common stock has been offered to the public for over forty years, and only one issue of convertible securities—by Burlington Northern —in early 1972.

Long-term debt. This represents the outstanding bonds and other long-term obligations. It usually consists of many separate issues, each of which has distinctive features, as discussed in an earlier chapter. Any capital structure ratio that shows 50 per cent or higher in bonds is excessively out of balance. The discrepancy is even greater than appears on the surface, since companies do not include guaranteed securities of leased lines in stating indebtedness. Such obligations are estimated by capitalizing annual

Table 28-6. CAPITAL STRUCTURES OF CLASS I RAILROADS, 1950–1970

(in billions of dollars)

	Amounts[a]					Percentage of Total[a]				
	1950	1955	1960	1965	1970	1950	1955	1960	1965	1970
Long-term debt[b]										
Equipment obligations	$ 1.9	$ 2.5	$ 2.4	$ 3.2	$ 3.9	8%	9%	9%	12%	14%
Bonds and other	7.4	7.3	7.1	6.7	6.9	31	27	26	24	24
Total debt	$ 9.3	$ 9.9	$ 9.5	$ 9.9	$10.8	40%	37%	35%	36%	38%
Preferred stock	1.8	1.2	1.1	1.0	.6	8	5	4	4	2
Common stock	6.0	6.6	5.5	4.7	4.7	25	25	21	17	17
Surplus										
Capital	c	.2	1.1	1.9	2.3	c	—	4	7	8
Retained earnings	6.4	8.6	9.6	10.2	9.7	27	33	36	37	35
Total surplus	$ 6.4	$ 8.8	$10.7	$12.1	$12.0	27%	33%	40%	44%	43%
	$23.6	$26.5	$26.8	$27.7	$28.1	100%	100%	100%	100%	100%

[a]Data may not add due to rounding.
[b]Includes long-term debt due within one year.
[c]Not available.

SOURCE: Interstate Commerce Commission, *Transport Statistics in the United States*, 1970, Part I, *Railroad Companies*.

rentals at 5 per cent (multiplying by 20). The importance of rental obligations is clearly shown in the example of the Penn Central, where such payments are 23 per cent of total fixed charges. Investors should prefer the securities of those companies, otherwise satisfactory, whose indebtedness, including capitalized rentals, does not exceed 40 per cent of total capital structure, and whose interest is adequately covered by earnings. They also prefer the long-term debt to consist increasingly of equipment obligations, which are serially retired from cash flow and whose interest rates are lower than those on bonds.

A stricter test of debt burden is the substitution of market for book value of common stock in the capital structure, which reveals the debt in relation to the going concern value of the company. Many roads whose debt appears reasonable on a book basis are found to be top heavy with debt in this more realistic sense.

The items comprising the funded debt should be arranged according to maturities, to disclose any large issues that must be paid in the immediate future. Early maturities do not cause difficulties in years of prosperity, when refunding can be readily arranged. But in years of recession, large maturing obligations have brought great embarrassment to many important companies and caused receivership in many instances.

Current liabilities. These include items payable within one year. The amount is of interest chiefly in relation to current assets, as previously discussed.

Deferred credits. These include a group of miscellaneous items payable at an indefinite time, usually more than one year in the future.

Reserves. These comprise principally accounts that have been set up for special purposes, such as insurance. The wide distribution of railroad property minimizes the risk of loss from fire and similar causes and enables the companies to act as self-insurers for a substantial part of the risk.

Capital surplus. This represents chiefly paid-in surplus from the sale of stock above par or stated value.

Retained earnings. Retained earnings, or reinvested profits, includes appropriations for specific purposes. The most popular purpose for segregation is "for addition and betterments," in which case the stated amount has been reinvested in property and cannot be paid out as dividends.

The unappropriated part of the retained earnings account is the amount from which dividends are declared and paid. It comprises (together with appropriated surplus) the accumulated undistributed earnings of prior periods, and forms a backlog for the payment of dividends in years of reduced earnings. Experience in some years of low earnings, however, has shown that a large profit and loss balance carries little assurance of dividends at such times. Numerous examples might be cited in which dividend rates have been reduced and, in important instances, have been entirely discontinued, despite large surplus accounts. The position of the cash account is more important than the size of the profit and loss account at such a time.

Railroad Bonds

Railroad bonds run the gamut of quality from the high-grade senior liens of the strong companies to the low-grade junior issues of weak companies on the brink of bankruptcy or which are bankrupt. The prime test of quality is earnings protection as measured by coverage of fixed charges. Additional important tests include (1) the ratio of debt to capital structure (discussed above), (2) the factor of safety, with an average of 8 to 10 per cent considered adequate and seldom achieved.

Highest-grade railroad bonds. There are virtually no railroad bonds of the very highest quality in 1973. In 1968 Moody's discontinued calculation of the Aaa rail bond average for lack of components. A search of *Moody's Transportation Manual* reveals only one or two. Bessemer & Lake Erie First 2⅞'s of 1996 qualify with interest earned over 600 times in 1971.

High-grade railroad bonds. These now include the senior mortgage bonds of relatively prosperous companies, as illustrated by the Atchison General 4's of 1995, the Norfolk & Western First Consolidated 4's of 1996, and the Union Pacific Refunding 2½'s of 1991.[6] Such bonds are considered junior only to equipment trust certificates, which enjoy the highest rating. But the decline in railroad earnings has moved the former highest-grade bonds down to the Aa or A level. Even equipment obligations rarely achieve an Aaa rating under conditions prevailing in the early 1970s.

The high-grade group also includes the divisional bonds secured by small properties which have been leased to large, important companies and whose interest payments are guaranteed by the latter. Only those divisional bonds that are secured by valuable property fall in this group. The Scioto Valley and New England First 4's of 1989 (guaranteed by Norfolk & Western) and the Hocking Valley First Consolidated 4½'s of 1999 (guaranteed by Chesapeake & Ohio) are good examples. Terminal bonds secured by valuable properties and guaranteed by prosperous companies, such as the Cincinnati Union Terminal Company First 2¾'s of 1974, are likewise in this group.

Bonds that qualify in the high-grade group are usually issued by companies which show earnings after taxes of 3.5 or 4 times all fixed charges over the preceding five years, and at least 2.5 times in the poorest year. In early 1973 bonds in this group provided income yields of between 7 and 8 per cent, depending on maturity.

Second-grade railroad bonds. These include issues that are acceptable investments but which are relatively less secure than the highest grade. They comprise the junior issues of the prosperous companies and in

---

[6]The Atchison General 4's of 1995 ($136 millions outstanding) are secured by a direct first lien on 11,917 miles of line (90 per cent of the system). All fixed charges of the Atchison, Topeka, & Santa Fe system were earned an average of 12.9 times (before taxes) during 1960–1966, but fell to 5 times in 1970–1971.

some cases, the senior issues of the weaker companies. Examples are the Atlantic Coast Line General Mortgage 4's of 1980, the Atchinson, Topeka & Santa Fe Adjustment 4's of 1995, and the Northern Pacific General Lien 3's of 2447.[7]

Second-grade railroad bonds are usually secured by an earnings factor ranging from 1.5 to 2 times fixed charges over the preceding five years. In early 1973, bonds in this class yielded between 8 and 8½ per cent.

Third-grade railroad bonds. These comprise the issues of companies which are still solvent but which show narrow margins of safety. They include issues such as the Morris & Essex First Refunding 3½'s of 2000, and the Chicago, Milwaukee, St. Paul & Pacific Income 4½'s of 2019.[8] These bonds are secured in most cases by a narrow margin of safety ranging from deficits in poor years to less than 1.5 times interest requirements in good years. Bonds in this class generally yielded 9 to 11 per cent in early 1973 or sold "flat."

Railroad Stocks

Like bonds, railroad stocks include a wide range of quality. In general, however, they have lost in relative investment status, reflecting the low earnings in the industry. Few offer any growth possibilities. Those with any attraction are purchased either for dividend income, or as special situations expected to benefit from mergers. Moody's annual averages (Table 28-7) show the price performance of railroad common stocks, their price-earnings ratios, and yields in the postwar period, as contrasted with the two other main categories.

Railroad stocks as a group have shown only modest growth in price for over fifteen years, although the performance of individual companies has varied widely. The general price-earnings ratios have lagged well behind those on industrial stocks; the high level in 1970–1972 reflected not so much prospects of higher earnings as the fact that as earnings decline, stock prices usually fail to decline as much. Along with those of utilities, the yields on railway common stocks are much higher than on industrials. But the average yield for the whole group is misleading because stocks paying no dividends are included. Without these, the average rate would be higher.

Toward the end of 1971 and in 1972, there were indications of some

[7]Northern Pacific is now a part of Burlington Northern, and Atlantic Coast Line of Seaboard Coast Line. But the bonds retain their original names and liens. The Northern Pacific General Lien 3's of 2047 are secured by a second lien on 4,800 miles of road, of which 2,542 miles are main line and 2,315 miles are branch line. They are also secured by land grants, of which there remained unsold 1,928,329 acres as of December 31, 1970. All fixed charges were earned an average of 3.2 times during 1960–1969 (before income taxes). Burlington Northern earned its fixed charges 1.8 times in 1970–1971.

[8]The Chicago, Milwaukee, St. Paul & Pacific General Mortgage Income 4 1/2's of 2019 have a second lien on all lines and their interest is payable only if earned. Fixed charges were earned an average of 2.5 times in 1960–1968 but were unearned in 1969 and earned only .27 times in 1970 and 1.25 times in 1971. In 1972, they sold "flat."

Table 28-7. PERFORMANCE OF RAILROAD COMMON STOCKS

	1945	1950	1955	1960	1965	1972
Price averages ($)						
125 Industrials	44	58	131	173	284	362
24 Utilities	26	31	49	70	117	80
25 Rails	40	34	70	62	95	91
Price-earnings ratios						
125 Industrials	16.1	6.8	12.4	18.0	17.3	17.7
24 Utilities	15.3	19.9	15.3	17.0	19.8	10.4
25 Rails	9.2	4.6	8.3	13.0	11.7	15.0
Dividend yields (%)						
125 Industrials	4.0	6.5	3.9	3.5	3.0	2.7
24 Utilities	5.0	5.7	4.5	3.8	3.3	6.1
25 Rails	5.5	6.5	4.9	5.7	4.3	4.1

SOURCE: *Moody's Mannual of Investments, Transportation.*

improvement in railroad earnings over the miserable performance in 1970. Prices of shares of the stronger companies rose to reflect the better outlook and the fact that passenger traffic was mainly the problem of "Amtrak" rather than that of the carriers. (See pp. 540–41). The yields on stronger equities declined from their 1970 levels.

Such data do not reveal the varying experience of individual stocks. Union Pacific and Norfolk & Western enjoy top rating among the invest-ment services; but their appeal is largely for income. The stocks of very large companies such as Chicago & North Western and Milwaukee are more attractive for speculation based on merger expectations, than for investment. Those of certain companies such as Seaboard Coast Line, Rock Island, and Milwaukee emerged for reorganization in the 1930s and have gained some investment recognition, but have been characterized by wide price and earnings fluctuations. Several "good-grade" companies such as Santa Fe Industries, Kansas City Southern Industries, and Southern Pacific are ap-propriate in portfolios seeking above-average current cash dividends.

"Investment-quality" preferred stocks are available in the railroad field, but again only in a limited number of instances. And investors demand a higher yield on these than on utility and industrial issues. In early 1973, such stocks yielded from 6 to 8 per cent; the lower yields were found on convertible preferred stock of some of the holding companies. Investors able to undertake the greater risks find attractive opportunities in the preferred stocks of the very strong carriers.

Consolidations

Joint control of competing lines is now permitted under the Transportation Act of 1920 as amended in 1940. Consolidations, whether by lease, stock purchase, or otherwise, must provide for the preservation of competition and the maintenance of existing routes and channels of trade and of com-merce. The arrangement must be in the public interest and the terms must be approved by the Interstate Commerce Commission. The merger process is long and complex.

A wave of railroad mergers began in the early 1950s. Carriers sought the economies of large-scale operation and the reduction of duplicating facilities. Each of the consolidations finally approved by the Commission up to 1973 was the result of long negotiations between the companies and protracted hearings before the I.C.C. The more important combinations were Norfolk & Western and Virginian (1959); Erie and Delaware, Lackawanna & Western to form Erie–Lackwanna (1960); Southern Pacific and Texas & New Orleans (1961); Southern Pacific and Central of Georgia (1963); Norfolk & Western and New York, Chicago & St. Louis (1964); Atlantic Coast Line and Seaboard Air Line to form Seaboard Coast Line (1967); Chesapeake & Ohio and Baltimore & Ohio (1967); New York Central and Pennsylvania to form Penn Central Transportation (1968); Great Northern, Northern Pacific, and Burlington to form Burlington Northern (1970); Illinois Central and Gulf, Mobile & Ohio (1971); Seaboard Coast Line and Louisville & Nashville (1971). The only merger case pending before the I.C.C. in early 1973 involved four proposals from different roads with respect to the Rock Island. Several other mergers were in the talking stage.

Combinations such as the above hold possibilities of substantial economies, but they have not all succeeded, as witness the dramatic bankruptcy of Penn Central in 1970. Investors must examine with great care any estimates or claims of economies of scale and improved earnings made by companies that propose to merge.

Recent Legislation

After extensive hearings on the "railroad problem" inspired by the decline in earnings in 1957 and early 1958, Congress passed legislation in 1958 that was aimed at remedying certain crucial aspects of the railroad situation. The Act (1) authorized government guarantees of up to $500 million of private loans to railroads, (2) authorized the I.C.C. to permit discontinuance of unprofitable interstate trains and services, (3) increased the authority of the I.C.C. to order fast adjustments in intrastate rates without waiting for state action, and (4) directed the I.C.C. not to require railroads to maintain rates higher than necessary merely to protect railroad competitors.

In October 1966, a new Federal Department of Transportation was established to include Federal railroad, aviation and highway administrations. The hope was that this would result in a more integrated national policy with respect to competing forms of transportation.

The dismal financial record of the railroads in the latter 1960s stimulated much action for reform and assistance. In 1970 an organization created by the Association of American Railroads, America's Sound Transportation Reviewing Association—ASTRO, proposed that the railroads be placed in a position of equality in a balanced national transportation system. Greater freedom of rate-making and management, dropping of unprofitable branch lines and services, government guarantees of loans for new equipment, Federal financial aid for way and plant improvements and the development of diversified transportation companies were all recommended. Such appeals, together with support from the Department of Transportation, led to the Surface Transportation Act of 1971. This bill also received the support of the railroads' chief competitors—trucking and waterway interests—which underscored the urgency of the situation.

The chief provisions of the proposed legislation were (1) Federal loans to railroads to expand and improve equipment and facilities, (2) rates adequate to produce a fair rate of return, (3) abandonment of nonproductive facilities, and (4) restoration of the investment tax credit; this last provision has been effected.

The Department of Transportation sent two bills to Congress in late 1971 which urged (1) permission for carriers to change rates without regulatory approval (within certain limitations) and (2) substantial Federal support of new capital expenditures.

Future Prospects

The outlook for the railroad industry in 1973 contained both favorable and unfavorable factors which may be summarized briefly as follows.

Favorable. Railroads still comprise the backbone of the nation's transport system and provide the most economical form of mass freight transportation. Congress will take some action on the deteriorating railroad situation, and the attitude of the Department of Transportation gives hope for more equitable treatment insofar as public policy is concerned. Operating efficiency, measured by such factors as gross ton-miles per freight train-hour, train speed, and mileage per freight car-day, continues to improve; diesel power has all but replaced steam; tractive power and freight capacity continue to increase. The carriers are introducing as many cost-saving measures as can be financed; yards are being modernized, and excess runs eliminated; modern methods of hauling, such as the use of trailer-on-flat-car (piggy-backing) and unit train equipment, are luring some traffic back to the rails.

The deplorable situation of unprofitable and unattractive passenger service may be substantially relieved by the operation of the National Railroad Passenger Service Corporation, created in October 1970. This quasi public company, Amtrak, has taken over the management of most of the intercity passenger service and has developed a network of routes that should speed up passenger service and eliminate unnecessary runs. Participating railroads buy common stock in the corporation. They turn over to it their intercity operations and are reimbursed for providing rights of way and for operating costs. Amtrak is financed by Federal grants, and Federal loans are available to the companies that operate the trains under contract with the managing organization. Better service should result. And much of the passenger deficit will be transferred to the government (a dubious change in the minds of many). Only four major carriers have not yet joined the new system.

Railroad earnings improved somewhat in 1971 and 1972. The weaker carriers that are reorganized or merged will have their debt reduced. In 1971 President Nixon signed a bill providing for $125,000,000 in Federal guarantees of loans by railroads undergoing reorganization. Some carriers (including the Penn Central) have already made use of this support. There is genuine national and official concern over the problems of the industry.

All of these factors, plus the restoration of the 7 per cent investment tax credit to be applicable in 1972, substantial increases in freight rates in 1970 and 1971, and an improved general economic situation, augur substantial gains for the railroad industry in the middle 1970s.

Unfavorable. The industry's share of intercity freight traffic had declined by 1971 to 38 per cent from the 67 per cent enjoyed in 1946. Competition from motor vehicles, pipelines, and waterways is still growing. Passenger traffic continues to decline. Both debt and fixed charges have increased in the early 1970s, leaving the carriers vulnerable to variations in operating earnings. The required capital expenditures for increased efficiency and safety have been difficult to finance except by borrowing. Operating expenses (especially wage rates and material costs) have increased at a more rapid rate than revenues; an operating ratio of 78 to 80 per cent reflects a general cost squeeze. The proportion of revenues absorbed by wages and benefits (46 per cent in 1971), although somewhat lower than its peak of 49 per cent in 1958, remains high. The rate of return made by the industry continues to be worse than meager. The vulnerability of the industry to recession in general economic activity places the marginal carriers in a precarious position. Since 1967 six major railroads—Reading, Central of New Jersey, Boston & Maine, Lehigh Valley, Penn Central, and Erie-Lackawanna have declared bankruptcy. The financial collapse in 1970 of the Penn Central, the second largest carrier in the country, was an enormous shock to investors, government, and the general public.

For many years to come, the railroads will provide the main medium of freight transportation. Self-interest alone will compel public policy eventually to give the carriers fair consideration. The future of the industry will depend upon the ability of management to improve service, to adjust to changing conditions, and to persuade Congress and government regulatory bodies (Federal and state) to adopt a policy toward the railroads that will enable them to earn an adequate return on the value of their net investment in properties. For the near term it appears that only a few major companies will achieve this objective.

REFERENCES

Association of American Railroads, Bureau of Railway Economics, *Railroad Transportation: A Statistical Record, 1921–1964*. Washington, D.C.: The Association, 1965.

———, *A Review of Railroad Operations*. Washington, D.C.: The Association, annual to 1969.

Banks, R. L., et al., *The Railroad Future: A Study of Prospects and Problems Through 1970*. Washington, D.C.: R. L. Banks and Associates, 1962.

Conant, Michael, *Railroad Mergers and Abandonments*. Berkeley, Calif.: University of California Press, 1964.

Daggett, Stuart, *Principles of Inland Transportation*, 4th ed. New York: Harper & Row, Publishers, 1955.

Fair, M. L., and John Guandolo, *Tedrow's Regulation of Transportation: Practice and Procedure before the Interstate Commerce Commission*, 7th ed. Dubuque, Iowa: Wm. C. Brown Company, 1971.

Graham, Benjamin, D. L. Dodd, and Sidney Cottle, *Security Analysis*, 4th ed., Chapter 19. New York: McGraw-Hill, Inc., 1962.

Guthmann, H. G., *Analysis of Financial Statements*, 4th ed., Chapters 11, 12. Englewood Cliffs, N.J.: Prentice-Hall, Inc., 1953.

———, and H. E. Dougall, *Corporate Financial Policy*, 4th ed., Chapter 17. Englewood Cliffs, N.J.: Prentice-Hall, Inc., 1962.

Kennedy, R. D., and S. Y. McMullen, *Financial Statements*, 5th ed., Chapters 27, 28. Homewood, Ill.: Richard D. Irwin, Inc., 1968.

Lochlin, D. P., *Economics of Transportation*, 6th ed. Homewood, Ill.: Richard D. Irwin, Inc., 1966.

Nelson, Scott, *Market Value and Financial Structure in the Railroad Industry*. Hartford, Conn.: Travelers Insurance Co., 1961.

Nielson, J. C., *Railroad Transportation and Public Policy*. Washington, D.C.: The Brookings Institution, 1959.

Norton, H. S., *Modern Transportation Economics*, 2nd ed. Columbus, Ohio: Charles E. Merrill Publishing Co., 1970.

Pegrum, D. F., *Transportation: Economics and Public Policy*. Homewood, Ill.: Richard D. Irwin, Inc., 1963.

Phillips, C. F., Jr., *The Economics of Regulation*, rev. ed. Homewood, Ill.: Richard D. Irwin, Inc., 1969.

Sampson, R. J., and M. T. Farris, *Domestic Transportation: Practice, Theory and Policy*. Boston: Houghton-Mifflin Company, 1966.

Stover, J. F., *American Railroads*. Chicago: University of Chicago Press, 1961.

Street, D. M., *Railroad Equipment Financing*. New York: Columbia University Press, 1959.

29 Bank Stocks and Debentures

SCOPE: This chapter discusses the investment position of the securities issued by commercial banks. The assets of banks are chiefly government and corporate securities and loans. Investors in bank securities are, therefore, delegating to others the placement of their funds.

The order of discussion is (1) classification of banks, (2) banking functions, (3) nonfinancial information, (4) types of statements, (5) income statements, (6) balance sheets, (7) bank stock analysis, (8) stock values, prices, and yields, (9) holding companies, and (10) investment position.

Classification of Banks

Banks may be classified as (1) *national* or *state,* depending upon the source of charter; (2) *commercial* or *savings,* depending upon the nature of operations; (3) *member* or *nonmember,* depending upon membership in the Federal Reserve System; (4) *insured* or *noninsured,* depending upon participation in Federal deposit insurance; and (5) *stock* or *mutual,* depending upon the nature of ownership.

National commercial banks are chartered by the Federal government and are subject to uniform regulation and supervision by the Comptroller of the Currency, as well as by the Federal Reserve authorities and the Federal Deposit Insurance Corporation. State commercial banks are chartered under state banking acts and are supervised by state authority and by the Federal Reserve and the F.D.I.C., depending on membership in these systems.

Commercial banks do a general banking business in accepting demand and time deposits, making a variety of loans and investments, performing trust functions, and offering a number of services to customers. Mutual savings banks accept time deposits and invest in selected bonds and mortgages, but do not make personal or commercial loans. They have no capital stock outstanding. They are chartered under special state legislation but are subject to Federal Reserve and F.D.I.C. supervision if they are members of these systems.

Membership in the Federal Reserve System comprises all of the national

**Table 29-1. DEPOSITS AND NET WORTH OF COMMERCIAL BANKS,
DECEMBER 31, 1971**

(dollars in millions)

	Number of Banks	Total Deposits	Net Worth
Federal Reserve Membership			
National (all members F.R.)	4,599	$314,085	$27,065
State			
Members F.R.	1,128	111,777	11,128
Nonmembers F.R.	8,056	112,084	9,018
Total	13,783	$537,946	$47,211
Extent of F.D.I.C. Coverage			
National (all insured)	4,599	$314,085	$27,065
Members F.R. (insured)	1,128	111,777	11,128
Nonmembers (insured)	7,875	109,161	8,538
Nonmembers (uninsured)	181	2,923	480
Total	13,783	$537,946	$47,211

SOURCES: *Federal Reserve Bulletin;* Annual Report of the Federal Deposit Insurance Corporation.

banks, and the state banks that have elected to join the system, together with a few mutual savings banks.

Most banks belong to the Federal Deposit Insurance Corporation and their depositors enjoy the protection of mutual insurance.

Investor interest is, of course, centered in the commercial banks. The smaller of these have a local following, but it is to the stocks of the larger commercial banks whose shares are traded in the exchange or over-the-counter markets that the following discussion pertains.

As of December 31, 1971, the 13,783 commercial banks in the United States had deposits outstanding totalling $538 billions and a combined net worth of $47.2 billions. Table 29-1 shows the relative importance of the various categories.

Banking Functions

The traditional functions of the commercial bank have been to make short-term loans to business, to accept deposits (in new funds or as created by loans) and thus provide checking and safekeeping services, and to provide miscellaneous services such as collection of items and trust functions. In more recent years, commercial banks have become "department stores of finance," through the development of a wide variety of personal, real estate, and business loans, trust and investment services, and facilities such as safe-deposit vaults. They have also become the most important owners of government securities. And through the use of the holding company, banks have extended their services to a wide variety of fields (see p. 556). The banking functions *per se* are regulated by Federal and state authorities with respect to liquidity and solvency (through regulation and supervision of loans and investments and through reserve requirements) and protection against unwarranted duplication and competition. In addition, the credit-granting powers of the banks are influenced by law, regulation, and moral suasion as the credit structure (in the opinion of the Federal Reserve) requires expansion or contraction.

The essential character and the growth of bank services and the imposition of a mass of regulation indicate that as a whole bank stocks should constitute a safe and stable medium of investment. During recent years the bank failure rate has been very low, but banks still differ in their attractiveness to the stock buyer. Numerous factors, some of a general character and some revealed by analysis of bank financial statements, must be considered by the would-be investor.

Nonfinancial Considerations

While the major emphasis in the analysis of bank stocks is given to examination of financial statements, their interpretation requires a knowledge of the size, character, economic stability, and growth of the community served, the types of industries in the bank's clientele, the types and degree of regulation imposed, and the connections of the management. The investor would prefer a growing bank in a growing and stable community, not dependent on any one industry or small group of borrowers, with deposits diversified both as to size and type, and with a management alert to the possibilities of new services and sources of revenue, whether by the bank itself or by its parent company.

Types of Statements and Financial Information

One disadvantage of many bank stocks is the lack of adequate financial information. Banks must publish "statements of condition" (condensed balance sheets) four times a year. Banks differ widely with respect to the publication of more detailed balance sheet information, and income statements are entirely a matter of discretion save for those whose shares are listed on organized securities exchanges. Policies governing the valuation of assets also differ considerably, although most banks lean toward conservatism. Book value and actual value of assets may differ substantially.

Fortunately, in recent years the tendency on the part of larger institutions has been to make available more detailed statement information, especially concerning income and expenses. And because of the highly liquid character of most bank assets, book values represent liquidating value much more closely than in the case of business corporations.

Another advantage is the availability of adequate industry data. The reports of the Comptroller of the Currency, the state bank authorities, the

Federal Reserve, and the Federal Deposit Insurance Corporation contain combined statistics that are useful in judging the trends and conditions in banking as a whole and in comparing an individual bank with its family. And a number of investment services and investment banking houses now issue comparative studies of considerable value.

Income Statements

The operating revenues and expenses of insured commercial banks for three years in the 1960–1971 period, are given in Table 29-2, together with the relationship of each item to total operating earnings. This group comprised 13,602 banks of the 13,783 commercial banks in the country as of the end of 1971.

Table 29-2. EARNINGS, EXPENSES, AND DIVIDENDS OF INSURED COMMERCIAL BANKS, 1960–1971

(in millions of dollars)

	1960		1965		1971	
	Amt.	*%*	*Amt.*	*%*	*Amt.*	*%*
Operating income						
Income on loans	$ 6,807	63.4%	$11,205	66.6%	$23,940	65.8%
Interest on U.S. Gov. obligations	1,790	16.7	2,225	13.2	3,396	9.3
Interest and dividends, other securities	579	5.4	1,285	7.6	4,282	11.8
Service charges on deposit accounts	590	5.5	843	5.0	1,232	3.4
Other service charges, commissions, and fees	219	2.4	304	1.8	989	2.7
Trust department income	460	4.2	690	4.1	1,258	3.5
Other operating revenue	279	2.5	265	1.7	1,267	3.5
Total	$10,724	100.0%	$16,817	100.0%	$36,364	100.0%
Operating expense						
Salaries, wages, and benefits	2,854	26.6	4,288	25.5	8,395	23.1
Interest on deposits	1,785	16.7	5,071	30.1	12,218	33.6
Other interest	87	.8	190	1.1	1,377	3.8
Premises expense, net			732	4.4	1,410	3.9
Other operating expenses	2,207	20.6	2,205	13.1	6,251	17.1
Total	$ 6,933	64.7%	$12,486	74.2%	$29,651	81.5%
Net current operating earnings	$ 3,791	35.3%	$ 4,331	25.8%	$ 6,713	18.5%
Recoveries and profits	449	4.2	209	1.2		
Losses and charge-offs	(371)	(3.5)	(267)	(1.6)	212	.6
Net additions to valuation reserves	(482)	(4.5)	(730)	(4.3)		
Profits before income taxes	$ 3,387	31.5%	$ 3,543	21.1%	$ 6,925	19.1%
Taxes on net income	1,384	12.9	1,029	6.1	1,689	4.7
Net income after taxes	$ 2,003	18.6%	$ 2,514	15.0%	$ 5,236	14.4%
Dividends and interest on capital	$ 832		$ 1,202		$ 2,231[a]	

[a]Dividends only.

SOURCE: Compiled from Annual Reports of the Federal Deposit Insurance Corporation.

These data reveal the chief sources of revenue and the chief expense items of commercial banks as a whole. The proportions vary somewhat for individual banks, depending on their size, location, and types of business emphasized. In 1971 income from loans provided 66 per cent of operating earnings, as a result of the great increase in loans in expansion of the 1960s and early 1970s. Income from securities grew in both absolute and relative terms, as a result of the high yields available. Trust department and service income is important but not predominant as a source of revenues.

Salaries, wages, and benefits require about 23 per cent of total revenues and constitute about 28 per cent of total operating expenses. Interest on time and savings deposits has grown to about 33 per cent of revenues and about 41 per cent of operating expenses, reflecting the rise in interest rates paid. Interest paid on debentures and other debt, expenses of operating the bank premises, and a host of minor items comprise the other expenses.

The net operating earnings are now only about 19 per cent of operating revenues, so that an operating ratio of 81 per cent is produced. The net operating earnings, which indicates the real earning power, is subject to further adjustments arising out of profits (or losses) on securities transactions and on recoveries (or losses and charge-offs) on loans. In addition, many banks charge earnings with substantial amounts for bad debts and securities losses, prior to actual liquidation experience with these assets. Variations in the handling of losses, recoveries, and reserves among banks makes comparison of their net profit before taxes somewhat difficult. Analysts recommend that in comparing banks the net operating earnings figure be emphasized.

Income taxes absorb about 5 per cent of operating revenues, leaving a net profit which now constitutes only about 14 per cent of revenues. This is a high net income margin as compared with business corporations, but is necessary because capital funds are so large in relation to operating revenues.

The unwillingness of many banks to issue a detailed income statement is an obvious handicap to the investor. Where no net income figure is reported, an approximation may be obtained by finding the difference between the total surplus and undivided profits in the balance sheet at two different intervals and adding back the dividends paid in the interim. An adjustment may also be necessary to allow for any surplus derived from sale of stock above par value during the period.

The larger banks of investment interest ordinarily distribute only a modest fraction of their profits as dividends, so that yields on bank stocks are low. The steady "ploughing back" of earnings is necessary if net worth is to keep pace with the expansion of deposits. The appeal of the stock in a sound and growing bank lies in the relative regularity of dividends plus the appreciation in book and possible appreciation in market value that follows the growth in net worth and earnings.

Balance Sheets

The bank balance sheet reflects the character of the bank's activities. The chief liability items are deposits. The chief asset items are cash, loans, and investments. The data in Table 29-3 show the combined (and condensed) balance sheets of all insured commercial banks as of year-end 1960 and 1971. Significant changes took place during this period both in the amount and the relative importance of balance sheet items.

Table 29-3. ASSETS AND LIABILITIES OF INSURED COMMERCIAL BANKS—AS OF DECEMBER 31, 1960 AND 1971

(in millions of dollars)

Item	1960	1971
Assets		
Cash and due from banks	$ 51,902	$ 98,691
U.S. Govt. and agency obligations	60,522	79,769
State and municipal securities	17,337	80,135
Other securities	3,161	9,263
Loans and discounts	119,878	347,869
Less: valuation reserve	2,356	6,443
Net loans and discounts	$117,522	$341,426
Bank premises, furniture, and fixtures	2,829	10,285
Other assets	3,050	13,891
Total assets	$256,323	$633,460
Liabilities and Capital		
Deposits		
Time and savings	$ 73,284	$276,905
Demand	155,709	262,279
Total deposits	$228,993	$539,184
Other liabilities	6,671	47,368
Capital stock	6,208	11,903
Surplus	9,916	19,899
Undivided profits and reserves	4,534	12,150
Capital notes and debentures	—	2,956
Total liabilities and capital accounts	$256,322	$633,460

SOURCE: Compiled from annual reports of the Federal Deposit Insurance Corporation.

    Cash. Cash, or the bank's *primary reserve,* consists of cash on hand, balances with other banks, cash items in process of collection, and legal reserves, which, in the case of members of the Federal Reserve System, consist of the required reserve balances held at the Federal Reserve Banks plus vault cash.[1] Primary reserves are maintained against cash withdrawals as a protection to depositors and for maintenance of general liquidity. Total cash of all insured commercial banks comprised 20 per cent of total assets in 1960 and 16 per cent in 1971.

[1]Until November 1972 the legal reserve requirements for all member banks were 3 per cent on savings deposits and 3 per cent on time deposits under $5 millions and 5 per cent over $5 millions. Against demand deposits, they were 17 to 17$^{1}/_{2}$ per cent for "reserve city banks" (in sixty-five cities) and 12$^{1}/_{2}$ to 13 per cent for "country banks."

    Effective in November 1972, the distinction between "reserve city" and "country" banks was eliminated, and required reserves against demand deposits, for all banks, were graduated from 8 per cent on the first $2 million up to 17.5 per cent on deposits over 400 million.

Investments and loans. These are called the "earning assets" of the bank, as they produce the bulk of the income. United States Government and agency obligations, the most liquid of the earning assets, comprised 30 per cent of total earning assets in 1960 and 15 per cent in 1971. They had reached their peak in 1946; in the postwar period, they declined in relative importance as a result of the substantial growth of commercial loans. Government obligations are not without price risk; the value of those that are marketable fluctuates with changing interest rates. Many banks minimize this risk by emphasizing the holding of short-term Treasury bills and certificates, or Treasury notes and bonds nearing maturity. Securities other than Federal issues consist of the state, municipal, and corporate bonds approved for bank investment. Banks hold permanently no stock except stock in the Federal Reserve Banks (in the case of member banks) and in affiliates.[1]

Loans and discounts. These represent the advances of the bank to its clients and include commercial, industrial, and agricultural loans, loans to brokers and others secured by securities, real estate mortgages, personal and consumer loans, loans to banks, commercial paper, and bankers' acceptances. Loans are usually shown net after reserve for losses. The proportion of total assets held in the form of loans, and the types of advances made, are major determinants of bank operating earnings. Reflecting the great demand for loans in the latter 1960s and early 1970s, this asset rose to 51 per cent of total commercial bank assets at the end of 1971 from 46 per cent in 1960. Banks that desire liquidity and, hence, concentrate on investments rather than loans, produce lower earning power but enjoy greater safety.

Secondary reserves. To assure liquidity, the bank's second line of defense consists of its secondary reserve of short-term Government securities, banker's acceptances, and commercial paper. These earning assets yield relatively low returns. Hence, a high proportion of primary and secondary reserves produce lower revenues, although greater safety is achieved. For all insured commercial banks, secondary reserves were about 20 per cent of total assets at the end of 1971.

Fixed assets. These are relatively small. Their importance varies considerably from bank to bank, depending on the type of premises and equipment and the method of valuation for balance sheet purposes.

Other assets. These include (1) *customers' liability on acceptances* representing claims against customers for whom the bank has accepted drafts and bills under letters of credit. This item is offset by a corresponding liability representing the obligation of the bank to honor such acceptances that are still outstanding; (2) *income accrued but not collected* representing the accrued interest on customers' loans and on securities that will be collected at a later date. Similarly, on the liabilities side of the balance sheet, a figure appears representing interest collected in advance but not yet earned; and (3) *prepaid expenses* and a variety of minor miscellaneous items.

Deposits. These represent the main liabilities of the bank. They are subdivided into (1) time and savings deposits, which are not subject to check, which bear interest, and on which the bank is entitled to require notice of withdrawal, and (2) demand deposits due to individuals, business concerns, governments, and other banks. The relative proportion of the two main types affects the operations of the bank in several ways—the interest expense, the required reserves, and the type of investments held. Because time deposits have a slower turnover, lower reserves are held for their payment, and when they form a large portion of total deposits, the bank is justified in holding more longer-term investments, such as bonds and mortgages. Where demand deposits predominate, especially amounts due to other banks, the bank must maintain higher reserves and more liquid earning assets.

The other liabilities of the bank are of minor importance and include borrowings from other banks, accrued expenses, taxes, and any reserves that represent liabilities rather than valuation and surplus reserves.[2]

Net worth. The net worth section of the balance sheet (often designated as "capital" or "capital funds") ordinarily contains four items: (1) the capital stock; (2) the surplus, representing permanently held accumulated earnings transferred from undivided profits and any premiums received from the sale of stock above par value; (3) the undivided profits, or "free surplus," into which current profits are credited and from which dividends are paid (national banks are required to have surplus equal to 20 per cent of their capital stock before they may declare dividends—surplus which is ordinarily obtained by the sale of stock at a premium over par value, or built up by transfers undivided profits); and (4) reserves including general, contingency, security valuation, and loan loss reserves (over and above the bad debts reserve allowed for income tax purposes).

A fifth category of items in the "capital funds" section consists of notes and debentures. Beginning in 1963, a number of larger banks have sold notes or debentures to increase their loanable funds and provide greater support to their deposits. Although these obligations represent debt, they are subordinate to deposits in their claims on assets, and so provide additional leverage in the capital structure (see p. 557).

Bank Stock Analysis

The investor in bank stock should be satisfied that the bank shows a satisfactory position with respect to (1) liquidity, (2) solvency or capital adequacy, and (3) earning power. Liquidity is the bank's ability to meet deposit obliga-

---

[2]The term *reserve* has several meanings in banking. First, there are the *legal reserves* of cash or deposits that must be maintained to satisfy the law; these are assets. Second, as we have seen, groups of assets are classified as primary or secondary reserves with respect to their purpose of providing adequate liquidity. Third, bank balance sheets often contain reserves similar to those found on business corporation statements: *valuation reserves*, such as reserves for depreciation or bad debts, *liability reserves*, such as reserves for taxes or dividends, and reserves that are in fact merely segregations of surplus.

tions at short notice. Solvency is the measure of its ultimate ability, possibly after a period of liquidation of assets, to meet its deposits. Earning power is of primary importance to the investor seeking income, price appreciation, or both. These three concepts are closely interrelated. A bank with sufficient primary and secondary reserves to meet its deposits if they were all withdrawn at once would be both liquid and solvent, but would produce little or no net earnings. A bank seeking maximum earnings would maintain only those reserves required by law and minimum daily needs, and would emphasize high-rate loans subject to greater losses or, in the absence of a demand for loans, medium- and long-term bonds subject to price variations. Such a bank would not be highly liquid; it might be solvent, given sufficient time to transfer its assets into cash. Its earnings would be high, if only for a temporary period. The problem of bank management is to steer a middle course so as to maintain liquidity adequate to satisfy the chief obligation of safety to depositors and, at the same time, provide an adequate return on the investment of the stockholders.

Tests of liquidity. The basic test of liquidity is the reserve ratio, or ratio of primary reserves to deposits. For all insured banks at the end of 1971 this ratio stood at 18 per cent. It tends to be higher for the banks in large cities holding deposits of other banks that are required by law to maintain higher legal reserves and whose deposits are primarily demand. Banks whose deposits are predominantly time and savings accounts feel safe with a lower reserve ratio. Banks whose assets other than cash are highly liquid also require smaller cash balances. This suggests an extension of the reserve ratio in the relationship between cash plus U.S. Government securities to deposits. This figure stood at 36 per cent for all insured commercial banks at the end of 1971. For the aggregate of seventy-three selected large banks whose shares are of considerable interest to investors, the range was 18 to 49 per cent.[3]

Another measure of liquidity is found in the ratio of loans to deposits. This shows the extent to which loanable funds are invested in earning assets bearing the highest risk. For all insured commercial banks the ratio stood at 63 per cent at the end of 1971.

Tests of solvency. The traditional test of solvency is the ratio of "capital funds" (capital stock, surplus, undivided profits, surplus reserves, and debentures) to deposits. Tradition has set this ratio at 10 per cent, but in recent years only the larger and more conservative banks have preserved this relationship. For all insured commercial banks at the end of 1971, the ratio was 9 per cent. For an aggregate of seventy-three large banks as of December 31, 1971, the ratio of capital funds to deposits showed a range of 7 to 20 per cent.[4] The net worth provides the cushion of protection to the bank's creditors. It also indicates the degree of leverage by which a modest

---

[3]The First Boston Corporation, *Data on Selected Commercial Bank Stocks*, 23rd ed., 1972. Data used by permission.
[4]*Ibid.*

rate of earnings on total resources is magnified into a respectable return on the owners' investment.

Whether the capital funds-to-deposits ratio is satisfactory can be learned only by examining other relationships. Where the bank is highly liquid, and its loans and investments are well selected and managed, the ratio can safely be much lower than the average. Rapid growth of deposits and a relatively larger increase in loans than in high-grade investments have caused a number of banks in the late 1960s and early 1970s to offer new stock and notes in order to improve the ratio. The size of this relationship also has an important influence on dividend policy. Transfers from undivided profits to surplus permanently impound funds which might otherwise be available for dividends. The investor should determine whether an attractive rate of earnings and of dividends is at the expense of solvency as indicated by an unsatisfactory net worth position.

Other measures of capital adequacy include the ratio of (1) capital funds to *assets at risk* (total assets less cash and U.S. Government securities), (2) capital funds to *deposits at risk* (deposits less cash and Governments), and (3) capital funds to *loans*. These measure the exposure of deposits to risk of decline in value of the earning assets in general, and loans in particular. Ratios for 1960, 1965, and 1971 are shown in Table 29-4.

Table 29-4. CAPITAL ADEQUACY RATIOS, INSURED COMMERCIAL BANKS

	(1)	(2)	(3)
1960	13.7%	17.7%	18.4%
1965	11.7	14.1	14.9
1971	10.0	12.6	13.6

SOURCE: Federal Deposit Insurance Corporation, annual reports.

The declines in these ratios reflect the increase in bank activity without a similar increase in capital. This has been one of the reasons for the issuance of subordinated notes and debentures in recent years.

Tests of earning power. The earnings record and prospects of a bank depend on all of the influences that govern the investment of its funds and the operation of its departments. Nevertheless, there are some useful specific clues.

The ratio of loans to investments, and the types of loans and of investments within these categories, have a marked influence on earnings. In general, investments are less remunerative than loans, and short-term loans and investments less lucrative than long term. Table 29-5 shows the pertinent relationships for all insured commercial banks and for seventy-three large metropolitan commercial banks for 1971.

Of course, banks differ considerably in the character of their earning assets. The investor must be satisfied that quality has not been sacrificed for earning power in the selection of the earning assets.

Special attention should be paid to the trend in the growth of deposits and of loans as indicators of management. The bank's earning power depends in large measure on its ability to obtain and hold deposits, and to invest these deposits in earning assets that produce a satisfactory income. The banks that show better-than-average earnings are those that are growing at a better-than-average rate, that emphasize loans rather than investments, and that have a lower-than-average ratio of capital funds to deposits.

Where sufficient detail is available, the bank's income statement may be analyzed in the same manner as that of the business concern, except, of

Table 29-5. COMMERCIAL BANK FINANCIAL RELATIONSHIPS, 1971

	Insured All Banks	Large Banks
Loans as percentage of assets	51%	52%
Range	—	16–72
Loan interest as a percentage of operating revenue (net after interest paid)	32	42
Range	—	27–67
Average yield realized on loans	7	7
Range	—	6–9
Return on securities	4	8
Range	—	6–9

SOURCES: All insured commercial banks: Federal Deposit Insurance Corporation, *Annual Report, 1971;* Large banks: The First Boston Corporation, *Data on Selected Commerical Bank Stocks*, 23rd ed., 1972. Data used by permission.

course, that different standards are used. The operating ratio is the relationship of operating expenses to operating earnings and, for banks as a whole, is about 81 per cent. A low operating ratio indicates management efficiency and the ability to withstand declines in revenues without making too heavy inroads into net operating earnings. A high operating ratio must be offset by larger revenue per dollar of investment.

Certain individual expense items, notably salaries and wages, and interest paid on deposits, have a marked effect on the operating ratio and on the net operating earnings. The former constitutes about 23 per cent and the latter 33 per cent of total revenues, and 28 and 41 per cent, respectively, of operating expenses, for all insured commercial banks in 1971. For the year 1971, the range among seventy-three leading banks was 12 to 47 per cent of operating revenues for the employment cost ratio and 21 to 55 per cent for the interest expense ratio. The latter reflects the composition of deposits between demand and time. When both of these costs are rising (as during 1962–1970, when there was a wave of increases in interest paid on savings accounts), profit margins tend to narrow.

The net operating earnings (before taxes) show the result of banking operations proper, prior to any special gains or losses on loans and investments. As a percentage of operating revenues, net operating earnings before income taxes and securities gains or losses were 19 per cent for all insured commercial banks in 1971. The range for seventy-three large banks was 6 to 25 per cent. But the overall earning power of the institution is better indicated by the relation between pretax net earnings and capital funds plus deposits. For 1971 the rate for all insured commercial banks was only 1.25 per cent. To earn a good return on its capital funds, a bank relies on the leverage provided by a substantial ratio of deposits to net worth. A capital funds-to-deposits ratio of less than 10 per cent is required to magnify a 1.25 per cent return on total funds employed to 14.0 per cent on net worth (before taxes). Banks with a capital funds-to-deposits ratio of more than 9 are likely to earn an inadequate rate on net worth. Banks with less than this ratio would, with the same net earnings, produce a very substantial return on the owners' investment but would be undercapitalized.

The adjustments to net operating earnings, representing (1) gains and losses on securities, and recoveries and charge-offs on loans that are recorded when realized, and (2) the additions to or reductions of valuation reserves, deserve close scrutiny. The size of these items depends somewhat on the original book value placed on earning assets. In addition, their amount varies considerably from year to year. For these reasons the basic earning power of the bank is measured by the reported earnings before rather than after these adjustments.

The percentage of operating revenues carried down to net income after taxes, coupled with the turnover of capital funds, produces the rate of return on the book value of the owners' investment, which in 1971 for all insured commercial banks, was 14 per cent. This has fallen considerably in the postwar period, having been 36 and 24 per cent in 1945 and 1950, respectively. The range for seventy-three large banks in 1971 was 4 to 20 per cent.

To the shareholder, earnings per share, and their trend and stability, is the crucial figure. For short-run analysis, per-share results are calculated from net operating earnings after taxes. For longer-run comparisons, the net after profits or losses on securities sales is valid. In common with industrial companies, some banks show earnings per share giving effect to the dilution that would result from the conversion of convertible notes and debentures.

Where, even in good years, a relatively low rate is earned on net worth, and only a fraction of net profits, say, 40 to 50 per cent, is declared in dividends, the resulting in-pocket return to bank stockholders is bound to be modest.

Stock Values, Prices, and Yields

The market value of bank stock is determined by the earnings and dividend record and prospects of the institution and the industry, by asset values underlying each share, by the general course of the stock market as a whole, and by the valuation placed on bank earnings in terms of the price-earnings ratio. Except in periods of generally low stock prices, bank stock has sold traditionally at 1.25 to 2.0 times book value (net worth divided by number of shares outstanding). The rationale is that book values are notoriously conservative and that the bank's assets are so liquid that book value is much more accurate a measure of realizable value than in the case of business corporations. Of the seventy-three metropolitan institutions reported on by the First Boston Corporation, the stock of only eight sold below book value in March 1972. The range was from 88 to 338 per cent of book value.

The price of bank stock in recent years has also increased from its former position in relation to earnings. In the 1950s ratios of 10 times or less were not unusual. As of September 31, 1971, for fifty-seven banks and holding companies, the average was 11.4 times and the range was from 7.2 to 20.7 times.[5] A considerable variation is to be expected, reflecting differences in the overall rate of earnings and in the relative importance of special adjustments and increases in capital reserves per share.

Prices of bank stocks are more stable than those of industrial concerns. Nevertheless, considerable volatility has appeared in recent years as indicated by Table 29-6 for nine New York City banks (weighted averages). The variations in banks stock prices and price-earnings multiples reflect the loss of prime investment status of the group.

Table 29-6. NEW YORK CITY BANK STOCK PRICES

	Market Price per Share			Earnings per Share	Price-Earnings Ratio (average)	Dividend per Share	Yield (average)
	Low	High	Monthly Average				
1955	$ 80.63	$ 76.14	$ 78.85	$ 5.78	14.93	$3.19	4.04%
1960	107.68	97.98	101.42	8.16	12.43	3.97	3.91
1965	140.53	155.78	147.14	9.81	15.00	4.90	3.33
1966	105.90	139.12	125.20	10.65	11.76	5.06	4.04
1967	132.75	145.53	138.29	11.59	11.93	5.35	3.87
1968	141.65	198.29	171.22	12.93	13.24	5.82	3.40
1969	148.82	191.43	171.93	13.19	13.03	6.40	3.72
1970	155.68	185.67	167.84	14.75	11.38	6.77	4.03
1971	163.27	194.51	175.87	15.26	11.52	7.28	4.14
1972	187.17	241.67	218.61	15.50	14.08	7.32	3.35

SOURCE: *Moody's Stock Survey.*

Because banks generally retain a considerable portion of their earnings, as a means of increasing their capital funds base, dividend yields tend to be modest. A bank does well to earn 12 per cent on its net worth, and if its stock sells at 1.5 times book value, and one-half of its earnings are declared in dividends, the resultant yield is 4 per cent. In only two cases of the fifty-seven banks previously mentioned was the yield as high as 6 per cent in September 1971. The range was 1.7 to 6.1 per cent and the average 4.2 per cent, with an average payout of 45 per cent. However, a modest

[5]M. A. Schapiro & Co., Inc., *Bank Stock Quarterly*, December 1971. This publication also shows "times diluted net operating earnings per share" for the twenty-four companies with convertible notes or debentures outstanding. Data used by permission.

dividend yield is likely to be compensated for by regularity of dividends and by appreciation possibilities. Several large metropolitan banks have had unbroken dividend records for over 100 years.

Bank Holding Companies

A company that owns or controls 25 per cent or more of the voting shares of one or more banks, or otherwise controls their boards of directors, must register with Board of Governors of the Federal Reserve System under the Bank Holding Company Act of 1956 as amended in 1970. The Board exercises broad regulatory control.

Legislation enacted in December 1970 placed one-bank holding companies under the regulation of the Federal Reserve Board, but holding companies are prohibited from controlling any subsidiaries unrelated to banking unless they had been acquired before June 30, 1968.

A number of bank holding companies have been formed in very recent years. By the end of 1970, only four of the twenty-five largest banks in the country had not adopted the holding company format. The usual procedure has been for the bank to be reincorporated as a holding company, at which time it exchanges its shares for those of the bank or banks to be controlled.

The holding company format has a number of financing advantages, including the issuance of commercial paper and longer-term notes and subordinated debentures. Perhaps the chief factor of interest to investors is a holding company's ability to engage in a number of approved activities that differ from and yet are "closely related to banking," namely, mortgage banking and loan servicing, investment and financial counselling, personal property and computer leasing, data processing service, title insurance, and credit insurance (for subsidiaries). Another appeal of the holding company is that it may be able to acquire a number of smaller banks and thus benefit from an expansion program.

The holding company provides many services for its bank affiliates, which while separately incorporated and enjoying legal autonomy, receive the benefit of examinations, operating and reporting advice, investment advice, aid in recruiting and training personnel, consultation on loan policy, and tax guidance, from their parent.

Certain differences between bank stock and stock of bank holding companies are of interest. A number of the latter are listed on organized exchanges and enjoy better marketability. In 1971 market prices were about the same in relation to earnings but dividend yields were generally lower than for bank stocks proper.[6]

The general approach to the analysis of bank holding company stock is similar to that of operating bank stock, except that consolidated statements are used. The important advantage of diversification lends a stability to the earnings of a bank holding company that many unit banks cannot enjoy. However, as nonbanking services become more important, the

---

[6]M. A. Schapiro & Co., *op. cit.*

consolidated statements become increasingly difficult to compare with the statements of operating banks and with those of other holding company groups performing a different variety of functions.

Investment Outlook

With the exception of very large city banks and holding companies, bank stocks are traded over-the-counter. Individual investors constitute the chief ownership, but an increasing number of institutional funds find bank stocks attractive, mainly for appreciation. Prices were depressed in 1963–1966 to reflect the squeeze on bank profits resulting from the higher rates paid on time and savings deposits.[7] And bank stocks, like others, suffered in the general market decline in 1966, rose moderately in 1967, and reached new highs in 1969. Earnings have increased since then, but these have been offset (until 1972) by lower price-earnings ratios. In 1971–1972, with earnings at new levels, the market was still satisfied with low yields on these securities. This situation reflected the chief appeal of bank stocks—for growth and future dividends rather than for generous current income.

The investor should not expect any unusual stability of price, any extraordinary yield, or any spectacular appreciation. Earnings on bank stocks as a group are largely determined by general economic conditions, especially the demand for business loans, the level of money rates, and the rates paid on deposits. The performance of individual banks reflects the degree of leverage employed, the liquidity, the types of loans and investments made, the ability to control expenses, and the variety of services rendered. Just as in the case of industrials, prices reflect differences in asset values, earnings, and dividends. Bank stocks are attractive to investors who are content with modest but regular dividend returns and who are interested in the appreciation possibilities derived from operation at high leverage.

Bank debentures. Notes and debentures, many of them convertible, have become an important source of financing in recent years, especially for bank holding companies. In early 1973, over $2 billions were outstanding. These are subordinated to deposits with respect to claim on assets. Their purposes have been to provide junior capital to support an increased volume of loans, to avoid the sale of stock at relatively low price-earnings ratios, and to benefit from the lower cost of debt capital. In early 1973, the yields and prices of bank debentures showed a wide range, depending on the value of the conversion privilege. "Straight" long-term bonds brought 6¾ to 7½ per cent yield.

Within the bank group there is a considerable range of quality and of appeal. While, in general, bank shares and debentures are recognized as conservative equities and bonds, their selection demands the same careful discrimination and judgment that are required of any other securities.

maximum rates on savings and time deposits see Chapter 4.

REFERENCES

American Bankers Association, *The Commercial Banking Industry*. Englewood Cliffs, N.J.: Prentice-Hall, Inc., 1962.

Comptroller of the Currency, *Instructions for Preparation of Income and Dividends Reports by National Banking Associations, Form 2127-A*. Washington, D.C.: U.S. Government Printing Office, 1961.

DURAND, DAVID, *Bank Stock Prices and the Bank Capital Problem*. New York: National Bureau of Economic Research, Inc., 1957.

EDWARDS, F. R., *Concentration and Competition in Commercial Banking: A Statistical Study*. Boston: Federal Reserve Bank of Boston, 1964.

First Boston Corporation, *Data on Selected Commercial Bank Stocks*. New York: The Corporation, annually.

FISCHER, G. C., *Bank Holding Companies*. New York: Columbia University Press, 1961.

GARCIA, F. L., *How to Analyze a Bank Statement*, 4th ed. Boston: Bankers Publishing Company, 1966.

GUTHMANN, H. G., *Analysis of Financial Statements*, 4th ed., Chapter 17. Englewood Cliffs, N.J.: Prentice-Hall, Inc., 1953.

Keefe Bank Stock Manual. New York: Keefe, Bruyette & Woods, Inc., annually.

KENNEDY, R. D., AND S. Y. MCMULLEN, *Financial Statements*, 5th ed., Chapters 30, 31. Homewood, Ill.: Richard D. Irwin Inc., 1968.

LENT, G. E., *The Changing Structure of Commercial Banking*. Hanover, N.H.: Amos Tuck School of Business Administration, Dartmouth College, 1960.

NADLER, MARCUS, AND J. I. BOGEN, *The Bank Holding Company*. New York: Graduate School of Business Administration, New York University, 1959.

PROCHNOW, H. V., ed., *The One-Bank Holding Company*. Chicago: Rand McNally & Company, 1969.

ROBINSON, R. I., *The Management of Bank Funds*, 2nd ed. New York: McGraw-Hill, Inc., 1962.

VAN HORNE, J. C., AND R. C. HELWIG, *The Valuation of Small Bank Stocks*. East Lansing, Mich.: Graduate School of Business Administration, Michigan State University, 1966.

30 Insurance Company Stocks

SCOPE: This chapter discusses the stocks issued by stock insurance companies. The order of discussion is (1) scope of the industry, (2) property-liability companies, (3) life insurance companies, and (4) market for insurance stocks.

Scope of the Industry

The insurance business consists of three main categories—life, property and liability, and health and accident. The division of these three types among companies is becoming less and less clear-cut as a result of mergers and acquisitions to form multiline companies, and because the health business not done by such organizations as Blue Cross and Blue Shield is almost entirely written by either life or property-liability companies.[1]

In addition, a number of company groups have been formed that involve parent and holding companies and subsidiaries offering life and property-casualty insurance and a variety of other services such as real estate and mortgage management, variable annuities, mutual funds, computer services, title insurance, and others. The consolidated statements of these groups, therefore, include a mixture of activities. The holding company structure provides greater diversification of services, income, and financial flexibility through the use of senior securities.

Life insurance companies write life insurance, annuity, and health contracts, and some have acquired affiliates in the property insurance field or are members of a group including property and liability companies. Of the 1,818 life insurance companies in the United States at mid-year 1971, about 9 per cent were mutual companies, owned by their policyholders, and 91 per cent were stock companies. Mutual companies, however, accounted for slightly over one-half of total life insurance in force and about two-thirds of total assets.

[1]Of the $17.8 billions in health insurance benefits paid in 1971 about $9.1 billions were provided by insurance companies. The balance was paid by Blue Cross, Blue Shield, and independent plans. See *1972-3 Source Book of Health Insurance* (New York: Health Insurance Institute).

In the property-liability insurance field, stock companies write about 70 per cent of the premiums and own 75 per cent of total assets. However, many are owned by life insurance, general holding, and conglomerate companies. Where several companies are controlled by a leading insurance corporation, the members of the "group" or "fleet" may each specialize in a particular type of fire or casualty business.

Data on the life insurance industry have already been presented in Chapters 3 and 23. Table 30-1 shows the relative importance of the two major categories of *stock* companies in 1970.

Table 30-1. COMPARISON OF STOCK INSURANCE COMPANIES, 1971
(dollars in billions)

	Life	*Property-Liability*
Number of stock companies	1,653	840
Total assets	$ 74	$49
Premiums written	21	25
Insurance in force	795	—

SOURCES: Institute of Life Insurance, *Life Insurance Fact Book 1972.* (New York: The Institute 1972); *Best's Aggregates and Averages: Property-Liability,* 33rd ed. (Morristown, N. J.: A. M. Best & Co., Inc., 1972).

Until about 1950 nonlife insurance was usually classified in two categories, fire and casualty, and these were written by different companies. These are now described as property-liability companies in recognition of the fact that various types of protection are now often combined in individual policies or written by the same companies.[2] The relative importance of the various types, in terms of net premiums written, is indicated by the data in Table 30-2.

Table 30-2. NET PREMIUMS, ALL PROPERTY-LIABILITY COMPANIES, 1970
(in millions of dollars)

	Amount	*Per Cent*
Auto bodily injury	$ 6,209	19.8%
Auto physical damage	4,321	13.7
Fire and extended coverage	3,147	10.0
Workmen's compensation	3,492	11.1
Homeowners' multiple peril	2,565	8.2
Auto property damage liability	2,750	8.8
Accident and health	1,909	6.1
Miscellaneous bodily injury	1,662	5.3
Marine	1,277	4.1
Fidelity and surety	562	1.8
All other	3,516	11.1
Total	$31,410	100.0%

SOURCE: *Best's Averages & Aggregates: Property-Liability,* 32nd ed. (Morristown, N. J.: A. M. Best and Company, Inc., 1971).

[2]For information on the structure and regulation of the property-liability industry see *Institutional Investor Study Report of the Securities and Exchange Commission,* Chapter VI. 92nd Congress, 1st Session, House Document No. 92–64, Washington: U.S. Government Printing Office, 1971.

Property-Liability Companies

Functions and characteristics. To the investor, a property-liability insurance company is a combination of an insurance underwriter and a closed-end investment company. The principal business is that of writing contracts under which fire and other risks are insured; this underwriting activity may or may not contribute anything to the net profits. In addition, the company invests funds representing capital, surplus, and premiums collected in advance on policies that run from one to five years. It expects to net a modest return on these investments, and may achieve a capital gain on its common stock holdings. The income and dividend position of the stockholder is thus affected by the company's ability to earn a sufficient premium income to cover the outlays associated with underwriting—commissions, administrative expenses, and losses—and to produce a respectable net return on investments. The solvency position of the stockholder is determined by the value and liquidity of the assets—chiefly the investment portfolio—and the relation of the capital funds to liabilities (reserves).

The profitable operation of underwriting is affected by the control of expenses and the premiums charged for and the losses charged to underwriting income. The property insurance business has a marked cyclical variation. Premium income rises with business prosperity, population, and the general price level. Losses are affected not only by ordinary and disaster burnings, hurricanes and other hazards, but also by the increased moral risk during depression periods. In addition, during periods of rising prices, the costs of restoring insured property rise and hence a squeeze is placed on income, collected as much as five years in advance. Premiums are established on the basis of the previous experience of the more efficient companies and are calculated for the majority of fire companies by the Board of Underwriters, a cooperative organization.[3]

The liability lines of business do not show the same degree of cyclical influence. The rates and loss trends of automobile liabilty, workmen's compensation, surety, and accident and health lines are affected by general economic conditions and special factors bearing on each segment of the business.

The results of the investment activity of the business are determined by the conservativeness of the portfolio and the variations in market value of the securities held. Although there is considerably less technical leverage than in the case of the commercial bank, the net gain from investing can be

---

[3]Fire losses in the United States, as reported by the National Board of Fire Underwriters, have run as follows:

Aggregate Fire Losses
(in millions of dollars)

1945	$ 484	1966	$1,497
1950	648	1967	1,707
1955	885	1968	1,830
1960	1,107	1969	1,952
1965	1,456	1970	2,264

Sources: The Spectator, *Insurance Yearbook* (fire and marine volume) and Standard & Poor's *Industry Surveys, Insurance.*

magnified considerably, depending on the relative importance of owners' investment to liabilities.

Property and liability insurance companies are examined and regulated by state authorities with the aim of assuring solvency and the soundness and adequacy of policy forms. Regulation of investment permits a substantial selection of common stocks. The result is that the property-liability company may obtain a higher, or more likely today, a lower current return on its portfolio than may the commercial bank, but it may also enjoy market price appreciation. It is, consequently, likely to show greater growth, and also, greater variations in liquidating value.

Investment policy. Property-liability companies have considerable freedom of choice above the minimum of cash or high-grade bonds required. Although regulations vary from state to state, in general, funds equal to minimum capital required must be invested in U.S. Government bonds and/or approved mortgages; funds equal to the unearned premium and the loss reserves must be invested in cash, government, and/or approved corporate bond issues. The remaining funds may be invested in both bonds *and stocks,* as long as the issuers are solvent and have maintained adequate interest and dividend records. Common stock and surplus may be invested 100 per cent in equities if reserves are fully backed by high-grade investments, if the "underwriting exposure" (as measured by the rate of net premiums written in relation to stockholders' equity) is low, and if the equity is large in relation to reserves.

Within the legal limits, the investment portfolios differ considerably. Since liquidity is of prime importance, funds equal to policyholders' claims (reserves) are held in the form of cash and bonds. But the stockholders' equity may be represented in one company by bonds alone, in another company by common stocks. The former would enjoy greater stability of income and less variation in market value; the latter, if the stocks were properly diversified, would (under ideal conditions) enjoy greater possible appreciation in market value, at the risk of stock market fluctuations. The investor in insurance company stocks may take his choice. He should insist, however, that those companies with below-average capital funds in relation to insurance risks show substantial conservatism in their investment portfolios.

The distribution of the investments of all stock property-liability companies is indicated in Table 30-4. Individual companies differ from the group as a whole. For example, common stocks may represent from 20 to 70 per cent of a portfolio.

Insurance companies are required to file annual balance sheet and income statements with state insurance departments. These are available to the public; together with the annual report to stockholders, which includes a list of security investments, they provide adequate financial information. The use of uniform accounting practices makes comparison of different companies easier than in the case of industrial concerns. One must now use consolidated statements in the analysis of most of the larger concerns, which have a number of subsidiaries in their "fleet." Group data on the industry are readily available in such services as *Best's* annual volumes, and in insurance trade journals and special studies by dealers specializing in insurance stocks.

Income statement. The income statement includes two or three sections or exhibits: underwriting, investment, and sometimes, surplus. Table 30-3 shows the aggregates for 840 *stock property-liability* companies in the United States for 1971, when after some years of loss, underwriting profits were enjoyed.

Table 30-3. COMBINED INCOME STATEMENT OF STOCK PROPERTY-LIABILITY COMPANIES, 1971

(in millions of dollars)

Underwriting Account	
Net premiums written	$24,841.2
Increase in unearned premium reserve	1,037.0
Net premiums earned	$23,804.2
Losses and adj. expenses incurred	13,808.8
Expenses incurred	9,316.2
Net underwriting profit	$ 679.2
Investment Account	
Investment income	$ 1,930.4
Investment expenses	145.7
Net investment income	$ 1,784.7
Net profit on sale of investments	192.9
Net investment profit	$ 1,977.6
Unrealized appreciation in book value of investments	1,439.4
Net investment gain	$ 3,417.0

SOURCE: *Best's Aggregates & Averages: Property-Liability*, 33rd ed. (A. M. Best & Co., Inc., 1972).

Net premiums written is the amount of premiums received on policies issued during the year less return and reinsurance premiums. *Net premiums earned* is the result of deducting from premiums written the increase in the unearned premium reserve. *Net underwriting profit* is derived by deducting losses and underwriting expenses—mainly acquisition costs and commissions—incurred during the year. It represents the portion of net premiums written that is applicable to the proportion of premium term that expired during the year. Since the expenses of a rising volume of business must be met immediately, and the larger premium volume is fully earned only in the future, a paradoxical situation is presented in which low underwriting profits or even losses may be reported in periods of expanded volume and high underwriting profits in a period of declining premiums written. After heavy losses in 1963–1965, 1966–1967 showed modest underwriting profits. The years 1968–1969 again showed an unhappy underwriting experience. Not only did an exceptionally large number of catastrophies occur, but rates on such large lines as automobile and home coverage insurance were inadequate. Some improvement showed in late 1970, but again, heavy storm losses and increasing accident claims provided a setback to earnings, and the industry as a whole did a little better than break even. Fortunately, the industry's expense ratio was reduced and much improvement was evident in 1971–1972 as a result of higher rates and lower losses.

Reported underwriting losses may be overstated or profits understated because acquisition costs are prepaid on new business (the addition to unearned premium reserve) that is not taken into income until the future. Analysts, therefore, "add back" to the reported net underwriting loss or profit an arbitrary percentage, such as 40 per cent, of unearned fire insurance premiums (35 per cent in the case of casualty companies) less income taxes at current rates on the amount added on.[4] In 1969 pressure from professional accounting associations, that insurance companies should apply "generally accepted accounting principles," led a number of companies to reflect this situation in their reports to stockholders. "Acquisition costs" are amortized against unearned premiums over the life of the policies, so that current underwriting profit is ordinarily increased, as are income taxes. Other companies continue to report on the "statutory" basis but indicate results separately on an adjusted basis. Thus, in its 1970 report, Aetna Life & Casualty Company disclosed that amortization of 22 per cent of the unexpired portion of premiums would still leave the unearned premium reserve at an adequate level. The Travellers Corporation presented operating statements on both the statutory and the adjusted basis.

The *net investment income* consists of the receipts from securities and other assets less investment expenses consisting of real estate repairs, expenses, and depreciation, and expenses of administration of the portfolio. To this figure is added actual gain (or loss) from the sale, redemption, or maturity of investments, to produce the *net investment profit* for the year. The *net investment gain* includes unrealized gains (or losses) on investments.

Book appreciation in securities is reported as additional investment income on official statements but is credited directly to contingency reserves or to surplus in many of the companies' reports to stockholders. Where shown as income (or loss), the change in portfolio value introduces an element that makes reported investment results unstable and to a certain extent unreliable.

Net operating earnings is another useful figure (not shown in Table 30-3). It is the total of net underwriting profit and net investment income.

The surplus exhibit, included in official statements but sometimes omitted from annual reports, shows the net change in surplus arising from underwriting and investment profits less income taxes, dividends, and any appropriations to special reserves.

Balance sheet. Table 30-4 shows the combined balance sheet of the 840 *stock* companies in the United States, at the end of 1971. The

---

[4]The adjustment for income taxes arises from the fact that, since all acquisition costs are recorded as expense at the time the commissions are paid, expense is overstated (and taxes understated) during a period of increasing volume; any underwriting profits that accrue in the future, as the unearned premiums become earned, are likewise overstated.

A further adjustment for taxes is used by some analysts, namely, a deduction of the capital gains rate on unrealized appreciation of portfolio value.

**Table 30-4. COMBINED BALANCE SHEET OF STOCK PROPERTY-
LIABILITY COMPANIES, DECEMBER 31, 1971**

(in millions of dollars)

	Amount	Per Cent of Total
Assets		
Cash	$ 1,147.7	2.3%
U.S. Govt. and agency bonds	3,468.7	7.1
Municipal (including revenue) bonds	13,717.3	27.8
Corporate bonds	5,199.5	10.5
Common stocks	17,188.3	34.8
Preferred stocks	1,565.6	· 3.2
Mortgages	135.1	.3
Real estate	688.5	1.4
Premium balances	3,693.2	7.5
Other assets	2,529.6	5.2
Total admitted assets	$49,333.5	100.0%
Liabilities		
Unearned premiums	$12,155.5	24.7%
Losses and adjustment expenses	16,190.4	32.8
Accrued commissions, taxes, etc.	721.0	1.5
Federal income taxes	324.4	.6
Funds held under reinsurance treaties	649.9	1.3
Other liabilities	1,984.2	4.0
Voluntary reserves	3.278.4	6.6
Capital	1,909.3	3.9
Surplus	12,120.4	24.6
Total liabilities	$49,333.5	100.0%

SOURCE: *Best's Aggregates & Averages: Property-Liability*, 33rd ed. (Morristown, N. J.: A. M. Best Company, Inc., 1972).

assets of fire or casualty insurance company include cash, securities (U.S. Government, municipal, and corporate bonds, and preferred and common stocks), mortgages, collateral loans, real estate, agents' balances (premiums in course of collection), and miscellaneous items. The proportions of the various items, notably cash and different kinds of securities, depend on the state regulations governing investments, the types of insurance written, and the investment policies of the company. Because their policies are written for one year only, and because their premium volume is three times as large as that of a fire company in relation to stockholders' equity, making the risk exposure high, the casualty companies, and multiple-line companies with a large casualty business, must follow a much more conservative investment policy. This shows up in the smaller percentage of common stock in their investment portfolios.

General indications of major investment policies of stock companies in the aggregate, 1965–1971, have been (1) a decline in holdings of Federal securities (from 14 to 7 per cent of assets), reflecting an increased cash flow and lesser need of liquidity; (2) a continued interest in tax-free municipal bonds (remaining at about one-quarter of assets); (3) an increase in holdings of corporate bonds (from 5 to 11 per cent of assets), mainly in the latter 1960s, when corporate yields became very attractive; and (4) a decline in the percentage of common stocks to total assets (from 39 to 35 per cent) as their yields have declined and those of other securities have increased. Equities are still, however, important as protection against the rising costs of repair and replacement involved in claims.

As indicated previously, individual property-liability insurance companies differ considerably within the group with respect to the character of their portfolios. In general, the companies have maintained adequate liquidity through their holdings of cash and marketable securities. The need for marketability to meet sudden large losses explains the small interest in real estate and mortgage loans. Bonds are carried on the officially reported balance sheet at their amortized value, and stocks and nonamortizable bonds at the market value. The "convention value" of the portfolio, therefore, differs somewhat from the actual market value at the year-end. In the reports to stockholders, all securities may be carried at market values as of the date of the balance sheet.

The total assets of the company appear on the published statement as *total admitted assets,* to include only those that are in accord with state law. The actual assets of a company may exceed the admissible assets by a small percentage.

The chief debts of the property insurance company consist of reserves. The reserve for unearned premiums represents the unearned portion of the full premium dollar collected, computed *pro rata* for the unexpired term of all policies outstanding. It is the amount that would have to be returned to the policyholders if all policies were cancelled or terminated. This reserve, calculated on an orthodox "statutory" basis, is overstated because, as previously noted, acquisition costs equal to 30 to 40 per cent of the unearned premiums have already been paid and losses and remaining expenses should not exceed 60 to 70 per cent of the premiums. Therefore, the custom in analysis of insurance statements and in some company reports is to allocate 30 to 40 per cent of the accumulated unearned premium reserve to the net worth of the company in determining the *"liquidating value"* of the capital stock.

Other liabilities are often designated as *reserves.* Those providing for unpaid losses and claims and incurred expenses are unique to the insurance business. Voluntary reserves are the part of the net worth earmarked for contingencies.

The total net worth, consisting of capital, surplus, and any voluntary reserves, is designated in the insurance business as *policyholders' surplus.*

Statement analysis. In selecting shares in property-liability insurance companies, the investor should be satisfied that the company is large and growing and that, either directly or through subsidiaries, it does a diversified business in a variety of fire and casualty lines He would then turn to an analysis of its statements to determine its safety, performance, and earning power in relation to the market price and yield available.

MEASURES OF SAFETY. While the ability to meet claims and losses is most important to the policyholder, it is also important to the stockholder seeking stability of asset values and earnings.

The first measure of safety is the composition of the assets. The higher the proportion of cash and high-grade bonds to liabilities, the less the hazard from variations in the market value of the portfolio. It also follows that a very conservative portfolio brings in lower investment income, but this may be offset, through careful selection of risks, by a favorable loss record.

A substantial portion of the stockholders' equity can safely be invested in common stocks provided the company is not operating at too high a degree of leverage, as measured by the relation of the net worth to debt (reserves) or to total assets. Normally, total net worth (not including equity in the unearned premium reserve) should exceed 30 per cent of total assets, and the more conservative companies show a ratio of much more. For the whole group of companies for which data are given previously, the ratio was 35 per cent at the end of 1971. In a company very conservatively financed, with respect to both type of investments and type of capital structure, a ratio of common stock assets to total assets of one-fourth and a ratio of net worth to total assets of one-half combine to produce a ratio of common stock assets to capital of 50 per cent. For the whole group of companies, this ratio stood at 99 per cent at the end of 1971. Another more specific test relates *investment risk* and *underwriting risk*. The former is measured by the ratio of cash items and bonds owned to reserves, together with the ratio of common stocks owned to capital and surplus. The latter is measured by the ratio of net premiums written to capital and surplus. The higher the underwriting exposure, the greater the emphasis on conservative investments. Table 30-5 shows the 1971 ranges of the three relationships for twelve property-liability companies.

Table 30-5. RANGES OF TESTS OF INVESTMENT AND UNDERWRITING RISK, 1971

	Range
Cash items and bonds as a percentage of reserves	**62–124%**
Common stock as a percentage of capital and surplus	**29–121%**
Net premiums written per dollar of capital and surplus	**$0.81–$2.70**

SOURCE: Company annual reports.

MEASURES OF OPERATIONS AND PROFITABILITY. Performance of a company with respect to its underwriting activities is measured by examining four ratios over a period of years: (1) The *loss ratio,* or ratio of losses and loss-adjustment expenses incurred to net premiums *earned,* indicates the company's ability to select risks. (2) The *expense ratio,* or ratio of underwriting expenses (advertising, commissions, and other expenses associated with acquiring new business) to net premiums *written,* indicates efficiency in writing new business. If the ratio is high, owing to an unusually careful investigation of risks, it should be offset by a low loss ratio. If it is low, the loss ratio is likely to be high. Expenses may also be related to premiums earned to indicate their effect on the reported statutory underwriting results. (3) The *loss-plus-expense ratio* combines the previous two ratios. Where this is 100 per cent, the company is just breaking even on its underwriting activities before "adding back" a portion of the unearned premium reserve. But even if this is the case, the company has had the use of funds representing premiums paid in advance, and hence its underwriting activities have contributed to earnings through the medium of investment income. (4) The *underwriting profit margin* is the ratio of underwriting profits or loss to premiums earned and indicates the extent to which underwriting activities are contributing directly to earnings.

Table 30-6. LOSS EXPERIENCE OF PROPERTY-LIABILITY COMPANIES, 1960–1970

	1960	1965	1966	1967	1968	1969	1971
Losses to premiums earned	63.6%	69.2%	66.1%	67.2%	68.8%	70.3%	66.7%
Expenses to premiums written	34.8	32.7	31.9	31.7	31.2	30.3	29.1
Loss-plus-expense ratio	98.4	101.9	98.0	98.9	100.0	100.6	95.8
Underwriting profit (loss) margin	.7	(3.1)	.8	.2	(1.1)	(2.0)	(2.9)

SOURCE: *Bests' Averages & Aggregates: Property-Liability*, 33rd ed. (Morristown, N. J.: A. M. Best Company, Inc., 1972), p. 135.

Table 30-6 shows the underwriting experience of the property-liability industry, 1960–1971. Net underwriting losses reached their peak in 1965. A decreasing loss ratio, accompanied by a somewhat lower expense ratio, produced modest profits in 1966–1967. Losses increased in 1969 due to the factors explained previously, but 1970 showed some improvement. A substantial underwriting profit was enjoyed in 1971. Individual companies show a considerable range of experience depending on the types of business written and on management competence. Table 30-7 shows the results in 1971 of selected major types of underwriting. The range in profitability is wide. The investor should carefully check the types of business written by a

Table 30-7. UNDERWRITING EXPERIENCE RATIOS, 1971

	Loss Ratio	Expense Ratio	Combined Ratio	Underwriting Profit (Loss) Margin
Group accident and health	89.1%	16.5%	105.6%	(6.0%)
Auto liability	74.2	26.2	100.4	(1.6)
Homeowners' multiperil	64.0	33.5	97.5	1.7
Workmen's compensation	76.7	20.6	97.3	2.0
Commercial multiperil	56.8	35.6	92.4	2.4
Auto fire, theft, etc.	63.4	29.7	93.1	5.2
Auto collision	62.9	27.0	89.9	9.0
Surety	36.9	51.5	88.4	9.3
Fire	53.8	35.9	89.7	10.2
Inland marine	53.6	32.8	86.4	12.1
Burglary and theft	47.1	39.4	86.5	14.3

SOURCE: *Best's Averages & Aggregates: Property-Liability*, 33rd ed. (Morristown, N. J.: A. M. Best Company, Inc., 1972), pp. 132–135.

company or group, their relative importance, and any indications of changing trends.

The returns from the *investment* activity of the company are shown by the ratio of net investment income to the value of the investment portfolio, without considering realized or unrealized securities appreciation.[5] For all fire and casualty companies as a group, the rate has varied between 4 and 5 per cent in the early 1970s. This is a modest return and indicates general conservativeness in investment policy. It also reflects the low yields on common stocks which comprise an increasing percentage of the portfolio. In 1971, realized and unrealized gains in portfolio value produced an additional 3.5 per cent on average portfolio value. Although such gains cannot be relied upon, they add a special appeal to fire and casualty stocks and in some years help to offset bad underwriting results.

Net investment income can be computed on a per-share basis for comparative purposes. It may also be used as the basis for showing the dividend payout ratio.

MEASURES OF TOTAL EARNING POWER. The net income (before taxes) reported in the income statement is the total of the "statutory" underwriting profit (or loss) and the net investment income, including gain on sale or maturity of securities. When adjusted by the reporting company or by the analyst, by the addition or subtraction of an appropriate proportion of the increase or decrease in the unearned premium reserve, the overall earning power of the company is indicated. A ratio of total net earnings to net worth can thus be developed, either before or after Federal income taxes.

The investor is primarily interested in per-share results. He will find these calculated in three different ways: (1) in company annual reports on the "statutory" basis; (2) this latter figure adjusted, in the financial services and broker house reports, by amending the underwriting profit (loss) as previously explained; and (3) in company reports that themselves use the adjusted basis, even though the company reports to state insurance departments on the statutory basis. In cases (2) and (3), deferred taxes on the unearned premium reserve increment are deducted from adjusted net earnings.

MEASURES OF ASSET VALUE. Asset value per share is especially significant in the case of insurance stocks because it approximates the realizable value at the reporting date; this is because the company is required to report its holdings of stock at market value close to the year-end, and because the book or amortized value of bonds is not too different from their market value. On published statements to stockholders, both bonds and stocks owned may be carried at market value as of December 31 instead of at "convention value." In either case, net asset value per share in insurance companies' statements is much closer to reality than in those of business corporations.

The net asset value or book value per share is calculated by dividing

---

[5]In the financial statements, bonds are carried at their amortized values and stocks at market value.

capital stock, surplus, and surplus reserves by the number of shares outstanding. The amount is affected by the method by which the portfolio is valued on the balance sheet. The calculation of "liquidating" or "adjusted book" value, however, requires two additional adjustments if these have not been incorporated in the company's reported figures (1) the addition of the equity in the unearned premium reserve, at an arbitrary rate such as 35 per cent or, more accurately, at a rate that reflects the actual experience of the company with respect to acquisition costs; and (2) the reduction at current tax rates of the equity in unearned premium reserve and of unrealized portfolio appreciation.

Stock values, prices, dividends, and yields. The market value of the stock of a property-liability insurance company is affected by (1) its liquidating value; (2) its earnings record and prospects, in both amount and stability; (3) its dividend policy; and (4) the condition of the stock market as a whole. In early 1973, the majority of the stocks were selling between 1.25 and 2 times equity value, although earlier, in periods of generally depressed stock markets, most of them had sold at substantial discounts. They were yielding very low returns on market price—in many cases below 2 per cent—so that their chief appeal had to lie in possible price appreciation. Such low yields reflected the modest percentage of investment income distributed, and the generally high level of stock prices.

When the investor buys the stock of an insurance company below liquidating value, he is purchasing a portion of a securities portfolio at a discount. But since the company is not going to liquidate, the market value is influenced more by earnings and dividends. A low market price in relation to asset value does not suggest a bargain unless profitable underwriting is in prospect.

Because of mergers and acquisitions and the growth of multiline and holding company groups, few "straight" property-liability companies remain on the scene. The analytical task becomes difficult where consolidated statements combine different types of insurance and, in some cases, a variety of other services. The investor must often rely primarily on final results: per-share earnings and dividends, price-earnings ratios, dividend yield, and price performance. He cannot appraise the separate activities unless the company chooses to publish separate information on these lines. Fortunately, a number of companies do so.

Life Insurance Stocks

Nature of earnings. In computing the premiums charged for life insurance policies, three basic assumptions are involved: (1) mortality experience at different ages, based on conservative mortality tables; (2) a rate of earnings on that portion of the premium that represents the addition to the policy reserve and is invested, mainly in securities and mortgages; and (3) a percentage of the premium designed to cover operating expenses—the "office load." Thus, profits are derived from (1) the ratio of actual mortality experience to that assumed in the premium calculation, (2) the interest earned in excess of the amount assumed in the premium calculation, and (3) any savings resulting from operations conducted at a lesser expense than was allowed for in the premiums collected. (*Growth* in profits is a function of these factors and of the volume and types of policies written.) The first of these has been very favorable over the past two or three decades, with the trend toward lower infant mortality and greater adult longevity. By reducing the assumed interest rates on new policies (to 2½ to 3 per cent) the companies have been able to enjoy, in recent years, an increasing net investment income derived from an increasing actual rate of interest earned. (See Chapter 23.) And the introduction of cost-saving devices and operations has kept the ratio of total expenses to operating income remarkably steady.

Investment characteristics. In the postwar period the life insurance industry has had a very substantial growth as revealed by Table 30-8. Many reasons explain this growth and its likely continuation: general growth of the economy, general increase in population, increase in young population and young families, increase in the percentage of personal income spent on insurance, decline in net premium cost (after participating dividends), introduction of new forms of policies such as the family-plan package, aggressive marketing, and increase in number of companies from 473 at the end of 1945 to 1,805 at the end of 1971. The last figures reflect the ease of entrance into the business and the possibilities of large profits to the shareholders of new stock companies.

Table 30-8. GROWTH OF LIFE INSURANCE INDUSTRY, 1945–1971
(in billions of dollars)

	1945	1955	1960	1965	1971
Gross National Product	$213.6	$398.0	$503.7	$684.9	$1,050.0
Life insurance in force	151.8	372.3	586.4	900.5	1,621.8
Life insurance purchases	14.6	48.4	74.4	142.2	207.8
Premium receipts	5.2	12.5	17.4	24.6	40.7
Investment income	1.4	2.8	4.3	6.8	11.0
Total assets	44.8	90.4	119.6	158.9	221.1
Disposable personal income per family	$3,200	$5,100	$ 6,100	$ 7,700	$10,800
Life insurance per family	3,200	6,900	10,200	14,700	21,800

SOURCES: Institute of Life Insurance, *Life Insurance Fact Book* (New York: The Institute, 1972); U.S. Department of Commerce, Bureau of the Census, *Statistical Abstract of the United States*, 1971.

The growth of the industry in terms of volume of business and assets has been accompanied by a steady growth in earnings. Serious government competition in the form of national service insurance of servicemen, Social Security, and more recently, Medicare, has not actually materialized. Indeed, such plans have stimulated private insurance by showing the advantages and need of adequate coverage. Even the threat of inflation, which makes each dollar of contracts less valuable, has encouraged increases in coverage as an offsetting factor.

Life insurance is not only a rapidly growing industry, but has also been outstandingly stable, as measured by the resistance to cyclical forces of new premiums written, insurance in force, and total income. Except for 1932 and 1933, life insurance in force has increased yearly since 1900.[6]

The investment practices of life insurance companies, and their regulation, have been discussed in Chapter 23. While in the long run the overall rate of earnings on investments varies with the conditions of the capital market (in addition to shifts in investment policy), a considerable lag exists between falling or rising money rates and investment earnings, because the investments are mainly long term and held to maturity. Thus, only *new* additions to the portfolio are acquired at higher or lower yields. In the meantime any spread between the assumed rate written into premium calculation and the actual rate earned tends to be perpetuated.

Other factors favoring the industry from the investment standpoint include lack of labor problems, inventory problems, and no threat of overcapacity. In addition, it has enjoyed special income tax treatment. From 1941 to 1957, only 15 per cent of net investment income was taxed at the 52 per cent corporate tax rate, or an effective rate of 7.8 per cent. Underwriting profits as such were not taxed. In 1959 a new Federal tax law was passed. The taxable portion of investment income (not required to maintain policy reserves) is determined on an individual company basis; it involves the application to reserves of an interest rate representing the average earning rate of each company in the current and four prior years. Taxable income also includes one-half of underwriting profits; the remaining half is taxable only to the extent distributed to stockholders. Federal taxes amount to about 27 per cent of net operating profits. Net long-term capital gains are taxable at the regular corporate rate.

We are concerned here with the analysis and evaluation of the shares of stock life insurance companies, which comprise 90 per cent of the firms but which account for about one half of life insurance in force and about 33 per cent of industry assets.

Income statement. The income statement of a stock company differs very substantially from that of an industrial corporation. Table 30-9 shows a condensed (and somewhat rearranged) statement of a hypothetical company.

Some of the income statement items need an explanation. *Supplementary contracts* are agreements by which the company retains the cash sum payable under a policy and makes payments in accordance with the settlement

---

[6]*Net earnings* of life insurance companies, however, have not shown the stability of insurance written and premium income. Porterfield attributes this to a combination of three factors: (1) the high leverage characteristic of the industry (large liabilities in relation to net worth), (2) the relatively low proportion of total income—3 to 5 per cent—brought down to earnings, and (3) the heavy proportion of fixed and partially fixed costs that characterize the industry. J. T. S. Porterfield, *Life Insurance Stocks as Investments*, Business Research Series No. 9., Chapter 8 (Stanford, Calif.: Graduate School of Business, Stanford University, 1956).

options chosen. Net investment income is the return from securities, mortgages, and other portfolio investments, less investment expenses and taxes. Net gain after income taxes is really not a true profit figure, since it stems in part from assumptions as to mortality, interest rates, and expense loading. A gain is reported only when mortality is less, expenses less, and interest

Table 30-9. CONDENSED INCOME STATEMENT, STOCK LIFE INSURANCE COMPANY

Income		
Premiums and deferred benefit contributions	$74,000,000	
Income from supplementary contracts	3,000,000	
Net investment income	23,000,000	$100,000,000
Distribution of income		
Death, accident, and health benefits	37,000,000	
Annuities and matured endowments	7,000,000	
Surrender benefits	4,500,000	
Payments on supplementary contracts	3,000,000	
Miscellaneous insurance deductions	2,000,000	
Increase in policy and special reserves	24,500,000	78,000,000
Operating costs		
Commissions to agents	7,000,000	
General expenses	7,000,000	
Taxes other than on income	2,500,000	
	$16,500,000	
Dividends to policyholders	2,000,000	18,500,000
Net operating gain before income taxes		$ 3,500,000
Income taxes		1,500,000
Net gain after income taxes		$ 2,000,000
Surplus to policyholders		
Surplus, January 1	29,000,000	
Net after income taxes	2,000,000	
Net gain from sale and maturity of investments	500,000	
Increase in market value of assets	2,500,000	$34,000,000
Less:		
Dividends to stockholders	800,000	
Increase in security valuation reserve	1,200,000	2,000,000
Surplus, December 31		$32,000,000

earnings greater than assumed in computing premiums. But even modest savings in these respects, compounded through the years by reinvestment, can add materially to stockholders' earnings. The "gain" does, however, indicate protection against adverse results that differ from these assumptions, and may be used to help calculate the per-share results.

In the statement in Table 30-9, premium income from life, annuity, and health insurance policies represented 77 per cent of total income, and net investment income 23 per cent. In 1971, for all life insurance companies, the latter (before income taxes) was 5.5 per cent on mean invested assets. For our hypothetical company, the figure was about the same. The rate for the industry rose for 23 consecutive years from its low of 2.88 per cent in 1947, reflecting rising interest rates in the capital market (especially 1969–1970) and the shift into corporate bonds and mortgages and out of Federal obligations. Such a high rate is very profitable because of the much lower assumed rates in most insurance and annuity policies at which reserves must be compounded.

In our hypothetical company, operating costs consumed 16.5 per cent of income. This operating ratio was 17 per cent for the industry in 1971, up from less than 14 per cent at the end of World War II. Use of data-processing equipment and strict cost control has helped, but the costs of selling, issuing, and administering new contracts are higher than those of maintaining old business, so that growth in insurance in force has imposed a penalty. Ratios vary, of course, from company to company, reflecting the types of coverage sold and the relationship of new to insurance in force.

Balance sheet. The assets of the insurance company show that it invests funds representing reserves and other policyholders' claims in bonds and mortgages, with some funds allocated to stocks, real estate, and policy loans. (See Chapter 23.) The main liability is policy reserves, or the amounts which (with interest), together with future premiums, will pay policy claims as they mature. Additional policyholders' funds consist chiefly of proceeds of policies left with the company. The security valuation reserve provides for possible future fluctuations in security holdings. Contingency reserves are established against changes in investment income and mortality. The unassigned surplus constitutes a large general reserve for unforeseen developments and for stabilizing dividends. A hypothetical condensed statement is shown in Table 30-10.

The substantial leverage represented by policy reserves and other customers' claims in relation to net worth (the last three items on the liability side) is evident in Table 30-10. Such obligations totalled $10.00 for every $1.00 of stockholders' equity. The book value per share was $45.50.

Analysis and valuation. The analysis of a stock life insurance company is a complicated procedure, and the investor should rely on the information provided by brokerage and investment banking houses that have made a specialty of insurance stocks. The main points to be checked include

General factors:

1. Growth in admitted assets, as reported to the state insurance departments and published in annual reports. The value of total real assets may actually be understated (see below).

2. Growth in capital funds, or total net worth, both as reported and as adjusted (see below). Capital funds in relation to reserve liabilities should also be checked against industry data and competitive companies.

3. Growth in insurance in force, premium income, and total income.

4. Composition of insurance in force, as indicated by the percentages of whole-life, endowment, term, group, and industrial insurance. The first type is usually the most profitable.

Table 30-10. LIFE INSURANCE COMPANY BALANCE SHEET

Assets	
U.S. Govt. and agency bonds	$ 11,000,000
Foreign and municipal bonds	15,500,000
Corporate bonds	175,000,000
Mortgages	180,000,000
Stocks	37,500,000
Loans to policyholders	40,000,000
Real estate	15,000,000
Cash and other assets	26,000,000
Total assets	$500,000,000
Liabilities	
Policy reserves	$400,000,000
Claims in process of payment	10,000,000
Policy dividend accumulations, deposits, and future payments	21,500,000
Taxes payable	4,000,000
Reserve for security fluctuations	9,500,000
Other liabilities	9,500,000
Contingency reserves	9,000,000
Capital stock (1,000,000 shares, $5 par)	4,500,000
Unassigned surplus	32,000,000
Total liabilities	$500,000,000

5. Amount of business other than life insurance, especially health and accident insurance, which has been generally profitable or has potential profitability.

6. Scope of the company's activities—whether it is a holding or parent company with subsidiaries or divisions in various lines of insurance and finance, or specializes in traditional life insurance and annuities.

More specific factors:

1. Size and trend of the net rate earned on portfolio. This is a function of the composition of the portfolio and its growth in periods of high or low interest rates. A high rate (say, 5½ per cent or more) is a great advantage to a company that has written policies based on assumed rates for reserve compounding of around 3 per cent.

2. Trend in the operating cost ratio. Insurance companies have offset rising labor costs by introducing computer techniques and have held the operating cost ratio to 17 per cent.

3. Annual growth rate in net gain from operations, after taxes. This reflects growth, mortality experience, portfolio earnings, and cost control.

4. Amount and trend of adjusted earnings per share. The entire cost of placing new business on the books (acquisition costs) is met in the first year, but will be recovered in future years. Therefore, new business has an earnings potential that is worth from $2 to $20 per $1,000 of increase in insurance in force during the year, depending on the type of policies

written.[7] This is added to net gain from operations to get adjusted earnings, both total and per share.[8]

5. Amount and trend of *adjusted book value* per share. Reported book value or *total equity* is the total of capital stock, unassigned surplus, and voluntary reserves (such as contingency reserves). Adjusted book value or equity is increased by the percentages of *total insurance in force* for each category as suggested in footnote 7.

6. Market price as a percentage of adjusted book value per share. As revealed by the data in Table 30-11, market price is usually higher than adjusted book value, reflecting growth and the high rate earned on total equity.

7. Market price to adjusted earnings per share. This is a refined price-earnings ratio.

8. Dividends as a percentage of adjusted earnings per share. The payout by life insurance companies is typically low.

9. Dividend yield. This is also typically very low.

Table 30-11 reveals the high market prices, in relation to both adjusted book values and earnings, and the low dividend payout ratio both of which produce a very low yield for the typical life insurance company stock.

Table 30-11. PRICE AND EARNINGS RELATIONSHIPS OF LARGE LIFE INSURANCE COMPANIES, 1971

	Range	*Average*
Adjusted earnings to reported earnings	—	125%
Market price to adjusted book value per share	80–250%	150%
Market price to adjusted earnings per share	7–22	13
Dividends as a percentage of net earnings	10–40%	25%
Dividend yield	.9–4.2%	2.0%

SOURCE: Standard & Poor's *Industry Survey, Insurance* (Current and Basic).

Market price performance. At their peaks in 1964, typical life insurance stocks sold at over 30 times adjusted earnings. The general price rise continued in early 1965; then these securities suffered a price decline to the low in 1966 that brought the price-earnings multiples into a more reasonable range (12 to 25). Prices rallied modestly to an interim high toward the end of 1968 that was still, however, well below the 1964 peak. The life insurance stock indexes then dropped more than the general market

[7]Standard & Poor's uses the following rates per $1,000 increase in insurance in force: $15 for ordinary life, $8 for term, $3 for group life, and $20 for industrial insurance.

[8]In very recent years various organizations have urged that life insurance companies adopt new accounting procedures for reporting earnings, by setting up more realistic reserves, by using actual rather than assumed rates of interest on reserves, and by writing off acquisition costs as policies mature or lapse—in other words, by adopting "generally accepted accounting principles." This would be in contrast with the customary rules for determining "statutory" earnings, at least in reports to shareholders. Such a practice would make the reports of different companies more comparable and would reduce the need for artificial adjustments.

and reached a ten-year low in October 1970. Since then, a modest recovery has sent the aggregate price-earnings ratio to a typical 16 times adjusted earnings in late 1972, although there is a wide range around this average. Dividend yields have remained very low, reflecting the policy of ploughing back most of the net investment income and any capital gains. They average (late 1972) around 2 per cent, within a range of 1 to 4.5 per cent. Shares of soundly operated life companies provide an excellent medium for long-term appreciation when purchased at prices commensurate with underlying values and earnings.

The Market for Insurance Company Stock

A few insurance stocks are listed: Those of most of the larger companies enjoy an active over-the-counter market, and their price quotations are found in the financial sections of the metropolitan dailies and in the financial journals and services.

Stocks of insurance companies are, in general, conservative investments offering regular but modest dividends (in some cases over a long period of years), diversification through a portfolio of selected securities, and the opportunity for long-term appreciation. The growth prospects derive from the ploughing back of any underwriting profits, capital gains, and part of the investment income. This results in growth in value per share, except under adverse general market conditions. But, as in the case of any securities, the results to the investor depend also on timing and selection—timing with respect to the course of the market as a whole and the outlook for the industry, and selection with respect to those companies showing the most favorable record and prospects.

REFERENCES

American Mutual Insurance Alliance, et al., *Property and Casualty Insurance Companies: Their Role as Financial Intermediaries,* a monograph prepared for the Commission on Money and Credit. Englewood Cliffs, N.J.: Prentice-Hall, Inc., 1962.

American Research Council, Inc., *Life Insurance: Annual Industry Study and Investment Forecast.* Larchmont, N.Y.: The Council, *annual.*

Best's Insurance Reports, Property-Liability. Morristown, N.J.: A. M. Best & Co., Inc., annually.

Best's Insurance Reports, Life-Health. Morristown, N.J.: A. M. Best & Co., Inc., annually.

BLAIR, B. F., *Interpreting Life Insurance Annual Reports,* rev. ed. Philadelphia: American College of Life Underwriters, 1960.

BRIMMER, A. F., *Life Insurance Companies in the Capital Market.* East Lansing, Mich.: Bureau of Business and Economic Research, Graduate School of Business Administration, Michigan State University, 1962.

Data on Selected Life Insurance Stocks and Fire and Casualty Insurance Stocks. New York: The First Boston Corporation, annually.

GUTHMANN, H. G., *Analysis of Financial Statements,* 4th ed., Chapter 18. Englewood Cliffs, N.J.: Prentice-Hall, Inc., 1953.

HUEBNER, S. S., AND KENNETH BLACK, JR., *Life Insurance,* 7th ed. New York: Appleton-Century-Crofts, 1969.

Institute of Life Insurance, *Life Insurance Fact Book.* New York: The Institute, annually.

Institutional Investor Study Report of the Securities and Exchange Commission, Chapter VI and Summary Volume No. 1, Chapters 2, 5. 92nd Congress, 1st Session, House Report No. 92–64. Washington, D.C.: U.S. Government Printing Office, 1972.

Life Insurance Association of America, *Life Insurance Companies as Financial Institutions,* a monograph prepared for the Commission on Money and Credit. Englewood Cliffs, N.J.: Prentice-Hall, Inc., 1962.

MEHR, R. I., *Life Insurance: Theory and Practice,* 4th ed. Austin, Texas: Business Publications, Inc., 1970.

MILTON, ARTHUR, *Life Insurance Stocks: The Modern Gold Rush.* New York: Citadel Press, 1963.

———, *Life Insurance Stocks: An Investment Appraisal.* New York: Timely Publications Corporation, 1965.

PHILO SMITH & Co., Inc., *Insurance Company Stocks.* Stamford, Conn.: The Company, 1965.

PORTERFIELD, J. T. S., *Life Insurance Stocks as Investments,* Business Research Series No. 9. Stanford, Calif.: Stanford University Graduate School of Business, 1956.

WIGHTMAN, E. C., *Life Insurance Statements and Accounts.* New York: Life Office Management Association, 1952.

Index

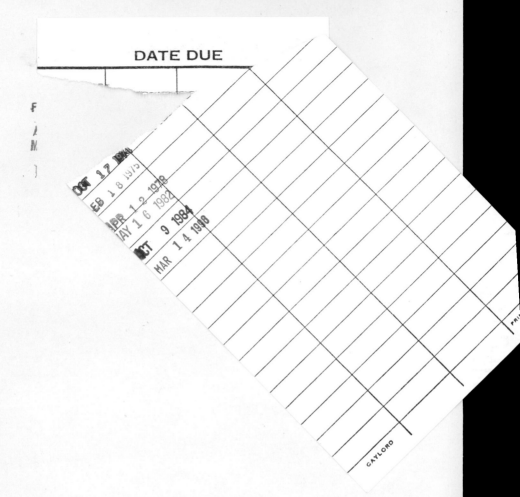